OUR MUSICAL HERITAGE

(From "Yankee Doodle" to Carnegie Hall, Broadway, and the Hollywood Sound Stage)

MARK EVANS

OUR MUSICAL HERITAGE

(From "Yankee Doodle" to Carnegie Hall, Broadway, and the Hollywood Sound Stage)

MARK EVANS

Published by Basset Books
An Imprint of Cultural Conservation

Our Musical Heritage © 2017 by Mark Evans. All rights reserved. Printed in the United States of America. No part of this book may be used or reproduced in any manner whatsoever without written permission except in the case of brief quotations embodied in critical articles and reviews. For information address Cultural Conservation, P.O. Box 3785, Pinehurst, NC 28374, or visit the publisher's web site for this book: www.culturalconservation.org

ISBN 978-0-9847679-4-6

Library of Congress Control Number: 2016906305

Book Design by Carol Ann Johnson

DEDICATION

In memory of six people who contributed immeasurably to my own musical heritage:

As always, first and foremost, my incomparable parents, Yale and Rea Evans, for a lifetime of infinite patience and encouragement in raising a composer. To list the ways in which they accomplished this would require a book of its own.

Two mentors, Irvin Talbot, Musical Director of Paramount Pictures for 45 years and his beloved wife Ethel. In the unlikely world of Hollywood, they were the symbols of enduring friendship and unwavering musical integrity.

Two teachers, Mario Castelnuovo-Tedesco, the Maestro in all things musical and Helena Lewyn, virtuoso at the piano and in life.

ACKNOWLEDGMENTS

BOOKS DO NOT WRITE THEMSELVES. As an author, I always find it a pleasure to thank those who aided this book's journey from idea to publication. My parents, in whose memory this book is dedicated, are always first on such a list. I would also like to express my appreciation to:

Sondra Nelson, friend and proofreader *extraordinaire* who can spot a missing comma or period a mile away. She always does so with patience and good humor!

Carol Ann Johnson, my favorite book designer, for bringing her considerable designing skills to this book;

Johnnie, Sharon, and Joshua Drakeford, dear friends who are always there in times of crisis. As I have often told Johnnie, one day the dictionary will simply offer a definition of the word "friend" as "Drakeford."

Robert B. Bronec, whose friendship, advice, and counsel, provided over many marvelous lunches, are appreciated beyond words, along with his constant devotion to the ideas and values that are essential for an exceptional musical legacy.

Brendan and Christine Walsh, my wonderful Irish friends in Sydney. Brendan, Australia's leading radio presenter of classical music, is a constant ally and advocate in spreading the word on behalf of true American music in an age of discord and confusion.

My colleagues, board members, and supporters of Cultural Conservation, the foundation dedicated to the principles espoused in this book, especially James Williford II, the Watsons, J. Raymond and Bruny, and Donnell G. "Buck" Adams.

Finally, there are dozens of musicians, writers, artists, historians, and teachers whose ideas have contributed greatly to the best of our past, present, and musical heritage and in the process, have given us all a legacy worthy of conservation, providing the reason I wrote the book you are about to read. It would be impossible to list them all.

However, a life devoted to words and music is not nearly so serene as many imagine. It is rather like seeking the perfect word or sound in the middle of a thunderstorm; you hope for inspiration, but what you really need is a good umbrella. Several very special and extraordinary friends have helped turn chaos into order in too many ways to mention here. But I thank them, including the late Mohsin Ali and his wife Dolores Gregory; the late Ted and Pat Dawes, The Buecheles, Dr. Walter and Frances; Virginia Nickel; Bernice Rappaport, Paulette Drakeford, The Holbrooks, Charles and Jewell, and Judith Greer Bender.

TABLE OF CONTENTS

DEDICATION i
ACKNOWLEDGMENTS iii
INTRODUCTION 1
THE CONCERT HALL 5
    The Founding Fathers 6
    The Innovators and Pioneers 16
    The Matinee Idol 25
    The Boston Classicists 28
    The MacDowell Affair 33
    The Individualists 36
    The Bandmasters 41
    The Maestros and Their Mentors 49
    How Opera in America Became Grand 56
    The Iconoclasts 65
    The Gershwin Phenomenon 73
    The Nationalists 75
    The Romantics 96
    The Italian-American Tradition 107
    The Intellectuals and their Pupils 115
    The Émigrés 122
    The Eclectics 137
    The Concert Hall Today 151
JAZZ 153
    The Ragtime Era 156
    Striding Through Harlem 158
    The Roaring Twenties 161
    The Swing Era 167

- Jazz Royalty I: A King and His Rivals 172
- Jazz Royalty II: The Duke and the Count 188
- "God is in the House" - The Legacy of Art Tatum 199
- To Be or Not to Bop: Gillespie, Parker, Monk, and Powell 203
- Oscar and Friends 214
- Hot Jazz Cools Off 219
- Singers and Swingers 228
- Jazz Goes to School 236
- Jazz Conquers the Globe 239
- The Future of Jazz 248

AMERICAN MUSICAL THEATER 253

- The Pioneers: Echoes of Operetta 254
- Irving Berlin and the Triumph of Tin Pan Alley 260
- Jerome Kern, Oscar Hammerstein, and a Make-Believe Show Boat 267
- The Brothers Gershwin: George and Ira 270
- The Improbable Duo: Rodgers and Hart 274
- The Voodoo That Cole Did So Well 276
- Destiny's Tot: Nöel Coward 279
- The Lions Roar: Dietz and Schwartz 281
- Broadway in the 1930s 282
- The Voices of Social Protest: Weill and Blittzstein 284
- The Triumph of the American Musical 290
- Some Enchanted Evenings: Rodgers and Hammerstein 290
- A Little Bit of Luck and an Abundance of Talent: The Collaboration of Lerner and Loewe 300
- Leonard Bernstein and Friends 306
- Jule 309
- A Most Musical Fella: Frank Loesser 312
- Giants on Broadway 320
- The Innovator: Jerome Moross 327
- Four Legends: Arlen, Harburg, Lane, and Mercer 328

The Shows of the 1960s and 1970s: Bock and Harnick, Kander and Ebb, Adams and Strouse, Jerry Herman, and Cy Coleman 333

Sondheim and Company 339

The Musical and the Twenty-First Century 345

FILM MUSIC 349

The Sound Of Silents 350

Silent No More 353

From Vienna to Hollywood: The Odyssey of Erich Korngold and Max Steiner 358

Culture Clash: Artists in Hollywood 367

Strings and Heartstrings: Alfred Newman at Fox 369

The Great Melodist: Victor Young 373

Frank Skinner: The Mainstay of Universal 376

Franz Waxman: A Place in the Hollywood Sun 379

Bronislaw Kaper: From Warsaw to MGM 383

Dimitri Tiomkin: The Russian Who Went West 384

The Double Life of Miklós Rózsa 387

The Americans: Copland and Thomson 391

The Bad and Beautiful Adventures of David Raksin 394

Hugo Friedhofer: A True Giant among Hollywood Pygmies 397

Citizen Herrmann: A Gulliver among the Lilliputians 400

The British Were Coming 404

The Italian Influence 408

The New Yorkers: Jerome Moross and Alex North 409

The Previn Journey: From Berlin to Beverly Hills 414

The Many Moods of Elmer Bernstein, Ernest Gold, and Laurence Rosenthal 416

Leonard Rosenman: Dodecaphony in Hollywood 419

A *Picnic* with George Duning 420

Soundtracks: The Records of the Movies 420

Henry Mancini: The Improbable Revolutionary 421

John Williams and the Symphonic Renaissance 424

Jazz and the Avant-Garde: 425

Jerry Goldsmith and Lalo Schifrin 425

The Rise of the Movie Musical 427

MGM and the Freed Unit 433

Broadway Goes To Hollywood 443

The Ghosts in the Dubbing Room 445

Broadway Composers in Tinseltown 447

The Masters of Movie Musicals 452

Wishing Upon a Star: Music and Animation 462

Film Music in the 21st Century: The Dollaristocrats 466

CODA 471

ABOUT THE PHOTOGRAPHS IN THIS BOOK 473

TABLE OF FIGURES 475

INDEX 503

INTRODUCTION

Mark my words . . . on music! That's a request I have frequently directed to audiences and readers alike. As a composer (and broadcaster) who has spent a lifetime in music, it should come as no surprise that words and music are my favorite subjects. In recent months, however, I have faced some harsh realities about those who may be listening to my words.

The genesis of *Our Musical Heritage* can be traced to a cool autumn afternoon when I was invited to appear as guest instructor at a college music class. I was on the campus of a fine Midwestern college with high academic standards. I had been invited by the college to present a lecture-concert on the history of film music, a specialty of mine, and a combination of anecdotes and demonstrations at the keyboard.

The chairman of the music department, a man of amiable disposition, invited me to visit his class as "professor for a day." He thought it would be an opportunity for his students to get to know me in an informal setting; I would not be the intimidating figure in a tuxedo seated at the concert grand, but a friendly visitor who might find a way to encourage the class to try new listening experiences in music. I told the students that I would be discussing several genres of American music: the Broadway musical, jazz, symphonic concert music, and film scores. "I'm not asking these questions to trap anyone," I explained. "But I'm going to mention several names. If you recognize a name, just raise your hand. It will be helpful for me to know if I'm telling you about familiar names." The students seemed pleased. "Cole Porter," I began, hopefully. Only one hand was raised, "Hoagy Carmichael." The class stared in silence. The composer of "Stardust" was an obvious unknown to the group. I had chosen Porter and Carmichael, both Indiana natives, since many of the students in the school were from Indiana.

"How about Art Tatum?" I asked. Tatum, who was to jazz piano what Babe Ruth was to baseball, brought no reaction. A number of the students were from Toledo, Tatum's hometown.

"Roy Harris?" I continued. Harris, whose *Third Symphony* was the first American symphony performed in Russia and China, had been one of my teachers. No one had a remote idea as to who he was.

Finally, I concluded. "Alfred Newman." A bright, smiling face appeared in the last row, and the hand of a sophomore shot into the air in enthusiastic recognition. "All right," I said, "tell me who Alfred Newman is. But there's one proviso. If the words *Mad* magazine are in your answer, then you can't answer." Like the flag of a vanquished frigate, the hand began its slow and depressing descent. Alfred E. Neuman, mythical poster child of *Mad* magazine was familiar to at least one student; Alfred Newman, the pioneer film composer was not.

In short, a class of music students had never even heard the names of several of the most important figures in American classical and popular music. Reaction by faculty members to this sorry story was hardly surprising. "My teenage son doesn't like music," one professor confided to me. "If I want him to the leave the house, all I have to do is play my Luciano Pavarotti recordings. He can't stand to be in the same room as Puccini."

Was this an isolated incident? Just a group of ill-informed students in a single school? Hardly. Over the next few months, I encountered dozens of such examples in my own travels and performances. At a national travel convention, representatives of cities around the country spoke with pride of their cultural achievements. "I've never been to Rochester," I explained to a pair of young and obviously upwardly mobile professionals representing that city. "But I've always wanted to visit Rochester, because I'm a lifelong admirer of Howard Hanson." (Hanson, perhaps the greatest champion of American music in the twentieth century, was a composer, conductor, teacher, and mentor to several generations of distinguished pupils, and for forty years, director of the Eastman School of Music in Rochester.) But the Rochester representatives responded to his name with a blank stare. One asked, "Who's Howard Hanson?"

A friend of mine, a recent college graduate, approached me at a party with a petulant frown. Friends of hers had performed a parody of "Oklahoma" at a debutante party and she had no idea what *Oklahoma!* was about. My explanation that "Oklahoma" was a musical by Rodgers and Hammerstein did not bring a smile to her face. This daughter of privileged and prosperous parents vacationed in Paris and Palm Beach, but she had never tried riding in "The Surrey with the Fringe on Top." She said, "Who were Rodgers and Hammerstein?"

A few days later, I received correspondence from a large university inquiring about articles of mine. The department secretary had managed to misspell many of the names of composers she mentioned. My favorite misspelling of hers is "Rock Monenoff," presumably distinguished from "Rock Hudson," "Rock Group," or "Rachmaninoff," the proper spelling of the celebrated Russian composer's name. On Irving Berlin's 100th birthday, I called a large store in Washington, D.C. They had no recordings of Berlin's music on sale. This situation is not limited to stores in the nation's capital. A friend of mine from Boston recently walked into a store and asked if the shop had any recordings of music by her favorite composer, Cole Porter. The clerk seemed puzzled, and then, asked "Is he new?"

Nor are these encounters with musical illiteracy only mine. While waiting in line for an embassy reception in Washington, D.C., I struck up a conversation with a married couple who proved to be opera buffs. He was Chinese, she was Filipino. She recounted a recent discussion with a young African-American professional who worked in her office. A few nights earlier, the Houston Grand Opera had presented a new and innovative performance of "Porgy and Bess."

She said, "I asked this young man if he had watched the performance and he replied, 'What's *Porgy and Bess?*'" (Coincidentally, this young man was not only missing an opportunity to experience wonderful Gershwin music, he was also ignorant of an important sociological milestone. Todd Duncan, the original "Porgy" in Gershwin's masterpiece, broke the color line as the first African American to sing at the New York City Opera.)

Does it matter? What happens to the students like the ones I spoke to on that Midwestern morning? They will become the upwardly mobile young professionals of tomorrow. Some, sadly, will make decisions affecting the entire future of music in America. They may even become powerful motion picture producers. The multi-talented André Previn, in his book *No Minor Chords,* recalls an encounter with one Jeffrey Katzenberg, formerly second in command at the studio carrying the name (if not the taste) of the late Walt Disney. Previn found Katzenberg ensconced in a palatial estate that "made Versailles look like a tool shed." While making ten phone calls (and probably ten mega-deals), Katzenberg revealed to Previn his plans to celebrate the 50th Anniversary of Walt Disney's *Fantasia* with a new version of *Fantasia*. "There's not a single piece of classic music that knocks my socks off," he declared. Then he informed the astonished Previn that his version of *Fantasia* would feature the only music worthy to survive the twentieth century, "The Beatles!" To his credit, Previn dissented from Katzenberg's musical opinion and declined his money.

It is easy to dismiss such anecdotes as evidence of a benign musical generation gap. But there is something more serious afoot. At a time when orchestras and opera companies are running out of money, when musical theater production is a pastime reserved for billionaires, when American jazz musicians are more at home abroad than at home, the future of American music is at stake. A generation of amiable musical illiterates is ill-equipped to make judgments about the survival of our musical institutions. We have been inundated with tales of students who cannot name their own senators, who cannot find another country on a map, who do not know when the Civil War was fought. Just as ignorance of our political past makes it impossible to exercise sound judgment in the present, ignorance of our musical past makes it equally impossible to save those institutions, which represent the very fiber of America's musical quilt. While rock stars become icons on postage stamps, Gershwin scholars are perceived as experts on a rare and exotic breed of musical style.

For example, throughout our lives, we hear the official songs of the U.S. military and other patriotic melodies, but how many of us know how and why these songs came to be? "The Army Goes Rolling Along" was written in 1908 by field artillery First Lieutenant Edmund L. Gruber as "The Caisson Song," reflecting the horse-drawn field artillery batteries. It was transformed into a march by John Philip Sousa. "The Marine's Hymn" was incredibly based on an aria by French composer Jacques Offenbach in his opera, *Genevieve de Brabant*. "Anchors Aweigh" was composed by Charles A. Zimmermann, bandmaster of the U.S. Naval Academy, with lyrics by a midshipman, Alfred Hart Miles. The U.S. Air Force Song, "Off We Go Into the Wild Blue Yonder," was composed by Robert Crawford, a musician known as "The Flying Baritone," and once rejected as a pilot during World War I. His song was chosen over 700 entries, including those by Irving Berlin and Meredith Willson. "Semper Paratus" the official Coast Guard marching song, was created by Captain Francis Saltus Van Boskerck.

"America the Beautiful" began as a poem by an English professor, Katherine Lee Bates, inspired by a trip to Pike's Peak. Eventually music was added by Samuel A. Ward and written on the shirt cuff of a friend by the suddenly inspired composer. "America the Beautiful" celebrates the beauty of the country, while the lyrics of "The Star Spangled Banner" by Francis Scott Key celebrate its struggle for liberty and freedom. Behind every song, every lyric, every symphony, concerto, stage musical, film score, or jazz improvisation is a story. Just as our national character has been shaped by American history, our country has also been molded by our musical history. As for "God Bless America," we should never forget the words of its verse: "While the storm clouds gather far across the sea, let us swear allegiance to a land that's free. Let us all be grateful for a land so fair, as we raise our voices in a solemn prayer." Mary Ellin Barrett, Irving Berlin's daughter, said it best. She says that no other singer, even the great Kate Smith, could sing those words with such conviction as Berlin himself. She writes, "He meant every word. He meant it then. He meant it thirty years later. It was the land he loved. It was his home sweet home. He, the immigrant who had made good, was saying thank you." To understand why we sing our National Anthem, why certain pieces of music are important in our lives, we need to know these stories, to remember them, and to pass them on as a legacy to be preserved and protected for all time.

Those who love good music—real music, music of the soul, the heart, the spirit; music of our history; music of our nation—have inspired *Our Musical Heritage.* For those yet to discover these musical treasures, this book has been written. *Our Musical Heritage* is many things; it is not a textbook. There are many fine books rich in historical detail. It is not an exercise in musicological analysis. Our academic institutions and conservatories are full of scholars eager to dissect the harmonic structure of lost chords, some of which should have remained lost for another hundred years. *Our Musical Heritage* is, rather, a personal journey, the exploration of America's musical past, and by a process of discovery, a link to our musical present. It is a chance for us to learn together, to look not just at dates, places, and facts, but to distill the essence of our nation's musical spirit from the music itself. Not every piece of music can be included nor every great musician; no itinerary, however ambitious, can include every city, every pathway, but that is the joy of musical adventures. This book is not the end of the story; it is the beginning

THE CONCERT HALL

For many years, American audiences and musicians alike asked a single question: who is going to write the great American symphony? I first became interested in this question while studying composition with Roy Harris, who could legitimately claim to have the answer. His celebrated *Third Symphony* was heralded around the world. Rafael Kubelik, the renowned Czech conductor, said of Harris's *Third Symphony*, "It captured everyone. At that time, I considered it the Symphony of America. It is not only truly American and contemporary, but has great symphony stature, a rare quality in music written today."

I discovered, as had many before me, that the answer wasn't easy. Many composers thought they were writing the great American symphony or for that matter, the great American opera. The great Czech composer, Antonín Dvořák composed his symphony, *From the New World*. It's a masterful piece of music, but it couldn't be more Czech in style if he had called it "Symphony from Prague." When Giacomo Puccini wrote his cowboy opera, *Girl of the Golden West*, audiences cheered. Puccini had written a marvelous opera, but it was no more indigenous to the American west than a delicious platter of Fettuccine Alfredo.

A host of American composers tried writing American symphonic and operatic works during the nineteenth century. They composed outstanding music, most of it clearly German and occasionally French in style. Were these compositions quintessentially American just because their creators were living and teaching in the United States? And what about composers from other countries who introduced clearly American elements into their work? Maurice Ravel and Igor Stravinsky absorbed aspects of American jazz and popular dances in their works, but no one would consider Ravel or Stravinsky "American composers."

What makes a work truly American? If an American composer writes in a style that is predominately European, is the music still American? In a musical melting pot, can any single style be legitimately described as truly American? The answer to these questions hasn't always been easy. Throughout history, even American composers have disagreed. In fact, Americans have been historically ambivalent about the role that musicians play in our society. Unlike doctors, lawyers, teachers, or politicians, musicians have never been regarded as essential to our culture. The role of the arts (and of artists) has been a subject of controversy since the founding of the American republic. In the early days of American music, even idea of teaching music in schools was regarded as highly controversial. Yet music is incredibly important. George Gershwin said that true music must repeat the thought of the people and inspirations of the time. To learn how American music evolved, how it developed, we need to go back to the beginning and see where it began.

6 | OUR MUSICAL HERITAGE

THE FOUNDING FATHERS

In 1788, Francis Hopkinson, a signer of the Declaration of Independence, sent a message to George Washington, who was about to assume his duties as first President of the United States. This message contained no political pronouncements, no advice or suggestions as to how Washington might cope with Congress or diplomatic intrigues. Instead, Hopkinson was celebrating Washington's inauguration in his own way, with a set of "Seven Songs" for harpsichord or fortepiano. The songs were enthusiastically received by the new President and received an equally warm reception at the home of Thomas Jefferson, whose daughter was so moved by the music and poetry that she burst into tears.

Figure 1 - Francis Hopkinson, designed an early American flag, helped design the Great Seal of the United States, signed the Declaration of Independence, and today is often considered to be America's first composer. (Engraving by James Barton Longacre after painting by Robert Edge Pine, used courtesy of Pennsylvania Historical Society. Public Domain)

As Washington was becoming the nation's first President, Hopkinson took the occasion to point out that he was probably the nation's first published composer. Historians had no trouble remembering the signers of the Declaration, but Hopkinson's musical efforts have faded in memory.

Within a few years, this nation had plunged into a period of explosive growth. A variety of wars, the Industrial Revolution, and continental expansion easily overshadowed musical developments. We may safely conclude that history will pay infinitely more attention to a man marching with a gun than sounding the trumpet or beating the drum that accompanies him. Yet, when the battles are over, very often it is the man with the trumpet or the drum who is best remembered. America's musical heritage and its history have been a riotous festival of improbability.

Two of the nation's earliest musical controversies began arguments that sound as if they were printed in yesterday's newspaper. A prominent composer accused a publisher of plagiarizing his work. Church choirs were divided over whether the most important melodic line should be given to men or women. (Can there be any doubt? The ladies won.) In retrospect, music has been an important part of this nation's history from almost the day the Mayflower approached the Massachusetts coast. Musicians have been ridiculed, ignored, threatened with lynchings and shotguns, and perpetually subjected to a prolonged state of unemployment. Yet somehow, in spite of it all, Americans have managed to sing and play their way through history as much as fight their way through it. The American composer, often neglected and maligned, has emerged on the world stage as a figure of consequence. How did this happen?

Long before the days of Washington, Adams, Jefferson, Franklin, or Francis Hopkinson, music had been a part of American life. In fact, when the very first settlers reached American shores, they brought music: a tradition of choral singing. The Pilgrims brought a book of thirty-nine psalm tunes with them on the Mayflower, *Henry Ainsworth's Book of Psalmes.* The Puritans, not to be outdone, brought a book of their own with a title alone that should have earned it a place in history: *The Whole Book of Psalmes, collected into English Meter by T. Sternhold, I. Hopkins, and others; conferred with the Ebrue, with apt Notes to sing them withal, faithfully perused and allowed according to the ordre appointed in the Queenes majesties injunctions: Very mete to be used of all sortes of people private for their solace and comfort: laying apart all ungodly Songes and Ballades, which tend only to the nourishment of Vyce & corruption of Youth.*

Some of the younger Puritans, not quite as afraid of "vyce" as their parents, proceeded to call the book only "Sternhold & Hopkins," a title that remained through several editions. The generation gap began almost at the inception of American musical history: in 1692, the second generation of Pilgrims replaced *Henry Ainsworth's Book of Psalms* with the new and easier *Bay Psalm Book*, insisting that their fathers' hymns were too complicated.

The earliest *Bay Psalm Book* contained no music, because there were no engravers available to print the hymn tunes. The early colonists took the interpretation of these hymns in deadly earnest. In 1647, the Reverend John Cotton published a treatise in Boston dealing with several of the issues of the day. Not only was there a question as to whether or not women should be permitted to sing the psalmes, but there were severe objections to the participation of "carnell men and Pagans," none of whom presumably belonged to the congregation.

Almost a hundred years after the arrival of the Mayflower at Plymouth, a minister named John Tufts, pastor of the church at Newbury, Massachusetts, entered the controversy. Since no actual notes were contained in the *Bay Psalm Book*, the deacon at each church would often sing the hymns, line by line, and the congregation simply echoed his melody. If the deacon had a good singing voice, the practice worked well, but if his voice was too low or too high for the rest of the congregation, some of whom had trouble staying on key themselves, there were problems. Furthermore, the deacons began changing the melodies, adding their own embellishments. Rev. Tufts decided that serious instruction was needed, so he wrote *A very plain and easy introduction to the whole Art of Singing Psalm Tunes.* He hoped that this work, the very first musical textbook in the English colonies, would clear things up. It didn't.

Almost immediately, suggestions that the congregations read music or eliminate the improvisation and embellishments were met with hostility. Supporters of the "note for note" method of singing were accused of everything imaginable, including attempting to introduce musical instruments into the church, using the names of the notes, which were thought to be blasphemous, concocting the whole scheme to make money, disrupting the younger generation, and worst of all, in the world of Pilgrims and Puritans, being under the influence of the Pope. *The Bay Psalm Book* (in New England) and *Sternhold & Hopkins* (in the other colonies) remained in force until nearly 1720, and during these years, the controversies over singing hymns remained the most crucial musical issue of the day.

In the following years, controversies continued to rage regarding music used for worship. It is hard to imagine the controversies today, but in their own time, such arguments stirred men's passions in heated intensity. The metrical style of psalmody, identified with nonconforming Puritans, became well established in the New World, as the hymns of the minority quickly became those of the new majority. In time, a new group came to regard the former Puritan dissenters as conformists, and these new nonconformists raised their own objections to prevailing style of singing and composing hymns.

In 1735, the Governor of Georgia, James Oglethorpe, invited two brothers, John and Charles Wesley, to the colonies. They left Oxford and set sail for the New World, bringing with them a "methodical" approach to study that would one day give new meaning to the word "Methodist." While on board, John Wesley discovered the hymns of the Moravians, a Pietist brotherhood with headquarters in Germany, and a patron, Count Zinzendorf, who composed over 2,000 hymns. Wesley eventually played a key role in "The Great Awakening," an intense religious revival, along with George Whitefield, who toured America, and Jonathan Edwards, a great New England orator. This evangelical enthusiasm manifested itself musically, as the Wesley brothers wrote words for numerous hymns. Perhaps the most extreme style of hymnody was provided by the unlikely collaboration of John Newton and William Cowper. Newton, a onetime naval deserter and slave trader, composed a hymn handed down from one generation to the next: "Amazing Grace." With Cowper, a poet who eventually lost his mind, he turned out several hundred hymns emphasizing exultation through salvation.

Figure 2 - John Newton, the composer of "Amazing Grace." (Photo courtesy of Cowper and Newton Museum, Olney UK.)

Each new religious group had its own ideas about music, especially those Protestants and Catholics who dissented from prevailing Puritan and Pilgrim doctrines. The Moravians built churches and established choirs in Pennsylvania in North Carolina. Their "trombone choir" ensemble so startled a group of attacking Indians during the French and Indian War that the Indians abandoned their attack. A young woman from England, Ann Lee, known as "Mother Ann," inspired a sect called the Shakers with her unique system of musical notation. Conrad Beissel, a one-time baker's assistant, devoted himself to music and wrote his own harmony textbook, dividing notes into "masters and servants."

Meanwhile, what is now the western United States had been colonized by Spain. In Texas, New Mexico, Arizona, and California, Catholics established missions where the

Indians made their own instruments and participated in their own orchestras. Religious plays with music inspired by the Catholic missionaries remained a part of our tradition long after the control of the territories passed from Spain to Mexico, and eventually, to the United States.

The sound of American music was changed forever by a Bostonian named Thomas Brattle, who brought the first organ to New England and gave the instrument to the Brattle Square Church in his will. In the early 1730s, Karl Theodore Pachelbel, a renowned German organist, came to New England and eventually went to New York, where he played that city's first recital, and finally, to Charleston, South, Carolina, where he became an important figure in southern musical life.

In 1734, Charleston was also the site of the first recorded operatic performance in the colonies, a ballad opera, *Flora*, or "Hob in the Well." Unfortunately, many leading citizens were convinced that the traveling actors or singers were lecherous scoundrels whose real motives were concealed by their theatrical make-up. A New York audience, convinced that a visiting acting troupe consisted primarily of pick-pockets, rioted and wrecked a theater in 1764. Acting troupes were banned in Boston and Philadelphia, as actors concluded that they could not find employment in those cities. Work was available in New York, but the audiences were dangerous.

Music masters began traveling across the colonies. Those who could earn a living teaching the harpsichord, flute, or guitar to wealthy colonists doubled as barbers, chimney-sweeps, or dancing instructors. Colonists assumed that the finest music came from Europe. George Frederick Handel would have been surprised to see an advertisement in Boston in 1766 that offered for sale "Handle's Oratorio." In 1770, William Tuckey, an organist, choirmaster, and composer from England, conducted the first American performance of Handel's *Messiah*, two years before audiences would hear the work in Germany. America also could boast of a new musical export. Mozart and Beethoven wrote works for a fascinating new instrument which appeared in 1763, the armonica, invented by an amazing and versatile Philadelphian named Benjamin Franklin. Franklin had collected a set of glass bowls and arranged them in order of size. He skewered them on a spindle, which rotated them in water. When a player wanted to produce a bell-like sound, he simply touched the wet rim of the glasses.

Figure 3 - The glass armonica, invented by Benjamin Franklin. (Photo by and courtesy of Vince Flango)

Franklin was not alone among the Founding Fathers in expressing an interest in music. Thomas Jefferson, who dreamed of establishing a private chamber orchestra on the grounds of Monticello, owned the finest collection of musical instruments in Virginia.

At least several of them could be played with equal facility by Patrick Henry who had mastered the violin, lute, flute, pianoforte, and harpsichord.

Francis Hopkinson enjoyed a distinguished career in public life as a Philadelphia lawyer and, following the War of Independence, as Judge of the Admiralty from Pennsylvania. He was not an imposing figure physically (John Adams described his head as "not bigger than a large apple"), but he had a keen mind, and his advice and counsel was very much in evidence at the Constitutional Convention. Like Jefferson, he was a collector, and his music library, including scores by Handel, Pergolesi, Scarlatti, Corelli, Vivaldi, Arne, and Purcell, is still in existence today. Hopkinson's most ambitious project was *The Temple of Minerva*, an "oratorical entertainment" which some believe to be our first American opera. The work included an overture, arias, and a collection of vocal ensembles singing the praises of the new alliance between the United States and France.

Hopkinson's chief rival for the claim of being the nation's first composer was a Presbyterian minister named James Lyon. Lyon's most famous work, *Urania*, was a collection of psalm-tunes, anthems, and hymns. Lyon, incidentally, was color-blind. He wanted to dress in solemn black, but instead would appear wearing the color of the "redcoats" worn by the British army.

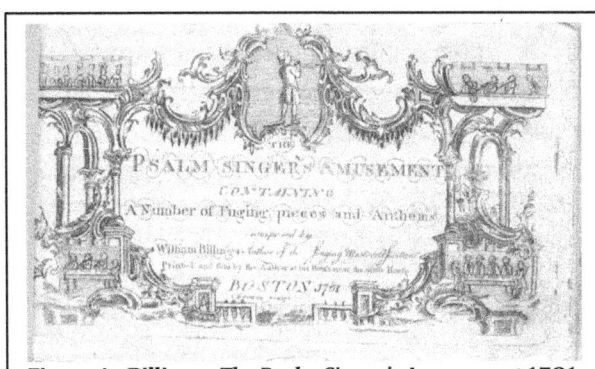

Figure 4 - Billings - *The Psalm Singer's Amusement* 1781. (Public domain)

The most interesting music of the day came from the pen of a Bostonian, William Billings. His friends said he looked like an unmade bed. His legs were of different length, he was blind in one eye, and those who knew him said that he spoke with an unusual voice of a "decided peculiar pitch." In 1770, he produced *The New England Psalm Singer* and began adding his own personal stamp to the nation's musical history. What he lacked in formal training, he made up for in enthusiasm. Billings believed in the music of joy. He was more concerned with the Resurrection than the Crucifixion. He sang his own music in a deep-bass voice so strong that colleagues protested they could hear no one else in the choir.

When critics suggested Billings' music was too gentle, too harmonious, he was quick to respond. He wrote a piece called *Jargon* containing dissonance worthy of the most experimental twentieth-century composers. (The text includes a phrase "Let horrid Jargon split the air, and drive the nerves asunder.") He also added a verbal explanation of the work; with his tongue planted squarely in his cheek, he wrote *A Manifesto to the Goddess of Discord*, which advised, "In order to do this piece justice, the concert must be made of vocal and instrumental music. Let it be performed in the following manner, viz.:

Let an Ass bray the base, let the filing of a saw carry the tenor, let a hog who is extremely weak squeal the counter, and let a cart wheel, which is heavy loaded, and that has long been without grease, squeak the treble, and the howling of a dog, the squealing of a cat, and what would grace the concert yet more, would be the rubbing of a wet finger upon a window glass. This last mentioned instrument no sooner salutes the drum of the era, but it instantly conveys the sensation to the teeth; and if all these in conjunction should not reach the cause, you may add this most inharmonious of sounds, 'Pay Me What Thou Owest.'" Not all Bostonians appreciated Billings' attitude. One hung a cat's tail on his door.

Billings could not have imagined that his own compositions, along with those of Francis Hopkinson, would be recorded two centuries later by Margaret Truman, the daughter of President Harry S. Truman. The music of Billings was hardly controversial in the 20th century, although a recital of songs by Schubert and Schumann presented by Margaret Truman provoked an unusual confrontation between President Truman and *Washington Post* critic Paul Hume, who wrote that Miss Truman had a small voice and sang flat. In what may remain the most famous response to any music critic, her father, President Truman, wrote Hume a letter, describing him as "an eight-ulcer man on four-ulcer pay." Truman also told Hume he would need "a new nose and a lot of beefsteak for black eyes," if the two men ever met in person. However, years later, after Truman left the White House, Hume visited him at home in Independence, Missouri, and the two played piano duets together.

Figure 5 - Former President Harry S. Truman returns to the White House to play the piano with President and Mrs. John F. Kennedy and Vice-President and Mrs. Lyndon B. Johnson in attendance. Music critic Paul Hume is nowhere to be seen. (Photo by Cecil W. Stoughton, courtesy of John F. Kennedy Presidential Library and Museum)

A major controversy of the day was launched by two men, William Little and William Smith, who published, *The Easy Instructor*, which explained "shape notes," a system of notation using triangles, circles, squares, and diamonds for the notes. Advocates of traditional European notation rejected the new system, criticizing the notation system and Billings' music alike as "too free, too revolutionary."

A more serious revolution was taking place in the colonies, however. From Lexington and Concord and the Boston Tea Party to the Declaration of Independence, Americans were rebelling against the tyrannical rule of King George III. One of the most popular tunes of the revolutionary movement was *Chester*, composed by William Billings. But it was completely overshadowed by another tune of more mysterious origins.

Historians have been arguing for years about the mysteries surrounding "Yankee Doodle." Many suggest that the words "Yankee" and "Doodle" were derived from the Dutch colonists of seventeenth century New Netherland. "Janke," which gave us "Yankee," meant "Johnny," while "Doodle" meant "fool." Other historians have suggested that "Yankee Doodle" was derived from a combination of two words, "Yankee" taken from "Yankoo," a tribe of New England Indians whose name meant "invincible," and "doodle" from "do little" or possibly "tootle."

The melody may have been brought to the colonies by the Dutch as well. But a melody quite similar to "Yankee Doodle" also appeared in John Gay's stage production, *The Beggar's Opera*, known throughout Great Britain. The melody turned up in an eighteenth century comic opera, *The Disappointment*, by Andrew Barton.

Figure 6 - "The Spirit of '76," originally titled "Yankee Doodle." an iconic painting by artist Archibald MacNeal Willard, was exhibited in the U.S. Centennial Exposition. (Public Domain)

One thing was certain: "Yankee Doodle" was originally meant as an insult, not a compliment. It was directed by New Yorkers, especially those of Dutch descent, at their New England neighbors. Eventually, the term was taken up by loyalists who supported continued British rule and disliked the rebellious and revolutionary colonists who joined groups such as the Sons of Liberty. In 1770, a New York Son of Liberty, Alexander McDougall, was denounced in a published satire called *The Procession*. McDougall was not only ridiculed in print, but in a lyric sung to the "Yankee Doodle" tune, which lampooned all colonial slogans. The lyrics were supplied by John Vardill, a loyalist who supported the British and disliked the rebellious Sons of Liberty. Dr. Richard Shuckburgh, a British military surgeon who lived in New York, wrote a series of scathing verses to ridicule the Connecticut Yankees who were fighting against the British redcoats. He chose the "Yankee Doodle" tune.

British troops played the tune to taunt the rebellious Americans, who soon turned the tables on the English after the battles of Lexington and Concord. "Yankee Doodle" became a rallying point for the Americans. "Yankee Doodle" followed the ragged, disorganized colonial troops wherever they went. The British would play "Yankee Doodle" as American troops approached and then add a few raucous, off-key sounds to insult their rivals. American troops returned the compliment by adding these musical "raspberries" to "God Save the King." American and British commanders eventually had to promise each other to prevent their troops from trading musical insults.

Nearly half of the two thousand British soldiers participating in the Battle of Bunker Hill were killed, along with some 460 colonial rebels. A more serious musical result of that battle was a solemn melody, *Bunker Hill*, composed by a Connecticut singing master, Andrew Law. Law was considered by many to be Billings' chief rival, but his restrained personal manner and conservative musical style left him at a disadvantage in competing with the flamboyant Billings. "Yankee Doodle" was there too, and it remained with the colonists through the battle of Yorktown which ended the revolution. By the time the colonists had won their independence from the British, "Yankee Doodle" had become a symbol of pride to a new nation.

"Yankee Doodle" had a life of its own. During the War of 1812, a British warship approached the harbor town of Scituate, Massachusetts. A boat filled with troops began heading toward the shore. But two teenage sisters, Rebecca and Abigail Bates, grabbed their father's fife and drum from the American Revolution and began playing "Yankee Doodle." The British naval commander assumed that they would be greeted by hostile troops and ordered his men to return to their ship. The two girls and "Yankee Doodle" actually saved their town.

Today, Andrew Law is remembered more for his innovations than his music: he put the melody of hymns in the soprano rather than the tenor, became one of the new nation's first writers on music, and was also one of the first composers to become actively involved in a copyright dispute. Law also made important contributions to musical life through his own singing school, in which he campaigned for "genteel pronunciation" in choral music and excluded patriotic or popular melodies from his published collections. Churches often started singing schools during this period, to train choral singers. The masters were often strict and students might be struck with a switch if they laughed too much in class. Earning one's living as a singing instructor was difficult.

Two of the better-known singing teachers are remembered today for other reasons: Noah Webster, who taught reading as well as music, became the father of the dictionary. Justin Morgan bred the horses that later acquired his name. The singing schools also generated some controversy. The year 1776 was not only the year of Independence, but also of the bass viol, which made its initial appearance. Some thought musical instruments were sacrilegious, as congregations identified themselves as "catgut churches" or "non-catgut churches."

By the conclusion of the War of Independence, singing schools could be found throughout the country. In 1786, a music society was organized at Yale. Harvard claimed to have its own singing society as early as Yale, a point that is accepted or rejected depending on where the historian making the observation happens to teach. Daniel Read, director of a Connecticut singing school, and Amos Doolittle, a prominent engraver, produced one of the nation's first musical publications, *The American Musical Magazine*, featuring compilations of tunes by American composers.

In the years following the revolutionary war, the fledgling nation that had broken away from Great Britain developed an attraction for a variety of European musicians. Among them were a musically prominent Dutch family, the Van Hagens, who contributed greatly to musical life in New York, and James Hewitt, former director of Court Orchestras during the reign of King George III. Hewitt is best remembered for the colorful titles of his program music, including a piano sonata called *The Battle of Trenton*, dedicated to George Washington and containing such sections as "Attack-Canons-Bombs," "Flight of the Hessians," and "General Confusion." Opposition to a strong central government was led in New York by the anti-Federalist Tammany Society. When Hewitt wrote an opera called *Tammany*, his severest critics were members of the opposing Federalist faction. Hewitt went on to compose a variety of other operas on historical subjects, including Columbus, William Tell, Robin Hood, and perhaps, the most colorful of them all, *The Wild Goose Chase*.

In Philadelphia, musical life was dominated by Alexander Reinagle, a friend of Karl Philip Emmanuel Bach, son of the great Johann Sebastian, and a virtuoso pianist by European standards. Pianos began replacing harpsichords in drawing rooms. Reinagle's pupils included Nelly Custis, step-granddaughter of George Washington. The general was in attendance when Reinagle and his friend, Alexander Juhan, played the first performances of four-hand piano music in the United States. Reinagle's talented colleague, Benjamin Carr, opened "Carr's Musical Repository," one of the first music stores in Philadelphia. Carr was also a composer, numbering among his works an incredibly long piano composition, which was intended to trace (in music) the history of England from William the conqueror to the Declaration of Independence. William Selby came to Boston from England, where he established himself as the leading organist-choirmaster in the city.

Another famous Bostonian was German-born Johann Christian Gottlieb Graupner. Graupner had known Franz Joseph Haydn in England and founded the first Handel and Haydn Society. While Americans were discovering the great classical pieces composed in Europe, political issues still caused the greatest controversies of the day. In 1798, Americans were divided over the French Revolution and how to deal with the new revolutionary rules of France. A piece of music, however, could unify all political factions.

In 1798, Philip Phile's piece, *The President's March*, won the wild enthusiasm of Federalist audiences, but the melody had no words. By popular demand, lyrics for *Hail Columbia* were created by Francis Hopkinson's son, Joseph, and sung by Gilbert Fox, a singer and engraver, who performed them for the first time in Philadelphia. According to First Lady Abigail Adams, the crowd demanded so many encores that their cheers could be heard a mile away. *Hail Columbia* might have become our National Anthem, but for another lyric, written a few years later.

The Star Spangled Banner has enjoyed an odd history from the moment of its first performance. In 1812, the United States found itself in another war against England, and although *The Star Spangled Banner* is generally thought to have been unfurled during the war, its melodic strains had been whistled much earlier, under decidedly different circumstances. The melody was originally a British drinking song. One of England's wilder and more boisterous associations was an organization called "The Anacreontic Society of London." This club, a group of eighteenth century artists and bohemians, often produced original tunes and lyrics, celebrating wit, harmony, and wine. Sometime between 1770 and 1775, Ralph Tomlinson served as President of the Anacreontics. He penned the lyrics for a song called *To Anacreon in Heaven*, inspired by "the convivial Greek bard."

John Stafford Smith, a well-known British composer, is generally credited with the melody, although some historians suggest that Dr. Samuel Arnold may have penned the tune. The last thing any of these spirited Englishmen expected was the emergence of their

Figure 7 - The Bombardment of Ft. McHenry inspired our National Anthem, *The Star Spangled Banner*. (Public domain - Courtesy of Maryland Historical Society)

drinking song as a national anthem for a new nation composed of former English colonists who had ousted the British king. But on June 1, 1798, the Massachusetts Charitable Fire Society celebrated its anniversary with a Boston banquet. A guest, a certain Mr. Thomas Paine (who later changed his name to Robert Treat Paine to avoid being confused with the well-known revolutionary author of *Common Sense*) was present. Paine subsequently received $750 from his publishers for the copyright to his original song, *Adams and Liberty*. The tune Paine selected was the melody of *To Anacreon in Heaven*.

Figure 8 - Francis Scott Key, a lawyer and poet, wrote the words for *The Star Spangled Banner*, our National Anthem. (Photograph used through courtesy of EyeonAnnapolis.net)

In one dynamic leap, the English drinking song had emerged as one of the new American patriotic tunes. An assortment of lyrics followed, by various writers, all using the familiar melody. *Adams and Liberty* was followed by *Jefferson and Liberty*, and ironically, a pro-Russian lyric extolling the Czar's victory over Napoleon

In 1814, Francis Scott Key, a Georgetown lawyer and amateur poet, was serving as a special envoy from President James Madison. He came to the British Fleet in Chesapeake Bay to secure the release of a non-combatant American, his friend, Dr. William Beames, who had been arrested. The British, concerned that Key might discover their plans to bombard Fort McHenry, below Baltimore, detained him. On the night of September 13, 1814, Key watched the American flag flying over Fort McHenry and wrote the first verse of *The Star Spangled Banner* on the back on a letter he had with him. Key had written another lyric for the *Anacreontic Song* once before, so his choice of melody should not be surprising.

After his release by the British, he went to Baltimore, where he recopied the verse and took it to the offices of the *Baltimore American*. The newspaper published Key's verse, announcing that it should be sung to the tune of *Adams and Liberty*. The new *Star Spangled Banner* was first performed on the spur of the moment by an actor and army private, Ferdinand Durang, in front of McConkey's Tavern in Baltimore, or more formally, on October 19, 1814, by a "Mr. Hardinge" at the Holliday Street Theater, next door to McConkey's. *Hail Columbia* and *The Star Spangled Banner* were rivals for the title of "National Anthem" until 1931, when *The Star Spangled Banner* was so designated in a proclamation by President Herbert Hoover.

The President's own anthem, *Hail to the Chief*, also dates from this period. Like *The Star Spangled Banner*, it has a British origin. Based on Sir Walter Scott's *Lady of the Lake*, the music was composed by James Sanderson, published in London and later in the U.S., about 1812. Historians believe that Martin Van Buren was the first President to be honored by its performance. Today, of course, it greets every entrance of the President of the United States.

THE INNOVATORS AND PIONEERS

American music, patriotic and otherwise, would not be the same without the contributions of Lowell Mason. Born in Massachusetts in 1792, Mason was a self-taught church musician who was intensely devoted to his art. In 1831, he was planning the music for the July 4 church service at the Park Street Church in Boston. Mason asked his friend, Samuel Francis Smith, to write some words, which could be sung to a hymn tune in honor of Independence Day. Historians suggest that Mason chose the tune; others insist that Smith selected the melody from a German songbook, assumed it was a German patriotic melody, and didn't recognize *God Save the King*. Certainly, the melody had been heard around the colonies. In fact, as far back as 1761, James Lyon's *Urania* had included the melody under the name *Whitefield's Tune* and opened with the words "Come, Thou Almighty King," Americans had used the melody of *God Save the King* for numerous patriotic lyrics, even including those in praise of George Washington during the revolution. In any event, Smith wrote new lyrics for Britain's hymn to its sovereign, and *My Country 'Tis of Thee* or *America* became one of the country's most enduring patriotic songs, beginning with its premiere on July 4, 1831.

Figure 9 - Lowell Mason, was responsible for introducing music into public schools in the U.S. He also composed hundreds of hymns and produced a famous setting of "Nearer, My God, To Thee." (Public domain)

Mason also single-handedly put the study of music into America's public schools. He began by conducting his own private classes and concerts featuring children. Opposing him were traditional academicians who insisted that music was an "entertainment," not worthy of recognition alongside reading, writing, and mathematics. Mason persevered. In 1834, he invited a dozen music teachers to a convention, and began trying to improve the level of musical instruction in the country. He urged adoption of a set of seven syllables, "do, re, mi, fa, so, la, si, do" to improve the accuracy of singers everywhere.

In 1837, after years of struggle, Mason finally persuaded the authorities in Boston to allow him to teach music when he offered his services without pay. (He was given a salary the following year.) Also in 1837, Oberlin College in Ohio began offering classes in music, the first college to do so. By 1849, Mason's conventions were drawing as many as a thousand teachers and he traveled the country preaching the gospel of musical instruction for every child. Mason's singular crusade advanced the cause of music education as no one else could. As a result of his efforts, there were hundreds of music teachers all over the country and children were introduced to good music at an early age. Those who grew up to become composers or conductors probably didn't realize how much they owed to one of America's great musical pioneers, Lowell Mason.

Figure 10 - Theodore Thomas, America's first major symphony conductor and first musical director of the renowned Chicago Symphony. (Public domain)

If you were to ask Americans today, even including those who are devoted to classical concert music, to name the conductor who was most influential in our musical history, many would name an international media star of the recent past, like Leonard Bernstein. Those more historically inclined would perhaps justifiably offer the names of the legendary maestros of the twentieth century, among them Arturo Toscanini and Leopold Stokowski. But we would be very safe in assuming that the most avid members of the audience at most symphony orchestra concerts wouldn't even recognize the name of Theodore Thomas. Yet in the nineteenth century, at a time when America didn't have any permanent symphony orchestras, in years that saw the country torn apart by the Civil War and emerging into what became known as the Gilded Age, nobody did more to advance the cause of concert music in this country than Theodore Thomas. Who was Theodore Thomas and why has he been forgotten by all but a number of music historians?

His biographer, Ezra Schabas, called him the "Johnny Appleseed of Music," a self-made man who strove and sacrificed to bring live symphony orchestra performances to America. He played pioneering roles in the creation of two major orchestras that are vital to America's musical culture today, the New York Philharmonic and the Chicago Symphony. Audiences today recognize many standard works by European composers and now regard them as classics. But American audiences often heard these works for the very first time in the nineteenth century, often under the baton of Theodore Thomas. At the time, they were new and contemporary compositions. Nor did Thomas limit himself to European masters. A new generation of American composers was beginning to make names for themselves with symphonic works in the European tradition. Thomas was a mentor and champion of many, despite resistance from concertgoers who assumed that domestically written music implied a lack of quality. In the 1880s and 1890s, Thomas was America's best-known conductor; when he died in 1905, he was considered an icon. Yet because recorded sound was in its infancy, after his death, his name and reputation faded quietly into our musical past. How did this happen?

In the early years of the nineteenth century, America was a small, but growing nation with little opportunity to hear the concert music written by such masters as Haydn, Mozart, and Beethoven. Just as our country was a nation of immigrants, it was also a nation of musical immigrants. In 1848, a group of twenty-three young musicians came to the United States from Germany. They were unhappy with conditions in Germany and began performing in America as "The Germania Society." They found it hard to earn a living through a musical ensemble. (Some things never change.) But they stayed in the United States, settled in various places, and became advocates for music wherever they went. As a result, the major supporters and teachers of concert music in the U.S. were predominately German for many years. "Good" music usually meant German music.

Johann Thomas was a musician who played and taught wind and string instruments in Germany and set out with his family for a better life in America in 1845. His ten-year-old son, Theodore, was a gifted violinist who joined his father playing in dance bands, theaters, and even saloons; he struck out on his own at only fourteen. It was an improbable beginning for one of America's great conductors. In the South, he billed himself as "Master TT—prodigy," standing at the door to sell tickets for his recitals and then dashing backstage to change in his concert clothes.

Thomas was always very serious about music. Early in his career, he played for a time under the baton of the flamboyant Frenchman, Louis-Antoine Jullien. Jullien was a showman who would have been right at home in today's high-tech era. Thomas detested musical theatrics. Fifty years later, he still called Jullien a charlatan.

Eventually, Thomas settled in New York, where he joined forces with William Mason, the son of Boston's music educator, Lowell Mason, to present chamber music through the Mason-Thomas Concerts. (New York audiences heard Mason on piano and Thomas on violin as part of a trio that presented the first American and possibly world performance of Johannes Brahms *Trio in B major*. Thomas turned to conducting as a last-minute substitute in 1859; he was successful. In 1862, he rented Irving Hall in New York, hired forty musicians and an amateur choir using his own funds, and presented his first major concert featuring the premiere of Richard Wagner's *Overture to The Flying Dutchman*. By 1864, as the Civil War drew to a close, Thomas was ready to change America's musical landscape with the Theodore Thomas Orchestra. Without Theodore Thomas, American audiences would have remained unfamiliar with the most important figures in European classical music.

Throughout his career, Thomas was a champion of new music. In 1866, American audiences heard Wagner's *Prelude* to Act 1 of *Tristan und Isolde* for the first time. Thomas was on the podium. He conducted the American premiere of Brahms *Symphony No. 2*. Today's audiences cannot imagine a Christmas season without hearing Tchaikovsky's *Nutcracker Suite*. Thomas led the very first American performance of the popular work. When the great Russian pianist and conductor, Anton Rubinstein, visited the United States, he said he was astonished by the quality of Thomas's orchestra, insisting that there was none better even in the major capitals of Europe. Thomas was a private man, not given to casual socializing. He favored modest and restrained gestures on the podium and he was known for an autocratic personal style.

When the German conductor, Dr. Leopold Damrosch, arrived in New York, he immediately became Thomas's rival. Unlike Thomas, Damrosch had considerable formal education and European credentials. He was the exact opposite of Thomas, intensely emotional in his music and manner of expression. When Thomas met him for the first time, it is said that he welcomed Damrosch to New York by declaring, "I hear, Dr. Damrosch, that you are a fine musician, but I want to tell you one thing: whoever crosses my path, I crush." In the modern era, Theodore Thomas would not have been of the school that desired to win friends and influence people. The operatic prima donna Adelina Patti was used to having her way as a diva. She was not pleasantly surprised when Thomas informed her, "I am the only prima donna here."

The New York Philharmonic was not a permanent orchestra at the time. Thomas conducted that orchestra's concerts as well for many years, but he believed intensely that orchestras should provide full employment for musicians. So Thomas actually found himself leading two major orchestras in America's largest city. Not all his efforts were successful. His uncompromising personality led to clashes with patrons, as when he became director of the new Cincinnati College of Music for a time. He struggled with finances, as when he became involved with the American Opera Company, an attempt to present major operas in English. (He survived bankruptcy and the failure of the company, which Thomas said had good intentions, bad management, and no money.) Thomas founded the Cincinnati May Festival in 1873, and for much of his life, he promoted and proselytized in the name of music. He traveled from New England to New Orleans, and in 1883, led the famous "Ocean to Ocean" tour that went as far west as San Francisco. Harold C. Schonberg, writing in *The Great Conductors*, observed, "Concerts were given everywhere—in parks, in railroad stations, in ballrooms, theaters, churches. Thomas preached music the way a traveling evangelist preaches religion."

The power of celebrity could often attract audiences that might be otherwise disinterested in classic music. The appearance of a great European virtuoso could always generate attention and controversy. Ole Bull was a renowned Norwegian violinist. His admirers compared him to Paganini, the dazzling Italian violinist who was considered the greatest violin virtuoso of his time. Bull's sister-in-law was the aunt of young Edvard

Grieg. Bull encouraged the young Grieg and he eventually became Norway's most celebrated composer. Bull had also performed in concert with Franz Liszt, then regarded as the world's greatest pianist. So when he came to the United States, Bull quickly attracted a large following. He spent several years in America, even purchasing a large tract of land in Pennsylvania to found New Norway, a colony for his fellow Norwegians.

After the death of Franz Liszt in 1886, Ignacy Jan Paderewski assumed the mantle of the most charismatic and popular pianist in Europe as well as the United States. While he had many rivals, he was so famous that even people who knew or cared little about classical music recognized his name. So an appearance by Paderewski virtually guaranteed huge crowds and thunderous cheers.

In 1893, Theodore Thomas persuaded Paderewski to appear at the World's Columbian Exposition in Chicago, only to find himself embroiled in a dispute over a competition between America's leading piano manufacturers. At the time, the great Polish virtuoso insisted on playing a Steinway piano, but since Steinway and other eastern manufacturers did not wish to participate in the event, Paderewski's piano had to be smuggled onto the fairgrounds.

Figure 11 - Ole Bornemann Bull, the famed Norwegian violin virtuoso who dazzled American audiences. (Photo by Abraham Bogardus, courtesy of Bergen Public Library (Norway) public domain, photo taken prior to 1908)

Thomas had always wanted a permanent orchestra financed in a major city. After years of frustration in New York, Thomas was asked by businessman Charles Norman Fay, "Would you come to Chicago if we gave you a permanent orchestra?" Thomas lost no time in replying, "I would go to Hell if they gave me a permanent orchestra." So in 1891, he left New York to found the Chicago Orchestra, and in 1903, he led the drive to establish Orchestra Hall, where the orchestra, renamed the Chicago Symphony, still plays today.

Figure 12 - Ignacy Jan Paderewski. In his lifetime, he was the world's most famous pianist and later Prime Minister of Poland. (Public Domain)

When Thomas died two years later, he was mourned as a musical legend. Many years later, an elderly Charles Norman Fay would celebrate the 50th anniversary of the Chicago Symphony with these words, "There were presidents from Grant to Theodore Roosevelt; Generals Sherman and Sheridan, Statesmen Root and Hay, Inventors Edison, Bell, McCormick... financiers... industrialists... all of them men of great achievement. But by far 'bigger' than any of them, the most powerful personalities I have known, as great as their work, were two musicians: Ignacy Paderewski and Theodore

Thomas."

Through his concerts devoted entirely to Wagner, his Brahms premieres, his first performances of works by everyone from Berlioz and Liszt to Dvořák, Tchaikovsky, Richard Strauss, and Edward Elgar, Theodore Thomas was a one-man crusade to introduce classical music to American audiences. In over 2,000 concerts, he left a legacy on which other conductors could build. His biographer Ezra Schabas said, "Unlike today's conductors, Thomas not only had to assemble an orchestra, train it, and conduct it well, but he had to create the opportunities for it to perform in a country not yet ready to listen." He concluded, "There were many nineteenth-century 'captains of industry,' but Theodore Thomas was the only real 'captain of musical enterprise.'"

In the early years of the nineteenth century, America changed profoundly. The Louisiana Purchase enabled a western and southern expansion. The historian Frederick Jackson Turner suggested that the settling of the American frontier was the most important historical event of the period. America's first presidents (except for John Adams) were wealthy Virginians and cultured intellectuals. With the election of Andrew Jackson of Tennessee, "Old Hickory," political power began moving to the west and the south.

Settlers of the American frontier had their own ideas about music as well as politics. They frequently resisted the traditions, opinions, and attitudes of their more cosmopolitan countryman in the country's larger cities. For instance, Lowell Mason's ideas about using seven syllables for singing received a cool reception in rural America. (In rural areas, people had become accustomed to a four-syllable system brought from England by early settlers.) Urban musicians adapted to Mason's ideas, but rural settlers continued to use the set of syllables beginning with "fa, sol, la," and became known as the "fasola" singers. This was only the beginning of differences of musical opinion between the urban easterners, who valued change, science, and intellect, and the rural southerners and westerners, who emphasized tradition, feeling, and a commitment to spirit.

It is important to remember that frontier audiences were often hearing classical or concert music for the first time. The four members of a string quartet touring the west were playing chamber music for an audience that hadn't heard such an ensemble before. They found themselves playing in a tent before an audience of cowboys armed with pistols and shotguns. It became clear that if the audience wasn't pleased with the music or the performers, the musicians might have to worry about more than a bad review.

In time, major differences would split American musicians and critics. One group believed that good music could only be written in "good taste," and "good taste" was synonymous with European tradition. The models for respectable culture could be found in the classics created across the ocean, especially by British and German masters. Attempts to write music with specific American themes were regarded with suspicion and skepticism. Other musicians believed that American music should be inspired by

American sources, ideals, and attitudes. But they weren't always sure how to achieve this goal. As the country grew, it began absorbing influences from immigrants with many musical traditions, including the homegrown influences of African Americans who were held in slavery in the American south. The conflict between art music and popular music, between the music of high culture and the music of the people, would continue throughout our musical history. It has dominated controversies throughout the twentieth century and continues to the present day. Composers were also torn between their desire to express themselves in a distinctly American way and the need to achieve approval from critics who measured their work against the standard of "good taste" as defined by Europeans.

Figure 13 - Stephen Foster. America's first writer of popular songs. (Public domain photo courtesy of Library of Congress)

One such composer was Stephen Collins Foster, born on the Fourth of July, 1826, in Pittsburgh. Foster's father had been a prosperous merchant who lost his fortune. His mother treasured the "polite arts" of the time, the genteel tradition of playing and singing graceful, sentimental ballads of the time. So Foster grew up in a household in which good taste was paramount, but finances were limited. As the composer of over two hundred songs, his musical instincts were divided between the respectable, sentimental ballads and the far more commercial, popular songs derived from a new form of entertainment, which appeared in 1843.

Minstrel shows featured white singers performing in black-face makeup created through burnt cork. Thomas Dartmouth "Daddy" Rice, a former woodcarver, composed "Jim Crow," the first American popular song to become popular around the world. Minstrel shows presented a caricature of the customs and behavior of black people, but among white audiences, the songs and skits of minstrelsy became incredibly popular, and often melodies from the minstrel shows found their way into American history. Ironically, the songs were billed as "Ethiopian." One such melody, "Zip Coon," resurfaced as "Turkey in the Straw." Dan Emmett's minstrel song, "Johnny Roach," referred to the South for the first time as "Dixie." On April 4, 1859, Bryant's Minstrels performed a new Emmett composition, "Dixie's Land," billed as "a plantation song and dance." Members of the cast strolled about the stage doing a bizarre dance to the music. "Dixie" would be re-invented as the Confederate national anthem, played at the inauguration of President Jefferson Davis, and would be reclaimed as a national song by Abraham Lincoln after the Civil War had ended.

Stephen Foster found the comedy of minstrel melodies and lyrics appealing. His first big hit was "Oh, Susanna" in 1847. Copyright laws did not protect composers at the time, and Foster's career reflected this situation. He offered his most successful song, "Old Folks at Home," to minstrel E.P. Christy for $15 and allowed Christy's name to appear on the published version as the author. When Foster changed his mind and asked Christy to put his name back on the music, Christy responded by calling him "a vacillating skunk." Foster's other major songs included "Camptown Races." "Jeannie With the Light Brown Hair," "Beautiful Dreamer," "My Old Kentucky Home," and "Old Black Joe," to mention only a few of his enduring compositions. Foster's career was marked by constant financial frustration, as he sold rights to future songs to pay his debts. Separated from his wife and daughter, and drinking to excess, he died in New York in 1864. Yet his music survives today, so much a part of Americana that it is difficult to realize that these songs all flowed from the pen of a single composer.

In contrast to Foster, consider the career of Anthony Philip Heinrich. In 1816, Heinrich arrived in the United States from his native Bohemia. Heinrich, like Foster, had his financial problems, and he wound up in Kentucky where he became known as "The Log Cabin Composer" and occasionally as "America's Beethoven." Heinrich was quite familiar with the classical works of Haydn, Mozart, and Beethoven. He formed a friendship with the great ornithologist John James Audubon and was captivated by the natural resources of his new country.

Heinrich was also fascinated by the descendants of native Americans. In 1831, Heinrich composed a work for orchestra, *Pushmataha: A Venerable Chief of a Western Tribe of Indians.* He also composed *Manitou Mysteries: The Voice of the Great Spirit* in 1845. These works were not performed during his lifetime; they premiered well into the mid-twentieth century. Heinrich was prolific, penning at least fifty works for orchestra, 400 songs, chamber music, and piano pieces. Heinrich did not try to quote actual Indian melodies in his pieces, but he tried to evoke the spirit of the Native American tribes. Despite the colorful titles of his works, his music was clearly steeped in the traditions of European classical concert music.

William Henry Fry took a far different approach to his identity as an American composer. Fry came from a prominent Philadelphia family. His grandfather had served under George Washington at Valley Forge. His father was the editor of *The National Gazette*, which paid considerable attention to music and literature. His brother Joseph translated Bellini's opera *Norma* into English, and William Henry Fry served as musical director for the American premiere of that operatic classic. When Fry began writing his own operas, such as his *Leonora* based on *The Lady of Lyons* by Edward Bulwer-Lytton, he used librettos in English written by his brother Joseph. For audiences accustomed to thinking of opera as a stage production always sung in French, Italian, or German, the very idea of operas in English was a shock. As for Fry's unabashed ambitions as an American composer, European musicians had their own ideas. The Philharmonic Society of New York, founded in 1842, was dominated by musicians from Germany who refused to consider Fry's orchestral pieces. Fry had to turn elsewhere for performances, but he refused to back down. He gave a series of lectures urging Americans to quit imitating the models of Handel, Mozart, and Beethoven and to find their own creative voices. Fry even called for the American composer to move away from European dominance in art as the founding fathers had moved away from the British crown politically. Fry's most controversial piece was his *Santa Claus* symphony, in which the orchestra emulated the sound of sleigh-bells and even quoted the Christmas carol *Adeste Fideles*. Fry called for unusual instrumentation, including a saxophone (perhaps the first time the instrument appeared in such a symphonic work by an American) and a toy trumpet. Conservative critics of the day dismissed the piece as an extravaganza not worthy of serious criticism or analysis.

George F. Bristow was a contemporary of Fry. Born in 1825, Bristow came to music naturally. His father was a British violinist who settled in America. Bristow himself joined the New York Philharmonic as a violinist in 1843 and remained in the first violin section until 1879. He left the orchestra briefly in 1853, joining Fry in a protest over the orchestra's devotion to the works of only "German masters, especially if they are dead." The Philharmonic did eventually perform his four symphonies and he also wrote a four-hour opera based on *Rip Van Winkle*. The opera was not truly American in style, but his choice of Washington Irving's story proved that American literature could be used as the basis for a serious opera.

Heinrich, Fry, and Bristow all made attempts to create a definitive identity for themselves as "American composers," free of a European model. Though they were inspired by American themes, their musical styles were still clearly under European influence. They were not the first American musicians to talk about the need for a national musical identity. Even Benjamin Franklin had criticized the trills and ornamentation in the music of George Frederick Handel as "monarchist affectations," and predicted that homegrown geniuses would one day create art, music, and literature of a decidedly American character. But some decidedly American critics disagreed.

These arbiters of taste were influential; they insisted that the influences of popular songs, folk music, or homegrown culture were clearly a pale imitation of the superior standards set in Europe. John Sullivan Dwight, a Boston music critic, was the most articulate of this group. Born in 1813, Dwight was a product of Harvard University and the Divinity School. He had no formal training in composition, but played both piano and flute as an amateur. Dwight was convinced that music was "the natural language of religion." A Unitarian minister, he translated "Cantique de Noël," by French wine merchant and poet, Placide Cappeau, which had been set to music by Adolphe Adam. The result was the beloved Christmas Carol, "O Holy Night." In 1852, he founded his own *Journal of Music* to expound his view. For Dwight, music was not always expected to be a means of expressing religion, but he thought it should always express culture and good taste. His idol was Beethoven. (One of the early writers for the journal, Alexander Wheelock Thayer, produced a celebrated biography of Beethoven.) Performers, according to Dwight, should behave with a religious reverence toward the masterpieces of Beethoven, playing them with the restraint and dignity of a New England Protestant clergyman delivering a sermon. Dwight was displeased when William Henry Fry called for homegrown geniuses to produce American masterpieces. But if a single musician embodied all the qualities Dwight disliked in music, it was Louis Moreau Gottschalk.

THE MATINEE IDOL

Louis Moreau Gottschalk was born in New Orleans in 1829. Gottschalk was Catholic, a flamboyant virtuoso pianist who drew upon the music of Creoles and African Americans as his sources of inspiration. His mother spoke and sang in French; he had an African-American nurse who introduced him to the folk songs of blacks from Africa and the West Indies. As a child in Louisiana, Gottschalk heard all kinds of music: arias performed by visiting opera companies, Army bands, Creole folk melodies, street musicians playing the violin, dance music imported from the Caribbean. At seven, he substituted for his teacher, Francois Letellier, as organist at a New Orleans church where he sight-read the music of the Mass and was declared a prodigy by an astounded press.

Figure 14 - Louis Moreau Gottschalk, a pianist, composer, and America's first matinee idol, direct from New Orleans. He performed for President Lincoln. (Portrait by Jacques Reich 1900)

Gottschalk's family sent him to Paris, where he formally studied piano, harmony, and musical theory. He also took lessons in Latin and Greek, horsemanship, and fencing. Eventually, he became the toast of Paris's literary and musical salons. Frederick Chopin heard him play the piano and predicted a brilliant future for the young American. Hector Berlioz became an early musical mentor, Jacques Offenbach played duets with him, and literary figures like Victor Hugo and Alexandre Dumas sang his praises. While in France, Gottschalk composed some of his most successful pieces. He drew upon the stunning new pianistic techniques developed by Chopin and Liszt, but also upon harmonies, melodies, and especially syncopated rhythms of the Creole and African Americans whose music he remembered from New Orleans. He used the melody of "Quan' patate la cuite," a familiar Creole folk tune, as the basis for his best-known piece. He called it *Bamboula*, the name of an African drum. He also wrote *La Savane*, based on a West Indian melody, and *Le Bananier*, a martial piece subtitled "chanson negre," and *Le Mancenillier*, inspired by a beautiful, but poisonous tropical tree (and the subject of a poem by Charles-Hubert Millevoye). Gottschalk was unapologetic about the American origins of his works. They were published and attributed to "Gottschalk of Louisiana."

Gottschalk toured Europe, winning the applause of adoring crowds wherever he went, especially in Spain, where he was decorated by the Queen and where he began composing music with Spanish themes. Then in 1853, he returned to the United States, the first American pianist and composer to become an international star and to play on the American concert stage after having been acknowledged as a first rate virtuoso in Europe.

Figure 15 - John S. Dwight, the conservative music critic and champion of German classicism in the New World. (Public domain)

Gottschalk was a showman. He knew how to please audiences and for his American concerts, promptly rewrote one of his Spanish works, *El Sitio de Zaragoza*, a grand national symphony for ten pianos, converting it into *Bunker Hill* with quotations from *The Star Spangled Banner* and *Yankee Doodle*. Gottschalk also incorporated quotations from popular songs by American composers like Stephen Foster into his work.

Gottschalk had enjoyed a lifetime of critical acclaim. He provoked a different reaction from an unsmiling John Sullivan Dwight. In Dwight's view, Gottschalk not only had the effrontery to play his own compositions, he did so at the expense of Northern European masters. For Dwight, Gottschalk embodied nearly all the musical traits to which he objected: he was a Catholic, a Southerner, a product of France, a champion of Italian operas, a performer of eclectic musical programs which included quotations from popular and patriotic songs, and worst of all, he had even suggested that Beethoven had not fully realized the potential of the keyboard in his piano works. As for Gottschalk, he viewed Dwight and his Boston allies as envious hypocrites, criticizing him unjustly for performing his own compositions instead of devoting himself to the work of long-dead European masters.

When Dwight dismissed Gottschalk's compositions as "trivial rigmarole," Gottschalk took his revenge. Borrowing a trick from Franz Liszt, Gottschalk substituted an unfamiliar piece by Beethoven for one of his own compositions announced on the program of his next Boston recital. Dwight dismissed the Beethoven piece as inferior to Chopin, proving Gottschalk's point. Gottschalk never revealed the hoax, but word of it spread, clearly proving that Dwight could be fooled by a musical label more easily than musical content. The feud between Gottschalk and Dwight, the differences between musical attitudes in Boston and New Orleans, underscored what would become a critical issue throughout America's musical heritage. Those who sought a classical tradition felt threatened by those who drew upon popular music for inspiration. This debate would continue well into the twentieth century. It continues today, even as the quality of popular music radically declined in the closing years of the twentieth century.

Dwight's criticism did not limit Gottschalk's career. He continued to play concerts, traveling to Cuba where he premiered his best-known orchestral work, *Night of the Tropics*. He also began conducting his famed "monster concerts," one of which involved 900 musicians. Over the years, Gottschalk staged music festivals in various countries calling for huge ensembles the size of several orchestras. (One, in Puerto Rico, featured a brass band, four pianists playing two pianos, and eight percussionists playing maracas and gourds.) Gottschalk was acclaimed for combining the rhythms of Latin America and the Caribbean with the orchestration of European concert music.

Gottschalk's output as a composer remained eclectic. He composed salon pieces like *The Last Hope* and *The Dying Poet*, which became staples for proper young women who played the piano in nineteenth century drawing rooms. He wrote two versions of a piece called *The Banjo*, which depicted literally the plucking of strings on an African-American banjo, all the rage during America of the 1850s, and including a quotation from Stephen Foster's *Camptown Races*. Though a Southerner, he sided with the Union during the Civil War, and one of his pieces, *Union*, was a thundering work, which included quotations from American patriotic songs. Gottschalk also performed for Abraham Lincoln and gave lessons to the brilliant young Venezuelan pianist, Teresa Carreño, who played an all-Gottschalk program for President Lincoln, as well.

It is impossible to imagine what Gottschalk might have accomplished had he lived a long and happy life in the United States. But in 1865, he went to California, where he and a friend, Charles Legay, were accused of corrupting two young girls who were students at a women's college in Oakland. Gottschalk was America's first musical matinee idol. Like Franz Liszt in Europe, the dashing virtuoso enjoyed the company of beautiful women wherever he went. Given Gottschalk's reputation with women, the newspapers had a field day and the man who had been welcomed only a few days before as "the world's greatest composer" had to flee California in the dead of night, never to return to his native country. Gottschalk went to South America, where he performed throughout Argentina, Chile, Peru, Uruguay, and Brazil, where he died suddenly of yellow fever in 1869. Gottschalk was acclaimed in all the South American countries he visited. He was welcomed by the presidents of the five nations he toured, and befriended by the Emperor of Brazil. When he died, the public mourned him as a national hero. He left numerous protégés and followers throughout Latin America. But by the early twentieth century, Gottschalk's music was nearly forgotten, dismissed and consigned to the "exotic periphery" of American musical history. But curiously, in the twentieth century, a Gottschalk revival began. His use of syncopations had not only anticipated the development of ragtime in the nineteenth century, but a fascination with the music of South America that appealed to twentieth century composers. In his own time, Gottschalk was considered shocking by his critics because he incorporated elements of popular music in what had been considered "classical" or "art music."

In the twentieth century, composers like France's Darius Milhaud drew upon Brazilian rhythms, while America's Aaron Copland was inspired by Mexican music in *El Salón México*. In the 1950s, Gottschalk's works were revived. He left a vast amount of music ranging from piano solos to dazzling concert works like the *Grand Tarantelle for Piano and Orchestra*. Yet even today, he remains a controversial figure. His biographer, S. Frederick Starr, observed that "the controversy over Gottschalk is part of the warp and woof over the larger debate over high culture and popular culture in America."

Gottschalk had walked a perilous tightrope between popular culture and high art. He anticipated the international celebrity of Americans like Leonard Bernstein by a full hundred years. Through his showmanship, he brought classical music to mass audiences that might never have discovered it otherwise. He also fought the elitist view that serious music must be serious all the time. His view that Americans should feel free to draw upon their own harmonies, melodies, and rhythms in concert music was validated by new generations in the twentieth century.

THE BOSTON CLASSICISTS

If any composer could be described as the complete opposite of Louis Moreau Gottschalk, it would be John Knowles Paine. It was Paine, not Gottschalk, who established a classical tradition of concert music in the United States. Paine was responsible for making music a respectable subject at American universities. His mentors and models were classical Germans, not romantic Frenchmen or Italians. He was a quintessential New Englander, and he trained and inspired a whole generation of pupils who became known as "The Boston Classicists." He did not look to American popular music or folk tunes as sources of melodic creativity. Not surprisingly, he won and retained the enthusiastic support of the ubiquitous John Sullivan Dwight. Paine was Dwight's idea of what a composer should be. He became so excited by the premiere of Paine's *Spring Symphony*, he stood up amidst a cheering crowd and opened and shut his umbrella to demonstrate to all present his unqualified approval.

Figure 16 - John Knowles Paine was America's and Harvard's first music professor. (Public domain)

Paine was born in 1839, in Portland, Maine, so he was a contemporary of Gottschalk. He was a descendent of the American Revolution's famed pamphleteer Thomas Paine. His grandfather was a fife major who made band instruments during the War of 1812 and eventually built the first church organ in the state of Maine. David Paine, an organist, and William Paine, a composer, were his uncles. His father manufactured musical instruments. By the time he was in his teens, Paine had already written a string quartet and given his first organ recital. He was sent to Berlin where he studied organ with Karl Haupt and orchestration with Friedrich Wieprecht. Paine became an ardent admirer of Bach in Germany and when he returned to the United States, he became active in performing the music of Bach and eventually founded the American Guild of Organists.

Paine's major concert work was his *Mass*, which he took first to Germany and then, in 1868, home in Boston, where it received its American premiere. Paine married Mary Elizabeth Greeley. He was invited to lecture at Harvard, but the prevailing view was that music was not an entirely respectable discipline and hence, the music professor should not be paid. In 1870, Paine persuaded the new President of Harvard, Charles W. Eliot, to organize a music department and to grant credits for classes in the history of music. Paine's arrival drew the wrath of well-established Harvard academicians, like the redoubtable historian Francis Parkman who paraphrased ancient Rome's hatred of Carthage with the slogan "Musica delenda est," or "Music must be destroyed." But Paine would not be intimidated; despite opposition of the Harvard faculty, Eliot agreed to Paine's requests. John Knowles Paine became an Assistant Professor on salary in 1873 and a full professor in 1875, the first to hold that title at an American university. He taught at Harvard for thirty years.

Paine also befriended Theodore Thomas, the most celebrated American conductor of the day. In 1876, Thomas was named musical director for the celebration of the American Centennial, the nation's hundredth birthday. For the inaugural ceremonies, he arranged for John Knowles Paine and Dudley Buck, two of America's leading composers, to be commissioned to produce new works. Buck, born in 1839, the same year as Paine, had also studied in Germany, distinguishing himself as an organist and choir director. Buck never found his place at a university, however, teaching privately, and concentrating on writing popular choral music. For the Centennial, Paine was asked to set the words of poet John Greenleaf Whittier to a hymn, while Buck was invited to base a cantata on a text by the poet Sydney Lanier. (Lanier, coincidentally, was also a flutist and composer who taught at the Peabody Institute in Baltimore for a number of years.) Thomas became a champion of Paine's music and introduced many of his works.

Paine's busy teaching schedule did not limit his continual composing. His works included an opera, *Azara*, symphonies, and symphonic tone poems inspired by Shakespeare's *The Tempest* and by paintings of the Isle of Shoals in New Hampshire. He also wrote an oratorio, *St. Peter*, and his best-known piece, incidental music for Sophocles' *Oedipus Tyrannus*, performed in Cambridge in 1881.

Through Paine's efforts, music became academically respectable. During his years at Harvard, he became the close friend of such important figures as Ralph Waldo Emerson, Oliver Wendell Holmes, Henry and William James, and George Santayana. He received an honorary M.A. degree from Harvard and an honorary Ph.D. from Yale. Paine retired from Harvard in 1904, and died the following year. Paine's musical style, heavily influenced by his teachers in Germany, was traditional. So with the passage of time, there were fewer performances of his music. His indefatigable energy on behalf of the musical arts, however, had a major impact on American music. His pioneering efforts on behalf of music education led to the acceptance of music as a legitimate course of study in colleges throughout the country. Many of these college music departments and conservatories were directed by his own pupils. Among those who became prominent composers were Frederick Shepherd Converse, Edward B. Hill, Henry T. Finck, Daniel Gregory Mason, John Alden Carpenter, and Arthur Foote, the first to earn a master's degree in music from

Figure 17 - George W. Chadwick (1913) was the Director of the New England Conservatory, was a composer, an influential teacher and author. (Public Domain)

Harvard. Paine and his pupils are often described as The New England School of composers. Their music is being rediscovered today after many years of neglect.

Unlike many of his colleagues, Arthur Foote was trained entirely in the United States, although the German influence in his work was clear. Foote was active as an organist, pianist, and composer. His music included large choral works, *The Farewell of Hiawatha, The Wreck of the Hesperus*, and *The Skeleton in Armor*, nearly 150 songs, organ compositions, a cello concerto, orchestral pieces, and chamber music.

George W. Chadwick was another important figure in New England musical circles. Chadwick turned his back on a career in his father's insurance company to pursue music. (One of his teachers was Dudley Buck.) After further study in Leipzig and Munich, he returned to Boston where he became Director of the New England Conservatory of Music, where he remained until his death in 1931. Chadwick liked to write descriptive music and his works were often inspired by rich imagery. Chadwick's works included three symphonies and colorfully titled orchestra pieces influenced by great works of literature, art, and, Greek mythology. Chadwick's pupils included composers Daniel Gregory Mason, Horatio Parker, Frederick Converse, and Florence Price.

Florence Price was the first African American woman to have a work performed by a symphony orchestra. George Chadwick, initially skeptical about the influence of black spirituals in concert music, eventually encouraged young Florence, who wrote 300 musical works, including a piano concerto and a symphony. Contralto Marian Anderson chose a song by Price, "My Soul's Been Anchored in the Lord," for her Lincoln Memorial recital. Price drew upon her African heritage, incorporating rhythms of dances such as the juba in her works.

Price's own pupil, Margaret Bonds, carried on her legacy. Bonds also studied with William Levi Dawson, another important black composer and with Roy Harris. She organized the Margaret Bonds Chamber Music Society to perform works by black composers. Bonds adapted texts by Harlem Renaissance poet Langston Hughes in *The Negro Speaks of Rivers, Shakespeare in Harlem*, and *The Brown King*, a cantata in honor of Martin Luther King. Price and Bonds were both trailblazers. Their music has been rediscovered in recent years.

Figure 18 - Daniel Gregory Mason, the composer and teacher who famously declared, "Thank God Wagner is dead and Brahms is alive." (Photo used courtesy of the George Grantham Bain Collection)

Daniel Gregory Mason studied with Chadwick after he found instruction from Paine lacking. The grandson of Lowell Mason, he joined the faculty of Columbia University in 1910 and taught there for thirty years. He is best remembered as a conservative who wrote in 1894, "Thank God Wagner is dead and Brahms is alive." Mason had little use for what he termed emotional excesses in music, praising throughout his career the ideals of balance, proportion, and classical beauty. Although he went to Paris to study with Vincent D'Indy, he had little enthusiasm for the music written by such innovators as Debussy, Ravel, or Stravinsky. His students recalled hiding scores of works by those composers when they heard him climbing the stairs to their classroom. His most famous work was written in 1928, the *Chanticleer Overture*, inspired by lines contained in Henry David Thoreau's *Walden*. Mason was also an articulate writer, who published many books on musical subjects. He died in 1953.

Figure 19 - Frederick Converse. His opera, *The Pipes of Desire*, was the first such work written by an American composer to be rewarded by the Metropolitan Opera with a premiere. (Public Domain)

Frederick Shepherd Converse studied with Paine at Harvard and privately with Chadwick in Boston, and with Joseph Rheinberger in Germany. He taught at the New England Conservatory of Music, wrote three symphonies and an opera, *The Pipes of Desire*, which had the distinction of being the first score by an American composer to be produced at the Metropolitan Opera House. His best-known works included a tone poem, *California*, and a symphonic poem, *Flivver Ten Million*, with movements based on various American subjects.

Figure 20 - Horatio Parker, Chadwick's most famous pupil, taught for twenty-six years at Yale, all the while, composing. (1913 photograph by Pirie MacDonald, Public Domain)

Chadwick's most famous pupil, Horatio Parker, was the son of an architect, a teenage organist. He followed in his teacher's footsteps, going to Germany for study with Rheinberger, finding time to compose overtures, cantatas, and a symphony which were given their German premieres in Munich. Parker's most famous work, *Hora Novissima*, was a cantata for chorus and orchestra based on the text of a twelfth century Latin poem by Bernard of Clairvaux. He also won first prize in a contest sponsored by the Metropolitan Opera with his opera, *Mona*. In 1893, Parker became Battell Professor of Music at Yale, where his pupils ranged from revolutionary Charles Ives to conservative Elliot Griffis. No one was more closely identified with the New England classicists than Edward Burlingame Hill, born in Cambridge, the grandson of a Harvard President, the son of a Harvard professor. Always known as "E.B. Hill" he graduated from Harvard, where he studied with Paine, subsequently worked with Chadwick, and joined the faculty in 1908. He taught at Harvard for 32 years. Unlike most of his Boston colleagues, Hill was drawn not to German, but French music. He devoted himself to writing instrumental music, including two suites inspired by the writings of Robert Louis Stevenson and based on poems from *A Child's Garden of Verses*, three symphonies, and symphonic poems based on such literary works as *Lilacs* and *Launcelot and Guinevere*.

Another New Englander was Amy Marcy Cheney, or as she is better known, Mrs. Henry Harris Aubrey Beach. Born in 1867 in Henniker, New Hampshire, she began composing in early childhood. When she was only two years old, she could hear her mother singing and immediately improvise a countermelody which could be played or sung at the same time. She taught herself to read when she was four. Her parents decided to have her trained locally in Boston instead of enrolling her in a European conservatory. As a young woman she made her debut as a concert pianist with the Boston Symphony and might have embarked on a promising career as a performer. But in 1883, she married a prominent Boston surgeon, twenty-four years her senior. Dr. Henry Harris Aubrey Beach insisted that she limit her performances to one per year with the funds donated to charity. So she remained at home and devoted herself entirely to composition. She did not resume public performance in a major way until after her husband's death in 1910, when she spent several years in Europe playing her own compositions. Critics of the day said she "wrote like a man," indicating that, unlike many other women who composed at the time, she was ready to tackle the larger musical forms, to write with the tough-minded energy associated with male composers, and to do both very well.

Figure 21 - Amy Marcy Cheney, known as Mrs. H.H.A. Beach, the first American woman to gain international fame as a composer. (Photograph courtesy of the George Grantham Bain Collection, Library of Congress.)

Her best-known works were her *Gaelic Symphony* based on Gaelic folk tunes and her *Piano Concerto*. She also wrote over 150 songs. Though she was regarded as "the finest woman-composer of her day," she had to endure the ridicule of some male colleagues who dismissed her conservative musical instincts and dubbed her "Mrs. Ha Ha Beach." Today critics have dropped the qualification. As a Beach revival is under way, Mrs. H.H.A. Beach has taken her rightful place alongside her male colleagues as a composer of consequence.

In the late nineteenth and early twentieth centuries, the New England classicists dominated the musical academies. Yet most of their music has been forgotten. Conductors and performers with a special interest in early American music occasionally revive their works, rediscovering particular pieces they find appealing. The composers of this era had generally followed John Dwight's model. They looked to Europe for approval, guidance, standards, and inspiration. Even when they composed music inspired by

American books, paintings, or places, their styles were essentially European, usually German. Many of these composers possessed fine technique and their works deserve new consideration today. But despite their considerable achievements in music and academia, John Knowles Paine, George W. Chadwick, and their various pupils and protégés would sadly be unrecognized by most American concert audiences today. Much of their music is certainly worthy of rediscovery.

THE MACDOWELL AFFAIR

Edward MacDowell was a composer who won the adulation of his countrymen. In the nineteenth century, he was universally recognized as the country's foremost composer. (One critic said his sonatas were better than those of any composer since Beethoven.) But In recent years, MacDowell has been regarded as a figure of music history not especially relevant to our time and place. MacDowell was born on December 18, 1861, in New York City, the son of a wealthy businessman who loved who loved music. Young Edward began piano lessons under the guidance of Juan Buitrago, a Colombian friend of his father's, and then he studied with a professional piano teacher, Paul Desvernine. He also had lessons from the celebrated Venezuelan concert pianist, Teresa Carreño. When he was fifteen, his mother took him to the Paris Conservatory. MacDowell, who wanted to be a concert pianist, was unhappy with the musical ideas and teaching methods in Paris. (One of his French classmates was a rebellious nonconformist named Claude Debussy.) MacDowell developed a dislike of French attitudes in music, which remained with him for a number of years.

Figure 22 - Edward MacDowell, America's most celebrated composer in the nineteenth century and his wife Marian. (Photo courtesy of The MacDowell Colony)

To get away from France, young MacDowell went to Stuttgart in Germany. Still searching for the ideal place to learn, he went next to Wiesbaden and then to Hoch's Conservatory in Frankfurt, where he became a pupil of pianist Karl Heyman. In Frankfort, MacDowell met composer Joachim Raff, the Conservatory's director, and the greatest influence on his musical life and career. MacDowell still considered himself in preparation for a career on the concert stage as a pianist. But he enrolled in one of Raff's composition classes, and when Raff challenged him to compose some "real music," not just exercises, MacDowell composed his *First Modern Suite* for piano.

Raff urged MacDowell to think about pursuing a career as a composer, and even sent the piano suite to Franz Liszt, who arranged for a public performance. Liszt became an enthusiastic supporter of MacDowell's and when MacDowell completed his *First Piano*

Concerto, Liszt recommended him to Brietkopf & Härtel, the famed German company that published not only his own works, but those of Bach, Handel, Haydn, Mozart, and Beethoven. MacDowell returned to America for a time, where he married one of his own pupils, Marian Nevins. He was prepared for a career as a struggling musician, but Marian used her inheritance to finance a return trip to Europe. The young couple divided their time between England and Germany, and eventually American musicians in Europe began visiting the rustic cottage in the woods near Wiesbaden when the MacDowells made their home.

In 1884 on a trip to London, the MacDowells attended a performance of *Much Ado About Nothing*, starring Henry Irving and Ellen Terry. MacDowell was inspired to write a tone poem about the play's leading characters, Beatrice and Benedick. But he abandoned the project and decided to incorporate the thematic material into his *Second Piano Concerto*, completed in Germany. In 1888, the MacDowells decided to follow the advice of their American admirers who urged them to return home. It would be hard to describe MacDowell's home as his native land at this point; he had left for Paris as a young American teenager seeking advance musical instruction; he returned after twelve years in Europe, absolutely committed to the ideal of German romanticism.

Not surprisingly, MacDowell decided to settle in Boston, home of the New England classicists, where the nucleus of German romantic composers could be found. MacDowell arrived with impeccable credentials, an established European reputation, the endorsements of Liszt and Raff, and performances of his piano music by his former teacher, the famed Venezuelan pianist, Teresa Carreño. On March 5, 1889, MacDowell appeared as soloist in New York City, playing his *Second Piano Concerto in D Minor*, under the baton of Theodore Thomas. He followed the New York premiere with a performance in Boston, and in the summer, with a triumphal appearance in France. Edward MacDowell was instantly established as America's foremost composer of serious concert music.

MacDowell remained in Boston for the next eight years, where he accepted private composition pupils and devoted himself to his own composing activities. He also wrote and spoke of his ideals in music, addressing himself to the controversial issues of the day. He particularly rejected the thesis advanced by the great Czech composer, Antonín Dvořák that Americans should consciously draw upon folklore and nationalist influences in their music. MacDowell, from the beginning, was a European at heart, in love with the forests, woods, and countryside described by the great European poets.

Even on the rare occasion when he drew upon an American source for inspiration, MacDowell was still under the influence of Germany. MacDowell asked one of his students, Henry F. B. Gilbert, to do research on the music of American Indians. MacDowell subsequently produced his *Indian Suite* for orchestra, incorporating themes of the Iroquois, Chippewa, Iowa, and Dakotans. MacDowell, however, was still true to his German tradition.

The source of MacDowell's "Indian themes" was a book Gilbert helped him rediscover, a German textbook on American Indian music, written by Theodore Baker.

In 1896, the trustees of Columbia University decided to establish a full professorship of music. The committee assigned the task of filling the position declared that Edward MacDowell was "the greatest musical genius America has produced." It was only logical that they offer the position to MacDowell, who accepted it with enthusiasm. He decided to develop a program to train composer-teachers and to develop instruction in music as an important element of the curriculum. MacDowell lectured on every musical subject imaginable, from the origins of Greek and Roman music to the influence of Asian scales. But MacDowell found the schedule exhausting and the bureaucracy and red tape of academic life frustrating. Many of his students lacked the drive and dedication he expected.

Seeking an escape from the pressures at Columbia, the MacDowells bought a farm at Peterborough, New Hampshire. Here, MacDowell could enjoy a serene surrounding. During this time, he composed some of his best-known pieces, including his *Woodland Sketches* for piano, which included *To a Wild Rose*. After two years, Columbia finally hired an assistant for MacDowell. But his troubles weren't over. While MacDowell was on sabbatical in Europe, Seth Low, the president of Columbia University, was replaced by Nicholas Murray Butler. Butler was a strong-willed man with ideas of his own regarding the role of music in a university. MacDowell's most fervent admirers knew him to have firm opinions on the teaching on music. It was inevitable that the two men would clash.

Problems began when Butler decided to reorganize the teaching of fine arts at Columbia while MacDowell was still on sabbatical. MacDowell had plans for a department of fine arts which would include not only music, but literature and the visual arts. Butler refused to implement MacDowell's plan, and MacDowell decided to resign in early 1904. A pair of student reporters asked MacDowell why he chose to leave Columbia. He told them.

When his remarks were reprinted by the New York newspapers, a public furor ensued. President Butler tried to explain MacDowell's departure by telling the press that the composer merely wanted to devote more time to his own work. MacDowell responded by insisting that he was leaving Columbia because the department under Butler, was to be turned into a "coeducational department store" emphasizing materialism over idealism. The whole episode became known as "The MacDowell Affair." While it may seem like a teapot tempest in the wake of today's politically charged atmosphere on college campuses, at the time it provoked a storm of controversy in musical and academic circles. Arguments over the direction of college music departments did not end with MacDowell's resignation. They continue today. As for the aftermath of the controversy, it is best to simply observe that the chair which MacDowell occupied at Columbia is today named after him.

MacDowell saw music as different from painting, which he regarded as far more literal. Music, he said, could express man's dreams through an intangible language he called "soul-language." He was not excited by the music of the baroque, with many voices moving in counterpoint and creating "complex polyphony." MacDowell wanted to use tones to express his dreams, the legends and ideals of poetry that inspired him in Europe. He wrote four piano sonatas: first, *Sonata Tragica,* inspired by the death of his teacher, Joachim Raff; the second, *Sonata Eroica*, also in G minor, influenced by the story of King Arthur; the third, *Norse,* based on Norse legends; the fourth, *Celtic*, a musical interpretation of Irish folklore. He also completed over forty songs for voice and piano, and often wrote the poetry for his own songs. His symphonic tone poems included *Hamlet and Ophelia, Lancelot and Elaine, Lamia, The Saracens*, and *Lovely Alda*. MacDowell could be sentimental, dramatic, and energetic.

Shortly after he resigned from Columbia, MacDowell was stricken by a fatal illness. His wife cared for him devotedly and he died on January 23, 1908. He was buried at Peterborough, where his wife established a colony for creative artists. Mrs. MacDowell personally supervised the summer colony until her death in 1958. Dozens of composers and writers have worked at the MacDowell Colony, producing numerous musical and literary works throughout the twentieth century, preserving his memory as a great teacher and sponsor of the arts. Edward MacDowell was the last composer of great stature to follow in the historic tradition of the gentleman musician. His legacy was the fine music he composed, and the standards of musical idealism to which many subsequent generations of composers and teachers aspired.

THE INDIVIDUALISTS

Figure 23 - Charles Martin Loeffler, an American who was at heart a French composer. (Portrait by John Singer Sargent - Public domain)

Not all composers conformed to the formula of the Boston classicists. After studying with John Knowles Paine, John Alden Carpenter went to London and Rome to study with the great Edward Elgar, the composer of *Pomp and Circumstance*. Carpenter returned to his native Illinois and decided to work for his father's shipping supply company. He served as vice-president of the family enterprise until 1936 and then devoted himself to composing. Carpenter was often described as an American "impressionist." He drew upon French influences and chose occasionally to absorb the rhythms of American jazz. He composed several ballets, one inspired by the great skyscrapers that were being built in American cities and even one by the *Krazy Kat* comic strip. His other works included a suite called *Adventures in a Perambulator* and *The Song of Faith* for the George Washington Bicentennial.

Charles Martin Loeffler, born in 1861, was an Alsatian violinist, a pupil of Joseph Joachim. After spending time in Russia and settling in Paris, he came to the United States. He settled in Boston where he became a favorite of Isabella Stewart Gardner, the city's most powerful patroness of the arts. Also in Mrs. Gardner's circle was Col. Henry Lee Higginson, founder of the Boston Symphony. Loeffler joined the Boston Symphony as first violinist in 1881, becoming the second concertmaster of the orchestra. He remained with the orchestra for 22 seasons.

In 1903, he retired to a farm in Medfield, Massachusetts, where he devoted himself entirely to composition. The Boston Symphony often introduced other works of Loeffler's, usually inspired by European poets ranging from Roman classicists like Virgil to the Belgian contemporary Maurice Maeterlinck. Loeffler is identified with the Boston Group because he was an important part of Boston's musical life during these years. Although an American citizen, Loeffler remained at heart a French composer. His greatest inspirations were the result of his efforts to recreate past memories and former times. His major works included an orchestral piece, *A Pagan Poem*, *Canticum Fratris Solis*, a work for voice and chamber orchestra based on St. Francis's *Canticle of the Sun*, and *Evocation*, for voice, women's chorus, and orchestra. Loeffler anticipated future generations of European composers who would settle in the United States, but remain true to their European musical origins.

Charles Tomlinson Griffes was a nonconformist. Born in 1884 in Elmira, New York, Griffes was a child prodigy on the piano, trained by Mary Selena Broughton, a thorough and blunt New Zealander who supervised his musical education, the books he read, the clothes he wore, and offered financial support enabling young Charles to go to Germany to study. Griffes enrolled in the Stern Conservatory. From the beginning, Griffes wasn't the typical student. As an American studying in Berlin, he submitted as his first composition, a song based on a text in French. His teacher promptly tore up the manuscript. Griffes eventually turned away from the conservatory for private instruction from Engelbert Humperdinck, the noted composer of *Hansel and Gretel*.

Figure 24 - Charles Tomlinson Griffes. He was a composer and a painter who was fascinated by the relationship of color and music, photography, and the culture of India and Japan. (Public Domain)

Griffes was a man of many talents. He was a gifted painter with a talent for etchings, watercolors, and drawings. He was fascinated by photography and the ideas of color, especially as it related to sound. When he returned to the United States, he abandoned the German style cultivated in Berlin and began experimenting with musical devices associated with the impressionist painters in Europe. These painters presented their momentary impression of a scene rather than depicting it literally. Griffes tried his hand using repeated note patterns (ostinatos), and chords that moved constantly in the same direction, practices forbidden by German classicists but explored extensively in France by Claude Debussy. Instead of confining himself to the scales practiced by most pianists, Griffes began following the lead of the controversial Debussy and using what were considered exotic "whole-tone scales."

Throughout his career, Griffes was a musical explorer, investigating colorful sounds from exotic locations around the world. Griffes's most famous works were a piano piece, *The White Peacock*, which he later orchestrated, and *The Pleasure Dome of Kubla Kahn*, a work for orchestra reflecting his interest in the music of Asia. Through Adolf Bolm, a dancer, he met Michito Ito, a Japanese pantomimist who introduced him to Japanese poetry. Griffes was fascinated by exotic sounds: he composed a dissonant piano sonata inspired by the complex harmonic colors of Russia's most daring composer, Alexander Scriabin. He also produced a work for string quartet based on Indian themes.

Griffes died tragically when he was only 35, in the spring of 1920. He left a legacy of interesting music and although his name is not widely known today, his works retain a host of admirers who still regard his music as a unique contribution to America's musical heritage. Griffes's interest in American Indian music was shared by his friend Arthur Farwell. It was Farwell who addressed himself to a major controversy in American music, the question of nationalism. Oddly enough, Farwell's uncompromising nationalism was inspired by an unlikely source: the Czech composer Antonín Dvořák.

Figure 25 - Antonín Dvořák, who was the most famous Czech composer, came to America to teach in New York and Iowa. (Public Domain)

Antonín Dvořák was born in 1841 in a Bohemian village near Prague. He was renowned throughout Europe, where one of his mentors was no less than Johannes Brahms. In 1892, he was invited to become director of the National Conservatory of Music in New York. He stayed in the United States for three years. His pupils included a number of noted composers, including William Arms Fisher, Harvey Worthington Loomis, Rubin Goldmark, and Henry Thacker Burleigh.

During his time in the United States, Dvořák was exposed to a good deal of Native American music. Burleigh, an African American, introduced Dvořák to Negro spirituals. After hearing Burleigh sing, Dvořák decided to absorb the musical spirit of these tunes. For a time, Dvořák lived in Spillville, Iowa, wrote a *Cantata to the American Flag*, and even considered writing a new "National Anthem for the United States." Dvořák's most famous composition was his symphony, *From the New World*, which incorporated elements of the spiritual "Swing Low, Sweet Chario*t*" in its score. The symphony, of course, wasn't American. It couldn't have been more Czech in style, tone, or spirit. Still, it indicated that a world-renowned composer took America's own music seriously, and felt it worthy to be used as the basis for his own musical inspiration.

One of Dvořák's most gifted pupils was Rubin Goldmark. Rubin Goldmark was the nephew of prominent Hungarian composer Karl Goldmark and steeped in traditions of nineteenth century Vienna. Goldmark drew upon American themes for inspiration, but his style was clearly that of a European. His works included a *Requiem* based on *The Gettysburg Address* and a *Negro Rhapsody*. To the chagrin of his pupils at the Juilliard School of Music, he remained a staunch musical conservative, but proved an outstanding teacher of such pupils as George Gershwin, Aaron Copland, Alfred Newman, and important teachers such as Philip James and Frederick Jacobi.

In 1893, when Dvořák's *From the New World* first appeared, Arthur Farwell was in an unlikely place for a musician. A native of St. Paul, Minnesota, Farwell was in the process of graduating from the Massachusetts Institute of Technology with an engineering degree. When he heard Dvořák's symphony in Boston, he decided that music was really his first love. He went to Germany to study with Engelbert Humperdinck, but also decided to take lessons from Alexander Guilmant, a renowned French organist in Paris. Farwell returned to the United States, joined the faculty at Cornell, and began acquainting himself with American Indian music.

Figure 26 - Arthur Farwell, a composer, teacher, publisher, and advocate of spirituals, folk tunes, cowboy songs, and the music of Native American tribes. (Photo by the Mojonier Studio, Hollywood, CA, 1921. Courtesy of the Arthur Farwell Collection, Sibley Music Library)

In 1901, Farwell launched the Wa-Wan Press. Publishers had rejected his Indian melodies, so he decided to publish them himself. Farwell borrowed some money, approached a local printer, and decided to publish two music books each quarter. To pay his lithographic and engraving bills, Farwell, began a career as a lecturer. He traveled from coast to coast, performing his own compositions based on themes derived from Native American tribes and proclaiming himself a champion of American folk music. Farwell became especially interested in the history and folklore of the southwest, and began a collection of folk songs originating in California during the state's Spanish and Mexican years.

In 1909, Farwell returned to New York where he joined the staff of *Musical America*, a publication devoted to concert music in the United States and the following year, he became Supervisor of Municipal Music in New York. The Wa-Wan Press continued for eleven years, publishing a wide variety of music by Farwell, his friend Edgar Stillman Kelley, and colleagues Arthur Shepherd and Henry Franklin Belknap Gilbert. The Press provided a forum for a group of young American composers who were breaking with academic tradition. The formal musical establishment in Boston ignored these upstarts, but the Wa-Wan Press published numerous collections of Negro spirituals, folksongs, cowboy melodies, traditional Native American music, and tunes from Spanish California. At the time, few formally trained musicians were aware of the real worth of these pieces.

Farwell remained a prolific composer. His works included a concerto for two pianos, *Mountain Vision*, inspired by his visit to the New Hampshire mountains, the *Rudolph Gott Symphony* (incorporating themes by his friend, Rudolph Gott), songs, chamber music, and orchestral pieces.

In 1921, Farwell provided the music for *The Pilgrimage Play*, depicting the life of Christ and presented in Hollywood at the outdoor Pilgrimage Theater. Farwell continued teaching in New York, California, and for twelve years, in East Lansing, Michigan, where he established his own music publishing company, printing and distributing his own music, even designing the covers for each work. Farwell wrote the music for a number of musical pageants and remained an important force in American musical life until his death in 1952. Unfortunately, Farwell's music was not recorded during his lifetime. An important part of his legacy was carried on by his best-known pupil, Roy Harris, an unabashed westerner who became America's most distinguished composer of symphonies.

Wa-Wan Press introduced new music by Farwell's colleagues Arthur Shepherd and Henry F.B. Gilbert. Shepherd, a native of Paris, Idaho, was sent by his English parents to the New England Conservatory where he studied with Percy Goetschius and George Chadwick. But he rejected the classical German training to explore the music of the French impressionists and began experimenting with the sounds of Celtic folk music. Each movement of his first symphony had a western title: *Westward*, *The Lone Prairie*, *The Old Chisholm Trail*, and *Canyons*. Shepherd also produced a *Fantasy on Down East Spirituals*, a violin concerto, chamber music, and orchestral pieces, and managed to find time to teach in Utah, New England, and eventually Cleveland where he was an important musical influence for many years.

As a boy, Henry Franklin Belknap Gilbert was so impressed by the Norwegian violin virtuoso, Ole Bull, that he built his own violin out of a cigar box. Gilbert was honored to be Edward MacDowell's first American pupil, but he struggled to support himself as a musician. Gilbert played the violin in dance orchestras, sold real estate, worked in a factory, grew silkworms, and even cut pies in a Chicago restaurant during the 1893 World's Fair. He went to Europe on a cattle boat to hear the premiere of Gustave Charpentier's opera, *Louisa*. He eventually met Arthur Farwell, with whom he shared an enthusiasm for folklore.

Gilbert's career had its frustrations. He devoted himself to writing an opera on the *Uncle Remus Tales* of Joel Chandler Harris, then discovered that the copyright had been awarded to someone else. He adapted the material of the opera into a *Comedy Overture on Negro Themes*. Gilbert was fascinated by the music of African Americans, folk themes from American Indian tribes, and Celtic melodies. In 1909, he completed his *Fish Wharf Rhapsody*, incorporating his attempt to depict literal sounds through music. Gilbert's most famous piece was the tone poem, *The Dance in Place Congo*, inspired by African

American and Creole dances in New Orleans. The work was premiered as a ballet pantomime at the Metropolitan Opera.

Charles Wakefield Cadman is best remembered for his song, *The Land of the Sky Blue Water*, but he also wrote two operas, *Shanewis* and *The Sunset Trail*. *Shanewis*, based on musical ideas from the Osage, Cheyenne, and Omaha tribes, was the first American opera to be performed for two seasons at the Metropolitan. (Its premiere occurred on the same day as Gilbert's *Dance in Place Congo*.) He also composed a suite, *Thunderbird*, inspired by Blackfoot Indian dances. Cadman was active in his native Pennsylvania as a music critic for years in Pittsburgh, but he eventually settled in Los Angeles, where he composed a *Hollywood Suite* with four musical portraits of Charles Chaplin, Mary Pickford, his mother, and the Hollywood Bowl. He remained a musical conservative until his death in 1946.

John Powell, born in 1882, was a brilliant pianist, a Virginian trained in Vienna under the world's most famous piano teacher, Theodor Leschetizky. Powell was one of the few Southerners to draw upon his background in writing music for the concert stage. He introduced his own *Negro Rhapsody* for piano and orchestra, and composed a *Sonata Virginianesque* for Violin and Piano, an overture, *In Old Virginia*, and a tone poem, *Natchez on the Hill*. Farwell, his colleagues, and successors, were all American composers searching for a national identity. Their experiments in using folk tunes, spirituals, and melodies from the cultures of African Americans, Hispanics, and various American Indian tribes proved that music indigenous to the American continent could become the basis for a whole new approach to creating symphonies, operas, ballets, and chamber music. They were dedicated composers whose explorations of the roots of American music would inspire subsequent generations to go further in establishing a truly American presence in the composition of concert music.

THE BANDMASTERS

Figure 27 - Louis Antoine Jullien, the flamboyant French conductor who pursued stardom by often conducting while facing the audience with a jewelled baton. (Caricature by Benjamin Roubaud, public domain)

While composers of serious concert music searched for audiences and for their own national identity, another group of musicians was making a real impact on crowds that gave them standing ovations. These were the nineteenth century bandmasters. One such bandmaster would emerge as the composer who captured the American spirit as no one else had succeeded in doing before or since.

In the early years of the nineteenth century, parts of America were devoid of true musical culture. By the end of the nineteenth century, legendary bands were not only appearing in parades, they had marched straight into the concert hall with a repertoire of decidedly American music. How did this happen?

In 1837, William Robyn, a young German, arrived in St. Louis hoping to support himself by teaching local citizens the numerous musical instruments he played. He found only four other musicians in the whole city, each of whom had to work at another trade (including barbering) in order to make a living. Robyn wrote in astonishment for a local band, consisting of a clarinet, a violin, and a bass drum playing the Christmas carol, "Adeste Fideles," as the sole music at a funeral. Robyn joined the faculty of St. Louis University where he taught at least twelve instruments, founded the school's Philharmonic Band and the St. Louis Brass Band, and eventually started an Oratorio Society.

Audiences of the day looked for quantity of sound as much as quality. Then, as now, showmanship could frequently trump artistry. In 1853, Louis-Antoine Jullien, a flamboyant conductor from France, arrived on American shores. Audiences had never seen anything like Jullien. His most famous (or infamous) orchestral performance presented *The Fireman's Quadrille*, a work in which in which a "fire" appeared to start on stage. To ringing fire bells, a group of uniformed firemen would hurry on-stage and douse the "fire" using real water from authentic fire hoses, all while the orchestra played furiously.

Jullien used a jeweled baton and donned a pair of gloves before he conducted Beethoven's music; an aide would deliver his gloves on a gold platter. On occasion, Jullien would whip out a violin or flute and suddenly begin playing along with the orchestra. He often conducted facing the audience instead of the orchestra, collapsing with exhaustion into a throne placed on stage for that purpose.

One of Jullien's less dramatic contributions to American music was the inspiration his success provided to a brash, enthusiastic Irish-American musician, Patrick Sarsfield Gilmore. Born in County Galway, Ireland in 1828, Gilmore settled first in Boston, where at only age twenty-three, he became bandmaster of the Boston Brigade Brass Band and also the Salem Band. When Gilmore led the Salem Band in the Inaugural parade honoring incoming President James Buchanan, *The Washington Post* reported approvingly that Gilmore's musicians were not only good, they were sober.

When Gilmore planned a concert in the Boston city limits with his Salem Band, the local musicians were furious that he was encroaching on their territory. A number of hotheaded brass players assembled with plans to meet Gilmore's train, smash his band's instruments, and use their fists to see that Gilmore's band would have

Figure 28 - Patrick Sarsfield Gilmore, the bandleader whose huge festivals featured 1000 instrumentalists and 20,000 singers. (Photo courtesy of George Grantham Bain Collection, Library of Congress)

swollen lips in the morning. Gilmore, however, was prepared. He hired a group of tough sailors and rough characters he found on the Salem waterfront. He arranged for these young toughs to follow behind the band as they marched into Boston. When the rival musicians launched their attack, Gilmore blew a whistle, and his army of waterfront brawlers appeared with brass knuckles, blackjacks, and belaying pins. The Boston bandsmen were so taken by surprise that they could do nothing but turn around and run as fast as their legs could carry them. While Gilmore's band acquitted itself as usual with a sober form of behavior to match their musicianship, his "waterfront plug uglies" celebrated with one of Boston's less glorious drinking sprees.

Gilmore observed Jullien's success in generating publicity and he determined to follow in his footsteps. In 1856, he promoted a musical competition. Gilmore, an accomplished cornet virtuoso, challenged Edward "Ned" Kendall, a celebrated master of the keyed bugle, to a musical duel. Kendall was called the "Paul Bunyan of New England." Both musicians took turns playing *The Wood Up Quickstep*, a relatively basic piece for the cornet, but requiring the technique of a dazzling virtuoso on the keyed bugle. Gilmore accelerated the tempo each time until establishing his superiority, then graciously sat down with the rest of the ensemble and allowed Kendall to conduct his band.

When Gilmore became director of the Boston Brigade Band, he gave annual concerts on the Boston Common. When he played a concert for the Boston Light Infantry battalion, he discovered an old camp meeting song, "Say Brother, Will You Meet With Us?" Gilmore copied the melody and had it arranged for his band. This was the beginning of a famous tune, "John Brown's Body." A few months later, Julia Ward Howe witnessed an army review disrupted by an enemy attack. She was inspired to write new words to the melody, including a chorus, "Glory, Glory Hallelujah." As Americans struggled with the controversy over abolition of slavery, "The Battle Hymn of the Republic" was born.

In appreciation for his support of the Union cause, a Union general sent Gilmore a silver goblet filled with gold coins. In a burst of enthusiasm, Gilmore wrote a tune with original words describing his feelings about the returning Civil War veterans. He published it under a pseudonym, "Louis Lambert." His song, "When Johnny Comes Marching Home," became one of the most memorable pieces of music to emerge from this era.

After the war, Patrick S. Gilmore began exerting an influence over the size of bands. He began promoting huge ensembles combining multiple bands and choruses. For an inauguration of the new Governor of Louisiana, he assembled a massive band with 500 musicians and a chorus of 5,000 children waving American flags. At the conclusion of the concert as the band played "Hail, Columbia," Gilmore lunged forward and pressed a button on the podium. Thirty-six cannons began firing on cue, booming in synchronization with the ensemble. As the cannons roared, the church bells of New Orleans began ringing. Those who heard this mammoth concert in Lafayette Square said it was a sound they would remember all their lives.

In 1867, Gilmore launched a new project, his "National Peace Jubilee and Great Music Festival." It took Gilmore over 750 pages to outline his concept. He wanted to build a coliseum big enough to seat fifty thousand people and present a musical festival before the President, Congress, and the Supreme Court. When he failed to gain support in New York, he took the idea to Boston. He won support from key figures in Boston's musical world. Eben Tourjée, director of the newly founded New England Conservatory of Music agreed to assemble a mammoth chorus. Julius Eichberg, a Swiss violinist and musical director of both the rival Boston Conservatory and the Boston Public Schools, agreed to provide a children's chorus of 20,000 voices. Carl Zerrahn, a prominent conductor, agreed to organize a 1,000- piece orchestra.

Gilmore also pursued financing for the project. John S. Dwight, ever the musical conservative, had no more use for Gilmore than he had for Gottschalk or Jullien. For once, Gilmore's Irish charm failed him. Dwight wanted nothing to do with the venture. But Gilmore obtained help on his own from music publisher Oliver Ditson, piano manufacturer Henry Mason, and finally Boston's wealthiest financier, Eben Jordan. Gilmore managed to mount a 939-piece orchestra (which he advertised as having 1000 players) and commissioned the Hook Brothers, who had built the largest concert organ in the nation, to build "the biggest concert organ ever built" for the Jubilee.

On June 15, 1868, the National Peace Jubilee opened in a huge wooden coliseum. The giant chorus sang "A Mighty Fortress Is Our God." A 600- piece ensemble performed Wagner's *Overture to Tannhauser* and Gilmore himself directed a performance of the *Anvil Chorus* from Verdi's *Il Trovatore*. Wielding a six-foot baton, he signaled the entrance of 100 uniformed firemen each carrying a hammer. He punched buttons that fired cannons outside the complex. To everyone's surprise, the Jubilee produced a $7,000 profit. Most Bostonians were delighted with the result, with the possible exception of John S. Dwight, who left town on the morning the festival started.

Four years later, Gilmore promoted the "World Peace Jubilee," an even bigger festival celebrating the end of the Franco-Prussian War, with 2000 instrumentalists, a chorus of 20,000 voices, and an auditorium seating 100,000 people. The highlight of the Jubilee, however, was a visit by the "Waltz King," Johann Strauss, Jr. and his fifty-six player orchestra from Vienna. The Viennese waltz captivated Americans in exactly the same way its lilting strains had captivated Europeans. Hostilities did not break out, as predicted, between the French and German musicians; even a touch of humor was added when one the of the giant choruses lost its place while singing Handel's "All We, Like Sheep, Have Gone Astray."

Gilmore became band director of the 22nd Regiment of New York, soon renamed "Gilmore's Band." Gilmore took his band on tour as far west as San Francisco. Although San Franciscans thought of themselves as highly cultured, they could be boisterous. When French piano virtuoso, Henri Herz played in San Francisco, he had to give his recital on a six octave saloon piano with half the notes missing. Gold miners paid for the tickets in gold dust, weighted by the ticket seller who had scales at the door.

Gilmore generated publicity by promoting a feud between rival cornet virtuosos Matthew Arbuckle and Jules Levy. Arbuckle was known for his singing tone and lyrical ballads written in his native Scotland. Levy specialized in pyrotechnics and could play notes faster than any other soloist alive. He liked to boast of his own prowess. When a friend asked if he would like to be President of the United States, Levy announced that becoming President would be a step down for him. Gilmore decided to promote a musical duel between the two musicians at Madison Square Garden. But when Gilmore broke up a fistfight between the two rivals, he accidentally tore some medals off Levy's chest and the furious Levy demanded a duel with Gilmore using pistols. Friends persuaded the two to settle the matter at a shooting gallery. Gilmore proved the better shot, and Levy had to buy Gilmore and his friends a sumptuous dinner at Delmonico's Restaurant. Gilmore had rivals, like the Italian bandleader Carlo Cappa, but when he died in 1892, he was the supreme bandmaster in America.

When the Gilmore Band performed in Philadelphia, it took turns performing with Offenbach's Orchestra. A young violinist with the orchestra spent considerable time away from the string section, listening to the sound of the concert band. He made up his mind that someday, he too would leave his mark on the world of bands. No one imagined that the young man would one day surpass Gilmore. Few would have believed that by the twentieth century, Gilmore's name would be unknown to many Americans. Yet within a few years, the young violinist playing in Offenbach's Orchestra would emerge as the American bandmaster universally recognized as "The March King" for all time. His name was John Philip Sousa.

Figure 29 - John Philip Sousa. He composed *Semper Fidelis* and America's national march, *The Stars and Stripes Forever,* and is known for all time as "The March King." (Portrait courtesy of United States Marine Corps)

There was considerable speculation regarding Sousa's nationality. A publicity campaign launched a widespread rumor that an immigrant ancestor of Sousa's had been eager to display his patriotism and added the letters U.S.A. to his name. The story is appealing but untrue. Sousa's father was Portuguese. Antonio Sousa was born in Spain, was a resident of England, and finally, became an immigrant to the United States. Sousa's press agent thought it good publicity to spread the tale that Sousa's ancestry could be traced to whatever country he was visiting at the moment. Sousa did nothing to discourage the rumors until years later.

Sousa's trademark in music was precision. He insisted upon a militantly steady beat, coupled with intense discipline of his players. Since he was widely regarded as even-tempered and fair, he often assumed a schoolmaster's attitude. He demanded constant repetition from his players until each member of the band phrased passages in an identical way. The result was a concert band of incredibly precise techniques. The first musical institution to taste Sousa's brand of discipline was the United State Marine Band.

From 1880 to 1892, John Philip Sousa devoted himself to the Marine Corps. Since the players were all older than the twenty-eight-year-old Sousa, he decided to grow a full black beard to make himself appear older. He retained the beard for nearly forty years. In 1888, Sousa wrote the march, *Semper Fidelis*, the official march of the Marines and the only official piece of music to be thus recognized by the U.S. Government. The following year, *The Washington Post* sponsored an essay contest. As part of the promotion, Sousa produced his *Washington Post March*, one of his most popular pieces. It was used for a popular new social dance, the two-step, and officially selected by an association of dance instructors. Sousa did not confine himself to marches. He also composed operettas, including *The Smugglers, Désirée, El Capitan, The Bride Elect,* and *The Charlatans*.

During Sousa's time as director of the U.S. Marine band, he led the ensemble at all state functions given by the President of the United States at the White House. He came into regular personal contact with Presidents Rutherford B. Hayes, James A. Garfield, Chester A. Arthur, Grover Cleveland, and Benjamin Harrison. In his book, *Experiences of a Bandmaster*, Sousa said of the various presidents that he served, "They were all very appreciative of music, and in this respect were quite unlike General Grant, of whom it is said that he knew only two tunes, one of which was "Yankee Doodle" and the other wasn't!" Although Sousa had a reputation for being a stern taskmaster, he did have a sense of humor. President Grover Cleveland got married while in the White House and the Marine Band provided music at his wedding. When Cleveland learned that Sousa planned for the band to play *The Student of Love* from one of his own operas, he told his aide, "Tell Sousa he can play the quartet, but he had better omit the name of it."

David Blakely was the manager of Gilmore's Band. When Gilmore died in 1892, Blakely made Sousa an offer of a salary of $6,000 per year and twenty percent of the profits if he would organize a private band. Sousa could not refuse the offer. He left the Marine Corps, personally auditioned every musician for the ensemble, and planned to organize a concert band, which would become universally recognized as the finest in the world. Among the musicians who appeared at the auditions was a young trombone soloist, Arthur Pryor. Sousa was so impressed with the young man that he made him his assistant. Pryor remained with Sousa for some years and finally left to form his own band.

Many of Gilmore's best members were quick to join Sousa. His title as "March King" did not come from his musicians or even from American critics. An obscure English journal devoted to brass bands said that John Philip Sousa was entitled to the mantle of "March King" as much as Johann Strauss, Jr. was entitled to be called "The Waltz King." That was all Sousa's American publishers needed to hear. Within a few hours, the title,

Figure 30 - *The Stars and Stripes Forever.* An early sheet music version of the most popular march ever written. (Public Domain)

"March King," was placed under Sousa's name on publicity posters. It was a title few around the world would dispute before very long.

Shortly after an exhausting tour, Sousa retired to Europe for a rest. While in Italy, he received the sad news of David Blakely's death. He boarded the S.S. Teutonic and set sail for New York. While pacing up and down on the deck, Sousa began hearing a melody in his head. He could not forget the melody. When the ship sailed into New York Harbor, he saw the American flag waving in the breeze. Sousa went to his office and began putting the melody on paper. He did not change a note, and sent it off to his publisher. Wisely, the publisher was quick to print it. The march was *The Stars and Stripes Forever*, the most popular and most stirring march ever composed by an American.

Sousa was characteristically modest about his achievement. He believed that most composers were influenced by a higher power and that they merely transmitted their inspiration to an earthly audience. Although Sousa's name is universally identified with marches and parades, his own band seldom marched. Sousa thought of his ensemble as a concert band, and his wind and brass players preferred to play sitting down. Sousa's dominance of the band world became clear when Herbert L. Clarke, Gilmore's last cornet soloist, decided to join Sousa permanently. He remained with Sousa for twenty years.

Sousa took his band on world tours. In France, he criticized the local habit of using string basses in concert bands, insisting that only wind instruments, not strings, belong in a band. An American journalist attacked Sousa for criticizing the French. Sousa responded by suggesting that the critic knew nothing about any bands, French or American. Sousa had strong ideas about the instrumentation of a band. In the early years of the twentieth century, local bandmasters used whatever instruments were available. (John S. Dwight declared that "all brass bands sound alike.") Patrick Gilmore began adding large numbers of woodwinds to his ensembles. By the end of his career, his band was two-thirds woodwinds. Sousa wanted an ensemble that would sound best in the concert hall. By 1898, his band included two woodwind players for every brass player. Sousa sought precision and the sound of the band as a single instrument. His instrumentation is considered standard for many school bands today.

Nothing could stop Sousa or even slow him down. He kept his band playing in concerts while on tour in Texas, when a swarm of black beetles hatched on stage, when hundreds of hats belonging to a vaudeville troupe fell from the rafters onto his musicians, and in Wales when the platform on which the players were seated collapsed. Sousa picked himself up off the floor and started the concert all over again.

In 1917, at the age of sixty-three, Sousa enlisted in the United States Navy. He disappeared from a box in the theater where he and his wife were attending a play. He returned without the beard he had worn for so many years. During this period, he also composed the score for *Land of Liberty*, a presentation included in a theatrical show, *Cheer Up*, celebrating the role of immigrants from numerous countries around the world who had contributed to the American way of life. Before he left the Navy, he managed to train nearly 3,000 musicians. By 1925, when trombonist Marv Lyons retired from the band, Sousa himself was the only member of his ensemble who had been associated with the original band.

Figure 31 - Victor Herbert, Irving Berlin, and John Philip Sousa, three of America's most renowned composers, joined forces on behalf of ASCAP in Washington, D.C. (Photo courtesy of George Grantham Bain Collection, Library of Congress)

Though Sousa could be willful and disciplined, there was one battle that he was destined to lose. For years, Sousa saw the development of recording equipment as the enemy of all live musicians. He refused offers to record his band and spoke up enthusiastically in favor of live music. Writing in *Appleton's* magazine, he said, "Canned music is as incongruous by a campfire as canned salmon by a trout stream." Sousa crusaded against recorded music for seventeen years. Dr. James Francis Cooke, editor of the famous music publication, *The Etude*, decided to introduce Sousa to the man most responsible for recording devices, Thomas Alva Edison. Edison made a few critical remarks about Mozart, Sousa disagreed, and the two quickly got into an argument about recorded music. The meeting between the two great historical figures ended in a chilly atmosphere.

Sousa took his responsibilities to his colleagues seriously; he became one of the founding members of the American Society of Composers, Authors, and Publishers, also known as ASCAP. The organization was the principal advocate for the rights of composers and lyricists to be paid when their music was performed

Sousa was best remembered by his men as a dignified bandmaster. But on one occasion he had to deal with a crisis beyond his expectations. In the 1920s, Sousa decided to appear as Santa Claus for the Salvation Army. Half- way across the stage, he lost his pants and found himself standing in long white underwear. Instead of pulling his pants up, Sousa merely called for help, and a colleague had to rush out and help him. Sousa never retired. When he died in March of 1932, he was in the midst of a busy schedule touring as a bandmaster and conductor. He once said, "Sincere composers believe in God. Anybody can write music of a sort. But touching the public heart is quite another thing."

In 1952, two decades after Sousa's death, twentieth Fox released a film about the life of the March King. The film was titled, not surprisingly, *The Stars and Stripes Forever*, and was loosely based on Sousa's own memoir, *Marching Along.* It starred Clifton Webb as John Philip Sousa. As often happens in Hollywood biographies, much of the plot of the film was fictional, with considerable screen time devoted to a romance between an imaginary protégé of Sousa's, portrayed by Robert Wagner and a singer played by Debra Paget. But in the final scene, the film presented the U.S. Marine Band marching in a contemporary setting and then superimposed over the scene the image of Sousa marching along into the sunset.

The film was incredibly popular; Webb was told by his friend, the eminent pianist Artur Rubinstein, that Sousa was still the best-known American composer throughout Europe. The message of the final scene was that every time a band marches anywhere in the United States, especially a military band, we are in certain ways celebrating and remembering the spirit of John Philip Sousa. His marches will undoubtedly continue to reflect the American spirit in the twenty-first century as they have since they were originally set to paper.

THE MAESTROS AND THEIR MENTORS

On March 30, 1881, Boston newspapers published a plan by philanthropist Henry Lee Higginson announcing his plan for a Boston Symphony Orchestra, a permanent ensemble that would be the equal of the best European orchestras. Higginson, who enjoyed a successful business career, had been developing his ideas regarding the Boston Symphony for twenty-five years. Higginson wanted to keep prices low so that he could gradually attract what he termed "A larger and less-educated class of society." Higginson subsidized the orchestra and served as its sole benefactor. His first musical director was George Henschel, followed by Wilhelm Gericke, Arthur Nikisch, and Emil Paur.

In 1906, Karl Muck became Musical Director for the first of his two terms, separated by four years when his colleague Max Fiedler was conductor. During World War I, Muck found himself in the center of a major political controversy. Muck was a greatly admired conductor known for thorough musicianship and minimal gestures. He was an intense man, a chain-smoker, and blunt in his self-expression. It was said that a violinist told him he had a pain in his arm and Muck allegedly snapped, "Cut if off." When the famed Polish pianist Paderewski was late

Figure 32 - In 1881, Henry Lee Higginson, a New England philanthropist, founded and subsidized the Boston Symphony. (Portrait by John Singer Sargent, Public Domain)

emerging from his dressing room, Muck said, "Tell the King of Poland I am waiting for him." Muck specialized in a German repertoire and although a Swiss citizen, had a personal relationship with Kaiser Wilhelm II of Germany. When the New York Philharmonic began opening its concerts with "The Star Spangled Banner," audiences were quick to notice the absence of the anthem at concerts of the Boston Symphony In fact, Muck never objected to playing "The Star Spangled Banner."

Higginson and Charles Ellis, the orchestra's manager, didn't want to embarrass Muck and felt the flames of controversy were being fanned by an outspoken newspaper publisher, John R. Rathom, in *The Providence Journal*. But Muck was widely criticized by everyone from Theodore Roosevelt to his musical rival Walter Damrosch. His brusque personality and identification with Germany didn't help. Rumors began suggesting that mysterious lights seen in the windows of Muck's home were secret signals to German U-Boats lurking off the New England coast. On Nov.2, 1917, Muck finally led the a performance of "The Star Spangled Banner," but when conducted it in New York, critics complained about the arrangement of the melody, not realizing that it had been arranged by Broadway's most celebrated composer, Victor Herbert. Eventually he was confined to an internment camp in Georgia and finally expelled from the country. He was succeeded by a French conductor in Boston, Henri Ribaud.

Figure 33 - Karl Muck, the German conductor who has the misfortune to be conductor of the Boston Symphony and a friend of Kaiser Wilhelm II when the United States went to war against Germany. (Caricature by Arthur George Witherby, known as "wag" and published in *Vanity Fair* 1899- Public Domain)

Figure 34 - Pierre Monteux, "Le Maître," returns to conduct the Boston Symphony with soloist Leonid Kogan and concertmaster Richard Burgin. This French maestro and teacher was the mentor to numerous prominent American conductors. (Courtesy of the Ruth Posselt-Richard Burgin Family Archives)

Pierre Monteux, the noted French conductor, teacher and superb baton technician, led the Boston Symphony from 1919-1924. Monteux took over the orchestra at a critical time. After Henry Lee Higginson had died, the orchestra was faced with a series of controversies over the dismissal of German musicians and with disagreements over unionization.

Figure 35 - Roland Hayes, the first black soloist with the Boston Symphony Orchestra, triumphed over prejudice on two continents. (Photograph courtesy of Carl Van Vechten Collection, Library of Congress)

This had severely lowered the morale of the musicians. Monteux hired new musicians and introduced new and modern works as the Boston Symphony played under his baton.

Roland Hayes, an African-American lyric tenor, became the first black soloist with the orchestra under Monteux's tenure. Hayes had an astonishing career. The son of tenant farmers who lived on a plantation where his mother has once been a slave, Hayes triumphed over racial prejudice on two continents. His appearance with the Boston Symphony came after a command performance before King George V and Queen Mary of England. Although he stayed in Boston only a short time, Monteux continued as a world-renowned conductor for decades. He also founded a school for conductors in Hancock, Maine; many of the world's foremost conductors were his pupils.

The conductor who left his mark on the ensemble to a greater degree than anyone else was the Russian Serge Koussevitzky. Koussevitzky had been a virtuoso on the double-bass in Russia. When he married the daughter of a wealthy tea merchant, the Koussevitzkys launched his conducting career by hiring the Berlin Philharmonic so that he could make his debut. He had also published the works of Russia's most eminent composers, including Alexander Scriabin, Sergei Rachmaninoff, Igor Stravinsky, and Serge Prokofiev.

Koussevitzky had a charismatic personality. When he appeared in Boston, audiences became quickly aware of his trademark opera cape, what one critic called his "Dostoevskian rages," and his malapropisms. Despite years in America, his accent and his struggle with English syntax never changed. Koussevitzky was an emotional conductor. He once told composer Howard Hanson that he had to look between the notes to find the music. His approach was very different than that of more analytical German conductors.

Figure 36 - Serge Koussevitzky, a Russian conductor who became the devoted champion of American composers. (Photo courtesy of George Grantham Bain Collection, Library of Congress)

Koussevitzky's efforts to communicate with the Boston Symphony led to an unconventional baton technique. Musicians said that they learned to follow his intentions rather than his hand signals. (One quipped, "When his hand reaches the second button on his jacket, that's the downbeat.") Koussevitzky founded the educational programs at Tanglewood.

He taught conducting for many years and became the mentor of many celebrated musicians, including the tenor Alfred Cocozza who later changed his name to Mario Lanza when he became a major movie star. Koussevitzky wanted to be succeeded by his favorite conducting pupil, Leonard Bernstein, when he retired, but Charles Munch was chosen as his successor. Koussevitzky had an enormous impact on American concert music, because he was a tireless advocate of new American composers, including Aaron Copland, Roy Harris, and Douglas Moore, among others. His Koussevitzky Foundation commissioned new symphonies and operas. From 1924-1949, the Boston Symphony rarely had guest conductors and not as many guest soloists as other ensembles. Musical life in Boston was simply dominated by a great star, Serge Koussevitzky.

Figure 37 - Leopold Stokowski, the charismatic conductor whose hands and accent fascinated audiences in Philadelphia. (Photo courtesy of Leopold Stokowski Papers, Kislak Center for Special Collections, Rare Books and Manuscripts, University of Pennsylvania)

The Philadelphia Orchestra was a major rival of the Boston Symphony. It was founded in 1900 by a German conductor, Fritz Scheel. Scheel spoke German at rehearsals and the end of the first season fired half the orchestra's personnel, replacing them with European musicians.

But the personality of the orchestra and characteristic "Philadelphia sound" came directly from another conductor who took the helm of the orchestra in 1912, Leopold Stokowski. He remained there until 1941, although he began to withdraw in favor of his co-conductor, Eugene Ormandy in 1936. Stokowski had been a young English organist with no real conducting experience when he had been engaged as conductor of the Cincinnati Symphony. After three years in Ohio, he arrived in Philadelphia and the legend began. Stokowski conducted without a baton, using widely expressive movements of his hands to convey his intentions to the orchestra. He wanted a full, rich, luxurious sound from the orchestra, and he got what he wanted.

The details of his personal life fascinated people. He was mysterious about his background. Was he really Leopold Boleslawowicz Stanslaw Antoni Stokowski, or simply Leo Stokes? Was his grandfather a Polish general who fought with Napoleon or was he the son of an Irish mother and English father with no ties to Poland? Historians spent years arguing about his true birth date and his family background. His legions of fans were mesmerized not only by his conducting, but his unique accent which critics said bore no relationship to the language of any specific country.

He constantly experimented with seating arrangements in the orchestra, moving musicians around to get the sound he desired. While members of the string sections in most orchestras used uniform bowings, following the lead of the concertmaster, Stokowski encouraged random bowings to produce a fuller, richer sound. He became

Figure 38 - Leopold Stokowski conducts the Philadelphia Orchestra in the 1916 performance of Mahler's Eighth Symphony. (Public Domain)

famous for his transcriptions of works by Bach; purists howled that he was applying nineteenth century romantic orchestral sounds to music written hundreds of years earlier. His advocates insisted that he was merely replicating the full sound of a pipe organ, his original instrument, through the orchestra. Stokowski was a great favorite of the ladies, with his grand gestures and mane of white hair. When the press devoted the same attention to his private life as they did to movie stars, he insisted that he hated publicity, although he seemed happiest in the spotlight.

Critics denounced him as a charlatan and a showman; supporters said he could produce sounds out of an orchestra equaled by no one else. George Szell, the legendary conductor who built the Cleveland Orchestra into an ensemble that could equal the best in the world, said bluntly, "When Stokowski stops acting the Apollo Belvedere and concentrates on the music, one realizes what a great musician he might have been." His friend and biographer, the distinguished pianist and teacher Abram Chasins described him as "the driven perfectionist pursuing a golden sound that he alone heard within himself and produced in his 'instrument,' the orchestra."

Stokowski played a considerable amount of contemporary music and took a serious interest in new music all his life. But his flamboyant personal style and ability to connect with the general public infuriated his critics and rivals. This was especially the case when he appeared in motion pictures like *100 Men and a Girl*, naturally playing himself in a film featuring the singing talents of child star Deanna Durbin. When he appeared on screen as musical director of Walt Disney's *Fantasia* and shook hands with Mickey Mouse, he was recognized by people everywhere who had no previous familiarity with classical music.

Stokowski continued to conduct until he was ninety-five. He defined the sound and style of the Philadelphia Orchestra for all time.

The most dominant conductor in America, however, could be found in New York. In 1926, Arturo Toscanini made his first appearance on the podium before the New York Philharmonic. In 1928, he became principal conductor of the merged New York Symphony and New York Philharmonic. Toscanini had spent seven years conducting the Metropolitan Opera beginning in 1908, but he had returned to Italy. Toscanini called himself a democrat in life, an aristocrat in music. His fiery temper and explosive rehearsals were legendary as he pursued meticulous clarity and reverence for the score in every performance.

Fascist gangs known as "Black Shirts" were followers of Italian dictator Benito Mussolini; they threatened violence against anyone refusing to submit to the Fascist regime. Toscanini detested the Fascists and the Nazis in Germany that they emulated. A musician was once asked if his colleagues weren't afraid to defy Mussolini. He admitted, "We're very afraid of Mussolini," but then added, "We're more afraid of Maestro." Toscanini's refusal to perform *Giovinezza*, the Fascist anthem, led to a scandalous incident in Bologna, when a Fascist punched him in the face. He left Italy after refusing to conduct *Giovinezza*, at La Scala.

New York musicians were terrified of Toscanini's initial debut. He was intense and emotional, exhorting the orchestra to make their instruments sing. He left the Philharmonic after the 1935 season, but in 1937 the National Broadcasting Company created an orchestra especially for Toscanini. The NBC Symphony became one of America's best-known orchestras through radio broadcasts and Toscanini remained its musical director until 1954.

Figure 39 - Arturo Toscanini, the fiery Italian maestro who said, "Not all of them hated me, only the bad musicians." (Photo Courtesy of U.S. Office of War Information)

Toscanini saw music horizontally, not vertically. Each instrument had its own musical line to express, to sustain, and most importantly, to sing. Charles O'Connell, musical director for recordings by RCA Victor, said, Toscanini "worships a Beethoven score as if it had come with the ink still wet from the hand of that great man."

When a musician didn't meet his standards, Toscanini would explode. The noted screenwriter Philip Dunne produced a documentary film on Toscanini and during a rehearsal, Toscanini became enraged by an oboist in the orchestra. Dunne apprehensively invited Toscanini and his family to view the completed film, but Toscanini walked out in the middle of the screening. Dunne was afraid that his film had somehow offended the Maestro, but Toscanini's son explained, "He's just mad at the oboist all over again." Toscanini once said that any fool could wave a stick in the air, but that making music was the real challenge.

While critics considered the three big eastern symphony orchestras, in Boston, Philadelphia, and New York, along with the Chicago Symphony, to be America's leading ensembles, a new rival appeared on the scene in Cleveland. Adela Prentiss Hughes was a pianist who decided to devote most of her time to promoting music. In 1918 she organized the Cleveland Orchestra and selected Nikolai Sokoloff to be its conductor. She continued to manage the orchestra for fifteen years. Sokoloff was known for efforts to promote equality for female musicians in symphony orchestras and paid them as much as men. He remained in Cleveland until 1932, and was succeeded by Artur Rodzinski and Erich Leinsdorf.

But the conductor most responsible for the mystique of the Cleveland Orchestra arrived in 1944. His name was George Szell. When he became conductor of the Cleveland Orchestra, he assumed total control of the ensemble and remained in total control for twenty-four years. Even today, people speak of "Szell's orchestra." Szell had a formidable musical background. He was born in Hungary and grew up in Vienna where he and lifelong friend Rudolf Serkin both studied piano with Richard Robert. He also studied composition with Eusebius Mandyczewski, a personal friend of Brahms. He emerged as a child prodigy, gifted in composition and a virtuoso pianist. But he chose conducting as his primary career and won the praise of Richard Strauss, conducting the first half of Strauss's *Don Juan* in its earliest recording. In Cleveland, Szell was determined to lead the best orchestra in America and to rival the best in Europe. He was an autocrat and a disciplinarian.

Figure 40 - George Szell, the brilliant conductor of the Cleveland Orchestra. (Photo courtesy of Carl Van Vechten Collection, Library of Congress)

Except for Toscanini, no other conductor insisted more on total obedience from his musicians. Szell quickly began firing members of the orchestra and replacing them with others of his own choosing. Josef Gingold, one of the world's finest violinists and teacher of many virtuosos served as concertmaster for many years with distinction. Szell imposed a military discipline on his ensemble and there was no mistaking the fact that it was definitely *his* ensemble. He was a meticulous baton technician who would severely criticize a musician he heard practicing, even a few minutes before a concert.

Szell pursued absolute technical perfection, clarity, and a classical repertoire. He had a photographic memory and specific ideas about the most minute details of any orchestra part. Szell's legion of admirers insist to this day that he was the finest conductor of the classic repertoire of Mozart, Beethoven, and Brahms, raising orchestral performance to a level rarely surpassed anywhere. But his personal style and temperament also led to detractors. When told that Szell was his own worst enemy, Rudolf Bing, director of the Metropolitan Opera, snapped, "Not while I'm alive."

Szell's literalist style was a polar opposite of the romantic approach taken by Koussevitzky and Stokowski. Like Toscanini, he placed great emphasis on each instrument playing a melodic line. Szell was devoted to chamber music and expected a hundred musicians to play together with the same clarity as a string quartet. His brilliance as a conductor led to the Cleveland Orchestra winning praise as one of America's finest orchestras; a number of leading critics said that it was *the* finest. Szell's autocratic approach did not win friends among a number of musicians who played for him or among rival conductors, especially when he said, "In Cleveland we begin to rehearse when other orchestras leave off." He pursued what he called "the most sensitive ensemble playing." To his critics, he was cold and detached, charges he denied. Szell responded by declaring that there are different nuances of warmth and that he could not pour chocolate over asparagus. To his admirers, he was the master of the German repertoire, his performances of Haydn, Mozart, and Beethoven unsurpassed by anyone, and a man who treated musicians he respected very well. Cleveland audiences remained proud of their orchestra. They stopped members of the orchestras and asked for their autographs as if they were sports stars. Fans would go to the airport and greet the orchestra returning from a tour as if they had won the World Series, shouting, "We're the best." Although there have been several fine conductors at the helm of the Cleveland Orchestra since Szell's death in 1970, he cast a long shadow. He gave his orchestra a characteristic sound that is remembered decades later. Irving Kolodin called Szell "irreplaceable" and wrote, "The size of his figure will grow as time recedes and the magnitude of his accomplishment emerges in ever and ever greater grandeur against its background."

HOW OPERA IN AMERICA BECAME GRAND

The art of opera has had a remarkable and often difficult struggle to achieve popularity in America. The men who organized and produced operas were often as colorful as the stars who shined upon their operatic stages. In 1844, Ferdinand Palmo, a prosperous restaurateur, took over Stoppai's Arcade Baths and turned it into an opera theater. Wealthy New Yorkers were nervous about going into what was considered an unsafe neighborhood, so Palmo provided transportation to and from his performances, guaranteeing audiences "police protection." Unfortunately, members of the orchestra, described by Palmo enthusiastically as "thirty-two professors," demanded to be paid on time and launched a strike in the middle of a performance. After the sheriff seized the box office receipts, the enterprise went bankrupt and the once well-to-do Palmo was rewarded for his efforts as an opera producer by the necessity of returning to his original vocation as a cook.

Figure 41 - Col. Henry Mapleson, a producer who charmed opera stars while fleeing his creditors, as he led the Academy of Music opera. He dismissed the rival Metropolitan Opera as "a yellow brewery." (Public Domain)

Several years later, a group of rich businessmen built the Astor Place Opera House in a better neighborhood, but the effort lost money and control of the property was assumed by William Niblo, a coffeehouse owner and caterer who knew something about how to attract crowds and sell tickets. Niblo presented trained dogs and monkeys instead of opera. The proprietors sued Niblo for violation of his lease in which he promised to present only respectable performances. Niblo responded that the dogs and monkeys had performed regularly before European royalty and privately were better behaved than certain Italian opera singers.

Not every effort to bring opera to New York ended in tragedy or comedy. In 1854, New Yorkers began flocking to the new Academy of Music, a huge opera house that seated 4,000 people and offered plush private boxes to elite families who could afford them. The opening season featured performances of operas by Bellini, Rossini, and Donizetti; eventually the Academy of Music would feature the American premieres of *Aida, Lohengrin, Die Walküre,* and *Carmen.* When the Prince of Wales visited the United States, a reception was held for him at the Academy. In 1878, the flamboyant Colonel Henry Mapleson took over the Academy. Mapleson had all the qualities required to be a successful stage producer. He could overpower the famous operas stars he brought to the Academy with charm and constantly avoid his creditors. (He once persuaded the soprano Adelina Patti to perform at a benefit to raise money to pay the salary that Mapleson owed her.)

But the Academy had competition. Boxes at the Academy of Music Opera House were considered a status symbol among the "old money" families of New York. They were next to impossible to obtain, even by self-made millionaires who could afford the $30,000 fee. In 1880, a year before Henry Lee Higginson announced the founding of the Boston Symphony, a group of these wealthy businessmen in New York met at Delmonico's restaurant to discuss the possibility of a new opera house in Manhattan The families of wealthy new industrialists were tired of being dismissed as "nouveau riche" by the long established members of New York society. So they that they would simply build a theater of their own.

The result was an opera house on Broadway and 39th Street. Although the new building featured a gas lit chandelier and two tiers of elegant boxes, Colonel Mapleson called it "a yellow brewery." In 1883, the new Metropolitan House opened with Christina Nilsson, a noted Swedish soprano, starring in *Faust* by Charles Gounod. Italo Campanini, who had previously sung for Mapleson at the Academy, portrayed the title role.

Under the direction of manager Henry Abbey, all operas at the Met were performed in Italian, even if they were originally written in French or German. The production of *Faust,* again starring Christine Nilsson, was also presented at the Chestnut Street Opera House in Philadelphia, beginning an eighty-year relationship between the Met and Philadelphia audiences. Because the first season in New York lost money, the Metropolitan's board engaged renowned conductor Leopold Damrosch as conductor for the second season. Damrosch specialized in the German repertory, so all the productions were then sung in German, even operas written originally in French or Italian. But when Damrosch died shortly thereafter, his young son Walter assumed his responsibilities.

To bolster Walter, the Met imported the demanding Anton Seidl, Richard Wagner's personal favorite conductor. Walter Damrosch served as Seidl's assistant, as the Wagnerian specialist introduced New Yorkers to *Tristan und Isolde*, *Das Rheingold*, *Siegfried*, and *Die Götterdämmerung*. Damrosch began a long association with the Met. Although Col. Mapleson promptly dubbed the Met's German performances "sauerkraut opera," the German years at the Met were successful; by 1886, the once dominant Academy of Music Opera House abandoned opera entirely for vaudeville shows and the personable Col. Henry Mapleson disappeared into history.

In 1891, original director Henry Abbey returned with co-directors Maurice Grau and John B. Schoeffel and promptly switched the dominant style of operas at the Met from Wagnerian music dramas to the lyrical, melodious Italian works. (Wagner's *Die Meistersinger* was even sung in Italian and billed as *I Maestri Cantori*.) They ushered in the "Golden Age" of the Met, with world-renowned opera singers, Jean and Édouard de Reszke, Lilli Lehmann, Emma Calvé, Lillian Nordica, Nellie Melba, Marcella Sembrich, Emma Eames, and Ernestine Schumann-Heink, among others.

In 1898, Maurice Grau became sole manager for five years; the urbane, Austrian-born Grau had started out to be a lawyer, but became involved in helping his uncle in theatrical production. Critics complained about sets and costumes, but Grau insisted that audiences came to see stars, and that crowds would flock to see guest casts in which everyone was a true opera star. Grau also had to deal with stars' egos and personal feuds.

Nellie Melba was a celebrated soprano, the first Australian to achieve worldwide fame in concert music. She regularly sang before the crowned heads of Europe. When she traveled, she handed out personalized tie pins as if they were medals, gave shops she patronized certificates of approval, and even had uniforms bearing the letter "M" made for her favorite music students.

Auguste Escoffier, the world's most famous French chef, created four separate dishes in her honor, Peach Melba, Melba sauce, Melba toast, and Melba Garniture. Melba's

Figure 42 - Nellie Melba, the Australian soprano who sang during the "Golden Age of the Met." (1914 Metropolitan Opera Photo in Public Domain)

Figure 43 - Enrico Caruso, the Neapolitan tenor who remains the most famous opera star of all time through the technology of recording. (Photo courtesy of the George Grantham Bain Collection, Library of Congress)

greatest rival at the Met was Lillian Nordica. Born Lillian Norton, the dramatic soprano who was called a "Yankee diva" had chosen a more exotic name because she believed that Americans wouldn't take a girl from New England seriously despite triumphant performances in Europe. Known as Mme. Nordica, she often sang opposite Jean de Reszke and was especially known for her interpretation of Wagnerian roles. Melba was furious to find Nordica sitting in the front row of one of her performances. She refused to go on stage unless Grau ejected Nordica. Grau refused, insisting that Nordica had paid for her seat with her money.

Grau's greatest triumph, however, was signing a contract with the famed and charismatic tenor Enrico Caruso. But since Grau was replaced by Heinrich Conried in 1903, it was during Conried's years that the renowned tenor made his debut at the Metropolitan Opera. Conried was a German impresario who intended to move the Met away from its emphasis on stars. For Conried, it was the music, not the celebrity of the soloist that was more important. However, there was a major exception to the rule, changing the face of opera in America forever.

Conried's business instincts made him realize that Caruso was unique. The Neapolitan tenor was so popular that audiences would flock to the box offices asking for tickets to hear Caruso sing without paying the slightest attention as to which opera would be presented. Caruso's fame came not only from his magnificent singing voice. He was a larger than life figure with a magnetic personality. He happened to achieve fame at a time when twentieth century technology was changing the nature of fame. Caruso became a genuine celebrity, enjoying the adulation and attention that is today lavished upon film and pop music stars. Newspapers reported his every activity.

While numerous classical musicians dismissed the new technology of phonograph records for their poor sound quality, Caruso embraced the new medium. The result was that he made a fortune not only as the highest paid opera star, but from not quite three hundred records he made for his wildly enthusiastic fans. It was said that his recording of "Vesti la giubba" from Leoncavallo's *Pagliacci* sold a million copies. He also appeared in a few silent films. People who knew nothing about music and cared little about opera still knew the name of Caruso, and while many of the figures of the "Golden Age" are remembered only by

Figure 44 - Heinrich Conried. He changed the emphasis on stars at the Metropolitan Opera, but suddenly found himself promoting the greatest opera star of all, Caruso. (Photograph of Conried by A. Radclyffe Dugmore 1906, Public Domain)

opera aficionados, Caruso's name is still remembered today. Long after his death, Hollywood made a movie, *The Great Caruso*, based on his life, starring a tenor who had idolized him—Mario Lanza. His legend survives today as a source of inspiration and comparison for today's finest tenors.

Conried's greatest impact on the Met, however, came from his efforts to elevate the music above the star by introducing new operas to the American people. In his first season, he decided to produce the first fully-staged production of Wagner's *Parsifal* in America. A huge controversy erupted, because Wagner had written the work to be performed only at the Festival Hall in Bayreuth, the Bavarian town which was home to the opera house built especially for the performance of Wagner's music and *Wahnfried,* the villa where he spent the last years of his life. His widow, Cosima, the daughter of Franz Liszt, now controlled the rights and when she objected, the New York newspapers had a field day covering the great battle between the supporters of Conried and those of Cosima. Conried won the legal fight enabling him to finally produce the work and he relished the publicity that enabled him to greet those arriving to claim their seats with a group of trumpeters playing themes from the opera.

Conried's greatest problem, however, was an unexpected competitor, the new Manhattan Opera House, launched by Oscar Hammerstein. Hammerstein was a prosperous businessman who had made money marketing cigars. He was driven by a desire to produce operas. Hammerstein was the scion of a family that would have the greatest impact on Broadway. His grandson, Oscar Hammerstein II, would later emerge as the most dominant lyricist and librettist in twentieth century American musical theater. The senior Hammerstein had the natural instinct of a showman. Since Conried was emphasizing new music and controversy in his productions, Hammerstein decided to place his emphasis on stars. Even when he produced new and challenging works like Debussy's, he attracted audiences with by announcing that the opera would feature the soprano Mary Garden. Garden had made her American debut with the Manhattan Opera House, singing the leading role in Massenet's *Thaïs*. She was born in Aberdeen, Scotland, but moved to America with her parents while still a child and grew up in New England.

Figure 45 - Oscar Hammerstein I started a family dynasty that impacted the entire history of Broadway. (Public domain)

Pelléas et Mélisande also generated publicity at the new Boston Opera House in 1908, when manager Henry Russell offered a prize of $1,000 to any journalist who obtained the first interview with Maurice Maeterlinck, the Belgian writer on whose play Debussy had based the opera. The reclusive Maeterlinck declined all interviews and had no intention of coming to Boston for the performance, but the public reacted the way audiences react today at the prospect of winning a lottery.

Meanwhile, in New York, Oscar Hammerstein not only recruited his own stars, he kept an eye on those who might be planning on singing at the Met. Luisa Tetrazzini created a sensation with her debut in San Francisco. So Heinrich Conried took an option on the services of the coloratura soprano from Florence, but when he failed to sign the Italian singer to a contract, Hammerstein stepped in. Tetrazzini, a serious rival of Nellie Melba drew crowds in New York. (Her colorful exit from Manhattan came after she won a lawsuit and announced, "I will sing in San Francisco if I have to sing in the streets, because I know the streets of San Francisco are free.")

Competition ultimately proved to be Conried's undoing. The directors at the Met took a bold step and invited the electrifying Arturo Toscanini to ascend the podium. Toscanini had conducted at the famed La Scala opera house in Milan, one of the world's most celebrated venues for performing opera. The manager at La Scala was Giulio Gatti-Casazza. New Yorkers suspected that Toscanini would not come to the Met without Gatti-Casazza, so he was engaged to replace Conried as manager. These two volatile Italian personalities would leave an indelible stamp on the Metropolitan.

The history of music might have been quite different were it not for several accidents in the life of Arturo Toscanini. He started his musical career as a cellist, but he was known for his photographic memory. He conducted a performance of Verdi's *Aida* in Brazil as a last minute substitute and by conducting the entire opera from memory, he created a sensation. Toscanini was famous for his fiery temper and his rages. (His wife would take a bag of cheap watches to his rehearsals, because he became so angry at the ineptitude of musicians that he would throw his watch on the floor and crush it beneath his shoes.) Toscanini had own method of dealing with the star power of the divas at the Metropolitan Opera. He told a soprano that stars only exist in heaven. Musicians were terrified of his explosions during rehearsals, but when they complained to Gatti-Casazza, he would simply say, "He abuses me too."

Toscanini seemed to know every note of every work he conducted. Although Italian, he corrected the pronunciation of French and German singers in their own languages. But everyone understood that Toscanini was not simply a temperamental conductor, he was a great musician. His performances reflected a burning intensity matched by almost no one. His piercing stare at a musician during a performance managed to elicit the finest musicality. So he was not simply feared, he was respected. In later years Toscanini responded to critics who talked about his temper. "Not all of them hated me," he explained, "Only the bad musicians."

In 1910, Oscar Hammerstein accepted a financial settlement from the Met and withdrew from operatic production leaving the Metropolitan Opera as the country's leading opera house. Toscanini left the Met in 1915 and returned to Italy. In another remarkable twist of fate, he had planned to book passage on one of the world's most glamorous ships, the *Lusitania*. (Jerome Kern, the great Broadway composer, also had a ticket to cross the Atlantic on the *Lusitania*.) Music history was changed forever when

Figure 46 - Giulio Gatti-Casazza. The undisputed master and manager of the Metropolitan Opera. (Photo used courtesy of The George Grantham Bain Collection, Library of Congress)

Toscanini sailed a week early on the *Duca degli Abruzzi* and Kern overslept and missed the *Lusitania's* departure. The Lusitania was sunk by a German submarine. The Germans regarded it as a military target and the sinking of the *Lusitania*, with a loss of nearly 1200 lives, began to sway public opinion in the United States in favor of entering World War I.

Meanwhile, Gatti-Casazza remained at the helm until 1935, setting the tone and style of the Metropolitan Opera for decades to come. Beniamino Gigli, sometimes considered a successor to Caruso, came to sing at the Met, along with Giovanni Martinelli, Amelita Galli-Curci, Giacomo Lauri-Volpi, Lily Pons, Lauritz Melchior, Giuseppe De Luca, Pasquale Amato, and the renowned Russian bass, Feodor Chaliapin, took the stage as well.

From 1935-1950, Edward Johnson managed the Met, with new American opera stars such as tenors Jan Peerce and Richard Tucker and baritone Robert Merrill in the spotlight. Jan Peerce came to public attention while working as a tenor soloist at New York's Radio City Music Hall. Arturo Toscanini had been looking for the ideal tenor to sing with the NBC Symphony and when he heard Peerce on radio, he invited him to audition.

Peerce first sang with Toscanini in 1938 and became the Maestro's favorite tenor. Peerce was a serious, dedicated performer and Toscanini never subjected him to any of his famous tirades. Peerce made his Metropolitan Opera debut in 1941. Toscanini chose him as tenor soloist for a filmed performance of *Verdi's Hymn of the Nations,* featuring the NBC Symphony and the Westminster Choir. Through radio and recording, Peerce reached millions of Americans who might never have listened to an opera singer. His recording of his signature song, "Bluebird of Happiness" in 1945, became one of the all time best-selling records by a classical singer.

Figure 47 - Jan Peerce, Arturo Toscanini's favorite tenor. (Photo courtesy of U.S. Office of War Information)

Peerce's brother-in law, Richard Tucker enjoyed a thirty-year career at the Met, but his success as one of the world's leading tenors didn't come easily. He was trying to run a small business in New York's garment district when he won second place in the Met's "Auditions of the Air." Eventually Edward Johnson offered him a contract and his 1945 debut launched his career. The two brothers-in-law had a strained relationship, presumably because Tucker believed Peerce hadn't been helpful enough at the beginning of his career, something Peerce always denied. But both were friends with the fun-loving baritone, Robert Merrill.

Merrill, once a shy boy who wanted to be a baseball player, turned to opera because his mother had always wanted to be a singer and insisted that he pursue a vocal career. Merrill could have continued as a successful radio crooner when he won the "Auditions of the Air" and made his Met debut in 1945. Merrill and Tucker, both from Brooklyn and with similar backgrounds, often sang in concerts together. Like Peerce and Tucker, Merrill recorded with Toscanini.

These American opera stars introduced opera to huge new audiences. Peerce and Merrill both starred in

Figure 48 - Robert Merrilll, the baritone who was famous for devotion to the Metropolitan Opera and the New York Yankees. (Photo courtesy of Robert Merrill)

productions of the Broadway musical, *Fiddler on the Roof,* and Merrill went to Hollywood to make a film and to Las Vegas to sing with Louis Armstrong. Merrill never forgot his boyhood ambition to play baseball. Despite his career at the Metropolitan Opera, Merrill took time out to record George Kleinsinger's *Brooklyn Baseball Cantata*, a work portraying an imaginary victory of the Brooklyn Dodgers over the New York Yankees. After the Dodgers left Brooklyn, Merrill supported the New York Yankees. Wearing a Yankee uniform, he sang "The Star Spangled Banner" at Yankee Stadium, proving that a real singer can perform the National Anthem without tricks or embellishments.

(Yankee manager Casey Stengel was duly impressed with Merrill's singing, but less so with Merrill's unrealized ambition to be a baseball player. He told Merrill's son that "There is no future in pitching like your father pitched.")

Figure 49 - Marian Anderson with Eleanor Roosevelt. The First Lady arranged for Anderson's historic concert at the Lincoln Memorial when she was banned from singing at Constitution Hall because of her race. (Photo courtesy of the Franklin Delano Roosevelt Library)

From 1950-1972, under the management of Rudolf Bing, the Metropolitan Opera presented gifted African American singers who finally broke the color line, starting in 1955 with Marian Anderson, an African-American contralto who had triumphed over racism and discrimination to gain worldwide acclaim. She never sought confrontation over racial issues, but in 1939, she was denied the opportunity to perform at Constitution Hall in Washington, D.C. Four years earlier, Constitution Hall had instituted a policy for "concerts by white artists only." The Hall was owned by the Daughters of the American Revolution.

When news of Marian Anderson's treatment became public, a huge protest was the result. First Lady Eleanor Roosevelt resigned from the Daughters of the American Revolution. Along with Marian Anderson's manager, Sol Hurok, and Walter White of the NAACP, she encouraged Secretary of the Interior Harold Ickes to arrange an open air concert for the contralto at the Lincoln Memorial. A crowd of 75,000 people attended the open air concert. In 1943, when Anderson finally performed at Constitution Hall, she insisted that the Hall abandon its segregated seating policies. In 1945, the renowned black baritone Todd Duncan became the first African American to sing with a major opera company when he appeared in a New York City Opera production of *Pagliacci*.

Figure 50 - Todd Duncan created the role of "Porgy" in *Porgy and Bess* and became the first black singer to star with a major opera company. (Photo by Van Damm, courtesy of Todd Duncan)

Numerous other African-American artists were then able to appear at the Met, including Leontyne Price, Shirley Verrett, Grace Bumbry, and George Shirley, among others. The Austrian-born Bing said that you didn't need wit to manage an opera, you needed style. Bing's style included leading the Metropolitan Opera into an age of twentieth century technology and managing the move from the famed Metropolitan House on Broadway into a new home at New York's Lincoln Center. Bing summed up his own managerial style by declaring, "Don't be misled, behind that cold, austere, severe exterior, there beats a heart of stone."

During the Bing years, a number of singers made their debuts at the Met whose popularity transcended the elite appeal of lesser-known opera stars, including Luciano Pavarotti, Placido Domingo, and Maria Callas, the latter a brilliant and temperamental soprano who was famously dismissed by Bing after her refusal to agree to an alternating schedule of performances at the Met. Callas, born in New York to Greek immigrant parents, launched her career in Greece and became a legend for the dramatic intensity she brought the roles she played. Bing was eventually succeeded by Schuyler Chapin. Tenor José Carreras, who later joined Pavarotti and Domingo in the famous "Three Tenors Concerts," made his Met debut under Chapin.

Figure 51 - Rudolf Bing often sat across from operatic divas in his office. The poodle sitting opposite him belonged to soprano Renata Tebaldi. (Photo courtesy of Metropolitan Opera)

Although the Metropolitan Opera received the most publicity for its stars, another important opera company, the New York City Opera, played a major role in popularizing opera with the American public. Founded in 1943, with Laszlo Halasz as director, the New York City Opera was quickly dubbed "the people's opera" by New York Mayor Fiorello LaGuardia. The New York City Opera lived up to that reputation by selling inexpensive tickets (costing as little as seventy-five cents to two dollars) and devoting as much as a third of its productions to American operas.

While modest budgets prevented the company, known as NYCO, from paying huge fees to international stars, it offered previously unavailable opportunities to two groups of musicians who might find closed doors at the Met: younger and lesser known singers at the beginning of distinguished careers and American composers who had to fight prejudice and apathy toward new operas from audiences who only wanted to hear familiar European classics. Halasz wasn't afraid of controversy, urging that at least one European opera each season be performed in English. Many of the singers identified with the New York City Opera continued their careers on the stages of the world. Four years after Todd Duncan's historic appearance in *Pagliacci,* NYCO became the first major opera company to present a grand opera by an African American composer, William Grant Still's *Troubled Island.* After Halasz left in 1951, NYCO continued to present world premieres of operas by American composers, including works by Aaron Copland, Douglas Moore, Norman Dello Joio, Jerome Moross, Jack Beeson, Carlisle Floyd, Gian Carlo Menotti, and Vittorio Giannini. The New York City Opera also produced opera house versions of Broadway musicals, ranging from Jerome Kern's *Show Boat* and Leonard Bernstein's *Candide.* No singer had a greater association with NYCO than Beverly Sills; hired by Julius Rudel in 1956, Sills spent twenty-three years as the star soprano of the New York City Opera and then succeeded Rudel as its director. But an aging audience, changing tastes, and a public less committed to classical music created a fatal challenge for the company. Increasing costs made the seemingly impossible happen in 2013. The New York City Opera, despite a stellar history, was forced to file for bankruptcy.

THE ICONOCLASTS

Charles Edward Ives enjoyed the strangest and most unique career in America's musical history. Ives was subject to ridicule and neglect during his lifetime. He lived long enough to see himself heralded as one of America's most original composers. Today, musical historians and critics consider Ives a legendary figure, among the most original spirits of his age. But in Ives' early years, no one would have imagined his remarkable musical odyssey.

Charles Edward Ives was born in Danbury, Connecticut, in 1874, the son of a bandmaster and Civil War veteran, George Ives. To understand the music of Charles Ives, it is necessary to understand his father, an imaginative musician who was curious about sound. George Ives was a bandmaster for the First Connecticut Heavy Artillery in the army of Ulysses S. Grant. In Danbury, he was the local music teacher, director of music at the Methodist Church, and a director of theater orchestras.

George Ives had an unusual fascination with sounds of all kinds. He built an instrument to play sounds he heard when he listened to church bells, sound that could not be played on the piano except in the cracks between the keys. He would play familiar tunes like "Swanee River" or "Old Folks at Home" on the piano in one key, while members of his family were instructed to sing in a different key. He experimented with glasses and bells, with the outdoor echo caused when he played his trumpet near water. When two bands, his own and another one, marched through town from opposite directions, their simultaneous playing of different tunes struck most listeners as noise. But to George Ives, the resulting cacophony was a source of inspiration.

Figure 52 - Charles Ives, the boldly experimental American composer who anticipated 20th century music in the 19th century and his wife, Harmony Twichell Ives, President of the Mark Twain Society. (Photo by Hallie Erskine, courtesy of the Charles Ives Society and the Irving Gilmore Library, Yale University)

As a teenager, young Charles Ives played the organ in church. His formal musical training was traditional. He studied organ with Dudley Buck and at twenty, enrolled at Yale as a pupil of Horatio Parker. But unlike the other New England classicists who turned to German symphonists for their models, Charles Ives drew upon his unique musical experiences with his father. For young Charles Ives, the hymn tunes he played in church, the martial band music his father liked, the tunes he heard at barn dances in New England played by country fiddlers, could all be used in composing concert music. His musical memories were filled with the sounds of marching bands, church choirs, and even the local stonemason who sang loudly off-key. Not only could they be quoted literally, they could be distorted, developed, combined into dissonant collages of sound.

Ives decided that he wanted to write boldly independent music, expressing an intensely personal style. He guessed correctly that critics, conductors, and respectable musical societies of the times were in no mood to appreciate his music. So he decided to pursue a career in the insurance business. Eventually, together with some friends, he started an insurance company of his own. Their apartment was initially nicknamed "Poverty Alley." But Ives became successful in his chosen field and over a twenty year period, he ran the nation's largest insurance agency. During the years between his twenties and his forties, he wrote most of his important music. He would come home after work, change clothes, and hurry to the piano to spend the rest of his time composing.

Ives experimented with polytonality, playing in two keys at the same time. He worked with tone clusters, groups of seemingly unrelated tones played simultaneously to produce surprising, percussive dissonance. For Ives, these sounds were as natural as the "triad" which served as the basis for most traditional music. He explored unusual meters, asking his players to play in different meters at the same time. When he put his music on paper, he used highly original methods of notation. Most composers notated music using an orderly pattern of evenly spaced bar-lines. To escape the "tyranny of the bar-line," Ives would use bar-lines when he wanted a particular pulse. Ives would use quotations from popular melodies and hymn tunes, often pitting one melody against another without adjusting them for the dissonances that would result. While many composers trained in the European tradition tried to adjust the natural rhythmic and harmonic idiosyncrasies of American music, Ives cared nothing for European traditions. Coping with this difficult style was complex enough, but Ives' pieces also made phenomenal technical demands on anyone attempting to play them.

Performers and conductors reacted in astonishment to his music. His works were full of sharp dissonances. His musical experimentation anticipated those of twentieth century European composers who would revolutionize contemporary music. Future generations would write approvingly of Europeans who experimented with different rhythms played simultaneously (polyrhythms), musical sections based on different scales played simultaneously (polytonality), startling groups of apparently unrelated tones which were sounded simultaneously together (tone clusters), and other avant-garde innovations. Ives tried these things entirely on his own. He worked on pieces over long periods of time, often thinking of his music as "works in progress" subject to major revisions after a period of years.

These efforts provoked outrage, skepticism, or laughter. Some musicians thought Ives was joking, unschooled in the rudiments of harmony. Ives insisted that he must write music as he heard it; and so he did. On rare occasions, Ives did hear a little of his music, performed by musicians he hired. But typically, he stored his scores in a Connecticut barn where he spent the summers writing music and contemplating the Berkshires or in a safe in the office of his insurance company. In the wintertime, he and his wife, Harmony Twichell Ives, would return to the New York apartment. Ives was a rugged individualist in all things; when someone suggested that he try wintering in a warmer climate, he scoffed, "Florida is for sissies."

In 1918, Ives' years of moonlighting caught up with him. A heart attack at forty-four left him physically depleted. Although he lived to be eighty, the major body of his musical work was behind him. Ives decided to publish his own music privately, so that those musicians who would accept his highly unconventional ideas might be aware of his writings.

Ives completed four symphonies, the first two of which were in a more romantic vein. Ives finished his *Third Symphony* in 1904, basing it on organ pieces and hymns he had played in the Presbyterian Church. The work is filled with quotations from familiar hymns: "What a Friend We Have In Jesus," "There Is A Fountain Filled With Blood," "Just As I Am Without One Plea," "Take It To the Lord," "All Through the Night," and an old Welsh battle song. Between 1909-1916, Ives produced his *Fourth Symphony*. This work called for a huge orchestra, including two pianos, an organ, a battery of percussion instruments, and a four-part chorus. Ives used quotations from dozens of familiar tunes, including "Yankee Doodle," "Turkey in the Straw," "In the Sweet Bye and Bye," the latter in quarter-tones, and even fragments of compositions of his own.

Ives loved patriotic themes; another of his works was a four movement symphonic composition for orchestra in which each movement represented a different American holiday: "Washington's Birthday," "Decoration Day," "The Fourth of July," and "Thanksgiving Day." As usual, the work is full of quotations of melodies ranging from "Nearer, My God, To Thee" to "Taps." The quotations are juxtaposed and jumbled in typical Ives fashion.

Ives' most famous orchestral work was a three movement suite, *Three Places in New England*, which he completed between 1903 and 1911. Each of the three movements depicts a different New England setting: *The "St. Gaudens" in Boston Common* (*Col. Shaw and his Colored Regiment*), *Putnam's Camp, Reading, Connecticut*, and *The Housatonic at Stockbridge*. In the second movement, Ives reconstructed a childhood memory: the sound of two marching bands passing each other at a Fourth of July picnic as they play different marches in different rhythms and different keys simultaneously. His other works included *Three Outdoor Scenes* (*Halloween, The Pond*, and *Central Park in the Dark*). His most puzzling work, *The Unanswered Question,* featured a continuous sound of muted strings, casting a musical cloud over sonorities played by other members of the orchestra.

Ives' New England heritage was apparent in his second piano sonata. *The Concord Sonata* was widely regarded as one of the most difficult piano compositions ever written. Ives portrayed the great literary figures of Concord in his sonata: Emerson, Hawthorne, the Alcotts, and Thoreau. His view of these writers was highly personal: Emerson is dissonant, Hawthorne reckless and filled with abandon, while the Alcotts were gentle as the hymn tunes the family sang. As always, Ives was imaginative and startling in his approach. Hawthorne's intensity was portrayed through tone clusters that could be produced by using a ruler on the piano. (The movement depicting the Alcotts also includes a quote from a piece the family undoubtedly knew: Beethoven's *Fifth Symphony*.) An optional flute could be used to express Thoreau's love of that instrument. Ives also published *Essay Before a Sonata,* a complex explanation of his musical philosophy. Ives' work reflected the transcendental idea that rejected any pedantic system or set of rules as applied to composition. For Charles Ives, rules were made to be broken.

Between 1888 and 1921, Ives composed *114 Songs*, which he published in 1921 in reverse chronological order. The songs reflected Ives' ideas of cowboy tunes, hymns, military marches, and ballads. They reflected the wide range of Ives' harmonic and rhythmic curiosity. Some were ferociously dissonant, others simple and folk-like. The song collections were distributed free of charge to anyone interested: librarians, music critics, performers. The public and the conservative music establishment generally ignored Ives. But a younger generation of composers began discovering his music and in particular, influential Europeans found out about Ives.

Nicolas Slonimsky, a Russian pianist and conductor specializing in avant-garde music, and Anton Webern, one of Europe's most controversial avant-garde composers, introduced Ives' music in Europe. Young Americans finally made a breakthrough for Ives in his native land. A prodigious teenage composer-conductor, Bernard Herrmann, discovered a copy of Ives' *114 Songs* in New York's 23rd Street library and wrote Ives a fan letter. Ives responded by sending his young admirer several scores, and Herrmann became a lifelong champion of Ives' music. He showed the songs to fellow composer Aaron Copland and determined that one day he would help bring Ives' music to the neglectful public. Herrmann saw Ives as a key figure in the cause of true American musical nationalism. Herrmann praised Ives music for its reflection of "the New England of granite Puritanism seen through a musical mind unique and extraordinary." Hermann declared effusively, "By Golly, Mr. Ives puts cowboy themes and hillbilly songs and camp meeting hymns into his symphonies. Those are the tunes of our country and we love them. Mr. Ives writes about everything from Nelly, the Poor Working Girl to the How and Why of Life. One of his sonatas is called 'Concord, Mass.' Now if that isn't American, what is? We know that Mr. Ives belongs among the immortals, and someday all the rest of America will know it. America will know it when it can appreciate the meaning of a new American tone, a new dissonance. His music is our music, it is not European."

But as Ives' music finally found its champions, the composer became more cantankerous and reclusive than ever. Pianist John Kirkpatrick introduced *The Concord Sonata* in 1939 to critical acclaim, though Ives refused to even attend the performance. In 1946, Bernard Herrmann, who had become conductor of the CBS Symphony, presented a movement from Ives' *Fourth Symphony* on radio, the first time that any of his music was broadcast over the airwaves. Paul Rosenfeld, an influential critic, praised Ives, while his friend Henry Cowell became his most important advocate, and ultimately, his biographer.

When Ives' *Third Symphony* was performed in 1947, the seventy-three year old composer was awarded the Pulitzer Prize. He was unimpressed. "Prizes are for boys," he snapped. "I'm grown up." Reporters loved the idea of the grand old man of American music finally being discovered. Ives refused to cooperate. He finally permitted a local photographer to take his picture, but he grumbled about the prize and eventually gave away the prize money. When his major orchestral works were finally played, he was too nervous to attend the performances, so he listened to radio broadcasts instead. Ives finally heard his *Second Symphony* played by the New York Philharmonic, fifty years after he wrote it. He would not attend the concerts, and even turned down a private performance at a rehearsal. But when he heard the music on the radio, he was so elated he danced a jig in his living room.

Ives died in 1954. After his death, his fame and critical regard for his music grew by leaps and bounds. The sharp clashes and jagged edges of his music reflected the spirit and tone of New England in a way truly his own. To Ives, the camp meeting, the hymn tunes, the circus parades were all as worthy of musical expression in the concert hall as the classic poems of Europeans. Ives had a capacity to evoke the past, the spirit of a bygone era in New England. Yet his music speaks directly to modern audiences.

Ives was personally conservative; he led the conventional life of a businessman because he would have been unhappy living the life of an artistic bohemian. He pursued an individual course in nearly total isolation from friends and admirers. It is all the more amazing that his music has survived and prospered in the modern age, becoming an important part of our nation's musical history. Ives reflected the true American spirit in music: individualistic, nonconformist, ready to explore new worlds and break with traditions, but never quite free from our historical past. Ives had sounded the trumpet for American nationalism. It would be a call answered by others.

Though perhaps the most influential, Charles Ives was hardly the only nonconformist in America's musical history. It would be hard to find more colorful, puzzling, or outrageously individual characters than those who have appeared in the development of America's music.

Foremost among these was New England's Carl Ruggles, described by Virgil Thomson as wiry, salty, disrespectful, and splendidly profane, a little like Popeye. Ruggles, born in 1876, near Buzzards Bay, Massachusetts, began his career as a violin prodigy who once played a recital for President Grover Cleveland. Eventually he settled in a converted schoolhouse in Vermont, where he wrote his pieces using colored crayons on large sheets of heavy butcher's paper.

Figure 53 - Henry Cowell (left) and Carl Ruggles (right), both major non-conformists who marched to the sound of their own drummers in American music. (Photo by Sydney Cowell, courtesy of the David and Sylvia Teitelbaum Fund, All rights reserved.)

Ruggles spent over fifty years supported by a patron, and in turn, he supported his wife and son, and composed ferociously dissonant, complex music not designed to please anyone but himself. He did not like to repeat a single tone until at least a dozen other tones had somehow been piled on top of it. Pupils of Carl Ruggles were not allowed to repeat a note in their compositions until they had used at least five other tones first.

On one occasion, composer Henry Cowell arrived at Ruggles' home and found him pounding a chord over and over, and singing a single note at the same time. When Cowell asked for an explanation, Ruggles said he was testing the chord for its lasting value. If he liked it, he thundered, it would stand the test of time. Nonconformists invariably need champions and one of the most active was Henry Cowell, an experimenter from the beginning of his own musical career. Cowell first shocked the public during the 1920s when he pounded his palms or forearms on a piano keyboard, producing a clanging, percussive sound that later earned the name "tone cluster." Ruggles remained a rebel throughout his life. He numbered among his friends other New England nonconformists, including Charles Ives and the poet Robert Frost. Ruggles was also an accomplished painter and could have actually had a career in the art world. (The artist Thomas Hart Benton painted a well-known picture of Ruggles seated at the piano.) No one ever accused Carl Ruggles of playing politics to advance his musical or artistic reputation. In fact, he was no respecter of musical tradition. While teaching at the University of Miami, he encountered a student who disagreed with his view that Sibelius was "a bad composer." The student asked Ruggles if Sibelius's haunting composition, *The Swan of Tuonela*, wasn't truly a great piece of music. According to his biographer, Marilyn J. Ziffrin, Ruggles scowled, chewed on his ever present cigar, and told the student that the bird in Sibelius's work was only a duck.

Cowell devoted many years to supporting the work of other composers, and still found time to turn out nineteen symphonies of his own, as well as a long list of compositions for band, orchestra, and chorus. Together with his wife, Sidney, he wrote a biography of Charles Ives, whose music he praised long before it was fashionable to do so.

Like Cowell, George Antheil made his initial impact on the American musical scene by shocking the public. He studied with Constantin von Sternberg, a Liszt pupil, and Ernest Bloch. Determined to pay his way to

Figure 54 - George Antheil, self-proclaimed "Bad Boy of Music," hard at work on a new score. (Photo courtesy of Arthur Antheil McTighe and Judith Donoher)

Europe in pursuit of a girl who interested him, Antheil developed an incredible virtuoso technique on the piano. In Paris, he lived in an apartment above Shakespeare & Co., a legendary book store run by Sylvia Beach, the first publisher of James Joyce. Antheil thus became the friend of literary and artistic bohemians in Paris, including not only Joyce, but Ezra Pound, Gertrude Stein, Pablo Picasso, Salvador Dali, and Ernest Hemingway. His percussive and dissonant new works, including The *Airplane Sonata* and *Sonata Sauvage*, created musical scandals in Germany, although in today's world, they would hardly shock modern audiences.

Antheil permanently earned the title, "Bad Boy of Music," when he composed *Ballet Mechanique*, scored for sixty mechanical pianos and percussion. When he returned to New York, the public wasn't ready for *Ballet Mechanique* either, with its anvils, bells, automobile horns, and buzzers. Antheil used the piano as a percussion instrument, instructing those playing his piano passages to perform them "coldly, without love." Nor were traditionalists and critics pleasantly surprised when another Antheil work, *Transatlantic*, featured the work's heroine singing an aria in a bathtub. Antheil was a prolific composer, writing concertos for the piano and the violin, a half-dozen symphonies, string quartets, and solo sonatas. Not all of his works were intended to be shocking. An early *Jazz Symphony* was written to compete with the concert works of Gershwin. His ballet, *Capital of the World*, was based on a short story by Ernest Hemingway and depicted the tragic fate of an aspiring young matador who dreams of fame and glory in the bullring, only to be fatally gored while practicing with a cynical older torero and using a chair mounted with knives to represent the bull's horns.

Antheil was a gifted writer and wrote numerous articles and even a murder mystery. He also collaborated with the glamorous movie star Hedy Lamarr to patent an invention for use in radio guided torpedoes. Their system of frequency hopping (spread spectrum) was designed to help the Allies overcome jamming of radio signals by the Axis forces during World War II. Both Antheil and Lamarr were named to the Inventors Hall of Fame as a result.

Eventually, Antheil settled in Hollywood where he wrote books (including one on criminology), ballets, symphonies, operas, and film scores. His best-selling autobiography was appropriately titled *Bad Boy of Music*.

Antheil's one-time pupil, Henry Brant, was born in Canada. An amazing orchestrator, he experimented with unusual combinations of instruments: a *Concerto for Flute* (accompanied by ten other flutes), a *Symphony* for toy instruments from the dime store, a brassy composition, *Millenium No. 22* for ten trumpets, ten trombones, eight horns, two tubas, and four percussion instruments. One of Brant's favorite devices was "antiphonal" music, with separate groups of performers placed in specific locations directed by the composer, playing in various keys, rhythms, and tempi. One work calls for five orchestras and three conductors; his *Consort for True Violins* calls for eight violins to be built especially for the piece.

Figure 55 - John Cage, the unpredictable and always startling non-conformist experimenting with a toy piano. (Photo courtesy of Schoenhut Piano Company)

One of the hardest composers to classify is the nonconformist, John Cage. When he saw every student in a college library reading the same book, he wanted to read something else. In 1938, Cage introduced the "prepared piano," a grand piano with strings decorated by bolts, nuts, screws, pieces of plastic, rubber, glass, and wood. Cage also "composed" *4:33*, a "piano piece" in which the pianist did not play a single note, and silence was the only "sound" heard by the audience for precisely four minutes and thirty-three seconds.

Laura Kuhn, Executive Director of the John Cage Trust, said, "John Cage is best known as a composer, but he was also a philosopher, a poet, a chess master, a visual artist, a diarist, a mycologist, and an enthusiastic macrobiotic cook." Cage was articulate. He apparently delighted in the controversy his life and music generated. Was he to be taken seriously? Today critics, historians, and musicians still cannot agree.

THE GERSHWIN PHENOMENON

On February 12, 1924, bandleader Paul Whiteman presented a concert that would change the history of American music. It was called "An Experiment in Modern Music." Whiteman called himself "The King of Jazz," although his dance band was not a true improvising jazz ensemble. (Jazz, had, in fact, evolved through the talents of numerous black American musicians before Whiteman appeared on the scene.) But Whiteman had decided to present his version of jazz in a concert hall, demanding all the dignity and respect accorded performances of European concert music. (James Reese Europe, a black bandleader, had presented a jazz concert in Carnegie Hall as early as 1912, but this didn't deter Whiteman.)

Figure 56 - George Gershwin. Decades after his sudden death in 1937, he remains one of the greatest icons of American music. (Photo courtesy Carl Van Vechten Collection, Library of Congress)

Whiteman also wanted to appear in Carnegie Hall, but because the Hall was booked, he settled for a smaller New York venue, Aeolian Hall. New York City. Two days before Whiteman's fabled Experiment, a rival bandleader, Vincent Lopez, used his dance band to illustrate the idea of "symphonic jazz," as presented in a lecture by Harvard professor E.B. Hill. But the lecture had little impact, while Whiteman's concert would have an impact no one could imagine. Whiteman was convinced that New York was a city that valued novelty over talent. He was determined to prove his point.

Whiteman's press agent announced that a committee of celebrated musicians would answer the question, "What is American music?" Curiously, the committee consisted of famed musicians: Sergei Rachmaninoff, Jascha Heifetz, Efrem Zimbalist, ironically, all Russian émigrés, and Alma Gluck, a native of Romania. A newspaper article announcing the choice of the judges also declared that special works were being created by leading composers for the concert: an American suite by Victor Herbert, a syncopated tone poem by Irving Berlin, and a jazz concerto by George Gershwin. Victor Herbert did compose a suite, but Berlin never supplied the announced tone poem. Gershwin, learning of this proposed project in the newspaper, began working on his own piece. Ira Gershwin suggested that his brother call the piece *An American Rhapsody*. But George Gershwin visited a museum, and influenced by the colorful titles of paintings by James Abbot

McNeill Whistler (including a portrait of his mother formally titled *Arrangement in Gray and Black*), he decided to call his composition, *Rhapsody in Blue*.

George Gershwin explained, "There has been so much talk about the limitations of jazz. Jazz, they said, had to be in strict time. It had to cling to dance rhythms. I resolved, if possible, to kill that misconception." While taking a train to Boston, Gershwin suddenly heard in his mind the entire thematic design of the rhapsody. The piece was orchestrated by Whiteman's pianist, Ferde Grofé, and premiered before a stellar audience filled with the most celebrated figures in music and theater, including highly influential critics who disagreed intensely about what Gershwin was doing. One, Lawrence Gilman, appeared in print the next day, declaring the *Rhapsody* to be "trite, feeble, vapid, sentimental, derivative, and stale."

The public did not agree. Gershwin received a standing ovation from the audience at Aeolian Hall. The *Rhapsody in Blue*, incorporating vigorous syncopations and "blue notes" used by improvising jazz musicians and introduced into the more classical format of a piano rhapsody, made Gershwin a celebrity. He was offered $10,000 a week to play it on the stage of the Roxy Theater. Themes from the *Rhapsody* were arranged for every instrumental ensemble imaginable, even including an orchestra of harmonicas. When Hollywood filmed Gershwin's life story, the film was titled *Rhapsody in Blue*. It has outlived its critics and remains a part of the standard repertoire today.

As a result of the success of the *Rhapsody*, Gershwin was commissioned by Walter Damrosch to write a piano concerto. On December 3, 1925, Gershwin played his own *Concerto in F*, with Damrosch conducting the New York Symphony. The *Concerto in F* was far more sophisticated than the *Rhapsody in Blue* in its formal structure. The three movement work followed a traditional concerto design, but the rhythms, dissonances, "blue notes," and syncopations drew upon jazz and popular dance music to supply an undeniable quality of vigor. The opening theme was an impassioned, lyrical melody; the final movement was a dazzling display of percussive rhythms and nervous energy. Gershwin's music was clearly a reflection of New York in the 1920s: combining elements of jazz and traditional orchestration in his own unique style.

Gershwin also composed a set of three piano preludes, which he performed himself. In 1928, Walter Damrosch conducted the premiere of another Gershwin classic, *An American in Paris*. Inspired by a vacation in France, Gershwin used French taxi-horns to depict the joyous chaos of French traffic, personally selecting the horns that would "honk" in tune with his musical ideas. The more lyrical sections reflected a loneliness and longing for home in the familiar Gershwin combination of symphonic orchestrations and the poignancy of the blues. Gershwin composed other concert works, including his *Rhapsody in Rivets* and the *Cuban Overture*.

Because George Gershwin gained his greatest fame in writing popular music, a number of self-styled "serious music" critics treated him with a mixture of envy and condescension. This was especially true in the case of his magnificent score for an opera,

Porgy and Bess. But Gershwin refused to allow his popularity to be used as an excuse to denigrate his work or to apologize for writing in an original style that would appeal to large audiences. His works have stood the test of time. They are widely performed today and nobody even remembers the critics who regarded his innovations as shocking. His contribution to American concert music was undeniable. Gershwin was unique in another respect; in our journey through American music, he appears as we consider musical theater, motion picture music, and jazz, as well as the concert hall. The songs he wrote with his brilliant lyricist-brother Ira are considered among the finest popular songs ever written. His versatility made him difficult to classify in his lifetime. Even today, decades after his sudden death in 1937, critics and historians debate and disagree over how he should be classified. The public, however, has already classified Gershwin as a genius and an icon; he is likely to remain so throughout music history. Gershwin once said, "My people are Americans. My time is now." This statement is as true today as when he first made it.

THE NATIONALISTS

The story of American music was rewritten by a group of twentieth century composers. These men broke with the traditions of the nineteenth century and blazed a trail that established them among the best-known composers in the world. Each of these composers developed a highly individual style; it is impossible to put labels beside their names.

As we meet these composers, we can discover many similarities and differences among them. They came from all parts of the country—from New England coastal villages to the western plains. Several devoted themselves to highly nationalistic styles, drawing upon cowboy rhythms and folk music. They regarded European traditions with respect, but they were unapologetically American in their styles, tastes, and outlooks. Others pursued an appeal to emotions, to a new romantic ideal. They explored new harmonic ideas, but retained a devotion to the emotional expression of the best nineteenth century composers as reflecting a standard that is classic and timeless. A number rejected nationalism and romanticism entirely. They were attracted by an appeal to the mind, to abstractions, to a classical tradition. Several were most at home in the theater, writing for the stage. Others were impossible to classify except as nonconformists, eclectics, or eccentrics. Still others were born in Europe but came to the United States to pursue their craft. All shared one thing in common: each in his own way made an important contribution to our nation's musical development.

In the early years of the twentieth century, American composers, like those in Europe, were faced with a dilemma. Music has been called an international language. Like a spoken or written language, music has its own vocabulary; groups of notes are put together to form chords. Melodies are often played against each other. Much of music is based on patterns of scales like the ones practiced by everyone who takes piano lessons.

It is a challenge to describe the composers' dilemma in terms that are non-technical. If you are not a musician, you may think this explanation is still too technical for your taste. If you are an experienced musician, you will undoubtedly find it an oversimplification.

Throughout the eighteenth and nineteenth centuries, nearly all music was based around "key-centers." A piece of music might be said to be written in "the key of C." In effect, this meant that the composer had constructed his melodies and harmonies based on the C major scale, the one you would play using only the white keys on the piano. A composer might allow his music to roam around to other key centers (and even a scale, which used nearly all the black keys on the piano). But if the music were written around a key center, in this case, the key of C, he would always return to the expected key center of C.

Leonard Bernstein used the example of a baseball player running around the bases. He would run around the base paths but always return to home plate. By the early twentieth century, composers in Europe (and several rather bold nonconformists in the United States) were staying away longer and longer from key centers. (If we put this in baseball terms, it is the equivalent of the base runner heading for the outfield, climbing the fence, and going outside the stadium to buy a hot dog instead of going back to home plate.) These musical experiments caused huge controversies. Some composers tried doing away with key centers entirely, while others (like the Austrian composer Arnold Schoenberg) decided to adopt a complex plan for artificial scales created by the composers themselves. Audiences and critics often scorned the new music with bitter arguments and even riots as the result.

The most respected American composers in the nineteenth century had always followed the lead of European composers, particularly those from Germany. But as European music erupted into chaos and confusion, Americans were faced with a dilemma of their own. The argument between the Boston classicists, who followed the European lead, and the Americans, who sought inspiration from our country's popular and folk music, had continued.

In the twentieth century, a group of American composers began producing works that were unlike anything to be found in Europe. Not all of these American composers agreed with one another regarding the best road to a uniquely American style of concert music. More often than not, they disagreed with each other. Several of the leading American composers of this period thought it was a mistake to pursue a new national style, while others embraced the idea with enthusiasm. When all was said and done, American concert music had been changed forever.

Aaron Copland was the trailblazer who found the road to American musical nationalism that had been sought in vain by others. Copland was born in 1900, on a drab street in Brooklyn, New York. He began studying piano with his sister. Because no other members of his family had demonstrated musical brilliance, his parents were skeptical about his pursuit of advanced studies. But he insisted and in his teens, he decided to become a composer. Copland took private lessons from Rubin Goldmark, the conservative taskmaster who had been a pupil of Dvořák and was one of the best-known teachers in New York. But Goldmark had little enthusiasm for music by modern Europeans like Debussy, Ravel, or Stravinsky, and Copland was already searching for new and different means of musical expression.

In 1921, Copland saw an advertisement in the magazine, *Musical America*, announcing a new summer school for Americans in France. He was so eager to attend that he became the first applicant to win a scholarship at the new American Conservatory at Fontainebleau. His composition instructor, Paul Vidal, proved to be as conservative as Goldmark.

But Copland took his meals in the company of two other musicians, a composer from Cleveland, G. Herbert Elwell, and a talented harpist, Djina Ostrowska. It was Ostrowska who began urging Copland to attend the harmony classes of Nadia Boulanger, a young instructor on the Fontainebleau faculty. Copland said he'd learned enough harmony from Goldmark and showed no interest. But Ostrowska insisted, and when Copland dropped in on one of Mlle. Boulanger's classes, he heard her lecture on Mussorgsky's opera, *Boris Godunov*. Copland was fascinated by her encyclopedic knowledge of the music of every historical period, her enthusiasm and energy, and especially, her awareness of all the latest developments in modern music. Copland made a virtually unprecedented decision. He decided to study composition with Nadia Boulanger in Paris. No major composers of any nationality had ever studied composition with a woman and no women composers were regarded as highly significant at the time. Nadia Boulanger was the champion of her late sister, the composer Lili Boulanger, who had died tragically at a very young age. Mlle. Boulanger was also an organist, pianist, conductor, analyst, and ultimately, maternal adviser to several generations of composers.

Figure 57 - - Nadia Boulanger – the legendary teacher of generations of 20th century composers. Her Paris salon became the gathering place for the "Boulangerie," her famed pupils who changed the face of contempory music. (Photo courtesy of la Bibliothèque Nationale de France)

About the time Copland began his studies with her, two other Americans, Virgil Thomson and Melville Smith, also became her pupils. In time, Mlle. Boulanger taught so many distinguished Americans that her first class became known as the "Boulangerie," the French word for "bakery." Virgil Thomson would later remark that every American town had two things: a five and ten cent store and a Boulanger student. Copland spent considerable time in Mlle. Boulanger's Paris salon, where he met all the important figures in European music, the modernists about whom he was so curious, including Stravinsky and Ravel, and even (to his astonishment), figures from the nineteenth century, including the elderly Camille Saint-

Figure 58 - Aaron Copland. Walter Damrosch said of him, "If a gifted young man can write a symphony like this at twenty-three, within five years, he will be ready to commit murder." (Photo courtesy of Aaron Copland)

Saens who died shortly thereafter. Copland spent three years in France. In 1924, Mlle. Boulanger planned a concert tour of the U.S. as an organist. She asked Copland to compose a *Symphony for Organ and Orchestra* for her to perform.

In 1925, Copland returned to the United States for the premiere. Conductor Walter Damrosch might never have accepted a new work from Copland, by his own definition, a "brash young man from Brooklyn." But he admired Nadia Boulanger, and the work was scheduled for performance. Copland, running late from the subway, came to the concert hall, hurried to the main entrance, pulled open the door, and was greeted by the thunderous blast of his own orchestration.

When the work was played before an audience, Damrosch told the audience, "Ladies and Gentlemen, I am sure you will agree that if a gifted young man can write a symphony like this at twenty-three, within five years, he will be ready to commit murder." Virgil Thomson told Boulanger he wept when he heard the work. When asked why, he said, "Because I didn't write it myself!" The success of the symphony led to other opportunities for Copland, including the enthusiastic support of Serge Koussevitzky, the prominent conductor of the Boston Symphony. Copland won numerous commissions and prizes, and joined his friend Roger Sessions to organize the Copland-Sessions concerts, a series of concerts devoted to contemporary music. (Sessions went to Italy for several years, and was of necessity, absent from most of the programs of which he was co-sponsor. After one such concert, a woman in the audience, obviously unaware of his absent colleague, approached Copland enthusiastically and said, "Mr. Copland, I can't tell you how much I enjoy your Sessions!")

In the late 1920s, Copland became interested in jazz and began experimenting with the use of snappy jazz rhythms in symphonic music. His *Music for the Theater*, a suite for small orchestra and piano, included jazz influences, as did his *Concerto for Piano and Orchestra*. Copland appeared as soloist in the Boston premiere of his Concerto. But he concluded that jazz was limited in means of expression to the blues and to swing. Some musicians (obviously including the most prominent figure in jazz to write major concert works, Duke Ellington) would challenge the assertion that jazz was so limited. But Copland had already absorbed jazz rhythms, which he regarded as the facet of jazz that most interested him.

Copland began writing music of a more abstract nature. Copland's more abstract pieces included his *Piano Variations*, the *Short Symphony*, and the *Piano Sonata*. Audiences, even musicians, found the abstract works more difficult to appreciate. When Copland asked Serge Koussevitzky if the *Short Symphony* was difficult, the conductor replied in French, "Not difficult, impossible!" The work was ultimately premiered in Mexico by Copland's friend, the Mexican composer-conductor Carlos Chávez. But years later, when an octogenarian Copland conducted a performance of his *Short Symphony* in Carnegie Hall, a violinist told him, "Mr. Copland, you taught American orchestras how to play in 5/4." Times had changed.

In time, Copland became concerned that his own music, and that of others, might be directed at too narrow an audience. As the champion of young composers, he helped organize festivals of American music at Yaddo, a retreat for artists in Saratoga Springs, New York. He became active in organizations devoted to the welfare of composers, the League of Composers and the American Composers Alliance. He wrote books, *What to Listen for In Music* in 1939, and *Our New Music* in 1941, designed to further the public's understanding of modern music. He taught, at Harvard and at the Berkshire Music Center in Tanglewood, Massachusetts. In his own music, he turned to themes and ideas that would be accessible to large audiences. His evocation of Mexico, *El Salón México*, was inspired by a visit to a popular Mexican dance hall. He wanted to capture the spirit of the Mexican people in his own original melodies. Copland was concerned that Mexican audiences might regard his efforts with skepticism. He was delighted when Mexican musicians told him his piece was "as Mexican as Revueltas," a reference to the Mexican composer Silvestre Revueltas, the equivalent of telling someone he was "as American as Gershwin." Copland scored films, including *Of Mice and Men*, *Our Town*, and *The Heiress*, and composed a work for narrator and orchestra, *A Lincoln Portrait*.

Of all Copland's works, his ballet scores won him the widest audiences and critical acclaim. His three stunning ballets, *Billy the Kid* (1938), *Rodeo* (1942), and *Appalachian Spring* (1944), firmly established Copland's nationalist style of composing. In these works, the composer was using the rhythms and harmonies that were distinctly American. Yet Copland was surprised to find himself writing a cowboy ballet in Paris.

When Lincoln Kirstein, a dance impresario, asked Copland to write the music for *Billy the Kid*, the composer was skeptical. "I was born in Brooklyn," he said. "I don't know anything about the Wild West." Kirstein told him that the ballet would be based on Eugene Loring's scenario about William J. Bonney, the real figure known as "Billy the Kid," a western desperado born in New York. Copland agreed, masterfully incorporating western styles, rhythms, and folk melodies like *Bury Me Not on the Lone Prairie* into the score.

Rodeo was written for choreographer Agnes de Mille, and presented the plight of a cowgirl (and a tomboy) who grows into a woman and finds true love as a western Cinderella. *Appalachian Spring* was introduced by choreographer Martha Graham and originally called for only thirteen instruments, although Copland later re-scored it symphonically. His use of country tunes and the distinctive sound of rural, homespun fiddlers was unmistakable. Curiously, the work was originally titled *Ballet for Martha*. When Graham told Copland she had decided to call it *Appalachian Spring*, she explained that the title came from a poem by Hart Crane. "Does the ballet have anything to do with the title?" he asked her. "No," she said, "I just liked the way it sounded." For years, admirers told Copland how they could visualize the scenes of pure beauty in the Appalachian mountains that they knew had been his inspiration in writing the work. Copland would smile and accept the compliment graciously.

One of Copland's best-known (and shortest) works is a fanfare he composed at the request of Eugene Goosens, conductor of the Cincinnati Symphony Orchestra. Goosens had asked British composers to write special fanfares, appropriately titled, to be played at concerts during World War I. Now, in the midst of the Second World War, he asked Copland for a fanfare. Copland's work, intended to last only two minutes, was scored for brass and percussion.

Copland faced two problems, how to make a traditional fanfare sound contemporary, and what to call it. Copland considered many titles, including *For a Solemn Ceremony*, *For the Day of Victory*, *For our Heroes*, *For the Rebirth of Lidice*, *For the Spirit of Democracy*, *For the Paratroops*, and *For the Four Freedoms*. He solved both his problems. Musically, its opening brass declaration is one of Copland's signature sounds. As for titles, *Fanfare for the Common Man* is universally recognized as a distinct expression of the American spirit.

Copland also turned out a *Clarinet Concerto* for Benny Goodman, known in jazz as the "King of Swing," and a clean, expansive *Third Symphony*. He also composed operas, including *The Second Hurricane* and, in 1954 on commission from Rodgers and Hammerstein, *The Tender Land*, the story of a farm family and the effect two drifters have on the family during the 1930s spring harvest time. In later years, Copland again turned to musical abstractions, experimenting with the twelve-tone techniques developed by

Arnold Schoenberg. When Copland's early music was played, he was regarded as a shocking rebel, challenging tradition. Today, his style is as recognizable as the most traditional of composers, but always in a highly personal manner. Copland has been an important influence on generations of younger composers. He was a musically adventurous spirit who wrote a number of most enduring concert works. The austerity, dissonance, rhythmic energy, and forthright clarity of his music have become a tradition all their own.

If Aaron Copland felt self-conscious about writing music with western or cowboy themes, the same could never be said about his friend, colleague, and occasional rival, Roy Harris. When Serge Koussevitzky, the distinguished conductor of the Boston Symphony Orchestra, was asked to comment about American music, he exclaimed, "I think that nobody has captured in music the essence of American life, its vitality, its greatness, its strength, as well as Roy Harris. I feel the genius of his art, which is great because it so colorfully portrays the life of our people."

Figure 59 - Roy Harris, born in a log cabin on February 12, Lincoln's Birthday, in Lincoln County, Oklahoma. As a symphonist, he aspired to become "The American Beethoven." (Photo by permission of John F. Kennedy Memorial Library, California State University, Los Angles)

Harris's own life was colorful, to say the least, and there has been no comparable figure in America's musical life, before or since. He was born on February 12, 1898, on Lincoln's Birthday, in a log cabin, in Lincoln County, Oklahoma. This coincidence was responsible for a lifelong identification with Lincoln. Harris used Lincoln's life and words as sources for his own inspiration.

Admirers described Harris as "America's musical Abraham Lincoln," an analogy which he did nothing to discourage. Unlike some composers who approached the American west as a place of exotic musical colors, Harris was a true westerner. His Scotch-Irish parents had built their cabin during the Cimarron frontier rush. One of his grandfathers had been a rider for the Pony Express. When he was still a boy, his family moved to California and young Roy Harris grew up on a farm. He went to Covina High School, but he described his true interests as "music, philosophy, poetry, the wonder of the clouds, mountain bird songs, and sunsets." After graduation, he worked on the family farm, drove a milk truck, and studied Greek philosophy. He entered the University of California, studying philosophy and economics. His ambitions to become a composer surfaced late; the University's principal expert on such matters refused to encourage him, insisting that Harris was too old to start a serious musical career, absent years of preparation during boyhood. Some years later, the same administrator offered Harris a position as head of the University's music department, a position that Harris, by now world famous, declined.

Harris began studying composition privately in Los Angeles, with Arthur Farwell. He had his first orchestral music performed when Howard Hanson conducted his *Andante for Orchestra* in Rochester, New York. The *Andante* was also awarded a prize, a performance by the New York Philharmonic. In 1926,. Harris borrowed a hundred dollars, quit his job as a truck driver, and headed east. He never looked back.

Instead, he won a Guggenheim Fellowship. At the suggestion of Aaron Copland, he went to Paris to study with Nadia Boulanger. Harris was not interested in formal exercises in harmony or counterpoint. He began an intensive study of the string quartets of Beethoven, and all his life, used Beethoven as a benchmark to measure his work and that of other composers.

While in Paris, he completed a *Concerto for Piano, Clarinet, and String Quartet*, which premiered with Mlle. Boulanger at the keyboard. He also composed a vigorous *Piano Sonata*. After three years in France, he returned home to find an American public ready, willing and able to appreciate his music. Robert Schumann, on hearing the music of Frederic Chopin, said "Hats off, gentlemen, a genius!" Harris's teacher, Arthur Farwell, paraphrased Schumann when he wrote of Harris, "Gentlemen, a genius, but keep your hats on." Now, the public agreed.

Like Aaron Copland, Harris acquired Serge Koussevitzky as an early mentor. "I am told you are the American Mussorgsky," Koussevitzky told the delighted Roy Harris, in his inimitable Russian accent. "You will write me a BIG symphony from the west. I will play." Serge Koussevitzky's singular comparison to Modeste Mussorgsky was appropriate.

Harris and Mussorgsky both embodied the fierce nationalist character of their countries. When a serious accident confined him to bed (preventing him from composing at the piano), he began developing the highly personal contrapuntal style which would mark so many of his works. Harris believed that music had been declining since Beethoven. He was fascinated by the long melodic lines of Renaissance and Baroque

Figure 60 - Roy Harris, composer, and his wife, pianist Johana Harris. Their musical marriage was a unique collaboration in which they traveled the country, all the while composing, teaching, performing, and lecturing to worldwide acclaim. (Photo by permission of John F. Kennedy Memorial Library, California State University, Los Angeles)

composers, culminating in the masterpieces of J. S. Bach. He was equally intrigued with modal scales, alternatives to traditional major and minor scales that did not shock or startle the ear, as did many artificial scales created by avant-garde Europeans. His approach to form frequently included fugues, passacaglias, chorales, and toccatas. If the forms were classical, brooding harmonic colors, western rhythms, and effusive energy were pure Harris.

Roy Harris wrote his first symphony in 1933. He also began teaching at the Juilliard School of Music, where he met and married Beula Duffey, a brilliant young Canadian-born concert pianist also on the faculty. A former child prodigy, she had joined the faculty of the Juilliard Graduate School at only 15. He changed her name to Johana as a tribute to Johann Sebastian Bach. His wedding present to his wife was a new *Piano Quintet*. As Johana Harris, she became the greatest interpreter of his music, and his collaborator in music and life for forty-three years. Johana Harris could have pursued her career as a concert pianist throughout the world. She was a virtuoso in interpreting the classics and a brilliant improviser. But she chose to specialize in her husband's music and devoted much of her life to being the champion of his music. The Harrises taught at numerous universities around the country and their fame spread around the world.

For years, critics had been asking, "Why doesn't someone write the great American symphony?" With the premiere of Roy Harris's *Third Symphony* in 1938, they stopped asking. Symphonies by American composers would typically receive a single performance. Multiple performances of the Harris *Third Symphony* followed throughout the world. Ironically, the work was almost never completed. Harris had been asked to write a violin concerto for Jascha Heifetz, at the time the world's most famous concert violinist. But in the midst of completing the concerto, he was informed by Heifetz that his manager thought it the wrong time to introduce a new concerto by a modern American composer. Harris decided to re-work the thematic material into a symphony. Heifetz's loss became Harris's gain. During the darkest days of World War II, a time capsule was buried in London to preserve the best of western culture if civilization didn't survive. The only work by an American composer to be included was a symphony by Roy Harris

Harris's *Third Symphony* is played in a single movement, divided into five sections: tragic, lyric, pastoral, a dramatic fugue, and a dramatic-tragic finale. The work seemed to capture the very spirit of rural and pioneer America, from the loneliness of the American prairie to the bright spirit and sounds of the pastoral countryside. The fugue was spirited, ambling, and confident. An emotional finale moved with the feeling of inexorable destiny and the inevitability of fate. The *Third Symphony* was the first American symphony performed by Arturo Toscanini and the NBC Symphony, and many years later, the only American symphony included in Leonard Bernstein's Bicentennial Tour with the New York Philharmonic. It was also the symphony by an American composer introduced in China by Eugene Ormandy and the Philadelphia Orchestra. Critics who disagreed on everything else seemed to finally agree that Harris had succeeded in a goal so many of his predecessors had found elusive. He had written the first truly great American symphony.

In 1941, Harris launched his *Folk Song Symphony* for chorus and orchestra. The work was based on folk themes: *The Gal I Left Behind Me*, a Civil War song; *Oh, Bury Me Not on the Lone Prairie*, a western cowboy song; the classic Negro spiritual, *De Trumpet Sounds in My Soul*; the southern mountaineer love song, *He's Gone Away*; and a melody often identified with Harris, *When Johnny Comes Marching Home*.

The folk song would be incorporated in Harris's music throughout his career. Although Johana Harris was an internationally renowned concert pianist, few people today know that she was also a gifted folksinger. In the 1940s, the Harrises presented a series of radio broadcasts devoted to the folksong, with Roy Harris providing the narration and Johana Harris the singing. This collaboration also resulted in him composing his *American Ballads* for piano, using original settings to varying degrees of melodies of tunes such as *Streets of Laredo* and *Black is the Color of My True Love's Hair*.

Harris was a natural symphonist and his future works were often cast in a symphonic vein. His *Fifth* and *Seventh Symphonies* were not influenced by extramusical sources. Both contained a good deal of counterpoint, mixed with tuneful quotations in the rhythmic and melodic styles identified with the composer: dance tunes, marches, hymns, and the wide, expansive melodic lines he preferred. (When Harris conducted his *Fifth Symphony* in Moscow, he became the first American composer to conduct such a symphony in Russia.)

Harris based his *Sixth Symphony* on the *Gettysburg Address*, and his *Ninth Symphony* on the Preamble to the United States Constitution and the poetry of Walt Whitman. Whitman was a regular source of inspiration to Harris. Aaron Copland described Harris's assertive, jerky rhythms as "blobs and yawps of sound." He compared them to the words in Whitman's poems. Harris did numerous settings of Whitman's poetry, which seemed ideally suited to his musical style. His *Eighth Symphony* was inspired by the City of San Francisco. Harris composed his *Tenth Symphony* for the 100th anniversary of Abraham Lincoln's assassination, combining his own original texts with those of Lincoln, adding men's and women's choruses to an orchestral sound of brass, percussion, and amplified pianos. (Harris became intrigued by the used of amplified pianos. He also completed a *Concerto for Amplified Piano and Orchestra*, premiered by Johana Harris, with the composer conducting. The work included an homage to Claude Debussy, another composer for whom Harris had tremendous admiration.

Until the end of his career, Harris continued to explore the form of the symphony. Though his sources of inspiration were many, each work reflected the composer's preference for big themes, both in his musical ideas and the philosophy that drove him to creation. His *Eleventh Symphony* was inspired by the ideas of war and peace, his *Twelfth Symphony* by the 300th Anniversary of the journey of Père Marquette, and his *Thirteenth* by the Bicentennial of the United States. (Harris was superstitious regarding numbers. He labeled *Symphony No. 13* as "14," but it was posthumously re-numbered as "13.") When he died in 1979, he left behind a large catalogue of music, commissioned by every major American orchestra and by leading soloists like cellist Gregor Piatigorsky and violist William Primrose. In addition to his symphonies, there were chamber music works, pieces for piano, and numerous choral compositions.

Harris was a composer with strong opinions. He once wrote, "The post Beethoven historical trough in which we find ourselves has descended even deeper than I had anticipated. I had thought we had hit rock-bottom with Stravinsky's *Le Sacre du Printemps* and Schoenberg's *Pierrot Lunaire*, both historically significant works, but with the advent of 'Musique *concrète*' and the tape assembly mosaics and all the other experiments in escapism from musical tradition, we still suffer from the postwar and presentiment of prewar psychoses that are leading creative music deeper and deeper into the wilderness of creative bewilderment."

He was a man of extraordinary personal magnetism. Johana Harris once described her husband as a child who would never grow old, an unquenchable optimist who loved beauty in every phrase of living. She said that the popular song, *Don't Fence Me In* described the law that governed her husband's life. He was a man of boundless energy, whose enthusiasm affected everyone with whom he came in contact: the pupils and apprentice composers who copied his music, the performers who interpreted it, and especially audiences. In a critical essay in praise of Harris, John Kreuger wrote, "There is another quality in the music of Roy Harris. This is almost indefinable. We hear it in the music of Bach and Beethoven. I hear it in Harris. For lack of a more complete term, I would call it 'the touch of the master.' There is a certain confidence and daring in the melodic turns, almost an arrogance in the selection of a sound, and a grandeur in the sweep of a form. As you study his music, you know instinctively that the man is fully aware of his Time; that he has absorbed its joys and its sadness and its searching spirit."

As a teacher, Harris disliked everything he regarded as pedantic. He had little regard for the use of harmony textbooks, especially those written by Ivy League college professors, which stressed the traditional rules and regulations of nineteenth century music. Instead, he started his pupils immediately on the study of the modal scales he used in his own music and expected even the most basic exercises in harmony and counterpoint to express their own creativity.

He called his famous wife Johana "Lady Jo" and she referred to him as "Papa." There was no doubt in the Harris household as to the guiding spirit of activity in life: the music of Roy Harris. Mrs. Harris often assisted him in editing his piano music. Their children and students (who often worked as apprentices and copyists) were expected to show the same devotion and enthusiasm for his music that Roy Harris displayed himself. Following his sense of wanderlust, Roy Harris pursued his musical ambitions in many places. But wherever the Harrises went, his incredible energy and optimistic self-confidence were infectious. Early in his career, he overheard someone in the lobby of a Boston concert hall make a disparaging remark about one of his symphonies. The man admitted that he hadn't actually heard the work and that he was relying on the opinion of his wife. Another composer might have walked away, but Harris confronted the skeptic and said, "I presume you're a businessman. Do you let your wife tell you how to run your business or do you make up your own mind?" Embarrassed, the man apologized, told Harris that he owned a shipping line and offered the Harrises free passage back to New York. Undaunted, Harris said, "I understand that you also have cruises to South America." The conversation ended with a new convert to Harris's growing fan club and a complimentary cruise for Roy and Johana Harris.

In recent years, a number of eastern critics with a neoclassic bent found it fashionable to dismiss Harris's conscious Americanism and its appeal to large audiences. These critics were frequently rival composers who taught at Ivy League universities and who did not appreciate the fact that when Harris told a pupil, "You're writing like an academic," he didn't mean the remark as a compliment. Harris would be delighted to be regarded as a composer of the people. He cultivated his own harmonic language, based on his analysis of acoustics. He had a capacity to infuse his music with vitality and energy, and these qualities were manifestations apparent in both his music and his personality, which casts a large shadow over the development of a national musical expression

Virgil Thomson was uniquely qualified to speak about the language of music, since he occupied a special place in contemporary musical history. He was internationally renowned as both a composer (with operas, ballets, orchestral works, chamber music, and film scores to his credit) and a critic (for *The New York Herald Tribune*). He was one of a group of American composers who emerged in the 1920s with a style so distinctly American that they liberated American music from an imposing European shadow. But Thomson's approach to music (and to life) was not like any friend or colleague. He was an original.

Virgil Thomson was born in Kansas City, Missouri, in 1896. (The sound of Midwestern church hymns can be heard clearly in his music.) Eventually, he went to Harvard and became the organist in King's Chapel in Boston. He continued playing the organ, off and on, until age 28, when he gave up the instrument because he was "tired of churches and preachers." He went to Paris because he said if he were going to lead the life of a starving composer, he wanted to do it where the food was good. He discovered, as had Melville Smith and Aaron Copland before him, the remarkable Nadia Boulanger who became his teacher.

Figure 61 - Virgil Thomson. A composer and critic, equally at home in Kansas City, Paris, or New York - inspired by hymn tunes and avant-garde poetry. (Photo courtesy of Virgil Thomson)

While in Paris, Thomson became friends with many of the leading French and American expatriate figures in music, art, and literature. Foremost among this group were the young composers who were called "Les Six," in particular Darius Milhaud and Arthur Honegger. Thomson also met Jean Cocteau, Pablo Picasso, F. Scott Fitzgerald, and the poet Gertrude

Stein. He maintained a lifelong affinity for Paris, and for many years, divided his time between apartments in the French capital and New York.

Thomson had definite ideas about being an American composer. "It never occurred to me to try to be American," he said. "I wouldn't have needed to try after 300 years in the country. But actually, the problem with my predecessors and with many of my contemporaries was not trying to be American, but trying to be European. They kept trying to write like a German composer or a Scandinavian composer or a French composer." Thomson's Americanism was quite different from the energetic New Yorker Aaron Copland or the expansive, sometimes brooding westerner, Roy Harris.

Thomson drew upon his roots in the churches of Kansas City, composing his *Symphony on a Hymn Tune*, a work which he would not hear in performance for twenty years. But he also became influenced by the wit and surprise of the French musicians and writers who had become his friends. Thomson always liked nonconformists. He encountered an avant-garde movement in Paris known as the "Dadas," and he wrote that all Americans were "a little Da Da." One nonconformist especially admired by Thomson was his close friend, the composer and pianist George Antheil, the self-professed "bad boy of music."

Antheil introduced Thomson to Gertrude Stein, the poet whose texts he began setting to music in 1926. Thomson collaborated with Stein on his operas, *Four Saints in Three Acts* and *The Mother of Us All*. *Four Saints in Three Acts*, an opera about Spanish saints, premiered in 1934, with an all-black cast, and ran for an unprecedented fifty performances, helping make Thomson famous. Thomson's wry musical wit was ideally suited to the Gertrude Stein text. The opera is full of energy identified with Midwestern religious zeal.

Their second operatic collaboration, *The Mother of Us All* revealed Thomson's flair for absorbing the rhythms and pulses of Middle America, blending them with Parisian style and turning out an entertaining piece of composition devoted to the life of Susan B. Anthony. Thomson, unlike numerous avant-garde composers, knew how to write tunes, melodies, and harmonies that communicated with audiences. His early *Sonata da chiesa* (or church sonata) contained a tango, as does a sequence in his film score for *The Plough That Broke the Plains*. In contrast to his early flirtations with French neo-classicism are his pieces based on American hymns, with gentle, folk-like harmonies that reflect his background as an organist. He could combine the sophistication of serious concert composer with the truthful simplicity of the American heartland: his work, like his persona, was part-Paris, part-Kansas City.

In the early 1930s, Virgil Thomson became part of the Federal Theater Project, and in the process, part of the theatrical circle surrounding the multitalented and prodigious actor-director-writer and all-around creative phenomenon, Orson Welles. At the time, Welles was a young man who had studied music, art, and magic before deciding to concentrate on acting. He became a serious theatrical producer at only twenty. The all-black cast in *Four Saints in Three Acts* inspired Orson Welles's legendary production of *Macbeth*. Thomson collaborated with Welles, providing music and sound effects for an all-black production, with the location of the Shakespeare classic moved from Scotland to Haiti. Welles, of course, would become the country's most prominent radio star and move on to Hollywood and his first film, the legendary *Citizen Kane*.

In 1938, Thomson pursued an entirely new creative avenue: ballet. George Balanchine called Thomson's ballet, *Filling Station*, "one of the oldest, if not the very oldest classical ballet with a specifically Native American theme." Thomson insisted on composing portraits of all the characters in the ballet, to introduce them to the audience. Gone were the images of fantasy and mythology identified with classical Russian ballets. The hero of this ballet is a filling station attendant. There were truck drivers, a nervous gangster, and an American family (with a henpecked husband). Instead of a typical Russian adagio, *Filling Station* featured a Thomson tango for the dance-duet between a rich young man and his girlfriend returning from a night at the country club.

Throughout his life, Thomson continued to display a flair for the theatrical, writing incidental music for stage plays and film scores along with his concert works. Late in life, he completed a full-length opera based on the life of Byron. He composed many songs, not surprising with a preference for French texts. Whimsical satire always appealed to Thomson. He once created a cantata based on the nonsense poetry of Edward Lear. He also composed string quartets, piano sonatas, and a number of orchestral tone poems, including *The Seine at Night, Wheatfield at Noon*, and *Sea Piece with Birds*.

One of Thomson's most original musical activities was his penchant for creating musical portraits of his friends. He composed around 150, depicting everyone from Aaron Copland to the Spanish artist Pablo Picasso, from the French composer Henri Sauguet to New York's colorful Mayor Fiorello LaGuardia. Thomson liked to have his subjects sit for their musical portraits as they would for a visual artist. He would not try to recreate a physical image of his subjects in sound, but used his musical instincts to capture their inner spirit in his own musical language. Thomson also created an unusual self-portrait, in the form of a cello concerto that received numerous performances. Not surprisingly, the work was based in part on the hymn tunes that were always a part of his musical character.

But Thomson also found time to write about music, as a clever articulate, highly opinionated music critic. He aimed his verbal barbs at such figures as Igor Stravinsky and Arturo Toscanini, scolding the latter for not playing enough works by American composers. In his fourteen years as music critic for *The New York Herald Tribune*, he regularly expounded his witty and occasionally acerbic views. He was a gifted writer who published his memoirs and displayed a decided ability as a raconteur. Despite his success, Thomson remained unaffected. In his nineties, the Francophile from Kansas City was honored by the nation (and the President of the United States), and decided to conclude his evening with a midnight dinner at a posh French restaurant in Washington,

D.C. Thomson, a noted gourmet cook himself, asked an astonished headwaiter if the restaurant could fix him a good plate of hash. The outraged waiter summoned the maître d'hôtel, to see what sort of person would make such a request, and Thomson repeated his request, this time in perfect French.

Figure 62 - Paul Bowles, composer and writer, who spent much of life living as an American expatriate in Morocco. (Photograph by Cherie Nutting, all rights reserved. The University of Delaware Library, Special Collections)

Reflecting upon his musical view, Thomson suggested that in the modern age, there is no avant-garde, that even the most extreme musical revolutionary is conventional at a time when it is fashionable, respectable, and even advantageous to be perceived as a revolutionary. Thomson called for composers to develop their gifts for the lyric theater. He himself played a vital role in the development of contemporary music, as both composer and critic, leaving a significant stamp on the American musical scene.

For many years, Thomson lived in an apartment in the Hotel Chelsea, a colorful New York residence that catered to bohemians and was frequented by an incredible assortment of writers, artists, actors, and musicians. He remained there for the remainder of his life. Paul Wittke described his apartment as a type of salon that attracted friends, admirers, and rivals from around the artistic world in search of debonair conversation and fabulous food, while Thomson held court like a maharajah. Wittke said, "From his command post in the Chelsea, Thomson directed and conscripted, admonished and advised by phone, usually from his bed, clad in expensive, bright pajamas, all those around him, a power broker with a wide reach." Those receiving his advice included his various distinguished pupils, including Paul Bowles and Ned Rorem.

Bowles was an unusual figure who spent over fifty years as an American expatriate in Tangier, Morocco. He was a versatile composer who wrote incidental music for ballets, documentary films, and plays, collaborating with major theatrical figures including Orson Welles, William Saroyan, and Tennessee Williams. He wrote major concert works for the piano duo of Gold and Fizdale. He was also a writer whose novels, short stories, and poetry overshadowed his music.

Bowles had studied with Aaron Copland, with whom he first traveled to Morocco, and also with Virgil Thomson (whose path he followed as a music critic for a time), Roger Sessions, and Israel Citkowitz. Copland said that Bowles never wrote a dull piece of music. His works were noted for wit and surprise, but he disliked formal study and described himself as intensely non-academic. Bowles pursued nomadic travel, going everywhere from Mexico to the Sahara Desert to India. His visits to Latin America inspired a number of his musical works, including a zarzuela, *The Wind Remains*.

In 1947, Bowles settled in Tangier and the following year, he published his first novel, The *Sheltering Sky*. Although he continued to write art songs and thought of himself first and foremost as a composer, he achieved greater public reputation as a writer. Much of his music is still being rediscovered.

Ned Rorem worked as Thomson's copyist for a year in exchange for orchestration lessons. He later studied with Bernard Wagenaar at the Juilliard School and emerged as one of America's most prolific composers. His output includes a remarkable ten operas, four piano concertos, three symphonies, as well as ballets. Rorem became America's best-known composer of art songs, with over five hundred such songs to his credit. He is also a prolific writer of many books, including his widely-read diaries and volumes of criticism.

Figure 63 - Ned Rorem, a Virgil Thomson pupil and one of America's best known composer of art songs. (Photo by David Diamond, used courtesy of the David L. Diamond estate - All rights reserved.)

Reflecting upon his musical view, Thomson suggested that in the modern age, there is no avant-garde that even the most extreme musical revolutionary is conventional at a time when it is fashionable, respectable, and even advantageous to be perceived as a revolutionary. Thomson called for composers to develop their gifts for the lyric theater. Thomson's time as a critic created problems for him after he left the *Herald-Tribune*. The composers, conductors, and performers who had been the target of his barbs were not eager to play his music or encourage others to do so. But he remained undaunted and positive. He himself played a vital role in the development of contemporary music, as both composer and critic, leaving a significant stamp on the American musical scene.

Another composer consistently identified with the "nationalists" in American concert music was Randall Thompson. Thompson was a native of New York City, his father the headmaster of a private school. He displayed great talent as a boy soprano, and began seriously studying both voice and the organ. At Harvard, he came under the influence of Archibald T. Davison and developed a lifelong devotion to

Figure 64 - Randall Thompson was one of America's leading composers of choral music. (Photo courtesy of University of Virginia Special Collections Library)

choral music. Following his graduation, he became a private pupil of Ernest Bloch. For three years, he lived in Rome as a Fellow at the American Academy and then returned to the United States, where he began teaching at a number of major universities. For a time, he served as director of the Curtis Institute of Philadelphia. He also taught at Harvard and the University of Virginia, remaining as a vital force in the American musical scene throughout his lifetime.

Thompson earned recognition as one of America's leading choral composers. His settings of eight choruses from Isaiah for unaccompanied mixed chorus, *The Peaceable Kingdom*, was especially dramatic. Thompson also adapted the writings of Thomas Jefferson in a four-movement work, *The Testament of Freedom*. Included was a stately opening movement, a rather ominous second movement, a quick-spirited march, and a dignified, graceful conclusion, the latter based on Jefferson's letters to Adams.

But Thompson also had a sense of humor. He also composed *Americana*, based on texts by the controversial writer and editor H. L. Mencken, each dealing with fundamentalism, spiritualism, temperance, capital punishment, and optimism, all excerpted from the popular magazine, *American Mercury*. Thompson's catalogue also included several symphonies, a pair of lyrical string quartets, a *Jazz Poem for Piano and Orchestra*, and a symphonic prelude, *The Piper at the Gates of Dawn*. In the 1960s, Thompson was still exploring the musical possibilities of the chorus: he completed an oratorio, *The Passion According to St. Luke,* and a cantata for women's voices, *The Place of the Blest.* Randall Thompson was known as a composer of taste and clarity, one who combined great energy with fine craftsmanship.

Douglas Moore was another American composer consistently identified with a form of nationalism. Moore, born in 1893 in Cutchogue, on Long Island, was a direct descendent of both John Alden and Miles Standish. Moore was a lifelong musical conservative. But unlike some of his predecessors, Douglas Moore was a highly creative and imaginative musician who could use a traditional approach to harmonic language to express American musical ideas in new and exciting ways. Moore studied with Horatio Parker at Yale, where he composed *Good Night, Harvard*, a traditional fight song for the Yale football team. He served in the Navy during World War I; during these years, he joined forces with John Jacob Niles to produce a collection of songs published as *Songs My Mother Never Taught Me*. Eventually, he studied in Paris with Vincent D'Indy and then went to Cleveland, where he became Curator of Music at the Cleveland Museum of Art. While in Cleveland, he joined an important group of young composers, Roger Sessions, Bernard Rogers, Quincy Porter, and Theodore Chanler, all pupils of Ernest Bloch. He also returned to Paris, this time studying with Nadia Boulanger.

Figure 65 - Edward Levy, co-director, Hanya Holm, co-director and choreographer, Douglas Moore, composer, and John Latouche, librettist, collaborating on a production of Moore's opera, *The Ballad of Baby Doe.* (Photo by Louis Mélançon, courtesy of University of Denver/Central City Opera House)

When he returned to the United States, the poet Vachel Lindsay encouraged him to devote his energies to depicting American themes in music. Moore responded in 1924 with one of his most successful pieces, *The Pageant of P.T. Barnum*. Moore's music depicted the images of Barnum's career in a romantic, expressive style, beginning with the sounds of his boyhood at Bethel, Connecticut, represented by country fiddles. Moore also wrote an expressive musical portrait of Joyce Heath, a 160-year-old black woman who was believed to be the nurse for the infant George Washington. He created a musical sequence depicting General and Mrs. Tom Thumb, complete with cap pistols and portrayed the famed singer Jenny Lind by a florid flute. Most notable was a circus march featuring the most out-of-tune clarinet ever to appear in an orchestra. In 1926, Moore joined the faculty of Columbia University, where he remained a distinguished teacher (and ultimately head of the music department) until his retirement in 1962.

Douglas Moore, like Roy Harris, felt most comfortable with American themes; but unlike Harris, whose natural métier was the symphony, Moore was happiest writing for the theater. Even his orchestral pieces had a decidedly theatrical quality. The titles of Moore's works reflected his unabashed Americanism: *The Down East Suite* for violin and piano; *The Ballad of William Sycamore* for baritone, flute, trombone, and piano; *Farm Journal*, a popular suite based on his score for the documentary film *Power and Land*; *Village Music*, another orchestral suite; and *Moby Dick*, a tone poem for orchestra, inspired by Herman Melville's classic novel. Moore also wrote orchestral works without plots or programs, but even when he wrote the more abstract *Symphony in A Major*, he acknowledged that the second movement was "inspired by a short poem of James Joyce which deals with music based on the coming of twilight." But Moore's true forte was writing operas. In 1934, he composed *White Wings*, based on a Philip Barry play about the resistance of street cleaners devoted to the horse and buggy in the age of the automobile. Moore had to wait fourteen years to hear his work performed.

In 1939, Moore completed *The Devil and Daniel Webster*, based on the story by Stephen Vincent Benét. In the Faustian tale with an American twist, Jabez Stone, a young New Hampshire native, sells his soul to the devil and is only able to redeem it when defended by the eloquence of Daniel Webster. Moore based his 1951 opera, *Giants in the Earth*, on a novel by O.E. Rolvaag, depicting the settling of the Dakotas by immigrants from Norway. Though he won the Pulitzer Prize for this effort, he surpassed it in 1958 with *The Ballad of Baby Doe*, considered one of the great classics of modern opera.

The Ballad of Baby Doe, with a libretto by John Latouche, was set in Leadville, Colorado. It retells the rise and fall of Horace Tabor, a real life silver king who lost his fortune when the country switched to the gold standard, and of his love for a young girl, Baby Doe, for whom he divorced his wife Augusta. The opera had sweep and pageantry and proved justifiably successfully without a dependence on European ideas. Moore continued writing operas, including *The Wings of the Dove* based on the Henry James' classic novel, and *Carrie Nation*, inspired by the real life story of the woman who led the drive for Prohibition of liquor by marching into saloons wielding a hatchet. Moore's music has proven to be direct, straightforward, undeniably American, and appealing to audiences everywhere. As a teacher and writer, he remained in the forefront of American music throughout his distinguished career.

The first graduate of the Eastman School of Music with a composition major was George Frederick McKay, a composer from the Pacific Northwest. Howard Hanson was at the very beginning of a long period of directing Eastman. With his Swedish family background and admiration for Sibelius, Hanson always welcomed the expansive influence and full orchestrations of the Scandinavian composers at Eastman. McKay's teachers there were the Norwegian Christian Sinding, famous for his piano piece, *Rustles of Spring*, and the Finnish composer Selim Palmgren. McKay was fascinated by a variety of musical influences—Civil War folk songs, fiddler's tunes, the music of Native American tribes in the Northwest, and even jazz he heard in Seattle. He wrote a suite for strings as a tribute to the folk music of Newfoundland.

McKay was incredibly prolific, composing around a thousand pieces, everything from major symphonies to string quartets, rhapsodies for concert band, music for the dance, works specifically for children, and compositions that incorporated American folk music. He was very interested in poetry and one of his symphonies was inspired by the writing of four major American poets.

McKay also was a dedicated teacher; he spent an incredible forty-two years on the faculty of the University of Washington, where he mentored student composers reflecting a variety of styles.. While at the University of Washington, McKay sponsored a lecture and full concert for his friend William Grant Still, the distinguished African American composer, at a time when prejudice and segregation limited opportunities for Still. McKay never tried to impose his own style or tastes on others. His pupils included William Bolcom, a composer and pianist fascinated by ragtime, Goddard Lieberson, who became a powerful executive and producer in the recording industry, avant-garde composer John Cage, and the thoroughly unpredictable Earl Robinson.

Figure 66 - George Frederick McKay, a major composer who spent a lifetime writing and teaching in the Pacific Northwest. (Photo courtesy of Fred McKay)

Earl Robinson, like McKay, was a product of the Pacific Northwest, but there the similarity ended. Robinson was trained as a composer of concert music, but he was also a political activist drawn to the voices of protest. He is best remembered as the composer of *Ballad for Americans*, introduced on radio by singer Paul Robeson, *The House I Live In*, a song made famous by Frank Sinatra as a plea for racial and religious tolerance, and *The Lonesome Train,* a Cantata about the death of Abraham Lincoln directed by the legendary poet laureate of radio, Norman Corwin. Robinson was also responsible for *Joe Hill*, a protest song that was adopted by labor unions. He was a folk singer, as well, who played the guitar. Robinson, like Paul Robeson, became deeply involved in the Communist Party and his career suffered greatly as a result. Robinson later became an advocate for environmental causes. He saw music as a way to express the ideas in which he believed.

William Schuman was born in New York City in 1910. He became known for his ability to draw upon the energy and vitality of American themes in his music. But Schuman entered serious composing in an improbable way. He absorbed many influences and musical styles before deciding to become a composer. He played the violin and in high school, was the only student in the New York Public Schools to play the double bass. He also led, arranged for, and even sang with his own dance band, Billy Schuman and his Alamo Society Orchestra. He also wrote numerous songs with his friend Frank Loesser, who went on to become one of the most successful Broadway composers. Loesser's first published tune was set to a Schuman lyric.

After spending time as a song plugger, Schuman began studying business. But at twenty, he heard his first live symphony concert. He was stunned by the enormity of the expansive sonorities produced by the orchestra. He quit his job at an advertising agency and decided to devote his life to music. Determined to become a composer, he studied privately with Max Persin and Charles Haubiel, earned two degrees from Columbia University, and began teaching at Sarah Lawrence. He also worked for two years under the guidance of Roy Harris, who, as teacher and mentor, influenced his musical outlook. In 1935, Schuman received his first New York premiere, with Harris in attendance to hear his *First Symphony*.

Figure 67 - William Schuman. A prolific composer and a major figure in American musical education. (Photo courtesy of Irving Gilmore Library, Yale University)

Schuman somehow managed to divide his time between an incredibly successful career as a composer and an equally dynamic career as an educational administrator. He served as President of the Juilliard School of Music, and then, in 1962, became President of the Lincoln Center for the Performing Arts. Schuman was comfortable with classical forms, writing symphonies, concertos, chamber music, brightly orchestrated and written, by his own description, through a process of singing, not improvising at the piano.

Schuman's works included ten symphonies, string quartets, violin and piano concertos, and many choral works. Schuman was never a musical snob. His biographers suggested that he used the word "arty" with all the distaste of a bishop using the word "atheist." His overtures included the popular *American Festival Overture*, the *Circus*

Overture, and a *William Billings Overture*. In the *American Festival Overture*, he introduced an orchestral version of the cry "Wee-Awk-Ee," a "call to play" he learned during his boyhood days and inspired by his memories of the streets of New York City. His compositions *Newsreel: In Five Shots* and *George Washington Bridge* are clearly nationalist in design, as is the *New England Triptych*, based on three choral works by William Billings.

Schuman's ballets have won an enthusiastic public. *Undertow*, *Night Journey*, and *Judith* reveal a somewhat darker tone of Schuman's work. He could be somber, as in *Credendum (Article of Faith)*, a symphonic work commissioned by the United States National Commission for UNESCO. He could be lively and unpredictable, as in the case of his baseball opera, *The Mighty Casey*. Schuman will be remembered as the first composer to win the Pulitzer Prize. He emerged as one of the major figures of his generation, and a vital force both in music education and contemporary American composition.

William Grant Still, like other noted concert music composers of his generation, created works with a distinctly American spirit. But Still, an African American, brought to his compositions stylistic elements that drew upon both American and African sources.

William Grant Still was born in Woodville, Mississippi, in 1895, and grew up in Little Rock, Arkansas. Still's career initially did not seem directed toward writing symphonies. He played the violin and clarinet, studied music at Oberlin College, was in the Navy during World War I, and he wrote arrangements for W.C. Handy, the composer of "St. Louis Blues."

Eventually, Still went to New York where he worked in the orchestra accompanying the first major black Broadway hit musical show, *Shuffle Along*, composed by Eubie Blake and Noble Sissle.

Figure 68 - William Grant Still. The first African-American to conduct and have his work performed by a major American symphony orchestra, with his friends, violinist Louis Kaufman and pianist Annette Kaufman. (Photo courtesy of Annette Kaufman)

In 1923, he began a two-year period of study with an improbable teacher, the French avant-garde composer Edgard Varèse, famous for dissonance and highly unusual orchestral combinations. Still was influenced by Varèse and began composing in a highly dissonant style. But he soon turned away from dissonance, adopting a lyrical and neo-romantic approach to music, often drawing upon his African-American heritage.

Still maintained a lifelong interest in opera and ballet. His ballet, *La Guiablesse,* written in 1927, was set in Martinique, while *Sahdji*, a 1931 choral ballet, based on a scenario by Alain Locke and Richard Bruce, was completed after Still studied African tribal history for over a year. The latter was produced at the Eastman School of Music under the direction of Howard Hanson. Hanson also conducted the premiere of Still's *Afro-American Symphony*, inspired by the poetry of Paul Laurence Dunbar. Throughout the 1930s, Still continued writing arrangements for popular bands, including one, "Frenesi," that became a hit of legendary proportions for the Artie Shaw dance orchestra. But he also composed concert works, often with African-American themes. His 1935 opera, *Blue Steel* presented the conflict between voodoo and traditional religion, with a black steelworker as hero. In 1938, he wrote *Troubled Island*, retelling the story of Jean Jacques Dessaline, the liberator and first Emperor of Haiti. When Still died in 1978, he left behind a legacy of many outstanding works, including five symphonies, numerous pieces for orchestra, piano, harp, violin, and various chamber ensembles, and an unusual composition for black and white choruses protesting racial bigotry and urging brotherhood, *And They Lynched Him on a Tree*. Still also broke down racial barriers as the first black American to conduct a major symphony orchestra (the Los Angeles Philharmonic) in 1935. Twenty years later, Still conducted the New Orleans Philharmonic, the first time a major orchestra in the American south featured a black conductor. Still was unapologetic regarding his musical style, despite neglect and criticisms from those who objected to the direct, emotional appeal of his music. He declared proudly that "intellect should be subordinate to inspiration," Rediscovery of his music in recent years validates his determination, not only as a trailblazer in racial matters, but as a rugged individualist who expressed himself without regard to fads and fashions.

Figure 69 - Howard Hanson, composer, conductor, teacher, educator and the indefatigable champion of American music. (Photo courtesy of Eastman School Photo Archives, Sibley Music Library)

THE ROMANTICS

A number of American composers were most inspired not by the need to express a national character or the intellectual stimulation of form, structure, and style, but by the need to express themselves in an emotional language that would move their audiences to excitement, laughter, or tears. These composers have often been described as "neo-romantic." There is no doubt about who led this movement.

Howard Hanson was one of the most important figures in American music throughout the twentieth century. His career encompassed all aspects of music, composing, conducting, and teaching. As a conductor, he introduced new music by virtually every major American composer of significance, premiering 1500 works by 700 composers at a musical festival he founded. He inspired and trained several generations of composers during a forty-year teaching career, and as Director of the Eastman School of Music, was in the forefront of music education.

As a composer, Howard Hanson was identified from the beginning as a leader among neo-romantic composers: "neo-romantic" because of a commitment to a form of emotional communication between the composer and his audience. He espoused this view in words as well as in music, and though it was a view that was often unfashionable, especially in avant-garde critical circles, Hanson remained true to his own ideals. Hanson declared that he embraced romanticism, which would find in this country, "rich soil, for a new, young, and vigorous growth." Hanson declared that his own music came "from the heart," and was a direct expression of his own emotional reactions.

Howard Hanson was born in 1896, in the Swedish-American community of Wahoo, Nebraska. His mother began teaching him to play the piano. He also studied the cello and by the time he was nine, he was trying to organize a string quartet. (When asked about his major contribution to American music, Hanson once quipped, "giving up the cello.") As a teenager, he played the organ, sang in church choirs, began conducting, and was high school valedictorian. He also pursued more advanced piano studies with Albin Peterson who told him, "What Grieg has done for Norway, you must do for Sweden." He pursued his musical education at the Institute of Musical Art in New York, under Percy Goetschius, and at Northwestern University. He started teaching in San Jose, California, at twenty, and became Dean of the Conservatory of Fine Arts.

In 1919, Walter Henry Rothwell, conductor of the Los Angeles Philharmonic, invited Hanson to conduct the premiere of his own composition, *Symphonic Rhapsody*. In 1921, Hanson won the coveted Prix de Rome with his composition, *Poem Before Dawn*, and went to Italy where he studied with Ottorino Respighi. While absorbing the warmly Mediterranean atmosphere of Italy, he continued to compose under the influence of Northern European composers. His first major symphony, the *Nordic,* was completed in 1932 in Italy, as well as a choral work, *Lament for Beowulf,* and a symphonic poem, *North and West.* Hanson's melodic and orchestral style won him the title of "The American Sibelius," fulfilling his teacher's ambition for him to express the essence of Scandinavia in American music.

In 1925, George Eastman, the Kodak inventor, was searching for a dynamic young musician to take charge of a music school he had founded in Rochester, New York. He invited Howard Hanson to assume this position. Hanson was responsible for leading the administration for many years, which established the Eastman School of Music as one of the world's finest music schools. Hanson wrote unapologetically that he was a neo-romanticist, though the movement was the poor stepchild without the social standing of her elder sister, neo-classicism. His second symphony bears the title *Romantic.* He composed seven symphonies in all, writing rich sonorities for full orchestra, singing melodic lines, and sometimes in stark, distant colors associated the Scandinavian landscapes.

In 1934, Hanson launched his opera, *Merry Mount*, a work based on Richard L. Stokes's libretto, an adaptation of Nathaniel Hawthorne's story, *The Maypole of Merry Mount*. The plot retells the conflict between Puritans and Cavaliers in seventeenth century New England. Hanson also adapted a *Merry Mount Suite* for orchestra containing an austere, somber *Overture*, spirited *Maypole Dances* and children's dances, and a lushly orchestrated love duet. (Typically, it is Hanson's preference for rich orchestrations that make his music accessible to large audiences, a factor that dubiously upset his critics while endearing his works to listeners. Hanson was a devotee of orchestral colors, even titling one of his orchestral works, *Mosaics*. Hanson was never far away from his roots in church music and the unabashed patriotism he had experienced in small-town America.

In 1943, Hanson dedicated his fourth symphony, a four-movement *Requiem*, to the memory of his father. It won the Pulitzer Prize. His fifth symphony was called *Sinfonia Sacra*, Hanson's expression of the story of the Resurrection as told in *The Gospel according to St. John*. He wrote works like the *Cherubic Hymn* in 1950 and *The Song of Democracy*, a dramatic setting of *An Old Man's Thoughts of School* and *Thou Mother With thy Equal Brood*, by Walt Whitman. In 1977, his seventh and final symphony was again inspired by Whitman.

Hanson's musical ideas and his conservative lifestyle made him an easy target for those who thought experimental change should be pursued for its own sake. The composer Elliott Carter, for instance, writing as a critic in 1940, praised Hanson's skill in composing his *Third Symphony*, but characterized the work as "reactionary." Long-time program annotator Michael Steinberg dismissed Hanson's *Romantic Symphony* as "Sibelian slush." When Steinberg attended a forum for music critics at Eastman, Hanson spoke to the various panelists. When he came to Steinberg, he, himself, made reference to Steinberg's barb. He told the audience, "Of course, Mr. Steinberg was quite wrong. It is my *Nordic Symphony* that is "Sibelian slush."

It is unfortunate that avant-garde critics and composers have tried to turn one of Hanson's great musical virtues, his ability to communicate emotionally with his listeners, into a musical vice. Hanson himself was far more open-minded than his critics, becoming the champion of such varied composers as Elliott Carter, Aaron Copland, Henry Cowell, Paul Creston, David Diamond, Roy Harris, Otto Leuning, George Frederick McKay, Douglas Moore, Quincy Porter, Wallingford Riegger, Elie Siegmeister, William Grant Still, Paul White, and Joseph Wagner, to mention only a few of those whose works were introduced at his festival of American composers. All of these composers wrote in vastly different styles, ranging from conservatives to self-proclaimed modernists. Hanson believed that they all deserved a hearing. Hanson also produced a book, *Harmonic Materials of Modern Music*, providing twentieth century composers with a highly original analysis of harmony based on acoustics rather than abstract theories.

In recent years, his music has undergone a well-deserved revival. And despite decades in Rochester, he has not been forgotten by his home town in Nebraska, where a sign has been posted which reads, "Welcome to Wahoo, Nebraska, the birthplace of Sam Crawford, first baseman of the Detroit Tigers during the glamorous days of Ty Cobb, Darryl Zanuck, famed Hollywood producer, and Howard Hanson. " Hanson's true legacy is the rich catalogue of music he composed and the achievements of the many composers he taught and guided.

Hanson's long-time colleague at Eastman, Bernard Rogers, has also been identified as a neo-romantic. Rogers, born in New York in 1893, joined the Eastman faculty where he headed the composition department and specialized in the teaching of orchestration. Rogers was initially interested in becoming a painter and later described his approach to composing in terms of a painter sketching his musical ideas. Asian art inspired several of Rogers' musical compositions. He studied with Arthur Farwell, with Percy Goetschius (like Hanson), and later with Ernest Bloch and Nadia Boulanger.

He joined the Eastman faculty in 1929. During his 36 years of teaching at Eastman, he numbered among his pupils many prominent composers, including David Diamond, Gail Kubik, and Burrill Phillips. His orchestral works illustrate the highly coloristic style he preferred. His catalogue included five symphonies, tone poems, and a suite for narrator and orchestra called *Leaves from the Tale of Pinocchio*. One of Rogers' works, *Once Upon a Time*, depicted through music the stories of five classic children's fairy tales. Rogers was frequently inspired by Biblical subjects. He composed an intense oratorio for solo voices, chorus, and organ called *The Passion*, which is devoted to last hours and death of Christ. His opera, *The Warrior*, retold the story of Samson and Delilah, based on a libretto by the poet-laureate of radio, Norman Corwin.

Figure 70 - Bernard Rogers (right) discussing the premiere of his opera, *The Warrior*, with fellow composer Deems Taylor, 1947. (Photo courtesy of the Bernard Rogers Collection, The Sibley Music Library)

For many years, composers of talent went to the Eastman School of Music in Rochester to work under Howard Hanson's guidance. Hanson became the champion of composers who chose to write in many different musical styles. But if one could describe a "Rochester school" of musical composition, it would be a group of composers who preferred lyrical melodies and emotional expression to intellectual theories about how to organize thematic materials.

One of the most interesting and unlikely of the Rochester composers was Alec Wilder. Alexander Lafayette Chew Wilder (Alec to his friends) was a Rochester native who studied informally with several Eastman faculty members, including Herbert Inch and Edward Royce. Wilder found Royce's approach be confining as a musical straitjacket. He did not get along particularly well with the school's strong-minded director, the venerable Howard Hanson. Wilder was a rugged individualist, a nonconformist who was totally impossible to categorize. He disliked bombast and preferred a gentle, pastoral quality in his music; this put him at odds with Howard Hanson whose powerful Sibelius-inspired symphonies were at the opposite end of the emotional spectrum. Wilder composed numerous pieces of chamber music, including string quartets and woodwind quintets, and works in larger forms like his cello concerto.

But Wilder was multi-faceted. He began writing music that combined improbable musical styles and instruments: jazz-oriented music for woodwinds and harpsichord. Wilder composed numerous sonatas and concertos for various wind and brass instruments. Wilder's most famous pieces were an outgrowth of his friendship with the oboist, Mitch Miller, who encouraged him to write his famous octets. The octets were scored for various woodwinds plus an improbable rhythm section consisting of harpsichord, bass, and drums. Each movement had a fanciful title: *The House Detective Registers*, *Bull Fiddles in a China Shop*, *Neurotic Goldfish*, *Walking Home in Spring*, *The Debutante's Diary*, *It's Silk, Feel It!*, *His First Long Pants*, and *Kindergarten Flower Pageant*, among others. He also wrote popular songs (including "I'll Be Around" and "It's So Peaceful In the Country") and scored films.

Wilder's music never made his name a household word, but it won him admirers who became devoted champions of his music, including the legendary cabaret singer, Mabel Mercer, pianist Marian McPartland, and Frank Sinatra, who (at the height of his fame) actually conducted a record album of Wilder's music. Sinatra didn't read an orchestral score, and never conducted, before or since the Wilder album.

Unlike many of his Eastman-Rochester colleagues, he did not confine his interests to concert music. Wilder was also an eccentric and a curmudgeon. He carried around a small pipe that children often used to blow bubbles. At the drop of a hat and when least expected, he would produce the pipe and send a stream of bubbles off toward the horizon. Unlike composers who described themselves as members of the *avant-garde* ("advance guard") of modern music, Wilder proudly proclaimed himself as a leader of the *derriere-garde*, those who found more value in a reassuring past than an uncertain future. At times, Wilder seemed to be a general without troops in this cause, but he allowed his own taste and talent to be his guide. He had a devoted group of friends and admirers and was loyal to them.

One of his best friends was the North Carolina pianist and composer Loonis McGlohon, with whom he often collaborated on songs over a twenty-year period. McGlohon summed up Wilder as "Erudite, witty, ill-mannered, well-mannered, rude, caring, Edwardian, hostile, loving, insulting, well-read, childish, intolerant, protective, eccentric, ill-kempt, critical, and one of the most fascinating people I have ever known."

Figure 71 - Alec Wilder, blowing bubbles, while a bemused Marian McPartland observes. (Photo by Louis Ouzer, courtesy of the Sibley Music Library, Eastman School of Music)

Wilder had no reservations about expressing his strong opinions on all subjects and even his greatest admirers would not describe him as tactful. He lived for many years in a small apartment in New York's Hotel Algonquin. Often, he wrote music for friends, gave them the original manuscript of his work, never bothering to keep copies for himself.

One of his greatest achievements was a book, *American Popular Song*, considered by many to be a definitive study of the works of American songwriters during the first half of the twentieth century. He was also true to his principles in an outspoken denunciation of rock music. Said Wilder, "The rock group has just played something on a TV show that is a dreadful insult to music, with lyrics that virtually exhort the kids to turn on to some drug. Following the usual hysterical audience response, the smiling 'host' holds up his hands and says, 'Wasn't that really super? And would you believe that these boys started to play the guitar only three weeks ago?' Three weeks ago, and they're already earning $500 a week each. Well, it's a familiar story in an age that's been conditioned to instant everything." This was highly unusual, because so many composers tripped over their own feet in a headlong rush to identify with rock music, which many privately detested, to save their careers.

Wilder refused to back down. Writing an essay in the *New York Times*, Wilder described rock stars as amateurs. He said that there were brilliant young music students who were neglected by the media because they were "too calm, too quiet, and too civilized to be good copy." He delivered a savage critique of the 1960s counterculture. He wrote, "Joy, innocence, compassion, style, discipline, excellence, humility, and perspective were not only choked off but derided." Through the end of life, he consistently marched to a different drummer. Because he was difficult to classify, he remains an elusive, enigmatic, but fascinating musical figure.

Under the leadership of Howard Hanson, the Eastman School of Music became a training ground for American composers. Unlike many other schools of music, Eastman (with Hanson as the prime mover) supported and encouraged composers who wanted to hone their craft using a musical vocabulary that was contemporary, but not beholden to the intellectual and mathematical dictates of the avant-garde. The Rochester composers were free to find their own individual musical paths and they chose to move in many different musical directions.

Figure 72 - H. Merrills Lewis, Louis Mennini, Wayne Barlow; seated, Howard Hanson, at the annual Festivals of American music. (Photo used courtesy of the Eastman School Photo Archives, Sibley Music Library)

Wayne Barlow studied with Hanson and Rogers at Eastman, and eventually joined the faculty in 1937. He taught at Eastman for 41 years. He won wide recognition for *The Winter's Passed*, a rhapsody for oboe and orchestra, which drew upon folk material from the North Carolina Appalachian Mountains. Throughout the 1940s and 1950s, Barlow wrote major works inspired by dance and choral themes. In the 1960s, he made an unusual entry into a new genre, studying and then composing in the area of electronic music.

William Bergsma was encouraged as a young composer, while still a teenager, by Howard Hanson. His work, *Paul Bunyan*, was written for puppets, dancers, and orchestra and and was performed many times. Eventually, he went to Eastman, studying with Hanson and Rogers, and later joining the faculty of the Julliard School of Music for many years. Another Bergsma ballet, *Gold and the Señor Commandante*, was also introduced by Hanson. Bergsma once said that everything he had to say about music was in his music. But Bergsma did make a statement when he wrote *The Fortunate Islands* for string orchestra, in response to a quotation from Sir Walter Raleigh that "the artist does not guide the ship, nor discover the Fortunate Islands." Kent Kennan was another pupil of Hanson and Rogers. He had his most popular early works, including *Night Soliloquy* (for flute with piano, strings, or wind instruments), and *Andante for Oboe and Orchestra*, introduced under Hanson's baton.

Ulysses Simpson Kay was the first black composer to win the prestigious Prix de Rome. But he began his career as a composer of serious concert music in an unusual way. His uncle was Joe "King" Oliver, the legendary jazz cornetist from New Orleans. Oliver insisted that Kay study the piano before pursuing jazz. Kay eventually entered Eastman like so many others, studying with Hanson and Rogers. His musical interests were varied. One of his compositions, *Portrait Suite*, was inspired by works of contemporary sculptors.

Umbrian Scene was a tranquil piece, inspired by the hills and valleys Kay saw in Italy. Theater Set was Kay's nod to the sounds of opening night at a Broadway theater. He also scored the film, *The Quiet One*.

One prominent Eastman faculty member who didn't train at Eastman was the prolific Samuel Adler. Born in Mannheim, Germany, Adler moved to Massachusetts with his family and studied at Boston University and at Harvard with Walter Piston, Randall Thompson, Aaron Copland, and Paul Hindemith. Adler's mother photographed a plaque on the hospital where he was born. The plaque declared that Mozart had once lived on the site, so Adler's mother was convinced that he would become a composer. She was not wrong.

Adler wrote over four hundred works, including *The Disappointment*, a reconstruction of one of the first American ballad operas written in 1767, and numerous operas, symphonies, chamber, and choral compositions. After Adler founded the Seventh Army Symphony Orchestra, Gen. Dwight D. Eisenhower told him that it was the greatest thing to happen to U.S.-German relations since the end of World War II. Adler taught at the University of North Texas before spending nearly three decades at Eastman and eventually on the faculty of Juilliard. He found time to write several books, including a huge textbook on orchestration, and to lecture and music schools throughout the country.

Louis Mennini and his younger brother Peter were both students of Howard Hanson and Bernard Rogers at Eastman. Their father was a former restaurateur and avid record collector. Louis Mennini was a prolific composer of chamber music and chamber operas, and also composed two symphonies, and a ballet. To avoid confusion with his brother, the better-known Peter changed his last name to Mennin. Even as a child, Peter Mennin wanted to write symphonies. He ultimately wrote nine, along with concertos for the piano, cello, and flute. Both brothers became educators. Louis Mennini joined the Eastman faculty, served as the first dean at the North Carolina School of the Arts, and founded the Virginia School of the Arts. Peter Mennin became director of the Peabody Conservatory in Baltimore and later, President of the Juilliard School of Music. He was known to believe in discipline and organization, and said of the Juilliard students, "Our job is to teach them how to do it, not how to enjoy it." He called discipline one of the necessary talents for a composer and said that any composer could find a reason not to write if he chose to do so.

Figure 73 - Joseph Wagner, conductor, teacher, and author. Lexicographer Nicolas Slonimsky called him "America's Most Undiscovered Composer." (Photo courtesy of Joseph Wagner)

Joseph Wagner has been described by Nicolas Slonimsky as America's most undiscovered composer—and deservedly so. Wagner, born in

Springfield, Massachusetts, in 1900, produced an impressive catalogue of music, but for some reason, his name is invariably absent from the lists of America's major composers, which include his colleagues Copland, Harris, Hanson, Thomson, and Moore. Wagner studied composition with Frederick Shepherd Converse and Alfredo Casella, and then with Nadia Boulanger, and conducting with Felix Weingartner and Pierre Monteux.

He was equally active as a composer and conductor, composing three symphonies, three ballets, including *Hudson River Legend*. He also composed a violin concerto and a choral work widely performed throughout the United States, *The Ballad of Brotherhood*. His own favorite work was his *Missa Sacra*. As conductor of the La Orquesta Sinfónica Nacional de Costa Rica, he was the first American to permanently lead a Latin-American orchestra. He taught at numerous universities and wrote two outstanding textbooks on orchestration and band scoring; his orchestration book was dedicated to Howard Hanson. He became intensely interested in the symphonic band and wrote numerous works for symphonic wind ensemble, one of the few American composers to make the symphonic band a major factor in his choice of instrumentation. Joseph Wagner was clearly a neo-romantic who absorbed nationalist influences as well. His music has been unjustly neglected, despite the enthusiastic admiration of many of his colleagues.

Ron Nelson, yet another Howard Hanson pupil, also became known as one of the country's leading composers for the concert band. (The Eastman Symphonic Wind ensemble was perhaps the nation's best-known concert band under the direction of Frederic Fennell.) Nelson's band works were inspired by many sources, often historic events of places in the United States. His compositions included *Savannah River Holiday*, *Sonora Desert Holiday*, and *Pebble Beach Sojourn*, as well as a *Mayflower Overture*. He also wrote a *Medieval Suite* as an homage to composers of that musical period and a widely praised *Passacaglia on B-A-C-H*, honoring J.S. Bach.

Figure 74 - Composers Martin Mailman and Ron Nelson, both alumni of the Eastman School of Music. (Photo courtesy of Ron Nelson)

Although Nelson is often identified as a band composer, he proved himself equally skilled in writing orchestral and chamber music. His orchestral *Sarabande: For Katherine in April* is undoubtedly one of the most expressive and haunting pieces of music written by a contemporary composer. Nelson also found time to teach, spending nearly four decades at Brown University.

Martin Mailman, like Ron Nelson, was an Eastman alumnus who gained wide recognition as both a composer and teacher. After studying with Howard Hanson, Bernard Rogers, Wayne Barlow, and Louis Mennini, he embarked on a career as a prolific composer. His works were scored for orchestra, concert band, chamber ensembles, and choirs. He also wrote for motion pictures and television, and composed a requiem for chorus, orchestra, and soloist.

Mailman was widely in demand as a teacher. He taught for many years as professor and composer in residence at the University of North Texas, and found time to present clinics and lectures at an incredible ninety colleges and universities, inspiring countless musicians in their studies of performance and composition.

In 1931, a group of young composers began holding meetings in the apartment of Aaron Copland. The group included Elie Siegmeister, Henry Brant, Israel Citkowitz, Vivian Fine, Arthur Berger, and two composers who would become legends in motion picture music, Bernard Herrmann and Jerome Moross. The sessions were stormy, often with artistic disagreements generating an intensity equaled only by disputes over religion or politics.

Figure 75 - Bernard Herrmann with Sir John Barbirolli. Famous for his film scores, he was also a renowned conductor and composer of works including his opera *Wuthering Heights* and his cantata *Moby Dick*. (Photo of recorded CD of *Moby Dick* courtesy of the Sir John Barbirolli Society)

Bernard Herrmann was undoubtedly the most original American musical personality to emerge in both film music and the concert hall. Though Herrmann has become a worldwide cult figure as a film composer, he maintained a lifelong interest in concert music and saw himself as a composer who happened to write for films, not as a film musician who occasionally composed for the concert stage.

Herrmann spent fifteen years as conductor of the CBS Symphony Orchestra. As a confirmed Anglophile, he led the orchestra in American premieres of numerous compositions by leading British composers. He rediscovered musical gems by neglected nineteenth century romantic composers and gave first performances of numerous contemporary works by fellow-American composers.

While devoting much of his life to composing and conducting for radio, television, and motion pictures, Herrmann found time to compose major concert works, including a turbulent, intense cantata, *Moby Dick*, inspired by Melville's novel. His concert pieces also included a symphony, the *Currier and Ives Suite,* and a magnificent opera, his masterpiece, *Wuthering Heights*. Herrmann's music often alternated in mood between furious, impassioned, thundering energy and a haunting, ethereal mood suggesting the peace and calm of an after-life.

Herrmann was drawn to themes and ideas that were larger than life. In 1938, he collaborated with the New England poet, W. Clark Harrington, to adapt *Moby Dick*, Herman Melville's classic novel as a work for male chorus and orchestra. He described *Moby Dick* as offering opportunities for all kinds of music: "New England-Hymns, the fiery exhortations and melancholy soliloquies of Captain Ahab, the white storms of the sea, the drunken

Figure 77 - Bernard Herrmann, an Anglophile, was the champion of British music in America. Pictured are (from left) Sir William Walton, Lyn Murray, Victor Bay, Bernard Herrmann, and André Previn. (Photo courtesy of The Queens Borough Public Library, Archives, New York *Herald-Tribune* Photograph Morgue Collection)

revelry of the Pequod's crew, tropical calms, and the omnipresent terror of the White Whale." For Herrmann, *Moby Dick* offered "a magnificent evocation of ocean, sky and man grappling with his epic fate."

Between 1943 and 1951, Herrmann worked on an opera, *Wuthering Heights*. His wife, the writer Lucille Fletcher, wrote the libretto. The work was meticulously based on Emily Brontë's text. Every word used in the opera was originally by Brontë and when additions were necessary, Brontë's poems were used to enable musical ideas. Herrmann described the work himself as neo-romantic, a "lyric drama," with three distinct musical themes introduced early in the opera and developed throughout the work. Herrmann wrote "Each act is a landscape tone poem which envelops the performers." Passionate arias reflected what Herrmann's biographer Steven Smith called the stunningly English quality of his scoring. Herrmann was an orchestral painter: the loneliness of the Yorkshire moors, the power and fury of the storms, the intensity of the characters' emotional relationships were all presented with the touch of a master.

Herrmann's other concert works included *For the Fallen*, an orchestral elegy, chamber music (a string quartet and a clarinet quintet), and *The Fantasticks*, a song-cycle to words by Nicholas Breton.

Herrmann's music, like the man, defied labels. While others followed fads and fashions in music, Herrmann drew upon the influences of the composers he most admired: Debussy, Delius, Vaughan Williams, and Sibelius. His music evoked an emotional spirit rarely found among twentieth composers.

Jerome Moross, like Herrmann, is today best remembered for his film scores. But he was primarily a concert composer with a great interest in theater and dance. His first orchestral composition to be performed

Figure 76 - Jerome Moross, a composer whose unique personal style incorporated the rhythms and harmonies of folk tunes and popular songs into major concert works. (Photo courtesy of Susanna Moross Tarjan)

was *Paens*, conducted by Bernard Herrmann in 1932. While pursuing a busy career composing and orchestrating for films, Moross always felt more comfortable in New York than in Hollywood. He remained devoted to concert music.

In 1941, CBS Radio commissioned Moross to write an orchestral piece. Moross decided to use a hobo tune, "Midnight Special," as one of the themes. He then decided to use the piece as the third movement of a four-movement symphony, which received its premiere under the baton of Sir Thomas Beecham in Seattle in 1943. During the 1960s and 1970s, Moross began actively writing chamber music, including sonatinas for clarinet ensemble, woodwind quintet, brass quintet and string bass, as well as a *Sonata for Piano Duet* and *String Quartet* and a *Concerto for Flute and String Quartet*.

He also chose an acclaimed radio play, *Sorry Wrong Number*, written by Lucille Fletcher, the former Mrs. Bernard Herrmann, as the basis for a one-act opera. Moross had always admired the work of Aaron Copland, and in his concert works, he frequently employed the harmonies, rhythms, and melodic designs of American folk and popular music, always expressing his nationalism with taste and style.

THE ITALIAN-AMERICAN TRADITION

Figure 78 - Paul Creston - composer, teacher, scholar, and linguist. He was deeply inspired by his desire to write music that reflected spiritual values. (Photo courtesy of Portland State University)

Like Howard Hanson, Paul Creston was regarded as a lyrical composer with neo-romantic instincts, but drawing upon a totally different musical tradition. Paul Creston was a unique figure among American composers. Born in New York City in 1906, he studied piano with Gaston Dethier and organ with Pietro Yon, but as a composer he was entirely self-taught.

He was born Giuseppe Guttoveggio, the son of a Sicilian housepainter who had relocated to New York City, where Creston grew up. He played the role of Crespino in a high school play, and his friends nicknamed him "Cress"; when he married, he changed his name to "Paul Creston." His father played Sicilian folksongs on the guitar, and as a child, he went with his family to Sicily, where he discovered the vitality of Italian song and dance. These influences remained with him throughout his musical career. All his life, he was devoted to music. In 1934, he began a thirty-three-year period as organist of St. Malachy's Church in New York. He was accomplished as a writer, scholar, and teacher.

However, Creston's greatest achievement was as a composer. His catalogue contained over one hundred works, including five symphonies, various instrumental compositions, and concertos for highly unusual instruments. Among his thirteen concertos were solo works for marimba, saxophone, trombone, and accordion. "In the hands of a master," he said, "every instrument can be beautiful." He won numerous prizes and awards, and found time to become active in scoring for motion pictures, television, and radio.

Creston received one of his greatest compliments when he scored the radio drama, *Lifeboat*, starring Tallulah Bankhead. The program was praised by legendary entertainer Al Jolson, but Jolson added that the sound effects, the thrashing of the oars and the movement of the waves, were too loud. There were no sound effects used in the broadcast. All of the "sound-effects" were actually Creston's music

Creston was an avid student of the origins of words. He taught himself to speak numerous languages, including Italian, French, Spanish, Portuguese, German, Russian, Turkish, and Swahili. He regarded music as a language; he even delivered a lecture comparing the historical, structural, functional, foundations of music and language as elements of communication.

It was not surprising that Creston had a particular interest in choral music. He was also a deeply religious man for whom personal and musical integrity was paramount. His interest in Gregorian chant was best recognized in his *Third Symphony*, a work in which each movement represents the "Nativity, the Crucifixion, and the Resurrection." Creston's music is marked by a singing lyricism and by a natural enthusiasm for dance rhythms. Song and dance may be described as key elements in Creston's work. His *Two Choric Dances* and *Invocation and Dance* are examples of orchestral works strongly influenced by the dance. (Creston's wife of many years, the former Louise Gotto, once danced with Martha Graham's dance company.)

Creston was also interested in modal harmony and in rhythm, which he had analyzed to a greater degree than perhaps any other composer, producing a textbook devoted entirely to the study of rhythm. But for Creston, the most important element in music was one he found lacking in much of twentieth century music written by colleagues, a spiritual quality present in the works of the masters he admired. Creston said he was not concerned with depicting nature or fairy tales in his works, but with musical ideas. Still, the warmth and vitality of his work set him apart from neo-classical colleagues whose goals in abstraction were unrelated to the spiritual inspiration so important to Creston. Paul Creston once autographed a copy of his book on rhythm by putting the word "philomusically" or "loving music" above his name. This was not an exaggeration; he not only loved music throughout his life, but enabled many others to love it as well.

The Italian tradition of lyricism and rich emotional expression was continued as well by the Italian-American composer Vittorio Giannini and his pupil and protégé, Nicolas Flagello. Giannini, born in Philadelphia, grew up in a musical family. His father was an opera singer, his sister Euphemia taught voice for four decades at the Curtis Institute, and his other sister Dusolina was a prima donna, a dramatic soprano who sang with the Metropolitan Opera and was widely successful throughout Europe and the United States. Dusolina

Figure 79 - Vittorio Giannini continued the Italian-American tradition of musical lyricism and founded the University of North Carolina School of the Arts, the "Juilliard of the South." (Photo courtesy of University of North Carolina School of the Arts Archives)

supported her brother's natural desire to compose operas and sang the lead in his opera based on *The Scarlett Letter*, adapted by Karl Flaster from Nathaniel Hawthorne's book. Flaster was a news reporter and a budding poet who met Giannini at a bus stop. The two became lifelong friends and collaborators. Their song, "Tell Me, Oh Blue, Blue Sky," became a staple in the repertoires of concert singers for decades after they wrote it in 1927. They remained prolific writers of art songs.

Giannini originally studied the violin in both New York and in Italy, but he ultimately decided to devote his life to composing and teaching. He composed operas. He produced an interesting catalogue of music, including a piano concerto, chamber music, and several symphonies, including his *Third Symphony*, a popular work for symphonic wind band. He wrote a major opera, *The Taming of the Shrew,* and shorter operas for radio, including *Beauty and the Beast* and *Blennerhassett*, based on Aaron Burr's plans to overthrow the U.S. Government, with a libretto by Philip Roll and Norman Corwin. Corwin was the literary star of the CBS Radio Network and widely admired as the foremost writer of radio plays. Giannini devoted fifteen years to *Christus*, a set of four operas presenting the life of Christ.

Giannini said that he desired to draw upon the principles of the great masters in his harmonic and melodic language. Unfortunately, many of his works were introduced at a time when tradition was dismissed or ridiculed by critics and academicians. He devoted much of his life to teaching at the Juilliard School, the Curtis Institute, the Manhattan School of Music, and was founding president of the North Carolina School of the Arts, a school that was established to become "the Juilliard of the South."

While many modern composers dismissed the idea of melody, Giannini stood as its champion. He insisted that a composer should pursue the ideal of beauty and not just attempt to shock an audience with capricious dissonance. He told his pupils that they could write fugues or canons at will, but not melodies, which required inspiration. He added provocatively, "Those composers who make a point of avoiding melody are those who, in most instances, couldn't if they wanted to, because it never comes to them."

He had many pupils who became prominent composers in their own right and an especially close relationship with Nicolas Flagello. Flagello grew up in a musical family in the Bronx in New York. His maternal grandfather had been a pupil of Verdi in Italy. Flagello was gifted as a child musician, playing the violin, the piano, and even singing. (He was billed as "The Little Caruso.") Eventually, he concertized widely as a pianist, but he decided to concentrate on composing and was inspired by his teacher, Vittorio Giannini, who taught him that musical ability was a gift from God. At the end of his compositions, Flagello would write the letters AMDG (Ad maiorem Dei gloriam,) the Latin motto of the Jesuits which means "To the Greater Glory of God."

Flagello was a facile, incredibly prolific composer, but like Giannini, he often faced neglect because he did not bow to self-proclaimed arbiters of musical tastes who believed that only followers of Schoenberg or Stravinsky were justifiably modern. One critic suggested that Flagello's style

Figure 80 - Nicolas Flagello. He aspired to challenge the most sophisticated musicians while inspiring the most modest listeners. (Photo courtesy of Maelos Music, Inc. - All rights reserved.)

would fit in the world of Hollywood film scores. It was not meant as a compliment. Flagello's style, like those of his teacher Vittorio Giannini, actually reflected a continuation of late European romanticism. Like Giannini, he was a proud and unapologetic romanticist. He said that he aspired "to fulfill Mozart's dictum that the greatest task for the composer is to challenge the most sophisticated musician while entertaining the most modest listener."

Flagello joined the faculty of the Manhattan School of Music. He wrote six operas, two symphonies, eight concertos, as well as chamber music, and works for orchestra and choir. Gradually, Flagello's music began to attract praise and attention. His most popular work was his oratorio, *The Passion of Martin Luther King*, a work, which included a musical setting of a portion of Dr. King's "I Have a Dream" speech. His opera, *The Judgment of St. Franc*is, received its premiere in Assisi, Italy. Unfortunately, Flagello's struggle for recognition and a debilitating illness led to his withdrawal from public life at the very time his music was being recognized for its true value. He was only sixty-six years old when he died in 1994.

Figure 81 - Norman Dello Joio, a composer who drew upon his heritage of Italian church music. (Photo by (c) Don Hunstein)

Norman Dello Joio was yet another composer who drew upon his Italian-American musical heritage. His family included three generations of Italian church musicians. Dello Joio developed an interest in Gregorian chant as a result of his boyhood studies as a young church organist. Later, he organized his own jazz band and drew upon jazz elements as well. His greatest influence was Paul Hindemith, with whom he studied composition at Yale.

His *Magnificat* was an orchestral work that clearly reflected his fascination with Gregorian chant, as did his *Variations, Chaconne, and Finale for Orchestra,* and "The Cloisters," one of seven orchestral vignettes he composed as *New York Profiles*. The latter also included movements called "Little Italy" and "Grant's Tomb," which quoted "The Battle Hymn of the Republic." When Dello Joio won the Pulitzer Prize in 1957, it was for *Meditations on Ecclesiastes,* once again drawing on a liturgical source for inspiration.

Dello Joio also wrote ballets, operas, and award-winning scores for television programs. He described himself as belonging to a generation that didn't think "triad" was a dirty word. What he meant was that there was still much to say musically, using a modern vocabulary that didn't reject or denigrate traditional harmony and counterpoint just because a composer was writing in a contemporary age.

Figure 82 - Vincent Perschetti. He amazed his students with his ability improvise in the style of any composer, or even in their styles. (Photo courtesy of Associazione Musicale Vincent Persichetti)

Vincent Persichetti, like Dello Joio, was a child prodigy on the piano and organ. Born in Philadelphia, the son of an Italian immigrant father and a German immigrant mother, Persichetti was a gifted improviser. When he found himself unprepared for a master class given by concert pianist Olga Samaroff, he whipped out a Bach organ prelude and played it at sight on the piano. Samaroff encouraged him to put his piano transcription of the work on paper. When pianist Eugene List performed it to critical acclaim, Persichetti found himself receiving a surprise offer to publish his first piece of music. It would not be his last. The prolific Persichetti went on to compose nine symphonies, numerous chamber and choral works, a piano concerto, and incredibly popular pieces for the concert band, the best-known of which, *Divertimento for Band*, received hundreds of performances.

In 1973, Persichetti was commissioned to compose a piece for the Inauguration of President Richard Nixon. Persichetti, who had once studied with Lincoln admirer Roy Harris, based his work on the text of Lincoln's Second Inaugural Address. Lincoln's description of the Civil War as "a mighty scourge" generated modern controversy when the Inaugural Committee thought the term could be applied by listeners to the Vietnam War. So Persichetti's "A Lincoln Address" was dropped from the program. Persichetti was known to pursue understated craftsmanship in his works, but he also drew upon many sources of inspiration. While in Rome, he heard the tolling bells of the Chiesa di San Pietro and Gianicolo, and reproduced them musically in his *Ninth Symphony*, a one movement work entitled *Janiculum*. Persichetti also spent many years as a teacher at the Philadelphia Conservatory and the Juilliard School of Music. His students were often dazzled by his ability to improvise at the piano in the styles of many other composers and to even create passages in their styles on the spur of the moment.

Samuel Barber has often been identified as a "neo-romantic." He was born near Philadelphia in West Chester, Pennsylvania, in 1910. He was one of the first students to enter the Curtis Institute of Music in Philadelphia, where he spent nine years, studying composition with Rosario Scalero, piano with the formidable Isabella Vengerova, and voice with Emilio de Gorgoza. Barber was always interested in vocal music. His aunt was Louise Homer. a celebrated contralto and star of the Metropolitan Opera. His inclinations toward lyricism were clearly the result of a musical outlook, which desired lines that can be "sung" by instruments as well as by the human voice.

Barber's name first came to public attention in 1933 when the Philadelphia Orchestra premiered his *Overture to the School for Scandal*. Two years later, the New York Philharmonic introduced his *Music for a Scene from Shelley*. Barber went to Europe where he not only composed, but gave recitals as a vocalist. He also made his debut as a conductor in Vienna, not learning until the morning after his concert that a cache of ammunition and weapons were hidden under the stage by a group planning to lead a labor uprising. On impulse, he rang the doorbell at the home of a man he always wanted to meet, the legendary conductor Arturo Toscanini. Toscanini was at home; the two spent an afternoon going through the score of a Monteverdi opera. Barber's reputation grew by leaps and bounds when Toscanini selected him to have a work premiered with the NBC Symphony. Barber's best-known piece, the lyrical and elegiac *Adagio for Strings*, was conducted by Toscanini, as was Barber's *Essay for Orchestra*.

Figure 83 - Samuel Barber, famous for his operas, art songs, the *Adagio for Strings*, and his neo-romantic style. (Photo courtesy of Carl Van Vechten Collection, Library of Congress)

Unlike many of his contemporaries, Barber had no problems writing in a musical language that was accessible to concertgoers. His neo-romantic style won him enthusiastic admirers throughout the world. Barber had a capacity for using dissonance as seasoning, rather than as the main dish. He continued to write for the voice in works like *Knoxville: Summer of 1915*, a nostalgic composition based on the texts of James Agee, for soprano and orchestra, and a cantata, *Prayers of Kierkegaard*, for mixed chorus, soprano solo, and orchestra.

One of Barber's more dissonant works was his *Piano Sonata*, introduced in 1950 by Vladimir Horowitz. His sonata is a popular showpiece for pianists desiring to plunge into contemporary music. He also completed concertos for violin and cello, and a rather dissonant *Symphony Dedicated to the Armed Forces*. His *Capricorn Concerto* is really a concerto grosso, a clever, wry piece for flute, oboe, trumpet, and strings, rather in the style of Stravinsky's fusion of contemporary rhythms and dissonance with classical clarity.

In 1955, Barber was commissioned to write a ballet for Martha Graham and the result was *Cave of the Heart*. Barber ultimately adapted his score into an orchestral suite, *Medea*. Barber devoted hours of intense concentration to his musical themes, relaxing only when the main themes of a new work were on paper. (He was so engrossed in the themes of his piano sonata that he became oblivious to a large wad of cotton placed in his mouth by a dentist, and didn't realize it was there until he sat down to dinner.)

Outside of music, one of Barber's greatest interests was literature. He was a connoisseur of poetry, using texts of numerous poets as inspiration for his choral works and prolific songs. Barber had a reputation for being meticulous and fastidious in his choice of texts. It was only natural for Barber to turn to the operatic stage. But he was determined to find exactly the right libretto.

Figure 84 - Gian Carlo Menotti. His operas, including *Amahl and the Night Visitors* and *The Consul*, won rare popularity among audiences of every age and musical taste. (Photo courtesy of Carl Van Vechten Collection, Library of Congress)

He turned to his lifelong friend and colleague, the noted opera composer Gian Carlo Menotti. Barber's music and Menotti's text resulted in *Vanessa*, a highly eclectic opera featuring rich full orchestrations, mixtures of song and speech—the lyrical lines associated with Barber, but also a generous amount of dissonance and adventurous harmonic ideas. Barber won the first of his two Pulitzer Prizes with *Vanessa*. The second was awarded for his *Piano Concerto*, which has been widely performed and won critical acclaim. Barber's second opera, *Antony and Cleopatra*, written in 1963, was far less successful, as problems with the lavish sets and staging by director Franco Zeffirelli seemed to mar Barber's long string of successes in vocal music.

Barber taught for many years at the Curtis Institute of Music. He was, from the beginning, a composer more concerned with the expression of lyricism than with musical ideology. His music was clearly the product of a mind which absorbed the advice of Toscanini, who used to demand this his orchestras respond to his fervent command, "Cantare, cantare," or "Sing, sing," Barber remained a potent force in the development of music until his death in 1981.

Barber's long-time colleague, Gian-Carlo-Menotti, always defied classification. Critics have always wanted to find a category into which Menotti can be neatly placed, but he is a powerful musical personality with many facets. Was Menotti an American composer? He was born in Italy, and remained an Italian citizen. He came to the United States as a teenager, where he met Barber when the two were students of Rosario Scalero at the Curtis Institute of Music. Menotti's operas have been produced on Broadway, suggesting to starched collar critics that he is really a writer of serious musical comedies. Menotti himself rejected this idea, however, dismissing Broadway as a place in which commerce, not art, is the dominating feature. Broadway critics always considered Menotti's work to be strictly operatic. Menotti clearly always had the capacity to blend influences of traditional Italian opera with what may be the surest sense of theatricality on the American stage. The result is a phenomenon. Menotti is difficult to classify, but easy for Americans to enjoy.

Born in Cadegliano, Italy in 1911, Menotti was the son of a wealthy exporter. At nine, he received a puppet theater as a present. He began writing his own plays, building sets, designing costumes. By eleven, he had composed a full three-act opera, complete with a tragic ending in which all the characters killed themselves by the end of the evening. When Menotti's mother took him to New York, a family friend, the conductor Tullio Serafin, introduced him to Rosario Scalero, who offered to take Menotti as a pupil. Scalero was a disciplinarian and Menotti learned his lessons well. At twenty-two, he completed an opera, *Amelia Goes to the Ball*, the tale of a pampered young woman whose efforts to attend a fashionable ball in Milan are constantly thwarted. The work was so well received that the young composer was offered a commission from NBC to write a new opera exclusively for radio. Menotti, again writing his own libretto, produced *The Old Maid and the Thief*. Two new companion pieces, *The Medium* and *The Telephone*, were launched on Broadway in 1947. *The Medium* is the terrifying tale of a fake spiritualist, *The Telephone*, a comedy about a phone continuously spoiling a marriage proposal. At first, the production was in constant danger of closing, but word spread, and the unlikely show featuring two Menotti operas became a hit.

Menotti achieved even greater success with his 1950 opus, *The Consul*, a tragic story about Magda, a woman who tries to escape with her child from a dictatorship. When her husband comes to her aid, he is arrested and she ultimately commits suicide. The true theme of the story is the bureaucratic nightmare facing refugees, as typified by the autocratic secretary in the consulate. Magda's aria, "To This We've Come," represented one of the most moving moments in contemporary opera. *The Consul* achieved worldwide success, although the composer was attacked by critics in Italy; some were communists who clearly saw the opera as critical of Iron-Curtain tyranny, while others objected to Menotti's continued residence in the United States.

In 1951, Menotti was commissioned to write a Christmas opera exclusively for television, *Amahl and the Night Visitors*, which became a regular feature of every holiday season. Faced with a deadline, he strolled through the Metropolitan Museum, stopping to view the painting *Adoration of the Kings* by Hieronymus Bosch. Since *The Three Kings* are so important to the Italian celebration of Christmas as Santa Claus is to the American celebration, Menotti hit upon the idea that inspired him: the story of a crippled child and his mother, their encounter with the three kings and the way in which the little child is miraculously cured. Other Menotti operas include melodramatic works, *The Saint of Bleecker Street, Maria Golovin,* and *The Most Important Man*, the latter dealing with apartheid.

Menotti wrote his own librettos and composed music in the *verisimo* style of Verdi; he could be as lyrical as Puccini, as surprising as Prokofiev. He founded the Festival of Two Worlds in Spoleto, Italy, in 1958, an American counterpart in Charleston, South Carolina, and an Australian version in Melbourne. He devoted much of his time to directing the festivals, a world-renowned musical presentation of the works of many composers. Near the end of his life, he divided his time between Monte Carlo in Monaco and a small village in Scotland, where purchased the estate of the Marquess of Tweeddale. Although he wrote instrumental works, including a *Piano Concerto*, a *Violin Concerto*, and a Mass commissioned by the Roman Catholic Diocese of Baltimore, it is for his operas that he will be remembered. For his devotion to Italian lyricism, Menotti suffered the slings and arrows of criticism from self-styled modernists who accused him of excessive sentimentality. Audiences cheered his works for their obvious emotional appeal. Menotti said that dramatic music must express love, compassion, wonder, and outrage, adding that true inspiration must come from God. As for his critics, he responded, "They often spoil my breakfast, but never my lunch."

THE INTELLECTUALS AND THEIR PUPILS

Not all composers believed that American composers should be consciously American. Walter Piston asked, "Is the Dust Bowl more American than, say, a corner in the Boston Athenaeum?" He was expressing his preference for form, structure, design, and thematic development, rather than a nationalist or emotional appeal. Piston was staking out musical territory for his generation of Boston classicists. Unlike their predecessors (and teachers), these composers were eager to embrace the new, dissonant harmonic language developed by twentieth European composers. The structures and designs associated with European classical music were still their models. Piston and his followers have been dubbed, "neoclassicists."

Figure 85 - Walter Piston, (center) the neo-classical icon whose music and pedagogy defined the study of music at Harvard for decades, with teaching fellow John C. Crawford and Music Department Chairman Randall Thompson. (Photo UAV 605 Box 11, courtesy of Harvard University Archives)

Piston concluded that there were creative opportunities in writing for small combinations of instruments, rejecting the huge orchestral sounds of the nineteenth century romanticists. He sought to apply a modern harmonic language to eighteenth century forms such as the sonata and the symphony.

Walter Piston was born in Rockland, Maine, and began studying the violin in Boston when he was a boy. He joined the Navy during War World I, took up the saxophone, and after the war, decided to become a composer. He enrolled at Harvard, where he studied with Archibald T. Davison and subsequently went to Paris, where he studied under Nadia Boulanger. When he returned from Paris, he began teaching at Harvard, where he remained on the faculty for thirty-four years, composing, writing several noted harmony, counterpoint, and orchestration textbooks, and teaching several generations of composers, including Elliott Carter, Leonard Bernstein, Irving Fine, and Arthur Berger. Piston was a man of many talents. His textbook on orchestration included detailed drawings of all the instruments: his own.

Shortly after Piston joined the Harvard faculty, he met Serge Koussevitzky, the celebrated Russian conductor of the Boston Symphony. Koussevitzky, whose battles with the English language were legendary, asked Piston "Why you no write symphony?" Piston expressed doubt that anyone would play such a work, if he composed it. "You write, I play," said Koussevitzky. Piston began a long association with the Boston Symphony, which commissioned several of his symphonies and performed many of works over the years.

Figure 86 - Roger Sessions, an amiable and popular teacher, often described as a "difficult" composer who delighted in dissonance and complexity to express his musicality. (Photo courtesy of Roger Sessions)

Piston's extensive catalogue of compositions included numerous works for orchestra and chamber ensembles. He was not especially drawn to writing for the voice or the theater. Oddly, one of Piston's most popular works is a rare piece of program music, a ballet, *The Incredible Flutist*. Piston's music depicted a flutist who comes to town with the circus and charms not only snakes, but the local merchant's daughter. Although Piston was identified with what Saint-Saens called "la music pure," the suite from *The Incredible Flutist* is one of his most performed works.

Piston believed that the ideal goals for a composer were structural cohesion and melodic clarity. He was acknowledged as a master of counterpoint and inclined toward emotional restraint. His eight symphonies reflected his belief in absolute music, without extramusical references. Piston rejected what he called the "self-conscious striving for nationalism," which he saw as an obstacle to a composer's capacity for individual expression. Piston believed that musical ideas could speak for themselves; there was no need to use music to express poems, paintings or plots that could already existed in words or as pictures. He saw form, structure, and design, not emotional moods, as the true reason for writing music.

Like Piston, Roger Sessions rejected the idea of nationalism as a musical ideal. As a friend and colleague of Aaron Copland, he helped organize the Copland-Sessions concerts to advance the cause of contemporary American composers.

But in time, Sessions came to specifically oppose the whole notion that American composers should be consciously American. Sessions would later declare "You create music and if it's genuine and spontaneous music written by an American, why then it's American music. These things have to come naturally. For me, nationalism is the wrong approach." In fact, internationalism might best describe Sessions' musical taste. He considered conscious nationalism to be a "mannerism," like an accent, which defined and limited what a composer could do.

Roger Huntington Sessions was born in Brooklyn, New York, in 1896, and shortly thereafter, his family, originally from New England, returned to Massachusetts. Sessions was widely regarded as a musical craftsman and teacher. He had a wry and witty sense of humor, a demeanor, which belied the complexity of his music. Sessions was described for years by critics and admirers alike as a complex, difficult composer, not easily understood or absorbed by the general public. He acknowledged this openly and explained that he simply wrote music as he felt it. If others regard him as complex, it was more their problem than his.

Sessions began composing early; by the age of twelve, he had turned out an opera. At only fourteen, he entered Harvard. After graduation, he studied with Horatio Parker at Yale, and taught at Smith College. But it was Ernest Bloch who exerted the greatest influence over Sessions. Initially, Bloch found the influences of many composers in Sessions' work and Sessions was inclined to regard this as criticism. But Bloch explained that he expected to find many influences in the work for a young composer and the two became fast friends. When Bloch became Director of the Cleveland Institute of Music, Sessions followed him to Cleveland and became his assistant. Sessions dedicated his music for the drama, *The Black Maskers* to Bloch. When Bloch was dismissed from his position Cleveland, Sessions resigned in protest. He spent considerable time in Europe, before returning to the United States. Sessions undertook an active teaching career, at the University of California, the Juilliard School of Music, and especially, for many years at Princeton University.

Sessions was an articulate writer, who wrote numerous textbooks and essays on music. His pupils composed in many styles, some pursuing careers in the theater and motion pictures, some (including famed film composer Elmer Bernstein) writing lush, romantic scores that were the antithesis of their teacher's dissonant, complex approach to music. When asked about this apparent paradox, Sessions quipped, "I don't encourage my students to compose in my style. I don't believe anyone does that quite as well as I do." Sessions opposition to nationalism was clear in his music as well as his writing. He clearly absorbed influences from Bloch, and from intensely serious European composers like Arnold Schoenberg and Igor Stravinsky. Mark Schubart, Dean of the Juilliard School, said of Sessions' music, "It is true that it follows the German conception of music as a grandly expressive art, rather than the French conception of it as a sensuous or coloristic one." Sessions' best-known works included his *Violin Concerto*, *The Idyll of Theocritus* for soprano and orchestra, a *Mass*, string quartets, nine symphonies, and an extremely complex opera, *Montezuma*. Sessions' music is often highly chromatic, dissonant, and very demanding, calling for great virtuosity on the part of the people who perform his works.

Composers like Walter Piston and Roger Sessions were succeeded by a variety of pupils who reflected, to widely varying degrees, the musical philosophies of their teachers. Two of Piston's most widely acclaimed pupils were Elliott Carter and Leonard Bernstein. One could not imagine two more different musical personalities.

Elliott Cook Carter, Jr. was born in New York in 1908. As a boy, he turned for guidance to several avant-garde mentors, including Edgard Varèse, Henry Cowell, and especially Charles Ives, who sold insurance to his family. Carter became an admirer of the twelve-tone technique developed by Arnold Schoenberg and carried on by his pupils. He regarded the Harvard music faculty as too conservative for his tastes, graduated in English literature, eventually switching to music as a graduate student under Walter Piston. Then he went to Paris for three years of study with Nadia Boulanger.

Figure 87 - Elliott Carter, mentored in his youth by Charles Ives, was still composing at 104. (Photo by Irene Haupt, courtesy of Music Library, University at Buffalo, All Rights Reserved)

Carter changed his style often, turning to an analytical "neo-classical" style and teaching for a time at St. John's College in Annapolis, Maryland, where he participated in Scott Buchanan's "Great Books" program, teaching mathematics and Greek philosophy as well as music. Carter developed the college's music program as a branch of physics and mathematics. Carter won the Pulitzer Prize two years in a row, both times for string quartets. He taught at numerous schools, including the Peabody Conservatory, Columbia University, Yale, and the Juilliard of School of Music. His major works included ballets, *Pocahontas* and *The Minotaur*, a piano sonata, a *Double Concerto for Harpsichord and Two Chamber Orchestras*, and a *Symphony for Three Orchestras*.

Carter's life showed astonishing personal as well as musical longevity. His early interest in music was inspired by attending the New York premiere of Stravinsky's then-controversial work, *The Rite of Spring*, conducted by Pierre Monteux. Carter heard the work again at a concert by the Boston Symphony in 2008. This time the concert was in celebration of his 100th birthday; also on the program was his own composition, *Interventions for Piano and Orchestra*. Carter composed forty new works in the previous ten years; since turning 100, he completed at least fourteen more. He died in 2012, only a month shy of his 104th birthday.

If Carter's analytical and intellectual approach to music was not directed at a large public, the same could not be said for Leonard Bernstein. In fact, what can one say about

Bernstein that has not already been said? The career of Leonard Bernstein has been a unique phenomenon in American music. A paradox of Bernstein's composing career was that he became best-known the public as the composer of Broadway shows like *West Side Story* and as a conductor and international celebrity.

But Bernstein also penned numerous pieces of concert music. His works included such varied fare as three symphonies, a clever song cycle, *La Bonne Cuisine*, based on French recipes, another song cycle, *I Hate Music*, and a one act opera, *Trouble in Tahiti*, completed in 1952 as a satire on suburbia.

Bernstein was always at home in the theater, writing ballets like *Fancy Free* and *Facsimile*, and in choral music, with works like *Chichester Psalms*. Bernstein's music is emotional, intense, and energetic. By his own definition, he was a musical eclectic, drawing upon an incredible number of influences, ranging from Copland to Mahler to jazz, somehow fusing them in his own personal style. His music, like his personality, was imposing, flamboyant and sophisticated, with an exceptionally sure sense of theatricality.

Figure 88 - Lukas Foss, a pupil of Serge Koussevitzky, was a composer, conductor, pianist, and teacher. (Photo by Jim Tuttle, courtesy of Music Library, University at Buffalo, All Rights Reserved)

Bernstein also saw himself as a commentator on the world stage, with compositions like *Slava: A Political Overture*. Yet his concert works were somehow overshadowed by the tremendous success of his stage musicals on Broadway and his general celebrity as a conductor and television personality.

Lukas Foss, like his friend Leonard Bernstein, was a protégé of conductor Serge Koussevitzky. Born in Germany, Foss fled the advent of the Nazi regime in Germany, as his family moved first to France, then the United States. Foss attended the Curtis Institute of Music, where he studied (like Bernstein) conducting with Fritz Reiner, and piano with Isabella Vengerova. At the Berkshire Music Center at Tanglewood, Massachusetts, Foss became assistant to Serge Koussevitzky, and later studied composition with Paul Hindemith.

When Foss became familiar with the music of Aaron Copland, he was inspired to try his hand at writing music in an "American" style, the idiom of his new country. Throughout his career, he proved to be a man of many talents: he served as official pianist of the Boston Symphony for six years, conducted major orchestras throughout the country, and taught at major universities, including U.C.L.A., where he was the successor to Arnold Schoenberg as teacher of composition. As a composer, he composed in all forms; his operas included *The Jumping Frog of Calaveras County*, inspired by a short story by Mark Twain and *Griffelkin*, an opera for children featuring a quotation from a work by Mozart.

Foss also composed concertos for various instruments, cantatas, works for narrator, chorus, and orchestras, and some highly experimental pieces. (One was his *Concerto for Improvising Instruments and Orchestra*, another was *MAP*, a musical game in which five players move about the stage playing according to Foss's "rules.") Though Foss was always open to musical experiments, he insisted that to have a "big foot in the future" a composer should always have a "big foot in the past," He remained an active musician able to move in many different directions.

Two of Roger Sessions' best-known pupils were David Diamond and Leon Kirchner. David Diamond was a native of Rochester, New York and began his musical studies in Cleveland. By the time he graduated from high school, he had written and heard performances of as many as one hundred compositions, all of which he ultimately destroyed. He studied with Roger Sessions. Eventually, he attended Eastman and studied composition with Bernard Rogers. When Howard Hanson introduced his *Psalm for Orchestra*, he became widely recognized. Diamond didn't grow up in a wealthy family and surmounted many financial obstacles to become a composer. (As a struggling musician, he once worked at a soda fountain on Broadway and even mopped floors to support himself while composing.) Later, he played the violin in the orchestra for the radio program, "Your Hit Parade." But he persevered and subsequently emerged as an extremely prolific and serious composer, one of America's major composers of symphonies, with eleven in his catalogue.

Figure 89 - David Diamond in Italy. His career took him from working in a Broadway soda fountain to renown as the composer of eleven symphonies. (Courtesy of the Estate of David L. Diamond - All rights reserved.)

Diamond had an intense, emotional personality and it was reflected in his music. An unproduced ballet based on *Uncle Tom's Cabin,* provided him the opportunity to go to Paris. There he studied with Nadia Boulanger, was introduced to Stravinsky, and met the composer he most idolized, Maurice Ravel. In 1944, he wrote his most famous work, *Rounds*, a major piece for string orchestra. Diamond wrote numerous string quartets, orchestral works inspired by *Romeo and Juliet* and *The Tempest*, and a major choral work, *This Sacred Ground*, based on Lincoln's *Gettysburg Address*. He continued to compose prolifically, creating, in addition to his symphonies, three violin concertos, concertos for cello, piano and numerous other instruments, ten string quartets, song cycles based on many sources, including the letters of Claude Debussy, operas, ballets, and even a sonata for the accordion.

He also composed musical elegies in memory of the writers and composers he admired most, novelist William Faulkner, poet e. e. cummings, and the noted French composer Maurice Ravel. Despite his huge musical output, he found time to write music for television, including Edward R. Murrow's series, "See It Now," and to teach for decades at the Juilliard School. Virgil Thomson, writing in *The New York Herald Tribune*, said, "Composers, like pearls, are of three chief sorts, real, artificial, and cultured." He added, "David Diamond is unquestionably of the first sort; his talent and his sincerity have never been doubted by his hearers, his critics, or by his composer colleagues."

Leon Kirchner, generally regarded like his teacher Roger Sessions as an "expressionist," was born in Brooklyn in 1919, but his family moved to California while he was still a boy. His piano teacher, John Crown, introduced him to Ernst Toch who encouraged Kirchner to pursue composition. He went on to study with Arnold Schoenberg at U.C.L.A., and then with Ernest Bloch at the University of California. He also studied piano with Schoenberg's friend and ally, Richard Buhlig. Kirchner completed his training in New York with Sessions, and eventually succeeded Walter Piston to teach at Harvard, remaining there for twenty-eight years. While at Harvard, he mentored many young composers and also created an extremely influential class in the analysis of chamber music while conducting the Harvard Chamber Orchestra.

Figure 90 - Leon Kirchner, as composer and teacher, he spoke out forcefully for modern composers to communicate on an emotional level with their audiences. (Photo by and (c) Lisa Kirchner)

Critics generally describe Kirchner as "emotionally intense." One of his early works to achieve recognition was his *Duo for Violin and Piano*, his first work to be published. Aaron Copland described it as a piece of music "expressing a creative urge so vital as to burst the bonds of ordinary control." His style reflects the tone and mood of music composed by Schoenberg's pupil Alban Berg. Kirchner once said that a great piece of music creates anxiety as the audience anticipates what will happen next.

He won the Pulitzer Prize for his *Quartet No.3 for Strings and Tape*. The introduction of an electronic component in a chamber work attracted considerable praise from critics. His other works included two piano concertos, chamber music, a concerto for violin, cello, ten winds, and percussion, and *Lily*, an opera based on Saul Bellow's *Henderson, the Rain King*. Kirchner adapted some of the material in his opera in a separate work entitled *Lily*, which included his own dramatic readings of Henderson's monologues. Kirchner declared himself an advocate of emotionalism in music, denouncing "quasi-arithmeticians" who worship complexity. He was unimpressed by composers in whose work, "idea, the precious ore of art, is lost in the jungle of graphs, prepared tapes, feedbacks, and cold stylistic minutiae." He criticized those who saw music only as a science, writing that music was a science, but "a science which must make people laugh, and dance, and sing."

THE ÉMIGRÉS

One of the most interesting aspects of our musical heritage was the arrival on American shores of many of Europe's most distinguished composers. Most of these men came to the United States because of oppression at home. The Russian Revolution and two World Wars made it necessary for musicians from all over the world to seek safety in the United States. Some became American citizens. All continued composing, and many enjoyed distinguished careers as teachers. To varying degrees, they involved themselves in America's musical life. Were these renowned figures American composers? Clearly, residence or academic activities in another country do not alter a composer's nationality. Although many continued writing music in their new home, their styles remained varied, and usually, European. But no discussion of our musical heritage would be complete without acknowledgment of these very important figures in contemporary concert music, many of whom left an indelible mark on America's musical horizon through their pupils.

Figure 91 Ernest Bloch, composer and renowned teacher. His pupil, Roger Sessions, praised him for expressing "the grandeur of human suffering." (Photo by Ernest Bloch II, 1956, Courtesy Old Stage Studios)

Not all composers, however, came to the U.S. as refugees. Some came for musical or economic reasons. Swiss-born Ernest Bloch trained a whole generation of American composers. In 1916, Bloch came to the U.S. as a conductor for the dancer Maude Allen. Bloch recognized that one of the works to be performed, Claude Debussy's *Khamma*, needed revisions to be performed by the small orchestra available. He asked Debussy's permission to adapt it; the normally outspoken Debussy gave his blessing and said that he trusted Bloch with his music because he knew him. When the Maude Allen troupe went bankrupt, Bloch found himself stranded in New York.

He stayed in the U.S. and built his reputation not only as a composer, but as one of America's most important teachers of composition. He served as Director of the Cleveland Institute of Music, and later, taught in New York and San Francisco. A long list of distinguished American composers and teachers were Bloch's pupils. It was Bloch who composed an epic rhapsody, *America*, as a musical homage to his new country; the piece won $3,000 prize offered by the magazine, *Musical America*, and was premiered simultaneously by the New York, Chicago, Boston, Philadelphia, and San Francisco Symphonies.

Among Bloch's best-known works were his compositions for strings: his four string quartets, a quintet for piano and strings, *Schelomo—A Hebrew Rhapsody* for cello and orchestra, and *A Voice in the Wilderness* for orchestra and cello obbligato. His skill in writing for strings came naturally. He had been a child prodigy on the violin and studied that instrument under Eugene Ysaÿe, the great Belgian virtuoso. During his lifetime, he was widely admired and critics suggested that "Bloch" be added as the "Fourth B" to the list of "Bach, Beethoven, and Brahms." A Society named in his honor included not only musical admirers, but the music-loving physicist whose name was synonymous with genius, Albert Einstein.

Although his most widely performed works, such as his *Sacred Service*, reflected the inspiration of Judaism, he had many musical interests, including a life-long fascination with Chinese culture. He never founded a "school" or "method" of composition, but encouraged each of his pupils to find his own way. His daughter Suzanne wrote of her father, "His capacity for joy, suffering, anger, and affection was immense." Bloch was also an accomplished photographer and left thousands of negatives of the pictures he had taken, including trees, landscapes, and portraits. Quite by accident, he discovered the coast of Oregon and spent the last two decades of his life with his wife and family in a home in Agate Beach, Oregon, surrounded by tall trees and the crashing waves of the Pacific Ocean. He said that great composers were not just masters of notes, but great men first, who expressed their message through music. Bloch wrote, "Bach, Beethoven, and Wagner never had any idea of amusing or diverting. They had a message to deliver to humanity through words and sounds. That is all that preoccupied them. When the public is wearied of the childish harmonic, instrumental, and rhythmic games with which our generation seems mostly concerned, the message of these great masters will still shine in all its glory, because, being purely human, it is eternal."

Figure 92 - Edgard Varèse, the French composer who came to America, was called "The Father of Electronic Music." (Photo courtesy of George Grantham Bain Collection, Library of Congress)

From France came the avant-garde composer, Edgard Varèse who planned to spend a few weeks in the U.S. in 1915, stayed seven years, and decided to become an American citizen. Varèse was active in writing percussive, experimental music, and pioneering in the use of electronic media. In 1921, Varèse teamed with the harpist Carlos Salzedo to found the International Composers Guild, the first American organization established to champion the cause of twentieth music. Varèse created a storm with his work *Ionisation*, which he scored entirely for percussion instruments, including sirens. He also pioneered in the use of electronic instruments like the theremin and the Ondes Martenot.

Figure 93 - Darius Milhaud, the serious composer of modern French concert music who was captivated by jazz in the 1920s. (Public Domain)

Darius Milhaud was a French composer who drew upon the music of the Americas, both North and South. Milhaud followed in the footsteps of French composers who wanted to break away from the influence of Germany. But he saw a danger in French composers following what he called "shimmering finery, vapors, and wistfulness." He was extremely prolific and could write music very rapidly. He was a leading member of the French group of composers known as "Les Six." Although the six composers were friends, each had his own style and his own goals.

Milhaud began experimenting with polytonality, the idea of music being played with two key centers at the same time. He was also strongly influenced by American jazz, the music he explored during a visit to Harlem while spending time in New York, and by the rhythms and dances of Brazil, where he spent much of his time during World War I.

Milhaud's ballet, *La Création du Monde*, actually preceded George Gershwin's *Rhapsody in Blue* as an effort to introduce jazz rhythms and harmonies into concert music. Milhaud liked to experiment. He composed *Scaramouche*, for either solo saxophone or two pianos. Another of his many ballets, *Le bœuf sur le toit (The Ox on the Roof)*, and his dance suite, *Saudades do Brasil*, reflected his interest in Brazilian popular music. He composed in large forms, writing concertos for piano, violin, and cello, numerous operas, the best-known of which was *Christophe Colomb*, twelve symphonies, and eighteen string quartets. But he found time to have fun, basing one composition on the textual description of agricultural and farming equipment.

Milhaud and his wife Madeleine, an actress, fled France and the Nazi occupation during World War II. He taught for many years at Mills College in Oakland, California after the war, and eventually devoted much of his life to teaching in the United States as well as France. Darius Milhaud once said that the most difficult thing in music is still to write a melody of several bars that can be self-sufficient. Conductor Robert Lawrence said that the keynote to Milhaud's character was his love of youth and of freshness in art and his life; his aversion to the static and pretentious.

The Dutch-born Bernard Wagenaar came

Figure 94 - Bernard Wagenaar, an urbane Dutch-born composer who numbered many of America's finest composers among his pupils at Juilliard. (Photo courtesy of Mary Louise Miller Spang W1933 Collection (MC 035), Marion B. Gebbie W1901 Archives & Special Collection Madeleine Clark Wallace Library, Wheaton College Norton, MA.)

Figure 95 - Sergei Rachmaninoff, the logical successor to Tchaikovsky. When this Russian composer settled in the U.S., his romantic style made him one of the most widely beloved composers in the world. (Public Domain - Courtesy of Pictures and Prints Collection Library of Congress)

to the U.S. in 1920, and became a U.S. citizen seven years later. He was an accomplished performer on both the violin and keyboard instruments and played in major symphony orchestras before devoting his full time to composing. His principal works, including four symphonies, string quartets, a violin concerto, and numerous other pieces were all written in the United States. Wagenaar spent over forty years teaching at the Juilliard School of Music, and he remained a critical influence on contemporary composers throughout the country.

But it was wars and revolutions that brought most composers to the U.S. Here was an adopted country where they could be free to compose as they pleased, and free to speak their minds without being arrested or murdered by dictators and their secret police.

Sergei Rachmaninoff, the last of the great European romantics, was a direct musical descendent of Tchaikovsky. He left his native Russia, controlled by the communists, never to return, after the Bolshevik revolution in 1917. After a number of years in Europe, primarily in Switzerland, he came to the United States in 1935, where he remained until his death in 1943. Although Rachmaninoff lived elsewhere, he was admittedly the most Russian of all composers, and considered himself a musical expatriate living in exile. Rachmaninoff had no sympathy for many of the experiments of modern composers. His romantic style, however, dazzled performers and audiences alike. His music is still beloved the world over. He remains the favorite composer of countless devotees of concert music and it is unfortunate that such a great composer is often dismissed by a minority of critics and academics because of his very popularity.

Like Rachmaninoff, Igor Stravinsky left his native Russia, settling in Switzerland, then in France, where he became a French citizen. Unlike Rachmaninoff, Stravinsky was not a musical conservative. He began his career writing ballets like *The Firebird* and *Petrouchka*, inspired by his teacher, Rimsky-Korsakov. But the primitive rhythms of *Le Sacre du Printemps* (*The Rite of Spring*) caused a riot in Paris when it premiered. Stravinsky settled in the United States in 1940, and became an American citizen in 1945. He became one of the towering figures of the neo-classic

Figure 96 - Igor Stravinsky. A composer of many changing styles, he became the icon of neo-classical music in the 20th century. (Photo Courtesy of Library of Congress, Public Domain)

Figure 97 - Arnold Schoenberg conducting an American class. Pupils here include Natalie Limonick, H. Endicott Hansen, Alfred Carlson, Richard Hoffman. He was a celebrated teacher and musical revolutionary, although his twelve-tone technique still remains controversial in the 21st century. (Photo by Richard Fish - Courtesy of the Arnold Schönberg Center, Vienna, Austria)

movement and a major figure in twentieth century music.

His presence in the United States undoubtedly increased his influence over numerous American composers who studied his every musical inclination intensely. Critic Cecil Smith wrote, "No young American composer can afford to ignore Stravinsky's insistence that expression without cogent or formal musical structure is not a proper musical aim." Stravinsky became an American citizen and wrote many major works in the U.S., including his *Symphony in Three Movements*, his opera, *The Rake's Progress*, his serial ballet, *Agon*, and his *Mass*.

One cannot imagine two less similar musical outlooks than those of Rachmaninoff and Stravinsky. The two were both renowned composers and Russian exiles. It was said that on rare occasions when they met, the conversation turned to what they shared in common, their sense of being Russian and living the lives of exiles, not their disparate tastes in music. In his later years, due to the influence of conductor Robert Craft,

Stravinsky surprised admirers and critics alike by adopting some of the twelve-tone techniques developed by his archrival, Austrian-born Arnold Schoenberg.

With the advent of the Nazis, Schoenberg left Germany for California, where he became an American citizen. Arnold Schoenberg taught a wide assortment of students, including many noted composers who were active film composers. His pupils found him to be a man of lively humor who could express admiration for composers whose musical

Figure 98 - Gerald Strang, Schoenberg's assistant, was also a prominent composer, teacher, and acoustics consultant, and pioneer in the field of electronic and computer music. (Photo courtesy of The American Composers Alliance)

styles were quite unlike his own. He praised George Gershwin, who returned the compliment by painting a portrait of Schoenberg. Students were often shocked that Schoenberg did not begin by teaching them his twelve-tone serial technique. He insisted on thorough studies of musical form and analysis, harmony, and counterpoint, usually based on the German classics. He insisted that his music represented neither anarchy nor revolution, but musical evolution. He wanted his major works, ranging from string quartets to his *Piano Concerto*, to be appreciated only for their musical appeal. He wrote," If a composer does not write from the heart, he simply cannot produce good music." Schoenberg insisted "I offer incontestable proof of the fact that in following the twelve-tone scale, a composer is neither less nor more bound, hindered, nor made independent. He may be as coldhearted and unmoved as an engineer, or, as laymen imagine, may conceive in sweet dreams—in inspiration."

Schoenberg taught at U.C.L.A., where the Canadian-born composer, Gerald Strang and the American pianist, Leonard Stein became his teaching assistants and editors of his published works.

After Schoenberg's death in 1951, they carried on his legacy. Strang had served as editor of *New Music Quarterly*. For twenty years, he composed electronic and computer music. Strang called his electronic works "Synthions" and his computer pieces "Compusitions." He shared Schoenberg's belief that great music must have an underlying sense of logic. Leonard Stein, a piano pupil of Schoenberg's friend, Richard Buhlig, became director of the Arnold Schoenberg Institute. He lectured on Schoenberg's works for decades throughout the world and performed all of Schoenberg's piano pieces.

George Tremblay, another Schoenberg pupil, was the son of a prominent Canadian organist and a highly skilled improviser on the piano.. Eventually, Tremblay published and widely taught his "definitive cycle" using a combination of two groups of six tones to create an extended series of scales for the composer to use. In doing so, he eliminated the techniques of inverting the notes of the scale (inversion) or using them backwards (retrograde,) used previously by many exponents of Schoenberg.

Figure 99 - Leonard Stein, a noted pianist, conductor, lecturer, editor and teacher, was also Schoenberg's assistant. Later, he served for many years as the Director of the Schoenberg Institute. (Photograph by Betty Freeman, Courtesy of Piano Spheres)

Figure 100 - Ernst Toch, distinguished as composer, teacher, and author of *The Shaping Forces in Music*. He told his pupils that all secrets of composition could be found in the music of Mozart. (Photo courtesy of the Irvin Talbot Collection)

Like Schoenberg, Viennese born Ernst Toch won distinction as a composer and teacher in Germany. In 1933, the Nazis ruined the scheduled premiere and publication of his piano concerto.

Like so many leading European musical figures who fled anti-Semitism and the persecution of the Nazis, he realized that he would have to find a way to emigrate to America. He was permitted to represent Germany at a conference in Italy. He never returned and instead went to Paris. He then sent his wife Lilly a cable signaling her to bring their daughter and join him. Eventually, the Tochs went to London and New York before settling in California.

Before boarding a ship to cross the Atlantic, he walked the fogbound streets of London to meticulously record the sounds of the chimes of Big Ben. He then composed a set of orchestral variations on the sounds of the famed British clock. Toch was extraordinarily imaginative. A 1930 composition, his *Geographical Fugue*, was written for a speaking chorus. The text was based entirely on interesting and unusual names of a number of real places around the world. American audiences were also drawn to *Pinocchio: A Merry Overture*.

Toch wrote many orchestral and chamber works, all the while teaching at the University of Southern California, composing prolifically, and writing an important textbook, *The Shaping Forces in Music*. His *Piano Quintet* was regarding as one of the major chamber music works of its time. In 1956, his *Third Symphony* won the Pulitzer Prize. Toch taught privately for many years, numbering among his pupils such prominent musical figures as Aurelio de la Vega, Hugo Friedhofer, Alex North, André Previn, and Leonard Pennario. Toch was a prolific composer throughout his life, writing numerous string quartets, seven symphonies, and works for the piano (including two concertos and fifty etudes.) He also scored motion pictures. Because traditionalists regarded him as an experimentalist and the avant-garde composers defined him as conservative, his music was neglected for a time. Happily, today, his legacy is being rediscovered.

Figure 101 - Ernest Kanitz, noted Austrian composer, spent several decades in Southern California as a teacher specializing in "modern counterpoint." (Photo courtesy of Ernest Kanitz)

Toch's successor at U.S.C. was a noted Viennese composer and choral conductor, Dr. Ernest Kanitz, a greatly admired professor who had a distinguished teaching career while turning out three symphonies and a steady stream of chamber and choral music, often in a neo-classic style. He also composed solo concertos for instruments ranging from the bassoon to the theremin. Kanitz said, "Music's foremost task is bringing messages to its listeners, which cannot be expressed in words, in stone or marble, or on canvas."

Ernst Krenek, like Kanitz, a Franz Schreker pupil, had distinctly different musical inclinations. Krenek wrote a jazz opera, *Jonny spielt auf* with an inter-racial plot, which made him a highly controversial figure. He came to the United States in 1937 and continued a extensive career as a composer, conductor, writer, and a teacher.

Figure 102 - Ernst Krenek explores electronic music as fellow composers Aurelio de la Vega and Beverly Grigsby join him. (Photo courtesy of Aurelio de la Vega)

After the Nazi invasion of Austria, he remained in the U.S., marrying American composer and former pupil Gladys Nordenstrom, and settling in Palm Springs, California, where he pursued a keen interest in electronic music. Krenek's output included five symphonies, four piano concertos, operas, and numberous chamber music works. Krenek explored neo-romantic, neo-classical, and serial styles. He said his pursuit of many musical styles in his career was the result of his pursuit of freer musical thought.

Figure 103 - Paul Hindemith a leading neo-classicist who combined a modern European musical vocabulary with the contrapuntal techniques of the Baroque era perfected by J.S. Bach. (Photo courtesy of Irving Gilmore Library, Yale University)

German-born Paul Hindemith was one of the leading neo-classicists of twentieth century music. He sought to combine a modern harmonic vocabulary with the musical techniques, which had been perfected by Johann Sebastian Bach. Hindemith composed his own set of Preludes and Fugues, the *Ludus Tonalis*, and his best-known opera, *Mathis der Maler*. The premiere of the opera was canceled on personal orders from Adolf Hitler; Wilhelm Furtwangler, the conductor who defended Hindemith, was sent into exile. After spending some time in Turkey, Hindemith settled in the United States, where he joined the faculty of Yale. He also became an American citizen. After the war, he returned to Germany for a hero's welcome. Hindemith divided his time between the U.S. and Switzerland, eventually settling in Switzerland, where he continued to compose and teach.

Not all Austrian or German composers were inclined toward neo-classicism. Erich Wolfgang Korngold was an unabashed romantic. A child prodigy, Korngold proved himself a composer of consequence while still a boy. The son of a prominent Viennese music critic, Korngold won plaudits from the most demanding musicians of his time. Gustav Mahler called him "a genius," Richard Strauss praised his assurance of style, mastery of form, bold harmony as "truly astonishing," and Giacomo Puccini called him "the greatest hope of German music." As a mature composer, Korngold gained fame for his operas, including *Die tote Stadt*, *Das wunder der Heliane*, and *Die Kathrin*. He began coming to the United States to score motion pictures, and in 1939, settled permanently in the U.S., like so many others, to escape the Third Reich. He became an American citizen. Ironically, in Vienna, Korngold's romantic works had been praised by critics while the experimental compositions of his

Figure 104 - Erich Wolfgang Korngold. When he died, Korngold thought his concert works would be forgotten, eclipsed by his years in Hollywood. Instead, his operas and instrumental works are more famous than ever. (Photo used with the kind permission of the Brendan Carroll Collection)

much older rival, Arnold Schoenberg, were dismissed or ignored. Korngold even composed four children's piano pieces satirizing the styles of the modernists, Schoenberg, Stravinsky, Bartók, and Hindemith. In the 1930s, the works of Korngold and Schoenberg and their followers were both suppressed by the Nazis. But in later years, it was Schoenberg who was cheered by critics and academics, while Korngold's post-romantic scores were mocked by those who thought music should be a cold, intellectual process. Sadly, Korngold did not live long enough to witness the rediscovery of his genius. In recent years, his concert works have undergone a tremendous revival, justified by his melodic and orchestral brilliance.

Figure 105 - Béla Bartók. A major Hungarian composer was inspired by true Hungarian folk music. (Public Domain)

From Hungary, Béla Bartók came to the U.S. in the 1920s on a concert tour. He was a pioneer in the collection of Hungarian folk music. When World War II broke out, he settled in the U.S., where he remained until his death. Bartok was often neglected during his lifetime. But during the last two years of his life in America, he gained wide recognition as a composer. Although a pianist, he wrote major works for strings over the years, including his six string quartets and *Music for Strings, Percussion, and Celesta*. He was an extremely prolific composer and wrote major works during his last years in the United States, including his *Concerto for Orchestra* and his *Third Piano Concerto*. After his death in 1945, musical historians declared him to be one of the major composers of the twentieth century.

Hungarian-born Miklós Rósza succeeded in doing the nearly impossible: writing distinguished concert music, including violin, piano, and viola concertos, while

Figure 106 - Miklós Rósza. He composed concertos for the violin, cello, and viola, among his many concert works, while always maintaining the highest artistic standards and the schedule of a film composer. (Courtesy of New York World Telegram and Sun Collection, Library of Congress)

simultaneously pursuing a successful career as a film composer. Rósza was always Hungarian in his musical outlook. (Even in high school, he had organized concerts devoted to the music of the older Hungarian composers he admired: Béla Bartók, Zoltán Kodály, and Erno von Dohnányi.) He declared his musical goal to be the creation of a Hungarian symphonic music that would go beyond simply adapting folk tunes. Rósza also became an American citizen.

European composers who arrived in Hollywood as refugees were often faced with a dilemma. Those who became extremely successful were often identified by critics as "Hollywood composers" and their concert works were simply dismissed. Others worked anonymously in the film industry, receiving little or no credit for their work, while they still faced a struggle to achieve recognition as composers of serious concert works.

Eugene Zádor was a Hungarian composer of great achievement, a pupil of Max Reger, and credentialed as a professor of music in Vienna. He fled Europe in 1939. He composed eleven operas, the best-known of which was *Christopher Columbus*. His work, *The Children's Symphony*, received a hundred performances.

Figure 107 - Eugene Zádor, was a prolific Hungarian composer who wrote important concert works while orchestrating film scores anonymously. (Photo courtesy of Leslie Zador)

Figure 108 - Eric Zeisl. His tonal and traditional style and his sudden death at the height of his creative powers at only fifty-three resulted in unjust neglect of his music. (Photograph courtesy of Barbara Zeisl Schoenberg)

Known as an extremely facile and highly skilled orchestrator, he decided to seek his fortune in the field of film scoring. He found himself in Hollywood contributing original music and orchestrations to over 120 films, always anonymously. Zádor was thus taken seriously as a composer of concert music, but even the most intense aficionados of motion picture music might not recognize his name. Like Miklós Rósza, whose film scores he often orchestrated, he was prolific, articulate, and consciously Hungarian in his musical style.

Eric Zeisl was an Austrian composer who fled the Nazis, as did so many. His teacher, Richard Stöhr, was a contemporary of Arnold Schoenberg, but he still believed in the traditional harmonic vocabulary of composers identified as "romantics." Zeisl also came to Hollywood, but his experience in the film capital was an unhappy one. He found himself anonymously scoring travelogues and unable to receive major film scoring assignments or screen credits. He became a prominent teacher and an active member of the European exile community that escaped Hitler, Mussolini, and Stalin. Zeisl's reaction to Hollywood was intriguing. He gave it a nickname, "Schein-Heiligenstadt." The name includes a pun on the German word for hypocrisy.

Mario Castelnuovo-Tedesco was one of Italy's most prominent composers. The eminent Florentine composer settled in California when he escaped Mussolini's Fascist oppression in his native country. He was an incredibly prolific composer. Fluent in a more than a half-dozen languages, Castelnuovo-Tedesco composed operas and wrote his own librettos in both English and Italian for his prize-winning masterpiece, *The Merchant of Venice*.

Figure 110 - Mario Castelnuovo-Tedesco, at his writing desk, where he orchestrated in ink. The Maestro's scores required few corrections or changes. (Photograph courtesy of Mario Castelnuovo-Tedesco)

He was inspired by Shakespeare, composing settings of all the songs in Shakespeare's plays and orchestral overtures to many of the plays. His early opera, *La Mandragola*, won the praise of Puccini. One of his last operas, scored for soloists, two pianists, and two percussionists, was *The Importance of Being Earnest*. To match the Oscar Wilde play upon which it was based, the score included dozens of satirical and amusing quotations from classical masterpieces that could be recognized by the audience.

His study of the English language gave him great familiarity with the King James Bible and he composed many works inspired by Biblical subjects. His *Second Violin Concerto* was called "The Prophets." He also wrote a seven scenic oratorios and cantatas and numerous choral works based on passages from the Old Testament.

He also composed concertos for the great virtuosos of his day, including Jascha Heifetz (violin,) Gregor Piatigorsky (cello,) and Andrés Segovia (guitar.) He is generally recognized as the premier composer of guitar music in the twentieth century. He wrote numerous solo and ensemble pieces for guitar, ranging from *Platero and I* for narrator and guitar to his splendid *Quintet for Guitar and String Quartet*. The second movement of his first guitar concerto was written as a farewell to his parents and his Italian homeland before he, his wife Clara, and their two sons left for the United States. It is one of the most poignant pieces written for the classical guitar. Castelnuovo-Tedesco also wrote large amounts of

Figure 109 - Mario Castelnuovo-Tedesco. Polish composer Bronislaw Kaper once said the word "composer" in the 20th century should be redefined to mean anyone who has studied with, is studying with, or will study with Castelnuovo-Tedesco. (Photo courtesy of Mario Castelnuovo-Tedesco)

Figure 111 - A gathering of composers at the Hollywood Bowl in 1948 included many prominent émigrés and their American colleagues. (L-R, George Antheil, Eugene Zádor, Arthur Bergh, Italo Montemezzi, Miklós Rósza, Richard Hageman, William Grant Still, Igor Stravinsky, Ernst Toch, Louis Gruenberg, Erich Wolfgang Korngold. (Photo courtesy of Leslie Zador)

piano and chamber music, all of great distinction. His own favorite composition for piano was *Cipresi*. It depicted the cypress trees in the Tuscan woods near his home in Italy. Another of his piano works, *Alt Wien*, contained an unusual tragic foxtrot movement.

With a twinkle in his eye, he referred to himself as "the father of west coast jazz." Although he never wrote or played a note of jazz in his life, the Maestro was the mentor and teacher of several generations of America's finest jazz composers and arrangers. Although he became an American citizen, he was a quintessentially Italian composer in his musical style, with some influences from Spain. For a time, critics ridiculed his work, filled with lyrical melodies and emotional expression as "old-fashioned," Today such critics are largely forgotten, while his music has enjoyed an unprecedented revival.

Mario Castelnuovo-Tedesco never believed in any arbitrary musical style or ideology. He said that he regarded music as an art capable of progress and renewal. Of his adopted country, the United States, he wrote, "I hope to be able to give the great country that has given me a haven, to America, the best of my life, and my art, just as I gave them for more than thirty years, in full and absolute conscientiousness, to my own country."

The presence of so many of the world's most distinguished composers in California contributed greatly to the state's cultural life. Though many had come to the United

States for the same reasons, their differing musical styles and old rivalries often stood in the way of their becoming a community. Rachmaninoff and Stravinsky were both Russian exiles, but their completely opposite musical views meant that they would never be close friends. Schoenberg's rivalry with Stravinsky was legendary, exacerbated by the fact that both men lived in Los Angeles. The two men had very different views regarding the ideal future path for contemporary music. They did not socialize together. Their musical disciples regarded each other with bitterness and suspicion. This was apparent to observers in 1945 during the rehearsals of a unique experiment combining the talents of several leading émigré composers in a collaborative effort known as *The Genesis Suite.*

The work was commissioned by Nathaniel Shilkret, a composer, conductor, and former child prodigy on the clarinet, who spent many years as a musical director for RCA Victor. Shilkret chose six episodes from the Book of Genesis to be set to music with narration. When he felt that he couldn't complete the project himself, he turned to Mario Castelnuovo-Tedesco whom he knew from their association at MGM. Castelnuovo-Tedesco agreed to write a movement depicting The Flood and brought his friend Ernst Toch into the project to write a movement depicting the rainbow following the flood. Toch, in turn, called Alexandre Tansman, who wrote the movement inspired by the story of Adam and Eve. It was Tansman who brought in Darius Milhaud and Igor Stravinsky. Milhaud chose to write a movement depicting Cain and Abel, while Stravinsky selected Babel as his theme. Shilkret then approached Schoenberg, whose "Prelude" depicting the chaos that existed before Creation would open the work.

Shilkret went to great lengths to keep Schoenberg and Stravinsky from attending the work's rehearsal at the same time, but his plans went awry and their supporters glared at each other from opposite ends of the auditorium. The nearsighted Schoenberg didn't initially recognize Stravinsky, while Stravinsky completely monopolized the available rehearsal time. When one of Schoenberg's pupils asked for his opinion of Stravinsky's piece, Schoenberg said, "It didn't end, it just stopped." *The Genesis Suite* was recorded under the baton of Werner Jansen. It never became part of the standard orchestral repertory, perhaps because the movements reflected such different styles on the part of the composers.

Figure 112 - Nicolas Slonimsky was a Russian composer, musicologist, historian, lexicographer, conductor, pianist, author, and extraordinary raconteur. (Photo courtesy of Electra Slonimsky Yourke)

Certainly one of the most colorful of the émigrés was the multitalented Russian, Nicolas Slonimsky. Slonimsky was simply "beyond musical category." A pianist, conductor, and composer, he became the champion of modern composers of many styles and tastes. He played and conducted their works at a time when they were often subject to neglect or ridicule. But Slonimsky became best-known to the public for his literary and analytical skills. He was a renowned raconteur. He was also the complete opposite of a pedantic scholar who bored or condescended to his audiences. He combined wit, humor, and irreverence with tremendous musical insight. Although a serious composer, he didn't think composers should take themselves too seriously.

One of his piano suites was inspired by Yellowstone National Park. In 1925, he became the first composer to set American advertising copy to music, even including the text of a promotion for Pepsodent toothpaste. He composed an encore song for the singers of art songs called "I Owe a Debt to a Monkey." Slonimsky had worked as an associate to fellow Russian conductor Serge Koussevitzky and attempted to help the famed maestro with his intense and often amusing struggles with the English language.

He was also a prolific writer and his many books offered a unique contribution not only to musical literature, but to our understanding of the true nature of music itself. His *Lexicon of Musical Invective* was a collection of critical reviews of the works of great composers when their works were heard for the first time. Compositions ranging from Beethoven's symphonies to Gershwin's *Rhapsody in Blue* suffered the slings and arrows of critics predicting that they would fade into a guaranteed oblivion.

In 1944, Slonimsky made an historic tour of Central and South America. The result was his book, *The Music of Latin America*, introducing composers of twenty countries and analyzing their works. Children are often told by their piano teachers to practice their scales, but even the most professional musicians were astonished by Slonimsky's *Thesaurus of Scales and Melodic Patterns.* This huge reference book contained hundreds of scales and their sophisticated analysis. Musicians who only knew major, minor, or even modal scales, were suddenly confronted with Slonimsky's "infra-inter-ultrapolation" and his "Phrygian polytetrachord." He also spent many years as the editor of *Baker's Biographical Dictionary.* As a lexicographer and teacher, he delighted in playing musical pranks on his musicologist colleagues when he thought they had too much starch in their collars. On one occasion, he made reference to a bogus cantata with a Czech title that contained no vowels to see if anyone could pronounce it or recognize it as the product of his imagination. His sense of ironic humor was ever-present throughout his life, whether writing letters to his devoted wife of many years, the art critic Dorothy Ardlow, or in compositions such as *51 Minitudes,* his satirical piano miniatures, including one based on "The Square Root of Beethoven's Fifth Symphony" or his variations on a Brazilian tune that require the popping of balloons in the final fortissimo. Critics called him "the greatest musical chronicler of our time." When he died at 101, he left a legacy that will not soon be forgotten.

Not all composers came to the United States from Europe. Carlos Chávez and Silvestre Revueltas, the best-known Mexican composers, also spent time working in the United States.

Today composers are still settling in the U.S. from around the world, and for the same reasons. After Fidel Castro's communist revolution in Cuba, musicians from that country, like Aurelio de la Vega, a leading Cuban composer and director of one of his country's most important music schools, settled in the United States. De la Vega had been a pioneer in music education in Cuba and founded programs new to all of Latin America. The Castro regime tried to erase his achievements in Cuba, but de la Vega embarked on a distinguished teaching career in California that lasted for more than three decades and resulted in his being named the most outstanding professor in the entire California State University system.

Aurelio de la Vega's catalogue includes compositions for orchestra, solo instruments, cantatas, ballet scores, chamber music, pieces for the human voice, and the results of a lifetime exploration of electronic music. He sought to explore an intensely personal style with a contemporary musical vocabulary. His works have been extensively performed throughout the United States, Europe, Asia, and most countries in Latin America except for Cuba following the communist revolution. He has been the subject of documentary film, *Aurelio: Rebel with a Cause*. Finally, in 2012, after being blacklisted for fifty-three years by the country of his birth, de la Vega's worldwide prominence was finally acknowledged by web sites purportedly associated with the Cuban government.

Figure 114 - Carlos Chávez, noted Mexican composer, recognized for his percussive music and complex rhythms. (Photo courtesy of the Carl Van Vechten Collection, Library of Congress)

Figure 115 - Silvestre Revueltas, a leading Mexican composer and teacher. He drew upon the rhythms and energy of Mexican folklore to create a unique personal style expressing the character of his people. (Photo courtesy of Fototeca Nacional de Mexico)

De la Vega is a man of many talents. He has been a prolific writer on many subjects, including not only the music but the visual arts of Latin America. He has even combined music and the visual arts in works such as *The Magic Labyrinth*. Known for his meticulous notation, the composer has produced "painted scores" with colors and visual shapes interpreted in sound. *The Magic Labryinth* was selected for inclusion in a Library of Congress collection along with works of such masters as Beethoven and Brahms.

True to his artistic principles and eschewing fads and fashions in a time of ubiquitous pop culture and commercialism, de la Vega declared, "The composer of art music is a crusader whose goal is not to kill or conquer, but to elevate beauty to such lofty

Figure 113 - Aurelio de la Vega, Cuban-American composer, teacher, art historian, writer, scholar, and a voice in the wilderness calling for integrity in the arts and the behavior of nations. (Photo by Lee Choo courtesy of Aurelio de la Vega)

heights that it shines like a gigantic beacon for all humanity."

The presence of so many composers from around the world has had a significance effect not only on our musical heritage, but on that of other countries. In some cases, these composers have absorbed American influences and taken them around the world. In others, they brought to the American music al melting pot the traditions, styles, and musical ideas of other nations, making an important contribution to our national musical attitudes. Their contributions should be remembered.

THE ECLECTICS

Most composers do not like to be classified or labeled or placed in neat categories that define or describe their style. (They seldom object to descriptions if the words "brilliant" or "genius" are used.) Academicians, scholarly writers, and musicologists delight in putting labels on composers and their work. The music written by certain composers, however, makes such labeling impossible. Their sources of inspiration are many; to mention only a few, their music draws upon jazz, folk tunes, popular songs, spirituals, and a collection of international influences often called "world music."

We can call them "eclectics," because they simply fit no category and defy classification. While they speak musically to large audiences, their versatility has often posed professionally challenges for them. Because their works represent a fusion of many genres and styles, the self-proclaimed arbiters of such styles are quick to object: does a work belong on the concert stage if members of the orchestra are playing non-traditional instruments? What about performances featuring elements of jazz improvisation? Critics are apt to dismiss "light" music as "not serious" and therefore undeserving of serious musical consideration. Jazz or folk musicians may be equally quick to declare such concert composers to be "inauthentic" because they cross the line and produce fully written or orchestrated scores. The public, typically, could not care less. As for the composers, they are artists we should meet and appreciate on their own merits.

Then there are those American composers who intentionally ignored trends and fashions in musical composition. They stuck to their principles, often drawing upon many musical styles and more often than not, felt comfortable with tradition instead of revolution. This would be a difficult path to pursue.

Charles Haubiel, an Ohio native, served in World War I and eventually settled in New York, where he studied with Rosario Scalero, from whom he derived a great interest in the polyphonic music of the Baroque, especially the works of J.S. Bach. His early works reflected this interest, including *Karma*, a set of orchestral variations expressing India's *Bhagavad Gita*. But Haubiel later turned to a combination of Romantic and Impressionist influences that led critics to dub his style "a combination of Brahms and Debussy." His *Metamorphosis* was a very different set of variations on Stephen Foster's "Swanee River" in the styles of composers from Gregory I to Gershwin. Haubiel was the founder of the

Composers Press and spent more than three decades publishing the works of American composers, including those who shared his unabashed musical conservatism. He once said one of his teachers, the pianist Rudolph Ganz, called him a "musical Bolshevist." Yet by the end of his long musical career, he declared atonality and most other musical "isms" to be psychologically unsound.

Philip James spent decades as Chairman of the Composition Department at New York University. He drew upon many sources of inspiration, ranging from Irish ballads to 16th century Italian paintings to the writings of Mark Twain's rival, Bret Harte. Music historian David Ewen said that Philip James wrote to "please the ear and the heart." Composer Frederick Jacobi had a similar view in mind when he wrote that music should give pleasure and not try to solve philosophical problems. Harl McDonald was a westerner who went east. Although he taught for many years in Pennsylvania, he was inspired by the Mexican songs he heard in his youth spent on farms and cattle ranches in California. McDonald advised composers not to ignore music of their own locales and said that there were "many undiscovered gold mines in people's back yards."

Deems Taylor might have led the conventional life of a composer if it were not for his other talents as a writer and commentator. Taylor had started to gain recognition as a composer when he wrote an orchestral suite, *Through the Looking Glass*, based on Lewis Carroll's classic tale. It musically depicted talking flowers and even included a fugue for the battle against the Jabberwock. Taylor was a gifted writer and became music critic of the New York World in 1921. He also wrote music for plays on Broadway, including *Beggar on Horseback* by Marc Connelly and George S. Kaufman. Both men invited Taylor to join them at the famous Round Table, a group of writers and wits who met for daily lunches and to exchange epigrams at the Algonquin Hotel, and included such other members as Dorothy Parker, Franklin P. Adams, and the acerbic Alexander Woollcott.

Figure 116 - Deems Taylor became so well known as a writer and commentator that his music was eclipsed by his activities as an author and broadcaster. (Photo courtesy of Carl Van Vechten Collection, Library of Congress)

Taylor wrote numerous best-selling books on music and became a leading advocate of music appreciation. In many ways, Taylor served as an ambassador from the musical world to the public at large. He continued composing orchestral works and operas, always in a romantic, dramatic, and accessible style. His compositions such as *Circus Day* and *A Christmas Overture* were easy for the public to understand; they made him popular, but their very popularity made it easy for other critics and academicians in search of dissonance to dismiss them.

Figure 117 - Robert Russell Bennett, seen with violinist Louis Kaufman. Bennett was a fine composer, but the public often only knew his reputation as the foremost orchestrator on Broadway. (Photo courtesy of Annette Kaufman)

Robert Russell Bennett was a prominent composer who drew upon many musical styles as sources of inspiration. But because of his tremendous success as a Broadway orchestrator, even many sophisticated concertgoers have little idea of his own creative works. Bennett, a native of Kansas City, Missouri, had to contend with infantile paralysis as a child. He studied music with his bandmaster father and decided to pursue a musical career. The public discovered Bennett through his prize winning *Abraham Lincoln Symphony*. A chance meeting with flutist-conductor Quinto Maganini on a transatlantic voyage led to Bennett's decision to study with Maganini's teacher, Nadia Boulanger, in Paris.

But Bennett's skill as an orchestrator led him down an unusual musical road that he'd never anticipated. He became the foremost orchestrator of the Broadway musical theater, arranging and orchestrating the musical shows of Jerome Kern, Irving Berlin, Cole Porter, Richard Rodgers, and Frederick Loewe, among others. For fifty-five years, he orchestrated all or part of over 300 musicals. The public seldom realized that while their favorite Broadway composers wrote the melodies in such shows as *Oklahoma!* and *Show Boat*, the orchestrations were done by highly gifted musicians such as Robert Russell Bennett.

As a composer himself, Bennett produced an impressive catalogue of concert works, occasionally incorporating elements of jazz and dance music. He had a natural sense of whimsy and an innate sense of American

Despite his many achievements, Bennett knew he would be remembered for his contributions to such shows as *Show Boat, Oklahoma!, South Pacific, The King and I, Kiss Me, Kate, My Fair Lady*, and *The Sound of Music*. Although there were fine orchestrators before Bennett, including the very respected Hans Spialek and many successors, Bennett is acknowledged as the inventor of the Broadway orchestral sound. He was a modest man who didn't take himself too seriously. When asked what Richard Rodgers would do without him, Bennett quipped, "Hire another orchestrator."

Alan Hovhaness was a unique composer whose musical accomplishments and life in general defy classification. Born Alan Vaness Chakmakjian, he was the son of an Armenian college professor and a mother who had a Scottish heritage. He eventually embraced his Armenian heritage and adopted the name Alan Hovhaness. An only child, he pursued a wide variety of interests ranging from painting to astronomy. Eventually, he settled on music, studying traditional composition at the New England Conservatory under Frederick Converse.

Figure 118 - Alan Hovhaness (standing) joins colleagues (from left) John Lessard, Virgil Thomson, Sylvia Marlowe, Vittorio Rieti. (Photo at the Rachmaninoff Society, courtesy of Alan Hovanhess, the official web site)

Hovhaness was an early fan of Jean Sibelius, Finland's greatest composer, and even traveled to Finland to meet Sibelius himself. Sibelius encouraged him, but Hovhaness had other musical interests as well. He became fascinated by the songs of Armenia and was inspired to write his early *Exile Symphony* about the persecution of Armenians by the Turks. Throughout his career, Hovhaness was intrigued and influenced by the music of countries whose melodies, harmonies, and rhythms, were little known by most Western composers. He admired the choral music of the Armenian composer-priest Komitas Vartabed, later studying the music of Egypt, India, and especially Japan.

Hovhaness was incredibly prolific throughout his life, writing vast amounts of music in many styles and winning unexpected allies. *Lousadzak*, a 1944 concerto for piano and strings, introduced a, "spirit murmur" combining various instruments from both Turkey and Armenia. They were played constantly without a relationship to the musical material performed by the other traditional orchestral players. It won him enthusiastic support of avant-garde composers John Cage and Lou Harrison.

Hovhaness also acquired the support of pianist Maro Ajemian and her sister, violinist, Anahid Ajemian, who became his champions, playing and recording his music. Many leading figures in the world of concert music didn't know what to think about Hovhaness. (He insisted that Aaron Copland and Leonard Bernstein had simply laughed at his composition style when he went to study briefly at Tanglewood.) But slowly, Hovhaness began gaining recognition around the world. His enormous catalogue of music made him impossible to pigeonhole. He scored *The Flowering Peach*, a play by Clifford Odets that ran on Broadway. He traveled to India and wrote a work only for Indian instruments and to Japan and Korea where he absorbed the sounds of the ancient court music of those countries. He wrote music for modern ballets choreographed by Martha Graham. He was inspired by nature and loved the mountains of Switzerland and Seattle, where he permanently settled. He wrote an incredible sixty-seven symphonies during his lifetime, as well as concertos for numerous instruments. What made Hovhaness so unusual was that he showed little interest in the battles over musical styles that preoccupied many other composers. The struggle between supporters of Schoenberg's serial techniques and Stravinsky's neo-classicism didn't capture his attention, nor did the efforts of American colleagues who tried to develop a true American style of concert music.

Hovhaness had a complicated personal life. He was disinclined to join groups or movements of composers. He married six times, the last time, happily, for twenty-three years to Japanese soprano, Hinako Fujihara. To sum up such a vast and unusual output of music is difficult, if not impossible. Speaking about himself, years earlier, Hovhaness had written, "I propose to create a heroic, monumental style of composition simple enough to inspire all people, completely free from fads, artificial mannerisms and false sophistications, direct, forceful, sincere, always original but never unnatural." He went on to declare, "It is not my purpose to supply a few pseudo-intellectual musicians and critics with more food for brilliant argumentation, but rather to inspire all mankind with new heroism and spiritual nobility." Ultimately, against all odds, he succeeded in his mission.

Walter Piston was invariably identified as a classicist with an intellectual style. But one of his pupils, Leroy Anderson, was quite the opposite. No one ever had a musical career quite like that of Anderson, who acquired many generations of admirers through his mastery of light music. Anderson was the son of Swedish immigrants who settled in Cambridge, Massachusetts. He attended Harvard, directing the Harvard University Band and studying composition with Walter Piston. Convinced that a musical career was a financial risk, Anderson was pursuing a doctorate in German and Scandinavian languages. He was a gifted linguist, mastering German, Swedish, Norwegian, Icelandic, Danish, French, Italian, and Portuguese.

Figure 119 - Leroy Anderson. One of America's most popular composers of light music. (Photograph used by special permission of Woodbury Music Company, All rights reserved.)

Anderson gambled on pursuing a musical career instead of being a language teacher. He never looked back. Arthur Fiedler, conductor of the Boston Pops Orchestra, discovered Anderson's skill at composing and arranging. He wrote a *Harvard Fantasy,* based on Harvard themes, for Fiedler and began writing original compositions for the Boston Pops. He wrote several of his most famous compositions, including *The Syncopated Clock* and *Promenade* while serving as Chief of the Scandinavian Department of Military Intelligence at the Pentagon during World War II.

During a Connecticut heat wave, he wrote his Christmas holiday classic, *Sleigh Ride;* he also composed such memorable orchestral miniatures as *Blue Tango, Belle of the Ball, Forgotten Dreams, Bugler's Holiday, Horse and Buggy, The Typewriter, Waltzing Cat,* and *Plink, Plank, Plunk!* Anderson tried his hand at larger forms of music, writing a piano concerto and the Broadway musical, *Goldilocks.* While American music critics tend to dismiss light music, audiences found his works unforgettable. Anderson's pieces served as themes for popular television programs: *The Syncopated Clock* introduced "The Late Show" for CBS for twenty-five years, while *Plink, Plank, Plunk!* was the theme for the popular game show, "I've Got a Secret." His unique ability to depict a clock, a typewriter, sleigh bells, and dozens of other musical effects, made him one of the world's most honored composers of light music. It would be hard to imagine a symphonic composer who gave audiences more pleasure. Anderson once said that he just did what he wanted to do and that it turned out that people liked it. He was being modest. John Williams, who succeeded Fiedler as conductor of the Boston Pops, said that Anderson's music is as young and fresh as the day it was written.

Morton Gould was another musician who defied easy classification. He was a composer, arranger, conductor, and pianist, and he projected a musical personality in his work that was quite unique. Gould began his musical life as a child prodigy and he studied composition with Vincent Jones of New York University. Jones introduced him to his own piano teacher, Abby Whiteside, an unusual pedagogue who stressed muscles from the back and upper arms rather than letting the fingers initiate and control physical action. Whiteside also stressed the emotional aspect of music and encouraged improvisation. She became Gould's teacher, mentor, and lifelong confidante.

Gould became staff pianist for the newly built Radio City Music Hall. At only twenty-one, he became musical director, composer, and conductor for a national radio program. Throughout his career, he accomplished something few other musicians did, before or since: he bridged the gap between music considered "classical" or "serious" music by its aficionados and popular music. Long before it was fashionable for artists considered classical musicians to cross over into other genres, Gould did so, moving full speed ahead.

In short, Morton Gould was never a musical snob. When Gould was inspired to incorporate unusual musical elements in his

Figure 120 - Morton Gould, composer, conductor, and pianist. His music transcended labels as he incorporated jazz, blues, popular music, and folk tunes into his concert works before it was fashionable. (Photo courtesy of Abby Burton)

compositions, he did so, regardless of what staid critics might write. Hence, his works included a *Tap Dance Concerto* for dancer and orchestra, and *Hosedown*, evoking the world of the firefighter, including crackling flames, fire alarms, and the most important fire hose. He wrote numerous pieces for piano, including a series of "caricatones," satirical impressions of different types of people, including a ballerina, a ventriloquist, a prima donna, and a child prodigy. His major works included his four symphonies, his orchestral symphonettes, including one devoted entirely to Latin-American dances, a *Cowboy Rhapsody*, a *Minstrel Overture*, and *Spirituals for String Choir and Orchestra*. His work *Venice* was scored for double orchestra and brass choirs, and was inspired by a visit to the Piazza San Marco with its pigeons, fireworks, and a history of multichoirs.

Gould was prolific. He wrote ballets *(Interplay, Fall River Legend* [retelling the story of Lizzie Borden] and *I'm Old-Fashioned: The Astaire Variations)*. He scored films, including the wide screen experimental films, *Cinerama Holiday* and *Windjammer*, and television programs such as *World War I*. His childhood memories of marching bands and military parades inspired him to write major works for the concert band. His fourth symphony became known as the "West Point." Gould achieved stardom and his name was known to millions of radio listeners. He even portrayed himself in the film *Delightfully Dangerous*, a 1944 Jane Powell movie that he also scored.

He was known as a man of wit to his friends, but he disliked self-promotion and the networking often practiced by composers in New York. In later years, he had to contend with the disastrous rise of rock music, which devastated the careers of many composers. In more recent years, Gould's work has been increasingly rediscovered and appreciated. His 1995 work, *Stringmusic*, won the Pulitzer Prize. He described music as the sound of the human condition, reflecting everything from the sounds of pain, of glee, of sadness, to a self-conscious organized sound.

Don Gillis was a prolific composer who enjoyed an unusual association with the most celebrated conductor of his time, Arturo Toscanini. Gillis was a trombonist, originally from Missouri, who was on his way to achieving recognition as a composer and conductor when he accepted a unique assignment in broadcasting as scriptwriter and producer for the NBC Symphony, the orchestra led by the fiery Toscanini. Gillis was a key individual in the eventual formation of the Symphony of the Air and also produced a radio program about Toscanini after the Maestro's death.

Figure 121 - Don Gillis with the most intimidating of conductors, Arturo Toscanini. (Photo courtesy of Don and Barbara Gillis Collection, North Texas University Music Library)

In addition, Gillis was a prominent music educator, holding positions at the famed Interlochen music camp and at various universities, finishing his academic career as composer-in-residence at the University of South Carolina. Despite his many activities in teaching and broadcasting, Gillis managed to write over 150 works including ten symphonies and six string quartets. Many of his pieces had colorful titles reflecting his interest in Americana and the influence of jazz. These included *The Alamo, Alice in Orchestralia,* and *The Panhandle*. His works often reflected a sense of musical whimsy and his natural sense of humor. Like Leroy Anderson and Morton Gould, Gillis wrote in an accessible and melodic style that could be easily understood by enthusiastic audiences. (He also wrote several books, including a satirical book on conducting called *The Unfinished Symphony Conductor.*) But the accessibility of his works should not be held against them. He wrote music that millions of people enjoyed and appreciated.

Any discussion about the relationship of jazz and traditional classical music must include reference to two extraordinary composer-pianists, Calvin Jackson and Donald Shirley. Neither of these musicians could be classified as a conventional jazz musician. In fact, both defy classification at all. But their work demonstrates that what has conventionally and conveniently been labeled as "jazz" has been absorbed into the musical mainstream and adapted in ways early improvisers might never have imagined.

Calvin Jackson was a composer, conductor, arranger, concert pianist, and jazz virtuoso. A native of Philadelphia, he joined a band while still in high school. (Dizzy Gillespie and Charlie Shavers were also members.) He received extensive classical training at the Juilliard School of Music in New York, with James Friskin on piano and Bernard Wagenaar in composition. Jackson was a member of a unique fraternity of extraordinary musicians who excelled at anything they tried.

Figure 122 - Calvin Jackson. A composer, conductor, and pianist in every genre. He was a true Renaissance man and under recognized genius. (*The Two Sides of Calvin Jackson* (c) by Reprise Records/Rhino Entertainment Company, all rights reserved.)

By the time he had completed his education, he was writing arrangements for top bands, including those led by Jimmy Lunceford, Benny Carter, and Coleman Hawkins. He befriended Teddy Wilson and Art Tatum. As a full-fledged concert pianist who could also improvise with ease, he was one of the few pianists not intimidated by Tatum's dazzling pyrotechnics, and the two enjoyed many after-hours sessions exchanging ideas. As a pianist, Jackson developed a unique style, executing at the keyboard passages he would imagine for orchestra. He had an incredible sense of humor in his playing, and was as likely to improvise a Bach-like fugue or a Rachmaninoff-inspired rhapsody on a popular tune as to burst into swinging jazz. He said that Rachmaninoff and Delius were his favorite composers.

Early in his career, he formed a two-piano team with Margaret Bonds, one of the first African American women to become prominent as a composer. Then, in the 1940s, Jackson became active as an assistant musical director at MGM, where he composed and orchestrated music used in fourteen musicals. Seeking to obtain recognition unavailable in the Hollywood Studio system, he returned to New York and then, at the suggestion of Oscar Peterson, moved to Toronto. Even when accompanying artists such as dancer Paul Draper and harmonica soloist Larry Adler, he dazzled audiences. Morgan Winters, writing in *New Liberty* magazine, described an evening in February 1950 and Jackson's effect on music listeners. He said, "The audience had come to the theater to see Paul Draper, but during the performance, they had caught the magic background notes of the piano player and had recognized the impact that only something close to genius can impart across the footlights." While in Canada, Jackson played concertos and conducted premieres of his ballets, *The Loon's Necklace* and *Maria Chapdelaine*, with the Toronto Symphony. He also had his own television program, featuring his trio and a twenty-one piece big band.

When he returned to the United States, he accepted a major challenge: to produce a version of George Gershwin's *Rhapsody in Blue* scored for piano and modern big band. In his own words, he prepared to "invite ridicule, risk censure, incite the faithful to an examination of hempen cord and strong oak with the avowed intention of stretching the neck of the offender." He told Gershwin's admirers, "If you love jazz and Gershwin as do I, you must have felt as though there was an enormously interesting and vital Huckleberry Finn being stifled in a boiled collar and tails."

For the remainder of his life, Jackson continued to compose, including a stunning *Piano Concerto* partly inspired by his 1941 visit to Brazil which included a chance meeting with the young John F. Kennedy, then serving in the U.S. Navy; the two Americans talked about changing the world sociologically as they celebrated their birthdays together. His trip to South America further inspired his *Copacabana Cakewalk*, a piano piece depicting the mosaic sidewalks of Rio de Janeiro. He also wrote numerous pieces for orchestra. Jackson admired the poetry of Carl Sandburg and this resulted in his *Carl Sandburg Suite*. Jazz and the classics became one under his skillful pen and deft fingers; Benny Green, writing in *The London Observer*, declared, "The currency of critical language has long been debased by misuse, but Calvin Jackson really is something unique." At the time of his death in 1985, Jackson was still undiscovered by mass audiences, but idolized and admired by those privileged to know him and his work.

Figure 123 - Donald Shirley. A pianist, organist, composer, linguist, painter, and musical philosopher. He combined the classics with spirituals, folk songs, and world music to create a voice unique in musical history. (Photo by Josef Astor)

By his own definition, Donald Shirley was not a "jazz musician," though he has been arbitrarily grouped with jazz performers on occasion. He was born into a prominent Jamaican family. A child prodigy, he was invited to study piano with Leopold Mittolovski at the Leningrad Conservatory in Russia. (Igor Stravinsky said, "His virtuosity is worthy of gods.") On returning to the U.S., Shirley studied organ and composition with Conrad Bernier and George Thaddeus Jones at Catholic University in Washington, D.C. He was a man of many interests and talents, holding doctorates, in music, psychology, and liturgical arts. He spoke eight languages.

For a time, he left his musical career to pursue his interests in psychology. But while doing research on juvenile crime in Chicago, he decided to perform an experiment, playing in a small club to test audience reaction to certain combinations of tones. His playing created a sensation. Shirley did not improvise in the conventional sense of a jazz musician, but he applied the full harmonic vocabulary and technical resources of European classical music to a whole new repertoire: spirituals, West Indian folk songs, popular tunes from Broadway, and jazz melodies. His *Porgy and Bess* suite featured the cello as Serena, the bass as Maria, the piano as Porgy, and renowned soprano Martha Flowers as Bess.

Duke Ellington selected him as soloist for a performance of his piano concerto, played in Carnegie Hall with the NBC Symphony of the Air. Shirley had an affinity for the music of Dule Ellington and Sergei Rachmaninoff. When he met Calvin Jackson for the first time, the two Renaissance men talked all night, especially of their mutual admiration for Rachmaninoff and the deep, sonorous Russian chords that fill his compositions. They shared an interest in creating music, which joined the techniques and forms of the classical concert world with rhythms, harmonies, and melodies of popular songs, jazz, and folk tunes. Even several of the most accomplished jazz pianists pounded the keyboard, but both Donald Shirley and Calvin Jackson had an exquisite classical touch, obviously derived from years of conservatory discipline.

Figure 124 - Donald Shirley after a performance of *New World's A Comin'*, with former Miss America, Jinx Falkenberg, composer Duke Ellington, vocalist Lena Horne, and her husband, musical director Lennie Hayton. (Photo courtesy of Donald Shirley)

Donald Shirley appeared with a trio that used bass and cello, not bass combined with drums or guitar. He composed highly sophisticated variations on the themes he selected, with a sound more clearly approaching chamber music than jazz. Shirley also composed a variety of original music, including a symphonic tone poem based on James Joyce's *Finnegan's Wake*, string quartets, concertos, an opera, and a set of piano variations inspired by the legend of *Orpheus in the Underworld*. When Shirley used improvisation to create these variations, he made no attempt to swing or play jazz. His approach to improvising was identical to that of the great nineteenth century European virtuosos, especially Franz Liszt. Al "Jazzbo" Collins suggested that Shirley represented the "suffusion" of classical music and jazz. While efforts to pigeonhole Donald Shirley may be futile, no one can deny the absolute brilliance of his creative output.

Astor Piazzolla was not typically identified as an "American composer." He was born in Argentina and his concept of "nuevo tango" made him the most recognized and often controversial figure in the development of Argentina's national dance. Although Astor Piazzolla was born in Mar del Plata, Argentina in 1921, his parents relocated to New York in 1936. He spent his childhood in New York, received his first bandoneon, purchased by his father for nineteen dollars in a Manhattan pawnshop, and made his first record there.

The bandoneon is a type of concertina, invented in Germany and brought to Argentina by German and Italian immigrants. It resembles an accordion, although both keyboards contain buttons. It became the instrument of choice throughout Argentina in the performance of tango music. Throughout his career, Piazzolla was always torn between his natural instincts as a tango composer and his desire to be taken seriously as a composer of concert music after the fashion of Stravinsky and Bartók. It was only when he embraced his heritage as a tango composer that he achieved his latter goal.

While in New York, Piazzolla met Carlos Gardel, the legendary singer, composer, and matinee idol of all Latin-America and Argentina in particular. Gardel's signature song was "El Día Que me Quieras," and Piazzolla

Figure 125 - Astor Piazzolla, creator of the Nuevo Tango and virtuoso of the bandoneon, with pianist Pablo Ziegler and singer, Milva. (Photo courtesy of Ziegler Music)

appeared in the film of the same title, playing a newspaper boy. Although he studied classical piano with Bela Wilda, an exponent of the music of Rachmaninoff, the bandoneon became his primary solo instrument. Gardel wanted Piazzolla to join him on a tour, but Piazzolla's protective father refused, insisting that Astor was too young. It was a fateful decision. Gardel and his lyricist, Alfredo Le Pera, were both killed in a tragic plane crash. Piazzolla would later say that had he gone on the tour, he might be playing a harp in heaven instead of the bandoneon on earth.

After the family returned to Argentina, Piazzolla was captivated by a radio performance of Elvino Vardaro's sextet playing the tango. Piazzolla was intrigued by the use of tango rhythms combined with new and unconventional harmonies and forms. He joined the orchestra of Anibal Troilo, the celebrated bandoneon soloist, and also began studying composition with Argentine concert composer Alberto Ginastera. His melodic and harmonic experimentation proved too daring for him to remain with Troilo. Piazzolla felt he was expanding the horizons of the tango; his critics accused him of trying to destroy the traditional tango. In 1953, his concert composition, *Buenos Aries,* won first prize in an important competition named for conductor Fabien Sevitzky. Its performance nearly generated a riot when fist-fights broke out over the use of the bandoneon in the orchestra. Piazzolla's final decision not to abandon the tango for contemporary concert music was inspired by an unusual source, the doyenne of contemporary music advocates, Nadia Boulanger. Piazzolla went to study with Boulanger in Paris and was reluctant to discuss his tango background. But when she persuaded him to play his tangos for her, she was duly impressed and told him that the tango represented his true path to self-expression.

Piazzolla went on to a legendary and often controversial career, bridging the gap between the dramatic, seductive melodies and rhythms of the tango with the harmonic vocabulary and generous use of dissonance found in the works of composers of concert music. He composed tangos for chamber music ensembles and performed them himself as soloist on his beloved bandoneon with his own quintet. He returned to New York and composed one of his most famous pieces to honor the passing of his father, *Adios, Nonino*. He was an incredibly prolific composer, writing around a thousand pieces of music and organizing numerous quintets, quartets, and chamber ensembles specializing in "nuevo tango," the "new tango."

In the 1960s, Piazzolla's "nuevo tango" was considered highly provocative in Argentine culture. In 1961, the newspaper *La Mancha* declared, "Piazzolla has dared to defy a traditional establishment greater than the state, greater than the gaucho, greater than soccer. He has dared to challenge the tango." Everyone from heads of state to taxi drivers in Buenos Aries had an opinion. When Piazzolla hailed a cab, the driver might refuse to charge him a fare out of respect or refuse to even accept him as a passenger as a protest.

Piazzolla also pursued the larger forms of composition, a "tango-opera," *Maria de Buenos Aries,* and a *Concerto for Bandoneon and Orchestra*, which he premiered as soloist with the orchestra conducted by Lalo Schifrin. His most popular pieces, such as *Libertango* and *Oblivion*, are played on concert programs along with the music of Bach and Beethoven. His collaborations with jazz musicians like Gerry Mulligan demonstrated the success of such unlikely combinations as the bandoneon and jazz saxophone. Perhaps the most defining characteristic of his music is the personal style he sought for so long. Anyone hearing a work by Astor Piazzolla is unlikely to confuse it with a composition written by anyone else.

Not all of Vittorio Giannini's pupils reflected the influence of Italian-American romanticism. David Amram studied with Giannini, but drew upon a host of other musical influences. Amram grew up on his parents' farm in historic Buck's County, Pennsylvania. He chose an unusual instrument, the French horn, as his primary means of musical expression, pioneering in the world of jazz as well as playing classical works in symphony orchestras. He joined the Army and finding himself in Paris, became part of the literary circle led by *Paris Review* editor George Plimpton. He eventually returned to the U.S., where he studied with Vittorio Giannini and Gunther Schuller, the latter an

Figure 126 - David Amram, composer, conductor, French horn soloist, teacher, writer, advocate for world music, comfortable in every musical genre, including symphonic works, jazz, and folk tunes. (Photo courtesy of David Amram)

exponent of "third stream" music, which combined jazz and classical elements. To support himself, Amram played at leading jazz clubs in New York with famed jazz bassists, Charles Mingus and Oscar Pettiford.

Amram became associated with the New York Shakespeare Festival, composing incidental music for twenty-five productions of Shakespeare and writing an opera, *Twelfth Night*. He became friendly with the "beat generation" writers in the 1950s, including Allen Ginsberg and Jack Kerouac, scoring and even acting in Kerouac's documentary film, *Pull My Daisy*. In 1957, he created the first jazz/poetry readings, performing them with Kerouac. Amram cultivated a multiplicity of interests and unlike many composers, never abandoned them. His prolific writing for plays and television productions led to his film scores for such motion pictures as *Splendor in the Grass*, *The Manchurian Candidate*, and *The Young Savages*. Amram was always a world traveler. He appeared as a composer, conductor, and performing musician in thirty-five countries. He also explored world music, examining the folk and native music of many countries from Brazil to Kenya. He continued to perform on the French horn, but also on the piano, flutes, whistles, and folkloric instruments he discovered during his travels. David Amram, always an advocate of passing the appreciation of music to new generations, devoted twenty-five years to conducting concerts for young people presented by the Brooklyn Philharmonic.

The colorful, prolific, and delightfully unpredictable Amram found time to write a hundred concert works for orchestra, band, choirs, chamber ensembles, and the operatic stage. His sources of inspiration ranged from a Navajo prayer and the writings of Thomas Jefferson and Henrik Ibsen to the jazz drummer Chano Pozo. He had an incredibly eclectic group of collaborators, including playwright Arthur Miller, director Elia Kazan, Harlem poet Langston Hughes, dancer Jacques d'Amboise, and musicians who excel in many genres ranging from folk music to jazz to chamber ensembles. Amram was the first composer-in-residence with the New York Philharmonic, chosen by Leonard Bernstein. He wrote several memoirs, including *Vibrations*, his autobiography, *Collaborating with Kerouac*, and *Nine Lives of a Musical Cat*. David Amram's appreciation of the music of the very English Frederic Delius came from an unlikely source—jazz saxophone virtuoso and bebop pioneer, Charlie Parker. His entire career reflects an energetic eclecticism that defies classification or category.

Frank Lewin was an extraordinarily talented and versatile composer whose work defied easy categorization. Born in Germany, Lewin arrived in the U.S. as a teenager with his family. He studied with several renowned teachers including Roy Harris and Paul Hindemith, and graduated from Yale. Frank Lewin's music was perhaps best-known to the public for his highly individual scores for important television programs such as *The Defenders* and *The Nurses*. He also wrote music for numerous feature and documentary films, displaying a mastery of scoring for small instrumental combinations in contrast to the big orchestras often preferred in Hollywood.

Figure 127 - Frank Lewin, preparing his Mass in memory of Robert F. Kennedy with soloists Sylvia Jones and Leo Geokie in 1969. (Photo courtesy of Miriam and Naomi Lewin)

He remained on the East Coast, living in Princeton for many years and scoring in New York. He often incorporated folk and popular music of every nationality in his scores, greatly emphasizing authentic use of melodies and instrumentation.

"Outdoor Drama" is the term usually applied to pageant-like productions depicting major events in American history. Lewin composed music for a number of outdoor dramas and also incidental music for presentations of plays by Shakespeare, Jean Anouilh, and Tennessee Williams. He conducted his own cantata, *Music for the White House*, at a state dinner hosted by President Lyndon B. Johnson. When he saw the train bearing the body of the recently assassinated Robert F. Kennedy pass through Princeton Junction, he was inspired to write his *Mass for the Dead, in English,* containing a moving setting of *The Lord's Prayer*.

Frank Lewin was a prolific composer of concert works, writing for a variety of instruments, including a concerto for the harmonica, a number of chamber and choral pieces, a widely praised opera, entitled *Burning Bright,* inspired by the novel and play of the same title by John Steinbeck, and song cycles (including one based on the light verse of poet Ogden Nash.) He also taught for many years at Yale and Columbia University, and found time to write a serious analysis of the music of Richard Wagner. His compositions were all eminently musical. The fact that his music never upstaged the dialogue in films, plays, and dramatic productions should not result in neglect, but recognition of his work as representative of a unique voice in American music.

THE CONCERT HALL TODAY

It would be rewarding to conclude our exploration of American concert music with an observation that America's concert halls are filled with the sounds of symphonies, operas, ballets, concertos, all by American composers. Sadly, this is not the case. It still remains difficult for American composers to obtain performances of new works, let alone repeated performances and recordings. But in the twenty-first century, we live in a world in which the works of some American composers are taken seriously. No longer does the label "American" suggest an inferior or second-class approach to musical composition. The works of composers like Copland and Harris, so revolutionary in their time, are now played around the world. New generations of composers are writing in many styles reflecting a basic truth. There is no single "American" style or "American" approach to composing. Our composers, like our people, are a diverse group with many styles, tastes, and differences of opinion. These are richly expressed on long sheets of score paper and in intense verbal conflicts on every musical subject we can imagine. Will American composers ever agree on the answer to that perplexing question, "What is an American composer?" Agreement is as likely on that subject as on the question of who should be the next President of the United States. But the question posed during the last century has been answered with a resounding chorus. Why doesn't someone write the great American symphony? Someone has. Many "someones," with movements reflecting the great American prairie, the cities and towns of the American landscape, the oceans and plains, the forests and deserts. What is included in the great American symphony? Everything from fugues to the blues, from jazz and popular tunes to stirring marches and hymn tunes. The composers whose works we have explored are only a few of those whose musical voices have contributed to this vast tapestry of sounds. Which pieces will survive in the standard musical repertoire? Those written by composers in the next century who have talent, luck, good fortune, not necessarily in that order, and a generous sense of the American spirit for adventure, non-conformity, and music.

JAZZ

During my music-student days, I once sat in on a session with a popular jazz band in Los Angeles. After the session, one of the band members, a budding young saxophone virtuoso, introduced me to a friend by declaring, "Meet Mark Evans, he plays groovy piano." I smiled and hoped I was receiving a compliment. When I returned home, I quickly whipped my jazz encyclopedia off the shelf to discover that, yes, indeed, "groovy" wasn't a bad thing to be if you were playing jazz. But clearly, jazz musicians had a vocabulary all their own. I couldn't imagine one of my strict European classical teachers telling me that I had "great chops." The milieu of jazz has often confused people, even those who are devoted to the musicians responsible for creating this elusive and uniquely American art form. Fictional portrayals of jazz musicians haven't helped. The jazz musician is typically depicted as a brooding, inarticulate eccentric drowning in a sea of drugs and depression. Critics, historians, and musicians themselves frequently find themselves arguing furiously over precisely what jazz is and what it is not.

Jazz is truly music of the people. How this uniquely American phenomenon evolved is a remarkable story. Because the lion's share of jazz has never been written down, musicians and scholars alike often have a hard time establishing who did what and when they did it. There are many things we do know about the history and origins of jazz. But whatever we say about jazz, someone is sure to turn up wanting to disagree with it. We do know around what period the music we call jazz started: the early twentieth century. The place was New Orleans, or so tradition has it. Small groups of black musicians combined African rhythms with uniquely American sounds sung by church choirs, played by marching bands, and explored by ragtime pianists, among others. In the process, they created the music we call jazz.

Twenty-first century jazz is a phenomenon heard, played, adored, and criticized worldwide. Jazz musicians have been heard and hailed in countries with no historical or musical connection to its sounds, styles, and rhythms. American jazz musicians have carried a musical message to Tokyo and Shanghai, to Paris and Stockholm, to Rio de Janeiro and Buenos Aries. Today, you will find jazz musicians born and raised in London, Montreal, Copenhagen, Rome, Prague, and Seoul. A jazz musician may be found expressing his art in the classrooms and concert halls of the world, or even in the Royal Palace in Bangkok, where the King of Thailand not only listens to jazz, but plays it himself. Jazz has played an important role in dance, theater, and films, and jazz has been the subject of books and television programs. Many jazz critics and historians believe jazz has earned the title of "America's Indigenous Classical Music." Although jazz musicians can point with pride to a rich legacy of performance and a technically astonishing repertoire, jazz has always been controversial. What is jazz and how did it originate? The question is deceptively simple. Louis Armstrong is alleged to have said, "If you gotta ask, you'll never know!"

Dr. Billy Taylor was a noted jazz pianist and teacher who devoted a considerable part of his life to being an ambassador from the jazz world to listeners and students everywhere. With an almost evangelical fervor, Taylor wanted to explain jazz to aficionados and novices alike and in the process, dispel many myths about America's unique contribution to remarkable art form. He wrote, "Jazz is an American way of playing music. It is also a repertory, which formalizes its various stages of development into classical styles that musically articulate authentic musical feelings and thoughts . . . as a musical language; it has developed steadily from a single expression of the consciousness of black people to a national music that expresses Americana to Americans as well as to people from other countries. Jazz emerged from the need of black Americans to express themselves in musical terms."

If you listen to a fine jazz performance, two elements are nearly always present. One is improvisation: simultaneously composing and performing. Not only is the musician composing a melodic line, frequently he is even creating the form or musical structure of the composition at the same time. When a jazz musician is improvising, he is, in effect, making up a new melody on the spot. His new melody may be based on a familiar tune or a set of musical chord patterns (called "changes" by players.) Those new to jazz or just mystified by it often ask the classic question, "Where's the melody?" The answer, of course, is that the melody is in the head of the jazz musician as he is playing it and you are hearing it for the first time.

The other ingredient is swing. Duke Ellington provided the answer when he wrote, "It Don't Mean a Thing If It Ain't Got That Swing." There is a reason why scholarly descriptions of swing usually fall short and leave the writer looking puzzled and confused. Harold Ross, the meticulous founding editor of *The New Yorker* magazine, was known to have said that "Nothing is indescribable." But Mr. Ross never tried developing a textbook definition of "swing." Swing is, in part, a tension produced by brilliant players who improvise slightly before or slightly after the conventional rhythmic pulse known as "the beat." This produces a musical tension that is hard to describe but apparent to the ear. Inflections affecting pitch and tone color, particularly the slightly off-key "blue notes," add to the elusive but appealing sound. When he alternates tension and relaxation over a steady, driving beat, the jazz musician swings. The most casual listener to jazz may not remotely be able to define swing, but he will recognize it when he hears it. This is why jazz fans are busy tapping their feet or hands and often seem lost in a private world of their own.

Jazz musicians frequently disagree about whether an individual musician swings. Many a fierce argument has been provoked over comparisons between various jazz performers. A jazz musician may possess great technique even though his detractors snap, "He doesn't swing." Similarly, fans may admire a rival musician with poor technique but insist, "He swings." The world of classical music, especially up to the twentieth century, had many musical stars who were accomplished improvisers. But they weren't jazz musicians and they didn't swing.

Johann Sebastian Bach was an accomplished improviser at the organ, but he was improvising classical fugues in church. The great English jazz pianist Sir George Shearing insisted that Bach would have been a great jazz musician if he had lived in the modern era. Franz Liszt was considered the world's finest piano virtuoso of the nineteenth century. He was master improviser who dazzled audiences with his technique. But he didn't swing and he wasn't playing jazz. In the twentieth century, the art of improvisation in the classical world virtually disappeared. There were exceptions. The American concert pianist Johana Harris was a superb improviser who would conclude her classical concerts with an improvisation combining themes of all the classical pieces she had played earlier, often adding quotations from popular tunes for good measure. But this wasn't a jazz performance either. Except for the most radical and revolutionary composers of concert music, classical musicians generally left improvisation to their twentieth century cousins—the jazz artists of the world. It is the combination of swing and improvisation together that generally creates jazz.

Among jazz historians, discussing the origins of jazz is a good way to provoke an argument. One reason for the controversy is that because jazz was African American in origin, the issues of race and nationality, always beacons for controversy, arise. Jazz was created by African Americans in this country, drawing upon their African heritage, but jazz was never African music. Its origins were more complex. Historian Frank Tirro has written, "Black society was every bit as complex as white, and the old stereotypes of the nineteenth century black American no longer suffice in depicting the environment from which jazz sprang. Black Americans were aware of and participated in the European art-music tradition. To deny this aspect of black American society in the nineteenth century in order to emphasize the African origins of jazz would be a disservice to both the historical facts and the splendid talents of the black American who achieved a great deal in the realm of European art music." Black Americans brought African rhythms to the United States and passed them down through generations. Complex rhythms, often combining two beats over three, and the off-pitch notes, later known as "blue notes," came directly from the African tradition. American blacks combined these elements of their African musical heritage with new influences heard in America. They also heard and absorbed other elements of music: folk tunes sung throughout the American South, hymns that were sung in church, work songs, and melodies from traveling minstrel shows. In addition, European classical music was performed in America. True African music was more complex than early jazz, which increased in rhythmic complexity as it developed. In America, black musicians combined elements of African rhythm with harmonic influences derived from popular songs, marches played by brass bands, ragtime, and especially "The Blues"—vocal music which evolved when work songs were combined with African-American religious melodies.

To see where jazz is going, we have to see where jazz has been. It is impossible to discuss the origins of jazz without exploring ragtime. Ragtime was played by American blacks on banjos, trumpets, and fiddles, for their holidays, picnics and parades.

THE RAGTIME ERA

Scott Joplin was the most gifted musician of the ragtime era. Joplin, a pianist, was born in Marshall, Texas, in 1868 and grew up in Texarkana. As a teenager, he left home to pursue the itinerant life of a musician, working on Mississippi riverboats, in gambling houses, and cafes, and at the great World Columbian Exposition in Chicago. Along the way, Joplin absorbed a variety of musical influences. He discovered the Fisk Jubilee Singers, a black choir that performed Negro spirituals before audiences throughout America and Europe, and "Blind Tom," an extraordinary sightless black pianist who could play virtually any piece, including the European classics, by ear.

Figure 128- Scott Joplin, the most gifted musician of the Ragtime Era. (Public domain)

Joplin's study of classical piano rendered him quite familiar with the European style of music. But when he played or performed his own music, he incorporated the lively irregular rhythms (syncopation) derived from African music and the other styles of musical expression being developed by African Americans. For a time, he settled in Sedalia, Missouri, where he composed *The Maple Leaf Rag*, which became a tremendous hit when it was published in 1899. Scott Joplin composed many other rags, waltzes, and marches, including *The Entertainer, Cascades, Elite Syncopations, The Chrysanthemum—An Afro-Intermezzo, Nonpareil*, and *Solace*, a mournful Mexican serenade. He also wrote an opera, *Treemonisha*. Although Joplin died in 1917, his opera wasn't fully performed or acclaimed until 1972. Ten years later, Joplin was honored with his name and picture on a U.S. postage stamp.

A number of ragtime musicians had studied musical notation and wrote down their compositions on paper. They influenced those ragtime performers who were skilled improvisers, but only played by ear. In turn, the "reading" musicians who notated their own ideas absorbed the lilting rhythms of those players who were natural improvisers. Other leading ragtime pianists and composers included James Scott, Arthur Marshall, Louis Chauvin, Joe Jordan, and a white friend of Joplin's, Joseph Lamb. Eubie Blake, one of the most remarkable of the ragtime musicians, was active as a performer long before he gained fame as a Broadway composer. He was rediscovered by an adoring public late in life, still performing at age 100.

The famed composer-bandleader W.C. Handy told jazz historian Leonard Feather that jazz evolved from music that could be heard "wherever slavery was practiced." In the early years of the twentieth century, New Orleans was a true melting pot--a cosmopolitan city populated by descendants of French and Spanish settlers, and especially by a large population of black people descended from both Africans and natives of the Caribbean islands. In the years before the Civil War, West Indian drummers had performed in an empty lot named Congo Square, which became the center of New Orleans voodoo dances brought to New Orleans as a West African religion in which chanting and intense drumming were used to accompany dancing. After the Civil War, New Orleans blacks formed their own brass bands; these bands would march to funerals in a somber style, but return playing lively, lilting ragtime melodies.

Figure 129 - Buddy Bolden, known in his time as New Orleans' premier cornetist and bandleader. (Public domain)

Certainly, many great jazz pioneers lived and worked in New Orleans. In the latter years of the nineteenth century, New Orleans most legendary cornetist was Charles "Buddy" Bolden. His band included the cornet, trombone, clarinet, guitar, string bass, and drums. His piercing cornet carried the main melodic line, while the trombone and clarinet improvised melodies of their own.

Buddy Bolden's specialty was a slow, mournful blues, and New Orleans aficionados said that when Bolden played, he could be heard for blocks away, even for miles.

Successors from the Buddy Bolden band, were trumpeter William Geary (Bunk) Johnson and cornet soloist Freddie Keppard. Keppard , who was an important figure in New Orleans jazz before World War I, eventually settled in Chicago. Emerging from Freddie Keppard's band as key figures in the development of the New Orleans style were Alphonse Picou and Louis Delisle (Big Eye) Nelson, two veteran clarinetists But the most colorful figure to emerge from New Orleans was a pianist.

Figure 130 – "Jelly Roll" Morton, the man who once claimed to have invented jazz. (Public domain)

"Jelly Roll" Morton has been called the first important jazz composer. Born Ferdinand Joseph La Menthe (or La Mothe), Morton was a Creole whose life story was embellished by a legend of his own making. In his early years, Morton became an admirer of Tony Jackson, a fabled ragtime pianist from New Orleans who played in a faster and more flamboyant style than the Midwestern followers of Joplin. Declaring himself "the inventor of jazz," "Jelly Roll" Morton could spin tales for hours about his musical accomplishments and improbable personal adventures. He was happy to tell anyone who would listen about how jazz was created, usually portraying himself as the most important character in the tale. He left New Orleans permanently in 1907, embarking on a colorful career that led him throughout the country as a pool shark, night club owner, vaudeville comedian, and professional gambler, to mention only a few of his vocations. At one time, Morton sold a "medicine" which consisted of Coca-Cola mixed with salt. He managed to play the piano while pursuing all of these activities. Separating fact from fiction regarding Morton has mystified and delighted his biographers. What remains certain, however, was his musical contribution: a pianistic style that emulated the sections of a band.

Morton did more than write tunes or simple piano pieces. When composing or arranging for band, Morton was very specific in his choice of instruments and his original musical ideas regarding the melody, harmony, and rhythm of each piece. From 1926 to 1930, in New York and Chicago, Jelly Roll Morton and His Red Hot Peppers made a number of recordings, which personified the best of the New Orleans style of jazz. (Trombonist Kid Ory and clarinetist Johnny Dodds were among the participants.) His compositions included the *Black Bottom Stomp*, *King Porter Stomp*, *Wolverine Blues*, *Milenburg Joys*, *Wild Man Blues*, and *The Pearls*. Morton regarded jazz, blues, and ragtime as three separate elements, with blues and ragtime defined by tradition. (The blues could be created according to a specific design and format: musicians could create a blues piece based on an eight, twelve, or sixteen bar theme, but the chord progressions were predetermined.) Jazz, in Morton's mind, allowed for improvisation, and he improvised on anything that suited his fancy, even including a French quadrille he claimed to have turned into *Tiger Rag*. He also improvised on operatic excerpts, marches by John Philip Sousa, and elements of Latin-American music that evolved into his "jazz tangos."

Morton's capacity for self-promotion led to inevitable controversy. Admiring critic George Avakian called him "a strange mixture of genius, musician, poet, snob, and braggart." But Duke Ellington said Morton's greatest talent was "talking about Jelly Roll Morton." W.C. Handy, famed composer of *St. Louis Blues,* who feuded with Morton for years, insisted that many of his claims about his own musical importance were untrue. Morton eventually faded into musical oblivion, only to be rediscovered in the last years of his life after his music has been dismissed as old-fashioned years before. He died in 1941.

STRIDING THROUGH HARLEM

While New Orleans had some of the greatest brass and wind players in the country, New York became the capital of innovation for pianists. In Harlem, a new generation of young black pianists brought a technical virtuosity to the keyboard that hadn't been seen in other parts of the country. These "Harlem stride masters" were highly competitive and many of the finest examples of pianistic skill would be on display at the private parties in which they had contests, like athletes trying to top one another. Foremost among the group were James P. Johnson, Charles Luckeyeth Roberts, Donald "The Lamb" Lambert, Stephen "The Beetle" Henderson, and Willie "The Lion" Smith. James P. Johnson, born in New Jersey in 1891, was considered "The Father of Stride Piano." Stride players used a lilting left hand providing a constant pulse emphasizing four beats Rural folk music and the blues were not their most important influences. James P. Johnson once played a "stomp" using the *Rigoletto Concert Paraphrase* by Franz Liszt. Johnson composed the dance tune that became a virtual anthem for the Roaring Twenties: "Charleston." There are millions of people who have danced to this melody or heard it performed on television or in films without realizing that James P. Johnson was the composer. The "shout" or "ring-shout" was an African dance that had survived in another form in black churches. A worshiper would "shout" his message and the congregation would respond. Johnson's most famous piano composition, the

Figure 131 - James P. Johnson. His composition, "Charleston," became the dance anthem of the Roaring Twenties. (Public domain)

Carolina Shout, became a challenge for pianists participating in the Harlem "cutting contests." These contests, conducted after hours, would pit the legendary Harlem stride musicians against each other like champion prizefighters, each convinced that he was the man of the hour. Johnson was also interested in writing concert music and wrote a variety of works employing black folk themes and rhythms, including *Symphony in Brown*, a piano concerto, and a symphonic suite based on W.C. Handy's *St. Louis Blues*. An entire concert in Carnegie Hall was devoted to his work.

Charles Luckeyeth Roberts, known as "Luckey" to his friends, was born in Philadelphia in 1891. He wrote numerous rags, which required great technical ability. Eventually, he became one of New York's best-known society pianists. Willie "The Lion" Smith earned his nickname during World War I, when he spent 33 days on the front lines with the 350th Field Artillery. James P. Johnson said that when "The Lion" walked into a room, "Every

Figure 132 - Willie "The Lion" Smith. Ferocious as a soldier in World War I and at the piano. (Photo courtesy of William P. Gottlieb Collection, Library of Congress)

Figure 133 - Thomas "Fats" Waller began as a church organist, but he gained fame when he wrote the popular song, "Ain't Misbehavin'." (Photo courtesy of New York World Telegram and Sun Collection, Library of Congress)

move was a picture." Smith's forceful style of speaking, his bowler, and the ever-present cigar made him a memorable personality. Smith became a regular in New York nightclubs from Harlem to Greenwich Village, but he was not truly discovered by the public until the 1930s.

James P. Johnson's protégé was Thomas "Fats" Waller. A minister's son, Waller was an organist who played in church and in theaters while still a teenager. While still young, he discovered ragtime. After winning a contest playing variations on Johnson's *Carolina Shout*, he began studying with Johnson. Waller was familiar with European classical music, for a time taking lessons from the renowned concert pianist, Leopold Godowsky. Waller wrote for Broadway, composed hit tunes including "Ain't Misbehavin'" and "Honeysuckle Rose," starred on radio in "Fats Waller's Rhythm Club." He had a light touch on the piano combined with a ferocious energy playing stride that made him one of the most impressive jazz musicians of his day.

The Harlem stride pianists never lost their sense of competition. Donald "The Lamb" Lambert was a brilliant musician although he couldn't read or write music and played entirely by ear. Lambert would adapt assorted pieces of classical music to his Harlem stride style, including "Pilgrim's Chorus" from Wagner's *Tannhauser*, "Anitra's Dance" by Edvard Grieg, "Elegy" by Jules Massenet, and the "Sextet" from *Lucia di Lammermoor* by Gaetano Donizetti. Eubie Blake once told Lambert's friend, the Danish jazz enthusiast Terkild Vinding, that he was booked to appear with Willie "The Lion" Smith and Lambert at the Newport Jazz Festival. Lambert put on such a dazzling performance that Blake asked Smith what they could do to possibly follow "The Lamb" on stage. Willie "The Lion" said, "I plan to talk a lot." Even hard times wouldn't diminish the competitive spirit of these remarkable pianists. By 1958, Lambert's best days were behind him. He was drinking heavily and living in a tiny apartment near the New Jersey bar where he was playing and where his career ended. A few years before Lambert's death in 1962, Vinding took him to hear Erroll Garner, at the time one of the most popular

Figure 134 - Donald "The Lamb" Lambert, an unfortunately forgotten giant of the stride era. Transcriptions of his dazzling solos have now been published in France. (Photo courtesy of Paul Marcorelles, all rights reserved.)

rising stars in the jazz world. When Vinding asked Lambert for his reaction, "The Lamb" said simply, "I can take him."

THE ROARING TWENTIES

By the mid-1920s, Chicago had supplanted New Orleans as the center of jazz activity. In 1917, the federal government closed Storyville, New Orleans' district of legalized prostitution, effectively ending employment opportunities for many local jazz musicians. To find new opportunities to play, many of these musicians boarded trains operated by the Illinois Central Railroad. They got off the trains in Chicago, thereby turning the Windy City into one of the most important jazz capitals of the Roaring Twenties. Among the musicians moving North from New Orleans was cornetist Joe Oliver. He personified the New Orleans style of jazz. He was born on a Louisiana plantation and absorbed spirituals, work songs, and the blues in his formative years. At the height of his popularity, he was the most admired cornetist in New Orleans. With his derby hat and charismatic style, he projected what modern day critics would have called "star quality." In Chicago, his reputation had preceded him. Two bands sent delegations to meet him at the railroad station when he arrived in the Windy City and both offered him jobs. He accepted them both. When he began working at two places at once in Chicago, trombonist Kid Ory dubbed him "King" Oliver, and remained the "King of Jazz" for the rest of his life. (The jazz world would always have its own royalty, hence the eventual triumphs of Edward Kennedy "Duke" Ellington, William "Count" Basie, and Lester "Prez" Young, the latter's more democratic title a nickname derived from being called "President of the Saxophone.") Kid Ory himself proved to be one of the most enduring products of the New Orleans era and his own bands remained active for many years after the New Orleans era ended. New Orleans clarinetists Jimmy Noone and Sidney Bechet both worked with Oliver and also moved to Chicago. Noone became better known because Bechet worked in large orchestras and eventually became a world traveler, taking American jazz to Paris and then around the world. He made a comeback in the 1940s and was finally recognized for his abilities in playing New Orleans jazz.

Figure 135 - Joe "King" Oliver. His band was the first black jazz band to be commercially recorded. (Public Domain)

In 1917, a Chicago band of white musicians, originally from New Orleans and led by cornetist Nick LaRocca, moved to New York and, as the Original Dixieland "Jass" Band, and began performing jazz at Resenweber's Restaurant.

Huge crowds of young New Yorkers flocked to hear them and LaRocca's group became the first band to record a jazz record. (It was around this time that recording companies began marketing their products under the label "jazz" instead of "jass.") The band had been

Figure 136 - Nick LaRocca. His Original Dixieland Jazz Band became the first to make a jazz recording. (Photo courtesy of James LaRocca)

founded only a year earlier by LaRocca and included Larry Shields (clarinet), Eddie Edwards (trombone), Henry Ragas (piano,) and Tony Spargo (drums). Their recordings of the comedic "Livery Stable Blues," "Original Dixieland One Step," "At the Jazz Band Ball" and "Tiger Rag" won popular acclaim. They sold over 1.5 million Victrola records and became the first jazz group to appear in a movie. In 1917, The Original Dixieland Jazz Band appeared in *The Good For Nothing;* two years later, the ensemble achieved another "first" when members entertained U.S. troops in Europe fighting in World War I. The band's success appeared to usher in the jazz age as the "Roaring Twenties" began to roar. Members of the band remained active in music for years; in 1957, drummer Tony Spargo found himself working with singer Connee Boswell in the same recording studio in which the Original Dixieland Jazz Band had recorded forty years earlier. LaRocca's son James is a trumpeter and prolific songwriter who records and plays traditional New Orleans jazz with his own twenty-first century "Original Dixieland Jazz Band."

Joe "King" Oliver was important in the history of jazz for two other reasons. In 1923, "King" Oliver's band became the first black jazz ensemble to be commercially recorded. A year earlier, Oliver sent for his protégé, Louis Armstrong, who had succeeded him in the Ory band. Armstrong joined Oliver as second cornetist. Louis Armstrong, born in New Orleans, claimed July 4, 1900 as his birthday. He was born in a neighborhood nicknamed "the battlefield" by local residents who knew it to be the toughest place in town. The family had no gas or running water. Louis was enthusiastic and impulsive as a boy, and eventually took the nickname "Satchelmouth" or "Satchmo," which remained with him throughout his

Figure 137 - Louis Armstrong, known as "Satchmo'" to the public, "Pops" to his friends, became an icon of jazz. (Photo courtesy of New York World Telegram and Sun Collection, Library of Congress)

career. He began singing for nickels and dimes on the streets of his native city at age seven. At thirteen, he celebrated New Year's Eve by borrowing a gun his mother owned and firing it in the street. He was arrested and sent to the Waifs' Home, where he was given a cornet and some lessons from Peter Davis, the music instructor at the Waif's Home. He had to leave it behind when he left the home.

Armstrong continued to play after his release and regarded "King" Oliver as his idol. Eventually, Oliver also became his friend and musical mentor. He also worked on riverboats that went to Memphis and St. Louis and gained musical experience with Fate Marable, a Kentucky-born pianist who supervised the music on shipboard. (Marable also played the steamship calliope, an instrument that could be heard on the river. Marable had to wear a raincoat and hat for these performances, because of huge amounts of water resulting from condensed steam.)

After Armstrong joined Oliver in Chicago, he met Lil Hardin, a pianist who had turned to jazz after classical studies at Fisk University. Their mutual interests were personal as well as professional. In 1924, Armstrong married Lil Hardin and went to New York to join Fletcher Henderson's band. But the following year, he returned to Chicago, where he formed his famous quintet, the Hot Five, with Kid Ory (trombone), Johnny Dodds (clarinet), Johnny St. Cyr (banjo and guitar), and Lil Hardin Armstrong (piano). Subsequently he added tuba and drums to the five, renaming the group, "The Hot Seven." The sixty recorded cuts known as the "Fives" and "Sevens" had enormous impact on jazz styles and helped launch Armstrong on a career that jazz historians regard as one of the most important in jazz history.

What distinguished Armstrong from a host of contemporaries? Composer and historian Gunther Schuller suggests it was at least four things: his choice of notes and the shape of his musical lines, his tone quality, his sense of swing, and the vibratos and shakes he used to color his musical sound. Says Schuller, "When on June 28, 1928, Louis Armstrong unleashed the spectacular cascading phrases of the introduction to *West End Blues*, he established the general stylistic direction of jazz for several decades to come." Armstrong's opening passages in his *West End Blues* solo demonstrated that jazz was more than popular or folk music and that jazz musicians could express themselves with melodic and rhythmic complexity comparable to that of European classical music.

In 1923, a young pianist from Pittsburgh arrived in Chicago. His name was Earl Hines. His father was a trumpeter, his mother an organist. He began working in Chicago at the Entertainer's Cabaret, playing a miniature piano on wheels that rolled from table to table. Unlike the New York stride players, Hines liked to play swinging melodic lines with his right hand, which sounded as if they had been originally created on a trumpet or horn. His "horn-line" style became highly influential.

One day, Hines was seated at the piano in the black union hall playing *The One I Love Belongs to Somebody Else*. Louis Armstrong was passing by, heard Hines, took out his instrument, and began an impromptu duet. "I knew right away he was a giant," said Hines. The two musicians began a friendship and in 1927 collaborated on recordings, like their celebrated performance of "Weather Bird," a tune by "King" Oliver. The following year, Hines launched his own big band, maintained it for twenty years, and then rejoined Armstrong. Hines and Armstrong were ideal collaborators. Once Hines tried to persuade a radio announcer not to drink while working; the announcer promptly dubbed Hines "Fatha." and the named stayed with him throughout his career.

Figure 138 - Earl "Fatha" Hines plays for Private Charles Carpenter. His trumpet and horn lines on the piano changed the jazz style of an era. (Photo courtesy of National Archives)

When Armstrong went to New York after the success of his "Hot Fives" and "Hot Sevens," he was astounded to hear his records played in shops and homes all along his travel route. White musicians in large numbers began moving into jazz during this period. White audiences had already discovered the blues. As early as 1912, W.C. Handy's "Memphis Blues" became a hit; Handy followed this success with his most famous composition in 1914. "St. Louis Blues" became an even bigger hit than "Memphis Blues." The mournful sound of the blues was everywhere. Music publishers were quick to note the success of blues singers like Bessie Smith. When Smith became a major star in the black community, publishers were eager to capitalize on the popularity of the blues by publishing "blues pieces." Following the African tradition, the harmony, time scheme and scales of the blues were not written. The signature of the blues was the "blue note," a sound that existed in between two notes on the piano. True blue notes could not be played on the piano, but they could be produced on instruments that didn't depend on a keyboard, like the trumpet or the saxophone.

Jazz and the blues developed separately, but jazz musicians were clearly influenced by the melodic and harmonic elements of the blues. Blues singers traditionally sang their solos without a conventional accompaniment associated with European music. So publishers began marketing printed compositions that attempted to make the blues sounds accessible, at least in part, to many who would otherwise not have heard them. Recordings of the blues were intended primarily for black audiences and ironically dubbed "race records." But white instrumentalists and singers and their audiences discovered them as well. Historian James Lincoln Collier has written, "There is no doubt that jazz was made in the first instance by blacks, that the majority of superior players have been black, and that most of the significant advances have been worked out by blacks. But the fact remains that whites have played important roles in giving jazz a shape."

The legendary jazz trumpeter "Bix" Beiderbecke is generally regarded as the first great white jazz musician. Leon Bismarck "Bix" Beiderbecke grew up in a German-American family in Davenport, Iowa, the son of prosperous parents. As a student, Beiderbecke loved classical music, particularly the works of Debussy and Ravel.

But he was totally captivated by the solos of Nick LaRocca of the "Original Dixieland Jazz Band" and spent hours copying them until he could duplicate them on his cornet. Young Bix's parents sent him to study at the prestigious Lake Forest Academy, a school near Chicago. Instead of concentrating on academic studies, Bix discovered the music of "King" Oliver, Louis Armstrong, and Emmett Hardy, a white trumpeter he admired. In 1923, he joined a band called the Wolverines and eventually recorded with them. Bix's trademark was his unusually lyrical and legato style of melodic phrasing. He worked in Chicago and with bands led by Frankie Trumbauer, Jean Goldkette, and Paul Whiteman.

Figure 139 - Bix Beiderbecke, a jazz musician who had a brief, but influential career in the early days of jazz. (Public domain)

He also turned his hand to composing. One of his pieces, *In a Mist*, showed the influence of Edward MacDowell. The stock market crash of 1929 ruined Beiderbecke financially. He was not widely known to the public, and when he died of pneumonia and alcoholism at the age of 28, he might have passed into obscurity. But a novel, *Young Man With a Horn* by Dorothy Baker, seemed to chronicle aspects of his life and he became a jazz age legend. Today, he is remembered, like the characters of F. Scott Fitzgerald, as a symbol of the jazz age, forever young, forever optimistic, forever part of the "Roaring 20s."

Among the most avid Beiderbecke fans were a group of young musicians attending Austin High School in Chicago. They were nicknamed the "Austin High Gang." The group included the McPartland Brothers, Jimmy on cornet and trumpet and Dick on banjo, Bud Freeman on tenor saxophone, Frank Teschmacher on clarinet, Jim Langan on piano, Dave Tough on drums, and a gifted teenage clarinetist, Benny Goodman. The group developed a style all its own. All the members became noted jazz musicians, and Goodman became one of the great legends of American music.

During this same period, an important new band was organized in New York by Phil Napoleon, a well-known trumpeter, and his associate, trombonist Miff Mole. The band changed its name every time it changed a record label. "The Original Memphis Five" reappeared as "Gene Fosdick's Hoosiers," "Pasternacki's Orchestras," "The Beale Street Serenaders," "The Tennessee Ten," "The Tennessee Tooters," and finally, "The Cotton Pickers." In 1925, cornetist Red Nichols assumed leadership of the group. Nichols led it for five years, later renaming it "The Five Pennies." The Nichols group became one of the most successful of the New York ensembles.

Jazz was not the only major musical development during the Roaring 20s. An incredibly talented group of young composers were revolutionizing American popular music. George Gershwin was one of Broadway's leading composers in 1924 when his *Rhapsody in Blue* was introduced to an enthusiastic audience by bandleader Paul Whiteman who led the historic concert in Aeolian Hall. While several classical musicians may have thought of the *Rhapsody* as jazz, they were decidedly mistaken. Gershwin had absorbed the harmonies and rhythms of jazz, but he had written a concert composition for piano and orchestra. (Unfortunately, Gershwin was dubbed "The composer who made a lady out of jazz." One suspects that Gershwin knew jazz was entitled to respectability without his help!)

Jazz began to travel around the nation and around the world. American phonograph records crossed the Atlantic and Europeans were captivated by the syncopated rhythms of improvised music. French listeners eagerly bought recordings by Louis Armstrong and went to live performances of jazz at the first European jazz club, *Le Boeuf sur le Toit*. Major European composers in capitals such as Paris or Berlin could be found in the audiences that were attracted to the effusive energy of instrumental jazz. Among the European composers who were attracted to jazz influences to varying degrees were Claude Debussy, Arthur Honegger, Georges Auric, Germaine Taillefaire, Darius Milhaud. Maurice Ravel, Igor Stravinsky, Sergei Prokofiev, Dmitri Shostakovich, Ernst Krenek, and Kurt Weill. among others. It is interesting to note that all of these composers wrote in varied styles and often disagreed with each other. But all were intrigued by American jazz.

In 1922, at the behest of French singer Yvonne George, Milhaud visited Harlem. When he returned to France, he brought with him a collection of "race records" on the Black Swan label. Milhaud then used obvious jazz rhythms when he composed his ballet, *La Création du Monde*. European concert music was going through a period of conflict and controversy, and twentieth century composers began rejecting the traditions of the previous era and experimenting with all types of new rhythms and harmonies. Ernest Ansermet, the distinguished Swiss symphony conductor, was just beginning his career. Ansermet was quick to sing the praises of Sidney Bechet, the New Orleans soprano saxophonist who went to Europe with Will Marion Cook's Southern Syncopated Orchestra. Ansermet dubbed Bechet "a genius." Chris Goddard wrote that Ansermet made "almost every important point which characterizes black, as distinct from European music, pointing out that the performance rather than the original

Figure 140 - Sidney Bechet, soprano saxophonist, Freddie Moore, and Lloyd Phillips. Conductor Ernest Ansermet called Bechet "a genius." (Photo courtesy of the William P. Gottlieb Collection, Library of Congress)

conception is the determining factor and stressing the broad sonorities and individual tone which each musician cultivated." The European concert composers who were influenced by jazz could copy the syncopated rhythms of the new American music; they could try to capture the sound of improvised "blue notes" on paper. But in writing down their music note-for-note, they weren't creating jazz, and their concert works, though often dazzling and exciting, didn't swing.

Not all composers who were interested in jazz were European. After the conclusion of World War I, many of America's most talented young composers went to Europe to study. Quite a number settled in Paris where they became pupils of Nadia Boulanger. Aaron Copland, Roy Harris, and Virgil Thomson were among the composers who followed this path; France was always a country that reflected an exceptional appreciation of American jazz, so the Americans in Paris, including these composers, suddenly heard jazz in a new light in a new European setting. Aaron Copland had certainly encountered jazz in his native New York, but he said that it seemed more special to him in Paris. Jazz became an important influence on many composers of concert music; less known is the fact that many jazz musicians began absorbing the harmonic influences of the concert composers. So Ravel might add jazz rhythms to his piano concerto, while years later, pianist-composer John Lewis of the Modern Jazz Quartet would incorporate the harmonic elements of Ravel's approach in his jazz. By the end of the 1920s, jazz had grown from its early days in New Orleans and Chicago to a phenomenon. The twenties, a time of peace, prosperity, irrepressible optimism, bold social change, and exuberant fun, ended with the Wall Street crash and gave way to The Great Depression of the 1930s. In the years that followed, the era known as The Roaring Twenties would live on in memory as "the jazz age."

THE SWING ERA

The years from 1935 to 1946 were among the most important in the development of jazz. Although there were many active bands in the 1920s, it was in the mid-1930s that big bands developed a performing energy and creative vitality that would propel jazz to the forefront of American music. These years became known as "The Swing Era." The early pioneers of jazz in New Orleans and Chicago would never have imagined the success, influence, or levels of popularity achieved by leaders, composers, and arrangers of the big band era. Several of the early big band leaders had ties to previous periods in jazz. Bennie Moten, a pianist who had studied with pupils of Scott Joplin, led a popular band in Kansas City. But the most important figure bridging the gap from the 1920s to the 1930s was Fletcher Henderson.

Fletcher Henderson and Don Redmon were both college graduates from middle-class homes. Unlike the early New Orleans and Chicago musicians, they had not grown up playing or listening to black folk music or the blues. Today, they might pursue careers in classical music. But because the world of classical music was highly segregated, opportunities in jazz were far more accessible. Musicians who started and developed their styles in the early days of jazz in New Orleans and Chicago created their own independent melodic lines when they played together. Listeners were hearing a group of soloists joining together as they improvised in small groups. Their music, although improvised and featuring the syncopated rhythms and "blue notes" of jazz, could be truly described as "polyphonic." This is the term associated with concert music of the Baroque period, the era of J.S. Bach. In Bach's works and in the early jazz improvisations, a listener would hear several melodies being played simultaneously, each as important as the other. But Fletcher Henderson, Don Redmon, and their colleagues wanted to develop ensembles that could play as a single unit. They sought opportunities for the jazz composer-arranger to achieve this by applying the concepts of part-writing and voice-leading, found in classical music, to their compositions and arrangements for the new "big bands" that were forming. The result was a new, dynamic, and thoroughly cohesive approach, which revolutionized the sound of jazz ensembles.

Fletcher Henderson arrived in New York as a young man from Cuthbert, Georgia, who had traveled north to study mathematics and chemistry. He worked his way through school by playing the piano in W.C. Handy's orchestra, eventually starting a band of his own. In 1923, a Henderson band recording, "The Dicty Blues," became a success and Henderson abandoned the idea of being a chemist.

Henderson's bands included some of the best-known jazz musicians of all time, including trumpeters Louis Armstrong and Roy Eldridge, and saxophonists Coleman Hawkins, Benny Carter, and Don Redmon.

Figure 141 - Coleman "Bean" Hawkins. After hearing his solos, musicians took the saxophone seriously during the swing era. (Photo courtesy of the William P. Gottlieb Collection, Library of Congress)

Coleman "Bean" Hawkins had studied the piano and cello as well as the saxophone. Until his time with Henderson, the saxophone had been primarily a novelty instrument played by white musicians. Hawkins had a unique musical gift. Jazz musicians improvise melodies over chords. He could take all the notes of a musical chord, notated vertically on a piece of score paper and instinctively know every possible note that could be used in an improvised melodic line played over that chord. His total mastery of "vertical improvisation" established the saxophone as an instrument for serious musical expression in the jazz idiom. Hawkins remained with Henderson for ten years and then left to join Jack Hylton's band in England. After five years in Europe, he returned in 1939 to record his version of "Body and Soul," widely regarded as one of the finest jazz solos of all time. He tried starting his own band, but his studious manner could not compete with the flamboyance of more commercial bandleaders. Hawkins would remain a major influence on dozens of jazz saxophonists who followed in his footsteps and emulated his tone, his phrasing, his sense of harmony.

Don Redmon, a former child prodigy, had been playing trumpet at age three, joined his first band at six, and was familiar with the technical idiosyncrasies of every instrument in the orchestra. After thorough musical training at conservatories in Detroit and Boston, he emerged as the first composer and arranger of significance in the world of jazz bands. When Louis Armstrong joined Henderson, he brought the driving syncopations and phrasing of his solo style to the ensemble, later absorbed by many of the other members of the band, and especially by its arrangers. The arranging style developed by Don Redmon and Benny Carter emphasized melodies that could be harmonized in "block chords" where each section would play the rhythm of the melody, but with a different melodic line. Henderson liked to offset the sections of brass and saxophones. In this "antiphonal" style, one musical section would express an idea that another section would answer. One section might play a series of jazz "riffs," simple phrases repeated over and over, contributing to the driving rhythmic swing of the ensemble. When Don Redmon left to become the leader of Detroit's popular band, McKinney's Cotton Pickers, Henderson himself assumed the responsibilities of the lead arranger for his band. Henderson was known as a gentleman. Big band historian George T. Simon remarked that Henderson might have been more successful were he not so gentle and genteel. But Henderson's personal manner made it difficult for him in the rough and tumble music business.

Henderson's band had its rivals. Drummer Chick Webb led a swinging ensemble at the Savoy Ballroom in Harlem. One night, a Webb colleague, Bardu Ali, attended an amateur contest at the Harlem Opera House and discovered a young singer performing Hoagy Carmichael's tune, "Judy." He had to virtually lock Webb in his dressing room to persuade him to audition the girl. Her name was Ella Fitzgerald and before long, she was known as the most popular jazz vocalist of all time.

One band that did not follow the Henderson lead was Jimmy Lunceford's. As a high school student, Lunceford received musical training from Wilberforce J. Whiteman, the father of bandleader Paul Whiteman. The senior Whiteman directed music for the public school system in Denver. He was a dedicated, hard-working musician who taught his students the values of discipline and practice. Lunceford learned his lessons well. When he became a well-known bandleader, he never allowed fame or extracurricular activities to distract him from his primary mission: making music. (Arranger Sy Oliver created a piece for the Lunceford band called "Hittin' the Bottle," which suggested that "everyone except Jimmy hits the bottle.") Oliver wasn't joking. Lunceford didn't drink nor do anything else to excess. He was a graduate of Fisk University and began his musical career in an unlikely way: as music instructor and athletic director of Manasa High

School, in Memphis, Tennessee. Several members of his band first encountered him as their sports coach. The nucleus of Lunceford's band began as a high school dance orchestra. Pianist Moses Allen, drummer Jimmy Crawford, and trumpeter Henry Clay all played in the band. While Lunceford was still a high school teacher at Manasa, he was impressed by two of the most gifted students, the group's pianist, Edwin Wilcox, and its alto saxophone soloist, Willie Smith. When Wilcox and Smith graduated, they went to Lunceford's own alma mater, Fisk University. Lunceford then joined the faculty. Eventually, both would become key players in Lunceford's band. Like his early mentor Wilberforce Whiteman, Lunceford saw himself as a teacher. He always tried to earn the respect of his players and he expected them to behave in ways that would earn the respect of the public. In the words of jazz historian and composer Gunther Schuller, "This was in startling contrast to the behavior ascribed to jazz musicians, then, and alas, even now, as rather vulgar, gin-guzzling inebriates, disreputable Don Juans, and worthless spendthrifts."

Figure 142 - Bandleader Jimmie Lunceford, photographer William P. Gottlieb, drummer Gene Krupa. Lunceford saw himself as a teacher and mentor to other musicians. (Photo by Delia Potofsky Gottlieb, courtesy of William P. Gottlieb Collection, Library of Congress)

Eventually Lunceford and his band traveled from Memphis to New York City, where they performed at the Cotton Club, an engagement that helped make the band famous. Jimmy Lunceford's band was known for its great precision. Unlike Duke Ellington's orchestra, which was an outlet for Ellington's talent as a composer, Lunceford's band was primarily a showcase for outstanding arrangers. Lunceford came up with an inspired idea: he asked trumpeter Sy Oliver to write arrangements for the band. Oliver, who had never formally studied arranging, wrote dozens of outstanding big band arrangements in a crisp, clean style and created what became known as "the Lunceford two-step," a smooth, lilting approach to swing. (Other bands depended on a newly-emphasized four-beat.) While most bands would swing directly on the beat or ahead of the beat, Oliver wrote arrangements that allowed the Lunceford ensemble to swing *behind* the beat. Oliver's arrangements were full of surprises, including transitions that might change key suddenly.

Oliver liked to experiment with unusual combinations of instruments, and on occasion, would do away with the rhythm section of the band and then bring it back into a piece to heighten the explosion of swing. Oliver, who gave up aspirations to practice law in order to be a musician, was known for his creativity and intelligence. (His nickname,

"Sy," was derived from the word "psychology,") When nearly twenty top bands participated in a marathon concert, it was the Lunceford band that stopped the show and received the ovation. Lunceford might have enjoyed a brilliant career for years, had not the tension and severe demands of his busy schedule taken a toll. Ironically, Lunceford suffered a fatal heart attack, while signing autographs in a music store. He was only forty-five years old.

Drummer Ben Pollack organized a band at the Venice Ballroom in California in 1926. The band made its first record late that year in Chicago, featuring clarinetist Benny Goodman and trombonist Glenn Miller among its members. Nearly every white swing

Figure 143 - Ben Pollack and the Californians. From left, Glenn Miller, Benny Goodman, Gil Rodin, Harry Green, Ben Pollack, Fud Livingston, Al Harris, Harry Goodman, Vic Breidis, and Lou Kastler. (Photo courtesy of Glenn Miller Archive, American Music Research Center, University of Colorado, Boulder, All Rights Reserved)

musician of consequence worked for Pollack at one time or another. America was at the height of the depression. Audiences longed for reassuring sounds, from crooners like Rudy Vallee and Bing Crosby, and "sweet bands" like those led by Guy Lombardo and Ozzie Nelson. But the driving energy of the swing bands would soon emerge. The Casa Loma Band, named for the Toronto hotel where it began performing, was considered the first white big band to concentrate on jazz. Under the leadership of Glen Gray, it, too, achieved great popularity among college students with its combination of swing arrangements and lyrical ballads. By 1934, Pollack's band was at its height. (When it broke up the following year, many of its members joined Bob Crosby.) Tommy Dorsey and Glenn Miller were starting bands of their own. Decca Records began releasing new recordings by Jimmy Lunceford and Duke Ellington's band completed a tour of Europe. That same year, another band was organized that would provide the spark of a revolution and launch the swing era. Its leader was Benny Goodman. In the process, he would set a new standard for excellence in jazz, achieve such popularity that it would provide a launching pad for numerous colleagues and rivals. But the man who became "The King of Swing" started his rise to the pinnacle of the jazz world with a humble beginning.

JAZZ ROYALTY I: A KING AND HIS RIVALS

Benny Goodman grew up in Chicago, one of twelve children of a poor, immigrant tailor. Together with two of his older brothers who took up the tuba and trumpet, he started studying music at ten. He was given a clarinet, and from the beginning, displayed extraordinary talent. Goodman studied at a famous settlement house, Hull House. Franz Schoepp, a demanding woodwind master from Germany, was his teacher. Another young Schoepp pupil, Buster Bailey, was black. Goodman and Bailey played duets together. Years later, Benny Goodman would take the lead in breaking down the color barrier that prevented black and white musicians from working together. Goodman's imitation of a clarinet solo by Ted Lewis led to his professional debut. By the time he was thirteen, young Benny Goodman, in a custom-made tuxedo, was a boy in a man's world. He escaped a background of poverty through talent, discipline, drive, and hard work.

Goodman encountered the riveting music of Bix Beiderbecke, King Oliver, Fats Waller, Earl Hines, and trumpeter Freddie Keppard, who concealed his technique from rivals when he played by covering his fingers with a handkerchief. In a profile of Goodman, writer Stanley Baron described the incredible era of jazz-age Chicago. "It was a world of bathtub gin, redolent weed, Irish cops, Italian gangsters, ice-cream pants, double-breasted blazers, raccoon coats, hot music pouring from golden doorways into the snowy streets, high black limousines, sudden brawls and shootings, and girls with spit curls who wore slinky dresses above the knee. In those speakeasy years, Chicago at night was a magical melting pot, and music supplied the fire under it."

Figure 144 - Benny Goodman with pianist Teddy Wilson and singing star Mel Tormé on drums. (Photo from Metronome magazine, copyright not renewed when Metronome ceased publication.)

Ben Pollack invited the teenaged Goodman to join his ensemble in California, and he stayed with the band when it performed in Chicago. One night, Goodman and Pollack improvised many clarinet and drum choruses together, using the tune "I Want To Be

Happy" as a point of musical departure. Years later, Goodman used a similar approach in his classic version of "Sing, Sing, Sing" performed in Carnegie Hall. At twenty, he left Pollack to begin freelancing in New York, working with groups like The Five Pennies, led by the Dixieland cornetist Red Nichols. Nichols also led a pit orchestra for stage musicals by George and Ira Gershwin, with Goodman, Glenn Miller, and the Chicago drummer Gene Krupa. Goodman also recorded with his one-time idol, Ted Lewis, whose recorded solos he had imitated as a child.

In 1934, Goodman was faced with a choice: the security of a job offer from Paul Whiteman's band or the challenge and struggle presented by the prospect of a band of his own. He decided to become a bandleader. Fortunately, John Hammond stepped into the picture. Hammond was a young record producer, the product of an Ivy League education and an enthusiastic jazz buff. He offered Goodman an initial opportunity to record and became Goodman's lifelong friend and advisor. Goodman eventually married Hammond's sister, Alice. Goodman admired the work of Fletcher Henderson, to whom he frequently paid tribute. Goodman adapted Henderson's style to his own and eventually Henderson joined him as an arranger.

In 1935, Goodman got the chance for which he'd been waiting, a weekly appearance for his band on a radio program broadcast coast to coast. Goodman's band was selected as one of three to play on the program, sponsored by the National Biscuit Company. For three hours, audiences could hear the work of three bands, the Latin stylings of Xavier Cugat, the pleasant but unspectacular work of Kel Murray, and Goodman. After 26 weeks on the air, Goodman was ready for a national tour. The tour had rocky start including a disastrous appearance in Denver during which audiences demanded that the band play waltzes or refund their money. Goodman persevered. The band was booked into the Palomar Ballroom in Los Angeles. Goodman began by playing what he was told the audience expected--the pleasant but unspectacular sounds of a "sweet band." Midway through the performance, Goodman called for a dynamic, swinging Fletcher Henderson arrangement. Fans, mesmerized by Goodman's crisp, driving swing, mobbed the bandstand. Goodman's band found itself sitting on top of the world.

The band appeared in New York at the Paramount Theater, sharing the bill with *Maid of Salem*, a movie about witches in New England. Goodman hoped he wouldn't be playing to an empty theater. When 4400 screaming fans stood in line around the block waiting for tickets, Goodman had his answer. Everywhere, young audiences wanted to dance to the music of Benny Goodman. A three-week engagement in Chicago had to be extended to eight months. The big band era was about to reach its peak; Goodman was officially dubbed "The King of Swing."

Goodman was a trailblazer in many ways. At the time, black and white musicians performed together privately and informally, but no leading jazz figure had organized an interracial trio for major public performances. In 1935, Goodman decided to form a trio featuring the brilliant black pianist Teddy Wilson and the hard-driving white drummer

Gene Krupa. Goodman first heard Wilson at a private party at the home of vibraphonist Red Norvo. Most of the guests were musicians. Teddy Wilson sat down at the piano and began improvising on the tune "Body and Soul." Wilson, the master of "swing piano," had an elegant classical touch and Goodman was so impressed that he picked up his clarinet and joined Wilson in an impromptu duet. Such collaborations became for jazz musicians what chamber music represented for their classical counterparts.

Goodman continued to shatter the color barrier. He expanded his trio to a quartet by adding another prominent black musician, vibraphonist Lionel Hampton; he also hired guitarist Charlie Christian and trumpeter Cootie Williams in his band. (When Williams left his longtime employer, Duke Ellington, for Goodman, bandleader Raymond Scott actually composed a piece called "When Cootie Left the Duke.") Eventually, Williams left Goodman to start his own band, as did other Goodman alumni like Gene Krupa and the legendary trumpeter Harry James. Goodman also discovered singers like Billie Holiday (the daughter of Fletcher Henderson's clarinetist, Clarence Holiday) and Peggy Lee. He also employed outstanding arrangers, including Fletcher Henderson's brother, Horace Henderson, Edgar Sampson, and Jimmy Mundy. Goodman, like Henderson before him, also benefited from the arranging skills of Lyle "Spud" Murphy. Murphy's storied career began

inauspiciously, playing clarinet and saxophone for tips in a two-piece band in a Mexican border town. Eventually, Murphy emerged as an unsung hero of the big band era, writing six hundred arrangements and one hundred compositions of his own for the top bands of the 1930s. He settled in California where he scored films at Columbia Pictures and published numerous books on arranging and orchestration. He also developed his own system of organizing tonal materials that he called the "equal interval system." When he died at 97, he had more than two dozen books to his credit, and a long list of prominent jazz composers and arrangers who had been his pupils. Goodman enjoyed a status and respectability often denied to musicians who played jazz. Carnegie Hall was home

Figure 145 - Carnegie Hall poster announces Benny Goodman's Historical 1934 Jazz Concert. (Photo courtesy of Estate of Benny Goodman and the Irving Gilmore Library, Yale University. Used by permission)

to classical ensembles including The New York Philharmonic conducted by Sir John Barbirolli. *Metronome Magazine* announced that Goodman's band would be replacing "Jack Barbirolli and his Philharmonic Cats, the regular band that played in that spot."

Goodman was always a perfectionist. He was never satisfied with his own playing and throughout his life, he always wanted to improve, though reviewers like George Simon called his band "the closest thing to perfection" they had heard.

Goodman also demanded a similar devotion to high standards from his musicians. He became famous for the "Goodman Ray," a cold, withering look he directed at those musicians who made mistakes or whose technique or dedication could not match his own. Goodman had a capacity to focus entirely on the music, sometimes oblivious to what was taking place in the outside world. Once, during a recording session, his musicians, complained about the cold, unheated studio, "We're freezing in here." Goodman thanked them and the musicians assumed he was going to raise the temperature in the room. Goodman returned a few minutes later wearing a sweater and went about his business. On January 16, 1938, Goodman took his band into Carnegie Hall, There, for the first time, a jazz ensemble played on the stage was that was the preserve of symphony orchestras. For the historic concert, Goodman invited a number of black friends to join in the fun. The concert started with "Don't Be That Way" by Edgar Sampson and then moved to "One O'Clock Jump" by Count Basie. Goodman provided his audience with a "twenty-year history of jazz," including his Ted Lewis impression and a tribute to Duke Ellington featuring Duke's musicians Cootie Williams, Harry Carney, and Johnny Hodges. The Goodman trio and quartet performed, and the evening's rousing finale was Louis Prima's "Sing, Sing, Sing," alternating thundering big band sounds with pulsating clarinet and drum passages. Incorporated in the performance was another tune, "Christopher Columbus," by Chu Berry and Andy Razaf, which had been arranged by Fletcher Henderson. This unusual combination came together in performance and was later written down by arranger Jimmy Mundy. *Down Beat* magazine declared that the concert had delighted the 3800 "Sophisti-cats" in the audience.

Figure 146 - Benny Goodman (third from left) with musical alumni, left to right, Vernon Brown, George Auld, Gene Krupa, Clint Neagley, Ziggy Elman, Israel Crosby, and Teddy Wilson at the piano. (Photo by Fred Palumbo, courtesy of New York World Telegram and Sun Collection, Library of Congress)

Goodman proved an enduring musical figure. He remained active as a soloist long after the big band era ended. At the height of his fame, he took time for studies with the world renowned classical clarinetists Simeon Bellison and Reginald Kell. Long after the big band era had passed, Goodman recorded concert works like Mozart's *Clarinet Concerto*. He recorded Bela Bartók's trio, *Contrasts*, with famed concert violinist Joseph Szigeti and Bartók himself at the piano. He also commissioned works by Aaron Copland

and Paul Hindemith, and performed and recorded works for classical clarinet in the later years of his life. But Goodman will always be remembered for his role in the big band era. In 1978, a cartoon in *The New Yorker* by Dana Fradon said it best. An aging monarch turns to his Queen and says, "If I had it to all over again, I would like to have been the King of Swing." Millions of people around the world, many of them musicians and colleagues, agreed.

George Simon, critic for *Metronome*, a leading jazz magazine, recalled the fare available in New York during the mid-1930s. The leading hotels all featured star big bands: Benny Goodman's band was featured at the Hotel Pennsylvania. A block away, audiences could hear Jimmy Dorsey at the Hotel New Yorker or move on to the Hotel Lincoln to listen to Goodman's rival, the brilliantly articulate clarinetist Artie Shaw. Woody Herman held forth at the Roseland Ballroom. Chick Webb's band headlined at the Savoy. Nightclubs like the Cotton Club presented the great Duke Ellington ensemble, while the yet undiscovered Glenn Miller appeared at the Paradise Restaurant. All across the country, hotels, ballrooms, and clubs presented bands. The leaders, arrangers, instrumental soloists and vocalists differed greatly in style and technique, but all were part of a national phenomenon. The whole country was dancing to the tune of the big bands of the swing era. Fans could buy dozens of new jazz records and hear their favorite bands on radio. Concerts were broadcast live, so thousands of people who couldn't actually be present could participate in the experience. Magazines like *Down Beat* and *Metronome* were devoted to the big band phenomenon. Big Band historian George Simon recalled that "the free, spontaneous communication between the big bands and the fans was a natural culmination of the music itself." Throughout the 1930s and mid- 1940s, big bands ranging from Glenn Miller's "sweet band" to Stan Kenton's highly experimental ensembles achieved wide popularity with a remarkable variety of sounds. Among those who won an enormous following were the bands of Tommy and Jimmy Dorsey, Woody Herman, Artie Shaw, William "Count" Basie, Lionel Hampton, and the man generally recognized as the most important jazz composer, Edward Kennedy "Duke" Ellington.

Figure 147 - Artie Shaw, proclaimed "King of the Clarinet" and famous for his tone quality. (Photograph courtesy of Glenn Miller Archive, American Music Research Center, University of Colorado, Boulder. All Rights Reserved)

If Benny Goodman was the "King of Swing," Artie Shaw was billed as "The King of the Clarinet." Shaw himself weighed in on the controversy when he said, "Benny played clarinet, I played music," suggesting that their titles should be reversed. Artie Shaw was a natural rival for Benny Goodman. An intense man by his own description, he had a difficult personality "cursed with seriousness." Shaw was a lifelong intellectual, an avid reader, and a musical explorer always searching for new ideas. Shaw grew up in New Haven, Connecticut. While attending Columbia University, he became active as a studio musician in New York. Shaw first attracted attention when he played swing in a concert accompanied by a string quartet. As a result, Shaw was able to start his own band. Shaw was initially known as a good clarinetist, but not as a challenger to Goodman. But when he started his band, he closeted himself in a practice room and began working on his technique for eight hours a day. He emerged from these sessions as a full-fledged virtuoso. Shaw did not pursue technique for technique's sake alone. He had definite ideas about music as a medium of expression. Shaw's first big band also included an unusual string section. Although the band didn't achieve a wide commercial success, fame would not elude Shaw for long. A subsequent band, launched in 1937, recorded Cole Porter's "Begin the Beguine" which established Shaw as the primary challenger for Goodman's crown.

While Goodman's partisans insisted that Shaw's idea of swing was no match for Goodman, Shaw's admirers insisted that Shaw's tone quality was far superior. Shaw's solos and the arrangements he preferred were more introspective than those of swing bands that depended on high volume and musical intensity. Shaw disbanded his large ensemble in 1939. Only a year later, he was back with a new band, this time featuring his

Figure 148 - Artie Shaw at the Palomar Ballroom, 1939. (Photo courtesy of Glenn Miller Archive, American Music Research Center, University of Colorado, Boulder, All Rights Reserved)

own quintet, "The Grammercy Five." One of his biggest hits, "Frenesí," was recorded with a studio orchestra. Shaw organized and disbanded several bands over the years. A complex man of many moods, Shaw was always outspoken. He protested in public regarding what he felt was stupidity in the music business and even lectured his audiences when he thought they needed the benefit of his opinions. He was unpredictable. When he hired vocalist Billie Holiday as the band's full-time singer, he became the first white bandleader to hire a black woman to tour the South at the height of segregation.

Over the years, he organized ensembles that featured major performers of the big band era, including popular vocalists Mel Tormé and Helen Forrest, guitarist Barney Kessel, and the charismatic and highly opinionated drummer Buddy Rich, one of the few musicians whose displays of temperament could rival Shaw's. No one ever knew what Artie Shaw would do next. When the mood struck him, he would take a sabbatical from performing to pursue other interests such as higher mathematics. He liked to experiment with unusual combinations of instruments, even incorporating the harpsichord into an ensemble. The public remained fascinated with his personal life and in particular, his penchant for marrying glamorous women. He married eight times. (The much married Shaw was the target of a quip by Glenn Miller. After making the film *Orchestra Wives*, Miller suggested a sequel, *Orchestra Leaders' Wives*, presumably starring two of the Shaw's former wives, screen legends Lana Turner and Ava Gardner.)

Shaw never ran away from conflict. The music industry liked to label musicians. Shaw, a rugged individualist, refused to cooperate. In the Navy, he entertained the troops in the midst of Pacific battle zones. Once when a group of actors led by Ronald Reagan launched an anti-communist movement in Hollywood, Shaw began singing the praises of the Soviet Union.

In 1954, Shaw gave up jazz and the clarinet entirely, declaring that he had taken his instrument as far as it could go. He devoted his time to pursuing his other interests. He could always surprise the public. In 1991, Shaw appeared in London, conducting a performance of his own *Clarinet Concerto* with Bob Wilber as soloist. He remained a perfectionist in everything, becoming one of the country's foremost marksmen. Shaw wrote short stories and an autobiography, *The Trouble with Cinderella*, in which he observed, "Nobody lives happily ever after." At the time of his death in 2004 at age ninety-four, his three-volume, thousand-page autobiographical novel remained unpublished. But at the height of the big band era, Shaw was a major force on the bandstands of America.

The Dorsey Brothers, Jimmy and Tommy, were major figures of the big band era. Jimmy played the clarinet and alto saxophone, Tommy played the trombone (although he originally also worked with the trumpet). In 1932, the brothers formed a pick-up group to record "I'm Getting Sentimental Over You." They formed their own band the following year, including Glenn Miller and Bob Crosby as sidemen. By 1935, Tommy, the more ambitious and opinionated of the two, was ready to go out on his own. He formed his own band and took "I'm Getting Sentimental Over You" as his theme song. Speculation and rumors about the alleged rivalries between the Dorsey brothers were widespread. Jimmy's band achieved major success with the vocal stylings of Bob Eberly and Helen O'Connell. Tommy's vocalists included Jo Stafford, Connie Haines, and Frank Sinatra, who credited Tommy Dorsey with teaching him (by example on the trombone) how to sing long musical phrases without ever taking obvious breaths; this was a key factor in the development of Sinatra's ballad style.

Figure 149 - Jimmy Dorsey and his band at the Panther Room, 1940 - (Photo courtesy of Glenn Miller Archive, American Music Research Center, University of Colorado, Boulder. All Rights Reserved.)

Sinatra's years with Tommy Dorsey proved to be an education for him. He absorbed Dorsey's smooth phrasing, his breath control, and his musical slides; Sinatra observed and admired Dorsey's leadership style as well. Dorsey was tough and demanding; he insisted on discipline for his players and he always insisted on outstanding arrangements.

Trumpeter Axel Stordahl became one of Dorsey's principal arrangers. He knew precisely how to write band arrangements incorporating Sinatra's voice. When Sinatra eventually left Dorsey, Stordahl arranged his first solo recordings, beginning a two-decade collaboration. Stordahl was responsible for much of the Sinatra sound that made him a huge singing star among the teenage "bobbysoxers" of the World War II era.

Figure 150 - Axel Stordahl, whose arrangements helped make Frank Sinatra a singing idol for the "bobbysoxers," looks on while Sinatra rehearses. (Photo courtesy of William P. Gottlieb Collection, Library of Congress)

Frank Sinatra, by the way, was fortunate in working with several of the finest arrangers in popular music. Throughout his career, Sinatra also recorded a number of albums featuring the swinging big band arrangements of Nelson Riddle.

Like Stordahl, Riddle was an alumnus of the Tommy Dorsey band. From the 1950s to the 1980s, he worked with the best-known vocalists in popular music, arranging for Nat "King" Cole, Ella Fitzgerald, Peggy Lee, Dean Martin, and Rosemary Clooney, as well as Sinatra. Jonathan Schwartz spoke of Riddle's "private melodies that whisper respectfully under the Gershwin or Kern or Rodgers on the table," and his "out and out passion that informs every bar of every arrangements." Riddle also became widely successful as a composer for films and television; his knowledge of the band styles of all eras was especially present in his award-winning score for the film, *The Great Gatsby*.

In later years, Sinatra also worked closely with another talented composer-arranger, Gordon Jenkins. Jenkins was unusually gifted at writing for lush string orchestras and his melodic and harmonic style tugged at the listener's heartstrings. Jenkins had written a number of suites following specific themes, especially his work, *Manhattan Tower*, which earned him the key to the city of New York. In 1965, Jenkins arranged the album, *September of My Years*, for Sinatra. It featured Ervin Drake's award-winning melody, "It Was a Very Good Year," and Jenkins' favorite composition of his own, "This Is All I Ask."

Figure 152 - Nelson Riddle, a Castelnuovo-Tedesco pupil, naturally incorporated his swinging, big-band style in his motion picture scores. (Photo courtesy of Nelson Riddle Collection, University of Arizona Fred Fox School of Music)

Tommy Dorsey also hired Sy Oliver, Jimmy Lunceford's top arranger, to write for his band. Oliver was one of the first black arrangers to play a major role in a white band. He was a master at creating a modern "big band sound," with sharp, punctuating brass; his presence as an arranger attracted many fine musicians to Dorsey's ensemble, including the colorful and controversial drummer, Buddy Rich. Big band fans followed the rivalry of the two brothers the way today's fans are intrigued by gossip about celebrities and sports stars. In 1945, long after the big band era had come to an end, the brothers reconciled and formed a combined "Dorsey Brothers" ensemble to perform for a special record for America's troops, known as a V-Disc. The recording featured "More Than You Know" and "Brotherly Jump." In 1947, United Artists released a fictionalized biography of the two brothers, *The Fabulous Dorseys*, with Tommy and Jimmy portraying themselves. The film featured many of their greatest song hits and traced their rise from their early days in Pennsylvania through their highly publicized separation and subsequent reunion. The brothers are still regarded as major figures of the big band era. The lives of Tommy and Jimmy Dorsey, despite their differences, followed parallel roads; they died within six months of each other, Tommy in 1956, Jimmy

Figure 151 - Tommy Dorsey leads a rehearsal in 1945. (Photo courtesy of Glenn Miller Archive, American Music Research Center, University of Colorado, Boulder. All Rights Reserved)

Figure 153 - Jimmy and Tommy Dorsey, brothers, rival bandleaders, and giants of the swing era. (Photograph courtesy of Glenn Miller Archive, American Music Research Center, University of Colorado, Boulder. All Rights Reserved.)

in 1957. The U.S. Postal Service honored them with a stamp in 1996.

In 1939, Glenn Miller led the most popular band in America with a number of hits, including his theme songs, "Moonlight Serenade" and "In the Mood." Miller came from a background in jazz bands and recording studios.

While employed by the Ray Anthony band, he developed what became his signature sound—a clarinet lead played over the saxophone section. Miller studied for a time with Joseph Schillinger, a teacher and musical theorist who believed that music could be taught through mathematics. (Schillinger's theories were published posthumously in two volumes that were as thick as telephone books.)

For a time, it was quite fashionable to explore the Schillinger system. Not only did bandleaders like Benny Goodman and Tommy Dorsey consult Schillinger, but major composers including George Gershwin and Vernon Duke studied with him. At one time, Schillinger insisted that he was a major influence on George Gershwin in *Porgy and Bess*, a claim that was later rejected by his brother Ira Gershwin after George's death.) "Moonlight Serenade," one of Miller's best-known compositions, "was inspired not by the moon, but by an assignment from Schillinger. An original lyric provided the title, "Now I Lay Me Down to Weep." This was considered too depressing for Miller's fans, so Mitchell Parish came up with an alternate lyric and new title, "Moonlight Serenade." Few couples who danced and fell in love to Miller's music during World War II had the slightest idea that Miller's classic theme had begun as an intellectual exercise using the Schillinger system.

Miller's "sweet band" style was incredibly acclaimed, but this style was more endemic to popular music than to the hard-driving jazz espoused by various other bands. In 1942, Miller disbanded his ensemble and tried to enlist in the U.S. Navy. Although turned down by the Navy, he persuaded the Army to accept him so that he could organize an Army band. In 1944, on a trip to entertain troops, he left England in a plane bound for France. The plane vanished over the English Channel never to be found. People still speculate today regarding the disappearance and fate of America's most

Figure 154 - Glenn Miller's legacy lives on after his plane vanished during World War II. (Photo courtesy of Glenn Miller Archive, American Music Research Center, University of Colorado, Boulder. All Rights Reserved)

Figure 155 -Glenn Miller was a trombonist, but a clarinet lead played over the saxophone section made his band with its signature sound the most popular sweet band in America. (Photo courtesy of Glenn Miller Archive, American Music Research Center, University of Colorado, Boulder. All Rights Reserved.)

famous bandleader. Glenn Miller's legend and musical legacy, and however, survived him.

Woody Herman, a native of Milwaukee, was a clarinetist whose career as a big band leader spanned several eras. He was a featured soloist with a band led by Isham Jones for several years. Jones tired of life on the road and decided to retire to a Colorado ranch to raise turkeys. The musicians of the band found themselves stranded in Knoxville, Tennessee, without a job. They agreed that they had a good ensemble and should stay together. Discussions about who should lead the band pointed to Woody Herman and composer-arranger Gordon Jenkins.

When Jenkins was offered a job orchestrating and arranging the score of a Broadway show, Herman emerged as the leader. By the time the group arrived in New York, the Isham Jones alumni had become "Woody Herman and the Band That Plays the Blues." Herman added new musicians in Manhattan and soon, the group was booked into the Roseland Ballroom. Management expected the group to play dance music, waltzes, rumbas, and foxtrots. Gene Lees, Herman's biographer, described the ballroom manager, Joe Belford, as looking like a lineman for the Green Bay Packers. But when he began shouting at Herman to play dance tunes, Herman just smiled and went on leading his band in a repertoire emphasizing the blues. One piece Herman's band did play was "The Woodchopper's Ball." It began as a "head arrangement," retained not through notation but in the musical memories of its improvisers. It was based on a single-note blues "riff," eventually organized by arranger Joe Bishop. Walt Yoder, a bassist with the band, suggested the title after seeing a wood chopping contest. When "The Woodchopper's Ball" was a last minute addition to a recording session, critics and fans reactions were wildly enthusiastic. Critic Marshall Stearns declared that the arrangement "cops the tops" and concluded, "Man, they're on their way." Stearns was far from wrong. Herman, now and forever "The Woodchopper," was indeed on his way to becoming a jazz legend. Herman's band had a huge hit and had found its audience.

Throughout his career, Herman organized several ensembles, the best-known of which were his three famous "herds." The original Herd included impressive musicians. Herman changed personnel gradually. He developed a close relationship with pianist-arranger Ralph Burns, who wrote many of the band's arrangements. His rhythm section included Chubby Jackson on bass and Dave Tough, the drummer whose career dated back to the 1920s' "Austin High Gang." Tough himself belied the stereotypical image of the wild-eyed, flamboyant jazz drummer. He was highly literate, with ambitions to be a writer. When not quoting H.L. Mencken or visiting museums to appreciate modern art, he accompanied poetry readings by Langston Hughes and Kenneth Rexroth. Herman also featured colorful brass soloists. Trombonist Bill Harris looked like a mild-mannered, bespectacled schoolteacher, but he was a notorious practical joker who delighted in appearing solemn and serious to his audience while his colleagues couldn't restrain their laughter at his antics. (Harris's most infamous stunt involved the addition of a "fourth trombonist" on the bandstand, a life-size dummy.) Harris also had a special crook made for his trombone enabling him to play the instrument sideways. He invariably shocked audiences with this stunt when Herman couldn't see what he was doing. Herman's trumpet soloists included Milton "Shorty" Rogers, widely praised as a jazz composer, and the Candoli brothers, Pete and Conte. Nicknamed "The Superman of the Trumpet," Pete Candoli would leave the bandstand and return dressed in a Superman costume made by his wife, leaping onstage with a barrage of spectacular high notes.

Figure 156 - Woody Herman - He led "The Band That Played the Blues" and collaborated with Igor Stravinsky. (Photo courtesy of Glenn Miller Archive, American Music Research Center, University of Colorado, Boulder. All Rights Reserved.)

Herman's most improbable collaborator was the legendary Russian composer of concert music, Igor Stravinsky. In 1945, *Down Beat* magazine announced that Stravinsky had started writing a composition specifically for the Woody Herman ensemble, *The Ebony Concerto*. Stravinsky had clearly developed in an interest in jazz, because he had been experimenting with ragtime rhythms more than two decades earlier. Many untrue stories have been told about the origins of *The Ebony Concerto*. The idea may have originated with Howard "Chubby" Goldfarb, Herman's lawyer. Goldfarb learned that Aaron "Goldie" Goldmark, a jazz musician, was working as representative for a publisher and happened to played Herman's recording of *Bijou* (*Rumba a la jazz*) for Stravinsky, who had been apparently impressed with the arranging style of Ralph Burns. (Burns was also a major admirer of Stravinsky.) When the work was completed, Herman told his colleague and rival, Benny Goodman, of the work's difficulty. A skeptical Goodman quipped, "It can't be that hard." Herman sent him a copy of the score, and the next time they met, Goodman said, "It *is* hard." Youthful jazz audiences who wanted to dance to bands that swing didn't know how to respond to the concerto. But it established once and for all that "serious" concert composers took jazz seriously.

Herman broke up his First Herd in December of 1946 when many of the big bands dissolved. But he never fully accepted the idea that big bands couldn't achieve their former glory. For the remainder of his career, he continually organized new ensembles; the name and personnel of the band might change, but the determination of Woody Herman never waned. He was back in 1947 at the height of the bebop era, with his legendary Second Herd. Herman and Ralph Burns were acquainted with Gene Rowland, a pianist and arranger. Rowland had experimented with an unusual sound using three tenor saxophones instead of two altos and two tenors. Rowland's saxophone-playing colleagues weren't working steadily, and Herman decided to hire the whole ensemble: Stan Getz, Zoot Sims, Herbie Steward, and Jimmy Giuffre. Alto soloist Sam Marowitz and baritone saxophonist Serge Chaloff also participated in a recording of Giuffre's composition, *Four Brothers*. In this piece, a lead tenor and baritone saxophone play the same melody an octave apart, while harmony is provided by two more tenors. The *Four Brothers* sound was copied widely and became a signature sound of Herman's Second Herd. The saxophone section became world-famous as a unit.

By 1949, Herman was losing money with a large ensemble, and he dissolved the Second Herd. In 1950, he was back again, this time with his Third Herd. Herman continually organized new versions of his "Herd" and led bands long after the swing era had faded into memory. The later years of his life were marred by a continuous financial crisis. He eventually discovered to his horror that his longtime manager had paid gambling debts with funds earmarked for taxes. Herman spent his last years trying to pay his debts. He died in 1987, remembered as one of the major figures of the swing and bebop eras.

Harry James was an alumnus of the Goodman band who became a legendary leader in his own right. James was the son of a circus bandmaster. He developed a formidable technique while still a boy. By the time he was a teenager, he was a promising virtuoso.

Figure 157 - Harry James - His soaring trumpet made him a star during the Big Band era. (Photo courtesy of the William P. Gottlieb Collection, Library of Congress)

From his years of exposure to the circus, he developed the instincts of showman. He developed an aggressive, assertive style of phrasing and a manner that attracted the attention of audiences wherever he went. After working with Ben Pollack and Benny Goodman, James struck out on his own in 1939. Among his discoveries was a singing Master of Ceremonies named Frank Sinatra. When Sinatra left him to join Tommy Dorsey, James replaced him with another discovery, Dick Haymes. James was not exclusively a jazz musician. He enjoyed showing off his amazing technique with trumpet solos like Rimsky-Korsakov's *Flight of the Bumblebee* and *Carnival of Venice*. When James recorded "You Made Me Love You," one of Judy Garland's biggest vocal hits, he became one of the major stars of popular music. His rich, full tone and vibrato became characteristics of the James style. He inevitably went to Hollywood, where he began appearing in movies and married actress Betty Grable. James's critics suggested that he was "commercial," a term used negatively by some jazz aficionados, but hardly a detriment in the music business. James insisted that he played the music he liked. If such music turned out to be pure jazz or popular music, he simply didn't care. Harry James continued to lead one of America's most popular bands. When the swing era ended, he remained in demand as a soloist and continued to lead bands until his death in 1983.

Ben Pollack's band helped launch quite a number of musical careers. Several of his leading musicians felt that Pollack was devoting too much time to his wife's singing career. The phenomenal success of Benny Goodman inspired the men to form a cooperative group of their own. Gil Rudin was elected to manage the business affairs of the band, but he believed that the designated "leader" of the band should be someone with a personality that would appeal to the public. The band hired Bob Crosby. Crosby, the younger brother of singing star Bing Crosby, was a personable vocalist in his own right. With Crosby in front of the band and Rudin managing things behind the scenes, members of the band found themselves in an unusually cordial working situation. But the band caused controversy with its highly individual style. Crosby's band played quite a number of arrangements in a Dixieland style, but scored for a larger ensemble. Crosby continued for lead bands for years after the swing era ended, also working with his smaller group, the Bobcats.

Stan Kenton was unlike any other bandleader, always musically adventurous, and in search of "new sounds." Throughout his career, he challenged his listeners to join him in pursuit of new music that drew upon the energy and inspiration of jazz and the rhythmic and harmonic complexity of contemporary classical music. Kenton grew up in California, where to the consternation of his mother, a classical piano teacher, he became obsessed with the idea of becoming a jazz musician. A noted jazz pianist advised him, "Only listen to two musicians, Louis Armstrong and Earl Hines, and try to emulate what they're doing." After working with several bands, he became convinced that only through leading his own ensemble could he achieve personal expression. Kenton led several bands throughout his career. His orchestras, as he preferred to call them, were each designed to reflect Kenton's latest musical concept. Kenton's characteristic sound presented high volume arrangements featuring thundering brass and complex orchestrations.

From the beginning, Kenton marched to his own drummer. His signature theme, *Artistry in Rhythm*, was inspired by the harmonies of Maurice Ravel and a musical motif from Ravel's *Daphnis and Chloe*. Kenton took himself and his music seriously. *Artistry in Rhythm* became a hit in 1943. Kenton began adding personnel and he chose wisely. His various bands and orchestras became a launching pad for several generations of musicians who frequently became stars in the own right. Foremost among them was the very gifted composer-arranger Pete Rugolo, who wrote many of the band's arrangements and became Kenton's most important creative collaborator. (Rugolo would become best-known to the public in later years for his imaginative scores for popular television programs including *The Fugitive* and *Run for Your Life*.)

Figure 158 - Stan Kenton, a lifetime in search of "new sounds." (Photo courtesy of CSULA, The California State University, Los Angeles, John F Kennedy Memorial Library)

Kenton's ensembles began performing and recording more pieces with "artistry" motifs, including *Artistry in Bolero* and *Artistry in Jumps*. In 1945, Kenton had hired Shirley Luster, a Chicago teenager. He changed her name to June Christy; her first recording with the band was *Tampico*, a major hit. In August of 1949, Kenton made plans for an incredibly ambitious series of concerts using strings as well as the usual brass and reeds. Top soloists joined the ensemble, including Art Pepper and Bud Shank on saxophone, Maynard Ferguson and Shorty Rogers on trumpet, Laurindo Almeida on guitar, and Shelley Manne on drums.

In 1950, Kenton launched his most unusual band, which he called "Innovations in Modern Music." This forty-three piece orchestra included a string section, French horns, a tuba, as well as expanded sections with more typical big band instruments: five trumpets, five trombones, and a five-piece rhythm section.

Kenton clearly had his eye on the concert hall. Several of the pieces played by the group were named after Kenton's star soloists, including his drummer Shelley Manne and vocalist June Christy. The group did not perform conventional dance band music. Kenton was fascinated by pure sound, the louder, the better. Bob Graettinger, a highly experimental arranger-composer, created concert suites for the band, *City of Glass* and *This Modern World*. Graettinger traveled with the band and studied the sounds of individual performers. Using a technique developed by Duke Ellington, he wrote parts designed to exploit the particular talents of specific players who happened to be working with Kenton.

Reaction to Kenton's experiments was mixed. Throughout his career, Kenton inspired the devotion of fans and admirers. He was known to treat his musicians well and those who worked for Kenton often said he was the first leader to give them the respect they deserved. In turn, they admired his desire to use jazz as a springboard to create a whole new style of concert music. Critics, however, were abundant. Audiences looking for fast dance music were not going to find it in Kenton's ambitious concert pieces, which related more to symphonic works by Bartók than an excuse for teenagers to dance the jitterbug. Criticism of Kenton's approach usually challenged him on two grounds: his use of highly detailed written scores and his departure from a steady, predictable jazz beat. Both of these were expressed by the pianist-teacher Lennie Tristano, who said bluntly, "Stan's writers don't generally write things that swing." Tristano also declared that Kenton's approach, which was that of the composer who created his scores in writing, didn't produce jazz comparable to that of the best improvisers.

Figure 159 - Stan Kenton brought an evangelical fervor to musical performances, composing, and arrangements. (Photo courtesy of CSULA, The California State University, Los Angeles, John F Kennedy Memorial Library)

Kenton could always respond to his critics; he was the most enthusiastic promoter the jazz world had ever seen. His jazz clinics brought jazz to college campuses and inspired countless music students to try their hand at a musical genre that hadn't previously been welcome in the groves of academe. Jazz historian Leonard Feather wrote, "Whatever the sideshow he introduced, be it the sword swallowing attempt of the arranger to incorporate the steel of Hindemith into the body of Hampton or the two-headed man who could talk simultaneously in the languages of Tanglewood and Birdland, he has never failed to draw attention to jazz." Eventually, Kenton would scale down the huge ensemble, not because of the controversy it inspired, but the costs it required.

Kenton called his next ensemble "New Concepts in Artistry in Rhythm." The nineteen-piece band featured arrangements by Gerry Mulligan, Shorty Rogers, and Bill Holman. While this group played a more conventionally swinging brand of jazz, Kenton always remained fascinated by the larger forms of concert music. Arranger-composer Johnny Richards supplied Kenton with his highly successful *Cuban Fire* suite. In the 1960s, Kenton had still another twenty-three piece ensemble dubbed the "Mellophonium" band because of the presence of an unlikely jazz instrument. (He officially called it the "New Era in Modern Music" orchestra.) He also helped create the Los Angeles "Neophonic Orchestra," again combining elements of jazz and concert music.

Until his death in 1979, Kenton remained enthusiastic in his pursuit of "new sounds." He continued to lead a variety of experimental orchestras surviving decades after many of his more conventional rivals had faded from the scene. Throughout his career, Kenton always continued to search for new combinations of instruments organized as jazz ensembles in concert. He declared himself always in search of something new and revolutionary in the world of jazz.

When Stan Kenton received an honorary doctorate from Drury College, he advised students to look forward, not back. At the beginning of a *Mark My Words!* radio interview, he said he had only two conditions: he wanted to be called "Stan," not "Mr. Kenton," and he wanted to talk about the future, not the past. "I'm not into nostalgia," he said. Despite a lifelong fascination with musical experimentation and years of expressing himself as an advocate of the future, not the past, Kenton saw the rock revolution for what it was. When jazz historian George Simon wrote his book, *The Big Bands*, he visited Kenton who declared, "You compare the Beatles' lyrics with those of some great writers like Johnny Burke, Johnny Mercer, Jimmy Van Heusen, or Sammy Cahn . . . are we kiddin' each other?" Kenton always wanted to challenge his musicians, his listeners, and himself. Whether his music was always swinging jazz or not, his legacy was undeniable.

JAZZ ROYALTY II: THE DUKE AND THE COUNT

The success of many of the white bandleaders, especially Benny Goodman's crowning as *The King of Swing*, must have been difficult for black bandleaders, many of whom had been working for so long with the additional barrier of racial prejudice in their path.

When Goodman's band achieved its tremendous success in 1935, Duke Ellington's had toiled for years to create a distinct and original voice in jazz. For 50 years, Ellington led a unique jazz orchestra that included some of the world's finest soloists.

Although Duke Ellington was best-known to the public as the composer of numerous hit songs, he was far more than a songwriter. He wrote over 5,000 compositions, including concert suites, theater pieces, motion picture scores, and music for sacred concerts. It is nearly impossible to summarize his career in a few words. He was a larger than life figure with a dynamic personality; his creative imagination led to praise from such classical music icons as Leopold Stokowski and Igor Stravinsky, who called him one of America's greatest living composers.

Edward Kennedy "Duke" Ellington was born in Washington, D.C., in 1899, the son of a butler, who once served in the White House. Even as a child, Ellington was displaying the charisma that would captivate audiences and musicians around the world. (He told his cousins, "I am the grand and noble Duke, crowds will be running to me.") His predictions would come true. When Ellington went to the White House, in which his father had once worked, it was to attend a formal dinner in his honor hosted by the man Ralph Ellison described as "another piano player of note, President Richard M. Nixon." Ellington was an urbane, articulate man of restless energy. He delighted in flowery speech and spoke with what one writer called "Ambassadorial elegance." A typical bandleader might tell the audience, "For our next number, we'd like to play one of our hits." Contrast this approach with that of Ellington. Long after the swing era had passed, he once introduced *Bourbon Street Jingling Jollies*, a movement of his *New Orleans Suite*, by informing the audience that his ensemble was about to express "the excruciating ecstasy we find ourselves suspended in when in the throes of the rhythmic joy of Bourbon Street." At the height of his fame, he was a world-traveler who took pleasure in the company of beautiful women, a substantial wardrobe (including forty-five suits and a thousand ties,) and gourmet cuisine. In his autobiography, *Music is My Mistress*, he devoted one whole section to memorable meals he enjoyed. Wherever he went — in hotel rooms, on trains, in cars, he was constantly composing, always sketching new musical ideas on paper.

Figure 160 - Duke Ellington, justly known as a musician "Beyond Category." (Photo courtesy of Glenn Miller Archive, American Music Research Center, University of Colorado, Boulder. All Rights Reserved)

He displayed talent for both art and music. He initially admired the work of the New York stride pianists, James P. Johnson and Willie "The Lion" Smith. In 1923, he went to New York. He led an ensemble for several years at the Kentucky Club and in 1927, moved to the Cotton Club where he remained until 1932. During this period, Ellington's orchestra began to achieve widespread recognition, in films, concerts, and especially, through nationwide radio broadcasts. Unlike other leaders who wrote for sections, Ellington often tailored pieces to the particular skills of his soloists.

They were an outstanding group: New Orleans clarinetist Barney Bigard contributed his musical imagination to Ellington classics like *Mood Indigo* and *C Jam Blues*. Jimmy Hamilton, who replaced Bigard in 1943, stayed with Ellington until 1968. Trumpeter James "Bubber" Miley developed a growling style that became a trademark of the Ellington ensemble and terminated any thoughts Ellington had of leading a "sweet band." (Rival bands actually sent spies to determine how Miley produced these sounds.) It was the sound of Miley's poignant, blues-driven trumpet that moved listeners emotionally when they heard Ellington's 1927 hit, *Black and Tan Fantasy*. The piece won the praise of a new audience for jazz, critics, writers, artists, and intellectuals, who declared that Ellington was creating a new music that showed the true artistic potential of jazz.

Charles Melvin "Cootie" Williams replaced Miley, and developed his own brand of "growling trumpet," which Ellington used to advantage in his *Concerto for Cootie*. Trumpeter William Alonzo "Cat" Anderson was a master of the plunger mute and half-valve techniques that enabled him to produced a rich, full tone in the highest register. Ray Nance, a master showman, played violin as well as trumpet. Trombonists included the Anglophile Joe "Tricky Sam" Nanton, whose "growling" sound matched Bubber Miley, and the fleet fingered Puerto Rican, Juan Tizol, a creative composer who provided Ellington such hits as "Caravan" and "Perdido." Baritone saxophonist Harry Carney was Ellington's protégé, personal driver, and close friend. He died only four months after Ellington, after a lifetime of devotion. Carney's childhood neighbor, Johnny "Rabbit" Hodges, soloed on alto and soprano saxophone. Hodges joined Ellington in 1928 and remained with Ellington's band virtually until his death in 1970, although he did take a four-year sabbatical to start a band of his own. In his eulogy for Hodges, Ellington said, "Never the world's most highly animated showman or greatest stage personality, but a tone so beautiful it sometimes brought tears to the eyes—this was Johnny Hodges. This *is* Johnny Hodges."

Ben Webster, who joined Ellington in 1940, was the first major tenor saxophonist in the group, but he left Ellington after a disagreement. In 1956, saxophonist Paul Gonsalves, a veteran of many years with Ellington, played one of the most famous solos in jazz history. At the time, Ellington's ensemble had been before the public for more than three decades. Some were suggesting that the Duke's music was old-fashioned and in decline. Audiences seemed uninspired and the evening was late when Ellington's orchestra took the stage at the Newport Jazz Festival. Audiences in Rhode Island and around the world went wild when Gonsalves improvised chorus after chorus in a performance of Ellington's *Diminuendo and Crescendo in Blue*. The episode became a legend and Ellington returned to the pinnacle of the jazz world. Over the years, Ellington also employed outstanding rhythm sections, including drummer Louis Bellson and bassist Oscar Pettiford.

To the public, Ellington became well-known as the writer of highly original songs that became classics: "Mood Indigo," "Sophisticated Lady," "Satin Doll," "Solitude," "Prelude to a Kiss," "I'm Beginning to See the Light," "It Don't Mean a Thing," and "In a Sentimental Mood," among others. His melodies contained the rhythmic and harmonic elements of jazz, including syncopations and blue notes. Their harmonies were often complex and surprising. Unlike songwriters who tried borrowing or adapting elements of jazz, when Ellington used them, they were part of his natural creative musical vocabulary.

Ellington was a raconteur who loved to tell stories about how his works were created. Sometimes, like Cole Porter, he had multiple stories about the origins of the same composition. For instance, the Duke insisted that he needed an extra number for a six piece recording session the next day and wrote "Mood Indigo" while waiting for his dinner. But clarinetist Barney Bigard, who later sued Ellington, said that he not only played "Mood Indigo," but actually developed the piece himself using musical ideas created by his New Orleans clarinet teacher, Leonard Tio, Jr. Ellington's biographer, James Lincoln Collier, also quotes New Orleans jazz expert Al Rose as having heard the piece performed by the A.J. Piron orchestra before Ellington played it.

"In a Sentimental Mood," another Ellington classic, also has a history. Ellington said he created the song so he could dedicate it to two girls who had quarreled at a party he attended in Durham, North Carolina. But several historians suggest that soprano saxophonist Otto Hardwick, who introduced the melody, also helped create it. Hardwick has also been credited by some with composing the complex bridge section of Ellington's "Sophisticated Lady," with the main melody written by Lawrence Brown. But Ellington himself recalled struggling for weeks over the "bridge" or middle section of the tune.

It was as an orchestrator and arranger that Ellington made his mark on musicians. The tremendous success of Benny Goodman's band launched the swing era and bands by the dozens began organizing to meet the new demand of young listeners eager for "hot music." Duke Ellington, however, was a leader, not a follower, and his approach to his ensemble was quite different than that of typical "swing bands." Many of these groups developed energy by alternating sections of their bands.

Ellington liked to experiment with counterpoint, offsetting melodic lines against each other. He would write passages combining various sections of the band on the same melodic line. (In works like the "Creole Love Call," he used a *vocalise*, a wordless melodic line sung by the human voice.) Ellington used more dissonance in his arrangements than the "sweet bands" and he liked to use provocative orchestral effects not associated with dance music. Most importantly, Ellington chose to feature primarily original music with an occasional standard tune to please audiences. Many of the popular swing bands did just the opposite, creating original hits, but emphasizing swinging versions of popular tunes the public already knew. Still, the tremendous success of the swing bands made jazz more commercially appealing. Throughout the swing era and for years after it ended, the Duke Ellington ensembles continued to set the standard for original jazz orchestration.

In 1938, the Stanley Theater in Pittsburgh booked an appearance by Ellington's band, to be followed by Count Basie's ensemble. Ellington agreed to audition a young pianist-composer named Billy Strayhorn. The twenty-three year old Strayhorn had extensive training in classical music at the Pittsburgh Musical Institute and had performed Edvard Greig's *Piano Concerto* while still in his teens. He was especially drawn to the music of Debussy and Ravel, but he also led his own jazz group, "The Madhatters." He had decided to take to Ellington and Basie the songs he had been writing. No one knows how Basie would have reacted, because the astonished Ellington hired him on the spot. When he was only eighteen, he had written "Lush Life," one of the most harmonically and melodically complex songs written and with a lyric one would have expected from the world-weary Nöel Coward, not a Pittsburgh teenager.

For thirty years, Strayhorn became Ellington's musical alter ego, composing and arranging in a style so similar to the Duke that Ellington called him, "my right arm, my left arm, all the eyes in the back of my head, my brain waves in his head and his in mine." The two men could not have been more different. Ellington, sixteen years Strayhorn's senior, basked in the spotlight; Strayhorn, quiet and retiring, was a shy man happiest among the friends who nicknamed him "Swee' Pea." While the public wasn't always aware of Strayhorn's exceptional musical gifts, his fellow musicians regarded him with the greatest respect. Singing star Lena Horne asked him to coach her to expand her knowledge of classical music. Benny Carter said of Strayhorn's work, "It made us all think differently about what we were doing." Dizzy Gillespie said, "All those sevenths, man, I never heard anything like those things until him."

Figure 161 - Billy Strayhorn, a gifted pianist and composer in his own right, was Ellington's musical alter ego. (Photo courtesy of The Carl Van Vechten Collection, Library of Congress)

In 1940, a contract dispute was keeping Ellington's songs off the radio and the Duke needed new songs quickly. Strayhorn responded with "Passion Flower," "Day Dream," "Chelsea Bridge," and "Take the A Train." The latter, dashed off by Strayhorn in a single afternoon after receiving instructions from Ellington, became Ellington's theme and to this day is often mistakenly credited to the Duke by his fans. One of Strayhorn's melodies, performed under several titles, eventually became "Lotus Blossom," which Ellington used to conclude his concerts.

Strayhorn collaborated with Ellington a number of songs and concert works. "Isfahan," added to the Ellington-Strayhorn *Far East Suite,* became a major jazz standard. Strayhorn, a heavy smoker, died in 1967 and Ellington paid tribute to him by recording a collection of his compositions, *And His Mother Called Him Bill.* At the end of the recording session for this tribute, Ellington sat alone at the piano playing Strayhorn's wistful melody, "Lotus Blossom." Harry Carney unpacked his baritone saxophone and Aaron Bell joined the duo on bass in a final elegy for the memorable Billy Strayhorn. Ellington saw jazz as a medium of serious expression. He wrote an estimated thirty-three concert pieces designed for performance in the concert hall, not on the bandstand. Though he avoided political controversy, he was a student of African-American history. He penned highly original concert suites inspired by many subjects, ranging from the *Deep South Suite* to the *Liberian Suite* to *The Queen's Suite.* The sole recording of the latter was presented to Queen Elizabeth II and was only available to the public on record after Ellington's death.

One of his concert suites, *Black, Brown and Beige,* was described by Ellington as "A Musical History of the American Negro." The *Harlem Suite* was commissioned by the NBC

Symphony; it premiered at the Metropolitan Opera House under the baton of the formidable conductor for whom the NBC Symphony had been created, Arturo Toscanini. Ellington was inspired by many works of great literature, including those of William Shakespeare, T.S. Eliot, and John Steinbeck. It was Steinbeck's writing that led to *Suite Thursday,* a work initiated by Ellington with additions by Strayhorn. Neither man heard the other's contribution until the work was actually performed. Ellington's interest in ambitious concert works remained long after the end of the big band era. Both Duke Ellington and Billy Strayhorn were interested in writing works that transcended musical boundaries. The Duke of Jazz met the reigning Queen Elizabeth II at a private reception and told her she was so inspiring, something musical would come out of it. "Something musical" turned out to be Ellington's work, *The Queen's Suite.* Two of the suites by Ellington and Strayhorn were musical expressions of the struggles and triumphs of African Americans: *Jump for Joy* (1950) and *My People* (1963), written for the Century of Negro Progress Exposition in Chicago. Both works called for choreography and narration as well as music. Near the end of his life, Ellington devoted his time to the now famous *Sacred Concerts* in which he used music to express his religious beliefs. He regarded these *Sacred Concerts* as his most important musical work.

Figure 162 - Duke Ellington (seated at the microphone) and Billy Strayhorn (seated to the left of the microphone) join colleagues in a radio interview with Willis Conover. (Photo courtesy of Willis Conover Collection, North Texas University Music Library)

Critics and historians alike spent years trying unsuccessfully to classify Ellington. To be sure, he earned worldwide praise. When British critic Stanley Dance delivered Ellington's eulogy, he called him, "a genius of the rarest kind." Blaise Cendrars, the French surrealist poet, was so stunned by Ellington's creativity that he declared, "Such music is not only a new art form, but a new reason for living." Ellington's music, derived from the heritage of black Americans though incorporating improvisation and instrumentation associated with dance bands, was far more complex than typical popular music. His interest in creating large concert pieces suggested an ambition to move into a symphonic genre. This created controversy on both sides of the musical fence. Jazz champion John Hammond suggested that Ellington was moving away from his jazz roots; he was rebuffed in print by his colleague Leonard Feather. Nor did classical music educators provide a red carpet to welcome Ellington to the concert hall. When Mark Schubart, at the time, dean of the Juilliard School of Music, said that Ellington's music required a totally different technique than that need to play serious symphonic music, the Duke was amused. He told an interviewer that "Classical music is supposed to be 200 years old. There is no such thing as modern classic music. There is great, serious music." In 1944, *Time* magazine music critic Winthrop Sargeant published an article provocatively entitled, "Is Jazz Music?"

Ellington responded. He said, "To attempt to elevate the level of the jazz musician by forcing comparisons of his best work with classical music is to deny him his rightful share of originality." On one hand, Ellington acknowledged that he shared with European symphonic composers a desire "to imbue my work with disciplined structure and orchestration." But he also pointed out how many contemporary composers of so-called "serious" music had been influenced by jazz, putting the shoe squarely on the other foot. Quipped Ellington, "I could no more compose like Brahms than he could beat out the jive in a 52nd Street nightspot."

After Ellington died in 1974, his music did not disappear. Composer-historian Gunther Schuller urged the establishment of a jazz repertory: performances of the finest recorded jazz by live orchestras. Ellington's son, trumpeter, Mercer Ellington, continued to lead the band in performing his father's music. A school in Washington, D.C. was named "The Duke Ellington School of the Arts." (The school opened with a concert led by Mercer Ellington and featured Duke Ellington's granddaughter, Mercedes Ellington, as a solo dancer.) Today, Ellington's works are performed and are considered as contemporary as the day they were written. Ellington was fond of telling audiences, "I love you madly." The world still feels the same way about his music.

Figure 163 - William "Count" Basie - His hard-driving bands used "head charts," improvising in their unique way on jazz riffs. (Photo courtesy of Glenn Miller Archive, American Music Research Center, University of Colorado, Boulder. All Rights Reserved.)

The only band to rival Ellington's ensemble for longevity was led by the remarkable Count Basie. William "Count" Basie was a pianist working as a vaudeville accompanist. He had once taken informal lessons from the slightly older "Fats" Waller, while working in a Harlem movie theater. He found himself stranded in Kansas City, where he eventually joined Bennie Moten's band. After Moten's band broke up, Basie organized his own ensemble and hired several of Moten's best players as members. A radio announcer suggested that Basie become "The Count" to match the royal title assumed by "Duke" Ellington. Basie's soloists, like the brilliant tenor saxophonists Lester Young and Herschel Evans, combined swing and spontaneity. Basie's bands included great soloists on the trumpet (Oren "Hot

Lips" Page, Buck Clayton, and Harry "Sweets" Edison) and trombonists (Dickie Wells and Benny Morton).

In contrast to the precision developed by Jimmie Lunceford, Basie led a band that concentrated on improvisation. The Basie band often used "head arrangements," those that were not written down but were based on riffs—short, pungent jazz phrases that could be repeated over and over. Musicians would remember the phrases and use them from one concert to another. Many of Basie's biggest hits, such as "One O'Clock Jump" and "Jumping at the Woodside," originated in this way. "One O'Clock Jump" was inspired by a riff created by "Fats" Waller and was so strongly identified with Basie that it became his theme. Basie did not actually "compose" the piece, which resulted from the collaborative efforts of several of his musicians, including Buster Smith and Buck Clayton. Basie's deceptively simple sound was derived from a style that had originated in Kansas City and the southwest, and was nearly always permeated by the feeling of the blues.

Basie's colleagues in his rhythm section were guitarist Freddie Green, bassist Walter Page, and drummer Jo Jones. Page provided a "walking bass" sound that led the beat, while Jones kept time in his own relaxed, casual way, often using brushes. Jones led other drummers in emphasizing the "high-hat" cymbal instead of the bass drum. The rhythm section enabled Basie to accompany soloists with his own brand of sparse, punctuating jazz. Though Basie could play stride piano in the style of his one-time mentor, "Fats" Waller, he became famous for his ability to generate absolutely ferocious rhythmic swing by playing only a few notes, wittily interpolated into an arrangement at exactly the right moment. Basie's rhythm section, which stayed together for many years, became known as the "rhythm machine." Basie would prove one of the most enduring bandleaders. Decades after the big band era was over, he was still presenting bands in his own familiar style: incredibly driving swing and his own witty, understated keyboard commentary at the piano. Nobody could swing with more vitality than the Count Basie band. Although Basie was overshadowed in early years by rivals, in retrospect, he remains one of the most important figures of the swing era. When asked by a reporter to describe the meaning of his music, Basie said "Pat your foot."

Figure 164 - Lionel Hampton, was the first major jazz musician to prominently use the vibraphone in his preformance, at The Aquarium, 1946. (Photo courtesy of William P. Gottlieb Collection, Library of Congress)

Lionel Hampton was the first jazz musician to prominently use the vibraphone. Hampton was taught to play the snare drum by a Dominican nun at the Holy Rosary Academy in Kenosha, Wisconsin. He eventually joined Les Hite's band backing Louis Armstrong at the Los Angeles Cotton

Club. As a drummer, Hampton was a natural showman; he could toss his drumsticks in the air and catch them without missing a beat. He applied this same sense of showmanship to the other percussion instruments he played. His idol, Jimmy Bertrand, had given him lessons on the xylophone and when he married the dancer Gladys Riddle, she became his business manager and encouraged him to feature the vibraphone. He formed his own band to showcase his skill on the "vibes" and was promptly discovered at the Paradise Cafe. Benny Goodman expanded his interracial Trio to a Quartet when he invited Hampton to join him. This led to a major recording contract and with Goodman's approval, he eventually formed his own band and achieved a huge success with his recordings of "Flying Home," especially a 1942 pressing featuring the saxophone virtuosity of Illinois Jacquet.

Hampton's band was one of the longest surviving jazz ensembles in history and over the years, a launching pad for an incredible variety of talent, including vocalists Joe Williams and Dinah Washington, bassist Charles Mingus, trumpeters Clark Terry and Art Farmer, and saxophonists Illinois Jacquet and Dexter Gordon, to mention only a few. Despite his carefree showmanship on the bandstand, Hampton was known not only for energy and enthusiasm, but his personal discipline. When he died at age 94, he could look back on a number of non-musical achievements as well, including numerous charitable activities and the development of public housing projects as well as a major role in Republican politics in New York. The University of Idaho's School of Music was named for him, the first instance of a major college music school being named for a jazz musician. Hampton and his bands always provided a sense of excitement to audiences and he will be remembered as the man who put the vibraphone firmly on the jazz map.

Benny Carter was equally at home on the saxophone or trumpet, a gifted composer and arranger, and the organizer of an international jazz orchestra in Europe. He organized his own band and like Jimmy Lunceford, achieved universal respect among musicians, even though his band never received commercial recognition comparable to his competitors. Carter initially planned to concentrate on theology; he was a quiet, affable man who didn't devote considerable time to promoting himself. During the swing era, he was considered, along with Johnny Hodges, one of the two major influences in playing the saxophone. In 1937, he spent a summer at a Dutch seaside resort leading a large interracial band at a time when such an ensemble would have been highly unusual in the U.S. Carter wrote arrangements for Fletcher Henderson and Benny Goodman, among others, and his sophisticated, complex arrangements outlasted his fame as a performer or bandleader. Eventually, Carter settled in Hollywood where he continued performing and devoted considerable time composing and arranging for films and television. He also turned to teaching as a visiting professor at Princeton. His incredible career spanned eight decades. Benny Carter may not have been as well known as jazz performers or bandleaders who craved public attention, but he enjoyed the greatest respect of musicians everywhere who nicknamed him "King."

Not all the big bands played improvisational jazz. During the swing era, American audiences were also captivated by Latin-American dance music. The rumba became the most popular Latin dance of the time and its best-known advocate was the colorful and flamboyant bandleader, Xavier Cugat. Born in Spain, Cugat moved to Cuba with his parents when his father was ordered to leave Spain because of his opposition to the Spanish monarchy. Tenor Enrico Caruso and violinist Xavier Cugat were talented artists and shared a gift for caricature. Caruso brought Cugat to the United States as an opening act for his concerts. Cugat settled in New York and eventually went to Berlin to study with the formidable violinist Franz Kneisel. But when critics didn't regard him with the same respect they gave the reigning virtuosos, Jascha Heifetz, Efrem Zimbalist, and Mischa Elman, Cugat left music and became a political cartoonist for the *Los Angeles Times*. A friendship with silent film star Rudolph Valentino led him to provide background music on the sets of motion pictures and brought him back to music. In the 1930s, he emerged as the leader of the world's best-known Latin-American dance band, initially specializing in tangos, boleros, and congas.

Xavier Cugat led the resident orchestra at the Waldorf-Astoria Hotel in New York throughout the 1930s and 1940s. He often played himself in numerous Hollywood movie musicals, including several starring swimming icon Esther Williams. He was a gifted businessman with an eye for commercial appeal. When the mambo and the cha-cha gained popularity, Cugat was there to record them. Many of the performers he discovered, including Rita Hayworth, Dinah Shore, and Desi Arnaz, became huge stars. He married five times, always to actresses or singers who appeared with his band: Rita Montaner, Carmen Castillo, Lorraine Allen, Abbe Lane, and Charo. He believed that to reach American audiences, Latin-American music had to be a visual experience. He was famous for employing beautiful vocalists and displaying a trademark Chihuahua, which he would whip out of his pocket during performances. He remained "The Rumba King" throughout his long career; years after the big band era had ended, he was still playing, popularizing, and recording the music of Latin-America.

Figure 165 - Xavier Cugat, definitely the best-known Latin-American bandleader of his time, doing a caricature of one of his favorite subjects, himself. (Photo courtesy of William P. Gottlieb Collection, Library of Congress)

As the 1940s drew to a close, a number of leading musicians began to work in small groups outside the milieu of the big bands. Alumni of the bands became influential as they explored new rhythmic and harmonic vistas for their instruments, especially Ellington bassist Jimmy Blanton, Goodman guitarist Charlie Christian, Basie saxophonist Lester Young, and the trumpeter

Roy Eldridge who emerged as one of the most admired soloists on his instrument since Louis Armstrong.

Jimmy Blanton inspired a whole generation of players to create fresh melodic lines on the string bass and not limit themselves to simply outlining chord patterns. Blanton has been called the father of modern bass playing. He was equally at home plucking the strings of his bass or using his bow to create melodic effects. After Blanton's death, his successor was the much admired Oscar Pettiford. Pettiford, who grew up in Minneapolis, was the son of a veterinarian who organized a family band that included his eleven children as members. Pettiford's mother was a music teacher. Pettiford was especially gifted in creating melodic lines for the bass. In his hands, the instrument became not just a source of rhythmic punctuation, but a true messenger of musical expression.

Figure 166 - Lester Young, known as "Prez." His admirers elected him "President of the Saxophone." (Photo courtesy of William P. Gottlieb Collection, Library of Congress)

Lester Young used a lighter tone than his rivals Coleman Hawkins and Herschel Evans. He had admired the work of Frankie Trumbauer, a colleague of Bix Beiderbecke in the 1920s and master of the C-melody saxophone, an instrument with pitch half-way between the alto and tenor saxes. Young tried emulating that sound on his tenor saxophone, and produced the lyrical tone, apparently without vibrato, that became his trademark. Young also held his instrument at a forty-five degree angle to the floor, a mannerism that seemed to impress audiences and was copied by others.

Roy "Little Jazz" Eldridge was the dominant trumpet soloist of the 1930s. Influenced by Red Nichols, and by saxophonists Coleman Hawkins and Benny Carter, Eldridge was known for his powerful, driving swing and high register. He worked with numerous big bands, including Fletcher Henderson. Drummer Gene Krupa led a big band, which had been upstaged by Jimmy Lunceford's group. To strengthen his ensemble, he played the drums and worked in a duo with singer Anita O'Day. He also hired Roy Eldridge who starred on trumpet.

Charlie Christian, a young guitarist, grew up in Oklahoma City where he absorbed the sounds of the blues. According to legend, John Hammond and Artie Bernstein brought him to Victor Hugo's, a restaurant where Benny Goodman was playing, and moved Christian's gear on stage during an intermission. The young guitarist turned up wearing a ten-gallon hat, pointed yellow shoes, a bright green suit with a purple shirt, and a string bow tie. Goodman was furious to find him on the bandstand. A skeptical Goodman called for "Rose Room" and was so impressed by Christian's playing that he allowed the version of "Rose Room" to last for forty-five minutes. Goodman expanded his Quintet to a Sextet to make room for the gifted guitarist. Christian spent only twenty months with Goodman, but made a major mark in the jazz field. In his hands, the guitar was transformed from a novelty instrument to a vehicle for melodic design. Christian frequently participated in private jam sessions with pianist Mary Lou Williams in the basement of the Dewey Park Hotel; many of the melodic lines he created eventually became part of the Goodman repertoire. Unfortunately, Christian suffered from incipient tuberculosis. High living didn't help matters and Charlie Christian, the guitarist whose use of ninth, eleventh, and thirteen chords captured the fancy of musicians everywhere, died suddenly in 1942.

At the height of their popularity, the big bands (and their members) were idolized by their fans. Audiences knew the names of musicians and were reported in one poll to be more familiar with the personnel of bands than with the names of nearly everyone in America except for movie stars and 1930s gangsters. But the era came to a close almost as abruptly as it began. America's entry into World War II, after the attack on Pearl Harbor on Dec.7, 1941, was the beginning of the end. A 20 percent amusement tax and gasoline shortages made it difficult for fans to travel outside the city to go dancing. (The Glen Island Casino and the Meadowbrook were forced to close.) Musicians were drafted; those who remained behind could demand high salaries that bandleaders were unable to pay. Then in 1942, a recording strike imposed by the Musicians' Union led by its powerful president, James C. Petrillo, caused chaos. When musicians were unable to record, the field was left open to vocalists. Singing stars like Frank Sinatra, Bing Crosby, Perry Como, Dinah Shore, Jo Stafford, and Peggy Lee became the major attractions on record and replaced the big bands on radio. Sentimental ballads appealed to troops abroad and their wives and families at home. When the strike ended and the war was over, the swing bands seemed to have outlived their welcome. In December of 1946, eight of the leading bands broke up, including ensembles led by Benny Goodman, Woody Herman, Harry James, and Tommy Dorsey. The swing era of big bands had come to an end.

"GOD IS IN THE HOUSE" - THE LEGACY OF ART TATUM

During the swing era, the brilliant technique of a number of soloists helped stimulate the transition from the swing style to the next important period in jazz.

Teddy Wilson remained active at the piano long after his historic association with Benny Goodman opened the door for racially integrated jazz groups. Wilson was urbane and impeccably polished, musically and personally. (His mother was chief librarian at Tuskegee Institute, where his father was head of the English department.) Goodman called him "the greatest musician in dance music today, irrespective of instrument." Whereas other pianists pounded the keyboard, Wilson had the light classical touch of a jazz musician who practiced Scarlatti sonatas after hours. Teddy Wilson continued to work with Benny Goodman until 1939; he also recorded with Lester Young, Ben Webster, Buck Clayton, Lena Horne, and Billie Holiday. For two years, he led a big band of his own and then concentrated on leading small ensembles. Wilson rejoined Goodman over the years for major events including Goodman's historic tour of Russia and appearances at the Newport Jazz Festival and at Carnegie Hall.

Wilson's quiet demeanor was in sharp contrast to that of many flamboyant showmen of the jazz world. He devoted much time to teaching and mentoring younger musicians, and to social causes. (He leaned left politically and was dubbed by the tap dancer Howard "Stretch" Johnson, the "Marxist Mozart.") Wilson's refined approach to the keyboard allowed him to play melodies in octaves ornamented by glittering passages of broken chords. He maintained a steady "swing" beat with his left hand, but he often managed to develop counter-melodies with his left hand as well. This gave his playing a sophistication that made him the quintessential piano soloist of the swing era. As a pianist, Wilson had few peers. In the early 1930s, Wilson formed a personal and musical friendship with another pianist who became a legend in his lifetime and remains so today. His name was Art Tatum.

Figure 167- Teddy Wilson - His lilting phrasing and light touch made him one of the most admired pianists of the swing era. (Photo courtesy of William P. Gottlieb Collection, Library of Congress)

Tatum was nearly blind, a pianist whose technique rivaled that of the world's finest classical virtuosos. Virtually every jazz pianists of his time or since regarded Tatum as the undisputed master of the keyboard. His complete command of every aspect of his instrument and his technically dazzling performances left even the best pianists staring in disbelief. Born in Toledo, Ohio, in 1909, Tatum absorbed a host of influences during his formative years: church music, recordings and radio broadcasts of the Harlem stride pianists, and a considerable amount of classical music. Tatum was also impressed by the solos and arrangements of musicians who performed popular music outside the realm of jazz. Foremost among them was Lee Sims, who created his solos and arrangements of popular music under the influence of classical composers such as Debussy and Ravel. Tatum had an outgoing personality, generous to young pianists and colleagues, but he disliked talking about his personal life. So the Tatum legend remains, recalled and embellished by those who knew him.

Figure 168 - Art Tatum - When Tatum appeared, other pianists whispered, "God is in the house tonight." (Photo courtesy of William P. Gottlieb Collection, Library of Congress)

There was nothing Tatum could not do technically

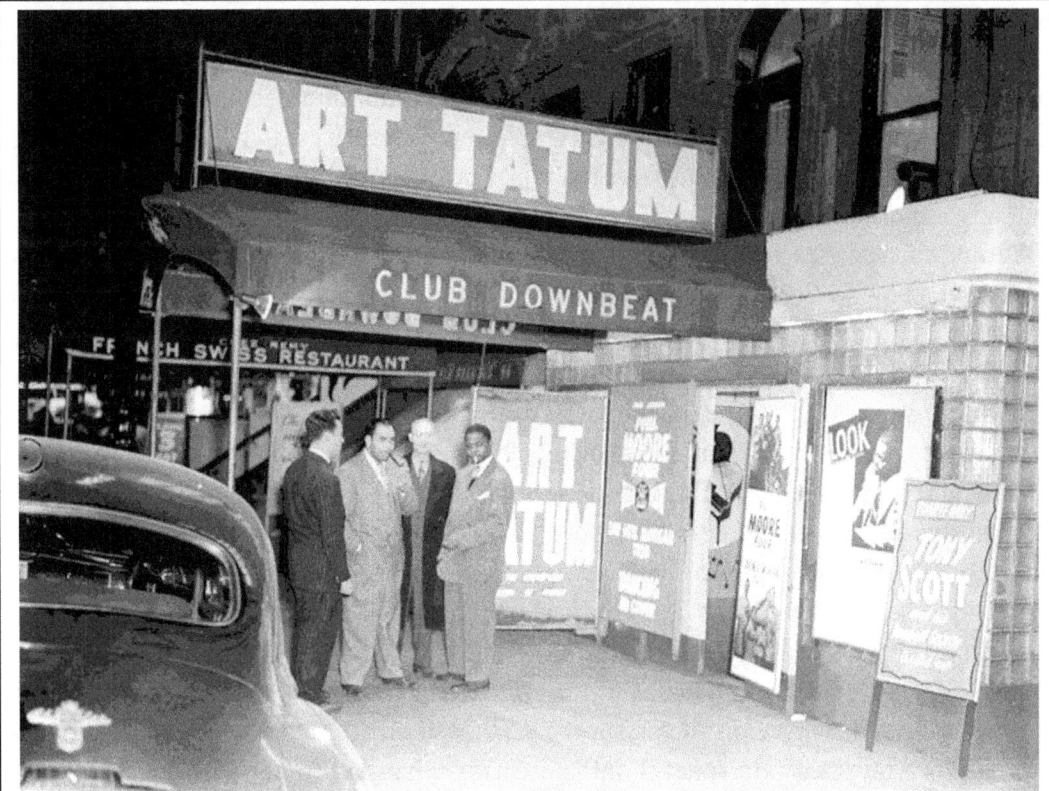

Figure 169 - Art Tatum and Phil Moore at the Club Downbeat, 1946-48. Tatum's dazzling left hand technique and right handed runs at blinding speed left even his most accomplished contemporaries speechless. (Photo courtesy of William P. Gottlieb Collection, Library of Congress)

on the piano. He joined singer Adelaide Hall as an accompanist, and eventually went to New York, where even the best pianists of the day responded in complete shock when they heard him. Tatum's gifts included a capacity to reharmonize the same melody in dozens of ways, each time choosing different chord progressions. He had an arsenal of runs, arpeggios, and musical embellishments that could turn anything, a simple popular tune, the blues, a rag, or a piece of classical music like Dvořák's *Humoresque,* into a stunning showpiece of virtuosity.

When Tatum arrived in New York, he was greeted by a "welcoming committee," the masters of Harlem stride, James P. Johnson, Willie "The Lion" Smith, "Fats" Waller, and Lippy Boyette, a pianist turned booking agent. The group went to Morgan's, a Harlem club, for a friendly duel. Tatum promptly played his version of "Tea for Two." Maurice Waller, "Fats" Waller's son and biographer, described what would be a typical Tatum performance: "Tatum's left hand worked a strong, regular beat while his right hand played dazzling arpeggios in chords loaded with flatted fifths and ninths. Both his hands then raced toward each other in skips and jumps that seemed impossible to master. James P. Johnson played his showpieces "Carolina Shout" and his version of Chopin's "Revolutionary Etude." Waller offered one of his most flamboyant solos, "A Handful of

Keys." When Tatum responded with an electrifying version of "Tiger Rag," the verdict was clear. Art Tatum was the undisputed champion of pianists, a crown he would retain for the rest of his life. An admiring "Fats" Waller said Tatum sounded like a brass band.

He also gave Tatum his most famous compliment when he said, "I only play the piano. But tonight God is in the house." Years later, jazz critic Barry Ulanov would quip, "Tatum, you can't imitatum!"

Tatum dazzled classical virtuosos as well, numbering Sergei Rachmaninoff, Leopold Stokowski, Leopold Godowsky, and Vladimir Horowitz among his admirers. The French playwright, filmmaker, and artist, Jean Cocteau dubbed Tatum "a crazed Chopin." On one occasion, he played for Ignacy Paderewski, the great Polish pianist and the most famous classical musician of his time, in the latter's private railroad car. Tatum could execute passages of great intricacy at unbelievably high speeds. But he could decorate and ornament a simple melody with stunning keyboard runs, all the while taking his left hand through a serious of harmonic modulations so quickly that few players could follow him. Many considered Vladimir Horowitz the greatest classical pianist of the century. The electricity, the exquisite tone quality, and the demonic fury he possessed were all legendary. Horowitz was known for closing concerts with dazzling transcriptions like his version of *The Stars and Stripes Forever* or his *Variations on Themes from Carmen*. Horowitz decided to develop such a showpiece based on an American popular song and selected "Tea for Two." He spent months creating what had to be the most technically difficult, demanding and dazzling version of "Tea for Two" ever set to paper, and then to test himself, played it for Tatum, who gave his approval. Tatum then responded with his own, equally complex version of "Tea for Two," which happened to be one of his major showpieces. "That's wonderful," said Horowitz, "every bit as good as my own. I took six months writing my arrangement. How long did it take you to do yours?" "That's not an arrangement," said Tatum, "That was an improvisation." Horowitz shelved his version of "Tea for Two" and didn't perform it in public.

Tatum never liked being described as a jazz musician. Although he worked with a trio for a time, he remained primarily a solo performer who drew upon many musical influences to create his own unique musical style. He inspired dozens of awe-struck pianists for generations to come. Pianist Billy Taylor, a Tatum protégé, recalled that his mentor gave impromptu lessons at the Hollywood Bar at 133rd St. and 7th Avenue in New York. Pianists like Bud Powell, Marlowe Morris, Dorothy Donegan, and Hank Jones absorbed the special fingering Tatum used to execute his dazzling keyboard runs. Nearly every jazz pianist (and not a small number of classical pianists) of consequence has a story or anecdote about his own initial reaction to Tatum's melodic and harmonic pyrotechnics.

Oscar Peterson, the Canadian virtuoso who became Tatum's friend and designated successor, never forgot his own first encounter with Tatum. As a teenager, Peterson developed a healthy ego and his demanding father, Daniel Peterson, decided that his gifted son needed a lesson in humility. He bought his son a recording of Tatum playing "Tiger Rag." Peterson could not even touch the piano for weeks. André Previn meticulously copied one of Tatum's classic versions of "Sweet Lorraine" until he could play it note for note. Years later, Peter Nero had a similar experience. Nero had studied at Juilliard and was guided by the duo-pianist team of Abram Chasins and Constance Keene, both friends of Vladimir Horowitz. Since he had classically trained to be a concert pianist, he could technically copy virtually anything he heard on a jazz record. But when he purchased an album entitled "The Genius of Art Tatum," he acknowledged his reaction as "very upset." On occasion, a brilliant pianist might dare to challenge Tatum. The bebop legend Bud Powell once made such a challenge. Tatum, although personally modest, told Powell, "Anything you do with your right hand, I'll do with my left." But Tatum's brilliance wasn't limited to speed alone.

What was also interesting about Tatum was his influence on non-keyboard performers. Tatum's capacity to reharmonize melodies with dozens of unexpected chords and changes of key were especially fascinating to saxophonists and trumpeters who saw in his work a whole new way of extracting chords from familiar pieces that could be used as the basis for their own improvisation. In recent years, concert violinist Itzhak Perlman declared that it was the discovery of Art Tatum's legacy that introduced him to American jazz.

Tatum died in 1956, but his music burns brightly in the memories of those who knew him and in the imagination of those discovering his work through recordings for the first time. Billy Taylor said, "Art Tatum was a genius whose mastery of time is still unmatched in solo jazz piano. His faultless subdivision of beats underscored his rhythmic security in improvisation. He was unquestionably the quintessential jazz pianist." Dave Brubeck said that there was about as much chance of another Tatum turning up as another Mozart. Count Basie dubbed him "The Eighth Wonder of the World." Teddy Wilson said that if you put the rest of the world's finest jazz pianists in a room and then had Tatum play, the rest would sound like amateurs. Oscar Peterson said that Tatum was the most complete jazz pianist of all time and he felt honored to be one of his humble and devoted disciples. He added, "I do not think we will see someone like him again."

TO BE OR NOT TO BOP: GILLESPIE, PARKER, MONK, AND POWELL

In the 1940s, a new approach to playing jazz turned the jazz world upside down. No one would have imagined the events that started a musical revolution. A number of young musicians began experimenting with music that was either too fast or too slow to be regarded as dance music. These musicians had a different attitude toward the music they played. They were primarily African American and wanted people to listen seriously to what they played rather than simply dancing to it. They saw themselves as artists, not entertainers. They created a style of music which became known as "Bebop" or "Bop" for

Figure 170 - 52nd Street: In the late 1940s, New Yorkers could hear the world's greatest jazzmen all in a few blocks. (Photo courtesy of William P. Gottlieb Collection, Library of Congress)

short. Many jazz historians have described bop as a rebellion against swing, but Billy Taylor has suggested that bop was actually swing's logical extension. Regardless of their intentions, these musicians sparked a revolution that changed the sound of jazz and the way it would be regarded forever. Though some of its leading players were still very young men when they died, the music they created at New York clubs like Minton's, The Onyx, The Five Spot, and The Three Deuces, continues to live in the memories of those who heard it and for generations of jazz fans discovering it for the first time. Throughout the 1930s and 1940s, an abundance of jazz clubs thrived on 52nd Street between Fifth and Seventh Avenues. While the bebop era began in Harlem, it moved downtown to 52nd Street where a listener could literally hear the greatest jazz innovators in the world all within the range of a few blocks.

The jazz revolution began inauspiciously. Teddy Hill was a saxophonist who fronted a band at the Harlem's Savoy Ballroom in the 1930s. Hill's band featured Roy Eldridge on trumpet and tenor saxophone soloist Chu Berry among others.

Then Hill hired a younger trumpeter, John Birks "Dizzy" Gillespie. The son of a South Carolina bricklayer, Gillespie had switched from trombone to trumpet, and eventually moved to Philadelphia where he absorbed the influence of his hero, Roy Eldridge. Gillespie quickly won a reputation as a dazzling technician and as the "bad boy of the bandstand." On one occasion, Hill ordered him to remove his foot from a chair. Gillespie promptly placed his foot on a music stand. From the beginning, Gillespie was fascinated by experimental harmonies. While working for the pianist-bandleader Edgar Hayes, he played an arrangement by Rudy Powell that contained an unusual chord, an E- flat major chord over an "A" in the bass. Gillespie played the chord over and over again, and even devoted a whole section of his autobiography to his discovery of "the flatted fifth." It was a sound that would help him launch a revolution a few years later.

In 1939, Gillespie joined Cab Calloway's band, where he became a trumpet star. Meanwhile, after his manager decided to concentrate his attention on another band, Teddy

Hill disbanded his ensemble. Henry Minton, the first black delegate in Local 802 of the Musicians' Union, owned a small club on 118th street in uptown Harlem. He asked Teddy Hill to manage the club. "Dizzy" Gillespie was not the only nonconformist who caused Hill problems. During the time he led his own band, Hill also had problems with drummer Kenny Clarke, who moved the ground beat of the rhythm section away from the drums and placed it on the large ride cymbal. Hill eventually fired Clarke. But when Hill accepted the offer to managed Minton's, he promptly dismissed the house band.

Figure 171 - Thelonious Monk, Howard McGhee, Roy Eldridge, and Teddy Hill at Minton's, the jazz club where bop was born. (Photo courtesy of William P. Gottlieb Collection, Library of Congress)

Despite having previously fired Kenny Clarke, Hill asked him to organize a new group to play at Minton's. Within a few weeks, some of the best big band players were turning up at Minton's to play in their own individual styles, experimenting with approaches that would have been unacceptable to the bandleaders who regularly employed them. Musicians working all over New York would drop in after hours for all-night jam sessions at Minton's. Foremost among the group was Dizzy Gillespie. Within a few weeks, Minton's would become a musical laboratory for several of the most experimental musicians in New York. No one would have imagined that Hill's hiring of Clarke and the arrival of Gillespie and his friends would spark a revolution. But that is precisely what happened.

Figure 172 - Thelonious Monk with his trademark beret and sunglasses, brought whimsy and unpredictability to the bop era as a composer. (Photo courtesy of William P. Gottlieb Collection, Library of Congress)

One musician, who was actually hired to work at Minton's, was the pianist and composer Thelonious Sphere Monk. Inevitably, Monk and Gillespie began exchanging musical ideas. Monk, described by Gillespie as "the most unique musician in our group," chose his own middle name, "Sphere," to prove he was not "Square." He was born in Rocky Mount, North Carolina, but he grew up in New York. Monk adopted what became the virtual uniform of the bop movement, a beret and horn rimmed glasses. Monk cultivated a sparse style of keyboard playing. Gillespie and Monk shared ideas regarding ways to alter the expected tones of chords and the chord progressions familiar to most swing musicians. Gillespie used chords containing notes a half-step away from the notes everyone expected. While Gillespie continued to work for Cab Calloway at the Cotton Club, he

Figure 173 - Charlie Parker, joined by Tommy Potter, Miles Davis, and Duke Jordan. Charlie "Bird" Parker was the leading saxophonist of the bop era. His speed and harmonic daring inspired generations of musicians. (Photo courtesy of William P. Gottlieb Collection, Library of Congress)

would devote his spare time to working out experimental chords and harmonic progressions for the jam sessions at Minton's. When the Calloway band took an intermission, Gillespie would join bassist Milt Hinton on the roof of the Cotton Club and outline his strategy for the late-night gathering at Minton's. Gillespie would call out the title of a standard tune, but arrange in advance to use a completely original set of chord progressions. These "changes" would frequently come as a surprise and a shock to musicians unprepared for the new, experimental way of playing. Though Dizzy protested his innocence, Calloway eventually fired Gillespie for allegedly hitting him with spitballs during a performance. Years later, Calloway and Gillespie reconciled and fellow trumpeter Jonah Jones admitted that he was responsible for the wayward spitball.

In 1941, Monk and Clarke discovered a little known saxophonist at Clark Monroe's Uptown House. His name was Charlie Parker. Parker was a native of Kansas City. After the death of his father, a song and dance man, Parker was raised by his mother. When she bought him a saxophone, he taught himself how to play. He married at only fifteen, and learned much of his technique from fellow Kansas bandleader Tommy Douglas and Henry "Buster" Smith, an alto saxophonist who made Parker his protégé and guided him musically. Parker also spent time copying recorded solos by Lester Young. His friends called him "Bird" or "Yardbird," allegedly because he liked fried chicken. Around 1941, Parker was working with Jay McShann's band and when Gillespie sat in with the band, the two musicians met. Soon Parker was a regular at the Minton's jam sessions, where he joined forces with Gillespie. Parker's approach to the alto saxophone left listeners speechless. Harmonically complex, technically facile, Parker could improvise at tremendous speeds. Gillespie said Parker's contributions were primarily in the areas of melody, accents, and "bluesy interpretation." Parker would introduce quotations from other musical compositions into the middle of an improvised melody.

At Minton's and in private jam sessions at the New York apartment of pianist Mary Lou Williams, they began experimenting with daring new sounds, playing fast pieces much faster than the swing bands and ballads at tempi slower than anyone had heard them before. They altered chords and often abandoned the melodies of familiar tunes. Instead, they created whole new melodies using only the chords of pieces they interpreted. Their jagged melodies were matched by an intense rhythmic complexity.

Mary Lou Williams recalled when this music was first heard in the 1940s, it sounded as if "Dizzy" Gillespie played a million notes in one bar.

Bop never attained the popularity of swing because it was music for listening, not dancing. When the bop pioneers performed ballads, they played at tempi many times slower than those used by the bands. But the real difference between swing and bop became clear when fast pieces were played. The bop players would swing at tempi two and three times as fast as the standard tempi preferred by swing bands. Bop players began accenting the second and fourth beats or "off-beats" of each musical measure. Since many of the top solos were never written down, musicians had to find some way to identify them. Dizzy Gillespie would sing a few "scat syllables" to the other musicians, often ending in

Figure 174 - Mary Lou Williams, pianist, whose New York apartment became the gathering place for bop musicians to experiment and turn the jazz world upside down. (Photo courtesy of William P. Gottlieb Collection, Library of Congress)

"bebop" or "rebop" to identify riffs or phrases of the pieces. Eventually, the period became known as the "bop era."

For admirers of classic swing, the sounds of bop came as a shock. The musicians who created these sounds didn't care about audiences wanting to dance to their music. They had their own ideas about musical performance and were determined to use jazz as a means of personal expression. Critics reacted derisively to the new music, which sounded strangely dissonant and experimental. Musicians unaccustomed to the new harmonic and rhythmic approaches were similarly startled. When Charlie Parker first started playing the saxophone, one of his idols had been Lester Young. One night, the great Lester Young himself visited Minton's and, unfamiliar with the repertoire or chord changes of the boppers, was virtually played off the bandstand.

"Dizzy" Gillespie was the organizer and motivational force among the bop musicians. He had a generous spirit and believed in sharing his musical discoveries and exchanging his ideas with colleagues. Some jazz musicians were inclined to protect their secrets, but Gillespie approached his view of jazz with an evangelical fervor. He liked to demonstrate his ideas on the piano and explained them to a wide variety of soloists on many instruments.

With brilliant technique and a capacity to hit high notes with ease, Gillespie established new standards of virtuosity for his instrument as Louis Armstrong had done two decades earlier. With Parker and his colleagues, he established bop as an energetic new movement in jazz suitable for performance by small ensembles and big bands. Gillespie and Parker both worked in a new big band organized by Billy Eckstine, which also featured some of the finest young jazz musicians, and a shy new singing star with a remarkable voice, Sarah Vaughan. The surprising rhythms and harmonies of bebop provoked controversy. The "flatted fifth" sound, which had fascinated Gillespie for years, became standard fare in the world of bebop. Jazz critic Gary Giddens wrote, "At the outset of bop, it was considered a terrible dissonance, a symptom of modern jazz's frantic assault on decency and good taste."

After leaving Charlie Barnet's band, bassist Oscar Pettiford frequented the jam sessions at Minton's regularly. In 1943, Gillespie and Pettiford led one of the first ensembles to perform bebop in public at a jazz club called The Onyx. Gillespie proudly recalled that audiences came to listen, not to dance. Parker and Gillespie were also booked to appear together on 52nd Street in New York, as audiences discovered the music that had once been the secret of musicians. In 1945, Gillespie and Parker appeared as members of a sextet at Billy Berg's jazz club in Los Angeles. Their arrival sparked so much controversy on the west coast that some compared their opening night to the infamous premiere of Stravinsky's *Rite of Spring*, a performance that caused a riot in Paris. In 1945, Parker and Gillespie joined forces for a series of historic records that completed the bop revolution and influenced many other musicians. The following year, Gillespie organized his own big band and kept it running for four years, even though the age of the great swing bands was over.

Figure 175 - "Dizzy" Gillespie admires a performance by Ella Fitzgerald with colleagues Ray Brown and Milt Jackson, while Danish jazz advocate Timmie Rosenkrantz watches. (Photo courtesy of William P. Gottlieb Collection, Library of Congress)

Gillespie was fascinated by the music of Cuba, and became the first musician of consequence to introduce Afro-Cuban rhythms to jazz. He stunned the jazz world again when he engaged Chano Pozo, a Cuban drummer, for his band. Luciano "Chano" Pozo Gonzales was a master of Afro-Cuban percussion who could also sing, dance, and of greatest importance, write music. The use of conga drums and Latin rhythms is widespread today, but Gillespie was the originator of the Latin influence in jazz bands. Pozo did not speak English, nor did Gillespie speak Spanish. When asked how they communicated, Pozo said, "Dizzy and I both speak African." Unfortunately, Chano Pozo was shot and killed in a Harlem bar under mysterious circumstances; his death was rumored to be the result of an argument over marijuana. Although he died young, Pozo left a legacy through the influence of Latin rhythms in pieces he co-wrote with Gillespie, including "Manteca" and "Tin Tin Deo," among Gillespie's biggest hits.

The most important pianist of the bop era was Earl "Bud" Powell. Born in New York, Powell studied seven years of classical piano before turning to jazz and appearing at

Minton's as a teenager where he met Monk and Parker. Stride pianists of the 1920s and the best keyboard artists of the swing era in the 1930s typically kept time with their left hands.

Figure 176 - Bud Powell was called "The Amazing Bud Powell" and with good reason. (Photo courtesy of Carl Smith, Budpowelljazz.com)

In contrast, Powell developed a percussive, pungent left hand that stabbed rhythmically as accompaniment. His right hand was capable of playing instrumental melodic lines on the keyboard. Just as Earl Hines had developed "horn lines" on the piano years before, Powell was capable of duplicating the complex and ornate melodies that Parker played. If Hines played trumpet-melodies on the piano, Powell played saxophone lines. Powell was also a composer and tunes like "Un Poco Loco" won him recognition as well. Blue Note Records dubbed him "The Amazing Bud Powell." No one listening to Powell articulating Bach-like lines at breakneck speeds in original pieces like "Tempus Fugit" would challenge the appellation.

The bebop movement produced its own repertoire of highly original compositions, full of irregular accents and harmonic surprises. The small ensembles and combos of the bop era produced a serious type of music that was jazz's equivalent of chamber music. A number of the pieces were created by Thelonious Monk. His most famous tune was "Round Midnight," a brooding, pensive melody. Monk also composed "Ruby, My Dear," "Blue Monk," "Off Minor," and "Straight, No Chaser." Monk was a rugged individualist, regarded as a nonconformist by some, an eccentric by others. Some critics called him the most original jazz composer since Duke Ellington. Others spoke skeptically of his pianistic style, with its long silences and nervous outbursts, questioning his keyboard technique. Monk was a rugged individualist, attracting attention for his wardrobe, including his trademark berets and sunglasses.

Another composer who made key contributions to the bop movement was Tadd Dameron. Dameron had been active as an arranger for the big bands of Jimmie Lunceford, Billy Eckstine, and Count Basie. Under Gillespie's the influence, Tadd Dameron absorbed the new rhythmic and harmonic techniques of bebop and began applying them to his arrangements. Gillespie, Dameron, and other bop musicians liked to create completely new melodic lines on the chord progressions of familiar tunes. They frequently chose tunes with complex progressions and added their own special brand of creativity. Musicians of the bop era would take familiar melodies known as "standards" and create entirely new improvised melodies, which even the composers of the original songs, might not recognize; the chords and the underlying harmony of the songs were the same, but the melodies were entirely different. The melodic lines created by the bop artists would reflect the startling rhythms, syncopations, and melodic surprises of the times. Charlie Parker took the harmonic foundation of "Cherokee," disposed of the melody, and created his own, "Ko-Ko." Parker's improvised melodic lines, played at breakneck speeds, set a new standard for jazz technique. Gary Giddens called "Ko-Ko" a "point of departure for the postwar jazz era," and compared its effect to Louis Armstrong's celebrated solo based on "West End Blues" in 1928. Parker based his classic melody, "Ornithology," on the jazz favorite, "How High the Moon." Tadd Dameron used Cole Porter's "What Is This Thing Called Love?" to create his own melody, "Hot-House." Gillespie turned the standard "Whispering" into his own original, "Groovin' High." Parker's original compositions were often transcriptions of his improvised melodies, written down so that other players could join him note for note before taking off on their own. His tunes did not sound like popular songs. They were jazz lines, having more in common with baroque instrumental classical music than with the tunes of Tin Pan Alley. Gillespie also wrote original pieces including "Salt Peanuts," "Con Alma," and the melody which came to symbolize the bop era, "A Night in Tunisia."

Figure 177 - Dizzy Gillespie, Tadd Dameron, Hank Jones, Mary Lou Williams, and Milt Orent discuss the state of jazz at Williams' apartment. (Photo courtesy of William P. Gottlieb Collection Library of Congress.)

Sadly, the personal habits and misfortunes of the founders of bebop brought the era to a close. Even as a young man, Charlie Parker had set in motion a chain of events that would influence his unhappy future. He began taking drugs, drinking heavily, and behaving badly to people when it suited his moods. (He once added Benzedrine to the coffee of an elderly junk dealer who had befriended him.) He went through stormy marriages and relationships with women, continued bouts with drugs and alcohol, and emotional instability. He died in 1955, at only 34. Parker's legend has only grown since his death. Several hundred recordings of his work have surfaced posthumously. Parker's biographer, Gary Giddens, described them as a treasure trove of historical and musical significance, comparing Parker's legacy to that of "Ellington in our time and the manuscripts in Schubert's attic." In 1988, Clint Eastwood, a true jazz aficionado, produced and directed the film *Bird* as a tribute to Parker. It starred Forest Whitaker as the brilliant but troubled jazz legend. Despite his death at such a young age, his mystique survives. Gary Giddens could declare that at least musically, "Bird Lives!"

Parker was hardly the only star of the bop era to confront serious problems due to personal behavior. Unfortunately, from the time Bud Powell turned twenty-one, he suffered periods of emotional illness and he augmented them with heavy drinking. The results were inevitable, and Powell died of problems caused by alcoholism in 1966. But he left behind a rich legacy of jazz recordings and reputation as one of the most influential jazz pianists of his day. Monk's career was nearly ruined when he was suspected, many believe wrongly, of carrying narcotics. He made a spectacular comeback in 1957, when he was booked into The Five Spot, a bar that featured avant-garde jazz. Monk helped launch the career of a new star when he hired the unknown John Coltrane as tenor saxophone soloist. Monk's reputation grew substantially over the years. When he died in 1982, he was widely regarded as a significant jazz composer and the Thelonious Monk Institute, founded six years later to encourage young jazz musicians, launched an international competition in his name,

While many of his colleagues fought battles with drink and drugs, Dizzy Gillespie occupied himself with music. Despite his reputation for a clowning style of showmanship, his zany antics on the bandstand, and his irreverent, mischievous sense of humor, Gillespie was at heart a serious musician. ("Dizzy like a fox," said one fellow musician.) With his trademark bent trumpet, he toured the world as a musical ambassador for jazz and inspired generations of musicians. He organized big bands during the 1950s for a State Department tour that in subsequent years, including a virtual "Who's Who" of jazz among his personnel: saxophonists Don Byas, Dexter Gordon, John Coltrane, and Paul Gonsalves; trumpeter Gerald Wilson; guitarist Kenny Burrell; drummers Shelly Manne, Cozy Cole, and Max Roach; vibraphonist Milt Jackson; trombonist J. J. Johnson; bassists Ray Brown and Al McKibbon; and pianists Al Haig, Wynton Kelly, John Lewis, Billy Taylor, and Lalo Schifrin. He also published his memoirs, titled appropriately, *To Be or Not to Bop*. Ironically, it was the "bad boy of bandstand" who proved to be the true survivor of the bop era. Gillespie also enjoyed a long and happy marriage,

Figure 178 - "Dizzy" Gillespie, famous for his bent trumpet, explored new harmonies and syncopated rhythms to spearhead the movement to bebop. (Photo by and courtesy of Roland Godefroy)

deep religious faith, and when he died in 1993, he could take delight in a life and career that established him as a true jazz legend.

By 1948, many the jazz clubs on 52nd Street were closing as musical activities concentrated there moved around the city. Little remains of the lost world of 52nd Street jazz today, because in the 1960s, the legendary clubs were razed to make room for banks and stores as part of urban renewal. Some in the post-bop era turned to playing "hard bop," an aggressive, sometimes abrasive sound delivering musical expression at blazing speeds and percussive energy. (Rhythmic punctuations by drummers were called

Figure 179 - Jazz fans, including widely admired bassist, Al McKibbon, wearing the hat, gather outside The Three Deuces, a popular jazz club of the 1940s. (Photo courtesy of The William P. Gottlieb Collection, Library of Congress)

"bombs.") The tradition of Charlie Parker and Dizzy Gillespie was carried on by an enthusiastic group of new musicians, many of whom were trained by the bop musicians who were members of the postwar bands of Earl Hines and Billy Eckstine. Trumpeter Fats Navarro appeared to be Gillespie's heir. More lyrical and known for a "sweeter" sound than Gillespie, Navarro became one of New York's leading trumpeters before he died of drug-related tuberculosis in 1950. One of Navarro's greatest admirers was a young trumpet soloist named Clifford Brown. Brown teamed with drummer Max Roach to form the Clifford Brown-Max Roach Quintet. (Also included were saxophonist Sonny Stitt on occasion, as well as Sonny Rollins on saxophone, and Richie Powell, the younger brother of Bud Powell, on piano.) Stitt, a prodigious saxophonist from Michigan, was dubbed "The New Bird," though he wanted to be regarded on his own, not simply as Parker's successor. The Quintet might have enjoyed a brilliant career for years. But in 1956, Brown, Powell, and Powell's wife were killed in a tragic automobile accident.

The trombone joined the bop movement when J. J. Johnson gained wide recognition as a soloist. Johnson, from Indianapolis, was an alumnus of the Benny Carter and Lionel Hampton bands. He began stringing together streams of eighth notes in bop style, adopting a sharp, staccato style full of leaps and breaks, avoiding the smoother, more legato style of his predecessors. Johnson teamed with Kai Winding, a native of Denmark raised in the United States, to form an unusual trombone duo. The ensemble became one of the big successes of the 1950s when they formed a quintet.

Associated with the bop movement were definite modes of behavior. Bop musicians dressed like conservative businessmen and tried to sound like professors except when they used their own private slang. The new "hip" attitude implied that the musician was silently aware of language and attitudes, recognized only by those musicians who shared a mutual understanding of their true meaning.

Leading bop pianists of the period included Tommy Flanagan, Hank Jones, Horace Silver, Wynton Kelly, Red Garland, and Phineas Newborn, Jr. Jones and Flanagan, along with Barry Harris and Sir Roland Hanna, were dubbed the "Detroit School" of jazz pianists, although each had a distinctly individual style. Jones and Flanagan were both

Figure 180 - Pianists Tommy Flanagan and Hank Jones join saxophonist Stan Getz in an ensemble. (Photo by Tad Hershorn, courtesy of the Institute for Jazz Studies, Rutgers University)

outstanding ensemble musicians. Both accompanied Ella Fitzgerald for a number of years. Barry Harris was also a fine accompanist and worked with Coleman Hawkins in that capacity. Harris developed his own teaching methods, inspired by the harmonic and melodic language of his major jazz influences, Bud Powell and Charlie Parker. The Detroit jazz world also included vibraphonist Milton "Bags" Jackson, one of the principals of the Modern Jazz Quartet, Duke Ellington's favorite guitarist, Kenny Burrell, trumpeter Thad Jones and drummer Elvin Jones, Hank Jones' brothers, and trumpet soloist and jazz educator Marcus Belgrave, Detroit's first official Jazz Master Laureate.

In the 1950s, jazz musicians explored many styles. Devotees of Dixieland suddenly insisted that only the original New Orleans style signified true jazz. Advocates of the latest changes or innovations in jazz responded that only "contemporary jazz" could communicate with audiences. But a number of highly independent jazz instrumentalists could not be classified as members of any "school" at all.

Like Earl Hines, Erroll Garner was a native of Pittsburgh. He developed a strumming left hand, which played chords in the manner of a guitarist accompanying a melody. Erroll Garner appeared to have little interest in the developments of bebop, intellectual theories about jazz, and controversies of the day. Only 5'2" tall, Garner was known to sit on telephone books while he played. His legions of fans were startled to learn that Garner didn't read music; he played by ear. One critic said that Garner imitated no one, but that everyone imitated Garner. Though he never learned to read music, Garner was also a composer; his tune, "Misty," became a popular jazz standard. . When asked why he never learned to read music after he became famous, Garner replied, "No one can hear you read."

Figure 181 - Erroll Garner - He became an international jazz star without reading music. (Photograph courtesy of William P. Gottlieb Collection, Library of Congress)

OSCAR AND FRIENDS

Few critics would argue that the dominant pianist of the 1950s was the logical successor to Tatum--the ultimate jazz virtuoso, Oscar Peterson. Peterson was a Canadian who spent years studying classical piano under the tutelage of a Hungarian concert pianist, Paul de Marky. Peterson's idol, not surprisingly, was Art Tatum. He developed the most formidable technique of any pianist since Tatum, who (years later) personally acknowledged Peterson as his successor.

Like Tatum, Peterson could execute the most dazzling runs in an ornamental style. But Peterson never tried to become a copy of Tatum. (He said, "Art taught me to play the instrument, not to let the instrument play me.") He had other influences, including his sister Daisy, a noted classical piano teacher, and Audrey Morris, a pianist and singer who encouraged him to be aware of the neglected verses and the meaning of lyrics in the tunes he played. Peterson also absorbed the lilting phrasing of Nat "King" Cole, and the percussive, driving swing of Bud Powell and the bop pianists. Peterson combined the ebullient energy of the swing era with all the harmonic and rhythmic innovations of bebop. Peterson's reputation had grown in Canada from the time he won an amateur contest at 14 and began making weekly appearances on radio in Montreal. Leading American jazz musicians like Jimmie Lunceford urged him to come to the U.S., but he remained in Canada until Norman Granz discovered him and invited him to join his *Jazz at the Philharmonic* concerts.

Figure 182 - Oscar Peterson, successor to Art Tatum as the ultimate jazz piano virtuoso, with bassist Niels-Henning Ørsted Pederson. (Photo © Claude Truong Ngoc / Wikimedia Commons)

Peterson made his New York debut in 1949 and audiences (including most rival pianists) have regarded him with awe and astonishment ever since. Peterson never saw his astounding technique as an end in itself, but as a means to express his musical ideas. His ability to swing at breakneck speeds sometimes caused critics to ignore the content of his expressive, creative, and eminently musical ideas. Unlike Tatum, who was never happiest working with ensembles or in a trio, Peterson formed a series of trios, initially with bassist Ray Brown and guitarists, including Barney Kessel, Irving Ashby, and Herb Ellis. Peterson worked with Ellis and Brown for five years. He said, "There was a love in that group which I would have to say showed in the music."

In the early 1950s, Peterson, Brown, and Ellis were booked into a Washington D.C. jazz club. Peterson and Brown enjoyed a mutual joke. Peterson would tease Brown with the idea that his hero, bassist Oscar Pettiford, was in the house. Brown would reciprocate by telling Peterson that Art Tatum was there to hear him play. Before a performance one night, Brown told a skeptical Peterson that Art Tatum was in the house. Peterson assumed Brown was joking as usual, but when he turned around, he was astonished to see that his idol, the most intimidating figure in jazz piano, was indeed present. The two met and went to an after-hours club. When Peterson was reluctant to play before his idol, Tatum told him there was a pianist he envied, an old man who could play only one chorus of the blues, but played it in a way that no one could duplicate. Tatum told Peterson that everyone must find his own way to make a musical statement. After hearing Peterson, Tatum said, "As long as I'm alive, I don't figure I'm going to let you have it. But you have it, and you're next after me." Tatum had a sense of humor. Jazz pianists of the day enjoyed testing their technical skills against each other like Wild West gunslingers at private parties. At one such party, Peterson put on a dazzling technical display. But then Tatum sat down at the piano and played a song with a private message for

Figure 183 - Art Tatum and Oscar Peterson - friends and great icons of jazz piano. (Photo courtesy of the Toledo Lucas County Public Library)

Peterson:"Little Man, You've Had a Busy Day." Peterson, despite admirers who insisted that he had taken Tatum's technique to a whole new level of his own, always deferred to his mentor and said he considered himself a humble musical disciple of the great Art Tatum. At the height of his own fame, Peterson had a similarly intimidating effect on other pianists, but he insisted that even he looked forward to growing daily in his mastery of a demanding musical instrument.

Figure 184 - Oscar Peterson at the piano with Voice of America host Willis Conover (Photo courtesy of Willis Conover Collection, University of North Texas)

When Ellis left in 1958, Peterson replaced him with drummer Ed Thigpen, forming the trio considered by many to be among the finest ever heard to play jazz. How good was the Oscar Peterson Trio? Conductor-composer André Previn, also an accomplished jazz pianist with stunning technique, took the members of his own outstanding trio, bassist Red Mitchell and drummer Frank Capp, to hear his friend Oscar Peterson one night. When Peterson unleashed his incredible technique on the keyboard, Previn quipped to his friends, "Can I fire all three of us?"

Ray Brown eventually tired of the constant travel required by a touring group and settled in Los Angeles, where he remained active in the Hollywood studio orchestras. Peterson continued to work in the trio format, with Niels-Henning Orsted Pederson on bass and Martin Drew on drums. In later years, Oscar Peterson emerged as an unaccompanied solo pianist. He often played in strict tempo, using a stride left hand in swing style, all the while stunning audiences with his brilliant right hand technique. Surprisingly, Peterson had his critics, who suggested that his eclectic style was somehow not original. In truth, Peterson had a distinctive style, entirely his own. He absorbed many musical influences, and was called by his biographer, Gene Lees, a summary artist: like J. S. Bach, he summed up all the best musical influences of his time. And though many try to sound like Peterson, he had a musical style which is easily identifiable and thoroughly original. His reputation as one of the world's best jazz pianists is well deserved.

Late in his career, Peterson suffered a stroke; but he fought his way back to the concert stage and could do more with one hand than most pianists could do with two. Peterson also devoted considerable time to composing, including works like the *Canadiana Suite,* the *Nigerian Suite,* and even an *Easter Suite,* using jazz to express the life and resurrection of Christ. When he died two days before Christmas in 2007, Oscar Peterson was one of Canada's most honored musicians and a musical icon throughout the world. While visiting Japan to receive an award, he found himself in conversation with a woman seated next to him at a banquet. She knew all of his recordings. Peterson learned that she was Princess Hitachi and that the royal family of Japan were among his biggest fans. So were millions of jazz aficionados throughout the world.

Figure 185 - Nat "King" Cole was an accomplished jazz pianist, but his pianistic skills were often eclipsed by his success as a singer. (Photo by William P. Gottlieb, courtesy of William P. Gottlieb Collection, Library of Congress)

Although Oscar Peterson always acknowledged Art Tatum as his hero, he was always profuse in praise of another pianist he admired, Nat "King" Cole. The twists and turns of a musical career led to Cole becoming famous as a singer; today he is better known to the public for his hit recordings as a vocalist and his considerable talents as a pianist are less recognized than they should be.

Cole was one of four brothers, Nathaniel, Eddie, Ike, and Freddy, all of whom became successful in musical careers. Nathaniel Cole became Nat "King" Cole when he acquired his nickname at a jazz club. Cole started the "King Cole Trio" displaying the piano skills he had acquired while absorbing everything from jazz, gospel music, and the classics from Bach to Rachmaninoff, during the years he grew up in Chicago. He eventually settled in California and his trio, consisting of piano, bass, and guitar instead of drums, gained wide popularity. He was one of the first artists to sign with the new Capitol Records company and the label's iconic building, resembling a stack of records with a needle at the top, was dubbed "The House That Nat Built." "Straighten Up and Fly Right," presumably based on a tale adapted from one of his father's sermons, was his first vocal hit.

As Cole achieved great popularity as a singer, he switched from jazz to standard popular songs, ranging from "The Christmas Song," which became a perennial holiday favorite, to the haunting "Nature Boy," to "Mona Lisa," to his musical signature, "Unforgettable." He was a pioneer in becoming one of the first black artists to host his own radio and television programs. Although a great number of jazz artists appeared on his television show for little or no pay, national sponsors were unwilling to support a show hosted by an African-American. Unfortunately, the show is now remembered more for the controversy it generated than the fine musical performances it featured. Cole's light-fingered, swinging style at the piano reflected the influences of Earl Hines and Teddy Wilson.

Figure 186 - The amazing Dick Hyman excelled not only as a jazz soloist, but as a composer and arranger in virtually every genre of music. (Photo courtesy of Dick Hyman)

The influence of Art Tatum was clearly present in the work of two other pianists who spent much of their careers in broadcasting. Dick Hyman studied with Teddy Wilson and like his mentor, worked with Benny Goodman. In his remarkable career, he proved himself equally adept as pianist, organist, arranger, musical director, and composer. He first gained attention on the staff of NBC in the 1950s. Hyman was classically trained and could emulate any jazz style virtually at will. He collaborated with critic Leonard Feather on a series of concerts devoted to the history of jazz. Hyman proved to be an important advocate for the legacy of great jazz musicians, lecturing, teaching, and combining their styles with his own, highlighted by dazzling technical displays.

Hyman recorded over 100 albums as a performer. His compositions covered a wide range of styles and forms, including ballets, a cantata based on the autobiography of Mark Twain, two piano concertos, his *Ragtime Fantasy*, and chamber music pieces. In more recent years, he composed, arranged, and conducted numerous film and television scores, including most of the major films written and directed by Woody Allen.

Like Hyman, Paul Thatcher Smith repeatedly stunned his audiences with an ability to play at electrifying speeds. A Californian, he worked in big bands led by Ozzie Nelson and Tommy Dorsey before settling permanently on the west coast. He spent a dozen years as staff pianist at NBC in Hollywood and accompanied a virtual "who's who" of vocalists, including Ella Fitzgerald. When Smith wasn't arranging or working in the studios, he found time to record as a prolific soloist; his technique enabled him to pay tribute to Tatum on recordings and in concerts. A friend once quipped that Smith looked as if he should be moving pianos, not playing them. But Smith managed to not only play them with technical brilliance, but to teach and write numerous instruction books on jazz piano. He also collaborated with his wife, Annette Warren, an accomplished singer, who dubbed the voices of major stars in Hollywood musicals.

Figure 187 - Paul Thatcher Smith, known for his brilliant technique and his wife, singer Annette Warren, made music together for decades. (Photo courtesy of Annette Warren Smith)

Nearly every living jazz pianist of consequence appeared on the radio program, *Marian McPartland's Piano Jazz*. McPartland was a British keyboard artist who had a completely unique musical career. Marian McPartland began her classical music studies in England at the Guildhall School of Music and was training to become a concert pianist.

To the distress of her family, she became captivated by American jazz and left school to join a piano quartet led by pianist and composer Billy Mayerl from whom she had been taking lessons in "modern syncopation." Eventually, she met and married Jimmy McPartland, a cornetist who was one of the pioneers of Chicago jazz, and a friend and colleague of Bix Beiderbecke. The McPartlands settled permanently in the U.S., first in Chicago, then in New York, where Marian McPartland led her own trio and became a leading advocate for women in jazz.

McPartland initially faced skepticism from those who doubted that an Englishwoman could be successful as jazz soloist in America. But she quickly proved that her critics were wrong. She formed a friendship with the composer Alec Wilder, recorded his music, and composed pieces of her own that were notable for their color, shading, and even the influence of that most English of concert composers, Frederic Delius. Her pensive approach to the keyboard and her rich harmonic progressions won her a wide following. When she died in 2013, at age 95, she could look back on decades of musical history and accomplishments not only as an internationally known performer, but as a leading jazz educator who had a great impact on the jazz careers of many musicians, especially women who wanted to enter the jazz world.

Figure 188 - Marian McPartland, pianist, broadcaster and advocate for women in jazz. (Photo courtesy of the Kurland Agency)

HOT JAZZ COOLS OFF

Just as bop had challenged swing, a new school of jazz musicians arose to challenge the advocates of bop. Bop, especially "hard bop," called for an aggressive style of playing, with virtuoso technique as an entry requirement for aspiring players. But this approach was uncomfortable for some musicians, whose personal manner was understated, relaxed, and not always inspired to play "hot music." Their answer was "cool jazz."

The "cool" school differed from "hard bop" as its name implied. Bop musicians emphasized speed, percussive attacks, driving rhythms, and an aggressive musical outlook. "Cool" players preferred the subjective, softer, shaded colors, and slow, brooding tempi.

Like swing and bop, cool jazz was the outgrowth of a number of events that brought a number of musicians together at the right time. Canadian-born arranger Gil Evans had always been fascinated by both jazz and the sounds of a variety of classical composers, particularly the French impressionists. He settled in Stockton, California, where he organized a band. Eventually, he turned the band over to its lead singer, Skinnay Ennis, who promptly arranged for the band to move to Hollywood to work on Bob Hope's radio program. Evans remained as the band's arranger, but Hope's producers disapproved of his interest in experimental harmonies. They hired Claude Thornhill as vocal arranger.

Figure 189 - Claude Thornhill, together with arranger Gil Evans, brought French horns into the jazz world. (Photo courtesy of William P. Gottlieb Collection, Library of Congress)

Thornhill was a product of conservatory training in Cincinnati and Philadelphia. He shared Gil Evans' fascination for the rich, full harmonies of Debussy and Ravel, and even introduced French horns into the ensemble.

In 1939, Thornhill decided to start his own band, with Gil Evans joining him as arranger. The band had an unusual group of instruments, incorporating six clarinets, two French horns, and tuba. Evans was free to adapt the melodic and harmonic innovations of bebop to a big band, but he did so according to Thornhill's instincts--a quieter, more introspective version of bop. Soloists were given softer accompaniments and more of a chance to be heard than in the other brassy, blaring big bands. Thornhill liked to use French horns to double the melody played by more conventional instruments. In Thornhill's band, the lines of Charlie Parker met the harmonies of Claude Debussy. Evans also began hosting meetings in his apartment attended by numerous young musicians, including Gerry Mulligan, George Russell, John Lewis, and Miles Davis.

While Thornhill and Evans were experimenting with a quieter, gentler reaction to bop, pianist Lennie Tristano was pursuing his own reaction to the driving swing of the late 1940s. Tristano, an individualist and nonconformist, was blind since childhood. He

Figure 190 - Lennie Tristano, experimental pianist and jazz teacher. (Photo courtesy of William P. Gottlieb Collection, Library of Congress)

moved from Chicago to New York where devoted himself to teaching. Tristano was a man of formidable opinions and classical training. He was concerned with developing "pure" melodic lines with shifting meters, while the rhythm section supplied few accents. Tristano also like to change keys, modulating constantly. With an interest in contemporary classical music, he drew upon unusual sources of inspiration for a jazz musician. In "Crosscurrent," he mixed meters and approached atonality in "Wow," his best-recognized compositions. Among Tristano's students were saxophonists Lee Konitz and Wayne Marsh, and guitarist Billy Bauer. Konitz, inspired by Tristano, developed an alternate style to Charlie Parker's, with longer melodic lines, fewer accents, and a more introspective attitude toward his music. In addition to joining Tristano, Marsh, and Bauer for recordings, Konitz also became a member of Claude Thornhill's band.

The "cool school" came together in 1949 and 1950 through a series of historic recordings called *Birth of the Cool,* launched by trumpeter Miles Davis. Davis grew up in East St. Louis, Illinois, the son of an affluent dentist. He began playing as a boy. While he was in high school in the 1940s, he had been exposed to the bop artistry of Dizzy Gillespie and Charlie Parker. After high school, he went to New York to attend Juilliard, but spent most of his time pursuing contacts with jazz musicians, especially Charlie Parker, with whom he later shared an apartment for a time. Though Gillespie and Parker were experimenting with their trademark delivery of countless notes at rapid speeds, Davis seemed to prefer a sparse, more contemplative style. When he formed a nine-piece band of his own, he engaged Lee Konitz on alto sax and Gerry Mulligan on baritone sax. Both Konitz and Mulligan were alumni of the Thornhill band, familiar with Gil Evans' arrangements, and Tristano's melodic and harmonic ideas. Davis was always a controversial and highly influential figure in jazz. He

Figure 191 - Miles Davis, trumpeter, led the "Birth of the Cool." (Photo by and copyright by Tom Palumbo)

suffered a period of heroin addiction, but broke the habit, and continued to play in small jazz ensembles, achieving his greatest success at the 1955 Newport Jazz Festival. One of Davis's most interesting experiments was a jazz oriented work, *Sketches of Spain*, arranged by Gil Evans, and adapted from a celebrated work for classical guitar, Joaquin Rodrigo's *Concierto de Aranjuez.*

It was during the 1950s that a number of pianists became similarly intrigued by lush harmonies, quiet introspection, and a contemplative approach to jazz. Foremost among these was Bill Evans. Born in Plainfield, New Jersey, Evans studied at Southwestern Louisiana College and eventually went to New York. In 1958, he began working with Miles Davis. Soon after, he formed his own trio with drummer Paul Motian and bassist Scott LaFaro. Evans liked to resolve melodic phrases simply rather than using streams of rapid notes. He sustained chords in the left hand without trying to use it for purely rhythmic purposes. Throughout his career, he liked to experiment with new approaches to music. His album, *Conversations with Myself*, featured him improvising both parts of a piano duet. He subsequently recorded jazz versions of piano themes by Bach, Chopin, Scriabin, Granados, and Fauré. He disliked being asked to explain his work, declaring, "You can't explain jazz to anyone without losing the experience. Words are the children of reason, and therefore can't explain it. Jazz has got to be experienced because it's not words, it's feeling."

Figure 192 - Bill Evans, famous for his harmonic voicings at the piano, said that jazz could not be explained—it had to be felt. (Photo courtesy of Institute of Jazz Studies, Rutgers University)

Among the "coolest" of the "cool school" jazz musicians were those who became identified with what came to be known as "West Coast Jazz." Quite a number of these musicians had backgrounds that included not only jazz, but classical concert music. Some were conservatory trained, fully comfortable with the European classics. Many were also alumni of the two big bands, led by Woody Herman and Stan Kenton, both of which survived the passing of the big band era. In 1950 at the conclusion of one of Kenton's tours, a number of his musicians decided to remain in Los Angeles.

Trumpeter Milton "Shorty" Rogers was one of the Kenton alumni who remained in California and recorded an album, *Modern Sounds by Shorty Rogers and his Giants*. (The "Giants" included Shelley Manne and Jimmy Giuffre.) All three musicians became associated with bassist Howard Rumsey, a member of the original Kenton band. Rumsey formed a combo to play regularly at the Lighthouse in Hermosa Beach, California. Under Rumsey's leadership, the Lighthouse became the leading west coast jazz club, frequently featuring musicians from the Kenton and Herman bands.

About the same time, The Haig, a small Los Angeles jazz club tried to improve its business by hiring a young publicist named Richard Bock. Bock engaged saxophonist Gerry Mulligan at the club. Mulligan, who grew up in Philadelphia, had been part of the "cool school" surrounding Gil Evans and Miles Davis, and had worked for drummer Gene Krupa. Mulligan's quartet featured trumpeter Chet Baker, bassist Bob Whitlock, and drummer Chico Hamilton. Significantly, the group did not include a pianist and created a sensation. Bock promptly launched Pacific Jazz, a new record label specializing in the new west coast groups. When eastern critics skeptically dubbed the new sounds coming from California "west coast jazz," the label stuck and the public asked for more.

No discussion of west-coast jazz would be complete without acknowledging the contributions of the amazing André Previn, a multifaceted musician who grew up in California. Composer, symphony conductor, film music prodigy, and concert pianist, Previn drew upon years of classical study (including seven years of composition study with Castelnuovo-Tedesco.)

He discovered jazz, was predictably dazzled by Tatum's pyrotechnics, and set about becoming an accomplished jazz musician himself. Determined to play longer runs than Tatum, he eventually switched to a driving bop style influenced by Bud Powell. Previn is one of the most technically facile jazz pianists, capable of executing any phrase on the piano at will.

He is also understated in his approach to the keyboard. Always innovative and surprising, Previn could turn even the most familiar melodies upside-down, as in the case of *Mack the Knife,* the often recorded melody by Kurt Weill. Previn was going to record the piece in a duet with trombonist J. J. Johnson. What could a musician do with *Mack the Knife* that hadn't already been done? Previn's solution: play the familiar melody in two different keys simultaneously.

Figure 193 - André Previn, the classical prodigy who made his mark as a jazz pianist and film composer before devoting his time to symphonic conducting and composing operas. (Photo by Bert Verhoeff / Anefo courtesy of Dutch National Archives)

Previn's jazz piano style changed over the years. After absorbing the pyrotechnical wizardry of Tatum and the rhythmic drive of Powell, he eventually turned to a softer, more introspective and personal approach to the piano. He virtually gave up jazz performance entirely after leaving Hollywood to pursue his worldwide career as a symphony conductor. Then, in a twenty-first century surprise, he began recording and playing jazz again.

It was also during the years of West Coast jazz that small ensembles created the jazz equivalent of chamber music. Not all the activity came from Southern California. Pianist Dave Brubeck was a pupil of Darius Milhaud, the distinguished French composer of concert music. (Milhaud had always enjoyed jazz, incorporating it into his own ballet, *La Création du Monde.*) Brubeck so admired his teacher that he named one of his sons "Darius." Brubeck's quartet featured alto saxophonist Paul Desmond, bassist Bob Bates, and drummer Joe Dodge. Eventually, Bates and Dodge would be replaced by Eugene Wright and Joe Morello. The quartet achieved incredible popularity during the 1950s, introducing jazz on college campuses throughout the country and issuing recordings of live concerts.

Figure 194 - Dave Brubeck startled audiences with daring jazz improvisations in unusual time signatures such as 5/4. (Photo courtesy of Carl Van Vechten Collection, Library of Congress)

Even many non-musicians are used to thinking of certain types of music as written with specific time signature: waltzes in 3/4 time and foxtrots in 4/4. (Audiences filled with listeners who have had no musical training will still count "one-two-three, one-two-three" when they hear a piece written in waltz time.) But no one knew how to tap his foot or when to clap when Brubeck appeared on the scene. Brubeck became identified with Desmond's composition, "Take Five," a piece in 5/4 meter that set the stage for many of Brubeck's future experiments in playing jazz with unusual time signatures. (Another Brubeck classic, "Blue Rondo a la Turk," was in 9/8.) Brubeck was also a composer. His best-known pieces included "The Duke" and "In Your Own Sweet Way." The quartet toured Europe and Asia as jazz ambassadors. At the height of his popularity, Brubeck's face appeared on the cover of *Time* magazine; he remained a jazz icon to a worldwide audience of admirers.

No ensemble achieved greater popularity than the George Shearing Quintet. George Shearing was one of England's finest jazz pianists. Blind from birth, Shearing proved one of the most enduring musicians to come from the bop era. Shearing worked in a seventeen-piece blind band led by Claude Bampton. He was discovered by critic and jazz promoter Leonard Feather who arranged for his first record date and for his arrival in the United States. Shearing was working with clarinetist Buddy deFranco in a quartet at New York's "Clique Club." He was offered a recording contract, but deFranco was obligated to another company. Feather suggested replacing the clarinet with an unusual combination, guitar and vibes. Bassist John Levy and drummer Denzel Best remained with Shearing, and they were joined by vibraphonist Marge Hyams and guitarist Chuck Wayne. The Quintet began recording with the song, "So Rare," which was followed by its biggest hit, "September in the Rain." Eventually, the "Clique Club" was renamed "Birdland," in honor of Charlie Parker. In 1952, Morris Levy, owner of "Birdland," asked

Figure 195 - George Shearing brought classical sensibilities to his solo jazz improvisations. (Photograph courtesy of The Institute of Jazz Studies, Rutgers University)

Shearing to play the theme for a "Birdland" radio program. Shearing didn't particularly like the theme and asked if he could write one of his own. Shearing remained dissatisfied with his own theme in progress until one night when he was seated at dinner, enjoying his favorite char-broiled steak. Suddenly, he jumped up and ran to the piano; in a few minutes, he had created an entirely new melody. He called it "Lullaby of Birdland," the theme which became his musical signature tune and a jazz standard which has been performed by virtually every jazz musician of consequence around the world.

Shearing's quintet made his name a household word among jazz aficionados. He developed the "quintet sound," with guitar and vibraphone doubling the piano part. On the keyboard, he adapted a style of "block chords" originated by pianist Milt Buckner. Shearing could swing in a lilting, lyrical style, and he perfected a delicate, pensive approach to ballads influenced as much by Debussy, Ravel, and Delius, as by jazz. Shearing was an accomplished classical pianist, and moved easily from jazz to Bach and Mozart. The Quintet remained active for twenty-seven years.

Then Shearing began working with smaller, more personal groups, including a series of duo-concerts with the multi-talented vocalist Mel Tormé. As a soloist, especially in the performance of ballads, Shearing had few peers. He had an incredibly sensitive touch, which explains his longevity in any style of musical expression he chose. While the public and the press still talk about his famous quintet, one can argue persuasively that his greatest musical achievements were his brilliant solos. He could take the simplest tune and turn it into a virtual jazz nocturne combining the best of both the jazz and classical worlds. When he was knighted by Queen Elizabeth II, he completed a remarkable journey from the pub in Battersea, where he began his musical career, to his status as one of the world's most renowned jazz musicians.

Figure 196 - George Shearing - Famous for his Quintet, but one of the finest ballad soloists in jazz history. (Photo by James Kriegsmann for Associated Booking Corporation, courtesy of George Shearing.)

John Lewis, together with vibraphonist Milt Jackson, drummer Kenny Clarke (later replaced by Connie Kay), and bassist Ray Brown (later replaced by Percy Heath) formed the Modern Jazz Quartet, or MJQ. The Modern Jazz Quartet was really the rhythm section of the Gillespie band playing small ensemble pieces to give the brass section a rest. Lewis was the son of an optometrist. He grew up in New Mexico, where he studied music and anthropology. He eventually went into the army where he met Kenny Clarke, through whom he became pianist and arranger for Dizzy Gillespie.

Settling in New York, he took two degrees at the Manhattan School of Music. He was thoroughly schooled in European music, and had a special affinity for the rich colors of French and Italian music, as well as Baroque counterpoint. Lewis became especially interested in applying European-influenced ideas about musical form and structure to jazz. His style was impressionistic and introspective. His sources of inspiration were long removed from Dixieland or the blues. His works include a four-part suite, *La Ronde*, and a series of movements inspired by the Italian *comedia dell'arte*. John Lewis's 1960 composition, *The Comedy: A Jazz Entertainment,* was performed in Paris by the Modern

Jazz Quartet with four ballet dancers. Lewis's best-known composition was *Django*, a mournful tribute to guitarist Django Reinhardt.

While Lewis was inspired by Paris and Venice, Milt Jackson, the group's bop-oriented vibraphonist, was clearly more influenced by his work in the jazz clubs on 52nd Street. The Modern Jazz Quartet was an important influence during the 1950s because they experimented with improvisation on themes that were included in larger formal concert pieces. Unfortunately, tension between Lewis and Jackson led to Jackson's departure, but the group did eventually reunite.

Ahmad Jamal is a native of Pittsburgh, where he began a storied musical career that took him to Chicago, New York, North Africa, and into the jazz history books. His uncle challenged three-year old Jamal to duplicate what he was playing on the piano. This led to piano lessons with pedagogue Mary Cardwell Dawson, the founder of the first black opera company in America. Jamal was entering classical

Figure 197 - The Modern Jazz Quartet combined the rhythms and harmonies of jazz with the genre of chamber music. (Photo by Tad Hershorn, courtesy of Institute of Jazz Studies, Rutgers University)

competitions, interpreting difficult Liszt etudes at eleven, and playing professionally by the time he was only fourteen. His keyboard creativity led to predictions of a brilliant future from no less than Art Tatum. Jamal eventually moved to Chicago and a performance at the Embers in New York led to a recording contract with John Hammond, the producer who had helped launch the careers of Benny Goodman and Count Basie.

Jamal achieved incredible success with his own trio at the Pershing Hotel in Chicago. His recording, "Live at the Pershing: But Not For Me," became a national bestseller for 108 weeks and made Ahmad Jamal a major figure in the world of jazz. Jamal had his own style, emphasizing unique chordal substitutions, counterpoint, countermelodies, and pedal point ostinatos at a time when many musicians emphasized speed and volume. His original group, "The Three Strings," was also called the Ahmad Jamal Trio, although Jamal never preferred the trio label and

Figure 198 - Ahmad Jamal. His use of contrapuntal lines in jazz has won him a worldwide audience of admirers for decades. (Photograph by Jacques Beneich, used by special permission courtesy of Ellora Management. All rights reserved)

always encouraged the unique creativity of the drummers and bass soloists with whom he played. Well into the twenty-first century, Ahmad Jamal received a host of American and international awards. He was named a Duke Ellington Fellow at Yale University, where he performed commissioned works with the Assai String Quartet and received an honorary Doctor of Music degree from the New England Conservatory of Music.

Critics have often praised Ahmad Jamal for his use of "time" and "space," although Jamal has said he prefers "discipline" to describe his approach. His "cool" approach to jazz won the admiration of his colleagues, particularly trumpeter Miles Davis. Stanley Crouch praised Jamal for the innovation of rhythmic surprise and energy associated with big bands in small musical groups. Having been trained to think orchestrally, Jamal has been able to apply this musical approach to his piano style. Jamal is also a thoughtful interpreter of ballads and considers the lyrics of the melodies he plays. Ahmad Jamal's career survived many different eras in jazz, including the age of big bands, the bebop years, and the high-tech electronic instruments of the twenty-first century. While he achieved his earliest success improvising on the melodies of other composers, for many years he has chosen to concentrate on his own compositions, now recognized as a major composer as well as performer in his chosen field.

Figure 199 - Randy Weston, a pianist who explored the musical heritage of Africa while building a reputation in jazz. (Photo by Ariane Smolderen, courtesy of Randy Weston)

The poet Langston Hughes said of pianist Randy Weston, "When Randy Weston plays, a combination of strength and gentleness, virility, and velvet emerges from the keys in an ebb and flow of sound seeming as natural as the waves of the sea." Weston, a tall, adventurous musician born in Brooklyn, took his musical career in a highly original direction when he moved to Africa and settled in Morocco. The six-foot-eight Weston once wrote a hit tune called "Hi-Fly," which he described as "A tale of being my height and looking down at the ground." Weston's father operated a West Indian restaurant frequented by famous jazz musicians. He carefully and deliberately educated his son in a subject he wouldn't explore in school: African culture and history.

Weston was influenced by many of the musicians he admired, especially pianist-composer Thelonious Monk. In Africa, Weston absorbed the rhythms of authentic African music. He also introduced American jazz, with its fusion of African and European musical elements, to African audiences. He performed in Morocco, but also before varied audiences in such countries as Tunisia, Nigeria, and Lebanon. Weston was inspired by his time in Nigeria to record *Uhuru Afrika* or *Freedom Africa*. This unique suite featured Weston's music, lyrics by the poet Langston Hughes, arrangements by Melba Liston, and soloists including soprano Martha Flowers, baritone Brock Peters, and narrator Tuntemeke Sanga.

Weston has been highly recognized with honorary doctorates and international awards. He called his autobiography *African Rhythms*. His music is and has been perhaps the most African-inspired of major figures in the world of jazz.

Sir Roland Hanna was a member of the band organized by Thad Jones, the younger brother of Hank Jones, in association with drummer Mel Lewis. Hanna was one musician whose claim to jazz royalty wasn't just honorary; he was knighted by the President of Liberia. Hanna trained classically at the Eastman School of Music and was highly skilled in incorporating European classical music into his improvisations. Hanna contributed greatly to many genres of music. He was a skilled accompanist for vocalists such as Carmen McRae and Sarah Vaughan (for whom he served as musical director). He toured the world as a jazz soloist, all the while exploring new ways of incorporating a jazz vocabulary into concert music. Hanna was also a gifted composer. Among his four hundred compositions was a jazz ballet, *My Name is Jasmine But They Call Me Jaz*. He combined jazz and chamber music in a *Sonata for Chamber Trio and Jazz Piano*. Sir Roland also appeared with the Detroit Symphony as soloist in his own work, *Oasis*, scored for piano and orchestra. His friend Jimmy Heath said that Sir Roland Hanna was "always raising the bar." He did this, in part, as a professor at Queens College in New York and by mentoring gifted young jazz musicians. Hanna saw music as more than a source of amusement or entertainment; he once said it was a helpmate to enable human beings to get through life.

Figure 200 - Sir Roland Hanna, renowned as a soloist and ensemble player in the jazz world, found time to compose four hundred original works combining classical and jazz elements. (Photo courtesy of Rahanna Music, Inc. All Rights Reserved.)

Phineas Newborn, Jr., was an amazing pianist from Whiteville, Tennessee, whose biography is nearly always recounted with bittersweet thoughts of what might have been. Newborn grew up in a Memphis musical family and developed a ferocious keyboard technique by mastering classical piano etudes by Franz Liszt. In the 1950s, he emerged as a major recording artist whose dazzling solos elicited loud cheers from the orchestral musicians who played with him. Newborn could shock audiences by playing complete melodic solos with his left hand alone and then playing with both hands in unison at high speed. His popularity took him to New York and Europe and he gained astonishing compliments from critics. Leonard Feather said that at his peak, Newborn was one of the three greatest jazz pianists of all time. No less than Oscar Peterson said that Newborn was the likeliest pianist to become his successor as he had succeeded Art Tatum.

Newborn's life, however, took a tragic turn when bouts with depression and an undiagnosed mental illness restricted his musical career. The rock music revolution didn't help matters. Suddenly, musicians with Newborn's flashing fingers and brilliant technique were no longer in vogue. In 1974, while preparing to record a comeback album, Newborn suffered a brutal beating; it resulted in broken fingers and required surgery. Nonetheless, he entered the recording studio shortly thereafter. Newborn died at only fifty-seven, back in Tennessee where he started. In recent years, Newborn's gifts have been rediscovered. He was a major musical figure in his time, but his admirers always wonder what his life and career might have been if good fortune had smiled upon him in proportion to his talents.

Figure 201 - Phineas Newborn, Jr., the dazzling jazz pianist from Tennessee whose career was sadly cut short by illness and circumstances. (Photo courtesy of Phineas Newborn, III)

SINGERS AND SWINGERS

Throughout jazz history, vocalists have played an important role in the development of swinging, singing melodic lines. But vocal art is deceptive. Since nearly everyone seems to like singing popular music, people sometimes mistakenly assume that anyone can sing jazz. The best pop and jazz vocalists were first and foremost accomplished musicians who used their voices like musical instruments. Their relaxed and often casual manner made such performances look easy. But don't be fooled. It was a lot harder than it looked ... or sounded!

To make matters more confusing, there is no precise definition of jazz singing. Nor do critics, even the best ones, agree as to precisely what constitutes jazz. Some vocalists specialize primarily in the blues, which for jazz encyclopedist Leonard Feather was an essential element of jazz singing. He credited Louis Armstrong and Ethel Waters for demonstrating that a blues-influenced jazz style could be applied to popular music. Feather suggested that phrasing, as much as improvisation, separates what he terms the "jazz wheat" from the "pop chaff." Whitney Balliett, known for his meticulous profiles of jazz musicians in *The New Yorker,* takes a more expansive view. Says Balliett, "The most popular definition of a jazz singer is that there is no definition. But there is. A jazz singer simply makes what he or she sings swing." Some popular vocalists perform with obvious influences from jazz: a driving, rhythmic swing and the ability to execute vocal improvisations worthy of the best brass or saxophone soloists.

In the 1930s, big bands featured vocalists too numerous to mention. Most bands elected to feature what were commonly described as "girl singers" or "boy singers." The best big bands featured vocalists who became strongly identified with the sound of their individual ensembles: Tommy Dorsey featured Frank Sinatra, Jo Stafford, Connie Haynes, and The Pied Pipers. Bob Eberly was a popular vocalist with the Dorsey Brothers original band. When the brothers went their separate ways, Tommy Dorsey hired Frank Sinatra, while Bob Eberly joined Jimmy Dorsey and was teamed with vocalist Helen O'Connell. Eberly would croon a melody with a Latin flavor, followed by Helen O'Connell's up-tempo version of the same song. Their duets, including such songs as "Tangerine" and "Green Eyes," became huge hits with audiences of the day.

When Glenn Miller asked Bob if he knew anyone who could sing in a similar style, Bob promptly suggested his brother Ray. Ray Eberle continued to use the family's original spelling of his name as he starred with Glenn Miller's ensemble, along with Paula Kelly and the Modernaires. Benny Goodman, though less inclined to emphasize singers, featured Helen Forrest and Peggy Lee. Herb Jeffries was the leading singer with Duke Ellington's orchestra.

Some who moved into other areas of entertainment are so identified with their later careers it is hard to imagine that they began on the bandstand. Dale Evans (long before she helped her future husband, cowboy star Roy Rogers, win the west in films and on television) sang with the Anson Weeks orchestra. Harriet Hilliard was a band singer before marrying Ozzie Nelson and becoming half of the television team, Ozzie and Harriet. Merv Griffin sang with Freddy Martin's band before becoming a talk show host and casino tycoon. Rosemary Clooney, Alice Faye, Betty Grable, Doris Day, Jane Russell, Janet Blair, Betty Hutton, Bing Crosby, Perry Como, Dick Powell, Tony Bennett, and Mel Tormé all began as band singers. Frank Sinatra was certainly the most emulated vocalist, an outstanding interpreter of ballads and a vocalist who could swing. But many of these big band performances could not remotely be described as jazz.

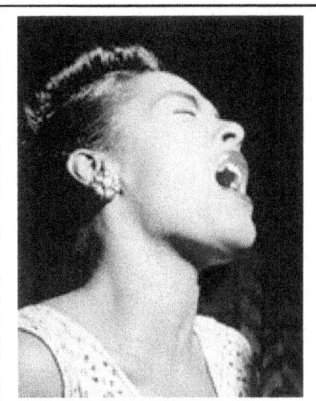

Figure 202 - Billie Holiday - "Lady Day." (Photo by William P. Gottlieb and courtesy off The William P. Gottlieb Collection, The Library of Congress)

While critics and historians delight in arguing over what constitutes a true jazz vocal solo, if asked to name the most important vocalists in jazz, they generally agree: in the big band era, most would choose Billie Holiday and Ella Fitzgerald. The two could not have been more different. Leonard Feather wrote that "the consistency of honey was as compatible with Ella's voice as was the aroma of vinegar with Billie Holiday's." Billie Holiday, dubbed "Lady Day" by Lester Young, lived through a sordid personal life, beginning with abandonment by her father and ending with her fatal addiction to heroin. Her rasping, blues-like delivery enabled her to infuse even the most ordinary popular tune with a sense of dramatic pain. She wrote the song, "God Bless the Child," to express the unhappiness of her own childhood.

In contrast, Ella Fitzgerald was known for the joyful exuberance of her voice and her stunning improvisations. Fitzgerald was discovered after winning an amateur competition at Harlem's Apollo Theater. In 1938, she enjoyed great success with the tune, "A-Tisket, A- Tasket," while singing with Chick Webb's band. The arrangement for this early hit was provided by Van Alexander, who had a long career as a well-known bandleader, arranger, and composer. Alexander also wrote an important textbook on arranging called *First Chart*. When bandleader Chick Webb died the following year, Ella Fitzgerald led the band for two years and then launched her historic solo career.

Figure 203 - Ella Fitzgerald everyone's favorite jazz vocalist, famed for flawless intonation and as the Queen of "Scat," welcomed to the White House by President Ronald Reagan. (U.S. Government Photo)

In the 1940s, Ella Fitzgerald began absorbing the bebop lines of Dizzy Gillespie, Lester Young, and Ray Brown. When she recorded "Lady Be Good" and "Flying Home," she established herself as "The Queen of Scat." The ability to sing wordless instrumental lines using syllables ("scat singing") became her trademark, as she improvised using her voice like an instrumentalist and injecting quotations from numerous other songs into her spontaneous melodic lines.

In the 1950s, she began recording a series of albums, each devoted to the "songbook" of a legendary composer or lyricist, including George Gershwin, Jerome Kern, Cole Porter, Harold Arlen, Irving Berlin, Duke Ellington, and Johnny Mercer. Mel Tormé paid tribute to Fitzgerald as "the world's greatest singer." Though especially identified with the swing era, she remained throughout her career a jazz icon whose style was emulated by dozens of other aspiring jazz vocalists. When jazz magazines published polls asking readers or expert judges to choose the best jazz vocalist in the land, Ella Fitzgerald was perpetually declared to be the winner.

The bop lines of Dizzy Gillespie and Charlie Parker were also absorbed by another important vocalist, Sarah "Sassy" Vaughan. Like her idol Ella Fitzgerald, Vaughan won an amateur contest at the Apollo Theater in Harlem and began her career as a band singer, with Earl Hines and Billy Eckstine. Mel Tormé called Sarah Vaughan "The Diva" because of the star-quality in her voice. Vaughan played the piano and could include the notes bop musicians added to chords

Figure 204 - Sarah Vaughan, known to her close friends as "Sassy." (Photo by William P. Gottlieb and used courtesy of The William P. Gottlieb Collection, Library of Congress)

in her vocal lines. She could move easily from a jazz sound produced in her throat to a high register head-tone associated with classical music. Her colleague Betty Carter said that Vaughan could have been an opera singer if she had chosen to pursue that path. Just as Ella Fitzgerald was the preeminent vocalist of the swing era, Sarah Vaughan was identified strongly with the sounds of bebop. She was credited as an early influence on Carmen McRae. When she was only eighteen, Carmen McRae wrote "Dream of Life," a song recorded by Billie Holiday. Like Vaughan, McRae came out of the bebop era, working at Minton's where bop originated. McRae was trained as both a pianist and singer, and worked with numerous bands, including those led by Benny Carter and Mercer Ellington. She often accompanied herself on the piano.

The world of jazz also produced outstanding vocal ensembles. Jon Hendricks grew up in Ohio and began singing on the radio as a teenager. His accompanist was family friend (and Toledo native) Art Tatum. Hendricks was a struggling songwriter in 1952 when he decided to perform a jazz piece as a *vocalise,* a wordless style of singing in which the voice emulates instruments. Hendricks chose "Four Brothers," a hit melody composed by Jimmy Giuffre and recorded by the Woody Herman band. Five years later, he recorded a second version of the tune, this time with colleagues Dave Lambert and Annie Ross blending their voices to sound like a saxophone ensemble. Their group, Lambert, Hendricks, and Ross, remained active for several years; when Ross became ill, she was replaced briefly by Carole Sloane, and then by Yolande Bavan. Hendricks also wrote lyrics to instrumental melodies, inspiring critic Leonard Feather to dub him "the poet-laureate of jazz." Dave Lambert was tragically killed in an automobile accident while helping a perfect stranger change a tire. Hendricks remained active in jazz, however. He actually created *Evolution of the Blues,* a show which traced the history of jazz from its beginnings to the bop era and even taught classes in jazz history.

Jackie Cain and Roy Kral (known universally as "Jackie and Roy") were perhaps the best-known duo among jazz vocalists. They were inseparable since they first collaborated in 1946, when they gained recognition as members of an ensemble lead by Charlie Ventura. They married three years later and in 1996, they celebrated fifty years together as a musical duo. (When they recorded an album of songs by André Previn with lyrics by Dory Langdon, Previn and Langdon declared, "'Jackie and Roy' is our favorite singer.") Their talents were recognized early

Figure 205 - Jackie Cain and Roy Kral, known as "Jackie and Roy," were collaborators for fifty-six years in a happy musical marriage. Photograph taken at Bach Dancing & Dynamite Society, Half Moon Bay CA, 1982. Brian McMillen (Used under Creative Commons license.)

by the composer Alec Wilder, whose music they often performed. The duo proved equally adept at performing jazz solos with or without words, often to highly inventive arrangements written by Roy Kral, who was also a pianist. Their unique sound was both cool and sophisticated. Roy died in 2002 and Jackie passed away in 2014, but their musicianship gave them a legacy that will not be forgotten.

Mel Tormé is quoted often here, because unlike many singers, he took the time and thought to consider and express reflections on the singing of American popular music as an author. Tormé was a multitalented musician, comfortable in performing many types of popular music, often with a strong emphasis on jazz. He was also a composer and included "The Christmas Song," a great holiday standard, among his works. As an arranger, he scored many of his own recordings. He was also a drummer, pianist, actor in numerous films and television programs, and a witty and ironic writer who wrote several works of both fiction and non-fiction. He was known for a mellow vocal sound that earned him the title of "The Velvet Fog," described in his autobiography as "a sobriquet he worked hard to outgrow." Tormé never described himself exclusively as a jazz singer, but no discussion of jazz vocalists would be complete without him. Tormé was versatile: as an Anglophile, he could interpolate quotations of music by Frederick Delius in a popular ballad and still engage in a scatting contest on television with the great blues singer Joe Williams. Williams, like Tormé, grew up in Chicago. Williams had a deep, rich vocal quality; he was a veteran of the big band era and from 1954-1960, he spent six years as the regular solo vocalist with Count Basie.

Figure 206 - Mel Tormé initially disliked his nickname, "The Velvet Fog." He was a brilliant vocalist, but also a drummer, composer, arranger, and author. (Photo courtesy of Alan Light)

Though Williams was best-known for his performances of the blues, he was also highly skilled in the art of scat-singing. The friendly contest between Williams and Tormé produced quite an exhibition of vocal virtuosity.

Mel Tormé's affinity for combining classical influences and jazz were never more apparent than in his collaborations with his friend George Shearing. With Shearing at the piano, Tormé would sing vocal lines that would swing, even though they were clearly inspired by one of his favorite musicians, J.S. Bach. Tormé began his career in Chicago, appearing as an actor and singer on radio before he was ten. Eventually he led his own group, the Mel-Tones, and worked with leading big bands (including Artie Shaw) throughout his career. Tormé was also the most articulate of all popular singers. He wrote an extensive book about his friends and colleagues, called appropriately, *My Singing Teachers*. He explained why breathing, diction, and intonation are all essential for a fine jazz performance. Tormé described scat as a craft that cannot be taught, but must be ingested by an unusual process of osmosis: "endless listening to jazz, trial and error, courageous ventures into uncharted territory, with mixed results on occasion, strict attention to intonation, made difficult at times by the very nature of that kind of singing—creative, experimental, haphazard."

Like Tormé, Carol Sloane is exceptionally articulate. She hosted her own radio program, worked as a jazz critic and reviewer for *Downbeat* magazine, and also teaches the elusive art of jazz singing to others. New England born Sloane identifies Carmen McRae as her principal influence. Like all good teachers, she makes clear the fact that one does not master the art and craft of jazz singing in ten minutes. She is a superb interpreter of lyrics, undoubtedly because she takes them seriously in an age when many vocalists cannot articulate a sentence that can be understood by an audience. Sloane once overheard an instrumentalist ask pianist Jimmy Rowles for the chord changes used in a particular piece. When Rowles began writing down the lyrics for the tune, the musician said he didn't need the lyrics. "How can you understand the tune if you don't know the lyrics?" demanded Rowles. Interestingly, she does not encourage her students to constantly sing scat syllables. In the early days of her career, she sang as an opening act for the legendary Oscar Peterson Trio. While performing Kurt Weill's "My Ship," she did everything but sing the melody as written. Peterson, seated at the piano, showed no reaction, and audience response was lukewarm. But when Sloane sang Weill's unadorned melody and allowed the lyric to deliver its message, the audience went wild and Peterson was beaming. Sloane learned from the experience that in jazz sometimes "less is more," and that a singer does not have to depend on scat to earn one's spurs as a vocalist.

Whole books can be written about the technique and style of jazz vocalists. Their road has not been easy, given the pressures at best, to perform accessible popular tunes, and at worst, the excesses of the rock music subculture. Their styles may differ, but the best jazz singers have one thing in common: they are first and foremost outstanding musicians, using the human voice like the musical instrument it can become in the hands (or perhaps, more appropriately, the vocal chords) of a master.

For many years, several instruments, especially the saxophone, were so strongly identified with jazz that they were unwelcome in classical circles, or at least treated with skepticism by concert musicians. (This was true despite the most innovative classical composers such as Claude Debussy, Jacques Ibert, and Paul Creston, who wrote for the saxophone.) Similarly, other instruments (especially the strings, other than the string bass) were so identified with the style and intonation of European concert music that they were not given a warm welcome by jazz musicians. A few instruments, notably the harmonica and the accordion, were not considered to have a true jazz sounds. But as always, pioneers and innovators appeared to break the mold and blaze new trails with their instruments where few had gone before.

The guitar often appeared in jazz ensembles. In the years following the death of Charlie Christian, several jazz guitarists had a lasting impact on their colleagues. Three of the best-known, Barney Kessel, Herb Ellis, and Joe Pass, all worked with Oscar Peterson.

Kessel, an Oklahoman, was known for his creativity in harmonizing melodies. He worked with bassist Ray Brown and drummer Shelly Manne, and played the guitar for vocalist Julie London when she recorded her signature hit song, "Cry Me a River" in 1955. Kessel spent a year with Oscar Peterson and Ray Brown on tour and he was replaced by Herb Ellis. Ellis, a Texan, was an alumnus of the Tommy Dorsey band. When the Dorsey band had a six-week break in its schedule, Ellis joined colleagues Johnny Frigo, a bassist and jazz violinist, and Lou Carter, a pianist, to form a trio, "Soft Winds," modeled on Nat "King" Cole's trio. Ellis grained wide recognition when he worked with Peterson. When he left the trio, his replacement was not another guitarist, but drummer Ed Thigpen. In the 1990s, Peterson, Brown, and Ellis reunited as a trio and proved that they still had the musical magic of four decades earlier.

Joe Pass, born Joseph Passalacqua, had one of the most unusual backgrounds in the jazz world. He was the son of a Sicilian steel mill worker and grew up in Johnstown, Pennsylvania. Pass developed an astounding technique, perfecting walking bass lines associated with the string bass, and a rich harmonic vocabulary that rendered his improvisations highly sophisticated. But in the 1950s, a heroin addiction sent him to prison and his career seemed to have ended almost before it started. But Pass triumphed over his addiction through the Synanon self-help program. He eventually recorded an album, *Sounds of Synanon*, with other jazz musicians, such as the gifted pianist Arnold Ross, who were also fighting drug problems there. Pass emerged as one of the world's leading jazz guitarists, able to play at the breakneck, lightning fast speeds that Oscar Peterson preferred. (Pass, when asked to compare his work with Peterson and his collaboration with other celebrated jazz pianists, praised the others while saying, "Playing with Oscar is an athletic event.")

Charlie Byrd was a Virginian who played jazz on an acoustic, non-electric guitar, in the finger style preferred by classical musicians. He studied with Sophocles Papas, a legendary pioneer in the advocacy of classical guitar music in Washington, D.C., and with Andrés Segovia, Papas's friend and the world's most famous concert guitarist. Byrd was best-known for his work in Brazilian jazz. His soft and gentle style of swinging jazz won him a worldwide audience.

The violin won acceptance in jazz when placed in the hands of Joe Venuti. Born in Italy, Venuti was brought to the United States as a baby when his parents settled in Philadelphia. In grammar school, he met guitarist Eddie Lang, who remained a lifelong friend and musical colleague. Venuti and Lang were members of Bert Estlow's dance band in the 1920s, where they allegedly joined other jazz musicians for improvising sessions in the men's restroom. Venuti eventually joined ensembles led by Paul Whiteman, Glenn Miller, and Benny Goodman. After Lang died in 1933, Venuti formed his own band. Venuti was famous for his practical jokes (including one legendary episode in which he filled the bell of another musician's sousaphone with flour) and his sharp, articulated phrasing. Venuti's records also influenced the French violinist Stephane Grappelli.

The classically trained Grappelli struggled through early years playing in cafés and on the streets of Paris. But by the mid-1930s, he had formed an ensemble with the famed guitarist Django Reinhardt and become one of the most influential jazz musicians on his instrument.

The harmonica made its way into jazz through the talents of Belgian-born Jean "Toots" Thielemans. Thielemans started playing the accordion as a small boy, but saw a performance by classical harmonica virtuoso Larry Adler in a movie and decided to take up the instrument himself. A man of many talents, Thielemans also learned how to play the guitar after being confined to bed by a respiratory illness. Thielemans worked with Grappelli and Reinhardt, who became his musical hero. He was fascinated by American jazz, worked with Benny Goodman and Charlie Parker, and eventually settled in the United States, becoming an American citizen. He spent eight years as a member of the George Shearing Quintet. Thielemans was also a composer. His *Bluesette* became a tremendously successful jazz standard. He proved that in the hands of a virtuoso, jazz passages worthy of the flute, clarinet, or saxophone, be brilliantly articulated on harmonica.

Figure 207 - Toots Thielemans, the Belgian harmonica virtuoso. (Photo by Jos L.Knaepen, courtesy of Veerle Van de Poel)

Art Van Damme was universally recognized as the master of jazz on the accordion. Van Damme's instrument was always popular, especially in Europe, but usually to express the pathos of cabaret ballads or the exuberance of the polka. Van Damme, unlike other colleagues who started on the accordion, never abandoned his instrument. Instead, he formed a jazz trio, eventually expanded to a quartet, and finally, a quintet, which became the mainstay of NBC radio and television for fifteen years.

During that period, Van Damme worked with most jazz vocalists and instrumentalists of consequence, ranging from Ella Fitzgerald to Dizzy Gillespie. What made Van Damme's approach to his instrument unique was his concept of tone and articulation. He used the bellows of the accordion to create a sound reminiscent of the wind section of the swing bands he admired. His melodic lines could have come from a fine jazz clarinetist. While never disrespectful of classical or

Figure 208 - Art Van Damme, regarded as the leading exponent of jazz on the accordion. (Photo courtesy of Sandra Mummert)

popular accordionists, Van Damme deliberately set out to develop a style of playing which most suited the jazz world. He succeeded to such an extent that he was universally identified as the world's leading exponent of jazz on his instrument.

JAZZ GOES TO SCHOOL

Jazz had comfortably moved into the concert hall in the 1940s through the efforts of Duke Ellington and Benny Goodman, among others. With equal vigor, it moved into the classroom, despite the raised eyebrows of a number of traditionalists who thought only European classical music belonged in academia. As leading jazz musicians began touring abroad and participating in newly organized jazz festivals, America's improvisatory music moved around the world. Most professional jazz musicians absorbed most of their training through experience, as traditions were handed down from one generation to another.

Innovations often came from new, rebellious young musicians eager to challenge the old order. There were jazz musicians who had trained in conservatories or in college music departments. But their studies in school were devoted primarily to European classical music. A small number of private teachers offered instruction in American jazz. These gifted teachers could articulate and notate the techniques of improvisation and paved the way for jazz to enter the classroom.

Teddy Wilson, John Mehegan, and Lennie Tristano were among the leading teachers of jazz in New York. Wilson offered jazz lessons at the prestigious Juilliard School of Music. His former assistant, John Mehegan, was a recording artist who also taught privately and became a prolific writer of new instruction books on jazz piano, complete with his own system of labeling chords. Lennie Tristano had a highly original approach to playing jazz piano and gained a reputation as a teacher among pianists in Manhattan.

One of the most accomplished jazz piano pedagogues could be found in Boston. The remarkable Sam Saxe could duplicate the most complex jazz solos on paper. He was a master transcriber who provided his students with note-for-note transcriptions of the best jazz piano solos on record. He was also one of the first teachers to

Figure 209 - Sam Saxe, one of America's finest piano pedagogues, was a major pioneer in the teaching of jazz. (Photo courtesy of Sam Saxe)

publish serious instructional materials for jazz pianists. He offered his pupils meticulous analysis of all of the elements of jazz, melody, harmony, and rhythm. All the while, he maintained a vast collection of original exercises enabling a student to master the finest jazz techniques.

Saxe had trained classically at the New England Conservatory of Music and with famed teachers Felix Fox and Hedwig Kanner. But he turned to jazz and played and wrote arrangements for major bands before deciding to concentrate on his special gift for teaching. The New England Conservatory invited him to become head of the popular piano department at the school at a time when offering instruction in jazz was highly unusual for strict classical conservatories.

After three years, he resigned to head west to Hollywood. During his forty-year teaching career, he coached and advised famous soloists and accompanists for such leading singing stars as Sarah Vaughan, Lena Horne, Mel Tormé, Betty Hutton, and Billy Eckstine. Many of the leading big bands during the swing years also featured Saxe pupils at the keyboard, including those led by Benny Goodman, Glenn Miller, Artie Shaw, Harry James, and Jimmy Dorsey. He was not well known to the public at large, although he was regarded as a virtual cult figure to his pupils, many of whom were famous recording artists. Claude Williamson, Arnold Ross, Joanne Brackeen, and Hampton Hawes were among his many accomplished piano pupils.

Sam Saxe's influence was apparent in others ways. In 1954, Elaine Lorillard, a socialite in Newport, Rhode Island, decided that jazz should be presented just like classical music—at a festival. She hired George Wein, a Sam Saxe pupil, to organize and run the series of concerts: the historic Newport Jazz Festival was the result. Four years after the groundbreaking festival was launched in Rhode Island, the Monterey Jazz Festival was organized in California.

Colleges and universities initially regarded jazz with suspicion. But jazz made its way into the college classroom in an unlikely way and in an improbable place. The pioneering efforts to teach jazz to college-trained performers began not in New York, New Orleans, or Chicago, but in Denton, Texas. In 1942, Gene Hall, an instructor at North Texas State College started teaching jazz and band arranging. Five years later, he organized what he called a "laboratory band" to train jazz musicians at the school. Eventually, Hall moved to Michigan State University, where he launched a jazz training program there. College music departments gradually became comfortable with the term "lab band" and it evolved into standard usage. Hall's successor at North Texas State, Leon Breeden, expanded the program to include twelve jazz bands. While classical music students journeyed to conservatories in major cities for training, jazz musicians were suddenly heading straight to Denton, Texas.

Not all colleges and universities were open-minded about jazz. Fred Katz, well-known as a jazz cellist on the west coast, joined the faculty of a local California college and found that he could only offer jazz courses through the anthropology department. Presumably, jazz was thought to signify "primitive culture." But at least one conservatory of music devoted its entire curriculum to jazz. The Berklee School of Music in Boston was founded in 1945 by Lawrence Berk. Berk was convinced that jazz instruction required a complete curriculum offered by a conservatory comparable to the best-known classical schools.

A similar experiment in specialized jazz training was developed by two unique schools on opposite coasts: the Westlake College of Modern Music in California (with a curriculum featuring studies in jazz arranging and composition developed by Dave Robertson) and the Music Inn, in Lenox, Massachusetts (with a faculty including Oscar Peterson, John Lewis, Dizzy Gillespie, Max Roach, Ray Brown, Bill Russo, Jimmy Giuffre, and Marshall Stearns). Although a number of prominent jazz musicians began their careers as students at these schools, unfortunately, neither of these schools survived. Dave Robertson, the pianist and arranger who served as Dean of Theory at Westlake, was quietly known in the jazz world for advice he gave to famous jazz stars, some of whom, "in the dead of night," asked him to ghostwrite music for their performances and recordings.

In 1952, Dr. Marshall Stearns founded the Institute of Jazz Studies. The Institute, now based at Rutgers University, collects numerous books and magazines devoted entirely to the subject, including Leonard Feather's extensive *Encyclopedia of Jazz*.

In 1960, Oscar Peterson decided to establish his own school, The Advanced School of Contemporary Music in Toronto. He was joined on the faculty by the members of his trio, Ray Brown and Ed Thigpen, along with trombonist Butch Watanabe and composer Phil Nimmons). Students hoping to pick up a few casual keyboard tricks from Oscar Peterson were in for a shock. Peterson was an inspiring but demanding teacher. Students at the school were amazed and surprised by Peterson's extensive curriculum, involving not only instrumental performance, but meticulous analysis of both written and improvised works throughout jazz history. Peterson gave extensive assignments requiring students at the Advanced School to listen to and thoroughly analyze every element of performances by the major historical figures in jazz.

When he told a class to listen to a performance by Duke Ellington's ensemble, a student might say, "I've already heard that piece." "Then what are the saxophones doing in the bridge?" Peterson would ask. "Why is the rhythm section, including the piano, not playing until the middle of the performance?" Peterson approached jazz as a serious art form, applying the same standards of form and analysis that conservatory students were expected to devote to concertos or chamber music.

The New School for Social Research in New York initiated an extensive jazz training program. In 1986, The School of Jazz at the New School was founded to provide students of jazz with a program in which they would be mentored by leading jazz professionals in Manhattan.

While many of the efforts to create schools of jazz modeled upon classical conservatories failed financially, the Berklee School of Music evolved into today's Berklee College of Music. Students flock to Boston to study with prominent jazz musicians such as pianist Ray Santisi, who joined the faculty over fifty years ago. Berklee also has its own publishing program and offers instruction in the latest elements of high technology that impact music.

In the 1950s and 1960s, critics and academicians finally began to take jazz seriously. Nobody had more enthusiasm in driving jazz onto college campuses than Stan Kenton. Kenton thought young musicians and young audiences were ideal targets for his endless quests for "new sounds." He started his own Stan Kenton Jazz Clinics in collaboration with Gene Hall. Kenton was a pioneer in offering instruction and concerts to new generations. His own bands made appearances on college campuses, making jazz seem "cool" and "hip" to younger audiences. On campus, Kenton took himself as seriously as he did off-campus. He modestly titled one of his pieces, *The Concerto To End All Concertos*.

Dr. Billy Taylor was known as an accomplished jazz pianist with impressive credentials. He grew up in Washington, DC. After he graduated from Virginia State University, Taylor became a protégé of Art Tatum in New York. During the bebop revolution, Taylor became a regular at Minton's, where he absorbed the harmonic and rhythmic innovations of bop. In his own solo work, Taylor combined elements of bop with smooth, elegant swing passages he heard Tatum play. He was a one-man ambassador of jazz, as pianist, composer, lecturer and teacher. Taylor led his own trio at Birdland, the jazz club where he worked with many jazz icons of the day. He could have simply rested on his laurels as a performer. But Taylor had the instincts of a teacher; like Kenton, he approached introducing jazz to new audiences with an almost evangelical fervor. So in 1964, he founded *Jazzmobile*, a modest outreach program, to introduce jazz to audiences "too young for nightclubs and too poor for concerts." Today, *Jazzmobile* provides workshops, recording facilities, and summer mobile concerts to thousands of young people who might never even hear a note of jazz otherwise.

Figure 210 - Billy Taylor, pianist and the greatest ambassador for jazz in the classroom and around the world. (Photo courtesy of Jazzmobile)

Taylor's modest outreach now entertains audiences of 350,000 annually and even sends jazz artists around the world to Europe, Japan, and Australia. Billy Taylor was also a prolific writer. He made numerous television and radio appearances. Taylor also wrote books (including an outstanding history of jazz piano filled with personal reminiscences) and remained continually active for the rest of his life on radio and television as a one-man ambassador of jazz, performing, composing, lecturing, and teaching. He was always pursuing his mission: to inspire an appreciation of jazz as "America's classical music," especially in young people who might otherwise not discover it.

JAZZ CONQUERS THE GLOBE

Jazz musicians performed in every corner of the world; they served as informal ambassadors for their musical art. This was the result of bands and soloists who achieved a popularity abroad that they often never achieved in their own home country. For instance, Pomping Vila was a brilliant young concert pianist in training at the Conservatory of Music of the Philippines when he heard a recording of "'Ain't Misbehavin'" performed by "Fats" Waller. He abandoned his ambitions for the classical concert stage and embraced the world of jazz. Eventually, he went to Hong Kong and then to Shanghai, where trumpeter Buck Clayton was leading a band. In Shanghai, an American named Jimmy James opened a plush nightspot, the famous Mandarin Club. Pomping Vila headlined there, displaying a personal style as a remarkable organist with a piano keyboard mounted on top of the electric organ. He was especially known for his dazzling footwork on the pedals.

He was influenced by the American jazz pianists, then working in pre-war Shanghai, Eddie Beal, Teddy Weatherford, and Palmer Johnson. Teddy Weatherford was often compared to Earl Hines. He spent much of his musical life introducing Asians to American jazz, living and performing in China, India, and Japan. Pomping Vila said that Palmer Johnson played more like Fats Waller than any other pianist. So a pianistic style created in Harlem in the 1920s circled the globe and came full circle when Pomping Vila settled in California after World War II had ended.

Figure 211 - Pomping Vila. He discovered American jazz in pre-war Shanghai as America's own music traveled the globe. (Photo courtesy of Pomping Vila)

Jazz had already become established in Europe through recordings and the performances of traveling musicians. But in the 1950s, jazz truly conquered the globe. Norman Granz took his *Jazz at the Philharmonic* concerts to Europe. The ever-industrious Woody Herman toured Latin America with his latest ensemble. Dizzy Gillespie, always intrigued by the sounds and rhythms of other cultures, appeared in the Middle East with a new band of his own. Willie Ruff, bass and French horn soloist, developed a program to bring one of the nation's most distinguished jazz programs to Yale, where he is on the faculty. In 1959, the Mitchell-Ruff Duo took jazz to the Soviet Union. Pianist Dwike Mitchell and French horn soloist Willie Ruff met as teenagers serving in the U.S. Army. Ruff was a classically trained French horn soloist; while in the service, Mitchell encouraged Ruff to play bass. They pursued separate paths (Mitchell the Philadelphia Music Academy, Ruff the Yale School of Music), but reunited as members of Lionel Hampton's band.

In 1955, they left Hampton and officially formed the Mitchell-Ruff Duo. Both musicians were equally accomplished in playing classical music or jazz. Mitchell and Ruff both knew that the Soviet government discouraged the performance of jazz with its American origins and emphasis on freedom and improvisation. Although they had been invited to appear in Moscow as strictly classical performers, the two versatile musicians took advantage of the opportunity to also play jazz for Russian audiences. They received a

Figure 212 - The Mitchell-Ruff duo featured Dwike Mitchell on piano and Willie Ruff on bass and French horn. Mitchell and Ruff gave historic performances of American jazz in the Soviet Union and China. (Photo courtesy of Willie Ruff)

wildly enthusiastic reception. Like their Soviet counterparts, the communist government in China never encouraged performances of improvised jazz. A number of American jazz musicians had indeed played in Shanghai before World War II. But when the communists took over the Chinese mainland, jazz was hardly part of the culture.

In 1981, the Mitchell-Ruff Duo was invited to make an historic trip to Shanghai. Jazz improvisation was new to Chinese audiences that had never been exposed to performers who could not only swing but make up music on the spot. They were stunned when a young piano student supplied a Chinese theme to the Duo. Mitchell and Ruff promptly improvised on the theme although they had never heard it before. Ruff is an accomplished linguist, fluent in seven languages. He further startled his hosts when they discovered that he spoke fluent Mandarin Chinese. Students in Shanghai wanted to know how Mitchell and Ruff created music on the spot. Ruff explained the Duo's music to the audience as "something created during the process of delivery," because there was no Chinese word for "improvisation." Fortunately, the music of the Mitchell-Ruff Duo didn't require translation.

Jazz also took to the airwaves. Ironically, the broadcaster most responsible for the popularity of jazz among international audiences was seldom heard in the United States. In 1955, *The Voice of America* began a series of broadcasts called *Music USA*. Since jazz was regarded as an American art form, countries behind the Iron Curtain didn't encourage listeners to appreciate the achievements of even the finest jazz musicians. Jazz fans throughout the U.S.S.R. and the countries that had been annexed into the Soviet orbit tuned in regularly to listen to *Music USA*. The host of the program, Willis Conover, was regarded as a jazz hero, an icon who became a symbol of jazz appreciation throughout those countries. Conover's name was a household word around the world, especially after he hosted jazz festivals everywhere from India to Brazil and inspired the White House tribute to Duke Ellington. Jazz fans called him, "The world's favorite American," but most Americans, including many jazz

Figure 213 - Willis Conover. Through the Voice of America, he became the voice of American jazz behind the Iron Curtain. (Photo by Voice of America)

aficionados, had no idea who he was, because Voice of America broadcasts were legally forbidden to air on American radio stations.

By the 1950s, jazz rhythms and harmonies were so familiar that a wide variety of musicians were drawing upon jazz influences without actually playing or composing jazz. Jazz was a natural source of musical ideas in the scoring of films, television, and theatrical productions. Choreographers began using jazz to inspire the creation of dances, even those with roots in ballet. In 1951, Alex North's film score for *A Streetcar Named Desire* was a landmark in the use of jazz. Valerie Bettis was one of the first modern dance choreographers to work with a ballet company. In 1952, she choreographed a ballet based on *A Streetcar Named Desire*, incorporating North's music. It was revived in the 1980s by the Dance Theater of Harlem.

A number of historians have described jazz as America's indigenous "classical music." Does jazz deserve the encomium? Books, plays, paintings, films, and musical compositions may be appealing at a given moment, but do they stand the test of time?

Throughout history, the most reliable criterion for considering works of art to be classic is their ability to endure. Carl Van Doren described classic books as those that "never need to be written again." This description could certainly apply to Beethoven symphonies, but can jazz be judged in the same way? Mortimer Adler called classics "rare, sustained achievements of excellence."

Certainly there is a rich legacy of jazz performance and composition. As jazz became accepted in the concert hall, organizers of new and experimental jazz orchestras commissioned composers to write new jazz works that could be added to programs of classic jazz works. Compositions premiered by Duke Ellington's orchestra, Stan Kenton's various ensembles, the American Jazz Orchestra led by John Lewis, and more recently jazz orchestra at Lincoln Center directed by Wynton Marsalis, might be written note-for-note by their composers. These notated works are created as precisely as a symphony or string quartet.

Such works represented a long journey from the days of small ensembles improvising in New Orleans or playing in small nightclubs on 52nd Street in New York. But it is the very nature of a jazz that sometimes causes confusion. Unlike traditional "classical" concert music, a classic jazz performance may exist only at the moment it emanates from its performing creator. Improvised jazz solos can be transcribed and concert works can be written down which are thoroughly based on jazz rhythms and harmonies. But like scenes viewed by a photographer, some may be preserved for posterity, however this does not diminish the value of those that are not.

Jazz soloists have often created melodies over chord structures of popular tunes. Leonard Feather calls these chord progressions, "the harmonic ski-trail over which ten thousand musicians have traveled." In Feather's words, "The improvisational bases of jazz are not melodies, but chord structures. Thus, the uninitiated listener who complains 'Where's the melody?' must be instructed in following the new melody created by the jazz man, based not only on the missing melody the listener is seeking, but on a harmonic routine identical with that original tune."

A jazz composition might be a melodic line based on familiar chords or a set of jazz figures (riffs) that are never written down; it could be a popular song suitable for improvisation that includes familiar jazz sounds such as blue notes or a full-notated concert work with as much detail as a Mahler symphony. In a jazz concert you may hear astounding improvisation or a virtuoso performance that has been as carefully planned as any classical piece of music. There are purists who insist that real jazz must be improvised. The subject is as controversial as politics and religion to true believers. Ultimately, we must always ask ourselves to evaluate the quality of the music. Many sounds in jazz are difficult if not impossible to notate. The most skilled musicians have sometimes failed in efforts to put selected jazz elements on paper. But we should never forget that music exists in the ear of the listener, not just on paper.

Today, many composers are writing works that combine elements of jazz and more traditional classical music. Duke Ellington established the tradition of original jazz concert works. Appropriately, his 100th birthday was celebrated in a concert presenting the New York Philharmonic and the Jazz Orchestra of Lincoln Center led by Wynton Marsalis. Both ensembles played the *Peer Gynt Suite*. The Philharmonic played Grieg's original, the jazz group played Duke Ellington's version of the same pieces. Duke Ellington and Billy Strayhorn arranged their own version of Tchaikovsky's *Nutcracker Suite*. The traditional *Dance of the Sugar Plum Fairy* became "Sugar Rum Cherry," while the *Waltz of the Flowers* became the "Dance of the Floreadores." The Philharmonic also played concert arrangements of Ellington classics.

Oscar Peterson composed jazz suites expressing serious themes. His *Canadiana Suite* applies jazz rhythms and colors to Western and martial moods depicting everything from the prairies to urban centers in Canada. Peterson also composed an *Easter Suite*, interpreting the birth, Crucifixion, and Resurrection of Christ through jazz.

John Lewis produced a variety of lasting works for symphony orchestra with jazz soloists and numerous small jazz ensembles. He was fond of writing fugues and drew upon the traditions of everyone from Bach to Debussy in his own unique jazz vocabulary. His most popular composition was "Django," a tribute to the guitarist Django Reinhardt. He would change the piece each time it was recorded. He also composed *English Carol*, a set of variations on the familiar Christmas carol, "God Rest Ye, Merry Gentlemen," for jazz quartet and symphony orchestra.

Composer Allyn Ferguson is best remembered by audiences for his symphonic film scores for a series of films made for television and adapted from literary sources, including *The Count of Monte Cristo*, *The Man in the Iron Mask*, *The Four Feathers*, *Les Misérables*, *A Tale of Two Cities*, *Ivanhoe*, and *The Corsican Brothers*. But Ferguson had also founded the Chamber Jazz Sextet, an ensemble combining elements of jazz and chamber music. He collaborated with poet Kenneth Patchen on a recording of jazz and poetry. Ferguson also created a jazz suite based on the Modest Mussorgsky's classical work, *Pictures at an Exhibition.*

Gunther Schuller, J.J. Johnson, James Giuffre, Lalo Schifrin, Billy Taylor, and André Hodeir are only a few of the composers who have written works combining elements of jazz and classical music. These are often labeled "third stream" compositions, but their composers usually resist having them labeled at all.

Duke Ellington referred to the French pianist-composer Claude Bolling as "my spiritual son." Bolling was a jazz prodigy on the piano, performing with such major figures as Lionel Hampton and Roy Eldridge at only fourteen. He became a prolific film composer and bandleader in France, eventually achieving worldwide acclaim. He also became the arranger for many of France's best-known vocalists, including Sascha Distel, Juliet Gréco, and Brigitte Bardot.

Bolling's *Suite for Flute and Jazz Piano,* recorded with famed flutist Jean-Pierre Rampal, achieved not only artistic praise, but an unlikely commercial success in the recording industry. Bolling went on to create other works combining traditional classical orchestral instruments and his jazz ensembles. These works were written for and performed by such noted soloists as violinist Pinchas Zukerman, cellist Yo-Yo Ma, classical guitarist Alexandre Lagoya, and trumpeter Maurice André. Although Claude Bolling's career has been primarily in France, his "crossover" works inspired many American performers and composers.

Figure 214 - Claude Bolling, a French pianist and composer, named by America's Duke Ellington, his "spiritual son." (Photo courtesy of Claude Bolling)

Invariably, efforts to produce larger, structured works in jazz bring charges from other musicians that such music isn't "real jazz."

These criticisms were even directed at such jazz icons as Duke Ellington. Cecil Taylor objected to the very idea of notating jazz; this protest underscores one of the most significant issues in the jazz world today. Critics and historians tend to speak of "the jazz musician" as if all jazz musicians were alike. However, this is complete nonsense. According to a study by the National Jazz Service Center, led by its dynamic president, the composer David Baker, jazz musicians no more think alike than do any group of diverse people. Jazz has become an international language. It has been adopted by a wide variety of people who invariably think of jazz as "their" music. So as jazz moved around the world and into different cultures, it was only natural for musicians to adapt various elements of jazz and to combine them with their own individual musical vocabularies.

Today, there are bands in Stockholm playing a Swedish version of New Orleans traditional jazz. A visitor to Japan can hear saxophonists emulating the riffs originated by Dizzy Gillespie and Charlie Parker in the 1940s. These musicians invariably bring their own creativity to jazz. With diversity comes a certain amount of controversy.

One of the most influential saxophonists of the 1960s, John Coltrane, experimented with harmonic ideas that had also intrigued composers of European concert music. Coltrane was an alumnus of the Dizzy Gillespie big band and spent several years as a member of a quintet led by his friend and frequent rival, Miles Davis. Nicknamed "Trane," he also worked with Thelonious Monk. Instead of conventional major or minor keys, Coltrane improvised melodies using modal scales. He began trying to produce "continuous" music, dubbed by critic Ira Gitler, "sheets of sound." Melodies from his 1957 recording, *Giant Steps,* were widely discussed and analyzed." Like so many jazz musicians, he fought battles with alcoholism and drugs. Eventually, he became interested in a spiritual revival and Eastern music, especially as played in India by sitar soloist Ravi Shankar. Coltrane began studying Indian music and in a subsequent recording, *My Favorite Things*, began working with bitonality, more than one key at the same time. In the 1960s, his recordings of "Impressions" demonstrated his skill at improvising solos that went far beyond the conventional length of jazz tunes in exploring modal scales, as did "Chasin' The Trane," a long blues solo without a conventional melodic theme. His interest in "free jazz," which bore little relationship to traditional scales and harmony, was controversial, but there is no denying that Coltrane was a major influence on generations of young saxophonists who hoped to follow in his footsteps.

Jazz musicians have always been a diverse group of people. An interviewer might ask a soloist to describe his art and receive a curt response, "I just swing." This never happened with bassist Charles Mingus who was always eager to expound on his theories and musical ideas. Like Coltrane, bassist Mingus was interested in modal scales, and also in "free jazz" moving away from conventional chords and written patterns. (In 1953, he joined Teo Macero, John LaPorta, and Teddy Charles to found the Jazz Composers Workshop.) Mingus was strongly influenced by Duke Ellington, but he became disenchanted with the idea of written jazz solos. Mingus was an opinionated, dominating musical personality who organized his own band, often teaching his pieces to m usicians by ear.

Of all the experimental jazz musicians who appeared in the 1950s and 1960s, none caused more controversy than saxophonist Ornette Coleman. When he appeared at "The Five Spot" in New York, Coleman improvised without references to traditional chords at all. His performance created a furor. Just like composers of avant-garde concert music in Europe, Coleman quickly divided the jazz world into two camps. Supporters of Coleman found his melodies "fresh and beautiful." (Coleman was praised by Gunther Schuller, president of the New England Conservatory of Music and a jazz composer and arranger who wrote for both Coleman and John Lewis, but others remained puzzled and confused.)

Coleman used no piano or guitar in his ensembles to provide harmonic support, introduced highly unusual rhythmic accents in his solos, and created as much controversy in the jazz world as Arnold Schoenberg had with his experiments in atonality years earlier in concert music. Like Coleman, pianist Cecil Taylor moved away from conventional key signatures, melodies, and meters. His solos seemed to have more in common with the avant-garde music of concert composers like Anton Webern than the stylings of Wilson, Tatum, or Powell.

Figure 215 - Ornette Coleman startled the jazz world by improvising without key signatures in an atonal style, the same one used by many experimental European avant-garde composers decades earlier. (Photo by Geert Vandepoele)

Not all musicians saw the future of jazz as an experimental journey away from traditional melody, harmony, or rhythm. One new style of jazz was inspired by melodies and rhythms south of the border . . . very far south, all the way from Brazil. What is intriguing is that Brazilian music became an interesting influence on American jazz, while music created in North America was simultaneously absorbed by leading Brazilian musicians. In 1958, a Brazilian singer, João Gilberto recorded two songs, his own "Bim-Bom" and "Chega de Saudade" by Antônio Carlos Jobim and Vinicius de Moraes. De Moraes was a former Vice-Consul who had left music for the diplomatic service and returned to his art after a nineteen-year absence. Critics suggested that these songs, introducing the new style of *bossa nova*, were written for singers who sang off-key. Gilberto responded by recording the incredibly successful "Desafinado," which means "off-key" in Portuguese, the language of Brazil.

In 1959, Gilberto's album, *Chega de Saudade,* became a major hit in Brazil, along with the motion picture, *Orfeu Negro* (*Black Orpheus*). The film score featured Brazilian songs by Jobim, Moraes, and guitarist Luiz Bonfá, whose haunting "Manha de Carnaval" ("Theme from Black Orpheus") traveled quickly around the world. Three years later, American guitarist and saxophonist Stan Getz recorded the album *Jazz Samba*, bringing Brazilian music to the center stage of the American jazz world. The album included compositions by Jobim, Bonfá, and the Brazilian guitarist Baden Powell. Powell was known to combine Brazilian phrasing and melodies with the influences of American jazz. In time, Brazil would attract such leading American jazz musicians as flutist Herbie Mann, trumpeters Kenny Dorham and Roy Eldridge, and saxophonist Coleman Hawkins.

Antônio Carlos Jobim emerged as the leading composer in the new Brazilian style. Jobim had been classically trained by a German pianist who admired the twelve-tone technique of Arnold Schoenberg. But Jobim was drawn to the stunning harmonies of Debussy, Ravel, and especially the music of Brazil's most prominent composer of concert music, Heitor Villa-Lobos. Jobim acknowledged drawing upon the melodies and harmonies of Brazil and the pulsating rhythms of Africa. The *bossa nova* won worldwide acclaim. In North America, songs like Jobim's "How Insensitive," "Corcovado," "Triste," and "Wave" became popular hit songs. One of Jobim's biggest hits, "The Girl from Ipanema," was scheduled for recording. João Gilberto's wife Astrud joined him unexpectedly in a duet, and the song became a sensation. With the popularity of the *bossa nova*, it was inevitable the popular performers of every type would record the songs. Many of these performances had no relationship to jazz. But the influence of Brazilian music (and the evolution of Brazilian jazz) played a significant role in a new style of jazz.

The *bossa nova* had evolved from the samba. Its melodies were long and full of surprises. The melodies often fluctuated back and forth from one tone to another in uneven phrases taking surprising turns. The harmonies were far more complex than those usually heard in popular music, while the regular, softly pulsating rhythms made such music ideal for jazz improvisation. Unlike the intense Afro-Cuban influence in jazz, which created a sense of energy and percussive excitement, the Brazilian style was more understated, more pensive, more romantic. Though the classic Brazilian tunes were quickly absorbed into the mainstream of popular music, the Brazilian style of the 1960s left a lasting legacy in the world of American jazz.

As jazz studies became academically respectable, it was only natural for jazz historians to draw conclusions about the musical revolution and evolution that jazz had caused. To this day, there are those who dislike all analysis of jazz, insisting that scholars are trying to impose an intellectual discipline on an art form that should be essentially free as a bird.

Leonard Feather developed an intriguing theory suggesting that jazz has gone through clearly defined periods of evolution that correspond to those of classical music, but shift sixty times as fast. The Renaissance was a period in which attempts to document and notate music thrived; in Feather's view, the Renaissance could be compared to the days of early jazz. The classic era of Haydn and Mozart emphasized clarity, form, and melodic line. Similar standards could be found in the era of the great swing bands. Beethoven tested the limits of harmonic and rhythmic resources of the day; so did the bop innovators playing in clubs in the 1940s. The romantic era in classical music was dominated by full-size orchestras required to play the symphonies of Brahms and Tchaikovsky. Stan Kenton challenged the jazz world with his huge ensembles and large-scale compositions. Debussy, Ravel, and the French Impressionists were boldly experimental in harmonic colors and placed less of an emphasis on the intense emotion of the romantic masters. The same could be said for John Lewis and the Modern Jazz Quartet. Lewis freely acknowledged his debt to Debussy and Ravel. In recent years, contemporary jazz has experienced periods of confusion and developments, which can also be found in the world of concert music. There is a tension between those who reject the past heritage of jazz and those who embrace it. Although Feather advanced his theory more than two decades ago, it still merits consideration today.

THE FUTURE OF JAZZ

It would be pleasing to conclude our journey through the jazz world by declaring that the legacy of jazz has been the product of evolution that each new period has somehow improved on the past and that jazz is guaranteed a brilliant and rewarding future. Unfortunately, two disparate sources seriously threaten such a conclusion. Academicians and commercial promoters have engaged in considerable mischief that threatens the jazz legacy. In the case of the commercial promoters, their efforts may indeed prove fatal.

Many of the finest classical performers today enjoy jazz whether they are able to play it or not. Every classical musician cannot improvise and there are many who resent those who can. A number of prominent composers of concert music dislike any music that appeals to audiences on an emotional level. So they instinctively dislike the popularity of jazz, which they regard as a threat to their cerebral approach to music. These composers and their musicologist advocates are usually in residence at college and university music departments. Because their own music often has little popular appeal, they respond by dismissing jazz as artistically insignificant and historically trivial.

Figure 216 - Duke Ellington at the White House - Jazz comes full circle. Duke Ellington is honored by President Richard M. Nixon as a guest in the White House where his father once worked as a butler. (U.S. Government Photo)

Consider the case of Duke Ellington Despite his iconic status in the world of jazz, Ellington had his critics who suggested that many of his large concert works were not truly jazz because they were precisely notated and actually belonged in the classical world.

So the very versatility that made Ellington special resulted in his having an ambivalent status among those critics who felt that jazz should have no role to play in the world of concert music. In 1955, the Symphony of the Air, a broadcast orchestra conducted by the venerable Arturo Toscanini, commissioned a new work by Ellington, *Night Creature*. Toscanini was a severely demanding conductor and his respect for Ellington would suggest that *Night Creature* would have been received with open arms by orchestras throughout the country. But because American symphony orchestras were unwilling to record it, the work had to wait years until it was finally recorded by French and Swedish orchestras.

Ten years after he received the commission from Arturo Toscanini's orchestra, Ellington was nominated for the Pulitzer Prize. But the full Pulitzer committee turned down a special award for Ellington, clearly because of his jazz roots. Ellington was gracious and quipped that at age sixty-six, "Fate is being kind to me. Fate doesn't want me to be too famous too young."

Because jazz was inextricably linked to the recording industry, commercial success and failure in jazz depended heavily on the attitudes of promoters, record company executives, and producers. The commercial promoters were in business to make money by selling records and sheet music. They were instinctively suspicious of any music that had serious or artistic pretentions. Unfortunately, this was doubly true because so many great jazz artists were African American. Promoters expected jazz musicians to be primarily entertainers. This attitude plagued many jazz artists throughout their careers; clearly, Louis Armstrong, Thomas "Fats" Waller, and Nat "King" Cole were affected by demands that they project a perpetually happy and entertaining personality. The urbane, intellectually adventurous jazz musicians who happened to be African American didn't fit the stereotype; and all musicians who tried to creatively stretch the musical boundaries of jazz were usually regarded with suspicion by a recording industry that wanted performers and music that were easy to pigeonhole.

The worst impact of commercialism on jazz came from the 1960s rock music revolution. Rock appealed easily to teenagers who suddenly had the money to buy records. Recording companies immediately measured all new music by a simple yardstick: could it appeal to a youth market? Many musicians responded to the new rock revolution with ridicule and anger, only to suddenly find themselves unemployed. Other musicians decided that they could preserve their careers by compromising or surrendering their standards in the hope that the new rock record producers would tolerate them. Jazz musicians, like their classical counterparts, faced a serious moral and artistic dilemma: should they stand up for their principles and risk their careers or should they jump aboard the rock bandwagon, even knowing where it would lead, in an act of self-preservation?

There were critics and performers of conviction. John Lewis responded to the new rock juggernaut with the observations, "They're show business entertainers, we're musicians." Famed jazz broadcaster Willis Conover agreed. He said, "Jazz is America's classical music. Rock is, at the moment, its spring fertility rite, a panting attempt to be honest. Music should express some feelings that go beyond lust and saving the whales. Some say rock is just another form of jazz, as Dixieland, swing, and bop were. My mind tells me this could be true. My heart tells me it's false." Leonard Feather described the new rock musicians as representing nothing more than the "Baser manifests of rhythm and blues music," consisting of "technically crude and harmonically dull performances by inferior singers, out of tune vocal groups and instrumentalists willing to prostitute their art for the financial interests of the big beat."

But not everyone stood tall in the face of professional insecurity and the huge financial rewards offered by pop record moguls who were taking over the recording industry and making unbelievable fortunes in the process. Many musicians succumbed to the commercial pressures. They altered their musical style or sang the praises of performers they knew in their hearts to be complete charlatans. One such performer was clearly Miles Davis. Once admired for his originality, Davis was the target of a scathing critique by Stanley Crouch, who accused him of "rejecting the beautiful to genuflect before the commercial." Many followed Davis's lead, trying to play "jazz –rock," not only emulating the musical styles of rock groups, but even copying their appearance and personal mannerisms.

Today, many young people are ignorant of our jazz heritage because they have been exposed to nothing but rock music. Jazz trumpeter Wynton Marsalis has been an outspoken critic of those who know nothing of our musical past and a strong advocate for the legacies of such historical figures as Armstrong and Ellington. Marsalis tells young jazz musicians that they will be better for "knowing what Louis Armstrong sang through his horn." Exposure to jazz is key to rectifying the situation. Jazz trumpeter Terence Blanchard recalls the rock music he heard in high school. He says, "We thought it was great music, but it wasn't. It doesn't stand the test of time. When we teach children jazz, we're teaching them to appreciate part of our heritage." Saxophonist Donald Harrison recalled that as a teenager, he could easily copy any of the sounds he heard on current pop records. But when he tried duplicating a Charlie Parker solo, he couldn't copy the first five measures. Harrison learned quickly that Parker's legacy, not current pop records, set the standard for jazz improvisation.

Duke Ellington summed up the importance of the jazz legacy by reminding us that each time we listen to a symphony or a great jazz work, we learn or experience something new. He said, "It is becoming increasing difficult to decide where jazz starts or where it stops, where Tin Pan Alley begins and jazz ends, or even where the border lies, between classical music and jazz. I feel there is no boundary line and I see no place for one if my own feelings tell me a performance is good. In the final analysis, whether it be Shakespeare or jazz, the only thing that counts is the emotional effect on the listener."

There can be no question that jazz does offer the composer or performer an opportunity to express a full range of emotions in ways that have lasting value. If jazz is indeed our classical music, will we preserve it? Jazz has undergone something of a renaissance: it is more popular than ever before and more appreciated than ever before. But musicians still face the same dilemma, how to preserve artistic integrity and creative independence in a commercial industry. Artistically, jazz is on solid ground. It is music that offers something each time you hear it. This is Ellington's description and it is clearly the classic definition of "classic." So jazz offers the promise of a rich and rewarding future, but only if we meet the challenge of recognizing and preserving its heritage.

How can I describe what jazz means to me, what it signifies in my own musical life? Summarizing any great musical genre is difficult. But describing one's jazz experiences is especially challenging; the two essential elements of jazz, improvisation and swing, imply constant change. Every pianist who plays a Chopin nocturne has a personal experience with the music. No two pianists will play it alike. But the notes of the nocturne will remain the same and each pianist will play the same notes, albeit with a different interpretation.

For centuries, great musicians have argued about whether there is a single "correct" interpretation of music. Concert pianist and teacher Ruth Slenczynska experienced this during her student days when one eminent teacher, Artur Schnabel, insisted that an artist should "set" an interpretation based on musical logic and not change it; another equally eminent teacher, Alfred Cortot, disagreed, encouraging her to improvise. The world of classical music has been filled by musicians of legendary virtuosity who believe they have found the definitive interpretation of the same collection of notes. The great (and highly opinionated) classical piano virtuoso Ethel Leginska did not seem in a mood for compromise when she told me, "Each time we play, we must play the same way." Presumably, this meant Mme. Leginska's way. Nor did Wanda Landowska, the eminent master of the harpsichord, seem interested in improvisation when she told her pupils, "You play Bach your way, and I'll play him *his* way."

Jazz musicians, however, do not have such arguments. They know that each performance is going to be different. Even the same player performing the same piece a hundred times will not play it exactly the same way. In fact, the more different, the more unique, the more improvisatory the performance, the more exciting the outcome! A jazz concert is like an athletic event or a night of election returns or even a bullfight. You think you know what is going to happen, but you really don't.

Oscar Peterson, whose jazz keyboard brilliance constantly set a standard for the rest of us, said that he embraced classical music whole-heartedly. But he also realized that jazz offered him the opportunity for total creative freedom. What is the jazz musician seeking through this musical freedom? Said Peterson, "All artists spend their creative lives trying to find out how high it is possible for them to climb before their time is over, and however majestic their achievements may seem to others, they are never satisfied. Only perfection will do." And Peterson goes on to observe that creating an uninhibited "off the cuff" musical composition in front of an audience is a dare-devil enterprise, not for the faint of heart; he says "it requires you to collect all your senses, emotions, physical strength and mental power and focus them totally onto the performance—utter dedication, every time you play."

When even the best jazz musicians begin to play, they must ask themselves, "Will this performance swing?" They may wonder if their fellow musicians (and their audience) will experience the driving rhythms, harmonic adventure, and melodic surprise that separate the best performances from the merely mundane. What makes jazz a unique element of our musical heritage is that it is the art form that always asks the question and the answer is different each time. Like life, jazz is full of surprises.

AMERICAN MUSICAL THEATER

When I was studying with the illustrious composer and teacher, Mario Castelnuovo-Tedesco, we discussed the creative paths that were available to an American composer. "You should leave the writing of operas to Italians," he said, "because we have been writing them for hundreds of years. And you should leave the symphonies to the Germans, because they are long-winded." To my surprise, the Maestro said he believed that American composers should explore the world of musical theater. I was startled by this advice, because the genre of Broadway shows was far afield from his usual areas of interest. But he understood instinctively that the American musical, like baseball and jazz, was a truly American invention.

But what is the American musical? We used to call them "musical comedies," but many of them aren't funny. We associate them with Tin Pan Alley. But the best musicals reflect a sophistication and literacy that transcend and surpass the popular song. The creators of our best musicals, Irving Berlin, Jerome Kern, the Gershwins, Cole Porter, Richard Rodgers (with his two partners, Lorenz Hart and Oscar Hammerstein II), Kurt Weill, Alan Jay Lerner, Frederick Loewe, Frank Loesser, Leonard Bernstein, among others, were far more than tunesmiths. They created a unique form of expression, part music, part theater, part poetry. I believe that some of the best music and lyrics of the twentieth century were written for American musical theater. Yet it all began by accident.

In 1866, a producer named William Wheatley was preparing to produce a melodrama by minor dramatist, Charles Barras. (One historian said that Barras had seen a performance of Weber's opera, *Der Freischutz*, and had never gotten over it.) Wheatley was approached by two impresarios, Henry C. Jarrett and Harry Palmer, who had a problem. The two had imported a troupe of dancers to perform the French ballet, *La Biche au Bois*. Their chosen theater had burned down. Wheatley made a momentous decision. He decided to improve Barras's melodrama by incorporating the stranded dancers and popular tunes of the day into the script. On September 12, 1866, he launched a five and a half-hour epic called *The Black Crook*. Critics panned Barras's play, but the public loved the music, the pretty French dancing girls, and the show's hit song, "You, Naughty, Naughty Men."

The rest was history. The show enjoyed fifty years of success, including eight revivals, the last one in 1929. Why was it a hit? For one thing, this extravaganza was sung in English, unlike most operas of the day, so the audience understood the lyrics. The music wasn't complex or sophisticated. Producers were quick to realize that a chorus line of pretty girls couldn't guarantee the success of a show, but it couldn't hurt. This was the inauspicious beginning of a new art form today called American musical theater. No one could have imagined that a fusion of opera, dance, and popular songs would lead to a whole new genre of American music, but that is precisely what occurred.

THE PIONEERS: ECHOES OF OPERETTA

In the years to come, audiences would discover many forms of musical theater. Some were heavily influenced by European opera, others by American popular song, and even jazz. It was this remarkable fusion of elements that made the American musical unique. For a time, American composers of comic operas, such as Reginald de Koven, absorbed the British influence of Gilbert and Sullivan. Viennese operettas were also popular. The term "musical comedy" originated in England, applied to *In Town* and *The Gaiety Girl* shows, which were imported from London to New York. Two key figures on Broadway were both Irish, but they couldn't have been more different. One, Victor Herbert, was born in Ireland and trained in Germany. The other, George M. Cohan, was a brash Irish-American vaudevillian.

Figure 217 Victor Herbert. Irish-born, he composed the scores for many of the most popular and successful Broadway productions of the early 20th century. (Photograph courtesy of Library of Congress, Public Domain)

Herbert was a cellist, a fine orchestrator, a bandmaster, and a polished musician. His wife, Theresa Forster, was an opera star; when the Metropolitan Opera hired her, she insisted that they hire her husband as a cellist.

In New York, Herbert produced a steady stream of classic shows, including *Babes in Toyland*, which took audiences to a land of fairies, magical moths, and dancing spiders. In 1905, he wrote the score for *Mlle. Modiste*; over the objections of its star, Fritzi Scheff, he insisted on including a song he had been keeping for years, "Kiss Me Again." It became the show's big hit. Herbert's most popular show was *Naughty Marietta*, which included "Ah, Sweet Mystery of Life" and "I'm Falling in Love with Someone." Herbert played an important role in another aspect of Broadway involving the rights of composers. He heard an orchestra in Shanley's Restaurant playing the music from *Sweethearts*, one of his own shows, without his permission. He protested and the result was a test case, which brought the newly founded ASCAP (The American Society of Composers, Authors, and Publishers) before the U.S. Supreme Court. ASCAP won the case and the decision by Oliver Wendell Holmes established the principle that composers should be paid for the performing rights to their music.

George M. Cohan was "born in a trunk" in Providence, Rhode Island. He was literally carried onto the vaudeville stage as part of his parents' act. Cohan claimed to have been born on the Fourth of July and if he wasn't, he should have been. Throughout his career, he loved to wave the flag at every opportunity. During World War I, his song, "Over There," not from any of his shows, became a virtual anthem for American troops. He

Figure 218 - Victor Herbert, at the piano, joined by colleagues and charter members of ASCAP, Gustave Kerker, Raymond Hubbell, Harry Tierney, Louis A. Hirsch, Rudolf Friml, Robert Hood Bowers, Silvio Hein, Alfred Baldwin Sloane and Irving Berlin. (Photo courtesy of ASCAP)

became famous for addressing his audiences, "My father thanks you, my mother thanks you, my sister thanks you, and as for me it goes without saying."

Cohan's biggest hit was *Little Johnny Jones*, in which he expressed his two great enthusiasms in life through songs such as "Give My Regards to Broadway" and "Yankee Doodle Dandy." Cohan stayed with these themes throughout his career. He would go on to produce shows called *Forty-Five Minutes from Broadway* and *George Washington, Jr.* Cohan decided he wanted to own his own little part of Broadway, "the top part," he said. He became an actor-manager. Though the public thought he was a universally beloved figure, he was considered a strike-breaking producer by actors who joined a union during the first Actor's Equity strike.

Victor Herbert's shows were full of romance and exotic settings like Egypt, Persia, Spanish New Orleans, and "The Land of Mother Goose." His characters, like those in European opera, were likely to be heroic and fantastic, not people you would see on the streets of New York. Cohan's shows spoke to the common man in language understood by everyone. Edwin Royle called musical comedy "lunch-counter art." It presented the thoughts and feelings of the people in words and music.

Around 1885, a number of music publishers set up offices in New York on 28th Street between Fifth Avenue and Sixth Avenue. The district became known as "Tin Pan Alley." There are various explanations as to the origin of the name. It was likely used initially in a derogatory way because the publishers' offices were filled with cheap upright pianos that had a tinny sound. When they were all being used (or pounded) at the same time, each playing a different tune, people thought they were hearing the sound of a group of people striking a collection of tin cans. One story relates that composer Harry Von Tilzer tried to make his piano more percussive by placing strips of paper on the strings and that the "tin can sound" was the description of a reporter who saw what he was doing. Several great composers started their careers working on the "Tin Pan" pianos.

Figure 219 - "Give My Regards to Broadway" by George M. Cohan became the anthem of Broadway. (Photograph used Courtesy of Abram Samuels Sheet Music Collection, The Trexler Library, Muhlenberg College)

By the 1920s, a creative tension or competition had arisen between these two attitudes. Many of the best musicals of the day were written by composers born in Europe who came to America. Their musical styles remained European, their lyrics and librettos clearly influenced by the tradition of opera. But they were challenged by a new group of young Americans whose traditions came from Tin Pan Alley and from the world of jazz. They all produced shows that had a major impact on the development of the American musical theater.

Figure 220 - "Over There" by George M. Cohan, literally inspired millions of Americans in World War I. (Photograph Courtesy of Abram Samuels Sheet Music Collection, Trexler Library, Muhlenberg College)

Gradually, radio and recordings surpassed the sale of sheet music as a way to introduce new songs to the public. In the 1950s and 1960s, the rise of rock and roll forced "Tin Pan Alley" into a decline, although several of the original buildings are still standing today.

Many songs from these pioneering music publishers became hits on their own. Other major hit songs came from two major sources, Broadway musicals and the movies. Together, the best tunes reflect the brilliant creativity of a unique group of composers and lyricists. Their work today is often described as "The Great American Song Book." Lists of the songs that are included are a source of controversy, rather like lists of the best presidents or baseball players. Nor is there total agreement regarding the beginning and end of the "Song Book's" era. But we should remember that American music and our daily lives over several generations would have been quite different without it.

For a time, it appeared that the Viennese waltz-operetta would dominate America's theatrical tastes. In 1907, Franz Lehar's phenomenally successful work, *The Merry Widow*, arrived in New York like a conquering heroine. The world of *The Merry Widow* was one of elegance, sentiment, charm, optimism, a view that love conquers all, and usually that the conquering would be done in 3/4 time.

Just two years later, audiences were delighted by Oscar Straus's popular operetta, *The Chocolate Soldier*. This work, inspired by George Bernard Shaw's *Arms and the Man*, told the tale of a warrior who would rather eat chocolates than fight. Shaw refused compensation for the rights to his play and told librettist Leopold Jacobson that the operetta must be advertised as a parody and not use his plot. Shaw characteristically expressed doubt that composers of the day had the skills to cope with his subject matter. When asked if he could think of a composer whose music was good enough to be paired with his words, Shaw declined and said modestly, "Mozart is dead."

Figure 221 - Franz Lehar, composer of the post-Strauss "Silver Age" in Vienna. He composed *The Merry Widow*, still today the most popular operetta of all time. (Photo courtesy of the George Grantham Bain Collection, Library of Congress)

Two composers from Middle-Europe settled in America and began producing their own homegrown versions of Viennese-inspired operetta: Sigmund Romberg and Rudolf Friml. Though the two composers enjoyed success during the same era, they were dissimilar. Romberg's prosperous Hungarian family wanted him to be an engineer. Friml, a native of Bohemia, never doubted his life would be devoted to music. Romberg achieved his Broadway success after a long struggle, while Friml became known much more quickly. Friml was inclined to be an intense, moody, serious musician. Romberg was known for his amiable disposition and the comical malapropisms that resulted from his life-long struggle with the English language. For Romberg, music was all-important. A colleague once tried to give him secret information during a card game by whistling Romberg's hit, "One Alone." Romberg didn't recognize the title of his own piece and said, "Who knows from lyrics?" Romberg was a violinist, while Friml excelled on the piano.

Figure 222 - Rudolf Friml, the composer whose romantic scores were among the most popular on Broadway in the 1920s, had his musical roots in 19th century operetta, as is clear in this 1905 sketch by Czech artist Alfons Mucha. (Public domain.)

Romberg eventually came to New York, where he began contributing songs to revues. He made his mark on Broadway with *Maytime,* a smash hit

Figure 223 - Sigmund Romberg - His scores, inspired by Viennese operetta, set the tone of romantic musicals in the years following World War I. (Publicity photograph-public domain)

musical. It was a sentimental tale about young soldiers in nineteenth century New York and a love story that spanned the generations that appealed to soldiers and their sweethearts at the outbreak of World War I. "Will You Remember?" was a question real soldiers, as well as Romberg's characters, were asking the girls they loved. *Blossom Time*, based on the work of Franz Schubert, added luster to Romberg's reputation. But his real success came ten years after his debut, with *The Student Prince*. By this time, he had contributed to forty shows. Ironically, Romberg's score was very nearly rejected by the Shuberts, the show's producers, who thought his Viennese style was "classic" and "too old-fashioned" for Broadway audiences.

The Student Prince was adapted by Dorothy Donnelly from a tale about a young German prince, Karl Franz, who falls in love with a waitress. But he must assume the duties of a king when his father dies and marry a princess who has given up her true love to marry him. The bittersweet ending upset the Shuberts, but they were forced to join the rest of the world in acknowledging Romberg's work as a classic. The score contained such memorable melodies as "Deep in My Heart, Dear," "The Drinking Song," and especially the sweeping "Serenade."

During the same 1924-1925 season, Rudolf Friml enjoyed his biggest hit *Rose-Marie*. Friml was born into a poor family in Prague, where he had been a child prodigy on the piano, a pupil of Antonín Dvořák at the Prague Conservatory, and accompanist for famed violinist Jan Kubelik. Unlike Romberg, Friml achieved success on Broadway quickly. In 1912, Victor Herbert refused to write a new show for his star singer, Emma Trentini, because he believed she had publicly snubbed him by refusing to sing an encore of his "Italian Street Song" at a benefit concert. Friml was chosen to replace Herbert as the composer of *The Firefly*. He turned out such melodies as "Giannini Mia," "Sympathy," and "Love Is Like a Firefly."

*Rose-Mar*ie contained Friml's best-known composition, "The Indian Love Call." *Rose-Marie* was set in the Canadian Rockies, featuring a romance between a fur-trapper and a singer who is half-Indian. The hero is falsely accused of murder, but the Mounties catch the real killer and the story has a happy ending. *Rose-Marie* was an important milestone for two other reasons. It was the first show to bring in a million dollars and Friml's lyricist was a young man named Oscar Hammerstein II, who would later emerge as the key figure in changes taking place throughout musical theater during the twentieth century.

Both Friml and Romberg followed their successes with other hit shows. Friml wrote the score for *The Vagabond King*, based on the exploits of the poet François Villon, and *The Wild Rose*. Romberg provided *The Desert Song*, *My Maryland*, and *The New Moon*. *The Desert Song* was written with librettist Otto Harbach and lyricist Oscar Hammerstein II. The show's hero was a young French soldier pretending to be the simple-minded son of the French commander, but secretly the leader of the rebellious Riffs in Morocco. Romberg's compositions included "One Alone," the martial "Riff Song," and "The Desert Song," the sweeping melody inspired by the show's title. *The New Moon* was set in French New Orleans and boasted such Romberg compositions as the stirring "Stouthearted Men," and such haunting melodies as "Lover Come Back to Me" and "Softly as in a Morning Sunrise," as well as the lush, lyrical songs, "One Kiss" and "Wanting You."

Figure 224 - Otto Harbach, lyricist and mentor to Oscar Hammerstein II in the early days of his career. (Public domain)

In time, the dominant musical figures of Broadway would bid farewell to the operetta. The sentimental tales of poets and princes sung by vocalists with operatic voices would be gradually replaced by shows that were under the influence of a new American art form, jazz. An elegant farewell to the age of the Viennese-inspired operetta came from an unlikely source. Noël Coward was an urbane British sophisticate, known for his suave manners and caustic wit. His irreverent, clipped speech and memorable one-liners seemed light years away from the world of *The Student Prince*.

But in 1929, Coward created *Bitter-Sweet*, a show that reflected not the modern jazz age, but the tender Edwardian romanticism of a bygone era. It tells the story of a young British aristocrat who must choose between the man her family prefers and her true love, a young jazz musician. Her aunt, Lady Shayne, tells her niece the story of her own lost, true love, also a musician; the story goes in flash-back to the world of Viennese operetta. The song that became Coward's musical signature, "I'll See You Again," contains the line, "What has been is past forgetting." Coward seemed to be bidding a nostalgic farewell to the world of operetta, a time of lyrical sentimentality, which the world would not see again. "I'll See You Again" came to him amidst the honking klaxons and shouting policemen in a New York traffic jam. Said Coward of his signature song, "I have heard it played in all parts of the world. Brass bands have blared it, string orchestras have swooned it, Palm Court quartets have murdered it, barrel organs have ground it out in London squares, and swing bands have tortured it beyond recognition, and I am still very fond of it and very proud of it." The wistful, nostalgic song, created so casually, was the top royalty earner in his catalogue for over sixty years.

IRVING BERLIN AND THE TRIUMPH OF TIN PAN ALLEY

If Coward waved good-bye to operetta, Irving Berlin helped push it out the door. Berlin, like Romberg and Friml, was an immigrant. But Berlin did not come from the polished world of classical conservatories. Born Israel Baline, he and his family immigrated to America from Byelorussia and settled in a lower East Side tenement in New York. At fourteen, he left school for the life of a singing waiter in the saloons of the Bowery and a restaurant in Chinatown. He worked at odd jobs, became a "song-plugger" for Tin Pan Alley publishers, and learned to play the piano, but only in one key, F-sharp major. One of his songs, "Marie From Sunny Italy" was finally published. His first real success came when he wrote the music and lyrics for "Alexander's Ragtime Band." This piece wasn't really ragtime. It wasn't jazz. But it was a hit tune that absorbed the syncopated rhythms and energy of a musical style far removed from operetta.

Figure 225 - Irving Berlin in 1906. Jerome Kern said that Berlin does not have a role in American music, he IS American music. (Public Domain)

In 1914, Berlin wrote the score for *Watch Your Step*, a musical show starring the great ballroom dance team of the day, Vernon and Irene Castle. Berlin produced "Play a Simple Melody," a duet in which two melodies are set against each other. One character sings, "Won't you play a simple melody, like the one my mother sang to me?" The other responds with a second, "Musical demon, sets your honey a dreamin', won't you play me some rag?" The musical argument between the two singers, two melodies, and two styles continues. The message is clear: ragtime (and the raucous, frenetic, up-tempo sound of Tin Pan Alley) is about to bid farewell to opera. Berlin's next two big hits couldn't have been more different: *Yip Yap Yaphank* was Berlin's revue of World War I Army life; he would write patriotic songs about his country for the rest of life. Producer Florenz Ziegfeld made a career of "glorifying the American girl" in his *Ziegfeld Follies*. The 1919 edition contained Berlin's hymn to the American girl, "A Pretty Girl Is Like a Melody." Berlin could be elegant, but his melodies were genuine American popular songs. The taxi horns of Tin Pan Alley would soon replace the violins of Vienna on Broadway.

Styles on Broadway were changing. So were audiences. The public, which once adored happy endings of operettas became less inclined toward sentimentality. After the leading man and leading lady embraced at the conclusion of one operetta, critic Burns Mantle grumbled, "It looks as though at the finish they might marry and raise duets." New names were appearing on Broadway musical theater programs. In 1914, *The Girl from Utah* opened in New York. The show, a hit in London, had new songs added, including "They Didn't Believe Me," by a young composer named Jerome Kern. The following year, *Hands*

Figure 226 - A rare view of many of America's leading popular composers and lyricists in 1920: from left, Gene Buck, Victor Herbert, John Philip Sousa, Harry B. Smith, Jerome Kern, Irving Berlin, George W. Meyer, Iving Bibo, Otto Harbach. (Photo by Al Aumuller, courtesy of New York World Telegram and Sun Collection, Library of Congress)

Up, a self-described "musico-comico-filmo-melodrama," opened. It introduced a new performer called Will Rogers and a song, "Esmerelda," by a young man from Yale named Cole Porter. A year after that, *The Passing Show*, a revue, introduced a song, "Making of a Girl," by nineteen year old George Gershwin. By 1924, the young Gershwin had composed *Rhapsody in Blue* and collaborated with his older brother, Ira, on a musical, *Lady Be Good*, which starred the brother and sister dance team of Fred and Adele Astaire. The show introduced Ira Gershwin's brassy, impertinent lyrics, the syncopations of the title song "Lady Be Good," "Fascinating Rhythm," and "Somebody Loves Me." A song that eventually became one of the Gershwins' greatest hits, "The Man I Love," was dropped from the show during rehearsal. Fred Astaire was an astonishing dancer, but his singing style was clearly non-operatic. New stars would appear in Broadway who might not produce pear-shaped tones; it seemed more important for them to know how to "sell" a song.

Another new team was prepared to challenge the Gershwin brothers for the songwriting crown on Broadway. In 1919, New York audiences went to the opening of a new show, *A Lonely Romeo*. The score included a song by composer Richard Rodgers and lyricist Lorenz Hart. The following season, the two were back with their own first full-length book show, *Poor Little Ritz Girl*. The Rodgers and Hart legend was secure by 1924, when their song "Manhattan" highlighted *The Garrick Gaieties*. Three years later, Rodgers and Hart provided the score for *A Connecticut Yankee*. Based on Mark Twain's classic tale of a modern man thrust back into the era of King Arthur's Camelot, the show introduced songs that became instant classics: "Thou Swell" and "My Heart Stood Still."

One of the biggest hits of the 1920s was written by Vincent Youmans. Youmans' life was hardly that of the struggling composer. His wealthy family owned a number of fashionable hat shops in New York. He went to private schools and took a job on Wall Street, but unexpectedly turned to music. In 1921, he made his Broadway debut with *Two Little Girls in Blue*. In 1925, Youmans composed *No, No, Nanette*, with lyrics by Otto Harbach and Irving Caesar. The show nearly closed in Detroit, but the producer asked for several new songs, and Youmans came up with "Tea for Two" and "I Want

Figure 227 - Vincent Youmans, who made his mark on Broadway with melodies of fine quality that are widely admired today, was devoted to fishing and sailing. (Photo courtesy of Vincent Youmans III)

to Be Happy." The plot concerned the exploits of a flapper who is the daughter of a Bible publisher. The show became a smashing success, inspiring a host of imitations. (*Bye, Bye, Bonnie* and *Yes, Yes, Yvette* were soon to follow.)

In later years, Irving Caesar declared that the lyric containing the words "Tea for Two" was originally only temporary. The song soon took on a life of its own around the world. In 1927, far from the lights of Broadway, the tune was transformed in an unlikely way.

When conductor Nikolai Malko and Russian classical composer Dmitri Shostakovich heard the popular tune on a record at Malko's home, Malko challenged his friend to transcribe "Tea for Two" for a symphonic orchestra in an hour or less. Shostakovich accepted the wager and won the bet for 100 rubles when he finished the task in only forty-five minutes. His version of "Tea for Two" became *Tahiti Trot*, a work performed in Moscow in 1928 and the following year used as an entr'acte in Shostakovich's ballet, *The Golden Age*.

Figure 228 - Irving Caesar early in his career with the junior partner in his Broadway publishing company, Incy, (pronounced "Inky.") (Photo courtesy of the ASCAP Foundation)

Irving Caesar had a remarkable career before and after "Tea for Two" and "I Want to Be Happy," the two lyrics he contributed to *No, No, Nanette*. Several years earlier, he had collaborated with his friend George Gershwin on the song "Swanee," without ever having seen the river which is the subject of the lyric. The two worked on the lyrics on a Manhattan bus ride after having lunch at Dinty Moore's restaurant. In the 1930s, it was Caesar who created "Animal Crackers in My Soup," the song that helped launch the career of the world's most famous child star, Shirley Temple. Caesar also produced a musical setting of "The Pledge of Allegiance," which was adopted officially by a resolution of the U.S. Congress. He wrote hundreds of songs during his career, married for the first time in his nineties, and when he died at age 101, he left the royalties from all of his works to the ASCAP Foundation to help deserving young composers. As musical styles changed for the remainder of the twentieth century, "Tea for Two," the unlikely hit, remained popular. Jazz piano virtuoso Art Tatum turned it into a dazzling piano solo as difficult as any etude by Chopin or Liszt. Bebop pianist Thelonius Monk used the chord structure of the tune for an entirely new jazz composition, while bandleader Tommy Dorsey recorded it as a cha-cha. By the end of the century, the song entered pop culture as bandleader Doc Severinsen would use the tune to punctuate failed jokes delivered by comedian Johnny Carson on television's "The Tonight Show," while children learned to recognize "Tea for Two" as sung by the animated Chipmunks and puppets such as The Muppets.

No, No Nanette became the first Broadway musical to circle the globe. It was performed throughout Europe, South America, New Zealand, the Philippines, and China. It was a show that stood the test of time. It was revived in 1971 on Broadway to great success.

Not every production for which Youmans composed the music after *No, No, Nanette* was commercially successful. But he invariably wrote hit songs of high quality. Whether the shows were hits or not, a score with music by Vincent Youmans always promised memorable melodies. Two of Youmans' best-known standards came from his last big Broadway hit, the 1927 production of *Hit the Deck.* One, "Hallelujah," was originally composed while Youmans was in the Navy; the other, "Sometimes I'm Happy" was originally in *Night Out,* a show that had not become a hit two years earlier. On the other hand, he also produced standards for shows that didn't prove to be financially successful. "More Than You Know" and "Without a Song," with lyrics by Billy Rose and Edward Eliscu, came from a show called *Great Day!* "Time on My Hands," with lyrics by Harold Adamson and Mack Gordon, came from *Smiles.* Lyricist Edward Heyman fondly recalled writing the lyrics for "Through the Years," title song for a show of the same name, in a single session while sitting in Youmans' moonlit New York apartment. Youmans also played a major role in the development of the movie musical in Hollywood. His songs in the film *Flying Down to Rio* helped launch the celebrated series of movies starring Fred Astaire and Ginger Rogers.

Youmans was a bon vivant, used by F. Scott Fitzgerald as the model for one of his characters in *Tender is the Night.* He delighted in sailing, fishing, and racing automobiles.

Sadly, in the 1930s and '40s, he was beset by an assortment of financial and health problems. He died in 1946; he was only 47 years old. Because he died at a young age and his major hit shows on Broadway were in the 1920s, Youmans is not as well remembered as his colleagues who lived decades longer. But the craftsmanship and skill apparent in his writing made him one of the giants of Broadway and Hollywood. This explains the survival of his songs as standards, performed and recorded by many generations too young to recall him at the height of his fame.

Composer Walter Donaldson and lyricist Gus Kahn were one of the most successful songwriting teams, producing a hundred songs together. Although they also worked with other collaborators, their work together made them especially well known. Donaldson, born in Brooklyn, began his career as a staff pianist on Tin Pan Alley. In the years just after World War I, audiences thought of soldiers returning from Europe when they heard Donaldson's "How 'Ya Gonna Keep 'Em Down On the Farm After They've Seen Paree?" with lyrics by Joe Young and Sam M. Lewis. Donaldson also teamed with lyricist George Whiting to write "My Blue Heaven." Gus Kahn was born in Koblenz, Germany and came to the U.S. when his family emigrated. He provided lyrics for bandleader Isham Jones, resulting in such hits as "It Had to Be You" and "I'll See You in My Dreams," the latter used many years later in 1951 as the title for a film about Kahn's life which starred Danny Thomas and Doris Day.

Kahn's first song with Walter Donaldson was "My Buddy." Many of their hits defined the music of the "Roaring Twenties," a time known as "The Age of Wonderful Nonsense." Songs such as "Makin' Whoopee," "Yes Sir, That's My Baby," "Carolina in the Morning," and "Love Me or Leave Me" had a life of their own and would be repeatedly recorded for decades. Musical styles changed, but the popularity of these songs remained. Donaldson and Kahn, like many successful songwriters from Broadway, went west to Hollywood and they contributed many songs to successful movie musicals.

The triumph of Tin Pan Alley, with its influences of ragtime and jazz, was never more evident than in the work of Broadway's leading black composers. Hubert "Eubie" Blake and Noble Sissle met while members of a Baltimore band. The two worked together in James Reese Europe's Society Orchestra and formed their own vaudeville act, "The Dixie Duo."

Figure 229 - Noble Sissle was a gifted songwriter who collaborated with his friend, pianist Eubie Blake. Sissle was a singer, a musician, and later in life a popular disc jockey in New York. (Photo courtesy of Carl Van Vechten Collection, Library of Congress)

At a benefit for the National Association for the Advancement of Colored People, Sissle and Blake joined forces with librettists Flournoy Miller and Aubrey Lyles to develop *Shuffle Along*. Inspired by a Miller-Lyles vaudeville sketch, the show presented a pair of political hacks trying to become

Figure 230 - "I'm Just Wild About Harry," originally a waltz, became a toe tapping hit in the 1920s and in1948, Harry S. Truman selected it as his campaign song when he ran for President of the United States. (Photo Courtesy of Abram Samuels Sheet Music Collection, The Trexler Library Muhlenberg College)

mayor of their town. Their plans are undone by a reformer, Harry Walton. Eubie Blake composed a waltz, *I'm Just Wild About Harry*, but he was persuaded to change it to a sprightly one-step. Blake was most comfortable writing rhythmic foxtrots and toe-tapping, up-tempo pieces. The show became a huge commercial hit, opening the first door for blacks in musical theater, not only as creators, but as members of an integrated audience.

Blake continued writing and playing the piano; he lived to be 100, and was rediscovered late in life as the last surviving ragtime pioneer. The sequel to *Shuffle Along* introduced a new composer, the master stride pianist, Thomas "Fats" Waller. In 1929, Waller composed the score for *Hot Chocolates* (with lyrics by Andy Razaf). The show introduced the popular *Ain't Misbehavin* and an unknown trumpeter who left the orchestra pit to appear on stage and play a solo. His name was Louis Armstrong.

The success of *Shuffle Along,* by Eubie Blake and Noble Sissle, paved the way for other musicals in the 1920s featuring black casts and paving the way to desegregate New York Theaters. One of the most prolific lyricists of this period was Andy Razaf, who provided the words for major hits by "Fats" Waller and Eubie Blake. He had perhaps the most unique background of any figure on Broadway. His maternal grandfather, John L. Waller, was a former slave who became a lawyer, journalist, newspaper editor, and eventually Minister-Resident and Consul-General to Madagascar. His daughter, Andy's mother, married the Grand Duke of Madagascar. After a French invasion toppled Andy's aunt, Queen Rànavàlona III, from the throne of Madagascar and resulted in the death of his father, Andy's mother fled to the United States, where Andy was born in Washington, D.C.

Figure 231 - Eubie Blake, pianist, composer, and the last surviving figure of the Ragtime Era. (Photo courtesy of Institute of Jazz Studies, Rutgers University)

Andreamenantana Paul Razafinkeriefo changed his name to the more easily remembered "Andy Razaf." He heard the young pianist Thomas Waller—not yet known as "Fats" and not related to his grandfather—at a 1923 piano competition and asked him to become his songwriting partner. Razaf and Waller wrote half the songs for the hit show *Keep Shufflin'in 1927.* Waller and Razaf wrote the scores for such shows as *Load of*

Coal and *Hot Chocolates*. Like many songwriting collaborators, Razaf and Waller were complete opposites. Razaf was quiet, modest, and disciplined, while Waller liked an abundance of good food, drink, and the Harlem nightlife. Razaf managed to keep Waller at a rented piano in his mother's New Jersey home for a while, but Waller eventually headed off to Harlem and nearly forget an improvised melody for a song which became one of their biggest hits, *Honeysuckle Rose*. He remembered it only after Razaf repeatedly hummed fragments of the tune to him over the phone.

"Fats" Waller liked to tell people that he was inspired to write "Ain't Misbehavin'" after missing his alimony payments and serving time in jail. But Razaf said that the producers of the revue *Hot Chocolates* needed an extra song and that Waller came up with the melody in just forty-five minutes after Razaf wouldn't let him leave his house in Harlem without finishing it.

Figure 232 - Andy Razaf, nephew of the Queen of Madagascar, became a prominent songwriter in America. (Photo courtesy of the Institute of Jazz Studies, Rutgers University)

One of the investors in the show was the notorious gangster Dutch Schultz. Schultz demanded a comedy song about blacks, but Razaf wrote his most poignant lyric, a song of despair about the racial obstacles placed before black Americans at the time. He called it "Black and Blue."

Razaf worked with other composers as well. He collaborated with a white Englishman, Paul Denniker, to write the hit "Sposin'" in 1929 and with Eubie Blake on "Memories of You" in their score for *Blackbirds of 1930*. For *The Kitchen Mechanic's Revue*, he provided lyrics to James P. Johnson, including those for a spoof of Cole Porter's style, "A Porter's Love Song: To a Chamber Maid." Despite his often lighthearted lyrics, Razaf had a serious side. He made notes for an opera based on the history of Madagascar, but when Waller died in 1943, he abandoned the idea.

MGM produced a short called "Honeysuckle Rose." It included a scene in which the hit by Waller and Razaf was composed by two white writers in jail. The scene didn't bother Waller, but Razaf was furious and protested in a letter to Louis B. Mayer who called him "ungrateful." Razaf responded, "I wonder how they would have placated Irving Berlin if they had presented a scene showing "Alexander's Ragtime Band" as being written by a colored boy behind bars." Later, Razaf protested apartheid in South Africa and communist atrocities in Fidel Castro's Cuba. He wrote and spoke about the need for black Americans to preserve their own history. He also created a book of original poetry, *The Trumpet of Sounds*. Though often neglected, Andy Razaf's lyrics received new audiences and earned him posthumous honors in the 1970s and 1980s.

JEROME KERN, OSCAR HAMMERSTEIN, AND A MAKE-BELIEVE SHOW BOAT

In the years following World War I, many composers, writers, and artists rejected the sentiments and ideals of the past. On Broadway, a revolution was coming. It was not led by a pair of wild-eyed revolutionaries, but by two of the most meticulous craftsmen ever to pick up a pen: Jerome Kern and Oscar Hammerstein II. Their magnum opus, *Show Boat*, would change the history of the musical theater forever. Kern was the composer acknowledged by Victor Herbert as the man best qualified to carry on his legacy. He was born into a prosperous New York family, which assumed he would go into the family business. When his father once asked him to buy two pianos, he purchased two hundred; the family concluded that he should pursue his real interest, music. Kern completed his studies in Germany and went to England. He remained a lifelong Anglophile. He started his career as an accompanist and during rehearsal breaks would begin playing tunes of his own. He succeeded in attracting attention.

Kern made an impact on Broadway with his contributions to a series of musicals known as the "Princess" shows, because they were produced at the Princess Theater. His collaborator for *Nobody Home* and *Very Good Eddie* in 1915 was the playwright Guy Bolton. Two years later, they were joined by the British humorist, P.G. Wodehouse, for *Oh, Boy*, which contained Kern's classic song, "Till the Clouds Grow By," and *Leave It to Jane*. These shows all reflected a more intimate approach to music and lyrics. They had American settings and themes; the songs were especially designed for specific characters. The boy and girl next door replaced the vagabond kings and merry widows of the operatic stage.

Figure 233 - Producer Morris Gest, writers P.G. Wodehouse and Guy Bolton, producer F. Ray Comstock, and composer Jerome Kern at the time *of Leave It to Jane* in 1917. (Public domain)

Jerome Kern had a remarkable gift for writing melodies that seemed to simply flow from his pen. He was probably the most lyrical of all Broadway composers. Although he could be every bit as rhapsodic as the creators of European operetta, he always managed to sound like an American: optimistic, unpretentious, and unaffected. He always managed to do something original. Kern's harmonies were neither experimental nor revolutionary, yet there was a certainty in his songs; his melodies and choice of harmonies and rhythms seemed so perfect that no one could imagine them being written in a different way.

The apparent simplicity in Kern's sweeping melodies was deceptive; he was said to labor for hours over a single modulation (a change from one key center to another.) He was a meticulous craftsman who made the results look easy, but they were the result of a master who took enormous care in completing his work.

In 1920, Kern wrote the score for *Sally*, a star vehicle for tiny Marilyn Miller, a story about an orphan who becomes a Ziegfeld girl and eventually marries a millionaire. The song-hit of the day was Kern's cheery "Look for the Silver Lining." The following year, Kern came up with "Good Morning, Dearie," featuring a blues melody based on *The Beautiful Blue Danube* and sung in counterpoint to the famous waltz. One of Kern's more interesting shows was *Sunny*, a 1925 production that included the familiar melody, "Who?" *Sunny* was important because it represented the first collaboration between Kern and Oscar Hammerstein II.

Hammerstein can be justifiably described as the single most important lyricist in American musical theater. He came from a theatrical family. His grandfather, the original Oscar Hammerstein, was impresario of an opera company, which rivaled the Metropolitan. His father was a theater producer; his uncle was a theater manager. Although he went to Columbia University to study law, it was inevitable that he would begin writing for the theater. Hammerstein's family introduced him to the perfect mentor, Otto Harbach, a leading Broadway librettist twenty-two years his senior. Harbach, known as the "professor," became Hammerstein's collaborator and teacher, suggesting ideas and titles for songs that young Hammerstein would develop; Harbach would then make his own changes to the lyrics. The two remained friends and collaborators for years. Interestingly, Hammerstein, years later, would assume a similar "mentor" role in the creative work of his protégé, Stephen Sondheim. When Harbach introduced Kern to Hammerstein, he found himself being eclipsed by his pupil. By 1927, Hammerstein had been the lyricist for both Rudolf Friml (*Rose-Marie*) and Sigmund Romberg (*The Desert Song*). But his collaboration with Kern on *Show Boat* was unique.

Figure 234 - Edna Ferber, whose sprawling, vibrant novel inspired Jerome Kern and Oscar Hammerstein II to write the score for *Showboat*. (Photo courtesy of Kevin C. Fitzpatrick, and the Dorothy Parker Society, dorothyparker.com)

Why was *Show Boat* so important? While other shows of the era are seldom revived, *Show Boat* has continued to delight generations of audiences since its 1927 premiere. It has enjoyed seven New York and four London revivals. Three separate films have been based on *Show Boat*, as well as a television program. Countless stock companies have produced the show around the country and around the world. There are numerous *Show Boat* recordings. To analyze *Show Boat* and tell the story of this remarkable show would take a whole book. (In fact, more than one has been written!) Summing up *Show Boat* in a few words is as daunting as adapting the show from the book on which it is based.

Show Boat was inspired by Edna Ferber's sprawling novel about life on a Mississippi river boat. Jerome Kern read the book and knew it was the basis of the musical show he was born to write. While attending the theater, he asked his friend, the acerbic critic Alexander Woollcott, if he could meet Edna Ferber. Woollcott turned around and barked, "Ferber, come here!" The writer, who was in the audience, met Kern and the rest was history. Ferber proved to be initially skeptical about her story being peppered with popular tunes and dancing girls. But Kern and Hammerstein were not to be denied. What made *Show Boat* revolutionary? Previous musicals seldom dealt with controversial subjects. *Show Boat* was a story about racial prejudice and miscegenation. The heroine, Magnolia, is a girl who lives on the Mississippi showboat. Her father, the well-meaning Cap'n Andy, and her domineering mother are shocked when she falls in love with Gaylord Ravenal, a dashing gambler. She marries the older and sophisticated Ravenal, but he turns out to be a charming scoundrel who eventually abandons her. Because the score of *Show Boat* had roots in operetta, it may seem traditional to contemporary audiences. But in 1927, *Show Boat* was anything but traditional.

Figure 235 - Helen Morgan, who introduced the song "Bill" in *Showboat* on Broadway and sang it in the 1929 and 1936 film adaptations. Ava Gardner performed it in the 1952 film, although her voice was dubbed by Annette Warren. (Photo by Carl Van Vechten, courtesy of the Van Vechten Collection, The Library of Congress)

Before *Show Boat*, writers of musicals would create the most outlandish situations to justify including songs that were arbitrarily thrown into a show. "That reminds me of a song I used to know" was enough to justify a "bell-note," a signal in the orchestra that someone was about to burst into song or that a chorus of dancing girls might suddenly appear on stage. *Show Boat* opened with a chorus of black stevedores lamenting their fate in life. For the first time, the racially integrated cast featured integrated black and white story lines. Most characters in musicals were unchanged by the end of the show. Magnolia was the first leading character in a musical to grow; by the end of the show, the dreamy-eyed ingénue became a mature, self-reliant woman with a grown daughter who followed in her mother's footsteps on the stage. All the characters were followed from the 1880s to what was then the present, the 1920s. Hammerstein found ways to cut Ferber's book, combining characters and adding elements of his own, so that the saga (which covers many years) could be reduced to a single evening's entertainment. Ferber had allowed Cap'n Andy to die in the book; Hammerstein kept him alive and reunited him with his daughter. Though some elements of the plot depend on unlikely accidental coincidences, the "book" or libretto of *Show Boat* presented for the first time a real drama with unified themes and serious subject matter. Hammerstein also devised the idea of a "Greek chorus" to comment on the action. The chorus consisted of the black workers who toiled on the docks, reminding us of the unifying force of the river. Man pursued his follies, but the river remained. (Years later, when someone would praise Jerome Kern for writing "Ol' Man River," Hammerstein's wife Dorothy said, "Jerome Kern wrote 'Dum,dum, dee,dee,' Oscar Hammerstein wrote 'Ol' Man River.'")

Kern composed a magnificently cohesive score. (The musical motif for the showboat, "Cotton Blossom," is an inversion of the melodic fragment of "Ol' Man River.") Few shows had as many hit melodies. *Show Boat* had a half dozen, including "Make Believe," "You are Love," "Can't Help Lovin' Dat Man," "Why Do I Love You?" and "Bill." Kern was taken by a performance of" Nobody Wants Me," sung by Helen Morgan in a revue called *Americana*. Morgan, cast in *Show Boat*, was given the song "Bill." The latter, written by Kern and P.G. Wodehouse, had been in and out of several shows. Rewritten by Kern and Hammerstein, it provided one of *Show Boat's* most poignant moments. Kern's melodies justified an early critic who described him as a composer of "Eiffel towering proportions."

During an out-of-town try-out, the original Magnolia, Norma Tertis, asked Kern and Hammerstein for a song for the second act. Hammerstein provided Kern with a set of lyrics containing every verbal cliché he despised. Kern was furious, until he realized that Hammerstein was playing a joke. He then produced a second set of lyrics for Kern, who was delighted, as theater-goers have been for years, with "Why Do I Love You?" When Hammerstein heard Kern play one of his melodies, he thought immediately of the phrase "Couldn't you? Couldn't I? Couldn't We?" But he couldn't decide what it was the young couple couldn't do. Eventually this melody became "Make Believe." *Show Boat* remained the crown jewel of musical Broadway in the 1920s. Kern and Hammerstein wrote songs for specific characters, specific dramatic situations. Though not everyone followed their lead, the path was clear. A new road had been charted for the American musical. *Show Boat* would remain the most revolutionary of shows for two decades, until the production of *Oklahoma!* (again written by Hammerstein, this time with composer Richard Rodgers.)

THE BROTHERS GERSHWIN: GEORGE AND IRA

In 1929, the stock market crashed and the United States found itself in the midst of the Great Depression. In the 1930s, a group of phenomenally gifted composers and lyricists, who had appeared in the 1920s, became the dominant force in America's musical theater. The nation was torn between the domestic trauma of the depression at home and ominous inevitability of war clouds on the horizon. Many musicals of the 1930s continued to feature plots whose main purpose was to entertain, to amuse, to make people laugh. But a new spirit was appearing in the theater, a spirit of biting satire, in which the sacred cows of the day were virtually barbecued on stage, with some of Broadway's foremost composers and lyricists to supply the seasoning. On January 14, 1930, the Gershwins unveiled the first major musical of the new decade, a revised version of their 1927 show, *Strike Up the Band*. The original plot, developed by playwright

Figure 236 - George and Ira Gershwin, New York 1928. As brothers and collaborators, they had a unique rapport that made a tremendous impact on America's musical history. (Photo used by special permission from the Gershwin Family Trusts)

George S. Kaufman, concerned a mythical war between the United States and Switzerland, a conflict started when the Swiss protested an American tariff on imported cheese. Since Kaufman wasn't interested in rewriting his original libretto, his friend Morrie Ryskind replaced him. The Gershwins' mother suggested changing cheese to chocolate in the new version; Ryskind agreed and also changed the tycoon's war against the Swiss into a dream sequence in the show. This time, *Strike Up the Band* was a hit.

The Gershwin brothers were a remarkable pair. Born in Brooklyn, raised in a tenement on New York's Lower East Side, the two remained close throughout their lives. The family, not as poor as popularly imagined, bought a piano so that older brother Ira could take lessons. Younger brother George, however, proved to be the one with musical talent. A gifted pianist, he would prove the most facile of all Broadway composers at the keyboard, actually starting his musical career as a song plugger and eventually, as rehearsal pianist for Victor Herbert. Ira Gershwin was the more retiring and reserved of the two, somewhat in his brother's shadow, though never to the degree suggested by the radio announcer who declared with a straight face, "We are now going to hear music by George Gershwin with lyrics by his lovely wife Ira." Fascinated by literature and rhyme, Ira was a natural wit who admired Gilbert and Sullivan. He turned to writing lyrics, which he described as "a precarious profession requiring the patience of a gem setter." His colleagues agreed, nicknaming him, "The Jeweler."

What set the Gershwin style apart from others was George's fascination with many styles of music, which were unrelated to Broadway or Tin Pan Alley. He tried his hand at writing instrumental concert works and turned out *An American in Paris* and his *Concerto in F* for piano. He was intrigued by the sounds of contemporary classical music. Though not a jazz musician, he absorbed major harmonic, rhythmic, and melodic elements of jazz. Listen to a Gershwin melody; the syncopations and "blue" notes originated in the improvisations of black jazz musicians of the time. Gershwin could create music easily by improvising at the piano. He wrote with an incredible facility that made his craft appear deceptively easy. In later years, Leonard Bernstein would observe this phenomenon as he asked his audience, in jest, "Why don't you run upstairs and write a nice Gershwin tune?"

Ira Gershwin longed to write lyrics for a show in which all the songs were integrated into a believable plot, a score that broke the mold of verse and chorus songs popular on

Tin Pan Alley. Lyricists like Ira Gershwin and Lorenz Hart were not dramatists, so they were dependent on their playwright-collaborators. Though the original production of *Strike Up the Band* failed, it launched a collaboration between the Gershwins and the acerbic playwright, George S. Kaufman, who curiously disliked musicals. (Irving Berlin noted that when he collaborated with Kaufman on a musical, the writer would leave the theater whenever the music would begin. Berlin tried to win Kaufman over by playing his own favorite composition, "Always," which Berlin had dedicated to his devoted wife Ellin. When Kaufman heard the line, "I'll be loving you, always," he suggested that Berlin change it to "I'll be loving you, Thursday.")

In 1931, the Gershwins, Kaufman, and Morrie Ryskind created the satirical show, *Of Thee I Sing*. The plot concerned the presidential campaign of one John P. Wintergreen and his Vice-Presidential running mate, Alexander Throttlebottom. Instead of addressing serious political issues, Wintergreen runs on a platform of "love," promises to marry the winner of a beauty contest in Atlantic City, falls in love with a secretary, and nearly causes a war with France by jilting the contest winner, a lady of French descent named Diana Devereux. Meanwhile, Throttlebottom turns up at the White House as a tourist; no one has the slightest idea who he is, and he spends the entire play trying to figure out what a Vice-President is supposed to do. The show contained vintage Gershwin tunes, including "Of Thee I Sing," "Who Cares?," and "Love is Sweeping the Country." When tearful audiences responded to Gershwin's music, the unsentimental Kaufman grumbled, "Don't they know we're kidding love?" The show became the first musical to win the Pulitzer Prize. The Gershwins were back with further Wintergreen-Throttlebottom misadventures in *Let 'Em Eat Cake* in 1933. This time, America's two favorite politicians were beaten by John P. Tweedledee and rather than accept defeat, they hatch plans for a revolution. Eventually, differences are to be resolved through a baseball game between the Supreme Court and League of Nations. Throttlebottom tries to umpire the game and his unpopular attitudes lead him to be sentenced to be guillotined.

Though he was successful with playful political satire, George Gershwin developed a desire to pursue the larger forms of composition identified with classical concert music. He wanted to write an American opera. One night, hoping to fall asleep, he picked up a copy of *Porgy*, a novel set in Cabbage Row, a black ghetto in Charleston, South Carolina. He knew he had found the subject for his opera. The book was written by DuBose Hayward, a white poet. Hayward and his wife, Dorothy, dramatized the novel in 1927. At one point, it appeared likely to be adapted into a musical by Jerome Kern and Oscar Hammerstein II, incredibly as a vehicle for charismatic entertainer Al Jolson to perform in blackface. Hayward agreed to collaborate with George Gershwin. When he began writing lyrics, it became clear that Ira's touch was needed. So Ira Gershwin began polishing Hayward's lyrics. When the poet's words ended in hard consonants, Ira would change them to singable vowels.

Porgy and Bess eliminated black-face make-up and vaudeville hoofing associated with black musicals of the day. Todd Duncan, a music professor at Howard University in Washington, DC, was invited to sing for Gershwin. After hearing his magnificent baritone voice, Gershwin said, "Will you be my Porgy?" Duncan confessed in later years that he thought of Gershwin as a Tin Pan Alley composer, hardly comparable to the composers whose works he usually sang — Schubert, Schumann, and Brahms. But he agreed, after hearing the score. Ann Brown, a Juilliard graduate, played Bess.

Gershwin spent time in Charleston, talking to local black residents, absorbing the atmosphere and rhythms of the local dialect. The storyline presented Porgy, a young man, although poor and crippled, who is devoted to Bess, the girl he loves, and his dangerous rival, a man called Crown. The work was more ambitious than anything that had been previously heard on the Broadway stage.

The real "Cabbage Row" was depicted on stage as "Catfish Row." There were duets, trios, and ensembles. When it came time for characters to speak to each other, Gershwin insisted on writing *recitatives* (as an operatic composer would) instead of using spoken dialogue. The score was an embarrassment of riches: the haunting lullaby "Summertime," the plaintive "My Man's Gone Now," the sweeping "Bess, You is My Woman Now," the joyous "I Got Plenty O' Nuttin'," and the finale, "Oh, Lawd, I'm On My Way." Ira Gershwin had particular problems writing a lyric for one melody. He generally created a "dummy" lyric, so he could remember the required rhythmic accents of the melody. George Gershwin suggested that he use the "dummy" title as the real one, and "It Ain't Necessarily So," expressing the views of the drug peddler known as Sportin' Life, was born.

Figure 237 - George Gershwin, Dubose Hayward, Ira Gershwin, discuss their score for one of the great American operas, *Porgy and Bess*. (Photo by VanDamm Studio, 1935, used by special permission from the Gershwin Family Trusts)

Porgy and Bess was inevitably controversial. It depicted black characters expressing a wide range of emotions—love, joy, and tragedy—for the first time. Porgy and Bess fell in love, but Porgy unwillingly killed Crown in a fight and was arrested. Bess joined Sportin' Life in New York, and when Porgy was released, he set out to search for her. This searching quality, the search by black Americans for a better world, permeated Gershwin's music. Critical reaction to the eclectic work was mixed.

A number of critics found *Porgy and Bess* too operatic to be a musical, too full of good tunes to be an opera. A number of African American musicians, including jazz icon Duke

Ellington and noted choral conductor Hall Johnson, criticized the work as an artificial attempt by a white musician to falsely portray black people. Even the public performances were marked by controversy. Todd Duncan refused to perform before segregated audiences in Washington, DC; theaters in the nation's capital were integrated for the first time as a result. *Porgy and Bess* was considered an economic failure in its day. In subsequent years, however, *Porgy and Bess* was revived, and it proved a huge success. Critics would recognize the melodic and harmonic genius of Gershwin; *Porgy and Bess* has been celebrated around the world more than any other opera written by composers with only classical credentials.

Throughout his life, Gershwin had thought he should pursue classical studies; on occasion, he approached world-renowned teachers, only to be told, "I have nothing to teach you." One such composer asked Gershwin how much money he made, and Gershwin told him. "I should be taking lessons from you," was the reply. Gershwin once said, "Life is a lot like jazz. It's best when you improvise." By following his own instincts, George Gershwin wrote music for the ages. He had a brilliant future.

But on July 11, 1937, George Gershwin died suddenly. His passing represented more than the loss of a brilliant individual composer; it signified the end of an era. Ira Gershwin would live on for many years, collaborate with other composers, and quietly champion the memory of his younger brother's achievement. One can only imagine the music that would have flowed from the pen of George Gershwin had he lived a long and full life.

THE IMPROBABLE DUO: RODGERS AND HART

The only team to challenge the Gershwins as the preeminent champions of Broadway during this era was Rodgers and Hart. *Time* called them, "America's Gilbert and Sullivan." Few would disagree. Richard Rodgers must be considered the single most important composer in the history of American musical theater. His collaborations, first with Lorenz Hart and years later with Oscar Hammerstein II, established him for sheer longevity as a dominant influence unrivaled by anyone.

Though people thought of Rodgers and Hart as a unit, the two men could not have been more different. Rodgers was a man who never struggled to achieve. Born on Long Island, the son of a doctor, he began playing the family's Steinway at age six. Early in his life, he discovered a fascination for musical theater. His older brother took him to see *Home James*, a varsity show produced by Columbia College. Among the students at Columbia at the time were future Broadway giants, including writers Oscar Hammerstein II, Morrie Ryskind, Herman Mankiewicz, Howard Dietz, and Lorenz Hart.

Eventually, Rodgers enrolled at Columbia where he was introduced to Hart. The two men were the original odd couple. Rodgers described the gnome-like Hart as wearing "frayed carpet slippers, a pair of tuxedo trousers, an undershirt, and a nondescript jacket." Said Rodgers, "All he needed was a tin cup and some pencils." Hart was a poet whose tremendous energy surmounted his mercurial nature. The two collaborators were opposite in every respect. Rodgers was serious, disciplined, meticulous, studious, and methodical. Hart was erratic, moody, inspired, and unpredictable. To make matters worse, Hart liked to drink; on occasion, he would simply disappear for days. He smoked cigars and on one occasion, he became so preoccupied with a lyric, that he set Rodgers' curtains on fire. But the collaboration not only worked, it sparkled. For twenty-two years, Rodgers and Hart produced an array of musicals unlike anything seen before on Broadway. Rodgers was a superb melodist who admired Jerome Kern, a master of both the lyrical song and sprightly tune. Hart's lyrics were wry, witty, impertinent, and clearly divorced from the style of the Viennese operettas, which had preceded them on Broadway.

Figure 238 - Richard Rodgers and Lorenz Hart - The disciplined, meticulous Rodgers and the mercurial, unpredictable Hart were improbable collaborators, but they produced one brilliant score after another throughout the 1920s and 1930s. (Photo courtesy of New York World Telegram and Sun Collection, Library of Congress)

A list of their best shows proved they were second to none. There was the fabulous *Jumbo*, the show that featured Jimmy Durante, an onstage circus, and hit tunes such as "The Most Beautiful Girl in the World," a production too expensive to be profitable. *On Your Toes* introduced "There's a Small Hotel" and "Glad To Be Unhappy." *On Your Toes* was the first Broadway show to integrate a real ballet into the plot. Rodgers wrote the music for *Slaughter on Tenth Avenue*, with choreography by George Balanchine. To avoid being shot by a pair of gangsters, the hero keeps dancing until the police arrive. Rodgers wasn't certain how to proceed with the ballet. Should he write music and expect Balanchine to make up steps or would Balanchine create the dance and insist that Rodgers write an accompaniment for his dancers? Balanchine settled the matter in his Russian accent by telling Rodgers, "You write, I put on!" The rest was history.

Babes in Arms premiered "My Funny Valentine," "Johnny One Note," "The Lady Is a Tramp," and "Where or When" in the same score. In *I'd Rather Be Right*, Rodgers and Hart worked with George S. Kaufman and Moss Hart to create a satire in which the romance of two young people depends on the ability of President Franklin D. Roosevelt to balance the budget, something Roosevelt was unable to do in real life. Unfortunately, the role of Roosevelt was given to the cantankerous George M. Cohan. When Rodgers and Hart played their score for Cohan, he said, "Don't take any wooden nickels," and walked out of the theater. Later, they learned he detested Roosevelt and tried to insert his own anti-Roosevelt lyrics into the show. Then came *The Boys from Syracuse*, a contemporary version of Shakespeare's *Comedy of Errors*, featuring "This Can't be Love" and "Falling in Love with Love."

In 1940, Rodgers and Hart created their most important score to date, *Pal Joey*. The hero of *Pal Joey* wasn't a hero at all, he was a heel. Rodgers and Hart set out to do something that had never been done on Broadway, develop a musical about hard-boiled, realistic characters who were at home on the streets. Since the characterization and lyrics were especially important, Hart took the unusual step of writing lyrics first for everything but the ballads. Although Rodgers usually wrote the melodies first, he set Hart's lyrics to music. John O'Hara adapted his own magazine stories from *The New Yorker* for the book. A new star, a brilliant and athletic performer from Pittsburgh, Gene Kelly, portrayed tough, opportunistic Joey, a small-time nightclub dancer with few redeeming qualities.

There were no sugar-coated, romantic figures in *Pal Joey*. Lorenz Hart had the perfect vehicle for his irreverent wit; Richard Rodgers was at his best. Joey could charm the ladies with "I Could Write a Book," while Joey's burlesque stripper girlfriend sang the satirical "Zip," an intellectual parody of real-life burlesque star Gypsy Rose Lee. "Bewitched, Bothered, and Bewildered" was another outstanding tune. The show was devoid of a happy ending. Though critics scoffed, it became a success. *Pal Joey*, like *Show Boat*, was a landmark. It proved that even the most improbable subject matter could be adapted in musical form, if in the hands of a master composer or lyricist.

THE VOODOO THAT COLE DID SO WELL

Not everyone spent the Depression years in poverty and disillusionment. Cole Porter spent the 1930s living a life beyond the envy of our wildest imagination. His colleague, Alan Jay Lerner, recalled that Porter "grew up with a platinum spoon encrusted with diamonds in his mouth." Said Lerner, "He grew up enjoying all the privileges of the rich F. Scott Fitzgerald envied so." Porter, like his lyrics, was witty, sophisticated, and wickedly amusing. He lived with style and in the grand manner.

He was born in Peru, Indiana, the grandson of a millionaire lumber magnate. The six-year-old Porter had his own pony. Although he had private tutors, he was more interested in going to the circus; his proudest possession was a toy theater. At Yale, his classmates came from the richest and most influential families in America. He wrote two football fight songs at Yale; after graduation, he was dispatched to Harvard Law School by his family. He secretly switched to studying music after the dean realized that he showed little interest in court decisions and legal theory. Years later, Porter would write, "A college education I would never propose. A bachelor's degree won't even keep you in clothes."

Eventually, he went to Paris where he dabbled in classical musical studies with composer Vincent D'Indy, amused himself, and met and subsequently married Linda Lee Thomas, an older divorcée and one of the world's wealthiest women, who became his mentor. While

Figure 239 - Cole Porter, an extraordinary composer and lyricist brought a dazzling sophistication to the musical theater with wit, style, elegance, and astonishing rhymes. But when asked to describe himself, he just said, "I'm Broadway." (Public Domain)

other composers were plugging songs and peddling their wares on Tin Pan Alley, Porter was indulging his every fancy in a palazzo in Venice and dashing off outrageous lyrics about his society friends on the French Riviera.

Porter was one of the uniquely talented men who wrote both music and lyrics. His melodies and incredible facility with words made him the personification of elegance on stage in the 1930s. As a melodist, he especially liked to write melodies in minor keys, often switching back and forth between the darker hues of the minor keys and brighter, happier sound of the majors. But though Porter wrote marvelous melodies, it was his facility with words that truly astonished his admirers. Porter's skills as a lyricist were unsurpassed. Alec Wilder said it best when he observed, "The light touch, the mordent turn of phrase, the fingertip kiss, the double entendre, the awareness of the bone deep fatigue of urban gaiety, the exquisite and lacy lists of cosmopolitan superlatives, these were the lyrical concerns of Cole Porter." Nothing about his lyrics was general or vague. He could always select the precise word needed. The targets of his wit were specific. This became clear early in Porter's career.

In New York, his music and lyrics attracted the attention of Louis "Doc" Shurr, a powerful agent. Shurr was known on Broadway as a man of expensive tastes who usually got what he wanted. He kept a mink coat in his office; every time he dated a showgirl, she was expected to wear the coat. Shurr arranged for Porter to meet a producer, Ray Goetz, determined to make his wife, Irene Bordoni, into a prominent stage star. Goetz had been trying to get Rodgers and Hart to write the score for a show called *Paris*. When they were unavailable, he turned to Porter, who came up with his classic song, "Let's Do It, Let's Fall in Love." Writing love songs has always been a challenge, because it is difficult to avoid clichés. Porter dashed off an astonishing list of zoological species that "did it," including birds, sea creatures, insects, and animals, everything from "electric eels" to "heavy hippopotami."

While other lyricists wrote about gazing at the moon or the stars, Porter created lines like these: "In shallow shoals, English soles do it, gold fish in the privacy of bowls do it. Let's do it, let's fall in love." He continued, "Chimpanzees in zoos do it, Some courageous kangaroos do it. Let's do it, let's fall in love." Porter was always willing to tease the rich. "The world admits bears in pits do it, even Pekineses in the Ritz do it, let's do it, let's fall in love."

Other lyricists might try placing their rhymes at the end of phrases. Porter was a master of internal rhymes. He would create lyrics with multiple rhymes in a single line.

Porter would rhyme "Penguins in their *flocks* on the *rocks*" with "little cuckoos in their *clocks*." Another of his early successes was *Fifty Million Frenchmen*. This show told the tale of a millionaire playboy who bets his friends he can win the affection of an American heiress in Paris. By curtain time (and a host of Porter songs), she abandoned the Grand Duke her parents wanted her to marry for her true love, who had, of course, also fallen for her. For *Fifty Million Frenchman*, he turned out "You Do Something to Me," with his most famous internal rhyme, "Do do that voodoo that you do so well."

Porter also included "The Tale of the Oyster." This song had started as "The Scampi," written in Venice to amuse his friend, Princess San Faustino, the former Jane Campbell of New Jersey. (Among his friends, Porter always seemed to include Americans who had turned into royalty through marriage to titled Europeans.) He turned the "scampi" into an "oyster" and the song, with its new lyric, became another Porter classic. Porter's oyster found his home life "awfully wet" and longed to travel with the upper set. After ending up as the appetizer on society's silver platter, the oyster winds up back where he started, older and wiser about society folks.

Porter frequently included in his lyrics specific, amusing, and often risqué references to his friends and foes or to events of the day. For *The Gay Divorce*, he tailored the melodic range of "Night and Day" to the vocal range of the show's new star, Fred Astaire. Porter usually wrote the lyrics before the music, but he reversed the procedure for "Night and Day." He wrote the lyric in a single afternoon while lying on a beach in Newport, Rhode Island. His friend Monty Woolley had heard the music by itself the day before and told him to throw it away. Porter insisted that his hostess for the weekend in Newport was Mrs. Vincent Astor, who said, "I must have the eave mended at once. That drip, drip, drip is driving me mad." According to the tale, Porter immediately thought of the lyric, "Like the drip, drip, drip of the raindrops" that started "Night and Day."

As always with Porter, whether thoroughly accurate or not, he had a great story to tell. *Jubilee* contained "Begin the Beguine" and "Just One of the Things." Porter never resorted to clichés. What other lyricist would think of lines like "A trip to the moon on gossamer wings?" Then came *Anything Goes*, the 1934 musical with "I Get a Kick Out of You" and "You're the Top." The latter song contains a list of Porter's superlatives, all rhymed. "You're the top, you're the Colosseum, you're the top, you're the Louvre Museum, You're a melody from a symphony by Strauss, You're a Bendel bonnet, a Shakespeare sonnet, You're Mickey Mouse." As usual, there were tips of the hat to Porter's friends. (On his list were "the eyes of Irene Bordoni," rhymed with "a night at Coney" and "a Berlin ballad," a reference to Irving Berlin, rhymed with "Waldorf salad.")

Director Howard Lindsay decided to rework the libretto by P.G. Wodehouse and Guy Bolton, and since the collaborators were unavailable, Lindsay took Russell Crouse, a Theatre Guild press Agent, as his writing partner. Lindsay and Crouse became a remarkable team, creating, among others, *Life with Father*, which set a record as the longest running non-musical play in Broadway history.

Porter was a world traveler; he told wonderful stories about how he was inspired to write his songs, inserting them into shows years later when needed. In 1936, for *Red, Hot and Blue*, Porter provided "It's De-Lovely." Sung by Bob Hope and Ethel Merman, this song's unusual title often provoked questions. On one occasion, Porter announced that he, writer-director Moss Hart, and bearded actor Monty Woolley were in Java, discovering a fruit known as the mangosteen. Hart said, "It's delightful," Porter added, "It's delicious," Woolley said, "It's De-Lovely," and a song title was born. On another occasion, Porter claimed that he, his wife, and Monty Woolley sailed into the harbor of Rio de Janeiro. Porter presumably said, "It's delightful," his wife added, "It's delicious," and Woolley, this time inspired by a few extra whiskey and sodas, piped up, "It's De-Lovely." Porter had an endless supply of such stories, usually as intriguing as his lyrics. Knowing Porter's disdain for the hackneyed phrases of most lyricists, Monty Woolley once bet Porter that he couldn't write a song that repeated the phrase "I love you" over and over again. Porter was writing the score for the 1939 musical, *Mexican Hayride*. He did, in fact, write a song called "I Love You." Porter composed such an interesting melody that he won his bet and collected $25 from Woolley.

Porter's charmed life did not go on forever. It was marred by a terrible riding accident when he fell off a horse. He was unable to walk for the rest of his life. He continued, however, to write marvelous music and stunning lyrics with all the dash and wit associated with his name. On one occasion, Porter gave a cast party and rewarded members of the cast with diamonds. No one would have doubted that they were real.

Figure 240 - Noël Coward, urbane, sophisticated, world-weary, playwright, actor, composer, lyricist, wit, bon vivant, was simply described by his colleagues as "The Master." (Photo by Allan Warren. Used by special permission. All rights reserved.)

When the decorator Billy Baldwin began working on the elegant eleven-room apartment Porter maintained at the Waldorf Astoria towers, he asked Porter for instructions. Porter told him, "Just remember, I'm Broadway."

DESTINY'S TOT: NÖEL COWARD

No American lyricist could rival Porter in writing sophisticated lyrics, but he was rivaled by his British friend Nöel Coward. After the success of *Bitter-Sweet* in 1929, Coward wasn't finished with musical theater. He had hardly begun. No discussion of musical theater during this period would be complete without considering the remarkable phenomenon known as Nöel Coward. Of course, we are talking about American musical theater, and Coward was the quintessential figure of British musical theater, but he made such an impact in the United States that to ignore him would be a glaring omission. Alexander Woollcott dubbed him "destiny's tot." In later years, Alan Jay Lerner would describe him as "Celebrity and Star, Chic and Elegance nonpareil, a geyser of quoted wit, both on stage and off." Apart from his many talents as playwright, actor, director, bon vivant, Coward was also a fine composer and remarkable lyricist. His style overflowed with what Alan Jay Lerner called "world-weary, glossy romanticism" highlighted by multiple rhymes and inverted adjectives. *Time* called him "the word wizard."

Coward said he came from a generation that took light music seriously. (His own attempts to study serious music ended when he was advised in school that musical theorist Ebeneezer Prout forbade the use of the musical intervals known as parallel fifths in harmony exercises. Coward observed that Debussy and Ravel used parallel fifths all the time and that ended his classical studies!) He was an instinctive natural composer, often moved by inspiration of the moment to produce memorable melodies of a sentimental strain. While writing *Conversation Piece*, Coward suffered a severe case of writer's block, preparing to abandon the project. He drowned the sorrows of the day in drink and fully intoxicated, discovered he had left the lamp on the piano turned on. He went back to the piano, sat down, and played a brand new melody in G-Flat major, a key unfamiliar to him. The song became "I'll Follow My Secret Heart," one of his biggest hits. Though Coward's melodies were heralded, it was his lyrics that set him apart from colleagues, friends, and rivals. Like his American counterpart Cole Porter, he had a unique ability to characterize human behavior in a few words, to distill the essence of people's attitudes, prejudices, and eccentricities in a single phrase, invariably sophisticated, mischievous, irreverent, and outrageously funny.

Coward's humorous lyrics were among the finest of all time. He defined the 1930s as no one else could. In 1932, Coward provided the music and lyrics for a revue, *Words and Music*, that contained "Mad About the Boy," in which a society lady, a street-walker, a schoolgirl, and a scullery maid present their impressions of a famous movie star who turns out to be an egocentric dolt. *Words and Music* also contained a song that had been introduced two years earlier by Beatrice Lillie in New York. He came up with the idea during a thousand mile drive across Indo-China. Only Coward would declare, "At twelve noon, the natives swoon and no further work is done, But mad dogs and Englishmen go out in the midday sun."

In 1938 in *Operette*, Coward declared, "The stately homes of England, we proudly represent, we only keep them up for Americans to rent." Also during this period, Coward produced a song not for a specific show, but mentioned here because it may be the funniest lyric ever written. Coward called "Mrs. Worthington" "a genuine cri de coeur," but confessed that it had been unsuccessful in discouraging "dreadful eager mothers from making beasts of themselves." But who can listen to these words with a straight face? "Don't Put Your Daughter on the Stage, Mrs. Worthington, Don't Put Your Daughter on the Stage. Though they said at the School of Acting, she was lovely as Peer Gynt. I'm afraid on the whole an ingénue role would emphasize her squint."

In "If Love Were All," Coward said he had just "a talent to amuse." But behind his public persona of urbane witticisms and debonair humor was a meticulous craftsman who could labor over his work for hours trying to achieve just the right turn of phrase. Late in life, Coward was knighted and was later asked if there were things he could do as "Sir Nöel" that he could not do as plain "Mr. Coward." Coward replied, "No, but there are many things I could do as Mr. Coward that I can't do as Sir Nöel." It was not without reason that his friends and colleagues referred to him as "the master." When his friend, the writer J.B. Priestley, asked, "What is all this nonsense about your being called "Master?" Coward replied with his usual modesty, "It started as a joke years ago and it became true."

THE LIONS ROAR: DIETZ AND SCHWARTZ

Figure 241 - Arthur Schwartz, originally an attorney, with lyricist Dorothy Fields. Schwartz's dark and haunting melodies were memorable, as was his long time collaboration with another lyricist, Howard Dietz. (Photo by Walter Albertin, staff of New York World Telegram and Sun, courtesy of Library of Congress)

Although Porter was the unchallenged master of elegance in American musical theater, other writers of the period also pursued their craft with taste, style, and polish. Howard Dietz and Arthur Schwartz were such a team. Dietz was an MGM publicity executive who invented the famed MGM lion that appears in the beginning of all MGM films. Alan Jay Lerner, his friend and colleague, wrote the introduction to Howard Dietz's memoirs, comparing him to every icon of sophistication he could possibly name. Lerner described Dietz as "the Fred Astaire, the Chevalier, the Molnár, the Lubitsch of lyric writers." Dietz, hospitalized at the time, told Lerner that when he read these words, he went home. As a young lyricist, Dietz received a letter on legal stationery from a practicing attorney, Arthur Schwartz, who explained that he was also a composer, suggesting that the two collaborate. Dietz, who had already worked with Jerome Kern, turned down Schwartz's initial request.

But in 1929, the two finally joined forces for *The Little Show*, described as "The Aristocrat of Revues." When producer Max Gordon asked Dietz and Schwartz for a new revue, the two set down some conditions: sketches would be written by Dietz with George S. Kaufman, all lyrics would be written by Dietz with music by Arthur Schwartz, and the production would star the brother and sister dance team, Fred and Adele Astaire. Gordon agreed, and the collaborators created a memorable score for *The Band Wagon*. In "The Beggar's Waltz," Fred Astaire portrayed a beggar who falls asleep outside the stage door of the Vienna Opera House and dreams that for one night he dances with the prima ballerina, portrayed by Tilly Losch. Later in the show, John Baker sang Dietz's lyrics set to

Schwartz's stunning melody, "Dancing in the Dark," while Tilly Losch danced on raked, mirrored floors, which reflected changing light patterns.

Like Porter, Schwartz liked to write melodies in brooding, minor keys that inspired dancers. Dietz and Schwartz were back in 1931 with another review, *Flying Colors*, this time featuring Clifton Webb and Tamara Geva dancing to the haunting "Alone Together." In 1934, Dietz and Schwartz came up with their first "book show," based on Pedro de Alarcón's Spanish tale, *The Three Cornered Hat*, retitled *Revenge with Music*. The show's most enduring melody, "You and the Night and the Music," contained the line, "filled me with flaming desire," a phrase so provocative that it was actually banned from being broadcast over the radio How times have changed!

Figure 242 - Howard Dietz, standing, with collaborator Arthur Schwartz and actress Cyd Charisse at the piano. Dietz, a brilliant lyricist, also was also the publicist responsible for creating Leo the Lion, MGM's roaring mascot and the studio's on-screen motto, "Ars Gratia Artis." (Photo courtesy of Robert F.R. Ballard)

Dietz, like Lorenz Hart, was legendary as one of the most facile and fastest lyricists. While other masters— Oscar Hammerstein, Ira Gershwin, Alan Jay Lerner, among others—took great pains and much time developing lyrics, Dietz made his job look easy. Alan Jay Lerner recalled an episode in which Dietz and Schwartz were taking a walk together. Schwartz challenged him to produce an instant lyric. He suggested the melody to "Jalousie." The melody of "Jalousie" would force the lyricist to think of words with accents on unusual syllables. But Dietz, with his lightning quick imagination, immediately thought of dancer Cyd Charisse. Within a few seconds, Dietz warbled to that exact melody, "Cyd Charisse! Up there on my mantelpiece! You're quite a shock there. We need a clock there."

BROADWAY IN THE 1930S

Other significant new voices of composers and lyricists were heard on Broadway during the 1930s, several with the enthusiastic encouragement of George and Ira Gershwin. The Gershwins were tremendously impressed with Vernon Duke, who came to Broadway with an unusual background. Born Vladimir Dukelsky, Duke had been a child prodigy in his native Russia, composed a full-length ballet at eight, and studied under the renowned composer Reinhold Glière. Another of Glière's older pupils, Sergei Prokofiev, became a lifelong friend and mentor. Duke fled the Russian Revolution, went to Constantinople, Paris, and then London, where he turned his hand to musical theater. The Gershwins encouraged his Broadway debut under his new name, Vernon Duke. Unlike other Broadway composers, Vernon Duke never found a permanent collaborator to write lyrics. His theatrical work included shows with lyricists Ira Gershwin, E. Y. Harburg, Sammy Cahn, John Latouche, and Ogden Nash.

In 1932, Duke wrote the music for a revue, *Walk a Little Faster*. The show ran only for four months; critics and the audience overlooked one melody introduced on stage by Evelyn Hoey who had laryngitis at the time. But "April in Paris" survived the show, and today, it remains one of the most performed standards of all time. The highly critical Alec Wilder declared it to be "a perfect theater song." Two years later, Duke wrote another major hit, "Autumn in New York," for the revue called *Thumbs Up*. He wrote yet another memorable song, "I Can't Get Started," sung by Bob Hope in the *Ziegfeld Follies of 1936*.

His 1940 score for *Cabin in the Sky* is regarded as one of his finest. It proved to be a sure-fire production. The story concerned a religious black woman whose prayers are answered when the Lord agrees to let her rascal husband have six months in which to redeem his soul, over the objections of Lucifer, Jr. "Cabin in the Sky" and "Taking a Chance on Love" both came from this show. Duke's melodies were lush and sophisticated, and full of harmonic surprises that have inspired jazz musicians and given his songs a life of their own outside of the theater. In 1946, he was the composer in an unusual collaboration. Light verse writer Ogden Nash provided the lyrics for *Sweet Bye and Bye*, a stage musical based on a libretto by humorist S. J. Perelman and renowned caricaturist Albert Hirschfeld. The show was not a commercial success, but Duke wrote one of most haunting but neglected melodies, "Round About." His incidental music for the play, *Time Remembered*, resulted in another gem, "Ages Ago." Stephen Suskin observed that Duke wryly described his complex melodies as "out of this world tunes, not heavenly, just non-commercial."

Figure 243 - Vernon Duke (left) with his collaborator Ira Gershwin. (Courtesy of New York World Telegram and Sun Collection, Library of Congress)

Vernon Duke was a remarkably versatile and talented man. While his popular songs were best-known to the American public, he also wrote an impressive collection of concert works, including concertos for piano, violin, and cello, as well as numerous ballets. He also found time to write poetry in Russian, and a perceptive and witty memoir, *Passport to Paris*. Duke also wrote a highly provocative book about the state of contemporary music, *Listen Here: A Critical Essay on Music Depreciation*. Duke was outspoken and had no reservations about turning his wrath on those he regarded as unjustifiably sacred cows of modern music, especially Igor Stravinsky and the icons of the avant-garde, Pierre Boulez and Karlheinz Stockhausen. After he married the American soprano Kay McCracken, they toured together presenting numerous musical performances. Since his death in 1969, Duke's music has remained an important element of our musical history.

His concert works have been rediscovered by new generations and his music for the theater is admired for its melodic and harmonic originality.

The Gershwins also encouraged Kay Swift, a composer and close friend of George Gershwin, when she wrote the score for *Fine and Dandy*. Lyrics were by her husband, the banker, James P. Warburg, writing under the *nom de plume* of Paul James. The show featured a virtuoso performance by Broadway's clown-comedian, Joe Cook, and tunes like the popular title song, "Fine and Dandy."

It was only natural that the depression and the troubling times would inspire satire. But it was generally satire of a gentle nature. No one questioned the patriotism of the Gershwins when they produced *Of Thee I Sing* or *Let 'Em Eat Cake*. Even Irving Berlin, the most unconsciously patriotic figure in America's musical theater, indulged in topical satire for the wildly successful revue, *As Thousands Cheer*. The show, based on a set of newspaper headlines, called for a sketch based on the "rotogravure" section of the paper, a look back at the 1883 Easter Parade. Berlin, dissatisfied with his melody, found a tune he had written and discarded in 1917. Its opening lyric began, "Smile and show your dimple, you'll find it's very simple." Berlin wrote a new lyric, and the result was *Easter Parade*. Berlin's show included satirical looks at the defeat of Herbert Hoover by F.D.R., Gandhi's hunger strikes, and the always controversial subject of race relations. But again, the satire was gentle. The same could not be said, however, for a new brand of politically charged musical theater that had originated in Europe and arrived in the United States.

THE VOICES OF SOCIAL PROTEST: WEILL AND BLITTZSTEIN

Nothing could be further removed from the insouciance and amusement of Cole Porter's world than the blistering social protest of Kurt Weill and Marc Blitzstein. The German-born Kurt Weill was a serious composer of orchestral, chamber, and operatic music. He had studied composition with Engelbert Humperdinck (famed for his opera *Hansel and Gretel*) and also with the acclaimed piano virtuoso Ferrucio Busoni. Weill had turned his hand to writing symphonies and chamber music, but he had a special love for opera. While still in Germany, he began collaborating with Bertolt Brecht, a dramatist who wanted to use the theater to make a political statement. Brecht was a communist and saw the stage as a platform to express his Marxist political views. Brecht and Weill were drawn into a German cultural movement called *Zeitkunst*, which encouraged artists to appeal to the general public as well as intellectuals. Brecht and Weill began developing *Songspiel,* a new form of musical theater combining a political text attacking capitalism or other political targets with appealing popular songs that gave the writers a chance to comment on the way characters were behaving on stage.

In 1928, Brecht and Weill collaborated on an adaptation of John Gay's play, *The Beggar's Opera*. This tale of thieves, scoundrels, and rascals was turned into *Die Dreigroschenoper* (*The Threepenny Opera*). The hero of this epic is Macheath, the bandit captain, who marries Polly Peachum, the daughter of a man who speaks of morality while seldom practicing it. Harold Paulsen, the actor playing Macheath, commissioned a Berlin tailor to design a costume for him; he turned up at the theater dressed as a flamboyant, Victorian dandy, complete with a lounging jacket, spats, a thin cane, and sporting a bright, blue bow-tie. The producers protested, while Paulsen insisted he would rather quit the show than change his clothes.

Weill found the solution, deciding to compose a "moritat," a song in the style of ballads sung about criminals at German street fairs. The song would reveal to the audience that Mackie Messer, the German version of Macheath, could cut your throat even as he smiled at you. Weill said he was sitting on a Berlin streetcar when the sounds of the traffic suddenly inspired him to think of a series of musical intervals that could be repeated over and over. In a few moments, he had the idea for his "Moritat." This song would prove to be one of the most enduring ever written by the composer. Yet Weill wrote it in one evening and almost as an afterthought. Brecht, a man with a huge ego and a casual disregard for facts or people that stood in his way, tried to take credit for coming up with the basic idea for the melody and even had himself recorded singing it. *The Threepenny Opera* contained Weill's unique parodies of everything from tangos to marches. Weill's wife, the singer Lotte Lenya, starred in the show, which became a huge hit in Berlin, received thousands of performances, and was made into a motion picture in Germany. The libretto and lyrics were translated into eighteen different languages.

In 1929, Weill and Brecht collaborated again on an opera about gamblers called *Happy End*. The collaboration did not end happily. Weill continued to work with Brecht on his opera, *The Rise and Fall of the City of Mahogany*. By the time the work was ready for production, Brecht and Weill had parted company. It was a bitter separation. While their lawyers battled each other during rehearsals, Brecht, showing little gratitude toward Weill, threatened to "throw that second-rate Richard Strauss down a flight of stairs." Not surprisingly, Weill's pro-communist political stance and the fact that he was Jewish made him an easy target for the anti-Semitic Nazis. He fled Germany for France.

Weill was unique in that he could absorb the styles and tastes of the countries he visited. In Paris, the German Weill proved a master at writing French music. He wrote the score for *Marie Galante*, a 1934 stage production with curious history. Weill's collaborator was the playwright Jacques Deval. "Deval" was a pseudonym for Jacques Boulerin, a colorful Frenchman who delighted in startling friends and foes alike with controversial themes and his own behavior. (During World War II, Deval served in the U.S. Army. After returning from the front, many of Deval's fellow soldiers gathered together wearing whatever clothing was available, but Deval managed to appear in uniform covered with medals he had secured from a Hollywood prop department.)

Weill's relationship with Deval wasn't happier than his association with Brecht. He told his wife Lotte Lenya that Deval was "the worst literary swine" with whom he had worked. *Marie Galante* closed quickly in Paris and there has been considerable speculation about lost songs and parts of the score. But one of the songs in *Marie Galante*,

"J'attends un Navire," became a favorite of the French resistance and established the German Kurt Weill as a master of the French style of music. The show also may have contained an orchestral performance of a melody written independently as "Youkali," one of Weill's most haunting tangos.

It was inevitable that Weill would come to New York. In 1933, *The Threepenny Opera* arrived on Broadway. An English adaptation of Brecht's intense and bitter libretto did not fare well with American audiences. Nor did critics provide a warm welcome. Richard Lockridge, writing in the morning *New York Post*, dismissed the show as "sugar coated communism." while John Mason Brown called it "appallingly stupid" in the evening edition of the same paper. The production lasted two weeks, and no one would guess that the brilliant score would survive the generations. Coincidentally, Brecht also fled Germany; despite a harsh view of America and his continued commitment to communism, he eventually wound up in the United State where he renewed communications with Weill. Coincidentally, in 1947, Brecht was summoned to testify before the House Un-American Activities Committee. With a straight face, he told the Committee he had never been a communist, lied about the political implications of his work, and left the U.S. the next day, never to return. He achieved his life's ambition when he obtained his own theater in communist East Germany. Brecht still retained an Austrian passport, all the while insisting on being paid in non-communist West German marks, which he deposited in a Swiss bank account.

Weill approached the Broadway musical theater from a different vantage point than almost any other composer. George Gershwin, whom Weill admired tremendously, was a master of the popular song who constantly tested the limits of traditional song forms. Most traditional popular tunes had a verse and chorus, with two repetitions of a theme, a "bridge" or "release" section, and a reprise of the theme. Gershwin used the harmonic and rhythmic vocabulary of his songs in the long, developmental forms of concert music, producing works like his *Concerto in F* and his opera *Porgy and Bess*. Weill came to Broadway with an impressive list of classical compositions. He was a musician who wanted to make a musical statement in the lighter, more commercial medium of Broadway theater without sacrificing his serious intent. Weill was not impressed by New York's fabled Metropolitan Opera. He wrote, "Metropolitan: worst example of opera museum on one side, musical comedy, which tries to be sophisticated and low-brow at the same time on the other side. Nothing between. Enormous field for musical theater. Collaboration between playwright and composer."

Just as Weill had turned himself into a composer of French musicals with ease, he quickly transformed himself into a unique and highly original Broadway composer. But he was determined to continue expressing his political views wherever he lived and the light-hearted, gentle political satire of the Gershwins had little appeal for him. The first of Weill's American shows was *Johnny Johnson*, an anti-war musical that did no flag-waving. The show was produced under the auspices of the Group Theater, led by Harold Clurman,

Lee Strasberg, and Cheryl Crawford. Paul Green, a Pulitzer-Prize-winning dramatist who lived and taught in Chapel Hill, North Carolina, provided the book and lyrics. The cast boasted an extraordinary array of talent—serious, dedicated, intense actors, many of whom went on to fame as teachers, directors, and stars: Sanford Meisner, Robert Lewis, Paula Miller Strasberg, Elia Kazan, Morris Carnovsky, John Garfield, Luther Adler, and Lee J. Cobb. The character of Johnny Johnson, played by Russell Collins, was a young man who joined the army in World War I, became a war protester, and eventually wound up in an asylum where the other inmates are political figures of the day. He ended up selling toys on the street while the country prepared for another war. Audiences were unprepared for this show; the subject matter was that of a serious play, but the content was clearly musical. There were no choruses, whistling tunes, or dancing girls. Instead, there were anti-war speeches and a leading man who didn't sing until the very end of the story. The production was also a transition for Weill, who began moving away gradually from his roots in contemporary German opera toward American music.

Weill's next opus, *Knickerbocker Holiday* was written with book and lyrics by Maxwell Anderson, a serious playwright. Anderson decided to turn Washington Irving's book about New York City under Dutch rule in the 17th century into a musical. A key role went to the great character actor, Walter Huston, who played Peter Stuyvesant, a cantankerous, authoritarian Governor of New York. Huston wanted to soften his character, who hobbled about the stage with a peg-leg, and suggested that he try to unsuccessfully charm a much younger woman who is in love the show's hero. When asked about his vocal range, the gravel-voiced Huston said, "I have none." After hearing Huston try singing on the radio, Anderson and Weill sat down in one evening and wrote "September Song." As he had done years before in *The Threepenny Opera*, Weill produced one of his greatest classics quickly and as an afterthought. The song became so successful, it overshadowed the show's love song, "It Never Was You," which has been unjustly neglected to this day. Huston "stopped the show" when he received thunderous applause and "September Song" made history.

In 1941, Weill collaborated with Ira Gershwin who was still mourning the death of his brother. Together with director Moss Hart, they created a highly unusual show, *Lady in the Dark*. The "lady in the dark" was Liza Elliott, a publisher of a women's fashion magazine who cannot sort out the men in her life: Kendall Nesbitt, suave, successful, but married; Randy Curtis, a movie star who is "a precious amalgam of Frank Merriwell, Anthony Eden, and Lancelot"; and Charley Johnson, one of her employees. She also has to put up with Russell Paxton, a tongue-twisting photographer. To solve her neuroses, she seeks the help of a psychiatrist. Throughout the play, she keeps trying to remember a song from her childhood. With one exception, the music appears only in a series of remarkable dream sequences. In the four dreams depicting a glamour fantasy, a surrealistic wedding, a bizarre circus episode, and her childhood, Liza encounters the truths of her life. At the end of the show, Gertrude Lawrence sang the song Liza couldn't remember throughout the entire evening, Weill's haunting "My Ship." But the show was nearly stolen by newcomer Danny Kaye, making his debut as Russell Paxton, and performing "Tchaikovsky." Kaye had an incredible facility for singing tongue-twisting lyrics and executing parodies of foreign accents. In "Tchaikovsky," Kaye rattled off an unbelievable list of names of real Russian composers, which had been meticulously compiled by Ira Gershwin. The Weill-Gershwin score was brilliant, but too experimental to have an immediate influence on other Broadway shows. Kaye went on to become a major star, often in movies with scores written by his wife, composer-lyricist Sylvia Fine.

Though Weill turned away from political protest for a time, the influence of *The Threepenny Opera* continued. Weill's music was admired by a composer named Marc Blitzstein. Blitzstein, born into a wealthy Philadelphia family, had been a child prodigy pianist. The two great rivals in European modern music at the time were Igor Stravinsky and Arnold Schoenberg. Stravinsky did not actively teach and encouraged young composers to study with his friend, the legendary Nadia Boulanger. Schoenberg taught throughout his life, both in Europe and the United States. Many composers studied with Boulanger in Paris or Schoenberg in Vienna, Berlin or Los Angeles. Blitzstein studied with both Boulanger and Schoenberg. He thought musical theater was serious business, not just entertainment. Like Brecht, he had a Marxist political message. The Federal Theatre Project, funded by the WPA, was supposed to present Blitzstein's work, *The Cradle Will Rock*.

Figure 244 - Blitzstein's work was a scathing attack on the capitalist system. (Poster courtesy of The Federal Theater Project)

Blitzstein's work was a scathing attack on the capitalist system. Far removed from the flag-waving days of George M. Cohan, Blitzstein was prepared to offer propaganda as opera. The characters were really caricatures: "Mister Mister," the despicable boss of Steeltown (ironically played by Will Geer, later to gain fame as the kindly Grandpa Walton on the television series, *The Waltons,*) his insipid wife and family, and their corrupt allies. The hero, Larry Foreman, was a militant union organizer. If Blitzstein's political views were simplistic, his score, heavily influenced by *The Threepenny Opera*, was dramatic and intense. Blitzstein described the work as "a labor opera composed in a style that falls somewhere between romance, realism, vaudeville, comic strip, Brecht, Gilbert and Sullivan, and agitprop." John Houseman later declared that Blitzstein's work was free of conflicts between his wanting to be a serious composer, a composer with a social message, and a Broadway winner, a creative struggle that would confuse his later compositions. The lyrics included a devastating satire on starving artists and their patrons, and a driving intensity culminating in a courtroom scene (inspired by Brecht and *The Communist*

Manifesto) in which the proletarian masses turn the tables on their "capitalist oppressors." The labor leaders warns, "When the wind blows, and when the final wind blows, the cradle will rock."

John Houseman and Orson Welles prepared to mount the New York production when the political nature of Blitzstein's work caused a firestorm in Washington, DC. Members of Congress were outraged that the federal government was financing a show celebrating labor unions and filled with Marxist rhetoric. The cast was served with an injunction, forbidding actors from participating. Armed guards were sent to padlock the theater, turn away patrons, and forbid the cast and crew from having access to the sets, costumes, or scores. Actor's Equity and the Musicians' Union demanded that actors be paid scale for the work, in effect, forbidding their members to participate in the production. Ironically, this militantly pro-union play was being scuttled by unions.

On the opening night, Houseman and Welles found themselves without a theater and faced with the seemingly impossible challenge of presenting a production in which no actor could appear on stage and no musician could play in the orchestra pit. But Welles was determined to see his work as a director validated. Actors were told that they could speak their lines and sing their roles while sitting in the audience. The only musician the company could afford was Blitzstein himself, playing on stage on a rented piano. An agent who specialized in distressed theaters provided access to the Venice Theater so that the play could open. When playgoers arrived at the Maxine Elliott Theater, Welles dramatically led a twenty-block parade of actors and the audience to the new location. Blitzstein himself sat on stage at the piano, while actors popped up and down in the audience, speaking and singing their roles.

Eventually, Orson Welles would present a full production of the work, through his newly founded Mercury Theater, after both Welles and Houseman were fired by the WPA for insubordination. It would be revived in later years when the political passions of the depression had long cooled. But to this date, the work remained controversial, especially as we look back objectively at Blitzstein's message. In recent times, the cultural critic and concert pianist Samuel Lipman described Blitzstein's opus as "the quintessential piece of 1930s communist agitprop" featuring "the pasteboard characters of a Marxist morality play," Blitzstein continued composing, including the operas and musical plays, *No for an Answer*, *Regina*, and *Juno*. In the 1950s, his new English adaptation of *The Threepenny Opera* received the recognition Weill's work had been denied in the 1930s. Blitzstein died under mysterious circumstances during a brawl with three sailors in a bar on the island of Martinique.

Shortly after the premiere of *The Cradle Will Rock*, audiences flocked to one of Broadway's unlikeliest hits, *Pins and Needles*, a show mounted by the International Ladies' Garment Workers' Union, and written by a young architect, Harold Rome, who turned to music when he was unable to find employment following his graduation from Yale. Sketches in the review were changed regularly to keep up with world events. The cast, real machinists, weavers, and cutters, all union members, had a taste of Broadway success. (Hitler, Mussolini, and several British Prime Ministers were all characters in the sketches.)

But a real revolution was coming on Broadway. It would come not from those intent on encouraging political protest or revolutionary rhetoric. It would come through a series of events, seemingly unrelated, that would change America's musical theater forever. Jerome Kern had remained active on Broadway. In 1933, he wrote the score for his last real hit, *Roberta*, with book and lyrics by Otto Harbach. This show, about the world of fashion, included such hits as *Smoke Gets in Your Eyes* and *Yesterdays*. Kern's farewell to Broadway came in 1939 with *Very Warm for May*. Although this show, written with Harbach's protégé Oscar Hammerstein II, proved a flop, it contained one of the finest Kern-Hammerstein songs since *Show Boat*, "All the Things You Are."

Figure 245 - Harold Rome switched from architecture to music and became the composer of hit Broadway shows. (Photo Courtesy of Irving Gilmore Library, Yale University)

Meanwhile, despite the success of their work in shows like *Pal Joey*, Rodgers and Hart were having their problems. Rodgers was driven to constant frustration by Hart's personal behavior. His alcoholism, his disappearances, and his mental state were making their collaboration a nightmare. After more than twenty years of working together, Rodgers' patience was at an end. In 1943, the Theatre Guild was going to produce a musical version of a play by Lynn Riggs, *Green Grow the Lilacs*. Oscar Hammerstein II had been interested in the play, but Jerome Kern was less than enthusiastic, so the Guild offered the project to Rodgers and Hart. This play, about a group of settlers in Oklahoma, excited Rodgers, who saw the immediate potential for a new and different type of musical score. Hart, however, rejected the idea totally. This time, Rodgers refused to withdraw. He asked Oscar Hammerstein II to collaborate with him on the show. When Jerome Kern learned of Hammerstein's enthusiasm for the project, always the gentleman, he stepped aside. The two teams that had provided so many wonderful moments on the Broadway stage were no more; Rodgers and Hart would never write another show together; nor would Kern and Hammerstein. The new team, Rodgers and Hammerstein would revolutionize the American musical theater in ways no one had even imagined. The greatest triumphs of the American musical were just ahead.

THE TRIUMPH OF THE AMERICAN MUSICAL
SOME ENCHANTED EVENINGS: RODGERS AND HAMMERSTEIN

Today, it seems only natural to speak of the American musical in terms of two distinct eras, before and after *Oklahoma!* Like *Show Boat*, *Oklahoma!* was more than a single show; it changed the way composers, lyricists, playwrights, and their audiences would look at the whole idea of musical plays on stage. Yet when the new team of Rodgers and Hammerstein began working together, no one might have suspected that the show would even be a hit. Rodgers had composed the scores for a string of hits, while Hammerstein hadn't had a true Broadway success in ten years. Rodgers was known for writing topical, contemporary shows about real people who lived in big cities and listened to jazz. Hammerstein had been the lyricist for *Show Boat*; he was a master of operettas with exotic settings and providing the words for lush, lyrical, romantic melodies. But Rodgers knew that Hammerstein was a master of his craft; he had been the collaborator of Rodgers' hero, Jerome Kern. Rodgers and Hart had to depend on librettists like Herbert Fields to provide "book" portion of their shows. Hammerstein would write the book as well as lyrics.

When Rodgers and Hammerstein began their collaboration, the formula for hit shows on Broadway called for stars with highly marketable names, tunes that would be guaranteed hits regardless of whether they fit the characters in the shows, and lavish production numbers. Rodgers and Hammerstein decided to change all that. They decided not to write the show as a vehicle for stars, but to fully develop the characters in the play and make them realistic. Comedy would come out of the characters and situations, not through jokes or funny songs thrown into the score. All the music and lyrics would be integrated into a story that would captivate the audience. The libretto placed a new emphasis on a coherent, cohesive book. Gone were the instant song cues and excuses to string together a group of unrelated tunes. When Rodgers worked with Hart, he generally wrote the music first, since he didn't want to wait for the unpredictable Hart to finish a lyric. With Hammerstein, the process was reversed. Although there were exceptions, like "People Will Say We're In Love," most Rodgers and Hammerstein songs began with the lyric. As a result, the pieces created by the new team possessed a new and refreshing lyricism, longer melodic lines, and a fusion of Hammerstein's poetry with Rodgers' music.

Hammerstein developed an unusual libretto. He took the original play, *Green Grow the Lilacs*, and used whole scenes and passages of dialogue from the original text. But he also developed the characters. *Green Grow the Lilacs* was the story of a group of settlers around the time Oklahoma achieved statehood. Curly was a boastful cowboy, unwilling to admit his feelings for Laurey, the girl he loves, who was equally reluctant to acknowledge that she felt the same way. There is a subplot involving Ado Annie, the girl who "cain't say no" to her male admirers. Hammerstein created a new character, Will Parker, who was only mentioned in the original play. Will and Annie became involved in a comedy triangle with an itinerant Persian peddler. The romance between Curly and Laurey was threatened by the dangerous Jud Fry. Two unusual musical pieces defined Jud's character. One, "Pore Jud is Daid," reveals Jud's stupidity through comedy; the other, the extraordinary "Lonely Room," is a soliloquy revealing Jud's madness as he dreams secretly of Laurey's golden hair. Broadway audiences expecting toe-tapping tunes were in for a surprise. Even the love songs were unusual. Laurey told Curly that if he continued to admire her in public, "People Will Say We're In Love." Curly asked Laurey to ride with him in "The Surrey With The Fringe On Top."

The staging of the show was also remarkable. Instead of a huge chorus, the show opened with a woman churning butter. This wasn't the first time a Broadway musical opened without an ensemble of chorus girls, but this was the opening that people would remember. Curly's first song, "Oh, What a Beautiful Mornin'" contained poetic lines: "There's a bright golden haze on the meadow" and "the corn is as high as an elephant's eye." When Rodgers saw Hammerstein's first lyric, he knew that their collaboration would be special indeed. Theresa Helburn of the Theatre Guild suggested that Rodgers and Hammerstein write "a song about the earth." The idea seemed improbable, but Hammerstein decided to try his hand at the lyric. The result was *Oklahoma!*, a rousing number that would become the show's title song.

Figure 246 - *Oklahoma!* became one of the greatest hits ever produced on Broadway and changed musical theater history forever. (Photograph appears courtesy of Rodgers & Hammerstein: An Imagem Company, www.rnh.com)

The name of the show was changed from *Away, We Go* to *Oklahoma!*, with an exclamation mark added to the title. Choreographer Agnes de Mille had a history of getting fired from Broadway musicals. But Rodgers and Hammerstein decided to take a chance on her after producer Theresa Helburn became enchanted by the dances de Mille created for Aaron Copland's western ballet, *Rodeo*. de Mille developed an astonishing dream ballet, after Laurey has agreed to go to a dance with Jud. In her dream, she imagined what it would be like to go with Jud instead of Curly. De Mille depicted the conflict between the dancing girls in Jud's imagination with Laurey's friendly neighbors. She awakened, to her horror, to find the terrifying Jud ready to claim her. The dream sequence introduced ballet as an integral element of the show.

Rodgers and Hammerstein, despite their fame, had great difficulties obtaining financing for the show. Investors were skeptical about the show with the "cowboy ballet" and the death of the villain in the second act. One remark variously attributed to Mike Todd, his secretary, and Walter Winchell, summed up people's attitudes: "No girls, no gags, no chance." To everyone's surprise, *Oklahoma!* became a huge hit. It broke all box office records and held the record for eighteen years as the longest running Broadway musical. The score was released as the first Original Cast Album on record. It won a special award from the Pulitzer Prize committee, since the Pulitzer Prize could not go to an adaptation of a play. Their show spoke to wartime audiences in a simple and direct way. The hardy farmers and cowmen who came to life on-stage in *Oklahoma!* had an

Figure 247 - Rodgers & Hammerstein moved the setting of *Liliom* to New England and created *Carousel*, one of the finest scores ever written for Broadway. (Photo courtesy of Rodgers & Hammerstein: An Imagem Company, www.rnh.com)

infectious optimism that inspired hope in all who heard them. Most importantly, *Oklahoma!* established Rodgers and Hammerstein as the true pioneers of Broadway.

Among the throngs congratulating Richard Rodgers on the opening of *Oklahoma!* was Lorenz Hart. It must have been incredibly difficult for Hart to see that his former collaborator had moved on to spectacular success with a new lyricist. Rodgers still tried to help Hart, by promoting a revival of *The Connecticut Yankee*. Sadly, Hart died less than a week after the opening. Hammerstein remained friendly with Jerome Kern. But in 1945, Kern went to New York to co-produce a revival of *Show Boat* with Hammerstein and to consider writing the music for a show to be produced by Rodgers and Hammerstein, *Annie Get Your Gun*. He collapsed on the street and was taken to a hospital on Welfare Island, the same hospital in which Stephen Foster had died. Kern was unconscious and couldn't be moved, so he was placed in a ward with fifty or sixty patients, primarily alcoholics, derelicts, and the mentally ill. A physician explained to other patients who Kern was and asked them to maintain a quiet atmosphere, virtually impossible under the circumstances. Yet not one patient disobeyed instructions. The nurse on duty extended her stay for twenty-four hours. Oscar Hammerstein later explained that this unlikely turn of events in a public hospital took place because Kern had "devoted almost all his lifetime to giving the world something it needs and knows it needs—beauty." Kern never regained consciousness and died shortly thereafter. He is remembered to this day as one of the most admired composers ever to work on Broadway or in Hollywood. Unlike the work of many other composers, his songs grow in stature with the passage of time. Many of his songs became standards because of their enduring quality.

After the death of Kern, Hammerstein busied himself with *Carmen Jones*, a show he dreamed of writing, a modern-day version of *Carmen*, with his lyrics in English, Bizet's music, and an all-black cast. Then Rodgers and Hammerstein turned their attention to their next project. Their team was initially skeptical when the Theatre Guild suggested a musical adaptation of *Liliom*, a fantasy by the Hungarian playwright Ferenc Molnár. *Liliom* was a serious, rather grim tale about a brash carnival barker who dies during a failed robbery and then returns to earth sixteen years later for a day to try to help his wife and daughter. He still loses his temper, slaps his daughter, and fails again to prove himself. Hammerstein considered setting the story in Budapest or moving it to another location, possibly New Orleans.

The melancholy ending posed another problem. But the major obstacle was the playwright, Ferenc Molnár, who had previously turned down requests from celebrated composers interested in adapting his work for the musical theater. Not only had he said no to George Gershwin, he also had once rejected a request from the most famous composer of Italian opera in the world, Giacomo Puccini. But he consented to a request from Rodgers and Hammerstein after seeing *Oklahoma!*

Rodgers and Hammerstein decided to move the story to the New England coast. They developed the idea of the carnival barker, renamed Billy Bigelow, doing a soliloquy and revealing the gentler side of his nature, his determination to help the child his wife is expecting. Though Billy seemed only capable of solving problems with his fists, this "Soliloquy" made him appear, for the first time, as a sympathetic character. He began singing about "My Boy Bill," full of bluster and bravado; suddenly, midway through the solo, he realized that the child might be a girl, and to take care of "My Little Girl," he was willing to do anything to make money, to "go out and make it or steal it or take it, or die." The operatic soliloquy was one of the finest pieces ever composed for an American musical.

After solving the problem of the ending, the rest of the show, renamed *Carousel*, became feasible. Rodgers decided to dispense with the Overture. Ever the innovator, he wrote a "Carousel Waltz," an extended musical composition depicting the intoxicating motion of the carousel.

The romance between Billy and the girl he loves, Julie Jordan, was in sharp contrast to the relationship between Julie's friend, Carrie Pipperidge, and the very respectable, very predictable Enoch Snow, with whom she fell in love.

Billy and Julie sang the stunning duet "If I Loved You," in which they talk about what life would be like if they were in love. Again, Rodgers and Hammerstein avoided the clichés

Figure 248 - Gordon MacRae and Shirley Jones performed the famous "Bench Scene" in the film version of the Rodgers & Hammerstein's masterpiece, *Carousel*. (Photograph appears courtesy of Rodgers & Hammerstein: An Imagem Company, www.rnh.com)

inherent in most love songs. When Julie sang "What's the Use of Wonderin'," she expressed her view that love in unquestioning. As in the original play, Billy was persuaded by his unscrupulous friend Jigger to participate in an ill-planned robbery, a crime made even more futile by the fact that Jigger had already won the money Billy expected to get through the robbery. Billy was accidentally killed, and sixteen years passed. When allowed to return to earth by heavenly Starkeeper, he discovered that his daughter, now a teenager, was shunned by her friends. This episode, like the dream-sequence in *Oklahoma!* was depicted entirely through ballet. Billy did finally find a way to help his daughter. The play concluded with a graduation scene, in which Julie and her daughter realized that Billy really did love them in his own way. Rodgers and Hammerstein produced their most inspirational song, "You'll Never Walk Alone," for a dramatic final scene. *Carousel* was Rodgers' own favorite show—and with good reason. It was a masterpiece.

At the height of their fame, Rodgers and Hammerstein were determined never to repeat themselves. Following the success of *Oklahoma!* and *Carousel*, they created one of the most unusual shows to appear on Broadway to date: *Allegro*. Unlike *Oklahoma!* and *Carousel*, *Allegro* was an original play; it was not adapted from an existing novel or drama. Agnes de Mille was invited to direct the play. The selection of a choreographer (and a woman) to direct a major Broadway musical was unusual for the time. *Allegro* was the story of Joe Taylor, a doctor whose personal life and professional obligations seemed to always prevent him from fulfilling his true calling in life. The show depended heavily on dance to deliver its plot; besides the usual singers and dancers, *Allegro* called for a "Greek chorus" to comment on the action taking place on stage. The set of *Allegro* was a wide open space, highlighted by projections on a cyclorama. Props and furniture were constantly moved on stage and off, without the usual breaks in action to allow stagehands to change scenery. *Allegro* broke ground in another way: it became controversial. Some critics and audiences considered it revolutionary and magnificent, the first musical to deal entirely with an idea rather than with a conventional plot. Others, expecting a sequel to *Oklahoma!* or *Carousel*, were disappointed.

No one, however, was disappointed by the next Rodgers and Hammerstein magnum opus, *South Pacific*. James A. Michener's book, *Tales of the South Pacific* on which the show was based, was a collection of short stories. Rodgers and Hammerstein initially

Figure 249 - *South Pacific*, starring Mary Martin and Ezio Pinza, combined characters from several stories by James Michener in a brilliant, well-crafted and most memorable musical. (Photo with permission of Rodgers & Hammerstein: An Imagem Company, www.rnh.com)

planned to use *Fo' Dolla*, a tale about the romance of an American sailor and a Tonkinese girl as the principal storyline. The American, in a situation not unlike that depicted in Puccini's opera, *Mme. Butterfly*, was caught between his love for the girl and his realization that his family and friends would hardly welcome her as his bride in Philadelphia society. Rodgers and Hammerstein concluded that the show needed a subplot; the conventional wisdom called for a comedic couple like "Ado Annie" and "Will Parker" in *Oklahoma!* Instead, they decided to focus upon *Our Heroine*, the story of a pretty, unsophisticated American nurse who falls in love with an urbane, older French planter, only to discover that he has fathered two Polynesian children. *South Pacific* would deal with serious subjects like war, life and death, and racial prejudice. So for comedy, they chose a third story, *A Boar's Tooth*, and its principal character, Luther Billis, an outrageous, but appealing enlisted man who tries to wheel and deal his way through the Navy.

The direction of *South Pacific* changed radically when Edwin Lester, a west-coast producer, offered Rodgers and Hammerstein an opportunity to obtain a contract with Ezio Pinza, the acclaimed opera star. They decided to cast Pinza as Emile deBecque, the French planter, making his story-line the principal one of the show. Opposite Pinza, as nurse Nellie Forbush, they chose Mary Martin. Martin had known Hammerstein for years, having once sung "Indian Love Call" from *Rose-Marie* at an audition for him, which she identified as a song he might not know. Hammerstein told her he did indeed know the song; he had written the lyrics for it. (Martin, with a traditional Broadway voice, was not an opera singer. On learning of their plan to have her sing opposite Pinza, she said, "Do you want two basses?")

South Pacific had sweep and quality; each song grew out of the characters and their points of view. There were boisterous, American tunes for Nellie, "A Cockeyed Optimist" and "I'm in Love with a Wonderful Guy." Mary Martin had the idea of washing her hair on stage; the result was "I'm Gonna Wash that Man Right Outta My Hair." Pinza was given two glorious arias, "Some

Figure 250 - Mary Martin, the All-American Broadway star from Weatherford, Texas and Ezio Pinza, the Italian operatic basso, singing the "twin-soliloquy," providing an enchanted evening for all. (Photo courtesy of Rodgers & Hammerstein: An Imagem Company, www.rnh.com)

AMERICAN MUSICAL THEATER | 297

Enchanted Evening" and "This Nearly Was Mine." The composer and lyricist solved the problem of Martin and Pinza's differing voices by not having them sing a major duet. Instead, they wrote a twin-soliloquy, one of the most remarkable musical scenes ever to appear on a Broadway stage. Nellie and Emile reveal their feelings for each other, but only through song and unheard by the other party.

Other problems were solved. How could the ocean (and the South Seas setting) be established on stage? Hammerstein wrote the lyric for "Bali Hai," describing the island of men's dreams. In ten minutes, Rodgers created the three-note musical motive that became the basis for the song's haunting, exotic melody, and this motive also represented the mystical island never actually scene on the stage. For Lt. Joe Cable and Liat, the Tonkinese girl he loves, Hammerstein wrote the lyric, "Younger Than Springtime." The melody was actually "My Wife," written by Rodgers and discarded during rehearsal of *Allegro*. One song, "You've Got to Be Taught," created a firestorm of protest, because it dealt with the causes of racial prejudice. Despite a wide assortment of threats and criticism, Rodgers and Hammerstein refused to remove it from the show. James Michener's book, *Tales of the South Pacific* won the Pulitzer Prize; so did its musical heir, *South Pacific*. Rodgers and Hammerstein had created still another landmark show.

Figure 251 - *The King and I* combined a favorite Rodgers & Hammerstein theme, East meets West through music. (Photograph appears courtesy of Rodgers & Hammerstein: An Imagem Company, www.rnh.com)

Broadway shows were often written with specific stars in mind. But in *Oklahoma!*, *Carousel*, and *Allegro*, Rodgers and Hammerstein had preferred to write the show and then find the ideal stars, often new actors with good voices who had yet to develop famous names. But following the success of *South Pacific*, they were approached by Fanny Holtzman, agent for the notable British musical theater star Gertrude Lawrence, and persuaded to adapt *Anna and the King of Siam*, Margaret Landon's novel, as a vehicle for her client. This was tale of an English schoolmistress,

Figure 252 - It is hard to imagine anyone other than Yul Brynner, not the first choice, as the King, as he and Gertrude Lawrence perform "Shall We Dance? in *The King and I*. (Photo courtesy of Rodgers & Hammerstein: An Imagem Company, www.rnh.com)

Anna Leonowens, who brought western customs (and the spirit of an independent woman) to 19th century Siam. The King, supreme ruler of his domain, combines the instincts of a dictatorial eastern patriarch with the curiosity of a child, eager to learn about western civilization. Hammerstein worked his usual magic with the book portion of the show, developing the subplot, the tragic story of Tuptim, a young girl destined to become one of the King's many wives, and Lun Tha, the man she loves.

Rodgers and Hammerstein had difficulties casting the role of the king; unavailable were their first choices: Alfred Drake, Nöel Coward (Gertrude Lawrence's favorite leading man), and Rex Harrison, who created the role in the non-musical film *Anna and the King of Siam*, (which had been brilliantly scored by Bernard Herrmann). The film, of course, did not contain any Broadway-style songs. Mary Martin suggested an actor with whom she had worked in a Broadway show called *Lute Song*. Yul Brynner arrived for an audition, guitar in hand. Balding, arrogant, and part

Figure 253 - Mary Martin and Theodore Bikel share a musical moment in *The Sound of Music*, the last Rodgers & Hammerstein collaboration, ended only by Hammerstein's death. (Photo appears courtesy of Rodgers & Hammerstein: An Imagem Company, www.rnh.com)

Mongolian, Brynner did not merely look like an actor who could play an Asian monarch. He looked and acted like the king. His imperious scowl and authoritarian manner was exactly the quality the authors had been seeking. Brynner's manner of international folk singing struck Rodgers as "savage" and he was quickly signed for the lead. He left his stamp on the role to such an extent that more than a half-century later, actors playing the king still imitate Brynner's voice, his movements, his mannerisms.

The ingenious libretto, written by Hammerstein in collaboration with director Joshua Logan, solved the show's most difficult problem, how to portray a love story between two people, the King and the schoolmistress, who because of culture, protocol, personality, could never acknowledge their feelings for one another; the classic song, "Shall We Dance?" depicted this perfectly.

The show contained some of Rodgers' most lyrical music since *Carousel*: the lilting "I Whistle a Happy Tune," the lyrical waltz, "Hello, Young Lovers," the spirited "Shall We Dance?," "Getting to Know You," a melody discarded from *South Pacific*, the beautiful "I Have Dreamed," and one of Rodgers' most underrated melodies, the haunting "Something Wonderful." Strains of this melody accompany the final scene as the King dies, and his young son Prince Chulalongkorn prepares to ascend the throne and institute the reforms his mentor, Mrs. Anna, so desired.

Following *The King and I*, Rodgers and Hammerstein returned to Broadway with several more shows, including *Me and Juliet*, the story of life backstage on Broadway, *Pipe Dream*, based on *Sweet Thursday* by John Steinbeck, and *Flower Drum Song* about conflict between the generations in San Francisco's Chinatown. They also wrote a television musical based on *Cinderella*. Then in 1959, they launched what proved to be their last show, *The Sound of Music*. Although in a very different setting, Austria in the 1930s, the story was similar to *The King and I* with a charming and unconventional governess joining a rather strange household while falling in love with its autocratic master while teaching his children. Rodgers and Hammerstein were introduced to the project by their friend, Mary Martin, who wanted to star in the vehicle. The saga of the Baroness Maria von Trapp and the Trapp family singers became one of the most successful shows of all time, including such tunes as "Climb Every Mountain," "My Favorite Things," and "Do Re Mi." The opening song was originally "Summer Music" changed to "The Sound of Summer," and finally, "The Sound of Music," which became the title of the show.

Rodgers liked to compose in his own personal style without the influence of historical or musical research. (When Bernard Herrmann heard that Rodgers and Hammerstein were writing *The King and I,* he offered Rodgers research materials he had gathered on the music of Thailand when he had scored the original non-musical film. Rodgers declined.) But for *The Sound of Music*, Rodgers broke his usual custom and did musical research for the show, using nuns as musical advisors so that his choral music would sound authentic. As the onstage Trapp family fled the Nazis in Austria and headed over the border to freedom and the curtain fell, *The Sound of Music* made history on Broadway.

Sadly, shortly after the show enjoyed its premiere and its rave reviews, Oscar Hammerstein II died, ending one of the greatest collaborations in the history of Broadway. *The Sound of Music* went on to become one of Hollywood's most successful movie musicals, starring Julie Andrews in the role created onstage by Mary Martin. Following Hammerstein's death, Rodgers wrote lyrics for a show of his own, *No Strings*, and collaborated with others, including Stephen Sondheim, Martin Charnin, and Sheldon Harnick. But his collaborations with Hammerstein were the high point of his career. Together, these two men invented a form of musical theater, which was emulated and imitated, but never equaled by others. The triumph of the American musical would have been impossible without the skills, talents, and energy of Richard Rodgers and Oscar Hammerstein II.

While the 1940s and 1950s were dominated by the Rodgers and Hammerstein shows, other talented composers and writers began developing musicals according to the new standard set by *Oklahoma!*: fully developed plots, integrated choreography, and songs that could only be sung by specific characters in specific situations. There were new faces, including the soon-to-be legendary team of Alan Jay Lerner and Frederick Loewe, the prodigious and experimental musical phenomenon—Leonard Bernstein, and a remarkably versatile composer-lyricist named Frank Loesser. Acknowledged masters of the musical theater like Irving Berlin and Cole Porter enjoyed their greatest successes during this period. The ever-creative Kurt Weill continued to surprise and amaze audiences. Their shows would insure that the triumph of musical theater in America would not be confined to one brilliant team or one era.

A LITTLE BIT OF LUCK AND AN ABUNDANCE OF TALENT: THE COLLABORATION OF LERNER AND LOEWE

Throughout their stellar collaboration, Alan Jay Lerner and Frederick Loewe were an unlikely combination. Lerner was born into wealth; his family owned the Lerner Shops, a women's wear chain. He was the product of private schools in England, an American prep school, Choate, and Harvard, where he began writing lyrics for the Hasty Pudding Club. Frederick Loewe was born in Vienna, the son of Edmond Loewe, an operatic tenor known for his performances in *The Merry Widow*. Filled with ambition to be a concert pianist, he went to study in Berlin, where he wrote a song, *Katrina* that became a huge hit. Eventually he came to the United States, where he claimed to have toiled at many jobs ranging from cowboy to riding instructor to boxer. In 1932, he took a job as pianist in the pit orchestra of *Champagne Sec*, a show that featured the debut of musical theater star Kitty Carlisle. Miss Carlisle recalled that Loewe would visit her dressing room regularly, promising that one day he would write the greatest show ever seen on Broadway. At the time, Kitty Carlisle was skeptical; every composer with ambitions made the same promise. Frederic Loewe would have the last laugh one day, but not immediately.

Loewe's debut as a Broadway composer, *Great Lady,* was not a success. In the summer of 1942, shortly before the premiere of *Oklahoma!*, Loewe was in the Lamb's Club in New York. He went searching for the men's room, took a wrong turn, and spotted Alan Jay Lerner sitting at a table. The future didn't look especially bright for either man. Success seemed to have eluded Loewe at 41, while the 24-year-old Lerner was still waiting for his big break on Broadway. The two struck up a conversation and decided to collaborate. It was a fateful decision.

The collaboration between Lerner and Loewe did not always go smoothly. Their friend, colleague, and sometime mentor, the director and playwright Moss Hart, said, "It is a surprising partnership in that both men are utterly unlike in temperament and lead totally dissimilar lives away from the work bench." Lerner was inclined to constantly seek perfection. André Previn said Lerner took longer to complete a lyric than an elephant takes to produce a baby elephant. Loewe was a facile pianist, who would create his melodies by improvising at the piano, often drawing on inspiration of the moment. Both men had complicated personal lives; Loewe was a bachelor and bon vivant who loved wine, women, and song. Lerner married eight times. The first seven marriages all ended in divorce. Unlike Rodgers and Hammerstein, who never quarreled about anything, Lerner and Loewe disagreed frequently, each declaring that he would never again work with the other. But somehow, they always reconciled and tried again. Their initial efforts resulted in *Life of the Party* for a Detroit stock company, which was followed by *What's Up*?, a star vehicle for the burlesque comic Jimmy Savo. Neither show achieved the success their creators desired. Next came *The Day Before Spring*, a musical about a beautiful young woman who must choose between her conventional businessman husband and the dashing cad who had been her college sweetheart. *The Day Before Spring* was only a moderate commercial success. But in 1947, two years later, the pair struck gold with *Brigadoon*, their first major hit.

Brigadoon was a fantasy set in Scotland. Lerner, who had always admired the work of James M. Barrie, was always drawn to plots dealing with time and immortality. He said the idea came to him when Loewe made the remark that "miracles can move mountains." In *Brigadoon*, Tommy and Jeff, two Americans, went on a hunting trip to Scotland. Tommy, who had doubts about his impending marriage, fell in love with a Scottish girl, Fiona, who lived in the enchanted village of *Brigadoon*. But no one, including Fiona, could leave the village because of a heavenly spell allowing the tiny town to come to life only one day in each century. Tommy returned to New York without Fiona, but could not forget her. In the end, he left his former life behind and through the miracle of his true love, managed to return to Brigadoon. The score of *Brigadoon* contains numerous songs of note, including "Come to Me, Bend to Me," "There But For You Go I," "The Heather on the Hill," and "Almost Like Being in Love."

Audiences expected Lerner and Loewe to continue writing together after the success of *Brigadoon*. Instead, they broke up. Loewe wanted to enjoy the financial rewards of his success; Lerner wanted to keep working, and collaborated with Kurt Weill on a new show, *Love Life*. Weill was a composer who thrived on social messages while Lerner was the quintessential romanticist. Lerner became fascinated by the New York countryside and wondered what it might have looked like before industrial development. He came up with the idea of a couple, Sam and Susan Cooper, who didn't age and lived through the history of their little town as it survived from the American Revolution to modern times. Lerner reunited with Loewe three years later to write *Paint Your Wagon*, a saga of American gold rush. Lerner, inspired by the stories of Bret Harte, developed an original plot: Ben Rumson was a poor miner who struck it rich. He sent his daughter Jennifer east to a fine school, separating her from Julio, the poor and uneducated young Mexican she loves. Eventually, the couple were reunited, and the gold-hungry residents of the town turned to a more realistic set of goals. The show had marvelous songs: Ben's wistful memory of his late wife, "I Still See Elisa," the stirring melody "They Call the Wind Maria," "Wandrin' Star," and "I Talk to the Trees." But *Paint Your Wagon* also had its problems. Lerner changed the plot constantly, to the frustration of choreographer Agnes de Mille. The show enjoyed a good run, but lost money.

The same would never be said about the next effort of Lerner and Loewe. On March 15, 1956, Alan Jay Lerner and Frederick Loewe launched their musical version of George Bernard Shaw's *Pygmalion*. *My Fair Lady* broke box office records, won deserved critical acclaim, and set the standards by which other musicals are judged. It happened through an odd combination of accident, fate, luck, and destiny.

Years earlier, Lerner was approached by Gabriel Pascal. Born in Transylvania, Pascal was a Romanian whose native language was Hungarian. Lerner characterized him as having an accent that defied description and national origin. According to legend, Pascal had presented himself to George Bernard Shaw and announced that he wanted the rights to film Shaw's plays. When he admitted to having only eight shillings in his pocket, Shaw declared him the only honest producer he'd ever met and gave him the rights. Pascal now wanted a stage musical based on his filmed version of *Pygmalion*, which had starred Leslie Howard and Wendy Hiller. The reigning royalty of Broadway, Rodgers and Hammerstein, had worked with the property for a year and concluded it could not be adapted into musical form. Pascal had approached E.Y. Harburg and Fred Saidy and suggested their collaboration with Cole Porter, only to be turned down again. Now he offered the project to Lerner and Loewe.

Although challenged by the opportunity to adapt a Shaw masterpiece, Lerner and Loewe quickly discovered that as a musical, *Pygmalion* was fraught with problems. As everyone knows, Shaw's play was the story of the imperious, aristocratic Professor Henry Higgins and his attempts to make a lady of Eliza Doolittle, a Cockney flower girl, by teaching her to speak proper English. The play contained no great romantic love story. Except for Eliza, the principal characters are all insensitive, arrogant men. There is no subplot. Lerner could invent one, of course, but unlike Hammerstein's creation of new characters in *Oklahoma!* or *South Pacific*, creating a subplot for *Pygmalion* meant rewriting George Bernard Shaw.

Figure 254 - Alan Jay Lerner proved up to the challenge of adapting George Bernard Shaw's *Pygmalion*. His lyrics combined with music by Frederick Loewe made *My Fair Lady* one of the greatest Broadway shows.

Faced with such daunting problems, Lerner and Loewe decided to withdraw, and turn their attention instead to a musical based on more adaptable material: Al Capp's popular comic strip, *Li'l Abner*. But following the death of Gabriel Pascal, Lerner and Loewe decided to abandon the Capp project and return to *Pygmalion*. Though Oscar Hammerstein II advised Lerner, "It can't be done," Lerner and Loewe managed to persevere. This time they succeeded, despite innumerable obstacles. Lerner based some of his ideas on the film version of *Pygmalion*. Loewe didn't write Tin Pan Alley tunes, but a collection of rich, elegant melodies and sparkling up-beat songs perfect for Shaw's characters. Lerner's lyrics seemed to spring from the pages of Shaw's words. Higgins, through song, imagined the horror of a woman in his life: "She'll have a booming, boist'rous fam'ly, who'll descend on you en masse. She'll have a large Wagnerian mother, with a voice who'll shatter glass." When Higgins declared, "I'd prefer a new edition of the Spanish Inquisition than to ever let a woman in my life," he was still the character created by Shaw.

The show they completed is so indelibly etched in the public's memory that it is difficult to imagine it as a work in progress. Yet Eliza's triumph as Lerner and Loewe's "fair lady" followed a rocky road. In fact, everything from the show's title to its casting to its songs could have turned out differently. The show was originally titled *Liza* or *Lady Liza*. The authors changed it to *My Fair Lady* reluctantly. Loewe wanted to call it *Fanfaroon*, after an obscure English word, which means "someone who blows his own trumpet." Michael Redgrave and Nöel Coward were the original choices to play Higgins. George Sanders, who dominated the film *All About Eve* through his portrayal of a caustic, sardonic character, was considered. Finally, Lerner and Loewe persuaded Rex Harrison to accept the part.

A young actress named Julie Andrews, starring in the period musical *The Boy Friend*, was selected to play Eliza. Though unknown in America, Andrews had a four octave range and impeccable diction, and the authors chose her over more experienced alternatives. Then Mary Martin, the legendary Broadway star, expressed interest in the role through her husband, producer Richard Halliday. Mary Martin, the all-American star from Weatherford, Texas, was a most unlikely actress to play the very British Cockney flower girl. But she was one of Broadway's biggest stars and had a commanding reputation.

After hearing a few of the songs Lerner and Loewe had written, Martin told Halliday, "The dear boys have lost their talent." Halliday compounded the affair by telling the composer and lyricist that their composition "Ascot Gavotte" wasn't remotely funny and that "Just You Wait" sounded as if it had been stolen from a Cole Porter musical. In later years, as Lerner and Loewe became known as Broadway icons, they never forgot the episode with Mary Martin. Whenever one had a problem with a lyric or melody, the other would slyly say, "The dear boy has lost his talent." So Julie Andrews, not Mary Martin, was cast opposite Harrison. Stanley Holloway, the great music hall comedian, portrayed Eliza's father, the outrageous Alfred P. Doolittle. Cathleen Nesbitt as Higgins' mother and Robert Coote as Higgins' best friend, Colonel Pickering, rounded out the superb cast.

Initially, the casting seemed flawed. Rex Harrison, the leading man, was not a conventionally trained singer. He went to an instructor who tried to turn him into an operatic tenor. Lerner and Loewe were horrified at this turn of events, only to be told that the instructor had been recommended by Mary Martin. Instead, Harrison began working with Bill Low, who helped him develop a style of singing and speaking his lyrics. Loewe composed the melodies that would allow Harrison to talk his lyrics on pitch. When Julie Andrews seemed to be struggling with her role, director Moss Hart spent a day and a half coaching her alone in the darkened theater. She emerged as a radiant and confident Eliza. Rex Harrison proved a volatile and demanding star, perfectly cast as the egocentric Higgins. The Shaw estate placed rigid requirements on Lerner, requiring that a specific number of words in the script had to be Shaw's. Though Lerner meticulously adapted Shaw's dialogue, Harrison checked every word against a Penguin edition paperback copy of the original play. He thundered, "Where's my Penguin?" so often that Moss Hart finally went to a taxidermist and ordered a stuffed penguin. The next time Harrison demanded "Where's my Penguin?," the stuffed bird was placed in front of Harrison while the cast roared with laughter.

The songs of *My Fair Lady* are so well known that detailed description is unnecessary. "Wouldn't It Be Loverly," "With a Little Bit of Luck," "Just You Wait," "The Rain in Spain," "I Could Have Danced All Night," "Show Me," "On the Street Where You Live," "Get Me to the Church on Time," and "I've Grown Accustomed to Her Face" all achieved musical theater immortality. ("Come to the Ball" was planned to be Higgins' major solo; it was cut after one performance in an out-of-town tryout. "Say a Prayer for Me Tonight," Eliza's anticipation of her visit to the Embassy Ball, was also dropped. Everyone but Lerner wanted to drop "On the Street Where You Live," but it survived and passed into legend.)

Everything about *My Fair Lady* seemed perfect, from Cecil Beaton's costumes to the choreography by Hanya Holm. When Rex Harrison performed, "I'm an Ordinary Man," he sang Lerner's lyrics, "But let a woman in your life and your serenity is through! She'll redecorate your home from the cellar to the dome; then get on to the enthralling fun of overhauling you." The words sounded as if they had flowed from Shaw's pen. The late Mr. Shaw was no longer available to insist that only Mozart was worthy enough to add music to his plays. But the reaction of the critics and of greater importance, the public, was nearly unanimous.

Critics raved about the performances, the music, the lyrics. The show won countless awards and was performed by stock companies all over the world in many languages. Lerner and Loewe had succeeded in doing what many thought impossible: adapting *Pygmalion* into one of the greatest hits in the history of musical theater. Kitty Carlisle, now married to Moss Hart, the show's legendary director, remembered her Broadway debut in the 1930s, when an unknown Frederick Loewe promised her that one day he would write the greatest musical produced on Broadway. At the time, the idea seemed preposterous and amusing. After the premiere of *My Fair Lady*, no one was laughing, except at the show's laugh-lines. *My Fair Lady* represented the pinnacle of Broadway's musical theater.

Following the stunning achievement of *My Fair Lady*, Lerner and Loewe teamed again for the phenomenally successful score for the movie *Gigi*. They returned to Broadway in 1960 with a new musical based on T.H. White's novel, *The Once and Future King*, about the life of King Arthur. They called it *Camelot*. After *My Fair Lady*, Lerner and Loewe were faced with an unenviable task. How do you write a sequel to a work universally recognized as a masterpiece?

Camelot bore similarities to *My Fair Lady*. Moss Hart, the master director who was so responsible for the success of *My Fair Lady*, would direct. Julie Andrews was back starring as Queen Guinevere, this time opposite another classical British actor, Richard Burton, as King Arthur. Burton, like Harrison, wasn't a conventional singer, but had the vocal range and technique to sing and speak his lyrics and a compelling and resonant speaking voice. Robert Coote was also back, as the bumbling King Pellinore, and a new star, Robert Goulet, was cast as Launcelot. *Camelot* retold the legend of King Arthur, the idyllic period of his Round Table, and how the peaceful days of Camelot were destroyed when Guinevere fell in love with Launcelot, the king's favorite knight.

The show contained marvelous songs including "If Ever I Would Leave You," an outstanding lyrical ballad, "I Loved You Once in Silence," and "Camelot," the title song. But history rarely repeats itself. Lerner was faced with problems with the "book" portion of the show, especially differences between the light and amusing first act and the second act, with its emphasis on a forbidden love affair and the development of war. The illness and subsequent death of director Moss Hart left Lerner and Loewe without a key mentor and the show without a strong guiding hand. Initial critical reaction to *Camelot* was mixed. But an appearance on Ed Sullivan's television program by Burton, Andrews, Goulet, Lerner and Loewe led to box office success, and the show ran for two years. After the assassination of John F. Kennedy, Jacqueline Kennedy compared the Kennedy years in the White House to *Camelot* and the label stuck. The show and its score remain popular today.

After *Camelot*, Loewe retired to an estate in Palm Springs, California. Lerner, without Loewe, like Rodgers without Hammerstein, never seemed to feel at home with other collaborators. In fact, Rodgers and Lerner decided to write a show together. The partnership was probably doomed from the start, with the mercurial and elusive Lerner seeking inspiration for lyrics while Rodgers, with his meticulous work habits and rigorous adherence to a schedule, waited for Lerner to decide he had achieved perfection. After a failed attempt to write with Richard Rodgers, Lerner teamed with his earlier collaborator Burton Lane for *On a Clear Day You Can See Forever*, a musical about reincarnation. He tried working with other partners: André Previn, Charles Strouse, John Barry, and Leonard Bernstein, among others, without achieving his former success. The Lerner-Bernstein collaboration was especially intriguing: the composer of *My Fair Lady* collaborating with the charismatic conductor and composer of *West Side Story*. But the result was *1600 Pennsylvania Avenue*, a musical about the upstairs residents of the White House and their downstairs servants, which did not achieve success. Lerner also wrote *A Celebration: The Musical Theatre*, a history of the genre to which he had contributed so much.

Lerner's lyric for "One More Walk Around the Garden," a song in *Carmelina*, a show he wrote with Burton Lane, said it best. He longed for "one more walk around the garden before he closed the garden gate," in other words, another hit, another *My Fair Lady*. But sadly, it was not to be. Lerner died in 1986; his much older collaborator, Loewe, died two years later. The wit, elegance, and style of Lerner and Loewe were never equaled by their predecessors or by their successors. One critic said of Lerner and Loewe, "We shall not see their like again. A pity. I've grown accustomed to their grace."

LEONARD BERNSTEIN AND FRIENDS

Like Rodgers and Hammerstein, Leonard Bernstein was an innovator. In many ways, he was the true successor to George Gershwin. His contributions to Broadway were quintessentially the voice of the urban New Yorker. Three of his four major shows, *On the Town*, *Wonderful Town*, and *West Side Story*, were celebrations of New York City, its energy, its multi-ethnicity, its loneliness. Like Gershwin, Bernstein used the elements of concert music, especially opera and ballet, to expand and explore the dimensions of the popular song.

Bernstein brought an impressive set of classical credentials to the Broadway stage. He was a product of Harvard and the Curtis Institute of Music, where he had studied conducting with the formidable Fritz Reiner and piano with the intimidating and autocratic Isabella Vengerova. He subsequently became the pupil and protégé of Serge Koussevitzky, the revered conductor of the Boston Symphony. As a pianist, conductor, and composer, the multi-talented Bernstein could pursue virtually any path he chose in music. When illness prevented Bruno Walter from fulfilling a conducting appearance with the New York Philharmonic, the youthful Bernstein substituted for him and emerged as an instant star. In 1943, Bernstein collaborated with the choreographer Jerome Robbins on a ballet, *Fancy Free*, the tale of three sailors on leave in New York City. The following year, Bernstein and Robbins turned the ballet into a full-fledged Broadway musical, *On the Town*. Their collaborators were the lyricists Betty Comden and Adolph Green.

Figure 255 - Leonard Bernstein was drawn to Broadway as a comoser despite objections from his classical mentors. (Photo by Al Ravenna, Courtesy of New York World Telegram and Sun Collection, Library of Congress)

The partnership of Comden and Green is one of the most remarkable in Broadway's history. The pair, native New Yorkers, were both born in the same year, attended New York University together, participated in the Washington Square Players, and formed a nightclub act, *The Revuers*, which included their close friend, Judy Holliday. Betty Comden was a brilliant nightclub performer with a dynamic singing voice. Adolph Green's public persona was that of a flamboyant, zany comedian who could dash off tongue-twisting lyrics for laughs. But privately, he had an encyclopedic knowledge of concert music and was known to be able to whistle, on demand, passages from the entire classical repertoire, including pieces written by the most obscure composers. Not surprisingly, Comden and Green wrote roles for themselves into the plot of *On the Town*.

The stage version of *On the Town*, like the ballet, featured three sailors falling in love on a twenty-four hour madcap tour of New York. The spirited "New York, New York" caught the fancy of Manhattan audiences. Bernstein's ballads, "Lonely Town" and "Some

Figure 256- Betty Comden and Adolph Green, with one of their later collaborators, composer Cy Coleman (left.) (Photo courtesy of Noble Music)

Other Time," reflected the loneliness of those without love amidst the cacophony and energy of the big city. Like Gershwin, Bernstein was influenced by jazz. The syncopations, the raucous dissonance of the taxi-horns, and the melancholy wail of the saxophone playing the blues, were all captured in the score. The score had a zest and zip to it that proved irresistible.

While audiences were delighted with Bernstein's Broadway debut, the same could not be said for his mentor, Serge Koussevitzky. Koussevitzky was a champion of new composers; he had literally launched the careers of new American composers of concert music like Aaron Copland and Roy Harris. But he regarded Broadway as a distraction and made clear to Bernstein that he would have to choose between his new fame on Broadway and his long-term goal to succeed Koussevitzky as conductor of the Boston Symphony. Bernstein abandoned his musical theater career until after Koussevitzky's death. Ironically, Koussevitzky's wish and Bernstein's ambition did not come to pass. Charles Munch, not Bernstein, was chosen to succeed Koussevitzky in Boston. Bernstein subsequently became conductor of the New York Philharmonic.

When Bernstein did return to Broadway in 1953, he wrote the music for *Wonderful Town*, an adaptation of the play, *My Sister Eileen*, with a book by Joseph Fields and Jerome Chodorov, and lyrics by Comden and Green. Like *On the Town*, *Wonderful Town* celebrated New York, as seen through the eyes of naive out-of-town visitors. Instead of three sailors, the visiting out-of-towners were two sisters, self-reliant Ruth and the more vulnerable and naive Eileen, who move to Greenwich Village from Ohio. Bernstein again demonstrated his ability to compose stunning parodies of other forms of popular music. The witty lyrics of Comden and Green were brash, irreverent, and satirical, as exemplified by "What a Waste," a song celebrating the fate of starry-eyed hopefuls who arrive in New York and find themselves unemployed: the prodigious writer who hasn't written a word, the gifted artist painting signs on a bus, the talented actress flipping flapjacks at Childs' restaurant, and the opera singer warbling at the Fulton Fish Market. Comden and Green knew their subject.

Three years later, Bernstein was back on Broadway with *Candide*, one of the most unusual productions of all time. The show was initiated by playwright Lillian Hellman, who wanted to adapt the classic Voltaire satire into a musical play. While Bernstein wrote the music, words were provided by a succession of lyricists: Dorothy Parker, John Latouche, who died suddenly, and Pulitzer-prize winning poet Richard Wilbur. *Candide* had been Voltaire's scathing response to what he regarded as the hopeless optimism of philosophers. In Voltaire's tale, young Candide and the girl he loves, Cunegunde, live in idyllic Westphalia, where they are taught by the pompous Dr. Pangloss that "this is the best of all possible worlds." After chaos and catastrophe befall them, they survive everything from piracy and slavery to the Spanish Inquisition. But they return home having learned that it is best to "let our garden grow," instead of making ponderous philosophical pronouncements.

Bernstein's music may be the most musically sophisticated, stunning satirical score to grace the Broadway stage. The score was a true operetta, filled with musical gems, each often paraphrasing its musical counterparts in the world of serious music Bernstein knew so well. He incorporated the dance forms, including the schottische, the mazurka, the waltz, the tango, and the gavotte, into the score. The sprightly, frolicking *Overture* was not just a collection of tunes in the show, but a full-fledged concert piece worthy of Offenbach. Symphony orchestras still perform it throughout the world. A musical highlight of the show was "Glitter and Be Gay," a dazzling aria sung by Barbara Cook in the role of Cunegunde, who surmounted her fall from grace and the loss of her true love by accepting jewels and a luxurious life as a rich man's mistress. Bernstein wrote one of the most brilliant parodies of an operatic aria ever heard in a musical. Wickedly alternating between her sorrow that she is no longer pure and secretly delighted that her jewels are real, Cunegunde sang florid cadenzas and proved that Bernstein was at his best combining everything from Rococo melodies to Latin dance music. *Candide* was a composer's musical, a virtuoso performance by Bernstein that surmounted even the commercial failure of the show.

Despite the brilliant score, the show ran only seventy-nine performances. It became a hit years later when revived in the 1970s on stage and in concert performances. In 1989, Bernstein supervised a concert recording of the show, declaring it the musical child of his life that needed special attention. Singer Jerry Hadley, who sang the title role in the recording, declared *Candide* Bernstein's most fitting legacy. "It's eclectic, it's witty, it's profound, it's irreverent, it's tongue-in cheek one moment and innocent and full of child-like wonder the next."

Bernstein declared that his great ambition was to write one opera, which could be understood by everyone. While working on *Candide*, he was also developing that work, *West Side Story*. This 1957 production was revolutionary in tone and scope. For several years, Bernstein and playwright Arthur Laurents had discussed the idea of a modern version of Romeo and Juliet, taking place in the streets of New York. Choreographer

Jerome Robbins used dance to create the highly stylized image of violent confrontation between two street gangs, the Jets and the Sharks, one Puerto Rican, the other self-styled as "American." The inevitable clash between these modern day Montagues and Capulets erupted when today's Romeo and Juliet, Tony and Maria, fell in love. Bernstein wanted to write his own lyrics, but he was so busy that the opportunity was given to a young lyricist, Stephen Sondheim, the protégé of Oscar Hammerstein II.

Bernstein saw *West Side Story* as a way to deliver a message. His own personal copy of *Romeo and Juliet* contained a handwritten note on the opening page, "An out and out plea for racial tolerance." Alan Jay Lerner praised Arthur Laurents for the libretto of *West Side Story* as "a triumph of style and model of its genre."

"West Side Story" didn't look or sound like any previous musical. Bernstein used the raucous dissonance and lonely lyricism he had first introduced in his film score, *On the Waterfront*, a work of similar tone. Sondheim's lyrics were terse, blunt, and realistic. Robbins's finger-snapping choreography set the tone for this show. Broadway audiences weren't used to seeing dancers depicting the rumble of street gangs, a dream sequence depicting the world without violence, and an ending worthy of a Shakespearean tragedy.

West Side Story contained melodies that were far more complex than those of the average Broadway show—"Somewhere" and "Maria" among them. There were simple and innocent tunes"—"I Feel Pretty" and "One Hand, One Heart"— and the rhapsodic "Tonight," added to the balcony scene at the suggestion of Oscar Hammerstein who urged Bernstein and Sondheim to write a soaring love song for the show's most romantic moment. In later years, Sondheim typically expressed some embarrassment over allowing any sentimentality in his lyrics for *West Side Story*.

In a key scene, Anita, Maria's best friend, demands to know how Maria could possibly love the boy who killed her brother. In "A Boy Like That," Bernstein reverts to pure operatic form. Maria's answer, "I Have a Love," is one of the purest melodies in any Broadway show. The operatic duet was often overlooked by critics praising the show's more popular songs. It is important not because it is operatic, but because it represents s remarkable fusion of music, dialogue, and drama. *West Side Story* was a musical landmark. It showed how serious a genre once dubbed "musical comedy" had become. It also established the preeminence of the choreographer on the Broadway stage. *West Side Story* was a musical landmark. It showed how serious a genre once dubbed "musical comedy" had become. It also established the preeminence of the choreographer on the Broadway stage. Bernstein proved that what was once called "musical comedy" could evolve into a serious and important art form.

JULE

While Bernstein was busy with *Candide* and *West Side Story*, his friends Betty Comden and Adolph Green were busy too. Only a few days before the premiere of *Candide*, their show *Bells are Ringing* opened on Broadway. Their collaborator was the composer Jule

Figure 257 - Composer Jule Styne (right) and lyricist Bob Merrill (left), collaborators on the hit show, *Funny Girl*. (Photo courtesy of Margaret Styne and Suzanne Merrill)

Styne. Styne agreed to work with them on *Bells are Ringing*, a vehicle for their old friend Judy Holliday. Broadway, a street that had seen its share of original characters and personalities, had never seen anyone quite like Jule Styne.

Born in London, as a child he jumped on the stage of the Hippodrome for an impromptu performance with Scotland's singing star Harry Lauder. His family moved to Chicago, where he was considered a piano prodigy. But when the famed pianist Harold Bauer told him his small hands would limit his potential as a concert pianist, he turned to jazz. He became the vocal coach for girlfriends of gangsters, even leading a band in the employ of the most notorious gangster of all, Al Capone, who once borrowed his baton to direct a performance of music by George Gershwin.

Eventually, Styne moved to Hollywood where he worked as vocal coach to the world's most famous child star, Shirley Temple, wrote hit songs, and formed a partnership with lyricist Sammy Cahn. Cahn proved to be the perfect lyricist to collaborate with Styne. He had grown up in a New York tenement and dropped out of school to eventually pursue a career as a songwriter. He told his wife Tita that in his neighborhood, there were two choices, "show business or the chair."

Cahn initially wrote lyrics for composer Saul Chaplin who went on to become a major producer and musical director at M-G-M. Cahn had earned quite a reputation as a writer of parodies and special material for stars, and was known for his ability to write numerous high quality lyrics with lightning speed. But he was at a low point in his career after moving to Hollywood when he and Styne were assigned to write the songs for the movie *Youth on Parade*. "I've Heard That Song Before" became a tremendous hit when introduced on screen by Frank Sinatra, and the team of Styne and Cahn was suddenly in demand. Cahn thus began his long association with Sinatra, writing first with Styne and later with Jimmy Van Heusen.

Styne and Cahn worked together for six years, creating a major hit Broadway musical, *High Button Shoes*, and countless hit songs for

Figure 258 - Sammy Cahn, the master of the finger-snapping lyric and the sentimental ballad, celebrating several of his most successful songs. (Photo courtesy of Tita Cahn)

films and recordings. (Included were "It's Been a Long, Long Time," "Five Minutes More,"

"Time After Time," "It's Magic," "Saturday Night Is the Loneliest Night of the Week," and "I'll Walk Alone," the latter proving one of the most popular ballads on the home front during World War II.) Styne and Cahn ended their partnership when Styne decided to concentrate on writing Broadway shows, while Cahn remained in Hollywood. The two reunited years later, in 1954, to produce the hit film theme, "Three Coins in the Fountain."

Styne was prolific. (He turned out some 1400 songs.) He spoke in a language described by Comden and Green as "Stynese, a machine gun style of speech understood only by Styne himself." His colleague, conductor Milton Rosenstock, said, "Jule is pure Chicago." His wife Margaret described him as "impossible, infuriating, inconsistent, irresponsible and illogical, exhilarating, exciting, irrepressible, irreplaceable, and never boring."

Styne's collaborators certainly never found him boring. One said in story conferences he could argue passionately against an idea he had enthusiastically promoted the day before. On one occasion, he asked writer Anita Loos to develop a scenario for a musical designed for the talents of Marlene Dietrich. After weeks went by, he called suddenly and told her, "Split Dietrich's character into three; Dietrich is out and the King Sisters are in." The versatile Miss Loos did as she was asked only to have Styne call her again weeks later and tell her that the three King Sisters were no longer in the picture and that she should rewrite her plot as a vehicle for vaudeville legend Sophie Tucker. When Anita Loos checked her contract, she discovered it had expired six months earlier.

Styne was famous for his volatile temper. He argued at the top of his lungs. In a single rehearsal, he once managed to spill three liquids, a pot of Postum on the orchestra, a pitcher of coffee on the conductor's musical score, and a container of cream on his own copy of the music. He was a man of boundless energy, a streetwise gambler, a character who could have been invented by the writer Damon Runyon, whose short stories were the sentimental tales of hustlers and gangsters always convinced that a new hit was just around the corner.

Styne's biggest Broadway hits were *High Button Shoes*, a 1947 show (with lyrics by Sammy Cahn) featuring Phil Silvers as a con man and *Gentlemen Prefer Blondes*, based on Anita Loos' classic satire of the 1920s. Anita Loos insisted on a faithful adaptation of her book depicting the adventures of Lorelei and her sensible brunette girlfriend, Dorothy. With lyricist Leo Robin, Styne wrote "Diamonds Are a Girl's Best Friend," the anthem of the gold-digging blonde, Lorelei Lee. The song was inspired by Anita Loos' memorable quote, "A gentleman kissing your hand may feel very good, but a diamond bracelet lasts forever."

Styne first worked with Comden and Green in 1951. They collaborated on the music for a revue, *Two on the Aisle*, starring Bert Lahr and featuring the directorial debut of Abe Burrows. Two years later, they collaborated again, adding songs to a musical version of *Peter Pan* that had been written originally by Moose Charlap and Carolyn Leigh. *Bells are

Ringing, the saga of a telephone operator whose good intentions lead her to meddle in the lives of people she meets on the phone, became a hit.

The show had a precarious beginning when Frank Sinatra, an old friend of Styne's from Hollywood, showed no interest in it. One melody, which Styne had written years earlier, finally got a lyric to match. It became the hit, *Just in Time*. Judy Holiday refused to sing ballads in the show. Styne taught her *The Party's Over*, the show's leading ballad, by promising her it was a counter-melody to the real ballad, sung by someone else. When she finally asked who was singing the real ballad, he said, "You are, you've been doing it for a week." Then Judy Holliday issued an ultimatum that she wouldn't go on unless given an "11:00 o'clock number," something to "stop the show" just before curtain time. Styne, Comden and Green obliged, and the show became a hit, to the relief and surprise of Richard Rodgers, who had invested in the show and was sitting in the front row as Styne nervously waited for audience reaction on opening night. Comden and Green continued to collaborate with Styne on shows like *Say Darling* and *Do Re Mi*. They also performed a stage version of their own work, *A Party with Comden and Green*, in 1958.

One of Styne's biggest hits was *Gypsy*, a 1959 musical based on the life of the burlesque queen, Gypsy Rose Lee, her sister, June Havoc, and their domineering stage mother, Rose. Stephen Sondheim, after the success of *West Side Story*, was slated to write the score, but Ethel Merman, starring as Rose, insisted on an experienced composer with a name: Jule Styne. Sondheim agreed to step aside and write only the lyrics. The result was the unusual collaboration of Styne, known as a writer of hit tunes, and Sondheim, who wanted every song to rise from the emotional impetus of character and plot. *Gypsy* did contain hit tunes. One song, *Betwixt and Between*, had been discarded from *High Button Shoes*. Sondheim wrote a new lyric for Styne's melody; it became "Everything's Coming Up Roses." The collaborators wrote an electrifying scene at the end of the show, "Rose's Turn," in which Rose declares that it is her time for glory now that her daughters have left her alone. It was staged with immense theatricality and declared to be "an aria" by the amazed Ethel Merman. Styne remained active in musical theater, collaborating again with Comden and Green on *Subways Are for Sleeping* (1961), *Fade Out, Fade In* (1964), *Hallelujah, Baby* (1967), and *Lorelei* (1971). His biggest hit after *Gypsy* was the 1964 show, *Funny Girl*, based on the life of Fanny Brice, with lyrics by Bob Merrill.

A MOST MUSICAL FELLA: FRANK LOESSER

Frank Loesser emerged during this period as a major figure in America's musical theater. Loesser was born into a musical family. His father, Henry Loesser, was an accomplished classical piano teacher, who once accompanied soprano Lili Lehmann; his half-brother Arthur Loesser was a famous concert pianist, critic, teacher, and author of *Men, Women and Pianos,* a widely-praised history of the instrument.

Though Frank Loesser could play any tune by ear, he developed an unfortunate inferiority complex because of his lack of formal classical training. Even after he became quite famous, his brother Arthur regarded his success financial more than artistic. His brash and brassy personal style served him very well on Broadway, but dismayed his relatives. He fostered an explosive temper; his daughter (and biographer) Susan Loesser said his tirades sounded as if they were coming from an obscene Rumpelstiltskin. Then, as quickly as the storm came, it would end. Loesser enjoyed the confident impertinence of Broadway. His motto for singers was "loud is good." He wasn't shy or retiring, and he expected singers to follow his example. But the brash Broadway composer-lyricist had another side to his unique musical personality; he would develop a personal style that revealed him to be a pure romanticist in private.

Figure 259 - The remarkable Frank Loesser had a major impact on Broadway as both composer and lyricist. (Photo courtesy of Frank Loesser Archives)

Initially, fame seemed elusive. Loesser drifted through a series of odd jobs: he sold advertising, drew cartoons and caricatures, worked as City Editor for a fledgling newspaper in New Rochelle, screwed on insecticide cans, and even became a process server. Although he declined to pursue classical music studies to impress his family, he began collaborating on songs with his teenage friends. (One, William Schuman, became a renowned symphonic composer and President of the Juilliard School of Music.) In 1936, Loesser contributed lyrics to Irving Actman's music for *The Illustrator's Show* on Broadway. The show closed after only five performances, but the exposure led Loesser to Hollywood as a lyricist. His first hit was the result of a collaboration with Alfred Newman, "The Moon of Manakoora." He began writing song lyrics for Jule Styne, Burton Lane, Hoagy Carmichael, and Jimmy McHugh among others. In 1939, he made his debut as a composer, writing both music and lyrics for "Seventeen," the title song of a Paramount film. During World War II, he joined the U.S. Army's Special Services Division and wrote his own music as well as lyrics for the soldier shows. Just about the time he considered himself a failure, he produced two major wartime hits, "Praise the Lord and Pass the Ammunition" and "The Ballad of Rodger Young."

In 1944, Loesser wrote "Baby, It's Cold Outside." He performed it with his wife, Lynn Garland Loesser, at a housewarming party. The tune was written as a duet for two characters who were identified in the score as "wolf" and "mouse." The singing voice of "wolf," sung by Frank, tried to persuade the "mouse," performed by Lynn, to remain indoors for a romantic rendezvous using the cold weather as an excuse. It would not be the last time that Loesser would use counterpoint, the technique perfected by Bach, to offset one voice against another. Their mutually flirtatious performance of the "call and response" lyrics created a sensation. (Loesser said the song became their ticket to caviar and truffles.) He would introduce himself as "the evil of two Loessers." At first, it was only performed by the Loessers themselves. But after pressure from MGM, four years later, he sold it to MGM for the film *Neptune's Daughter* and it won the Academy Award. Only Lynn Loesser was unhappy over the song's success. She was deeply hurt that her husband had sold "their special song" and that it was suddenly being performed by everyone else.

Figure 260 - Frank Loesser at his desk, hard at work. (Photo courtesy of Frank Loesser Archives)

In *Neptune's Daughter*, Ricardo Montalban, a devoted husband in real life, but often cast as a Casanova in the movies, sang the "wolf's" lyrics to Esther Williams' "mouse." Williams tried to resist Montalban's charm by declaring that her family would worry if she didn't hurry home. Traditionally the "wolf's" lyrics are sung by a male voice. But the roles were also reversed in the same film with "wolf" Betty Garrett singing to "mouse" Red Skelton. "Baby, It's Cold Outside" has survived decades of changing musical styles. Every possible combination of singers have performed and recorded it, including the best-known stars of stage and screen. Perhaps the most unusual partnership teamed ballet dancer Rudolf Nureyev singing the role of the "mouse" and resisting the advances of Miss Piggy, the porcine puppet star of The Muppets, cast ironically as the "wolf."

In 1948, Frank Loesser made his Broadway debut as composer and lyricist with *Where's Charley?* The show was a musical adaptation of Brandon Thomas's often performed 1892 comedy, *Charley's Aunt*. With a book and direction by George Abbott and choreography by George Balanchine, the show became a huge hit, at the time the tenth longest running show on Broadway. *Where's Charley?* features the antics of two Oxford students, Charley Wykeham and Jack Chesney, and their efforts to woo their very proper English girlfriends, Kitty Verdun and Amy Spettigue. Charley was expecting a visit from his wealthy aunt, Dona Lucia d'Alvadorez. When she failed to arrive from Brazil ("where the nuts come from"), Charley masqueraded as Dona Lucia, engaging in slapstick clowning in skirts and trousers, fending off the amorous attentions of Kitty's pompous guardian. *Where's Charley* launched the career of Ray Bolger, whose performance of Loesser's "Once in Love with Amy" stopped the show nightly. Other Loesser songs included "Make a Miracle," "My Darling, My Darling," and "Better Get Out of Here," expressing the dilemma of the unchaperoned heroes and the objects of their affection.

Loesser's next opus was a Broadway classic, *Guys and Dolls*, based on a collection of stories by Damon Runyon. One of the tales, *The Idyll of Miss Sarah Brown*, would provide the principal story line, the improbable romance between a Salvation Army sister and the man whose soul she tries to save, the elusive gambler Sky Masterson. A secondary plot would involve Nathan Detroit, proprietor of "the oldest established floating crap game in New York," and his girlfriend, Miss Adelaide, to whom he has been engaged for fourteen years.

Initially, a Hollywood writer, Jo Swerling, was selected to write the book, but producers Cy Feuer and Ernest Martin discarded his work and hired Abe Burrows, then actively writing the radio series, *Archie's Tavern*. Burrows and Loesser met at a party, discovered their mutual interest in writing parody songs, and the rest was history. Burrows' script and Loesser's lyrics captured the true spirit of Runyon's outrageous characters, small-time gamblers and hoodlums with colorful names: "Nicely-Nicely Johnson," "Harry the Horse," "Benny Southstreet," and "Big Julie." These people had their own code of honor and their own traditions. They spoke the language of the streets. Burrows and Loesser captured the pulsating rhythms, the urban energy of Runyon's unforgettable characters and the legendary George S. Kaufman agreed to direct *Guys and Dolls*.

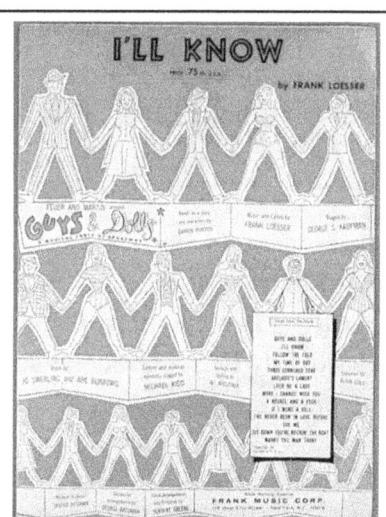

Figure 261 - "I'll Know," one of the fine love songs from *Guys and Dolls*. (Photo courtesy of Frank Loesser Enterprises)

One reason for the enduring success of *Guys and Dolls* was Loesser's ability to write from his characters' point of view. Even in the most outrageously funny situations, he took them as seriously as they always seemed to take themselves. ("Adelaide's Lament" depicted the outrage of a woman whose plans to go to Niagara Falls were derailed when Nathan Detroit got off the train to visit the racetrack at Saratoga for the fourteenth time.) Loesser introduced his readers of the Racing Form with a contrapuntal ode to gambling, the "Fugue for Tinhorns." There were love songs—"I've Never Been in Love Before," "I'll Know," and "If I Were a Bell," There were comedy classics—"Take Back Your Mink" and "Sue Me." Loesser provided the driving, swinging "Luck Be a Lady" as Sky Masterson rolls the dice on the most important bet of his life, and the rousing "Sit Down, You're Rocking the Boat." "More I Cannot Wish You" was poignant and memorable. Frank Loesser couldn't have wished for a greater success than he achieved with *Guys and Dolls*. In 1950, the "musical fable" opened to rave review, ran for 1200 performances, and it remains a classic of the Broadway stage.

After writing the score for a movie musical, *Hans Christian Andersen*, Frank Loesser began writing one of his most important works, based on Sidney Howard's 1924 play, *They Knew What They Wanted*. This work for musical theater, entitled *The Most Happy Fella*, was special. *Where's Charley?* had been Victorian, light, satirical, and traditional.

Guys and Dolls had broken new ground, as Loesser applied the musical vocabulary of Tin Pan Alley to such classical forms as the fugue. But *The Most Happy Fella* was a true opera.

Figure 262 - "My Heart is So Full of You," sung in *The Most Happy Fella* by operatic star Robert Weede to soprano Jo Sullivan in the original New York production. (Photo courtesy of Frank Loesser Enterprises)

Loesser avoided using the term; but this show was clearly a landmark in the total integration of music, lyrics, and libretto. Originally, Loesser's friend, the playwright Samuel Taylor, was going to write the libretto, but he couldn't tolerate Loesser's Broadway lifestyle, parties, and late hours. He urged Loesser to write his own libretto and Loesser took his advice.

The Most Happy Fella was a love story. Like *South Pacific*, it told the tale of love between two unlikely people: Tony, an aging Italian immigrant who lives in California's Napa Valley, and Amy, his mail-order bride. Tony is wealthy, but shy and uneducated; to please Amy, a San Francisco waitress he dubs "Rosabella," he sends her a photograph of Joe, his handsome farmhand, pretending that it is his own. Loesser added comedic characters to the original play, developing and expanding his plot for four years. There were finger snapping, toe tapping tunes, "Standing on the Corner" and "Big D," for example, but also rhapsodic arias like "My Heart Is So Full of You" and "Somebody, Somewhere." "Joey, Joey," expressed Joe's wanderlust in a haunting melody. Loesser used spoken dialogue, but also used operatic recitative in which dialogue is sung. There were so many musical pieces that the *Playbill* program originally didn't list titles of songs, because they were fully integrated into the story.

Starring in the show were Robert Weede, a renowned operatic baritone, and Jo Sullivan, a marvelous soprano who became the second Mrs. Frank Loesser. As the plot developed, Rosabella had to choose between Joe, the man she thought she loved, and Tony, who remained devoted to her and her baby. Though some critics were unfortunately baffled by Loesser's eclectic style, Loesser deserved nothing but plaudits for this stunning work. To some extent, Loesser faced the same dilemma as George Gershwin had faced two decades earlier. Classical music critics would smile and nod their heads as long as a complete score fit their personal notions of operatic style. Broadway pundits knew a hit song when they heard it, but were puzzled when characters sang music and lyrics that sounded operatic. So instead of praising Loesser for developing a brilliant new musical form, there were those who criticized him, albeit unfairly.

After trying his hand at the Broadway version of grand opera, Loesser turned to a folk opera, *Greenwillow*. This musical celebrated the long, lost days of rural Americana. Based on a novel by B. J. Chute, *Greenwillow* presented a mythical country village that exists in no particular place or time. The quaint characters and lack of plot made it difficult to adapt in musical form. It did not become a commercial success, although it retained a cult following among Loesser fans. Loesser's score for *Greenwillow* reflected a charm that surprised those who didn't think of Loesser as sensitive and introspective.

The same could not be said for Loesser's next musical, a huge commercial hit, *How to Succeed in Business Without Really Trying*. Producers Cy Feuer and Ernest Martin wanted to produce a show based on the book of the same title, a humorous "how-to" book about success in business. They approached Abe Burrows and Frank Loesser, both of whom said "no plot, no romance, no deal." But they relented and a plot was created, the saga of J. Pierpont Finch, who rises from window-washer to Wall Street legend by following the advice of a little book. He manages to impress J.B. Biggley, the pompous corporate tycoon who runs the World Wide Wicket Company, to fall in love with a secretary, and in the process, to overcome the machinations of the boss's nephew. Finch is both innocent and clever, both idealist and schemer. With tunes like "A Secretary Is Not a Toy," Loesser was back in the milieu of *Guys and Dolls*. One song, "I Believe In You," became popular as a love song outside the show; but in the show, Finch sings it to himself in the mirror. *How to Succeed in Business Without Really Trying*, the improbable tongue-in-cheek satire of corporate America, won the Pulitzer Prize. The role of Finch was played skillfully by Robert Morse, while his stuffy boss was portrayed by the one-time college idol of the 1920s, Rudy Vallee. Ironically, decades later, Morse would come full circle and be recognized by new audiences on the television series *Mad Men*, as "Bert Cooper," the staid senior partner of a New York advertising agency.

Frank Loesser was also a businessman. He formed his own publishing company, Frank Music, and published not only his own work, but that of others. Two of his protégés, composer-lyricists Richard Adler and Jerry Ross, wrote and produced memorable scores of their own. Adler was the son of famed classical piano pedagogue Clarence Adler, but he was drawn to popular music and especially the shows of Broadway. Jerry Ross had written "The Newspaper Song." It was performed by singer Eddie Fisher. Adler and Ross met in 1950. By 1953, their song, "Rags to Riches" had become a smash hit for vocalist Tony Bennett and the two collaborators wrote the score for a popular Broadway review, *John Murray Anderson's Almanac*. This attracted the attention of one of Broadway's most successful directors, George Abbott. Abbott invited the pair to write the score for his next major production.

So in 1954, they wrote *Pajama Game*, based on a book by Richard Bissell. *Pajama Game* contained tunes like "Hernando's Hideaway," a tango parody. The big song in *Pajama Game*, the saga of an Iowa factory strike, was "Hey, There," sung by John Raitt's character, a plant manager, who tries to talk himself out of an attraction to a pretty girl who is also a member of the union's Grievance Committee. Interestingly, Richard Bissell had his own opinions of what took place behind the scenes, as *Pajama Game* became a musical. He wrote *Say Darling*, a book subsequently turned into a musical by Jule Styne, Betty Comden, and Adolph Green.

Figure 263 - Richard Adler (seated) and Jerry Ross (at the piano), the brilliant team whose brief collaboration, cut short by Ross's sudden death, produced Broadway classic shows. (Photo by Paul Radkai, courtesy of Janie Ross Coulter.)

A year later, Adler and Ross were back with *Damn Yankees*, based on Douglas Wallop's Faustian tale of a middle-aged man who is so devoted to the Washington Senators, a perennially dismal baseball team, that he sells his soul to the devil for a chance to return to his long, lost youth and help the team beat the hated New York Yankees. He manages to become involved with the devil's seductive temptress, Lola, who sings to him, "Whatever Lola Wants, Lola Gets," another Adler-Ross tango. The new team of Adler and Ross seemed destined to become the next important writing partnership on Broadway. They had the two top running shows on Broadway and their future as a team couldn't have seemed brighter. But Ross died suddenly at the age of only twenty-nine, leaving Adler to continue his musical career alone. The musical theater world would always wonder about the shows the pair might have created in years to come.

An admiring writer once described Adler and Ross as "two young Loessers." Like their mentor, the team had an instinctive feel for the brash, finger-snapping style of urban America. But Loesser also took an interest in the creative work of another composer who couldn't have been less like himself: Meredith Willson. Unlike many figures on Broadway, Willson was a true Midwesterner. He had been born in Mason City, Iowa, and loved to reminisce about childhood, a world of innocence and optimism, of band concerts and barbershop quartets in a small town. Willson had been a musician all his life; as a flutist, he had performed with John Philip Sousa's band and during the silent film era, in a theater orchestra led by Paramount's venerable musical director, Irvin Talbot. Willson had written music ranging from serious compositions for a symphonic orchestra to the popular song, "May the Good Lord Bless and Keep You."

Although well-known on radio, Willson had never written a Broadway show. Loesser encouraged him to write a musical about his Mason City memories. Willson came up with *The Music Man*, a love story about a fast-talking confidence man, Harold Hill, and his attempts to sell band instruments and uniforms to the unsuspecting residents of his Iowa hometown, renamed River City. Hill's natural antagonist was the town's pretty (and eternally unmarried) librarian, the only one capable of determining that he knew nothing about music. Willson's "Seventy-Six Trombones" became the show's big hit march, while "'Til There Was You," proved to be its most successful ballad. In "Ya Got Trouble," Hill persuaded the people of River City that public morals were threatened by the appearance of a pool table in town and that only he had the solution.

It is hard to believe that Robert Preston, who created the role on Broadway, was not the first, but the last choice to portray Harold Hill. Danny Kaye, selected first by the producers, turned it down, and a long list of others (including comedian Jackie Gleason) were considered. But Preston, like Yul Brynner in the *The King and I,* made the role his own. He performed with such unabashed energy and the mischievous charm of a likeable confidence man that nearly every performer today who sings "Ya Got Trouble" sounds as if he is doing an imitation of Preston. Producer Kermit Bloomgarden originally wanted Moss Hart, a director whose success with *My Fair Lady* virtually guaranteed a successful production at the time, to take charge of *The Music Man.* But Hart, ever the Manhattan sophisticate, thought the show was too full of "Iowa corn" to draw New York audiences. He advised Bloomgarden to drop the project entirely, but Bloomgarden didn't listen. He hired Morton da Costa to direct and *The Music Man* became a tremendous hit, with Robert Preston recreating the starring role of Harold Hill in a film adaptation and Shirley Jones replacing Broadway's "Marian the librarian," Barbara Cook. on the screen.

Figure 264 - Meredith Willson never forgot his roots in Mason City, Iowa. He turned his hometown into River City, the mythical setting of his biggest hit musical, *The Music Man.* (Photo courtesy of Mason City Public Library)

Willson went on to write other shows, including *The Unsinkable Molly Brown,* the story of a real-life survivor of the Titanic and her silver-mining husband, and *Here's Love*, the latter a musical adaptation of the classic film, *Miracle on 34th Street.* Frank Music published all of Willson's music.

Frank Loesser died in 1969. Ironically, it was his music, not the esteem in which his brother was held by classical musicians that would remain with the public. After some neglect, his music is now enjoying a spectacular revival. *Guys and Dolls*, *The Most Happy Fella*, and *How to Succeed in Business Without Really Trying* remain among the most enduring Broadway classics. *Pleasures and Palaces*, a rare Loesser commercial flop, has been revived. *Señor Discretion Himself,* Loesser's last show, unproduced at the time of his death, was finally introduced to audiences. Based on a short story by Budd Schulberg, it contained such undiscovered songs as "I Cannot Let You Go" and "You Understand Me." Loesser always said he wrote for the present, not for posterity. But it appears that posterity will indeed always appreciate Frank Loesser for his unique contribution to our musical history.

GIANTS ON BROADWAY

Oklahoma! was a milestone in the history of musical theater. Music, book, and lyrics were unified in a fully integrated musical entity. But not everyone was convinced that this new format, with specific songs written for specific characters, was essential. One skeptic was Irving Berlin, the preeminent writer of an unprecedented list of hit songs. Cole Porter once said that composers did not sit down to write hit songs, except for Irving Berlin who could not help himself. Initially, Berlin was not persuaded by the idea of the integrated musical, with specific songs written only for specific characters and situations. He had written scores with hit songs added to scenes at the drop of a hat, or perhaps in Berlin's case, a top hat. But Rodgers and Hammerstein had changed the rules, and now musicals would be evaluated as whole dramatic entities, regardless of how many superb tunes might be included.

Lyricist Dorothy Fields had become fascinated by the idea of a musical based on the life of Annie Oakley. Joseph Fields, her brother, had written a screenplay about Oakley, the fabled sharpshooter. Oakley beat the best male marksman of the day, Frank Butler, in a contest, and then married him. Fields offered the idea to Rodgers and Hammerstein, who decided that they would produce the show, but turned the score over to Jerome Kern. However, Kern died in November of 1945.

Figure 265 - Irving Berlin, composer of *Annie Get Your Gun*, attends auditions with producers Richard Rodgers, Oscar Hammerstein II, and choreographer Helen Tamiris. (Photo by Al Aumuller. Courtesy of New York World Telegram and Sun Collection, Library of Congress)

Rodgers and Hammerstein approached Irving Berlin. Since Berlin wrote his own lyrics, the Fieldses would have to agree to write only the libretto. They did, and the result was *Annie, Get Your Gun,* a hugely successful show starring Ethel Merman, and later, on tour, Mary Martin. Berlin produced a score bursting with energy and enthusiasm. The songs magically fit the characters and situation; they were also, not surprisingly, the kinds of hits Irving Berlin seemed to write without difficulty: "The Girl That I Marry," "You Can't Get a Man With A Gun," "Doin' What Comes Natur'lly," and at the suggestion of Richard Rodgers, a "challenge song" for Annie and her husband, "Anything You Can Do, I Can Do Better." When Rodgers proposed the idea, Berlin agreed. Director Joshua Logan went home to his apartment and heard the phone ringing: it was Berlin, who already had written the song on the way home to his apartment in a taxi. Berlin also wrote a song for a scene change, extolling the virtues of show business. (Annie Oakley spent years touring in Wild West Shows.) Berlin thought Rodgers, Hammerstein, and Logan didn't like the song and was prepared to discard it. When they insisted it belonged in the show, they learned that his secretary, unimpressed by the piece, had nearly lost it under a phone book. It went back into the show, and "There's No Business Like Show Business" became one of the biggest hits of all time as well as the unofficial anthem of everyone on Broadway.

In 1949, Berlin was back on Broadway with *Miss Liberty*, but this show did not prove a success, despite good quality songs. Undeterred, Berlin returned to the formula of *Annie Get Your Gun*, a new star vehicle for Ethel Merman. In *Call Me Madam*, Merman played a character based on the socialite "hostess with the mostess," Perle Mesta, named by President Truman to be Ambassador to Luxembourg. "You're Just in Love," a duet featuring two distinct melodies sung simultaneously, was the highlight of the show. Berlin had used the same device in "Play A Simple Melody" in *Watch Your Step*, a show he had written in 1914. Berlin tried another of these contrapuntal duets in "An Old Fashioned Wedding," written in 1966 for the revival of *Annie Get Your Gun*. The basic premise called for Berlin to create a lyrical melody and a sprightly rhythm song that could each be sung independently and then performed together in a duet. The formula proved to be magic on stage.

Berlin's last Broadway show, *Mr. President*, premiered in 1962 and sadly, was not a commercial success. He never officially retired, but seldom appeared in public. There were major tributes to him on his hundredth birthday. He died in 1989, still the personification of the American dream. Several of his songs, including "Easter Parade," "White Christmas," and "God Bless America," became unofficial holiday and national anthems. As Jerome Kern said, "Irving Berlin has no place in American music, he is American music."

Berlin's success with *Annie Get Your Gun* motivated Cole Porter, who had not enjoyed a major hit on Broadway for several years. Producer Arnold Saint-Subber had been inspired by the backstage bickering of the brilliant married actors Alfred Lunt and Lynne Fontanne. He wanted to create a show about two feuding Shakespearean actors. Together with Lemuel Ayers, he planned to produce the show, and asked writers Bella and Samuel Spewack to do the libretto.

The leading characters were Fred Graham (a star modeled to some extent on the flamboyant and charismatic Orson Welles) and Lilli Vanessi, his volatile wife, deeply in love but unable to get along. The story would include a "show within the show," a musical version of *The Taming of the Shrew* in which the two leading characters perform. The plot thickened when gangsters arrived backstage to collect a debt from Bill Calhoun, another actor who was a member of the cast. Initially, the show was offered to composer Burton Lane, but he turned it down. Bella Spewack insisted that Cole Porter, considered by some to have his best shows behind him, was the ideal composer. Porter, initially resistant, agreed, and the result was *Kiss Me, Kate*, one of his finest and most successful scores.

Kiss Me, Kate included a variety of musical styles: the rousing "Another Op'nin', Another Show," "I Hate Men," in which the shrewish Lili uses a pewter mug as a

Figure 266 - Cole Porter in 1955 receiving an honorary doctorate from Williams College. He composed the score for *Kiss Me, Kate* on a Bechstein piano, today residing in the Williams College chapel. He received another honorary doctorate from Yale University five years later. (Photo courtesy of the Irving Gilmore Library, Yale University, Cole Porter Papers, Box 50, Folder 307s)

percussion instrument, "Wunderbar," a Viennese waltz, "Why Can't You Behave?," and "Always True to You in My Fashion." The show's major ballad was "So in Love." Porter also had his fun with the Bard of Avon, using such Shakespearean phrases as "I've Come to Wive It Wealthily in Padua" and "Where Is the Life That Late I Led?" In the latter, Fred laments the loss of his bachelorhood: "Where is Fedora, the wild virago? It's lucky I missed her gangster sister from Chicago." Only Porter, with his usual double-entendres and wickedly ironic sense of humor could have his leading man lament the loss of Lisa "who gave a new meaning to the Leaning Tower of Pisa." Finally, Porter wrote "Brush Up Your Shakespeare," an outrageous comedy song for the gangsters, mangling Shakespearean syntax with malapropisms and the slang of small-time hoodlums. Broadway pundits were not optimistic about *Kiss Me, Kate*. They considered Porter past his prime, recalled that major stars had turned down the leads, and expected the worst. When *Kiss Me, Kate* became a huge hit, Porter fooled everyone. Like Irving Berlin, he proved he still had the old magic.

Porter's next Broadway show, *Out of This World*, a tale of Greek gods on earth, was a commercial failure. ("From This Moment On," the show's most enduring hit, was cut during a Philadelphia tryout!) But in 1953, he wrote *Can-Can*, a tale of a young judge who falls in love with a can-can dancer. Some of Porter's best tunes were in the score: "C'est Magnifique," "I Love Paris," and the ever-popular "It's All Right with Me," which became standard fare for singers and jazz musicians everywhere. Porter's last Broadway show was *Silk Stockings*, a 1955 musical version of *Ninotchka*. The Abe-Burrows-George S. Kaufman-Leueen MacGrath book ridiculed Soviet communism at the height of the Cold War, while Porter produced another popular song, "All of You." Porter's wife Linda died shortly before the opening of *Silk Stockings*; four years later, doctors amputated his leg. He never wrote another Broadway show, and died in 1964.

Nothing could offer greater contrast to the optimism of *Oklahoma!* or the unabashed entertainment of *Annie Get Your Gun* and *Kiss Me, Kate* than the work of the serious, innovative, and unpredictable Kurt Weill. In 1943, the same year that *Oklahoma!* opened on Broadway, Weill's most conventional musical, *One Touch of Venus,* premiered. The show was inspired by an 1891 British novel, *The Tinted Venus*, in which the mythical goddess of love, Venus, comes to earth and falls in love with a meek, mild-mannered barber. Irene Sharaff, a noted costume designer, suggested the idea to Weill. Initially, Weill saw *One Touch of Venus* as a vehicle for Marlene Dietrich. When Ira Gershwin turned down the project, he engaged the famed light-verse writer, Ogden Nash, as lyricist. Humorist S.J. Perelman wrote the libretto, replacing earlier collaborator Bella Spewack. Nash and Perelman drank and dined their way through lunches at the Harvard Club and wrote the script about a heavenly statue that comes to life.

When Dietrich announced that the role was too provocative for the mother of a teenager, she withdrew. The role was offered to a skeptical Mary Martin. To persuade Martin that she could play Venus despite her wholesome, all-American image, Martin's husband asked Mainbocher, a celebrated couturier, to design a complete wardrobe for her. Irene Sharaff was supposed to do the costumes, since the show had been her idea. But she was in Hollywood at the time. Martin was taken with Weill's song, "That's Him," in which Venus explains her love for the barber, as well as the Mainbocher wardrobe, and agreed.

Included in the score were "West Wind," "Foolish Heart," and one of Weill's most memorable melodies, the haunting beguine, "Speak Low." Though *One Touch of Venus* was the most tuneful and therefore commercial of Weill's shows, he managed to include two ballets: "Forty Minutes to Lunch," in which Venus proves love is not dead by arranging a romance between a boy and girl of her choosing, and "Ozone Heights," in which the goddess debates the merits of life in the suburbs and life in the heavens. Mary Martin was convinced that the show's success was due in part to the fact that every time she walked on stage in a new Mainbocher original gown, the audience burst into applause for the designs even before she opened her mouth.

The tremendous commercial success of "Speak Low" might have misled audiences into thinking that Weill was about to spend his time thinking about writing hit songs. Quite the opposite. Weill continued to dream of totally integrated music, lyrics, dialogue, and dance in a new musical theater form closest to the operas of his Berlin days, complete with stories that would fuel the politics of protest. He began writing a folk opera, *Down in the Valley*, for radio broadcast.

When the project stalled, he turned to *Street Scene*, a Pulitzer-Prize winning play by Elmer Rice. Weill had seen the play in Berlin and approached Rice ten years earlier, but the writer thought it was too soon for a musical adaptation of his work. By 1947, Rice was more amenable to the idea. Weill and Rice invited Langston Hughes, a leading African American poet, to write the lyrics. Hughes took Weill to visit tenements, slums, nightclubs, and the various black neighborhoods in New York. Weill, with his uncanny ability to absorb the rhythms, melodies, and pulses of the cultures he encountered, was in his element. Weill saw *Street Scene* as an eclectic mosaic of operatic and popular music, a "musical melting pot" reflecting the races, languages, and cultures of the inner city. The show presented through music the emotions of what Weill called "young love, passion, and death." Weill used elements of jazz, Italian opera, and choral music to express the emotions of his characters.

Figure 267 - Kurt Weill (center) with author Alan Paton and playwright Maxwell Anderson collaborating on the musical version of *Lost in the Stars*. (Photo by Hagelmeyer, courtesy of New York World Telegram and Sun Collection, Library of Congress)

Sam and Rose, the principal characters, yearned for a better life. Rose's mother paid for a love affair when she was killed by a jealous husband. The songs and arias reflected the frustration and yearning of these people. Sam's major solo was the melancholy "Lonely House." A janitor sang the jazz inspired "I've Got a Marble and a Star." Two women asked, "Ain't It Awful, The Heat?" Hughes's lyrics reflected the reality of the urban condition. *Street Scene* was the extension of the milieu developed by George Gershwin in *Porgy and Bess*, and anticipated the same mood of Leonard Bernstein and Stephen Sondheim's *West Side Story* in years to come. Unfortunately, *Street Scene* had to compete with such Broadway successes as *Finian's Rainbow* and *Brigadoon*. Its harsh reality offered little optimism to audiences and no happy ending. As a Broadway show, it was not a financial success. As an opera, it enjoyed an extraordinary run, and critical acclaim.

In 1948, Weill collaborated with Alan Jay Lerner on a musical show, *Love Life*. But he was soon turning his thoughts again to opera. In 1949, Weill's folk opera, *Down in the Valley*, was first professionaly performed with a libretto by Arnold Sundgaard by the colorfully named Lemonade Opera Company. Weill used a number of American folk songs to depict the tragedy that befalls Brack and Jennie, a young couple in love, when Brack tried to protect Jennie and was accused of murder. This was not a Broadway musical; Weill's ideas about musical theater remained intellectually demanding and reflecting a seriousness of purpose.

Weill turned to social protest again, collaborating once more with his old friend Maxwell Anderson in *Lost in the Stars*. Anderson adapted Alan Paton's novel, *Cry the Beloved Country*, a scathing protest against apartheid in South Africa. This tragedy of a black, South African minister, Stephen Kamalo, and his family, confronting racial prejudice, asked more questions than it answered. In 1950, *Lost in the Stars* was hardly the hopeful and upbeat entertainment expected by post-war Broadway audiences. Rouben Mamoulian, who had directed *Porgy and Bess*, was the director and he suggested Todd Duncan, the original Porgy, as ideal for the role of Stephen Kamalo.

Lost in the Stars has elements of a Greek tragedy. There is a chorus commenting on the action, and the choral pieces like "Train to Johannesburg" added an intensity and energy to the score. Kamalo searched for his son Absalom, who dealt with the futility of his life, agreeing to join a gang. He was accused of killing a white man; the other gang members lied and were acquitted, but he told the truth and was sentenced to death. Kamalo performed the dramatic and prayerful soliloquy, "Oh Tixo, Tixo Help Me." Kamalo wondered aloud if the Lord has left him. His faith challenged, he asked if he and his people were "Lost in the Stars." In the end, he was visited by Jarvis, a British planter and father of the murdered man, who finally realized that he and Kamalo had much in common and spoke of brotherhood.

Weill's choral and orchestral scoring was brilliant, and *Lost in the Stars* was a powerful dramatic statement. Weill had many plans and began collaborating with Anderson on a new musical adaptation of *Huckleberry Finn*. But he would be haunted by the fateful line from "September Song"—"and the days grow short." In 1950, he suffered a heart attack and died suddenly while the production of *Lost in the Stars* was still running. Lyrics from *Lost in the Stars* were placed on his tombstone.

Weill was not forgotten. Two years after his death, a concert devoted to *The Threepenny Opera* was performed at Brandeis University. The concert premiered a new English translation by Marc Blitzstein and was conducted by Leonard Bernstein. Broadway producers immediately wanted to produce a new version of Weill's classic Berlin success, but each wanted to change the plot, alter the location, update the orchestrations, and "modernize" Weill's original ideas. His widow, Lotte Lenya, refused, however, until two young producers. Carmen Capalbo and Stanley Chase, agreed to a production that would be true to Weill's original intentions. In 1954, *The Threepenny*

Opera opened in Greenwich Village. The production broke attendance records and ran until 1961.

In its Americanized version, "Moritat," now dubbed "Mack the Knife," became a huge commercial hit and an enduring standard. When Weill dashed off his original "Moritat" in Berlin, he never could have imagined that the English language version of this song would achieve worldwide popularity lasting into the twenty-first century and be performed in every style imaginable by pop singers, operatic soloists, symphony orchestras, and jazz ensembles. Audiences now discovered the rest of Weill's fabled score: the tangos, the ironic waltzes, the street songs from Berlin of the 1920s that spoke to audiences of the 1950s. Lotte Lenya recreated her original role as Jenny, performing "The Pirate Song." Also included were the ironic satire of "The Jealousy Song," the cynical "Useless," the disillusioned "Barbara Song," and Macheath's urgent "Call from the Grave."

The success of his best-known work from Germany, long denied in America, was now a reality. Sadly, Weill did not live to enjoy his biggest success. In subsequent years, Weill's reputation has grown. There are societies devoted to his music, revivals of his scores, and even entire shows, like *Kurt Weill from Berlin to Broadway*, devoted to his music. Though much of Weill's music is beloved on Broadway, he was always something of a visitor there. At heart, he was a serious composer of concert music, eager to use his skills writing opera and orchestral music to develop a new form of musical theater. His music reflected intense musical integrity, an enthusiasm for true experimentation and innovation. While his insisting on injecting politics into his scores worked against them, he still proved that musical theater could speak to large audiences without sacrificing musical values, a lesson often lost on musicians of today.

Weill's highly innovative scores did not result in a school of followers. When composers on Broadway talked about the elements of classical music, they usually had something else in mind. Nothing could have offered greater contrast to Weill's classical influence than the scores of Robert Wright and George Forrest. In 1944, they wrote lyrics for *Song of Norway*, a musical based on the life of Edvard Grieg that turned Grieg's melodies into popular songs. They tried the same approach with the music of Alexander Borodin and tales from *The Arabian Nights* in *Kismet*, and eventually, the music of Sergei Rachmaninoff in *Anya*, a musical version of *Anastasia*, the fable of the Russian Grand Duchess who vanished during the Russian Revolution.

Turning well-known classical melodies into show tunes offered unusual challenges. Audiences didn't have to be persuaded to like songs based on classical melodies they already loved. On the other hand, recognition could proved to be a doubled-edged sword. During *Anya*, the show's leading character, apparently suffering from amnesia, recognizes a phrase from a familiar piece of music. When she declares that she has heard the music before, a few critics and classical music enthusiasts in the audience smiled and were quick to share their amusement when they sat down to write their reviews: they'd all heard it before, too, in the original work of Rachmaninoff.

THE INNOVATOR: JEROME MOROSS

One composer who did draw upon experience in the world of concert music was Jerome Moross. Trained as a classical composer, Moross had a unique ability to adapt the flavor of folk music to opera and ballet. In 1949, Moross teamed with lyricist John Latouche to create *Ballet Ballads,* an unusual trio of one-act plays, each set by a different choreographer. The plays depicted *Susanna and the Elders*, *Willie the Weeper*, and *The Eccentricities of Davey Crocket*. Moross was often drawn to Americana.

The collaboration between Moross and Latouche was not unlike that of the short-lived team of Richard Rodgers and Alan Jay Lerner—in both instances, a brilliant, disciplined composer and a gifted, but elusive lyricist. John Latouche was a poet and Moross's daughter, Susanna Moross Tarjan, wrote that "It was often hard for my father to get lyrics out of Touche, and much of their correspondence consists of Jerry asking Touche to produce work and Touche assuring Jerry that there were good reasons why he, Touche, hadn't."

In 1953, Moross and Latouche were back with *The Golden Apple,* filled with much music (and far less dialogue). No one had ever seen anything quite like *The Golden Apple* on Broadway. This unusual show transferred the great Greek classics of Homer, *The Iliad* and *The Odyssey* to Angel's Roost, Washington, a small American town at the turn of the century. The first act of *The Golden Apple* was based on *The Iliad*, the second on *The Odyssey*. The style and tone of the show were

Figure 268 - Jerome Moross (in the center), choreographer Hanya Holm, and lyricist John Latouche during a rehearsal of *The Golden Apple,* a highly experimental musical show that deserved a longer life. (Photo courtesy of Susanna Moross Tarjan)

perfectly compatible with Broadway. But instead of typical stage dialogue linking the songs together, Moross and Latouche came up with their unique version of operatic *recitative* or "sung speech." The experimental show won critical acclaim when it opened off Broadway, but when it moved uptown to Broadway, it did so without advance sales or advertising. In the hot New York summer, audiences weren't lining up to buy tickets if they didn't already know about *The Golden Apple*. So it passed into history, rediscovered by those who are fascinated by unjustly neglected musicals. One of the songs in the show, "Lazy Afternoon," achieved a life of its own outside the show.

Moross had a great affinity for Americana and decided to write a work for the theater that would depict the history of the Civil War through music. After years of research, he teamed with children's book author Edward Eager as his lyricist and wrote *Gentlemen, Be Seated*. He considered the minstrel show America's only original and indigenous form of musical theater and the decision to use this form for *Gentlemen, Be Seated* led to controversy and to the show's eventual downfall. Minstrel shows were originally performed in blackface. Susanna Moross Tarjan said that her father was naive enough to believe that since no white performers were in blackface and that one of the stars of the show, Avon Long, was an officer in the NAACP, the show would be acceptable in 1963. Unfortunately, the show was threatened with demonstrations by civil rights activists. To make matters even more complicated for a commercial endeavor, it was premiered by the New York City Opera. *Gentlemen, Be Seated* was not a conventional opera, but it wasn't a traditional Broadway musical either. The critics pounced. But Moross never lost his affinity for Americana. He became widely known as a film composer; as nearly everyone knows today, his score for *The Big Country* would be acclaimed as one of the finest to grace a western film.

Nearly every composer who has bridged the gap between opera and Broadway musical comedy has been subjected to the same unjust criticism; the classical critics howl that any production containing real songs doesn't belong on the operatic stage; those who consider themselves aficionados of Broadway bellow that a show with sung dialogue or complex musical forms belongs in an opera house and this is a polite way of saying that the production lacks commercial appeal and is guaranteed to lose money. Both groups of critics often fail to appreciate efforts of composers and lyricists to develop an entirely new musical form. For some reason, this treatment is not applied to the creators of rock operas. In the twenty-first century, we may well ask why the vast sums of money earned by rock operas and rock musicals mysteriously obviate the artistic objections of critics on both sides of the musical fence.

FOUR LEGENDS: ARLEN, HARBURG, LANE, AND MERCER

In the years following *Oklahoma!*, a number of interesting shows opened on Broadway. Often, these shows might feature music and lyrics of extremely high quality, but ultimate success depended on the validity of the "book" or libretto. During the 1940s and 1950s, audiences had an opportunity to attend premieres of musical shows by a group of remarkably talented men whose lives and careers seemed interwoven: Harold Arlen, E.Y. Harburg, Burton Lane, and Johnny Mercer.

The career of Harold Arlen was unusual. Arlen was an extraordinarily talented composer, widely respected by his colleagues, and considered an inspired craftsman, a rugged individualist, and a "songwriter's songwriter." Yet his greatest recognition and successes came from motion pictures. His Broadway shows frequently were based on librettos that drew criticism, and the shows were often plagued with the backstage intrigues that can upstage the finest scores. Discovered by the Gershwins, Arlen had an

Figure 269 - Harold Arlen. On Broadway and in Hollywood, colleagues said that Arlen was their musical role model. (Photograph courtesy of the Carl Van Vechten Collection)

even greater affinity than his mentors for the music of African Americans, especially the blues. He went on to write many classic popular songs, especially for motion pictures.

A native of Buffalo, Arlen had a natural affinity for jazz. He absorbed the "hot licks" or "riffs" of the day, even before studying the work of the great musical theater composers. Harold Arlen began his career as a vaudeville singer, pianist, and bandleader. While working as rehearsal pianist for Vincent Youmans, he created a piano vamp that turned into the hit song, "Get Happy." Arlen was always drawn to the syncopated rhythms, blue notes, and phrases created by black composers, especially the melodic lines of the true improvised blues. He was the only white composer of note to gain a reputation in Harlem by contributing regularly to the Cotton Club revues. He contributed to such shows as *Life Begins at 8:40*, *Hooray for What!*, and *You Said It*. Black admirers considered Arlen's style closest to the roots of African-American music. While at the Cotton Club, Arlen gained a friend and mentor in lyricist Ted Koehler. Eventually, he headed for Hollywood where he gained new collaborators: Ira Gershwin, E.Y. Harburg, and Johnny Mercer. With these lyricists, he wrote for motion pictures, creating such classic tunes as "Over the Rainbow" for *The Wizard of Oz*, "That Old Black Magic," "The Man That Got Away," "Blues in the Night," and "One for My Baby."

Edgar Yipsel (E.Y.) Harburg grew up in the poverty of New York's Lower East Side. A gifted student, he formed a friendship with classmate Ira Gershwin, who shared his love of light verse and introduced him to the recordings of Gilbert and Sullivan. Harburg eventually formed an electrical appliance business, but the lure of musical theater was too strong. Harburg, throughout his life, was a social activist, drawn to radical politics and protest movements of the time. As a lyricist, Harburg had something in common with composer Kurt Weill. The projects he liked best were those that gave him an opportunity to deliver a social or political message. When his business failed, Harburg followed Gershwin's advice and teamed with composer Jay Gorney to contribute songs to Earl Carroll's reviews, including the unofficial anthem of the depression, "Brother, Can You Spare a Dime?" Eventually, Harburg, too, headed to Hollywood.

In 1944, following the success of *Oklahoma!* and *Carousel*, Arlen's agent, Nat Goldstone, presented him with a play by a little known husband and wife playwriting team, Lilith and Dan James. The play was devoted to the exploits of Dolly Bloomer, a Civil War crusader for women's rights, abolition of slavery, and abolition of the hoopskirt. Arlen asked Harburg to join him in converting the play into a musical. Harburg agreed on the condition that Fred Saidy and Sig Herzig, screenwriters, work on the book. The show, *Bloomer Girl*, was to be produced by John Wilson. Central to the plot was a romance between Dolly Bloomer's abolitionist niece and a southern slaveholder who changes his view of slavery by the end of the show.

Bloomer Girl could boast its own "civil war" behind the scenes. Choreographer Agnes de Mille created a *Civil War Ballet*, depicting the tragedy of the war through dance. Harburg and producer John Wilson hated the idea and Wilson eventually announced that the ballet would be cut. Harburg demanded that de Mille tell him where the wit and humor were in the ballet. An outraged de Mille responded, "In war?" and told Wilson that if he wanted to buy *Oklahoma!*, he was a little late. De Mille worked secretly on revisions and when the show opened for tryouts, the audience was mesmerized as lead dancers James Mitchell and Lidia Franklin took the stage. The ballet "stopped the show." After thunderous audience applause, Harburg and Wilson apologized to de Mille, and *Bloomer Girl* became a hit.

Arlen's next major musical, in 1946, was *St. Louis Woman*. His collaborator was Johnny Mercer. In 1930, Harburg and Ira Gershwin were providing lyrics for Vernon Duke's music for that year's musical revue, *The Garrick Gaieties*. An aspiring actor and singer, Johnny Mercer auditioned, only to be told the show needed girls and songs. Mercer submitted a song and acquired E.Y. Harburg as a mentor. The two men could not have been more different.

Mercer was a Southerner, a native of Savannah, Georgia. He came from a socially prominent family (one ancestor had been a brigadier general under George Washington). But family traditions and exclusive prep schools couldn't keep Mercer away from the theater. *St. Louis Woman* was based on *God Sends Sunday*, a play based on a novel by Ara Bontemps and Countee Cullen, leading figures of the African American cultural movement known as the Harlem Renaissance. Unfortunately, the show was plagued by problems. MGM wanted Lena Horne to star in the show, but advance publicity persuaded Horne that the plot, featuring gamblers and jockeys of 19th century St. Louis, was racially demeaning, and she declined. Then Countee Cullen died suddenly, leaving the libretto dependent on Bontemps, who was primarily a novelist. One evening, a casual collaboration between Mercer and Arlen resulted in the show's best-known song, "Come Rain or Come Shine."

St. Louis Woman featured the dazzling tap dancers, the Nicholas Brothers—Harold and Fayard, as rival jockeys, and the Broadway debut of Pearl Bailey. The Nicholas Brothers were acknowledged by fans, friends, and rivals throughout their careers as among the finest dancers of all time. Their astonishing aerial leaps and splits amazed audiences; they managed to combine the graceful hand movements associated with classical dance and the fast and furious rhythms of tap. Pearl Bailey went on to become a major star. But despite all efforts, *St. Louis Woman* ran for only 113 performances.

In the following year, 1947, Harburg enjoyed his biggest hit, *Finian's Rainbow*. Fred Saidy joined Harburg to provide the book, while music was composed by Burton Lane. *Finian's Rainbow* was a fantasy. Its central character, Finian McLonergan, stole a crock of gold from the leprechauns of his native Glocca Morra, Ireland, and arrived in the United States with his daughter, Sharon. Og, a leprechaun was in hot pursuit. The trio shared a series of adventures while Sharon fell in love with Will Mahoney, an American in Rainbow Valley, Missitucky. Harburg, always eager for a social protest and political statement, included a scathing parody of two real members of Congress; both were Mississippi Democrats and notorious racists: Sen. Theodore Bilbo and Rep. John Rankin. In *Finian's Rainbow*, Sen. Billboard Rawkins, clearly a composite of the two well-known politicians, is turned black and then white again, by magic. Eventually, the crock of gold and Glocca Morra are revealed to be only in Finian's mind. But there was nothing artificial about the love songs, "If This Isn't Love" for Will and "Look to the Rainbow" for Sharon. There were marvelous lyrics including "When I'm Not Near the Girl I Love, I Love the Girl I'm Near" for Og. Everyone left the theater whistling the haunting "How Are Things in Glocca Morra?"

Figure 270 - Harold and Fayard Nicholas, the Nicholas Brothers, dazzled audiences through their incomparable appearances on stage and screen. (Photo courtesy of Rigmor Newman)

Harburg and Saidy collaborated with composer Sammy Fain in 1951 as they tried to recapture their magic with *Flahooley*, a fantasy about a laughing doll in a world of dolls that cry. The show seemed to have everything: the sparkling soprano voice of Barbara Cook, the exotic vocal range of Peruvian singer Yma Sumac, the Bil Baird marionettes, and of course with Harburg, a political message. In this show, the villains parodied followers of Sen. Joseph McCarthy as Harburg's political protest. But the show failed.

Figure 271 - Composer Burton Lane and lyricist E. Y. Harburg achieved their greatest success on Broadway with a musical combining Irish folklore and Southern social satire. (Photo by L. Arnold Weissberger, All Rights Reserved, courtesy of Ernie Harburg.)

Sammy Fain, by the way, was a veteran songwriter whose 1927 hit, "Let a Smile Be Your Umbrella," with lyrics by Irving Kahal and Francis Wheeler, journeyed to Hollywood in 1929 for an early film musical, *It's a Great Life*. Fain was a gifted melodist. *Flahooley* and another Fain show with splendid songs,

Figure 272 - Sammy Fain, a gifted melodist, wrote many of the most memorable songs heard in the movies. (Photo by George Mann, courtesy of Dianne Woods, the George Mann Archive.)

Christine, surprising audiences with the marvelous singing talents of Maureen O'Hara and Morley Meredith, didn't succeed commercially on Broadway.

Fain had learned that a huge hit could come from a show that closed far too soon. In 1938, a Fain-Kahal musical, *Right This Way*, ran for just nineteen performances. But two songs from the show, "I Can Dream, Can't I?" and "I'll Be Seeing You," proved to be huge hits. "I'll Be Seeing You" became the favorite ballad of couples parting as soldiers went off to fight in World War II and remained one of the most popular songs throughout the war. "I Can Dream, Can't I" sold a million records for the Andrews Sisters, who revived it in 1949. Fain enjoyed his greatest success in the movies. After the death of his longtime collaborator Irving Kahal, he eventually teamed with lyricist Paul Francis Webster to write such spectacularly successful movie themes as "Secret Love," " "Love Is a Many Splendored Thing," "A Very Precious Love," and "A Certain Smile."

In 1954, the same year that Harburg teamed with Sammy Fain to write *Flahooley*, Harold Arlen began work on one of his most unusual shows to date: *House of Flowers*, based on a short story by Truman Capote and starring a black cast. *House of Flowers* was the tale of a bordello in Haiti. The principal characters were Mme. Fleur, who ran the establishment (and named the resident young women after flowers), and her newest protégé Otillie, who created problems when she fell in love with Royal, a young man whose grandmother practiced voodoo.

Diahann Carroll made her debut in the show. The role of Mme. Fleur was offered to a provocative singer with an inimitable feline voice, Eartha Kitt. But when Eartha Kitt turned down the leading role of Mme. Fleur, Pearl Bailey was cast. Gradually, in rehearsal, Bailey emerged as the dominant star, and the show moved away from its original design and evolved into a vehicle for Pearl Bailey. Rehearsals were dominated by intense disagreements between Bailey and director Peter Brook. Both Brook and choreographer George Balanchine resigned. At one point, Capote threatened to withdraw when he heard a rumor that Johnny Mercer would be asked to rewrite his lyrics. Arlen's songs were of high quality. (One melody, originally composed for Judy Garland in the movie *A Star Is Born*, had a new lyric. It evolved as *The Honey Bee*, a distinctive, haunting song for the character of Otillie.) But *House of Flowers* could not be saved, although it has acquired a cult following after its commercial failure.

The problem of stars, libretto revisions, and behind the scenes warfare seemed to repeat itself with Arlen's show, *Jamaica*, in 1957. Harburg and Fred Saidy became intrigued with the idea of a Calypso musical, the tale of a young fisherman, Koli, who lived on a mythical Caribbean Island and Savannah, the girl he loves, who longs to go to another island, Manhattan. Koli would be played by Harry Belafonte. But when Belafonte developed a throat problem, producer David Merrick decided that the show required another star; he cast Lena Horne as Savannah. As usual, Arlen and Harburg wrote fine songs, like the lyrical "Coconut Sweet." Harburg also managed to inject his usual social message in the lyrics, this time a protest against nuclear proliferation. During rehearsals, Merrick and director Robert Lewis turned the show into a star vehicle for Horne. Songs and plots were adjusted to take maximum of advantage of Lena Horne's box-office appeal. Arlen was hospitalized at the time, leaving Harburg to feud with Merrick and Lewis, who locked him out of the theater. Harburg felt his original concept had been totally destroyed. He was so bitter and angry that he refused to even attend the opening night. Ironically, *Jamaica* became a major Broadway hit.

In 1959, Arlen reunited with Johnny Mercer, to create *Saratoga*, a musical based on a novel by Edna Ferber. This was a story of a New Orleans fortune hunter and the gambler she loved, as they pursued wealth and romance during the Saratoga racing season. Director Morton DaCosta, with a string a recent hits, was engaged to write the libretto. Despite valiant efforts by Mercer and Arlen, DaCosta found it difficult to cut Ferber's sprawling novel. Critic John Chapman dubbed it "the most complicated music-show plot since Richard Wagner wrote *Siegfried*." Praise for the songs could not save *Saratoga*. It was Arlen's last Broadway show. Nor could Arlen's music save *Free and Easy*, an attempt to revive the score of *St. Louis Woman* in a new form, a "blues opera." A bitter feud between producers Robert Breen and Stanley Chase erupted, destroying any chance of success for this project. Arlen, Harburg, and Mercer won and maintained the respect of their colleagues. The songs they wrote often survived the shows themselves and remain classics to this day.

Harold Arlen's love of jazz, E. Y. Harburg's desire for social protest, Burton Lane's special gift for melody, and Johnny Mercer's Southern heritage, all left a lasting impact on Broadway.

THE SHOWS OF THE 1960S AND 1970S: BOCK AND HARNICK, KANDER AND EBB, ADAMS AND STROUSE, JERRY HERMAN, AND CY COLEMAN

In the 1960s and '70s, events taking place throughout the country, and especially in New York City, affected the development of musical theater. Escalating ticket prices, rising crime rates, and the incredible costs of production were negative influences. Traditional musical theater faced a new and threatening challenge. Would it drown in a raucous sea of rock music designed to appeal to a teenage audience? Producers, eager to draw upon the financial rewards of sounds that would be promoted through a lucrative

Figure 273 - Jerry Bock and Sheldon Harnick - Their lyrical style resulted in a huge success for *Fiddler on the Roof*, a show which broke the record as the longest running musical on Broadway, a record which lasted for ten years. (Photo courtesy of Broadway to Vegas)

record market, discouraged composers who did not feel stylistically comfortable with the songs that would be listed among the Top 40 or promise huge profits if they were written to hit "the top of the charts."

Despite these influences, a number of significant new composers and lyricists emerged during these years. Lyrical melodies were the hallmark of Jerry Bock and Sheldon Harnick. The pair collaborated with George Abbott and Jerome Weidman to produce the Pulitzer Prize-winning musical, *Fiorello,* based on the life of New York's favorite mayor, Fiorello LaGuardia. Their Loesser-like score was refreshing and communicated easily with audiences. The team reunited for *Tenderloin*, a musical set in the 1890s and starring the Shakespearean actor Maurice Evans.

Bock and Harnick also wrote the charming and delightful *She Loves Me*, a gentle Middle-European romance set in Budapest of the 1930s. The show contained many beautiful melodies, including "Dear Friend" and "Ice Cream," a chance for multitalented soprano Barbara Cook to display operatic virtuosity. The show was adapted from Miklós László's play, *Parfumerie*, which had in turn inspired Ernst Lubitsch's film, *The Shop Around the Corner*. The tale of co-workers who fall in love as anonymous pen pals while unable to stand each other in person was irresistible. Unfortunately, the charm of the show, without flamboyant choreography or a line of chorus girls, had to compete with louder voices on Broadway: the brassy sound of more commercial musicals and the amplified drumbeats of rock music.

Bock and Harnick achieved their greatest success with *Fiddler on the Roof*, which set the all-time box office record for a Broadway musical. Based on *Tevye and His Daughters*, a group of stories by Sholem Aleichem, the show starred Zero Mostel. Leonard Nimoy, not yet known to audiences as "Mr. Spock" in the television and film versions of *Star Trek*, was Mostel's understudy at the time. *Fiddler on the Roof* contained many haunting melodies and "Sunrise, Sunset" took on a life of its own as a father reminisces about watching his children grow into adults. The show's record lasted for ten years until it was broken by *Grease*, a rock and roll musical. Bock and Harnick couldn't have chosen a more different property for their next production, an experimental show starring Julie Harris, *The Apple Tree,* and followed it by a more traditional musical, *The Rothschilds*. Bock subsequently withdrew from the theater, while Harnick began working with other collaborators, including Richard Rodgers. Bock subsequently withdrew from the theater, while Harnick began working with other collaborators, including Richard Rodgers and Michel Legrand, and also composed music as well as lyrics on his own.

For pure entertainment, audiences cheered the work of Jerry Herman and Cy Coleman. Herman had written off-Broadway shows and special material before making his Broadway debut with *Milk and Honey*. He became known for writing toe-tapping tunes. His big hits were *Hello, Dolly*, based on Thornton Wilder's play, *The Matchmaker*, and *Mame*. The efforts of the effusive Dolly Levi to land her man, the penurious and very rich Horace Vander Gelder, proved a star vehicle for Carol Channing.

Though the role was subsequently played by Ginger Rogers, Mary Martin, Pearl Bailey, and Ethel Merman, many believed the real star of the show was the brilliant director-choreographer, Gower Champion. He staged the show's most dazzling scene (introducing the title song) with an army of waiters racing around the stage carrying platters while Dolly descended a red-carpeted staircase. Ironically, rival

Figure 274 - Jerry Herman with two of his favorite leading ladies, Angela Lansbury, the original Mame, (left) and Carol Channing, the original Dolly (right.) (Photo courtesy of Jerry Herman)

producer-director Harold Prince is alleged to have suggested to David Merrick that he jettison the title song, "Hello, Dolly," from the show because the show-stopping scene in which it was introduced had no relationship to the plot and believed that there was no reason for the dancing waiters to sing to Dolly, "It's nice to have you back where you belong." Of course, Merrick didn't listen to the advice and the song became not only the show's biggest hit, it became one of Broadway's most popular songs because anyone could sing or whistle it.

Mame, Herman's subsequent effort, with a libretto by Jerome Lawrence and Robert E. Lee, proved an equally ideal vehicle for Angela Lansbury and a host of other *Mames*. It was based on Patrick Dennis's book, "Auntie Mame," featured a delightful, but wildly eccentric woman, her misadventures and her effect on her own family and friends.. Mame's life was turned upside down when her young nephew came to live with her. Herman's score, as usual, containing toe-tapping tunes including the title song, "Mame." Herman also wrote a memorable and pensive ballad, "If He Walked Into My Life" for the leading character.

One of Herman's favorite shows was *Mack and Mabel*, a musical about the stormy relationship between director Mack Sennett (played by Robert Preston) and the silent film star he discovered, Mabel Normand (portrayed by Bernadette Peters). The 1974 production came at a time when rock musicals were taking over the world of Broadway and the show closed after only eight weeks. However, a revival at the Nottingham Playhouse, starring Dennis Quilly and Imelda Staunton was well received.

When the British ice dancing team of Jayne Torvill and Christopher Dean won the World Championship in a dazzling performance skating to the Overture from *Mack and Mabel*, audiences everywhere discovered Jerry Herman's score.

A West End Revival in 1995 (complete with a new happy ending for Mack Sennett and Mabel Normand) also provided a happy ending for one of Herman's most tuneful shows, including such memorable songs as "Movies Were Movies" and "I Won't Send Roses." Herman, criticized on occasion for being too commercial, responded with an attitude Irving Berlin would have understood. He said that being too commercial was like being accused of being too pretty. The tremendous success of shows like *Hello, Dolly* and *Mame* represented a major shift from the plot-based shows of Rodgers and Hammerstein. A hit show seemed likelier to emanate from the appearance of an established star who would guarantee activity at the box office than from a traditional Broadway love story featuring younger, lesser-known performers.

The versatile Cy Coleman began his storied career as a child prodigy giving piano recitals at Carnegie Hall. He eventually formed his own jazz trio and was quickly in demand at nightclubs and on recordings. Together with lyricist Carolyn Leigh he wrote popular song hits including "Witchcraft" and "The Best Is Yet to Come." His "Playboy's Theme" became the signature music for Hugh Hefner's "Playboy's Penthouse" television program. Continuing his collaboration with Carolyn Leigh, he wrote the music for *Wildcat*, the musical that presented Lucille Ball in her Broadway debut. The tuneful march, *Hey, Look Me Over*, became the hit song of the show. Coleman and Leigh joined playwright Neil Simon to write *Little Me*, a show that starred the incredibly versatile Sid Caesar.

In 1964, Coleman met famed lyricist Dorothy Fields at a party. He asked her if she would like to collaborate with him. Fields had been writing the book and lyrics for shows since before Coleman was born and had worked with Jerome Kern, Jimmy McHugh, and other musical luminaries, but she hadn't worked in the theater for a number of years. When Coleman suggested that they work together on a new show, she allegedly said, "Thank God someone asked." The partnership between the legendary veteran and the young jazz pianist worked, and the result was *Sweet Charity*. With songs such as "If My Friends Could See Me Now" and "Big Spender" and a script by Neil Simon, the show starred Gwen Verdon and featured the choreography of Bob Fosse.

Figure 275 - Cy Coleman was a classical child prodigy and jazz pianist, but he made his greatest mark on Broadway. He teamed successfully with lyricist Dorothy Fields. She had been writing lyrics on Broadway before he was born. (Photo courtesy of Noble Music Inc.)

Figure 276 - Composer John Kander and lyricist Fred Ebb enjoyed many years of happy collaboration together, resulting in shows such as *Cabaret* and *Chicago*. Photo by Marc Mellon, courtesy of the Friars Club)

It was a huge hit. Coleman and Fields continued to work together until her death ten years later. Other Coleman shows included, *I Love My Wife*, a surprisingly operatic *On the Twentieth Century* (with lyrics by Comden and Green), *Barnum*, *Welcome to the Club*, and *City of Angels*. Coleman retained his pianistic skills. In Hollywood, scoring the Dick Van Dyke comedy, *The Art of Love*, Coleman sat down at the piano and performed his own memorable solo in a chase sequence, which combined a parody of Mozart with the "hurry-music" of an old-time silent film.

Composer John Kander and lyricist Fred Ebb wrote many shows, including *Flora the Red Menace*, which began their long association with actress-vocalist Liza Minnelli, *The Happy Time*, *Zorba*, *Chicago*, and *Kiss of the Spider Woman*, among others. Their biggest hit was undoubtedly the Weill-influenced *Cabaret*, a portrait of decadent Berlin during the era of the Weimar Republic in the 1920s. *Chicago* was a Prohibition era musical that retold the murder trial of Roxie Hart, accused of killing the man she loved in an era of bootleggers and scandals. Choreographer Bob Fosse collaborated on the show's libretto with Ebb. His trademark style incorporated bowler hats, canes, and chairs into pulsating dance routines that featured dancers with turned-in knees and shuffling feet. Kander and Ebb welcomed input from their favorite stars, Liza Minnelli and Chita Rivera.

Like Kander and Ebb, Charles Strouse and Lee Adams chose a variety of subjects for their musicals, often inspired by pop cultural icons. When rock and roll star Elvis Presley joined the army, they wrote a spoof of rock and roll singers and their fans, *Bye, Bye, Birdie*, a musical about a boxer, *Golden Boy*, and *Applause*, a stage musical version of the movie, *All About Eve*, Joseph L. Mankiewicz's devastating portrayal of the rivalry between two actresses and the intrigues that take place in the theater. Lee Adams' lyric, "You only come alive at night, you learn to kill with sheer delight," spoke volumes about more than one

Figure 277 - Charles Strouse at the piano with lyricist Lee Adams (left,) and playwright Clifford Odets (right,) during collaboration on *Golden Boy*. (Photo courtesy of Charles Strouse)

member of the cast of a Broadway show. Charles Strouse enjoyed one of his biggest hits when he teamed with lyricist Martin Charnin in the phenomenally successful *Annie*, based on the popular comic strip, as dozens of little girls (whose mothers had never heard Noël Coward's "Don't Put Your Daughter on the Stage, Mrs. Worthington") dyed their hair red and prepared to belt out Strouse's tune, "Tomorrow."

Figure 278 - Harvey Schmidt and Tom Jones, both Texans, seen here with Anne Bancroft, wrote *The Fantasticks*, which ran off-Broadway for forty-two years. One of the most popular musicals in history, the show continued for over 17,000 performances. (Photo courtesy of Harvey Schmidt)

Harvey Schmidt and Tom Jones proved it didn't take a cast of thousands to produce a hit. They created *The Fantasticks*, based on a play by Edmond Rostand. It received its premiere at the Sullivan Street Playhouse, a tiny Greenwich Village theater. The show featured a boy and a girl who fell in love, their fathers who try to keep them apart, and a roving bandit, El Gallo. Twenty years later, the show was still running at the same theater! Jones and Schmidt went on to write other hit shows, including *I Do, I Do*, the perennial two character standby of theaters across the country, based on Jan de Hartog's play, *The Fourposter*.

Some unusual subjects turned up as Broadway musicals. British composer Lionel Bart wrote *Oliver* based on Charles Dickens' *Oliver Twist*. Bob Merrill, a former child actor, director, and agent, turned to the plays of Eugene O'Neill for inspiration. He wrote *New Girl in Town* based on *Anna Christie* and *Take Me Along* based on *Ah, Wilderness*. Merrill's most successful show was *Carnival*, based on the movie *Lili*, known for its Academy Award winning score and title song by Bronislaw Kaper. Merrill, however, produced his own music and lyrics, completely independent of Kaper's film score, and the show became a hit.

Mitch Leigh and Joe Darion teamed to create *Man of La Mancha*, a musical based on the classic Don Quixote, with "The Impossible Dream" becoming the favorite showpiece for every tenor who liked to hit high notes. *1776* turned the signing of the Declaration of Independence into an improbable Broadway hit. Its sprightly score was by Sherman Edwards, a former history teacher. *A Chorus Line,* with music by Marvin Hamlisch and lyrics by Edward Kleban, broke box offices records with an unsentimental look at the private lives and personal turmoils of dancers auditioning for a chorus line on Broadway.

It was during this period that directors and choreographers became greater stars than the composers or lyricists who provided scores. Gower Champion maintained a long association with producer David Merrick, culminating in *Forty Second Street*, a stage version of a 1933 Busby Berkeley film. The show became a huge hit, but sadly, Champion died on the morning of its premiere and Merrick himself announced the news to a stunned cast and audience after the opening. Its success became part of his legend and legacy. Bob Fosse, who choreographed many shows, most notably *Cabaret,* changed the whole style of Broadway choreography, moving from the classic elegance of Agnes de Mille to a style inspired by the movement and rhythms of the streets, with an emphasis on jazz, Latin dances, and highly provocative poses and costumes. Fosse's style shocked some audiences. Choreographers emerged as the most potent force in musical theater. Often to make up for meager scores and inept lyrics, dancers were kept in constant motion on stage. Wit, grace, and style had been replaced by a dubiously artificial enthusiasm usually praised by sycophantic critics as "energy."

A host of rock musicals appeared to dominate Broadway, most notably *Hair*, which thrived on publicity regarding a nude scene and political harangue worthy of the "first hippie musical," and *Jesus Christ, Superstar*, an inexplicable attempt to use the life of Christ as a vehicle for mixing pseudo-classical and rock-pop sounds. Composer Ned Rorem described the latter, by Andrew Lloyd Webber, as an "indigestible stew" of musical styles, borrowed from a wide variety of popular and classical composers. These shows were legendary financial successes. The artistic merits were dubious at best. But Lloyd Webber emerged as the dominant figure in the creation of rock operas, a genre which sent the traditional American musical into virtual oblivion. His most successful shows, including *Cats* and *The Phantom of the Opera*, mixed operatic with pop and rock influences that made them part of a commercial juggernaut. They broke records on Broadway and the West End, and encouraged imitators everywhere. Similar success was achieved by composer Claude Michel Schönberg, lyricist Alain Boublil, and librettist Herbert Kretzmer with *Les Misérables*.

SONDHEIM AND COMPANY

Figure 279 - Stephen Sondheim. He revolutionized American musical theater with new forms and styles. (Public domain publicity still)

One musical figure emerged, however, who provided a different type of challenge to anything traditional in American musical theater. His name was Stephen Sondheim and his challenge came in the form of a desire to experiment, to explore, to question. Stephen Sondheim's intellectual approach to composition and lyricism has always been controversial in the world of the American musical. One suspects that it is a controversy he relishes. Stephen Joshua Sondheim entered the world of musical theater in a manner unique in the annals of Broadway. He was the chosen protégé of the most important lyricist and librettist in American musical theater history: Oscar Hammerstein II.

Sondheim's tutelage began when his mother bought

property adjacent to Hammerstein's farm in Bucks County, Pennsylvania. Sondheim became friendly with the neighboring Hammerstein family and Hammerstein became a virtual surrogate father to the young man next door. Sondheim aspired to be both composer and lyricist. Although Sondheim is both praised and criticized for being analytical and intellectual in his approach to musical theater, he has described himself as "a great audience who cries easily." He cried profusely because he was so moved by seeing the premiere performance of Rodgers and Hammerstein's *Carousel*.

As a teenager, he completed an early effort at musical theater and took it to Hammerstein. Convinced that he was a phone call away from a Broadway production, Sondheim received a rude awakening. Instead of plaudits and praise, Hammerstein gave him withering criticism. For several hours, he meticulously dissected Sondheim's work. "You don't believe this," he said of Sondheim's efforts to write of bucolic scenes and warbling larks that seem to populate Hammerstein's lyrics. Having torn Sondheim's work apart, Hammerstein then showed him how it should be reconstructed. Hammerstein hadn't forgotten the guidance he had received early in his career from Otto Harbach. Now, he assumed the role of mentor and teacher, and Sondheim learned his lessons well. To this day, he credits this "seminar with Hammerstein" as the beginning of his true training in musical theater. After Oscar Hammerstein apparently demolished his dreams of conquering Broadway, Stephen Sondheim could have simply quit. He didn't; many years later, in 1994, *New York* magazine published a major article about him asking outrageously "Is Stephen Sondheim God?" What happened in the years between Hammerstein's critique and the idolatry of Broadway was both improbable and extraordinary.

Sondheim went to Williams College and subsequently studied composition with Milton Babbitt, an avant-garde composer who was also a mathematician. He responded well to an analytical approach to music; he has said that creating form out of chaos is "the reason we write." Sondheim had a lifelong fascination with puzzles and games. He began collecting games of every era; in later years, his double-crostic puzzles would mystify readers of *The New York Times* on a regular basis. This fascination with word puzzles extended to his lyric writing. The complexities of lines with internal rhymes intrigued him. After writing television scripts for the series *Topper*, Sondheim began his career with the landmark *West Side Story* as a lyricist. He agreed to write only lyrics because the show provided an opportunity to work with composer Leonard Bernstein. Though set to write the full score of *Gypsy*, he again agreed (on Hammerstein's advice) to work with composer Jule Styne, after Ethel Merman insisted on a "name" composer.

Sondheim struck out on his own in 1962 with *A Funny Thing Happened on the Way to the Forum*, The book, by Burt Shevelove and Larry Gelbart, was adapted from plays by the Roman playwright Plautus. "Forum" was essentially a burlesque comedy in togas, with Zero Mostel as Pseudolus, a slave who tries to win his freedom by procuring a beautiful courtesan for his master. Sondheim quickly moved away from the model of his mentor Hammerstein. Instead of using songs to move scenes along or amplify their meaning, Sondheim used them so the audience could rest from the constant physical comedy and slapstick of the play. The whole show and its cast were introduced by an opening number, "Comedy Tonight," which set the mood of the day.

Sondheim's next effort, *Anyone Can Whistle*, starred Lee Remick, Angela Lansbury, and Harry Guardino, and was based on a book by Arthur Laurents. The tale was unusual: a small town with a domineering woman as mayor tries to encourage tourism with a fake miracle, only to have the hoax exposed by a psychiatrist, a nurse, and the patients of a mental institution. The show failed, but has acquired a following over the years, especially as Sondheim's star ascended through other works. In the title song from *Anyone Can Whistle*, Sondheim wrote the words, "What's hard is simple, what's simple comes hard." This conflict would be apparent in numerous other Sondheim shows and in his unique and complex career.

With the death of his mentor Hammerstein, Sondheim was faced with a choice. Richard Rodgers took him for a walk in the woods and invited him to become his new collaborative partner. Sondheim saw himself as the composer as well as lyricist of musical shows; he had already written musicals of his own after working with such famed musical figures as Leonard Bernstein and Jule Styne. On the other hand, he was being asked to step into the shoes of his mentor, the most venerated lyricist on Broadway. The invitation had come from the most influential composer in musical theater history. So Stephen Sondheim said "Yes" and the new team of Rodgers and Sondheim was born. Things did not go smoothly.

The collaboration between the two resulted in *Do I Hear a Waltz?* The show was based on Arthur Laurents' play, *The Time of the Cuckoo*, which had also been filmed as *Summertime* starring Katherine Hepburn and Rosanno Brazzi. The tale of a rather naive American spinster who falls in love with a charming (and very married) Italian sophisticate on a Venetian vacation seemed a natural for musical adaptation. Although *Do I Hear a Waltz?* contained fine music and lyrics, the Rodgers and Sondheim collaboration did not end happily.

Both men had strong personalities. Sondheim would (in a famous and controversial quote) describe his late mentor Oscar Hammerstein II as a man of "limited talent and infinite soul" and Rodgers as a man of "infinite talent and limited soul." Not surprisingly, the two did not part on friendly terms and would not work together again.

Sondheim's next show, a solo effort combining his own music and lyrics, was *Company*. In 1970, it changed musical theater history, much as *Oklahoma!* had altered the state of the art years earlier. *Company*, based on a series of plays by George Furth, concentrated on the dilemma of a bachelor whose married friends try to straighten out his life. What made *Company* unusual was its lack of plot. *Company* was a musical about an idea, a concept, a new form. Stephen Sondheim was not, like Hammerstein, a "cockeyed optimist." He seemed happiest dealing not with affirmation, but with ambivalence.

In *Company*, Bachelor Bobby can't find happiness with any of the women in his life; he can't resolve the confusion of his psyche. Bobby's friends describe their view of marriage as "Sorry-Grateful." Sondheim, a complex individual, seemed happiest writing about people torn by conflicts, not certain about who they were. The characters of *Company* were often hard-edged New Yorkers. Elaine Stritch performed "The Ladies Who Lunch" toasting the bored, jaded friends for whom the cost, not the gift, is the thing. Sondheim displayed his lyric writing skills in the tongue-twisting "Another Hundred People." In one musical scene, the traditional choral sounds of wedding music are offset by the ramblings of a nervous bride who doesn't want to get married. In the end, bachelor Bobby sings "Being Alive," a plea for someone to provide meaning in his life. At the conclusion of *Company*, he is still searching. Sondheim has made his statement and nothing is resolved.

Follies was a tribute to the lavish shows of yesteryear, but tinged with the bitter reality of what happens when we try looking back. *Company* presented the interaction of a New York bachelor and his married friends. *Follies* presented the interaction of two former stars of a Ziegfeld-like revue, their husbands, and the youthful ghosts of their distant past. The score contains numerous pastiches of the scores prevalent in the days of the Ziegfeld Follies. Sally, one of the former Follies girls, is married to a salesman. She has never forgotten Ben, the prominent and successful man who married her roommate. *Follies* is a show about disillusioned, unsatisfied people.

Again, Sondheim probes the psyches of his characters. We are provided with an unhappy wife who asks her husband, "Could I Leave You? Yes. Will I Leave You? Guess!" The tough-as nails survivor (not unlike the Elaine Stritch character in *Company*) was back again, portrayed by Yvonne de Carlo who sings, "I'm Still Here." Sally sings of unrequited love in a torch song, "I'm Losing My Mind." Of special note is the song, "The Story of Lucy and Jessie." Phyllis, the former Follies girl who seems to have the world as her oyster, is unhappy. She sings of two girls, now and then: "Lucy is juicy but terribly drab. Jessie is dressy but cold as a slab. Lucy wants to be dressy. Jessie wants to be juicy. Lucy to be Jessie and Jessie Lucy." Of course, Phyllis is both girls, ambivalent about her past and present. She declares, "Lucy wants to do what Jessie does, Jessie wants to be what Lucy was." Again, Sondheim delights in the psychological complexity of his characters. *Follies*, like *Company* offers no happy endings.

A Little Night Music was Sondheim's most conventional and popular show, with a score consisting entirely of waltzes. (Typically, the orchestral mood is more reflective of Ravel's *La Valse* than the waltzes of either Johann Strauss or Richard Rodgers.) *A Little Night Music* is a Viennese operetta, Sondheim-style, based on Ingmar Bergman's film, *Smiles for a Summer Night*. The show contained Sondheim's major hit song, "Send in the Clowns." One reason for the popularity of *A Little Night Music* was that both the songs and the plot reflected a sense of romance that still greatly appealed to audiences.

Sondheim, as likely to relax by listening to twelve-tone, serial chamber music as pop songs, moved gradually away from whistling melodies to musical lines that might be found in contemporary operas. Quartal harmonies (based on fourths), rather than thirds abound in his work. His harmonic vocabulary is often closer to the musical language of those who primarily compose abstract symphonies or woodwind quintets for the concert hall. Sondheim's approach to harmony wouldn't be considered startling in the world of avant-garde concert music, but it proved distinct and unusual when tested on the ears of Broadway audiences accustomed to hit tunes that were easy to whistle.

His most enigmatic work, *Pacific Overtures*, was inspired by Japanese Kabuki theater. It traced Japanese-American relations over a period of years and celebrated a dissonant, seemingly atonal style of composition. Sondheim has also been fascinated by the morbid side of life. (He reportedly enjoys playing a murder mystery game with friends in which all try to solve an imaginary murder.) *Sweeny Todd*, a musical version of *The Demon Barber of Fleet Street,* is a darkly Dickensian tale, which allowed Sondheim to explore his fascination with the macabre. Central to the plot is a barber who does away with the people he considers evil by baking them in an oven.

Sondheim reunited with writer George Furth to adapt George S. Kaufman and Moss Hart's *Merrily We Roll Along*. The show failed, and ended Sondheim's longtime collaboration with director-producer Harold Prince. Sondheim began an association with writer-director James Lapine to produce *Sunday in the Park with George*. This show was inspired entirely by a single painting by Georges Seurat, *Sunday Afternoon on the Island of the Grande Jatte*. For practical purposes, Sondheim was writing an opera.

Next came *Into the Woods*, another Sondheim-Lapine collaboration, an "adult fairy tale." Interaction between Cinderella, Little Red Riding Hood, and Jack (of Beanstalk fame) was used to probe psychological attitudes about parents, children, fears, and insecurities. Sondheim's fairy-tale characters were (to no one's surprise) mature, complex, and ambivalent. Sondheim also wrote *Assassins*, taking as his unlikely inspiration, the lives of those who tried or succeeded in assassinating U.S. Presidents. His 1991 show, *Passion*, was based on the novel *Fosca* by Iginio Ugo Tarchetti and the film *Passione d'Amore*. While some critics would characterize *Passion* as operatic, Sondheim disagrees. Although he described the songs in *Passion* as being somewhere between aria and recitative, with an occasional recognizable song, he specifically declined the operatic label. He said, "There's enough dialogue so that no one could mistake *Passion* for an opera. I hope." Analysis of Sondheim's work has become a virtual profession for certain musicologists who seldom turn their attention to Broadway. But despite constant comparisons to opera, Sondheim himself has never been eternally devoted to classical grand opera.

Nor is Sondheim a tunesmith. He has displayed little interest in writing hit songs. It is pointless to list hit tunes from Sondheim's shows. There are few. (Even "Send in the Clowns" deals with disillusionment and disappointment.) When Jule Styne protested that a Sondheim lyric for *Gypsy* was so specific for a female character that "Frank Sinatra will never sing this," Sondheim's reply was, typically, "So what?" Sondheim's importance in musical theater derived not from his ability to write hit tunes, but from a capacity to write theatrically.

He has written operas, integrating increasingly complex musical forms. He would likely disown the label of "opera composer," since he has admitted that he is not an "opera buff" and has rarely seen an opera that he didn't think could be shorter. Sondheim is universally recognized as a brilliant lyricist, a meticulous technician. (He is not without self-confidence in this area. having criticized Lorenz Hart's work as "sloppy," and being the only major composer or lyricist from Broadway to teach musical theater seminars at Oxford.) Sondheim delights in the intellectual analysis of craft; Irving Berlin would doubtless have wondered why anyone would have wanted to indulge in such analysis. When Ira Gershwin was asked, "Which came first, the music or the lyrics?" he quipped, "The contract." Sondheim would probably respond to such a question with an hour of serious discussion.

Sondheim's lyrics and music reflect his personality: the lyrics are full of double meanings expected from someone who is devoted to puzzles, riddles, and word games. If Sondheim's virtuoso technique is his strongest point, he is also unsentimental and analytical. (Typically, he has expressed embarrassment over a few of the lyrics of *West Side Story*, those that are most romantic in tone.) His melodies reflect a harmonic and rhythmic complexity associated with contemporary classical music.

Sondheim's supporters consider him in a class by himself, pointing the direction of musical theater of the future, shows presenting serious subjects and songs depicting situations rather than just facilitating a plot. His critics suggest that his emotional restraint appeals to an elitist audience more interested in an exposition of ideas than in being entertained. A Sondheim show is always intellectually challenging. But its characters may prove to be hard-edged, realistic, vulgar, and morbid. Why does Sondheim, who seems supremely confident in his comments on musical theater, his own creative output and everyone else's, seem fascinated by ambivalence? Musicologists will have a field day for years with this subject.

Sondheim's pervasive influence as an innovator cannot be denied. It is clear that the definitive perspective on the music and lyrics of Stephen Sondheim has come from Sondheim himself. In 2010, he wrote the commentaries and analysis to accompany the first of two volumes of his collected lyrics, *Finishing the Hat.* (The concluding volume, *Look, I Made a Hat,* was published a year later.) The first volume included "attendant comments, principles, heresies, grudges, whines and anecdotes," while the second promised "amplifications, dogmas, harangues, digressions, anecdotes and miscellany."

Sondheim did not disappoint. There have been Broadway memoirs and collections of music and lyrics, but no one has produced or is likely to produce anything like these two books. Sondheim's reminiscences, his unsentimental analysis of his own work (and his critique of even the most sacred cows of musical theater) are ironic, funny, caustic, and full of verbal pyrotechnics. He has described selected lyrics by Lorenz Hart as "mediocre," suggested that Noël Coward could be "posturing," and surprisingly characterized the worldview of Irving Berlin as "banal." Even his mentor, Oscar Hammerstein II, didn't escape the Sondheim critique; Sondheim declared that certain Hammerstein lyrics could be "verbose and nonsensical." Sondheim has never spared his own work; his self-criticism, is usually highly specific and analytical. Most intriguing and certainly a reason for applause is the reluctance of musical theater's great experimenter to fall prey to the temptation to seek acclaim by genuflecting before the rock-pop juggernaut.

Sondheim explains, "Rock and contemporary pop are not part of my DNA; worse, I find them unsatisfying when applied to the kind of musicals I like to write because of the limited range of their colors." In the final analysis, will Sondheim's shows be more admired than loved, more likely to provoke analysis than inspiration? Will Sondheim inspire a school of followers? Or will he remain, like Kurt Weill, a serious, uncompromising iconoclast? Only time will tell.

THE MUSICAL AND THE TWENTY-FIRST CENTURY

It would be delightful to conclude a discussion of the American musical with the observation that our musical theater, like the mindset of Emil Coué, is day-by-day, every day, getting better and better. But the realities of history do not justify such a conclusion. The social, political, and cultural upheavals of the 1960s have taken their toll. During the "golden age" of musical theater, from *Show Boat* to *My Fair Lady*, the quality of music and lyrics and (eventually) librettos was paramount. The impact of shows like *Show Boat* and *Oklahoma!* led to the evolution of a uniquely American art form, a fully integrated theatrical presentation of music, lyrics, drama, and dance.

One reason the American musical was not always taken seriously was that, like most things truly American, it drew from a plethora of eclectic influences. To the serious music critic, even the most ambitious works of George Gershwin and Kurt Weill were somehow "too commercial" or "too popular" to be regarded as "serious operas." To Tin Pan Alley, attempts to introduce musical forms more complex than a 32-bar song were highly suspicious and belonged on the operatic stage where they could safely claim to be art while losing money. In fact, musical scenes like those created by Rodgers and Hammerstein for *Carousel*, Frank Loesser for *The Most Happy Fella*, Leonard Bernstein for *Candide* and *West Side Story*, or Kurt Weill and Ira Gershwin for *Lady in the Dark* weren't conventionally operatic or conventionally popular; they were the epitome of a new form, the American musical in all its creative glory.

But mischief was afoot. In the years following World War II culminating in the 1960s, a number of figures in the theater assumed that only shows with political or social messages had meaning. Hammerstein's lyrical call for tolerance in *South Pacific* was replaced by the radicalism of the 1960s: the blaring sound of rock music dispensed with the need for witty, stylish, elegant lyrics, or music composed by skilled craftsmen and inspired melodists. Noël Coward spotted this trend early. He protested what he dubbed "the new religion, mediocrity," and added, "Nowadays, a light comedy whose sole purpose is to amuse is dismissed as trivial and insignificant. Since when has laughter been so insignificant?" He added that the stage should be a place for extraordinary people." Coward blasted, "the absurd notion that only inarticulate oafs are interesting."

Musical theater historian William Hyland observed that "the gap between the music of Rodgers and Berlin and rock and roll grew even wider until it was a chasm. And into this gap came television with its own insatiable appetite for visual effects, for charismatic personalities, and for new music and new performers. Bad music was driving out the good." As the quality of popular music declined in general, it also declined on Broadway. The need to sell records, to appeal to the fashions and fads of the moment, became dominant. The emphasis on movement and dance inevitably led to shows whose primary appeal was not their music, lyrics, or plot, but their movement. Shows were viewed (and financed) because of choreographer-directors, not scores. Alan Jay Lerner, writing his own history of musical theater, concluded, "The bankable part of the theatrical team is now the director. This in itself is an unhealthy symptom. The theater flourishes when it is a writer's theater, as it has done since Offenbach arrived in Paris."

Changes in style are inevitably trumpeted as progress, and criticism, even when coming from such august sources as Coward or Lerner have been dismissed as the ramblings of an older generation not eager to see their work (or fame) eclipsed by younger, more talented rivals. Younger perhaps, but hardly more talented. It is ironic that today's blockbuster Broadway hits tend to be "rock operas" which represent spectacles more than scores. Choreography and special effects are not new to the musical theater. In fact, just as the American musical began its evolution from the spectacle of *The Black Crook*, it has declined to the spectacle of today's successes.

Of course, there are exceptions. One critic, unkind but accurate perhaps, declared that after the "golden age" of the American musical, "the amateurs took over." Howls of protest, of course, will come from those convinced that a work by the genius of the moment has eclipsed all that has preceded it. But such scores usually have only two points in their favor: they are "contemporary," implying that those who are immune to their appeal are simply out of date, and they achieve commercial success. It is important to remember the distinction between a great show and successful show. While some masterpieces have been successful, others have achieved only limited profits. While some mediocre shows have flopped, others have become enormous commercial successes. The American musical would suffer a sad fate if its greatest classics were remembered only by scholars and historians, rather like the obscure popular favorites of other eras which are eclipsed in the public memory and recall fondly only by somnabulatory musicologists.

One trend that stands directly opposed to this sorry state of affairs is the revival. In recent years, Broadway has seen an abundance of revivals of classic shows like *Show Boat, Oklahoma!, Guys and Dolls, Carousel, South Pacific, The King and I,* and *Kiss Me, Kate,* which have proven unqualified successes. Of course, these shows (and others of the era) are also revived throughout the country in summer stock companies and on college campuses. They are not revived because they are old, but because they represent the superb product of men and women of taste and talent, whose creative efforts transcend time.

When Mario Castelnuovo-Tedesco suggested to me improbably that the American musical was the ideal vehicle for an American composer, what did he mean? I suspect he felt that way because the musical (at its best) was a typical American invention, born of Viennese operetta, British music halls, immigrants from Ireland, Austria, Germany, Hungary, and Russia, the sounds of jazz from New Orleans to Chicago, the folk-songs of African Americans, and even the Italian operatic tradition of which the Maestro was so proud. From this musical melting pot, a remarkable group of composers, lyricists, and playwrights fashioned a musical genre quite unique with skill, technique, imagination, and not insignificantly, a touch of magic. Will the best of our musical theater survive or be eclipsed in a cacophonous torrent of high-tech noise and special effects, politically correct scripts, and audiences incapable of knowing the difference? If Oscar Hammerstein II were here, the original cockeyed-optimist would probably say "absolutely, yes." Let us hope he would be right.

FILM MUSIC

When Alfred Hitchcock, the master of suspense films, directed a scene taking place on a lifeboat in the water, he considered using no background music. Said Hitchcock, perhaps rhetorically, "Where does the music come from in the middle of the ocean?" To which David Raksin, the distinguished film composer replied, "Let him tell me where the camera comes from in the middle of the ocean, and I'll tell him where the music comes from."

Where motion picture music comes from is actually an easy question to answer. It comes from the pens of the talented composers who have written the scores that give life, energy, and emotion to the movies, which have captivated the American public (and audiences around the world) for generations. For me, discussions of film music are highly personal. My own discovery of motion picture music came early, when I attended a screening of the movie *Anastasia*. I was captivated not only by the stellar performances of Ingrid Bergman, Yul Brynner, and Helen Hayes, but by the music. When the scoring credits appeared on the screen, I saw a name that was new to me, "Alfred Newman." I soon became aware that Newman had scored many films, including such classics as *The Song of Bernadette* and *Captain from Castile*. Like the oenophile who has tasted his first wine, I realized that music added an element of incredible importance to movies. But more than that, a film score could contain such beautiful music, a lyricism and emotional appeal often lacking in what is described (curiously) as "serious" contemporary concert music.

I soon became aware of the different genres of motion picture music. I became an enthusiastic collector of recordings of the great background scores: the classics by European born composers who settled in Hollywood, Erich Wolfgang Korngold, Max Steiner, Miklós Rózsa, Franz Waxman, Bronislaw Kaper, and their American counterparts, David Raksin, Bernard Herrmann, Hugo Friedhofer, Jerome Moross, Alex North, and Elmer Bernstein, among others. I was equally enchanted by the movie musical, a production in which music (in the form of lyrical songs and dazzling dances) moved from the background to the foreground. The movie musical might be an adaptation of a great Broadway hit or an original production never seen on the stage.

I grew up attending recording sessions at Universal Studios, where I met many of my boyhood heroes. My eminent teacher, Mario Castelnuovo-Tedesco taught several generations of film composers; I also acquired a distinguished musical mentor, Irvin Talbot, for forty-five years the musical director of Paramount Pictures. Finally, I wrote a book about film music, "Soundtrack: The Music of the Movies," Miklós Rózsa honored me by writing the introduction to the book; I also received guidance from Bernard Herrmann, David Raksin and especially Irvin Talbot, to whose memory the book was dedicated. So film scores have been a part of my musical life almost since the very beginning. Film music has had a remarkable history. Since our discussion is devoted to America's musical heritage, we will not be able to pursue in detail the great British, French, Russian, German, and Italian scores. But around the world, as in the U.S. movie music has had an influence far beyond the limitations of the screen. Legend has it that directors would always begin shooting a scene on the set with the phrase, "Lights, Cameras, Action." But perhaps "Lights, Cameras, Music." would be more appropriate.

THE SOUND OF SILENTS

A good place to begin the story of motion picture music (and an exploration of its functions) is at the beginning. In a darkened movie theater, an audience sits spellbound when a fragile young woman appears on the screen. In the midst of a raging storm, a tall, mysterious man enters. He wears a black cape and though he smiles a sly, diabolical smile, he is clearly a cad who is up to no good. As he twirls his mustache, he demands an overdue mortgage payment. Viewers know that danger is just around the corner because they hear ominous chords played on the piano by a musician who accompanies every silent action on the screen with a musical commentary. In the silent film era, audiences were thrilled and delighted by such scenes. The helpless heroine waiting for rescue, tied to the railroad tracks with a speeding train just moments away.....the hapless hero dangling from a rooftop overlooking a busy street scene teeming with traffic...the poignant gaze of the little tramp, heading down life's highway with nothing working out quite as he expected. These were scenes that represented the very essence of entertainment in the first two decades of the twentieth century.

The motion picture started modestly, not as a serious art form, or even as a commercial enterprise, but as a scientific experiment. On October 6, 1889, Thomas Edison introduced the cinto-phonograph, a device enabling viewers, one at a time, to view a moving picture accompanied by a phonograph record, which could only play for a few minutes. Charles Pathé in Paris and Oscar Messter in Berlin used a subsequent invention, the Berliner gramophone, to attempt synchronization of the filmstrip and gramophone record. But most pioneers in the world of film worked with silent moving pictures.

In France, the Lumière brothers began producing silent moving pictures and presenting them to the public in a carnival atmosphere. In 1895, they invited an audience to the basement of a Paris café. A pianist provided music for their film program, establishing a new tradition of live background music. On February 20, 1896, their first performance in England was incredibly successful. Within a few months, major British music halls began scheduling movie performances. Since live performers in the music halls required musical accompaniment, the musical halls already had orchestras, which could also provide accompaniment for silent films. Not only did the music drown out the noise made by the early projectors, it set the mood for each scene. A pianist, organist, or a full orchestra would compensate. When silent films became popular in the United States, they were invariably accompanied by musicians.

In small towns, the accompanist might be an organist, who might combine familiar classics and his own improvised themes. Composers wrote appropriate action, love, and suspense themes for scenes or characters in silent films. Among the most famous were Giuseppe Becce, who later continued to spend four decades scoring sound films, and John Stepan Zamecnic, an American trained by Antonín Dvořák in Prague, who composed his "Mysterious Burglar Music." Zamecnic's theme influenced "Mysterioso Pizzicato," often credited to composer J. Bodewalt Lampe, a theme for villains which has been parodied in countless movies and cartoons.

William G. Blanchard, emeritus professor of music at Pomona College, recalled his early days as a silent film organist as "an attempt to put under the control of one individual all the colors of the orchestra." Blanchard and other theater organists played pipe organs that provided a throbbing tremolo so characteristic of the era, and a plethora of percussion effects: snare drums, xylophone, cymbals, bird whistles, fire sirens, and gunshots, all of which add color and excitement to scene. In large cities, theaters would employ whole orchestras to accompany the films.

Figure 280 - William G. Blanchard at the console of a large theater organ. (Photo courtesy of William G. Blanchard)

Composer David Raksin recalled his father, a silent film conductor, using a baton with an electric bulb on its tip, so musicians could follow the conductor in the dark. At a moment's notice, they might have to change music as dictated by what was taking place on the screen.

Irvin Talbot was conducting an orchestra for the Missouri Theater when he received the opportunity to go to New York as a conductor for Paramount Pictures and as an associate of their leading musical director, Dr. Hugo Riesenfeld. When he accepted the invitation to join Paramount Pictures, he began his forty-five year career with the studio during which he emerged as one of the most distinguished of Hollywood's conductors, Conductors would be provided with cue sheets telling them the approximate length of each scene and the mood, comedy or drama. Hugo Riesenfeld, David Mendoza, Ernö Rapée, and Irvin Talbot would select music from an orchestral library, choosing themes that would be appropriate for a furious chase sequence or a romantic encounter between the leading man and leading lady. Irvin Talbot recalled, "The most popular misterioso theme was *The Slimy Viper*." For important epics like Cecil B. DeMille's *The Ten Commandments*, he assembled scores that were bound and distributed to other conductors around the country that might not have the expertise or time to catalogue their own musical sequences. Theaters also featured live performers on stage, before or after the movies. Irvin Talbot set the record for training conductors during the silent film era; he conducted more scores and vocal numbers for composers than any other conductor in the film industry. At the Paramount Theater in New York, he led orchestras accompanying performances by a stellar cast of entertainers, many of whom were just beginning to make their names as stars. There were opera singers like Luisa Tetrazzini and James Melton, popular vocalists like Bing Crosby and Kate Smith, Broadway stars including Ethel Merman, Gertrude Lawrence, and Fanny Brice, vaudevillians like Eddie Cantor, George Jessel, and Bob Hope, France's musical hall star Maurice Chevalier, and even the gravel-voiced man who would become America's best-known purveyor of gossip over radio and in print, Walter Winchell.

Figure 281 - Paramount Theater in New York. The Paramount Theater, like many of the 1920s "movie palaces" featured a full-length vaudeville show as well as motion pictures accompanied by a live orchestra. (Photo courtesy of the Irvin Talbot Collection)

Theater organists or pianists began using collections of music specifically created for silent movies: The Sam Fox Moving Picture Music Volumes by J.S. Zamcenik (1918) and the Kiniobibliothek by Giuseppe Becce (1919). Inevitably, producers of films began asking composers to write music specifically for their films. As early as 1908, the renowned French composer Camille Saint-Saens wrote a score for harmonium, piano, and strings for the film *L'Assasinat du Duc de Guise*. In 1915, director D.W. Griffith produced The *Birth of a Nation*. Carl Elinor prepared an original score, but Griffith discarded Elinor's score and replaced it with a series of pieces selected from the symphonic repertoire by Joseph Carl Breil. Griffith used compositions by Grieg and Wagner, (including *The Ride of the Valkyries*, patriotic tunes, and a romantic melody *The Perfect Tune*, which later became the theme of the *Amos and Andy* radio program.) The conflict between composers and the producers and directors of films began in the earliest days of films. Producers and directors, often with little musical knowledge of their own, had the power to impose their will on composers. Some composers resisted, others acquiesced. This struggle has continued to the present day.

Some of America's finest composers were asked to score films, including Charles Wakefield Cadman, (*The Rubaiyat of Omar Khayam*, 1918) Frederick Shepherd Converse

(*Puritan Passions,* 1923) and Mortimer Wilson (*The Thief of Baghdad,* 1924). George Antheil, the "Bad Boy of Music," collaborated with noted French artist Fernand Léger on the 1924 film, *Ballet Mécanique.* In Europe, some of the world's leading composers of concert music, including the most experimental and daring musicians of the day turned their hand to films, including Eric Satie, Arthur Honegger, Jacques Ibert, Paul Hindemith, and Dmitri Shostakovich. But the silent film era came to an abrupt end on October 6, 1927, with the premiere of a film called *The Jazz Singer.* The sound film era began, and music would play a more important role than in ever in the world of motion pictures.

SILENT NO MORE

1927 was a year to remember. Charles Lindbergh became the nation's hero when he boarded his plane, "The Spirit of St. Louis" and flew it across the Atlantic Ocean. Babe Ruth hit 60 home runs for the New York Yankee team regarded by many baseball fans as the best of all time. On October 6, a new film, *The Jazz Singer* opened before an audience astonished to hear Al Jolson shout, "You ain't heard nothin' yet folks, listen to this." What the folks listened to was Jolson singing one of his hit tunes, *Mammy,* as the silent film era came to an abrupt and improbable end.

Even before the turn of the century, inventors were aware of the principle of photographing sound of filmstrips. Eugene Augustin Lauste, a French immigrant to the United States and a former Edison employee was one of the pioneer developers of photography and sound for the movies. In 1911, he exhibited what may have been the first sound film in the United States. But for sound films to succeed commercially, it would be necessary to coordinate sound and music, and to amplify the sound so audiences could clearly hear it in theaters. Producers were faced with a choice between two competing systems, sound-on-film and sound-on-disc. This was not unlike the initial rivalry between promoters of Beta and VHS systems in the early days of videocassette recorders six decades later.

Figure 282 - Irvin Talbot. For forty-five years, he set the highest musical standards conducting the Paramount orchestra. (Photo courtesy of the Irvin Talbot Collection)

The photoelectric cell, patented in 1920, was a key element in a sound-on film system developed by inventor Lee De Forrest. Sound impulses could be converted to light patterns and recorded as a continuous soundtrack. In 1924, Lee De Forrest decided to test his approach. He collaborated with conductor Irvin Talbot on a unique experiment. Leon Rothier, a basso from the Metropolitan Opera, recorded *The Marseillaise* and *The Shadow Song* under Talbot's baton while being photographed under the inventor's supervision. William Fox used a different sound on film system, the German Tri-Ergon for a 1927 sound film, *What Price Glory? Fox Movietone News,* the first sound newsreel, released the same year, used the same technique.

In contrast, Warner Brothers opted for Vitaphone, a sound-on-disc system, used in the studio's films *The Jazz Singer* and *The Lights of New York.* Initially, producer Harry Warner could not believe that sound could be coordinated with photography. At a Bell Laboratories demonstration, a skeptical Warner peeked behind the movie screen to see if someone had hidden an orchestra there to fool him. On August 6, 1926, Warner Brothers teamed with the Vitaphone Corporation for an important premiere: a concert featuring such musicians as concert violinists Efrem Zimbalist and Mischa Elman, concert pianist Harold Bauer, and opera star Giovanni Martinelli, followed by a screening of *Don Juan,* starring John Barrymore and accompanied by a musical score assembled by Major Bowes, David Mendoza, and William Axt, and recorded by the New York Philharmonic under the baton of Henry Hadley, synchronized by the Vitaphone. Audiences and critics alike were enthusiastic.

Competition among the major studios began in earnest. Clearly, producers of movies wanted to be first on the market with the best sound systems. Actors who were only concerned with their appearance had to begin worrying about how their voices sounded. Singers, whose talents were not highlighted during the silent era, had wonderful new opportunities through the new sound medium. In 1928, Paramount released its first sound film, *Warming Up,* starring Richard Dix. Irvin Talbot assembled the score, timed it in the projection rooms, and hired five members of leading symphony orchestras in New York and Philadelphia to record the music. Paramount's first recording studio was a Baptist Church in Camden, New Jersey, selected for its excellent acoustics. Musical directors like Irvin Talbot were pioneers with no precedent to guide them. They had to be creative. The score of *Warming Up* included pistol shots; Talbot realized that actual pistol shots would cause the recording stylus to jump, so he arranged for the sound of the pistol to be simulated by a drummer. The recording equipment was primitive by today's standards. Recordings were completed on a pair of sixteen-inch disks, so if one failed, the entire recording might not be lost. No one could have remotely imagined such phenomena as stereophonic sound or the digital sound revolution that would revolutionize sound recording a century later.

In 1928, Paramount music executive Nat Finston headed for Hollywood (accompanied by a musical staff which included pianist Ray Turner) to start the studio's music department. Turner, became one of the film industry's leading pianists for four decades, dazzling more people than almost any other pianist in history through his uncredited solos and accompaniments in movies. Irvin Talbot and Max Terr remained in New York to complete assignments, including the score for *A Shopworn Angel,* a film which initially received a lukewarm reaction from exhibitors and critics. The film was turned over to Irvin Talbot, who assembled a dramatic score and incorporated a popular song by Fred

Coots, "A Precious Little Thing Called Love." The picture became a hit. Jesse Lasky, who, along with Adolph Zukor, headed the studio, credited Talbot with saving the picture. So in 1929, Paramount sent Irvin Talbot to join his colleagues in Hollywood, where he pursued a long and distinguished career as Paramount's musical director. It would be perhaps the first, but certainly not the last time musicians would be asked to save a film. Composer Bernard Herrmann once declared that music supplements what technicians have done, but mostly, what they are unable to do.

Studios were faced with a new dilemma. Now that sound had arrived, what could they do with it? *The Lights of New York* was an all-talking film. *Blackmail*, a British feature crafted by a young English director named Alfred Hitchcock, was planned as a silent movie, but quickly converted to sound. Some movies were planned with wall-to wall music (or should we say, screen to screen?) Others avoided music and concentrated on dialogue. Some of the most successful films were based on America's popular music: including *Broadway Melody* and *King of Jazz*, both in 1930, and *42nd Street*, in 1932.

Movie musicals were a new genre of film which called for the most technically advanced coordination of sound and film. A new group of technicians, "music mixers" became highly skilled in controlling the various microphones used in films. Initially music and sound were recorded simultaneously; eventually these two elements would be recorded separately. Paul G. Neal, one of Hollywood's most experienced music mixers,

Figure 283 - Irvin Talbot conducting the musical score for a sound film in the early days of Paramount Pictures. (Photo courtesy of Irvin Talbot Collection)

recalled that in the early days of sound musicals like *The Rogue Song*, he would have to arrange microphones to record the film's star, Lawrence Tibbett, singing to the accompaniment of an orchestra, But while Tibbett was singing, he was also moving around the sound stage while two cameras simultaneously photographed the entire scene. Recording the sound and photographing the scene at the same time presented all kinds of problems that hadn't existed in the silent film era.

The animated cartoon offered marvelous opportunities for sound and music. In 1923, a young man named Walt Disney arrived in Hollywood from Kansas City. He recalled in later years that he only had one shirt and two pairs of socks, but he had unlimited dreams and ambition. Together with his brother Roy, Disney founded a new movie studio. Unlike Warner Brothers, Paramount, or the other new studios in California, Disney chose to specialize in animated cartoons with original characters. Disney's new animated star, "Mortimer Mouse" was soon renamed "Mickey." By 1928, Mickey was starring in his third film, *Steamboat Willie*, when sound arrived. A soundtrack was quickly added to the film, including a version of *Turkey in the Straw*, improvised by Mickey and Minnie Mouse when a goat swallowed their written score. A year later, the Disney Studio released the first in its *Silly Symphonies* series, featuring an animated *Skeleton Dance* accompanied by Grieg's *March of the Dwarfs*.

Figure 284 - Walt Disney, whose Magic Kingdom, on screen and in life, all started with a mouse. (Photo courtesy of New York World Telegram and Sun collection, Library of Congress, public domain)

The Disney 1933 classic, *The Three Little Pigs* was released in the midst of the Depression. It featured a song, "Who's Afraid of the Big, Bad Wolf?" composed by Frank Churchill and Ann Ronell. In the middle of the Depression, audiences were eager for a positive message. The song improbably became an unofficial anthem for Americans inspired by President Franklin D. Roosevelt's reminder that "The only thing we have to fear is fear itself." (Another animated film, Pat Sullivan's *Felix the Cat* also contained a hit tune, "Felix Kept on Walking.") Producers began to realize that movies could create hit songs. This proved a mixed blessing for composers. Obviously, a greater demand for songs increased the demand for their talents. But producers, eager for commercial success, would insist upon "a song I can whistle" even if the film's central theme was the execution of a convicted axe-murderer. This conflict between artistry and commerciality has remained in films until the present day.

Walt Disney was not the only producer developing animated films with memorable musical scores. Max Fleischer was Art Editor of *Popular Science* magazine. In 1915, he invented the rotoscope, a device that enabled animators to draw frame by frame over filmed action. In 1921, even before Walt Disney arrived in California, animator Max Fleischer and his young brother Dave started their own studio. The first Fleischer studio was in a basement apartment in New York. Dave, a former clown, became the model for a new animated star, Koko the Clown, who delighted audiences when he emerged from a bottle of ink in the Fleischers' *Out of the Inkwell*. The Fleischers' first employee, Charlie Shettler, remained with the studio for its entire twenty-year existence.

In 1926, the Fleischers collaborated with Lee De Forest, an early pioneer in sound-on-film recording and the self-proclaimed "Father of Radio." The result was *My Old Kentucky Home*, the first cartoon using synchronized sound. The Fleischers also released cartoons combining animation and live action. Music was important in these productions, providing exposure for future jazz legends Louis Armstrong, Cab Calloway, and Don Redmon.

Some of the best-known composers of concert music were naturally attracted to scoring films. In Germany and Austria, Karol Rathaus, Paul Dessau, Hanns Eisler, and Frederick Hollander gained recognition as film composers. Hollander provided the music for *The Blue Angel*, a film which did not contain background music, but introduced Marlene Dietrich in a sultry performance as she sang the haunting theme, *Falling in Love Again*, and a chorale theme based on music from Mozart's *The Magic Flute*. In Italy, the silent film composer, Giuseppe Becce, employed his lyrical operatic style for sound films. In the 1920s, Dmitri Shostakovich began scoring sound films, although his best-known film scores would be completed years later. France's leading composers were also drawn to the new medium. Eric Satie and a group of his colleagues known as "Les Six," especially, Darius Milhaud, Georges Auric, and the Swiss composer Arthur Honegger were particularly interested in films. Honegger's score for the controversial *L'Idee* featured an early electronic instrument, the Ondes Martenot. Banned for left-wing political ideology, the film inspired Honegger's orchestral depiction of a railroad train, *Pacific 231*.

Sounds developed by concert composers sometimes became models for particular types of scenes in the movies. Igor Stravinsky's depiction of a carousel in *Petrouchka* was often imitated. George Gershwin's orchestral traffic jam in *An American in Paris* was copied for years by composers trying to depict the vitality of a great metropolis. But composers of serious concert music had a problem if they talked about art to producers who were interested in making money and selling tickets. Arnold Schoenberg composed an imaginary film score strictly employing his twelve-tone technique; but when Schoenberg was asked to score a film in Hollywood, he demanded a fee of $100,000 and a guarantee that not a note of his music would be changed. It was the second demand that ended Schoenberg's film scoring career before it started. The conflict between composers' pursuit of musical integrity and the producers' desire to achieve the greatest commercial success would plague the development of even the finest motion pictures. Soon, every Hollywood studio had its own music department, and the composers and conductors they hired would redefine film music as a unique specialty, changing both the sights and sounds of motion pictures forever.

In what has been called the "golden era" of film music, the 1930s, '40s, and '50s, the major studios maintained their own permanent orchestras. These were usually symphonic ensembles with permanent musical directors. Conductors such as Alfred Newman at 20th Century Fox and Irvin Talbot at Paramount could depend on many of the world's finest musicians in their orchestras. Concertmasters of studio orchestras included accomplished soloists like Louis Kaufman at 20th Century Fox and Lou Raderman at MGM. The woodwind section might feature flutist Arthur Gleghorn or French horn specialist Alfred Brain, both of whom had played under the renowned Sir Thomas Beecham in England.

Whole books could be written about the studio musicians; audiences would be astounded to learn that the film scores they have come to love and admire were being sightread by these musicians who had never seen the actual printed scores before the recording session. Pianists such as Ray Turner and Harry Sukman would be called upon to play solos as difficult as the most complex concert works. When scores called for jazz musicians, the veterans of the big band era were available as well as many well-known jazz stars. Bassoonist Don Christlieb spent fifty-two years in the studios. In his memoir, *Recollections of a First Chair Bassoonist*, he observes that performing musicians almost never received on-screen credit for their work or even public recognition of any type. The same could be said for a large number of orchestrators and arrangers who contributed to film scores in countless ways, often actually ghostwriting musical cues or creating full scores from sketches created by the composer. In Hollywood, only those behind the scenes often knew the unsung heroes of the film scoring world.

Though their contributions were great, the public would sadly not recognize their work, except in rare instances, such as Herbert Spencer's scoring of the Andy Griffith television show or Leo Arnaud's theme for the Olympic Games, *Bugler's Dream*.

FROM VIENNA TO HOLLYWOOD: THE ODYSSEY OF ERICH KORNGOLD AND MAX STEINER

During the 1930s, several European émigrés settled in Hollywood and elevated film scoring to a sophisticated art. These greatly accomplished composers of symphonic and operatic music brought technical mastery and emotional intensity to film scores. Foremost among these composers were Erich Wolfgang Korngold and Max Steiner, mainstays of the music department at Warner Brothers.

Erich Wolfgang Korngold was born in 1897, in Brno, now part of the Czech Republic. The family moved to Vienna when Erich was small, and he grew up in Vienna where he was quickly recognized as a musical genius. His father, Julius Korngold, was Vienna's most powerful music critic; he selected his son's middle name in homage to Mozart. It was a wise choice. At six, Erich Korngold began composing at the piano. The first

Figure 285 - Erich Wolfgang Korngold. The greatest musical prodigy of the century who became a pioneer film composer. (With the kind permission of the Brendan Carroll Collection)

musician of prominence to sing his musical praises was the formidable Gustav Mahler, a composer and conductor not easily impressed. His brilliance won the enthusiastic plaudits of Richard Strauss and Giacomo Puccini. At 11, he composed a musical pantomime, *Der Schneeman*, (The Snowman), which was introduced by the Vienna State Opera in a command performance for Emperor Franz Josef. By the time he was eighteen, he had two operas, *Der Ring des Polykrates* and *Violanta* to his credit. At 23, he composed his masterwork, *Die tote Stadt* (The Dead City). Korngold's lush style of orchestration, his sweeping, lyric melodies, were a direct outgrowth of the Viennese romantic style. His biographer Brendan Carroll calls him "the last prodigy." But he was also truly the last of a line of eminent composers whose musical hearts beat squarely to the rhythms and emotional impulses of Imperial Vienna.

Ironically, one of Korngold's teachers was Alexander von Zemlinsky, also the only teacher of Arnold Schoenberg, whose modernist disciples would challenge Korngold later in his career. A newspaper poll in Vienna declared Korngold and his rival, the much older Schoenberg, to be among the city's most eminent composers. The rivalry would have serious consequences for Korngold. In 1921, Schoenberg announced to his pupil Josef Rufer, that his discovery of the twelve-tone serial approach would sustain supremacy of German music for a century. Schoenberg's approach called for the composer to arrange twelve notes of the chromatic scale in a fixed order of his own choosing and to base all melodies and harmonies on this scale or its permutations. The leading opponent of Schoenberg's approach was Julius Korngold, and young Erich shared his father's view. The rise of the musical serialists and more ominously, the Nazi Third Reich in Germany cast a shadow on Erich Korngold's apparently charmed musical life, one in which his compositions were all published, performed, and praised.

In 1934, Korngold was invited by his colleague, the Viennese director, Max Reinhardt, to adapt Mendelssohn's music for the Warner Brothers film, *A Midsummer Night's Dream*. Korngold came to Hollywood. He said he knew nothing about film music; he not only learned quickly, but made up his own rules that were to inspire the admiring imitation of others. For *A Midsummer Night's Dream*, Korngold had to produce recordings of Mendelssohn's music, which were played over loudspeakers during the shooting. He also conducted music, which was recorded during photographic sessions, as well as more conventional background music added after the film was completed. He also invented a brand new technique, "conducting" the actors' speeches to be added to music not yet

Figure 286 - Erich Wolfgang Korngold conducted his film scores as if he were spontaneously conducting the score of one of his operas. (Photo used with the kind permission of the Brendan Carroll Collection.)

recorded by the orchestra. Korngold was a phenomenal pianist, a gifted improviser. His admirers said he had a unique way of making a piano sound like a full orchestra. At the time, composers in Hollywood nearly all used stopwatches and composed their music using mathematically correct timing sheets that would enable them to coordinate musical sounds with precise actions appearing on the screen. But Korngold did not use a stopwatch or pay attention to highly complex timings of film sequences. At night, he would have a projectionist run a scene over and over, improvising and creating themes at the piano. A veteran of European opera houses, Korngold would conduct a film recording session like a live performance of an opera.

Although he scored *Give Us This Night*, a musical, at Paramount, where he worked with Irvin Talbot, he returned to Warner Brothers for the remainder of his film scoring career. Among the Warner features of the period were many swashbuckling adventure stories, often starring Errol Flynn, costume films awash with pirates and sword-wielding heroes who specialized in rescuing leading lady Olivia de Havilland from impending disaster. Korngold's credits included *Captain Blood, Anthony Adverse, Another Dawn,* and *The Prince and the Pauper*. Korngold's approached each picture as seriously as he would approach an opera. In *Anthony Adverse*, a specific theme represented each character, mood, or idea. Korngold's method, treating a film as an opera without words, resulted in an exceptionally high standard of music. His biographer Brendan Carroll said quite accurately that Korngold "created intensely romantic, richly melodic and contrapuntally intricate scores, the best of which are a cinematic paradigm for the tone poems of Richard Strauss and Franz Liszt."

Korngold was never typical of composers who worked in films. Because of his prominence in European concert music, he was given a generous contract that allowed him to only work on films of his choosing, an option unknown to most composers in the studios. Ironically, he resisted working on some films, which are so identified with his music that today, it is impossible to imagine them without his trademark scores. He once wrote to producer Hal Wallis, "*Robin Hood* is no picture for me. I have no relation to it, and therefore, cannot produce any music for it. I am a musician of the heart, of passions, and psychology: I am not a musical illustrator for a ninety percent action picture." Korngold insisted that his resolve was unshakable. But the *Anchluss,* Hitler's annexation of Austria, made it clear that it was impossible for the Korngold family to remain in Vienna. He took his family, including not only his wife and children, but his parents, and moved permanently to California. The rest was musical history. Korngold wrote specific pieces for *Robin Hood,* such as the *Archery Tournament* and *The Battle and Finale*. His stirring march for Robin Hood's merry men is unforgettable. A flirtatious scene between Robin and Maid Marian was slyly dubbed by studio musicians *Robin Hood in the Vienna Woods*. The studio realized that the *Robin Hood* score was something special, arranging a unique recording of a symphonic version with narration by Basil Rathbone. Ironically, the recording was never commercially released, because executives thought such a record would be "non-commercial." It would emerge only decades later, not on a record but on a compact disc.

Korngold's scores began as symphonic overtures, with brilliant brass fanfares and long, sweeping string melodies such as those he used for the swashbuckling classic, *The Sea Hawk*. No one could write better heroic music, for the concert stage or the movie theater than Erich Wolfgang Korngold. Korngold was ever the unabashed romanticist. He once declared that the finest "film score" of all-time was the second act of Puccini's *Tosca.* He could be lyrically reflective. In writing an accompaniment to a love scene in *Juarez,* he experimented with music below the pitch of the actors' voices. For *Between Two Worlds*, a remake of the play *Outward Bound*, he created an ethereal background for strings and harp. He used brooding melodies for high strings to set the mood for *Devotion*, a film about the troubled lives of the Brontë family.

When appropriate, Korngold would compose a piece of concert music for a motion picture. He wrote *Tomorrow*, a tone poem for orchestra, women's chorus, and solo contralto voice for *The Constant Nymph*, a movie about the life of a composer. For *Deception*, he completed a one movement cello concerto. Korngold's last major score for Warner Brothers was his 1947 work, *Escape Me Never,* including a ballet *Primavera*.

When it became clear that the film needed a popular song, the studio considered hiring a songwriter for the task. Korngold simply dashed off his only popular tune, *Love for Love*. That same year, Jascha Heifetz played the premiere performance of Korngold's stunning *Violin Concerto*, based on themes from *Another Dawn, Juarez, Anthony Adverse,* and *The Prince and The Pauper*. The concerto proved that Korngold's film music was of such high quality, it could easily move into the concert hall under the very highest standards.

Korngold was a man of strong principles. Early in his Hollywood career, he was shocked by a deadline that called for him to write an hour of music in just three weeks, for *Captain Blood*. To make his job easier, he adapted some material from *Prometheus* and *Mazeppa*, by Franz Liszt, and insisted that the screen credit read "Musical Arrangements by Erich Korngold," Once, Korngold visited the home of Sigmund Romberg, famous for his Broadway operettas and known to borrow musical ideas from the classics. When a young composer, also present, asked if all the leather-bound volumes of scores in Romberg's library were of his own compositions, Korngold quipped, "Not yet," When asked if he considered the public's taste in scoring films, Korngold replied, "absolutely not." He wrote, "Never have I differentiated between my music for films and that for the operas and concert pieces. Just as I do for the operatic stage, I try to invent for the motion pictures dramatically melodious music with symphonic development and variation of the themes." Korngold enjoyed a friendly rivalry with his Warner Brothers colleague, Max Steiner. Once Steiner reminded him that the two had been working for some years at Warner Brothers and then observed, "My scores have been getting better, while yours have declined." Korngold said instantly, "That's because you've been emulating me and I've been emulating you."

After World War II, Korngold returned to the world of concert music. European critics, however, were now completely in the camp of Schoenberg and his pupils. Korngold's romantic style was regarded as old-fashioned. Nor could his music attract the attention of admirers as it once had because the composer was a child being constantly compared to Mozart. After a prodigious career equaled by almost no one else in music history and a tremendous success in films, it seemed that the times and tastes of the century had simply passed him by. A critic responded to his magnificent *Violin Concerto*, which had incorporated some material from his film scores, with the now infamous review, "More corn than gold." When he died, at only sixty, Korngold was convinced he was forgotten.

Happily, a revival of his music has taken place. His concert music is played throughout the world, and his film scores are universally regarded as among the finest ever written. In 2002, André Previn conducted a recording of several of Korngold's film scores and provided the definitive answer to Korngold's misguided critics. He said, "What it actually comes down to is that a great deal of film music began to sound like Korngold, as opposed to Korngold sounding like Hollywood." Erich Korngold's musical language, before and after his time scoring Hollywood films, was consistently romantic and directed at the hearts, not the minds, of his audiences. There are many composers, including some functioning today, who try in vain to sound like Korngold. But pale imitations do not replace the original. If Korngold had lived a long and full life, he undoubtedly would have been delighted to see the renaissance and rediscovery of both his concert works and films scores. At the height of his film scoring career, Korngold enjoyed completed freedom to determine the style and placement of music in motion pictures. His work demonstrated the high level of achievement possible when an outstanding composer is given the facilities of a major studio and the freedom to follow his best instincts.

Like Korngold, Max Steiner began his musical life as a child prodigy in his native Vienna. Maximilian Raoul Walter Steiner was named for his grandfather, the impresario who built the Theater an der Wien and persuaded Johann Strauss, Jr. to compose operettas. His father Gabor Steiner operated five theaters in Vienna and opened the "Venice in Vienna" exhibition that featured the Reisenrad, a historic Ferris wheel still operating today, as its main attraction. Young Max Steiner was trained by some of the most celebrated teachers in Austria, including Robert Fuchs, Herman Graedner, and Gustav Mahler. He also studied conducting with Felix Weingartner. At only fourteen, he composed an operetta, *Beautiful Greek Girl*. His father declined to produce the work, so young Max submitted it to one of his father's competitors who mounted a production, which enjoyed a successful one-year run before demanding Viennese audiences. Steiner eventually moved to London, where he became active as a conductor of stage musicals. In 1914, producer Florenz Ziegfeld invited him to come to the United States, where he quickly became one of the leading conductors, orchestrators, and arrangers on Broadway. Steiner remained in New York for fifteen years. He had a flare for sweeping sentimental melodies, and was right at home with those Broadway composers, whose works were heavily influenced by European operettas, including Victor Herbert, Sigmund Romberg, and Jerome Kern. He also worked with George Gershwin. Vaudeville theaters began closing in New York with the advent of the stock market crash, the depression, and the introduction of sound films. Steiner had served as conductor and orchestrator for Harry Tierney's musical, *Rio Rita*. Tierney urged RKO Studios to hire Steiner as musical director for the film version.

Figure 287 - Max Steiner – He composed over 300 film scores. His score for *The Informer* established the coordination between music and images on screen. (Photo by and courtesy of Alexander Courage)

As a result, in 1929, Steiner set out for Hollywood, initially as an orchestrator and conductor. He asked Roy Webb, a colleague from his years in New York, to join him as his assistant. Webb would later become a prominent film composer himself. Steiner went to work at RKO studios, and was assigned to work on the movie, *Dixiana*. Steiner began arranging music for films. Most of the scores used music that was already printed and was recorded by a small orchestra using only ten players. Steiner found the musical situation in Hollywood chaotic. Producers had no idea what to do with dramatic music in films. They understood the need for music if the film were a musical. But for dramatic pictures, they kept asking, "If there are no musicians visible on screen, where is the music supposed to be coming from?" RKO decided it didn't need background music for its dramas, and therefore, didn't need a regular music department. Steiner very nearly accepted a conducting job in Atlantic City and might never have returned to Hollywood. Instead of releasing Steiner from his contract, RKO suddenly decided to hire him on a month-to month basis as head of their music department. He never looked back. The studio couldn't find an available composer to score *Cimarron,* so they asked Steiner to write the score himself.. He was so prolific, writing under the pressure of intense deadlines, that it is virtually impossible to precisely catalogue how many motion pictures contained his work.

To make matters worse, recording techniques, which are now standard were just being invented. Steiner often had to conduct music while the director supervised shooting of the film. Music and dialogue were recorded while the actors were being photographed. If an actor forgot his lines, the music had to be re-recorded. If a musician hit a wrong note, the actors had to go through their dialogue again. A director might demand fifty takes of a scene before being satisfied. Dramatic films of the day didn't contain much music. Steiner changed all that. In 1932, nearly a third of the film *Symphony for Six Million* was accompanied by Steiner's music. *Bird of Paradise*, another 1932 release, was underscored by wall-to-wall Steiner music. Steiner served as musical director for the Fred Astaire-Ginger Rogers films, *Flying Down to Rio, The Gay Divorcee, Roberta, Top Hat,* and *Follow the Fleet.*

Steiner's greatest contribution to films of the day, however, came as a result of his unique innovations in coordinating music and the visual image. In 1933, Steiner completed the score for the famous horror film, *King Kong.* Studio executives worried that the image of a giant gorilla might make audiences laugh. But Steiner's score, recorded by an eighty-piece orchestra, contained a vast number of musical sound effects, all invented by Steiner. Its throbbing, pulsating quality made it an immediate classic. No one could doubt the impact of Steiner's score for *King Kong.* The acerbic pianist Oscar Levant quipped that the film should have been titled "Music by Max Steiner with accompanying pictures." At the time, directors were skeptical about full-length dramatic scores for pictures that did not have an overtly musical plot. John Ford's *The Lost Patrol* was supposed to have only a minimum of music, but when Ford's film wasn't received enthusiastically at previews, the studio decided to ask Steiner to provide a comprehensive score. From the early days of film scoring, composers were asked to compensate for ineffective writing, acting, or direction. Steiner's music for *The Lost Patrol* was the first dramatic score to be nominated for an Academy Award.

In 1935, Steiner composed the score for *The Informer*. In this film, he achieved one of his foremost ambitions in Hollywood: to coordinate the visual image and musical pulse in a dramatic film. Animated cartoons had always depended upon such coordination, but Steiner wanted to take the combination of music and visual image to an entirely new level. For scenes requiring absolute coordination, Steiner became a foremost exponent of the click-track technique. Carl Stalling and Scott Bradley had been the first to use this technique in cartoons; Steiner and Roy Webb pioneered its application to feature films. The click-track was a device that made it possible to achieve mathematical precision as music and film were synchronized. Decades before the advent of computers and today's digital technology, music cutters would punch holes in the soundtrack on the edge of the film, relating metronomic tempi to those of a film projector. The conductor could then lead an orchestra through a sequence while listening to "clicks" that acted like a metronome. Click-track technique eliminated the element of chance from scores. In *The Informer*, (directed by John Ford), Steiner provided an important underscore for the decline and fall of Gypo Nolan, an Irish informer who betrays a friend for the money to pay his passage to America. Steiner's brass and drum chords followed Victor McLaglen's lumbering walk as Gypo goes to his doom. Film scoring would never be the same. Steiner's ability to "catch" the smallest physical action on the screen would be emulated by many other Hollywood composers.

In 1937, Steiner joined the staff of Warner Brothers. He composed the famous fanfare used for virtually all Warner films except those scored by Korngold. He would remain at Warner Brothers for 30 years and score over 300 films in his career. Max Steiner enjoyed his busiest and most important year to date in 1939. He wrote the *Symphony Moderne*, a lush movie-concerto composition based on themes by concert pianist Max Rabinowitsch. Then producer David O. Selznick asked Steiner to score *Gone with the Wind*. Selznick, like most producers of the time, had definite notions about music. He was famous (or infamous) for bombarding composers (and everyone else who worked for him) with memos filled with mandates, orders, and instructions, despite the fact the composers who scored his films knew far more about music than he did. Selznick told Steiner he wanted little original music, with much of the score based on themes of the old South. He insisted that a small string ensemble play the themes for his approval before Steiner continued. In case Steiner couldn't meet his deadline, Selznick engaged Franz Waxman, another prominent film composer, to write a "back-up score." Selznick's fears were groundless. Steiner's two volume score was the length of an opera. He created seven principal character themes, for Scarlett O'Hara, Rhett Butler, Melanie Wilkes, a love theme for Melanie and Ashley Wilkes, another love theme for Scarlett and Ashley, Scarlett's father, Gerald O'Hara, and finally, the nostalgic, memorable melody for Tara, the O'Hara's plantation. Despite wide acclaim, Steiner had to face two ironic surprises regarding his score. Music was the only element of *Gone with the Wind* not to win the Academy Award, which went to the score for *The Wizard of Oz,* and David O. Selznick could not obtain release of the score on record. Record companies believed that the public would have little interest in a background score.

Steiner went on to score dozens of classic motion pictures, including his two Oscar-winning score of the 1940's, *Now, Voyager* and *Since You Went Away*. The theme from *Now, Voyager*, with lyrics by Kim Gannon, became a huge popular song hit under the title *It Can't Be Wrong*. *Since You Went Away* was a film dedicated to the families left behind as young American soldiers left to fight World War II. Thousands of young girls identified with Jennifer Jones as she raced along a railroad platform following the train carrying the boy she loved (portrayed by Robert Walker) off to war. Steiner quoted such popular songs as *I'll Be Home for Christmas* and Irving Berlin's *Together*, combining them with military bugles; he combined themes from various characters with an orchestral imitation of a train. His emotional music and the poignancy of the scene had an unforgettable effect on audiences of the day. Steiner was also responsible for the music in such classics as *The Charge of the Light Brigade, The Life of Emile Zola, Jezebel, Dark Victory, All This and Heaven Too, Casablanca, The Adventures of Mark Twain, Saratoga Trunk, Life With Father, The Treasure of the Sierra Madre, Johnny Belinda, The Adventures of Don Juan, The Fountainhead,* and *The Glass Menagerie*.

Because Steiner and Korngold spent many years as colleagues at Warner Brothers, it is easy to think of them together. But it is important to remember that when Steiner arrived on the west coast, he was forty-two years old, and had spent two decades working in the field of light music. So when Steiner began working in Hollywood, he brought with him a major influence: popular music as defined by the composers of Broadway. While Korngold remained steeped in European concert music, Steiner's approach emphasized themes that could be sung, lyrical melodies assigned to each character of consequence and developed according to the composer's taste and inclinations. When Steiner arrived in Hollywood, traditions of film scoring as we know them did not exist. Many were invented by Max Steiner. In time, he would become known as the quintessential Hollywood film composer. Steiner, with his background in Viennese operetta and Broadway musicals leaned naturally toward a musical style derived from rhapsodic 19th century European composers. The more dissonant harmonies and experimental rhythms heard in the music of composers like Igor Stravinsky and Sergei Prokofiev did not appeal to Steiner, at least in his own work. His musical style and technical innovations became a model for numerous others.

Despite Korngold's success, composers whose backgrounds were primarily in the area of classical concert music were regarded with suspicion by producers and studio executives. "Carnegie Hall" music was considered elite, intellectual, and possibly confusing to a large public audience. This view did not prevail in England, France, Germany, Italy, or Russia. But in Hollywood, the conflict between Broadway and Carnegie Hall would be played on many stages. Steiner rarely read scripts, preferring to confront the actual film, which might prove more or less than he expected from a written document. He sketched his music and then turned it over to orchestrators, including his long-time colleagues Hugo W. Friedhofer (later a major film composer in his own right) and Murray Cutter.

Steiner's approach, including *leitmotifs* or themes for major characters, close coordination between music and the physical movement of characters, and the use of many sweeping, lyrical melodies in a romantic style became the dominant influence in Hollywood for many years In later years, some of Steiner's critics would try to dismiss his attention to synchronization by dubbing it "mickey-mousing" and decry his unabashed sentimentality and lush orchestrations. But Steiner had no apologies. He directed his music at a viewer's heartstrings and was not overly sympathetic to intellectual analysis of his music. He believed firmly in the romantic, lyrical style, and today it is impossible to even imagine films like *Gone With the Wind* or *Casablanca* without the characteristic Max Steiner sound. He continued to score films until 1965. When he died in 1971, his colleague, composer David Raksin, praised the lyricism, beauty, wit, and grandeur of his music. He set the tone and style for the rise of the symphonic Hollywood film score.

CULTURE CLASH: ARTISTS IN HOLLYWOOD

Not every European composer of concert music received a warm welcome in Hollywood. Each new arrival had to cope with the ignorance and egos of an assortment of producers and directors, and especially the all-powerful moguls who ran the studios. Consider the fate of Ernst Krenek. Krenek was born in Vienna, the son of a Czech soldier who served in the Austro-Hungarian army. He had all the credentials to score motion pictures in America. (Gustav Mahler's daughter, Alma, whom Krenek later married, had actually asked him to complete her father's last unfinished symphony and he did work on two movements.) Krenek was drawn to the dissonant atonal experiments that were taking place in Europe at the time. Much of his reputation came from the overwhelming success of an opera, *Jonny spielt auf* that combined elements of jazz and modern dissonance with a plot featuring a then controversial inter-racial romance.

Krenek later became drawn to the twelve-tone techniques advocated by Arnold Schoenberg; the Nazis thoroughly disapproved of Krenek and he decided to leave Europe for the United States. When he arrived, he needed immediate employment and was agreeable to orchestrating or even copying music just to earn a living. A group of composers at MGM, including Bronislaw Kaper, Miklós Rósza, and John Green, went to the studio's most powerful producer,

Figure 288 - Ernst Krenek at work. (Courtesy of Archives and Special Collections, Vassar College Library)

Figure 289 - A luncheon at MGM as composers adjust to life at Hollywood's largest studio. From left, Eugene Zádor, Charles Wakefield Cadman, studio executive Nat Finston, actor and composer Lionel Barrymore, Mario Castelnuovo-Tedesco, Daniele Amfitheatrof. (Photo courtesy of Leslie Zádor)

Irving Thalberg, to persuade him to hire Krenek. Thalberg, to no one's surprise, had never heard of Krenek or his most famous opera, but the group remained undaunted. Kaper decided to give Krenek credit for writing Verdi's *La Traviata* and *Rigoletto*. Thalberg was increasingly impressed as the list of Krenek's operas grew longer and longer. But Kaper became so enthusiastic that he threw in Mascagni's *Cavalleria Rusticana*. Thalberg exploded when he heard the name of Mascagni's opera and announced that the publisher of *Cavalleria Rusticana* had sued him for using a few notes from the opera in a movie and that he wanted nothing to do with its composer. Poor Ernst Krenek was punished and not hired for an opera he had never written.

Krenek was not alone. The distinguished composer Ernst Toch, like many other leading intellectuals in Germany and Austria, fled the Nazis and settled in California. While refugees did escape Hitler's concentration camps and the scourge of war, adjusting to life in Hollywood wasn't easy. Toch's grandson, Lawrence Wechsler, recalled a popular story of the time. Two dachshunds were said to meet under the palm trees in Santa Monica. One would confide to the other, "Here it's true, I'm only a dachshund, but back in the old country, I was a St. Bernard." Toch did score several films in Hollywood, where he became a close friend of Paramount's Musical Director Irvin Talbot and his wife Ethel. While serious musicians like Irvin Talbot treated him with great respect, he had to contend with important figures in Hollywood who neither knew nor cared about music or culture. Shortly after his arrival in America, Toch had a conference with a powerful film director who gave him instructions. The director struck a single note on the piano and barked at the astonished composer, "THIS IS THE NOTE I WANT TO FEATURE IN YOUR SCORE." Toch wondered how he could work for such an ignoramus.

Hollywood producers didn't know much about concert music, but they understood the impact of a famous name. Louis B. Mayer, at the height of his power at Metro-Goldwyn-Mayer, invited Igor Stravinsky into his office. He sat at an enormous desk and began talking about how he controlled every activity in the entire studio from that desk. "I understand that you are the world's greatest composer," he said to the obviously pleased Stravinsky, who bowed courteously. "What would your fee be to score a motion picture at MGM?" said Mayer. Stravinsky thought for a moment and then quoted a fee quite modest for today, but substantial at the time. Mayer said, "That's a lot of money, but if you are the world's greatest composer, we will pay it." Stravinsky bowed again. "Now," said Mayer, "how long will it take you to complete a score?" "How much music do you need," said Stravinsky. Mayer replied, "One hour." Stravinsky said, "One hour of music will take one year." Mayer arose from his desk and said, "Goodbye, Mr. Stravinsky."

Mario Castelnuovo-Tedesco was one of Italy's most distinguished composers when he joined the MGM music department for a time. He was shocked to learn that he would not be allowed to orchestrate his own music. He protested that choosing the instruments to play his music was as integral to its creation as selecting the colors was the prerogative of a painter. He was given permission to orchestrate his own work, but this was considered an exception to the rule. While there were many changes in Hollywood over the years, the problem of the studio bosses and executives never changed. Several decades later, André Previn, a Castelnuovo-Tedesco pupil, was working at Warner Brothers. The studio was run by Jack Warner who mistakenly assumed that Previn, born in Berlin, was actually Monsieur Previn, a Frenchman. On his morning walk around the studio lot, Warner would effusively greet Previn daily by inquiring, "Howya doin', Mon Sewer!" At major studios, prominent composers could be subjected to the criticism of the wives, relatives, or even children of producers. 20th Century Fox's musical director Alfred Newman summed up the situation by declaring simply, "In Hollywood everyone knows two jobs, his own and the music."

STRINGS AND HEARTSTRINGS: ALFRED NEWMAN AT FOX

While some composers chose to create musical backgrounds that could "catch" bits and pieces of action, another group of composers elected to write mood music that would reflect the emotions of screen characters. Foremost of these was Alfred Newman. In

Figure 290 - Alfred Newman, composer, conductor, and creator of the "Fox String Sound," with a collection of his Oscars. (Photo courtesy of Thomas Newman)

contrast to Steiner's emphasis on music synchronized with physical action (for instance, the limping music for a limping leading character in *The Informer*), Newman chose to develop individual themes to identify with the emotional moods of principal characters.

Alfred Newman was born in New Haven, Connecticut in 1901. He was a child prodigy on the piano, a pupil of Sigismond Stojowski; he also studied composition with Rubin Goldmark and George Wedge. As the eldest child (with nine brothers and sisters), he began providing financially for his siblings in his early teens. He was hired as a young concert pianist to perform before films were shown at the Strand Theater, earning the praise of many noted musicians, including the most famous pianist in America, Ignacy Jan Paderewski. Grace LaRue, a vaudeville star, heard him play at Reisenweber's Restaurant, and chose him as her accompanist. This led to an assignment in a pit orchestra for the Broadway musical *Hitchy-Koo* and a meeting with conductor Bill Daly who encouraged Newman's conducting.

At 17, Alfred Newman was the youngest conductor on Broadway, musical director for the shows of George Gershwin and Jerome Kern, among others. Newman might have had a promising career as a symphony conductor, especially since Fritz Reiner arranged for him to appear as guest conductor with the Cincinnati Symphony. But fate stepped in. Irving Berlin suggested to Joseph M. Schenk, head of United Artists, that Newman go to Hollywood as arranger and orchestrator for his musical comedy film, *Reaching for the Moon*. Newman decided to spend three months in Hollywood. He remained in California for the rest of his life.

Newman's initial scores, like his classic *Street Scene,* reflected the influence of George Gershwin. The sound of the wailing trumpet, the mournful yearning of the blues reflected the loneliness amidst the electric energy of New York City. It became a model for all big city scenes in movies for years. Newman clearly admired the scores of Erich Wolfgang Korngold, and in swashbucklers like *The Prisoner of Zenda*, he moved stylistically from the sound of Broadway to a symphonic style influenced by Richard Strauss (with a nod to

Figure 291 - A Party at the Home of Alfred Newman. 20th Century Fox colleagues include, from left, Franz Waxman, Alfred Newman, Bernard Herrmann, Ken Darby, Vinton Vernon, Alex North, Hugo Friedhofer. (Courtesy of Hugo Friedhofer)

Korngold). Samuel Goldwyn came to depend on Newman for musical expertise. Newman scored numerous films for Goldwyn, including *Wuthering Heights*. The theme he wrote for Catherine Earnshaw proved typical of his melodic style: wide leaps, rich harmonies with doubled third and sixths, and a style of orchestration that supplied a restless, yearning quality to his characters. When Schenk and Darryl F. Zanuck formed a new company, 20th Century Pictures, Newman became their musical director, and when the company merged with Fox Films, Newman became the studio's General Music Director. As a powerful studio executive and as composer-conductor, Newman set the style and tone for music in all Fox motion pictures for decades. (He personally composed the fanfare played at the beginning of each Fox film and gave audiences the sense that when a Fox film opened, something momentous was about to take place.)

Newman's influence made Twentieth Century Fox a studio of great musical importance. He was an accomplished conductor, a "workaholic" perfectionist who demanded the most of himself and his staff. Newman was not afraid to hire bold, experimental young composers and give them an opportunity to test their innovations on Fox films. Bernard Herrmann, David Raksin, Hugo Friedhofer, and Alex North, among others gained recognition at the studio during Newman's tenure. Newman had an innate sense of theater, and could infuse a screen sequence with tremendous power, pathos, or joy. His capacity to evoke emotion was unparalleled among film composers. He was unapologetically romantic and lyrical. Some critics objected to Newman's unabashed emotionalism, but his music transcends such criticisms. Among his best scores were *The Mark of Zorro* (1940), with assistance from Hugo Friedhofer, *How Green Was My Valley* (1941), *Blood and Sand* (1941), *Leave Her to Heaven* (1945), *Dragonwyck* (1946), *The Razor's Edge* (1946), *Captain from Castile* (1947), *Prince of Foxes* (1949), *David and Bathsheba* (1951), *The Robe*(1953), *The Egyptian* (with Bernard Herrmann,) *Anastasia* (1956) and *The Diary of Anne Frank* (1959).

Newman's personal style was unmistakable; he developed a virtual encyclopedia of screen scoring techniques. Newman composed leitmotifs, developed them, transposed them to various keys, augmented and diminished them, played them in all tempi, and inevitably scored them for a yearning, expressive string orchestra. Newman's melodies, with wide leaps, created a sense of longing in the listener, a need for resolution. Against his main themes, he would create countermelodies. Pianist and wit Oscar Levant once quipped that Newman always composed themes for the husband, the wife, and the "other woman," Levant said that the "other woman's theme" was somehow more interesting than the wife's theme. Newman often alternated between major and minor keys, instilling in his audiences a fluctuation between joy and sorrow. The famous "Fox string sound" was Newman's creation. Together with his orchestrators, particularly Edward B. Powell, he wrote his most expressive music for strings playing in a high register. The strings created a breathless, surging quality that made any Newman score easy to identify. This was clearly evident in the sequences like *Catana's Theme* in the 1947 swashbuckler, *Captain from Castile.* The bold brass passages in the martial *Conquest* sequence and the stirring dialogue between strings and brass in the film's main title reflected the symphonic film score at its best. Violin solos highlighted through the "Fox string sound" often came from the bow of the remarkable Louis Kaufman. Kaufman was one of the most sought after violin soloists in Hollywood. He was a well-known recitalist, sharing the concert stage with his wife Annette, a gifted pianist. Kaufman played chamber music with the great virtuosos of the world (including Jascha Heifetz, Fritz Kreisler, Gregor Piatigorsky, Pablo Casals, Mischa Elman, Efrem Zimbalist, and Vladimir Horowitz.) Hollywood discovered him and the Kaufmans settled there as he provided violin solos for hundreds of film scores.

Newman's favorite among his own scores was *The Song of Bernadette*, a landmark in motion picture music. *The Song of Bernadette*, based on the book by Franz Werfel, relates the story of the miracle at Lourdes. Newman searched for inspiration for the famous "vision scene" in which a young French girl, Bernadette Soubirous, sees a vision of the Virgin Mary, whom she calls "the beautiful lady," in the grotto at Massabielle. Closeted in his studio bungalow, he ate, slept, and drove himself to succeed. He considered the great classics, Wagner's *Grail Music*, Schubert's *Ave Maria*, and even Gregorian chant, to no avail. Finally, he decided to score the scene from Bernadette's point of view, depicting the sounds of nature and a vision of unparalleled beauty rather than as an obvious religious experience. Newman's use of a musical theme reflecting innocence in the face of profound events was a trademark. He used a similar approach in the final scenes of *The Diary of Anne Frank*, reflecting a longing for peace and tranquility rather than the tragedy which befalls the film's leading character.

Other Fox films of the times owed much of their dramatic intensity to Newman's scoring: the eerie atmosphere of the Gothic mansion, *Dragonwyck,* (and a waltz reflecting the wide-eyed wonder of Miranda Welles, the leading character), the soaring walk into the sunset in W. Somerset Maugham's *The Razor's Edge*, the menacing implications of murder in *Leave Her to Heaven*, the folk-like nostalgia for the Welsh countryside in *How Green Was My Valley,* the poignancy of the recognition scene between grandmother and granddaughter in *Anastasia.* Newman could move easily from Biblical epics like *David and Bathsheba, The Robe,* and *The Greatest Story Ever Told* to modern settings like those of his final score, *Airport,* which looked back to the mood and tone of *Street Scene,* completed so many years before. Newman managed to fuse the styles of Broadway and European concert music. He won fifty nominations for Academy Awards and nine Oscars. In addition to his activities as a composer of original scores, he found time to act as musical director for some of Hollywood's finest adaptations of Broadway stage musicals. Newman retired from Fox in 1960, and freelanced until his death in 1970. He confessed that he was terrified whenever confronted by the blank page, yet he was among the most prolific of all film composers. His brothers, Emil and Lionel were also composers. Younger brother Lionel Newman joined 20th Century Fox as a pianist and conductor and remained for forty-six years, succeeding Alfred Newman as head of the music department and working on over 200 films. Lionel Newman served as musical director for many of the films of Marilyn Monroe and won an Oscar for his contributions to the film version of *Hello, Dolly*. As a composer, he also scored numerous television programs, including *Hong Kong*. "Again" was originally one of the themes he wrote for *Road House*, a 1948 film, but it became a major hit song for decades. The Newman family's involvement in film music has continued through several generations. As a conductor, composer, and discoverer of musical talent, Alfred Newman left an indelible mark on the art of film scoring.

THE GREAT MELODIST: VICTOR YOUNG

As the scores of Korngold, Steiner, and Newman dominated the Warner Bros. and Fox music departments, other studios took similar approaches, engaging émigrés from Europe or American composers who were comfortable with a style derived from Broadway as their leading staff composers. In the 1930s, Paramount maintained a busy music department with a studio orchestra under the masterful guidance of the meticulous Irvin Talbot, called by composer Lyn Murray "the best cue-catcher in the business." More often than not, the orchestra would be recording scores by Victor Young, who spent two decades scoring films, most of which were produced under the Paramount banner.

Victor Young was one of the most gifted melodists ever to work in Hollywood. He wrote so many beautiful melodies and apparently created them so easily that a few critics were unfortunately inclined to dismiss his work as facile and sentimental. Young was born in Chicago. His parents were Polish. When he was ten, his mother died, and he and his sister joined his grandparents who were still living in Warsaw. In Poland, he continued the violin studies he had begun in America, this time with a pupil of Tchaikovsky, Roman Statlovsky. He

Figure 292 - Victor Young. Friends said he looked like a prizefighter, but he is still regarded as one of the greatest romantic melodists ever to score films in Hollywood. (Photograph courtesy of Bobbie Fromberg)

was interred by the Russians and Germans during World War I, but after the war, he and his sister returned to Chicago, where he joined the Chicago Symphony.

In the 1920s, he became active as a violinist in theater orchestras, eventually graduating to conducting and arranging scores. By the mid-1930s, he was a highly successful conductor and arranger for radio and for major record companies like Decca. Hollywood beckoned and Young settled in California where he became the mainstay of the Paramount Music Department as the studio's single most active regular composer. When people spoke of "The Hollywood Sound," they often meant "The Paramount Sound," and that was a clear reference to Victor Young.

Young was one of the most prolific songwriters ever to provide music for films. He poured long, romantic, melodic lines into his scores, usually scored for a lush, full string ensemble by his regular orchestrators, Leo Shuken and Sidney Cutner. (Shuken was one of Hollywood's most enduring orchestrators; after the death of Sidney Cutner, he continued working with a new collaborator, Jack Hayes, and the phrase "Orchestrations by Shuken-Hayes" would appear in music credits for decades.)

Like his friend Max Steiner, Victor Young became known as the quintessential "Hollywood film composer." His approach to films was neither analytical nor intellectual. His sentimental, expressive melodies did not appeal to cynics or acerbic critics. He did not cultivate the mannerisms of a temperamental composer. (After listening to his music, fans might have expected him to look like the leading man in one of the films he scored. He didn't fit the part. He was 5'4" tall, stocky, and there was nearly always an ever-present cigar in his mouth. A skeptical producer said that Victor Young looked more like a prizefighter than a musician.) But he knew how to establish a bond directly with audiences on an emotional level, inspiring tears and laughter as required by the plots and storylines of films to which he added depth and dimension. He had the musical spirit of a complete romantic.

Young's finest score was clearly his work for the 1944 epic, *For Whom the Bell Tolls*. The film featured stellar performances by Gary Cooper and Ingrid Bergman, and was based on the classic novel by Ernest Hemingway. But it was Young's music that gave the film much of its dramatic intensity. Though his personal and musical background was Polish, Young had a remarkable affinity for the music of Spain and Mexico. In *For Whom the Bell Tolls*, a saga of the Spanish Civil War, Young introduced Sevillian, Andalusian, Moorish, Catalan, and Aragonese elements. The use of cathedral bells and a Spanish guitar increased the Spanish flavor of the music. Young's usual love theme was present, executed by Louis Kaufman's solo violin over a background of strings playing tremolo passages in their highest register. The melody, "The Earth Moved," was intense and Young's score became the model for other composers writing for films with Spanish settings.

Young's other major scores included *Golden Earrings, Love Letters, Samson and Delilah, The Bullfighter and the Lady, The Quiet Man, The Greatest Show on Earth, About Mrs. Leslie, The Brave One,* and *Around the World in Eighty Days,* among others. *The Brave One,* one of his last scores, had a touching plot reflecting the unlikely friendship between a young Mexican boy and the bull he helps raise. Eventually, the bull is sent to meet his fate against a great matador in Mexico's largest bullring. The boy tries to stop the fight, but he is too late. The crowd, however, seeing the even match between the bull and the matador, calls for an *indulto*, a rare pardon for the bull. The scene is an emotional one, but it is many times more emotional because of Victor Young's soaring music. Colleagues would marvel at his ability to turn out one beautiful melody after another.

Although widely recognized for his abilities as the songwriter who created "Stella by Starlight," "When I Fall in Love," "My Foolish Heart," "A Ghost of a Chance," "Alone at Last," "A Hundred Years From Today," and many other hits, Young did not use his songwriting talent for its own sake.

When he scored films, the creation of lush, lyrical melodies came naturally to him. But he used his themes primarily as a basis for development, altering his melodies to correspond to every shade and hue of emotion in the film. Unlike songwriters of a subsequent era, Victor Young saw melodies as themes designed for his variations, not simply to be played over and over again to achieve a hit record. He once described film scoring as requiring the exactitude of an Einstein, the diplomacy of a Churchill, and the patience of a martyr. Clearly, he was able to draw upon all of these qualities in his twenty-year career, contributing to some 300 motion pictures.

As one of the busiest film composers, he was subjected to the major pressure of studio deadlines. His niece, Bobbie Fromberg, recalls him dashing back and forth between two grand pianos as he simultaneously worked on scores for two films at once. For rest and relaxation, he hosted three-day card games in which the participants included most of the prominent film composers who played poker.

When he died suddenly in 1956, friends knew that the film scoring world had suffered a great loss. At his best, he added depth and vitality to films in the most direct way possible: he communicated with his audience. One cannot listen to a Victor Young song or watch a film that he scored without being affected emotionally. He left behind a legacy of memorable melodic creation.

During his busy years at Paramount, Victor Young found time to act as mentor to the brilliant pianist and composer Harry Sukman. Sukman, a former child prodigy from Chicago, had studied with Rudolph Ganz and had accompanied a number of the world's leading concert artists when he began working as a pianist-conductor in radio.

Figure 293 - Harry Sukman, pianist and composer, known for his keyboard virtuosity and rich, melodic style of scoring for films and television, accepting a well-deserved Academy Award from presenters Sandra Dee and Bobby Darin. (Photo courtesy of Susan Sukman McCray.)

Eventually, Sukman began scoring films, beginning in the science fiction genre. He won an Oscar for his musical direction for *Song Without End*, a film biography of Franz Liszt. It was Sukman's performance of Liszt's *Hungarian Rhapsody No.2* at a party that persuaded producer David Dortort to choose Sukman to write the music for the popular western television series, *The High Chaparral*. Dortort asked Sukman if he could write Mexican music. Sukman's daughter, Susan Sukman McCray recalled that Sukman replied, "Are you kidding?" The rest was history.

He also composed background scores for such classic television programs as *Dr. Kildare* and *The Eleventh Hour*. Sukman was a versatile composer, with credits ranging from *The Singing Nun* to *Salem's Lot*. Sukman, like Victor Young, was a highly lyrical composer with a special gift for melody.

FRANK SKINNER: THE MAINSTAY OF UNIVERSAL

Like Victor Young, Frank Skinner had a great gift for lyricism and was the musical mainstay of a major studio, Universal. Skinner grew up in an Illinois farming family that didn't entirely approve of his decision to make music his career rather than his hobby. As a child, he was accomplished on the cornet, then took up the piano, and he and his brother, a drummer, played together on steamboats that navigated the Illinois River. He eventually studied at the Chicago Musical College. He became a skilled arranger and settled in New York for ten years, composing and arranging around 2,000 popular songs. Although he never thought of himself as a pedagogue, he also wrote two fine books, *Frank Skinner's Simplified Method for Modern Arranging* and *Frank Skinner's New Method for Orchestra Scoring*. Years later, in Hollywood, he wrote one of the first true textbooks on composing for motion pictures, *Underscore*, filled with examples from one of his own scores for a film with an Irish theme. Skinner explained that he called his book *Underscore* because he thought that the word was much more appropriate to describe music's contribution to films than the widely used term "background music." He said that music was supposed to bring out every possible story value, even expected to make up for lackluster acting or deficient dialogue.

Beginning in 1938, he joined the music department of Universal Pictures, where he remained for twenty-eight years. Skinner scored an incredible variety of movies during his years at Universal. In many ways, he became the symbol of the studio's approach to music. In recent years, much attention has been paid to Skinner's scores for Universal's horror films, such as *Son of Frankenstein.* On occasion, Skinner collaborated on scores with another veteran Universal composer, Hans J. Salter. They were an unusual pair. Skinner, of course, had entered film music from the world of dance bands and American popular music. Salter had trained in Vienna with Franz Schreker and Alban Berg, and left behind a world of operas and chamber music when he fled the Nazis to settle in Hollywood. But the two were friends and worked well when they happened to share assignments.

Figure 294 - Frank Skinner - Film composer, big band arranger, and author. His talents enabled him to score every genre of film at Universal Studios for decades. (Photo courtesy of Frank Skinner)

Frank Skinner was an incredibly versatile composer who could score anything the studio handed to him. A brief mention of only a few of his films underscores his versatility: musicals (*100 Men and a Girl*, starring soprano Deanna Durbin), a series of Sherlock Holmes movies, comedies (including those of W.C. Fields and the team of Abbott and Costello), *Harvey*, based on a classic play about a man who claims to have a giant rabbit as his friend, and *Bedtime for Bonzo*, which is widely remembered because it co-starred future President Ronald Reagan with a chimpanzee. In the 1950s, Skinner scored many mature dramas such as *Written on the Wind, Man of a Thousand Faces,* and a whole group of motion pictures produced by Ross Hunter featuring elegance, romance, suspense, elaborate sets, fashionable costume designers, and plots that would tug at the heartstrings, including *Magnificent Obsession, Interlude, Imitation of Life, Portrait in Black, Back Street,* and *Madame X*. Skinner did not care for dissonance for its own sake. He liked lush, full orchestrations and melodies that were guaranteed to provoke an emotional response in the audience. In an industry filled with temperamental composers and artists, Skinner was known as an affable, modest, and often self-effacing figure; as a result, he did not become nearly as well known to the public as many of his less-accomplished colleagues.

Figure 295 - Joseph Gershenson, for many years, conducted and supervised numerous musical scores as the director of Universal Studios' music department. (Photograph courtesy of Joseph Gershenson)

Many of Skinner's scores, like those of others on the staff at Universal, were conducted by the director of the studio's music department, Joseph Gershenson. Gershenson began his career as a violinist playing duets with a pianist accompanying silent films and continued as a theater orchestra conductor. When he joined Universal in 1940, he became their principal music executive, managing staff assignments and conducted many of the scores, invariably listed as "Music Supervisor" on the screen. For three decades, he oversaw the multiple changes and innovations in the world of Hollywood film music.

Figure 296 - Russ Garcia, the amiable composer-arranger who gave up life in Hollywood to pursue his dreams in New Zealand. (Photo by Kaiwhakahaere)

Another mainstay of the Universal music department, Russell Garcia, had perhaps one of the most unusual careers in Hollywood. Garcia's major breakthrough in the entertainment industry came when he substituted as composer-conductor for a radio program, *This is America*, and impressed the show's director, Ronald Reagan. Reagan's wife at the time, Jane Wyman, recommended Garcia to NBC. At Universal, Garcia was known by his nickname, "The Guy with the Nicest Disposition." Garcia wrote music for numerous films and television programs and became known as one of the industry's leading arrangers, responsible for successful recordings with leading stars, including Louis Armstrong, Stan Getz, Ella Fitzgerald, Margaret Whiting, and Mel Tormé, among others. He also wrote two extremely successful textbooks for aspiring composer-arrangers.

Then in 1966, at the height of his success, Garcia and his wife, lyricist-singer Gina Mauriello Garcia, long-time members of the Bahá'í Faith, decided to give up their possessions, sell their home, and depart on a boat, sailing the ocean to spread their faith. The Garcias knew nothing about sailing and couldn't swim; two days after their departure, they had to return after being caught in a hurricane. But they tried again and after sailing around the world as traveling teachers, in 1969 they settled in New Zealand where Garcia became recognized as a composer, arranger, and lecturer, and where he completed his opera, *The Unquenchable Flame*. The Garcias also spent time teaching primary school children the values they could learn through music and stories. Russ Garcia was one of the few Hollywood musical figures to walk away from the fame and fortune of the movie colony because he had a very different sense of values.

Roy Webb, like Frank Skinner at Universal, was identified for many years with a single studio, RKO. When Max Steiner left RKO for Selznick International and later for Warner Brothers, Webb spent twenty years as the mainstay of the studio.

Roy Webb, a native New Yorker, was influenced by show business career of his older brother Kenneth Webb. He wrote the fight song for Columbia University and worked on Broadway as an orchestrator for the team of Rodgers & Hart. Webb was a prolific film composer. He gained recognition for his scores in the *film noir* genre, dark suspense films including *The Spiral Staircase* and Alfred Hitchcock's *Notorious*. He was extremely versatile. *The Enchanted Cottage* was a haunting film about a disfigured pilot and a homely maid whose love for each other appears to transform them in an enchanted seaside New England cottage. Webb adapted his music in the form of a piano concerto performed at the Hollywood Bowl. Although Webb scored over 250 films and was nominated for seven Academy Awards, his music is little known today by the general public. Webb and his wife were devastated by a fire that burned down their home in 1961, destroying the composer's entire library containing his film scores and numerous concert works. He stopped composing as a result. Webb was a quiet, modest man and since he didn't pursue publicity, his great contributions to motion picture music have been widely neglected and should be rediscovered.

Figure 297 - Roy Webb, pioneer film composer, spent two decades scoring motion pictures at RKO. (Photo courtesy of Roy Webb)

FRANZ WAXMAN: A PLACE IN THE HOLLYWOOD SUN

Franz Waxman was one of the leading exponents of the Middle-European style. Waxman was a musical explorer. He drew upon an eclectic set of musical influences to pursue many different styles and approaches. Bernard Herrmann once said that Waxman was never satisfied with himself, and that his constant pursuit of perfection was the mark of a true artist. Franz Waxman was born in Upper Silesia, Germany, the son of an industrialist who was unenthusiastic about a musical career for his son. But Waxman was undeterred. He worked as a bank teller to pay for music lessons, and then moved to Dresden, and later Berlin to pursue his studies in conducting with Fritz Zweig and theory with Hugo Strelitzer. He began a musical career as a pianist-songwriter, working with the Weintraub Syncopaters, a jazz band. Waxman began writing arrangements for the band. He also played four-hand piano duets with Gretel Walter, the youngest daughter of renowned conductor Bruno Walter at composer Frederick Hollander's avant-garde Tingel-Tangel Theater. Frederick Hollander discovered Waxman there and gave him a key assignment: to orchestrate and conduct Hollander's score for a film, *The Blue Angel*. The movie featured

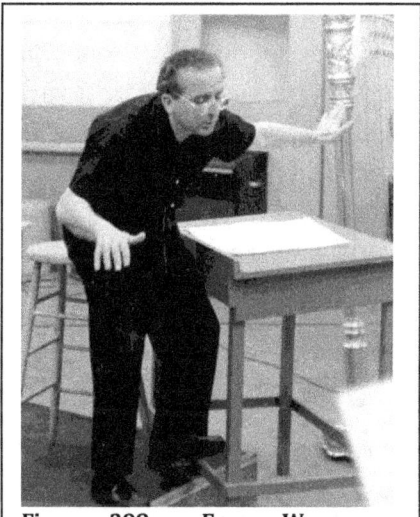

Figure 298 - Franz Waxman - Composer, conductor, and founder of the Los Angeles Music Festival. Waxman was the first to win the Academy Award two years in a row. (Photo by and courtesy of Alexander Courage)

Marlene Dietrich's sultry performance singing Hollander's song, *Falling in Love Again*.

Erich Pommer, producer of *The Blue Angel* and director of UFA Studios, a major Berlin film company, then gave Waxman his first major opportunity to write an original score of his own. In his first film score, for Fritz Lang's 1934 version of the Ferenc Molnár classic, *Lilliom,* Waxman proved himself an innovator by creating an echo effect created through recording in an empty Paris theater, and by choosing an electronic instrument, known as the Ondes Martenot to create the appropriate mood.

Waxman then joined Pommer in the United States to work on a musical, Jerome Kern's *Music in the Air.* Waxman settled in Hollywood, where he met director James Whale, who was working on a sequel to the film *Frankenstein.* In 1935, Whale was impressed with Waxman's "unearthly" sounds in *Lilliom,* and selected Waxman to work on *The Bride of Frankenstein.* Waxman developed individual leitmotifs for the principal characters, Dr. Praetorius, the monster, and the monster's mate. The music included an exciting chase sequence, a funeral march, and the most unforgettable episode, a chilling orchestral passage in which the relentless pounding of timpani suggest the beating of a heart. Waxman's score would be used again and again by Universal Studios in their serials, and his approach to the film became a model for composers trying their hand at horror or science fiction films. Waxman also became known as a master composer who could create suspense, resulting in many future assignments to create a sense of terror through music.

The score for *The Bride of Frankenstein* won such acclaim that Waxman was named Music Director at Universal when he was only twenty-nine years old. He remained at Universal for two years, working on fifty films before he left for seven years at MGM, he eventually joining Warner Brothers. 1947 was a banner year for Franz Waxman. He embarked on his most ambitious project, founding the Los Angeles Music Festival, a series of concerts devoted to contemporary music. Under Waxman's baton (and his leadership) the Festival premiered new music by the major composers of the twentieth century: Claude Debussy, Arthur Honegger, Benjamin Britten, Sir William Walton, Miklós Rózsa, Sergei Prokofiev, Dmitri Shostakovich, and Igor Stravinsky (who conducted first American and world performances of his own works). He also began to achieve major recognition as a composer of concert music as the result of his contributions to the film *Humoresque.* The film called for a major work for violin and orchestra to be played by a great concert virtuoso. Isaac Stern recorded the *Fantasie* Waxman composed. It was based on themes from Georges Bizet's great opera *Carmen;* the *"Carmen" Fantasie* took on a life of its own on the world's concert stages and led to performances of other concert works by Waxman including variations on themes from *Auld Lang Syne* and Wagner's opera *Tristan and Isolde.* Throughout the 1940s and 1950s, Waxman remained one of Hollywood's most influential film composers. He remained drawn to the sounds of the full symphony orchestra, but always using orchestration to heighten the emotional mood in his films. One of his most important scores of the period was *Rebecca.* In this gothic tale, Waxman created leitmotifs to intensify the emotional distress of a young bride whose life is overshadowed and threatened by the memory of her husband's deceased first wife. When the new Mrs. De Winter says, "Last night I dreamed I went to Manderley again," Waxman immediately introduces a menacing motif associated with the character of Rebecca. Waxman always chose his instruments carefully. A choral opening for *Dr. Jekyll and Mr. Hyde* represented the triumph of man's best instincts over his worst. A single trumpet in *Pride of the Marines* depicted the loneliness of a soldier going off to war.

Waxman was extraordinarily versatile. Despite his association with films of terror and suspense, he also scored such comedies as Jack Benny's *The Horn Blows at Midnight* and *The Philadelphia Story*. Waxman also excelled at swashbucklers like *Prince Valiant* and *Taras Bulba*. He was a superb melodist. While his serious concert works, (including his oratorio, *Joshua*, his *Sinfonietta for Strings and Timpani*, and his song-cycle, *The Song of Terezin*) were closer to his heart, he could hold his own with the best songwriters of his day. "Lisa" in Alfred Hitchcock's *Rear Window*, "The Wonderful Season of Love" in *Peyton Place*, "Rosanna's Theme" from *Hemingway's Adventures of a Young Man*, and the title song from *Beloved Infidel* were only a few of the rich melodies that flowed from his pen.

The high point of Waxman's career came in the early 1950s, when he became the first composer to win two Oscars in successive years, for *Sunset Boulevard* in 1950 and *A Place in the Sun* in 1951. In both films, Waxman's music played a key role in creating dramatic tension. *Sunset Boulevard* is the tale of Norma Desmond, a forgotten silent film star who leads a bizarre existence nourished by pathetic delusions of grandeur. Since Norma Desmond dreamed of her former glories in the age of Rudolf Valentino's tango dancing, Waxman used a tango theme to represent Norma and took the theme through numerous developments and permutations to underscore the tragedy of the film.

A Place in the Sun, based on Theodore Dreiser's novel *An American Tragedy*, relates the experiences of a poor young man played by Montgomery Clift, torn between his feelings for a girl with a similar background, played by Shelley Winters, and his infatuation with a beautiful socialite portrayed by Elizabeth Taylor. Waxman used a chromatic melody with wide leaps, played on a wailing saxophone, to introduce an implication of jazz in the score. A three note pick-up forms an ascending series of notes to characterize the longing of the young man as he looks up to the girl he idolizes. Waxman took great care with the score, personally selected saxophonist Ted Nash to play the solos. A sharp disagreement with director George Stevens led to the replacement of some of his cues by pieces composed by others. But the score remained clearly Waxman's. The most celebrated sequence in the film was a stunning orchestral fugue used to accompany a frenzied chase. Waxman conducted the west coast premiere of Dmitri Shostakovich's *Symphony No. 11*, noticing a similarity between a symphonic fugue in the Russian's work and his own cinematic fugue completed several years before. Since Shostakovich had never seen the film, it was clear that both musicians had independently explored similar melodic and contrapuntal ideas.

Figure 299 - Puccini in Japanese. Soprano Michiko Sunahara, center, joined by Franz Waxman and Irvin Talbot to her right. A team was required to suggest that Shirley MacLaine was singing opera in Japanese. (Photo courtesy of Irvin Talbot Collection)

Because Waxman was so versatile, his works were not as easily identifiable as those of some other composers. In *Sayonara*, he experimented with Japanese instruments. For *The Spirit of St. Louis*, he wrote "airplane music," with percussive xylophones, cymbals, and pizzicato strings. The main title of Waxman's score for *The Nun's Story* began with a series of stunning orchestral chimes. Scenes of the Michigan woods in *Hemingway's Adventures of a Young Man* were augmented by Waxman's woodwind solos echoing bird songs. Waxman could move easily from the dissonance and tension of horror and suspense films to the gentle innocence of the New England countryside in *Peyton Place*.

Waxman was involved in one of the most demanding technical sequences when he scored *My Geisha*, a film required to persuade audiences that actress Shirley MacLaine was singing two Puccini arias in Japanese. Conductor Irvin Talbot and music editor John C. Hammell developed a "click-track" set of timings based on an Italian recording to which MacLaine had been photographed "lip-synching." Japanese soprano Michiko Sunahara then recorded the arias in Japanese and Waxman recorded the accompaniments to fit her vocal tracks, which had to match the photographed performance by MacLaine. The scenes involved days of recording in two countries, but audiences just thought it was a touch of Hollywood magic.

When Waxman died in 1960, he left behind a rich legacy of 154 film scores, as well as many achievements as a composer and conductor of concert music. He was one of the major figures in the rise of the symphonic film score.

BRONISLAW KAPER: FROM WARSAW TO MGM

Metro-Goldwyn-Mayer, or MGM as it was popularly known, had one of Hollywood's most renowned music departments. Bronislaw Kaper spent twenty-eight years at MGM, scoring many of the studio's most important films. Like Max Steiner at Warner Brothers, he was first and foremost an exponent of the Middle-European Romantic style.

Kaper was born in Warsaw, Poland, in 1902. His father, a businessman, urged him to study law, but Kaper was drawn to music. He dreamed of being a concert pianist and prepared to perform Chopin's E-minor piano concerto for his senior recital at the Chopin Music School. A serious case of stage fright convinced him to reject a lifetime of performances before audiences. Throughout his Hollywood years, however, he remained accomplished at the keyboard, earning the consistent praise and admiration of his friend, the illustrious piano virtuoso Artur Rubinstein. Kaper went first to Berlin to study, began arranging music for films and musicals, and decided to concentrate on a career as a composer. In 1933, he fled the Nazis, and settled in Paris where Louis B. Mayer heard one of his songs and immediately invited him to come to Hollywood. Kaper arrived in California in 1935, where he became known as one of Hollywood's most elegant melodists. When Kaper turned out the popular title song, "San Francisco," for the classic film written by Anita Loos and starring Clark Gable and Jeanette MacDonald, Mayer immediately typecast Kaper as a tunesmith.

But by 1940 he was finally allowed to begin scoring dramatic films, and he proved a versatile master of the cinematic medium. Kaper's melodies frequently became popular songs. In 1941, he wrote "While My Lady Sleeps" for Nelson Eddy in *The Chocolate Soldier*. Six years later, he penned "Green Dolphin Street," which ironically (given Kaper's European classical background), joined the standard repertoire for jazz musicians around the world. His theme from *Invitation* was also widely performed. Kaper scored virtually every type of film during his many years in Hollywood including epics, like *Mutiny on the Bounty* and *Lord Jim*, and films of great dramatic intensity, like *The Brothers Karamazov* and

Figure 300 - Bronislaw Kaper. He excelled at scores of wit and charm during nearly three decades in the Music Department at MGM. (Photo by and courtesy of Alexander Courage)

Green Mansions, for which he adapted the music of Heitor Villa-Lobos. But he excelled at films combining light comedy with an almost operatic sense of romance.

Foremost among these motion pictures were several scored by Kaper in the early 1950s, *Lili,* with the haunting title song that was instrumental in winning Kaper his Oscar, *The Glass Slipper*, a version of Cinderella, and *The Swan*, Ferenc Molnár's tale of what it truly means to be a princess. Kaper's haunting waltzes for all three films proved that no composer had greater flair for films expressing the wit and charm of the Central European world he had left behind. His light touch remained evident in films from *Auntie Mame* to *A Flea In Her Ear*, his final film in 1968. Throughout his career, Kaper remained a bon vivant in his personal and musical life. He added elegance and charm to motion pictures for more than three decades and had an indelible impact on the way films were scored.

DIMITRI TIOMKIN: THE RUSSIAN WHO WENT WEST

While Igor Stravinsky never undertook a Hollywood film scoring career, several of his distinguished colleagues who remained in Russia wrote major scores for films. These included Sergei Prokofiev, who produced concert works based on his scores for *Lieutenant Kije*, a movie about a mythical soldier, and *Alexander Nevsky*, an historical epic featuring the memorable "Battle on Ice." Dmitri Shostakovich contributed to over thirty films, the most popular of which were his scores for *The Gadfly* and Russian adaptations of Shakespeare's *Hamlet* and *King Lear.* Aram Khachaturian was a masterful Armenian composer who scored numerous films. His romantic style, reflected in his ballets such as *Spartacus* and his incidental music for the play entitled *Masquerade*, made him an ideal composer for motion pictures. Prokofiev, Shostakovich, and Khachaturian were all denounced under the years of Stalinist tyranny in the Soviet Union.

Ironically, the Russian composer who became best known for scoring films was not a composer of Russian concert works, but a remarkable musician who came to Hollywood and built a reputation for writing thoroughly Russian music for westerns. His name was Dimitri Tiomkin.

Tiomkin received his training in the St. Petersburg Conservatory directed by the famed composer Alexander Glazounov. He began his colorful career as a concert pianist; he was a pupil of Felix Blumenfeld, the teacher of Vladimir Horowitz. He frequented a coffee house, "The Homeless Dog," which catered to bohemians and intellectuals, discovering a copy of Irving Berlin's "Alexander's Ragtime Band," printed on page torn from a New York theater magazine and used as wrapping paper. This led to his first awareness of American popular music. Tiomkin departed Russia after the communist revolution and the assumption of power by the Bolsheviks. He went first to Berlin, where he studied with Ferrucio Busoni and his pupil Egon Petri, toured the United States, and gained considerable recognition in Paris. He also married the dancer Albertina Rasch and composed ballet music for his wife's choreographic works.

Figure 301 - Dimitri Tiomkin (far right) joins colleagues at Paramount, from left, Richard Hageman, Boris Morros, Albert Coates, Irvin Talbot, Pietro Cimini. (Courtesy of The Irvin Talbot Collection)

While in Paris, the Tiomkins became close friends of George Gershwin and Tiomkin gave the European premiere of George Gershwin's *Concerto in F*. Gershwin wrote parts of *An American in Paris* at the Tiomkins' home. The Tiomkins headed for Hollywood after the 1929 stock market crash, and by 1930, it was Mrs. Tiomkin who was working in the new medium of sound film musicals. She persuaded MGM to hire her husband to write the ballet music for *Rogue Song*, starring famed opera singer Lawrence Tibbett. By 1937, Tiomkin was well-known enough to score *Lost Horizon,* James Hilton's epic tale of the lost paradise, "Shangri-La," and he never looked back. His main title, with a continuous melody depicting the eternity of "Shangri-La" left director Frank Capra and much of the audience in tears. Tiomkin wrote a sequence entirely for bells; he used a chorus of human voices to add to the "other-worldliness" of the mood. Tiomkin went on to score many classic Hollywood films and worked with some of the film industry's best directors, Frank Capra (*Mr. Smith Goes to Washington*, *It's a Wonderful Life*, and *Meet John Doe*), Alfred Hitchcock (*Strangers on a Train* and *Dial M For Murder*), Howard Hawks (*Red River* and *Land of the Pharaohs*), George Stevens (*Giant*), and William Wyler (*Friendly Persuasion.*)

Tiomkin was always happy when he was painting on a large musical canvas. He wrote for large symphonic orchestras, but instead of Steiner's combination of Vienna and

Broadway, Tiomkin's approach was quintessentially Russian. He was clearly influenced by folk music, by the brooding contrasts and a swinging pendulum of musical emotions so clearly found in Russian music.

In 1946, David O. Selznick asked Tiomkin to score *Duel in the Sun,* launching the composer on the road to fame as a composer of westerns. None of Tiomkin's western scores really sounded like the music of the American west, but they reflected Hollywood's view of the west, moods of conflict and power. For the love scenes between Gregory Peck and Jennifer Jones, Tiomkin wrote a love theme and a "conflict theme" and then arranged for them to clash contrapuntally in a thematic development often found in Russian symphonic music. Tiomkin went on to score numerous other westerns, including *High Noon* and *The Alamo. High Noon* began and ended with soft music, quite the opposite of Tiomkin's usual symphonic fare, and a song, "Do Not Forsake Me," which is repeated to remind the hero, Gary Cooper, and the audience, of the approaching showdown at high noon. The song became a tremendous popular success as did Tiomkin's thoroughly Russian melody, "The Green Leaves of Summer" which was introduced in *The Alamo.* (Tiomkin's use of a trumpet played by Mexico's astonishing trumpet virtuoso Rafael Méndez over strumming guitars was one of the high points of the film.)

Tiomkin's inimitable Russian accent (which even comes through on the pages of his autobiography, *Please Don't Hate Me*), his illegible musical notation which drove copyists and orchestrators to distraction, and his colorful personality only added to his mystique. Tiomkin had an independent spirit and fought for more opportunities for black musicians in studio orchestras. He told publicist Dave Epstein, "My fight is for a certain amount of dignity, not just for composer, but for all artists responsible for this picture." There were rumors that his "High Noon" theme was derived from a Ukrainian folk tune. He could apply the most Russian sounds to the most American situations and make the audience believe in their validity; one could hear echoes of Scriabin in *Duel in the Sun,* of Prokofiev in the documentary *Rhapsody of Steel.* When he used the piano in his scores, like the ominous passages anticipating a murder in *Angel Face,* a motion picture in the *film noir* genre, or the suspenseful *36 Hours,* his phrases and harmonic colors clearly reflect Rachmaninoff. Dimitri Tiomkin's most famous

Figure 302 - Dimitri Tiomkin spoke English and scored the most popular westerns with his inimitable Russian accent. (Photo by and courtesy of Alexander Courage)

Hollywood moment came when he accepted an Oscar for his tuneful and dramatic score for *The High and The Mighty.* Tiomkin said, "Ladies and Gentlemen, because I am working in this town for twenty-five years, I like to make some kind of appreciation to very important factor which makes me successful and adds to quality of this town. I like to thank Johannes Brahms, Johann Strauss, Richard Strauss, Richard Wagner, Beethoven, Rimsky-Korsakov..." Tiomkin never got to thank his most obvious influences, Tchaikovsky and Rachmaninoff, as the audience dissolved in laughter and master of ceremonies Bob Hope quipped, "You'll never get on <u>this</u> show again." Tiomkin did return, however, to win his fourth Academy Award for *The Old Man and the Sea.* When musicologists wondered how scores by the great European masters might sounded if they had worked in Hollywood, they could look to a hundred scores by Dimitri Tiomkin. Tiomkin meant no disrespect to the icons of classical music. He was proudly acknowledging his debt to the great masters of the past.

THE DOUBLE LIFE OF MIKLÓS RÓZSA

Foremost among the exemplars of the romantic European tradition was Miklós Rózsa, regarded as one of the finest composers to ever write for motion pictures. Rózsa, a Hungarian, was not the typical Hollywood film composers. Just as Erich Korngold personified the tradition of Strauss and brought the sound of Viennese concert music to the screen, Rózsa had fully absorbed the rhythms, melodies and harmonies of Hungarian folk music, and the concert works of his fellow countrymen, Béla Bartók and Zoltán Kodály. Despite a career of worldwide success and distinction in film scoring, like Korngold, Rózsa never ceased to think of himself as a composer of concert music. He continued to write concert, symphonic, and chamber works throughout his time in Hollywood. He was one of the few composers who managed to successfully lead a double life creating prolifically for both films and the concert hall. He titled his autobiography *Double Life,* inspired by the name of one of his films. But Rózsa never planned to be a film composer. Born in Budapest, he was the son of an industrialist and spent part of his childhood in the mountains of rural Hungary. An early age, he discovered the authentic Magyar folksongs, which were quite different from the Gypsy melodies associated with Hungarian music by the public. Throughout his musical career, Rózsa always drew upon his Hungarian heritage.

Figure 303 - Miklós Rózsa through his 'double life,' scaled the heights of both film scoring and concert music. (Photo by and courtesy of Alexander Courage)

To please his father, Rózsa agreed to study chemistry; to please his son, Rózsa's father agreed that he could also study music. Rózsa left Budapest for Leipzig, where he studied composition with Hermann Grabner, the successor to noted German master of counterpoint, Max Reger. In 1929, Rózsa graduated from the conservatory, and his first chamber music work was published by the prominent publishing house of Breitkopf & Härtel. At the suggestion of the distinguished French organist, Marcel Dupré, he decided to seek his musical fortune in Paris. Faced with the dilemma of earning a living as a composer, he turned for advice to his friend, the Swiss composer Arthur Honegger. He was surprised to learn that Honegger was scoring films, and was so impressed with his friend's score for *Les Miserables*, that he decided to try his hand at writing for motion pictures. As an unknown composer, however, he received no offers, so he remained in Paris for several years, writing concert music. One of his ballets attracted the attention of Jacques Feyder, a French director who asked him to dinner. During the meal, a glamorous woman with a German accent asked Rózsa if her songs were ready. Rózsa was startled to learn that he had failed to recognize Marlene Dietrich, and that he was to receive his first film scoring assignment for a film starring Dietrich, *Knight Without Armour*.

Rozsa eventually moved to London, where he became associated with a flamboyant family of Hungarian motion picture producers, the Kordas, scoring their major films, including the historical drama, *The Four Feathers*. A curious aspect of Rózsa's career was that he scored a certain genre of films so brilliantly that he became typecast, like an actor, asked to continually work on motion picture of similar style and tone. Eventually, he would move on, only to become typecast as the composer of yet another group of movies. So it is easy to divide Rózsa's career, like that of some well-known painters, into distinct periods. Before arriving in Hollywood, he gained recognition scoring exotic fantasies. His early successes in California set the standard for scoring films of psychological terror and suspense. Then came his contribution to the dark, brooding movies known as *film noir*. Finally, he became known as the master of the historical film, specializing in Biblical epics and costume dramas of all periods.

When Rózsa arrived in America, he was completing the music for Alexander Korda's classic, *The Thief of Baghdad* (1940). Remarkably, Rózsa very nearly didn't score the film, because its director, Dr. Ludwig Berger wanted a score by Oscar Straus, the noted Viennese composer of operettas. Korda told Rózsa and conductor Muir Mathieson that Berger was the sole arbiter regarding music in the film. He told Berger he could use the light-hearted (and totally) inappropriate music Straus had written, then cleverly arranged for Rózsa to constantly play his own music in a room near Berger's office. Berger overheard Rózsa and quickly changed his mind. Rózsa also collaborated with Sir Robert Vansittart, a prominent British diplomat and poet, who provided lyrics for his music. The outbreak of World War II determined Rózsa's fate: he remained in California. Rózsa continued working for the Kordas, scoring such films as *Lady Hamilton*, *Lydia* and *The Jungle Book*, based on Kipling's tales. His score became the basis for the first American film score to be commercially recorded by a major film company. Rózsa's approach to *The Thief of Baghdad* and *The Jungle Book* mixed a conscious orientalism and brilliant orchestrations (inspired by Rimsky-Korsakov) with the intense contrapuntal chromaticism that became a Rózsa trademark.

In the 1940s, Rózsa became firmly identified with films expressing psychological terror. He gained this reputation by writing the intensely dramatic score for Billy Wilder's dark thriller, *Double Indemnity,* starring Barbara Stanwyck and Fred MacMurray. For this film, about adultery and a conspiracy to commit murder, Rózsa provided the ideal score: dissonant, ominous, and suspenseful. A studio music executive was critical, however, telling Rózsa contemptuously that his music belonged not in Hollywood, but in Carnegie Hall. When Rózsa said he took the reference to Carnegie Hall as a compliment, the executive sarcastically responded that it wasn't meant to be. He predicted that the studio's top executive, Buddy DeSylva, would discard the score, rendering Rózsa unemployable in the future. When DeSylva praised the score enthusiastically at a preview, this same music executive smiled at Rózsa and said, "Buddy, don't I always get you the right man for the job?"

Double Indemnity led to Rózsa's assignment as the composer of Alfred Hitchcock's *Spellbound,* for which he won his first Oscar, in 1945. In the film's most terrifying scene, Gregory Peck, obsessed with the color white, enters Ingrid Bergman's room carrying a razor and discovers that she is sleeping under a white coverlet. Rózsa's intense, passionate music featured terrifying, shrieking tremolos in the strings interrupted by muted brass. In this score, he also used an electronic instrument, the theremin, which Rózsa proudly declared he had made the official Hollywood mouthpiece of mental disorders. Producer David O. Selznick was furious when he learned Rózsa had used the theremin again in a film he had not produced. Selznick was one of the most powerful producers in Hollywood. He was unaccustomed to having anyone talk back to him. So he telephoned Rózsa to berate him for using the electronic instrument in *The Lost Weekend*, a grim movie about alcoholism. Rózsa declared he had not only used the theremin in *The Lost Weekend* but the piccolo, the trumpet, the triangle, and the violin, and hung up.

A man of fierce pride and musical integrity, Rózsa was an urbane, polished figure, known for his kindness and cultured disposition. He was an art collector, a bibliophile, and a gentleman. But he had no patience for charlatans or obnoxious producers he considered to be "vulgarians." When the multi-lingual Rózsa first arrived in Hollywood, he dealt with their abrasive crudities by protesting that he didn't speak English. When David O. Selznick asked Rózsa to participate in a type of "contest" he was conducting to among several composers he was considering to score *Duel in the Sun*, Rózsa told him he had no intention working for Selznick on this or any other picture again. Even writing his best work, Rózsa had to stand up against studio bosses. *A Double Life* was a film about an actor, portrayed by Ronald Colman, who becomes obsessed with his role as Othello. Rózsa decided to use the music of the 16th century Venetian composer Giovanni Gabrielli as a source of inspiration. Studio executives tried to force Rózsa to discard his opening music as "too modern." But director George Cukor supported Rózsa and told him, "If you change one note, I'll kill you!" Rózsa subsequently told the studio bosses they could jump in the lake, "the nearest one being Toluca." When he won his second Oscar, the studio bosses changed their tune and were eager to take publicity photos with him. He refused.

Rozsa also wrote the music for three films produced by Mark Hellinger, *The Killers* (1946), *Brute Force* (1947) and *Naked City* (1948). These were stark dramas about crime, violence, and the underworld. Rózsa broke with Hollywood traditions, producing music that reflected brutality with forceful power. His musical motif for *The Killers* eventually became the best-known musical phrase on television, the ominous theme that opened the police detective program, *Dragnet*, starring Jack Webb. Rózsa eventually adapted the music from the Hellinger films in a concert suite, *Background to Violence*.

In 1949, Rózsa wrote the music for *Mme. Bovary*, with a stunning symphonic waltz to depict the emotions that draw Emma Bovary inexorably into a love affair. Then, in 1951, with *Quo Vadis, Rózsa* began scoring the historical epics that would remain his trademark for the rest of his career. Throughout the 1950s and 1960s, producers of major historical dramas asked for the music of Miklós Rózsa, What set Rózsa's music apart from other composers in this genre was his intense historical research. He spent weeks and months studying the instruments, harmonies, melodies, and history of the various musical periods, learning all he could about the music of the Greeks and Romans (*Quo Vadis, Julius Caesar, Ben-Hur, King of Kings*), the medieval era (*Ivanhoe*), the Pilgrims, (*Plymouth Adventure*), 12th century Spain (*El Cid*), and the romantic era of painter Vincent Van Gogh (*Lust for Life*). It was never his intention to reconstruct the actual music of these periods, but to use the harmonic and orchestral colors of the periods to shape and form his own music. Each of Rózsa's scores sounds distinctly like Rózsa. Hoever, his pursuit of authenticity, combined with his own singular musical creativity made his historical scores unique.

Figure 304 - Miklós Rózsa, a rare composer who retained his principles and musical integrity while achieving great public recognition and commercial success. (Photo from the collection of Janos Sebestyen courtesy of Robert Tifft)

Throughout his years in Hollywood, Rózsa never became a "Hollywood composer," During many a musical summer he retreated to the village of Santa Margherita Ligure in Italy where he devoted himself entirely to music of his own choosing. He continued his "double life" as a composer of serious concert music, including a wide variety of orchestral pieces (usually reflecting his Hungarian spirit), chamber music, and concertos for piano, cello, viola, and violin. His *Violin Concerto*, written especially for Jascha Heifetz, was also the basis of a film score, *The Private Life of Sherlock Holmes.* Nor was he apologetic about working in Hollywood and pursuing high standards. When challenged that a true composer cannot limit the length of his musical ideas to the timings of a film, Rózsa observed that Michelangelo limited his creativity to accommodate the size of the Sistine Chapel.

Rózsa also had a sense of humor. Though he fought studio executives who considered him a dangerous modernist, he rejected many of the avant-garde and academic theories about writing music He made an oblique commentary about the followers of Schoenberg with his sole excursion into twelve-tone music, a theme for the Devil in *King of Kings.* For Rózsa, it was an "in-joke," In his memoir he wrote, "For me twelve-tone music is a stillborn idea and thus naturally and admirably suited to the Devil, the 'Spirit of Negation," the "Father of Lies," I didn't expect a cinema audience to get the message but thought it might rehabilitate me with the avant-garde. No such luck."

Rózsa's film scoring career seems to come full circle in 1977 when he was asked by French director Alain Renais to score his film, *Providence*. He was especially pleased that Renais was familiar with his concert works as well as his work for films. At one point during the collaboration, Renais told him that he didn't want any synchronization between music and visual images on the screen. Rózsa was delighted; the approach, of course, was completely the opposite of that pursued by Max Steiner, who "caught" as many pieces of action on screen as he could. For *Providence,* Rózsa composed a little piece for piano and strings which the composer titled *Valse Crépusculaire* (Twilight Waltz.) The idea for the piece came to him while walking in the narrow streets Montparnasse, recalling his early days in Paris as a young composer forty years earlier.

Rózsa set the standard for composers of the Middle-European school. He always saw himself a composer who wrote music for films, not as a "movie-composer." He was one of the few composers to pursue his "double-life" successfully, achieving incredibly high standards in both his film scores and in his music for the concert hall.

THE AMERICANS: COPLAND AND THOMSON

Inevitably, there was a reaction to the style of Middle-European romanticism in films. A number of composers, all American-born and well aware of the more dissonant styles of concert music and the rhythms and melodic designs of jazz began scoring motion pictures.

For westerns, for the realistic stories of urban America, for tales influenced by our nation's folklore, a distinctly American style was absolutely appropriate. This style was strongly influenced by Aaron Copland, although he himself scored only a few films. In 1939, Copland, already established as a major composer of concert music, was invited to score *The City*, depicting American life for the New York World's Fair.

The following year, Copland wrote the score for the filmed adaptation of John Steinbeck's classic, *Of Mice and Men,* the latter conducted by Paramount's masterful musical director, Irvin Talbot. Also in 1940, Copland provided the score (again conducted by Irvin Talbot) for the movie based on Thornton Wilder's classic play about life in a small New England village, *Our Town*. For the open countryside, Copland used open brass, solo winds, and quiet strings. His music became livelier as the leading characters visit the local soda fountain, somber and austere for scenes in the village cemetery. The serenity and stability of Grover's Corners, New Hampshire was clearly reflected in Copland's music. Copland's style in these scores was typical of his concert music, the lean, occasionally stark melodic lines, pure harmonies, folk-like nationalism He adapted excerpts from his film scores in a suite, *Music for the Movies*.

Copland's style could be described as a reaction to what had become accepted as the "Hollywood sound." lush orchestrations and a sweeping melodic style derived from Middle European symphonic and operatic literature. But Copland was not so much reacting as composing for films in the same way he wrote for the concert stage. Copland never settled in Hollywood. He scored *The North Star*, a filmed tribute to Russia, which faded from popularity as the Soviet Union was transformed from wartime ally to Cold War adversary.

Figure 305 - Aaron Copland scored only a few films and protested the excesses of Hollywood, but he influenced film scoring through his pupils and admirers he influenced. (Photo by and courtesy of Alexander Courage)

In 1949, Copland was invited to score another film based on the work of John Steinbeck, *The Red Pony*. The principal figure of the tale is Tom Tiflin, who lives with his parents on a California ranch and his reaction to the life and death of his beloved red pony. Copland captured the spirit of cowboys and ranch life, not as done typically in Hollywood, as a musical epic with Russian overtones, but with tuneful and triadic music. Nature, directness, and simplicity were reflected by folk tunes. Copland never tried imitating the wind or the birds; his short phrases were models of clarity. Busy woodwinds accompanied the frying eggs and crackling bacon as dawn came to the ranch. The awkwardness of a trotting horse was augmented by a basic time stream of five, alternating 3/4 and 2/4 measures. The tone of an imaginary army was accompanied by a melody for toy trumpet and tuba. Copland made his score seem "western" through the irregularity and ambling, awkward line of his melodies, a free-wheeling angularity. He used dissonance to depict the harsh realities of life on the ranch, such as the sequence in which Tom fights off some preying buzzards.

The same year, Copland scored a major Hollywood production, *The Heiress*. It was not a happy experience for Copland. His music made a major contribution to film, an adaptation of Henry James' novel, *Washington Square*. This was the story of a shy, plain girl who is betrayed by a dashing opportunist in pursuit of her considerable fortune. In a key scene, Olivia de Havilland rushed out of her house, but audiences responded to an ostensibly tragic scene with laughter. When Copland's music was added, his dissonance reflected the bitterness and despair of her mood. The audiences laughed no longer. Unfortunately, Copland's opening music was replaced in part (without his knowledge or permission) by an arrangement of the song, "Plaisir d'Amour." While this was typical of the way composers were treated by producers and directors in Hollywood, Copland was shocked. Unaccustomed to such behavior, he ran an advertisement disclaiming responsibility for the episode and won an Academy Award for the score anyway. Copland, an independent-minded fellow, was only given one more film scoring assignment, eleven years later.

Copland's friend and colleague Virgil Thomson also tried his hand at scoring films during this period. In 1936, director Pare Lorentz asked Thomson to score his documentary, *The Plough That Broke the Plains*. Like Copland, Thomson approached motion pictures exactly as he approached concert music. For this movie about the desolation of the American terrain during the Depression, Thomson created a mood of pathos and loneliness, punctuated by hymns, folk-like tunes, homespun harmonies, and sparse orchestrations.

Also included were orchestral settings of cowboy melodies, including "I Ride on Old Paint" and "Git Along Little Dogies." In one remarkable sequence depicting the devastation of the land, Thomson used the dance music associated with the carefree 1920s, a tango. Played at a very slow tempo, the dance portrays triumph turned to tragedy.

Thomson took a similar approach for another Lorentz documentary, *The River*. He drew upon quotations from tunes like "Dixie" and "A Hot Time in the Old Town Tonight," the hymns that always seem to appear in Thomson's works, and a musical imitation of hammering sounds from a factory. Thomson returned to film scoring in 1948, for Robert Flaherty's *Louisiana Story*, depicting the dilemma of a Cajun trapper confronting the arrival of oil derricks and machinery. Thomson used authentic Cajun melodies and even wrote a fugue for a battle between a young boy and an alligator. Thomson was always uncomfortable with Hollywood film scoring and he never became active as a Hollywood composer. Though Copland and Thomson scored only a few films, they demonstrated that a new American style of scoring could add new musical dimensions to the movies. Alex North, a Copland pupil, became one of the most important American film composers of the 1950s and 60s. And other American composers of similar inclinations stayed in Hollywood and pursued a new, individualistic American style. Foremost among these composers were David Raksin and Hugo W. Friedhofer.

Figure 306 - Virgil Thomson made his mark in motion pictures scoring documentary films. (Carl Van Vechten collection. Courtesy of Library of Congress Public Domain)

THE BAD AND BEAUTIFUL ADVENTURES OF DAVID RAKSIN

David Raksin, was known to his friends and colleagues as perhaps the most articulate of all film composers. A man of verbal as well as musical brilliance, he combined his superb musical talents with the instincts of a teacher who could explain and analyze the true functions of music in motion pictures. Armed with an ironic sense of humor, a predilection for puns, and a sharp wit, he was always aware of the dilemma of writing Hollywood film scores: the pursuit of art in a land of commerce. A native of Philadelphia, he was raised in a musical family. His father was a composer and conductor in the silent film era, directing theater orchestras. He graduated from the University of Pennsylvania, where he studied with Harl McDonald, and went to New York, where he joined Benny Goodman's band as a saxophonist. He sold a complex arrangement of George Gershwin's *I Got Rhythm* to Al Goodman, a Broadway conductor. Through Al Goodman he met pianist Oscar Levant. Levant introduced him to Gershwin, who in turn recommended him for a job as an arranger at a major publishing house, Harms.

In time, Raksin was summoned to Hollywood by Alfred Newman to work with Charlie Chaplin on the score for *Modern Times.* Chaplin wanted to write his own score for the 1936 film, but he was not a trained musician. He could whistle, sing, and pick out melodies on the piano. Raksin notated, developed, harmonized, and expanded Chaplin's ideas.

Chaplin's perspective came from the English music hall; Raksin understood modern jazz and sophisticated contemporary concert music. The two men inevitably clashed, but Newman praised Raksin's sketches, Chaplin agreed to continue the collaboration. Raksin and Edward B. Powell orchestrated the score, which contained the haunting and sentimental melody, *Smile.* Raksin remained intensely loyal to Chaplin, declaring that Chaplin's musical approach was right for the types of films he made. He was always careful not to claim credit for Chaplin's musical themes; but at the same time, he was proud of the contributions he made to Chaplin's work, without which the successful score for *Modern Times* would have been impossible.

Figure 307 - The team from *Modern Times*: Charles Dunworth, conductor Alfred Newman, star Charlie Chaplin, composer David Raksin, sound engineer Paul G. Neal, orchestrator Edward B. Powell. (Photo by Autrey, all rights reserved. Courtesy of David Raksin and Paul G. Neal)

Raksin remained an orchestrator

at 20th Century Fox, writing ballet music and arrangements. Then in 1944, he was given an assignment that would change his own career and the art of film scoring forever. *Laura* is the story of a hard-boiled New York detective (portrayed by Dana Andrews) who becomes fascinated by the portrait of a beautiful woman, Laura Hunt (Gene Tierney), whose murder he is investigating. He finds himself falling in love with her, requiring an obvious musical accompaniment of great importance. *Laura* was reportedly a motion picture with problems. Fox's Musical Director Alfred Newman was too busy to do the score; it was offered to the outspoken Bernard Herrmann, who reportedly declared that if it wasn't good enough for Newman, it wasn't good enough for him either. So the assignment fell to David Raksin. Raksin stunned everyone by challenging studio boss Darryl F. Zanuck. A key scene, in which the detective falls in love with Laura while listening to her music and looking at her portrait, despite the fact that he is investigating her murder, was nearly cut from the film. No one ever spoke up to studio bosses, but Raksin did, to the astonishment of a music executive so obsequious that he was known by the unflattering nickname of "hinge-head."

With the scene remaining in the script, the film's autocratic director, Otto Preminger, wanted a sophisticated, haunting theme for *Laura*. Ira Gershwin had turned down Newman's request to use his late brother's classic, *Summertime,* so Preminger settled upon Duke Ellington's *Sophisticated Lady*. Of course, Raksin wanted the opportunity to write his own theme. Raksin was given only a weekend to produce something original. He struggled all weekend, to no avail, his thoughts on a letter he had just received, in his words, "from a lady with whom I was in love and to whom I was married." On Sunday night, he put the letter on the piano, read it, realized that the lady was saying "goodbye," and began improvising. In a few moments, he played the opening notes of what would become "Laura," the most popular melody every to emerge from a motion picture score.

Reactions to *Laura* were enthusiastic. Mail poured into the studio requesting copies of the melody, inquiring about lyrics to the tune and asking for Raksin's autograph. Raksin objected to early attempts to write lyrics to his melody and eventually asked that Johnny Mercer be engaged. Raksin compared Mercer to a world-famous high-wire walker, dubbing him "The flying Wallenda of lyricists" Mercer succeeded where other had failed. "Laura" became one of the most recorded songs of all time. But Raksin never played the melody all the way through in the film

Figure 308 - *The Timeless Melodies of David Raksin*. The composer's photo, substituted for iconic picture of Dana Andrews gazing at a portrait of Gene Tierney and listening to "Laura." (Photo courtesy of Susan Andrews, used by special permission. Collection (c) 1996 by EKay Music, Inc. All rights reserved)

and disapproved of its use as a typical "love theme" when the film was remade years later as a television special. Producers and directors never learn. Incredibly, while planning a television version of *Laura,* producer David Susskind considered a plan to hire a composer to write a new "theme from *Laura,*" and only later relented to use Raksin's famed melody.

Raksin emerged from the experience of *Laura* as a major film composer. His approach to his many future films was always highly original and frequently experimental. *Forever Amber* was a drama set during the English Restoration period. Raksin originally considered using authentic 17th century English music. Instead, he decided to use period instruments (including the oboe d'amore and the lute). Like Sergei Prokofiev's *Classical Symphony*, Raksin's score for *Forever Amber* reflected a respect for the past while remaining modern. Raksin composed a distinctive melody over the accompaniment of a bass scale. The melody represented Amber, while the bass scale became the "cantus firmus" of a sequence described by Raksin as a "quasicaglia," neither a passacaglia or a basso ostinato, but "combining the worst features of both." Raksin's opening music for the film consisted of thirty-two variations on a ground bass, and he declared his score contained "more canons than a Balkan uprising." *Forever Amber* included such pieces as "The Anacron Overture" (a pun derived from Luigi Cherubini's "Anacreon Overture,") "The King's Mistress," a spirited fanfare, "The Wench," some sensitive melodic writing, and a furious, contrapuntal accompaniment to the great fire of London.

Figure 309 - Two composers known for the scores for films starring Dana Andrews: David Raksin *(Laura)* and composer colleague Leith Stevens *(Night Song)* at an awards ceremony. (Photo by and courtesy of Alexander Courage)

Raksin always tried never to do the same thing twice. In *Force of Evil*, he produced an amazing final sequence opening with a chromatic solo played by the alto saxophone. Gradually, woodwinds enter, creating a tapestry of polytonal and polytriadic chords. Raksin was never afraid of dissonance, but his dissonances grew out of his complex melodic lines. When he scored *The Bad and the Beautiful.* a saga about an unscrupulous producer and the people whose careers he affected, he again created a remarkable melody. The melodic line, characterized by wide leaps and sophisticated harmonies, was anything but a "Tin-Pan Alley" tune. People were initially startled by the range and scope of this unusual melody, but eventually Raksin's theme was recorded and became one of his most memorable creations.

His other scores included films of every type: his taste and talent, combined with a seriousness of purpose created problems for him on occasion. For *Carrie,* he produced a dramatic score with complex thematic development only to have the score's most important sequences shredded by studio executives. He had a similar experience with *Separate Tables*, creating an elaborate fugue on a nine-tone row, only to have the sections of the score arbitrarily cut by executives without regard to the structure or design of the music. A versatile composer, his credits included everything from animated cartoons (*The Unicorn and the Garden*), dark, brooding crime dramas (*Al Capone*), westerns (*Will Penny*), and perhaps his most unusual score, *The Redeemer*, a movie about the life of Christ, for which he penned an extraordinary tribute to Johann Sebastian Bach.

Raksin never stopped learning or teaching. When Arnold Schoenberg settled in Los Angeles, Raksin took time out to study with him. Raksin was always attracted to musical complexity; some colleagues smiled when told that Schoenberg, known himself for an extremely complex approach to composition, pointed to one of Raksin's pieces and said, "Don't you think this is just a little bit complicated?" Later, David Raksin taught regularly at several universities, conducting classes not only in film music, but in subjects as far-reaching as urban ecology. He was also a gifted writer and wrote an extensive memoir, *The Bad and the Beautiful*, titled after his favorite film theme. He continued actively composing concert music and articulating his belief in film scoring as an art capable of high standards and polished craftsmanship until shortly before his death in 2004. His musical deeds of a lifetime matched his words.

HUGO FRIEDHOFER: A TRUE GIANT AMONG HOLLYWOOD PYGMIES

Figure 310 - Hugo Friedhofer, called by David Raksin, 'the most learned of us all." (Photo courtesy of Hugo Friedhofer)

David Raksin was generous in his praise of those composers whom he admired; he admired none more than his longtime friend and colleague, Hugo W. Friedhofer. Raksin called Friedhofer "the most learned of us all and often the most subtle." Friedhofer was considered a master by his most accomplished colleagues. Raksin declared, "Hugo Friedhofer was a paradoxical figure. On the one hand, he was surely one of the most learned, most accomplished members of our profession, a fine composer, a master of the orchestra, quick to perceive what was required of the music for a film and sure-footed in providing that music. But there was also the man who knew too much, the virtuoso of self-doubt who never seemed to have learned to take "yes" for an answer." Raksin was not alone. Henry Mancini said of Friedhofer, "An affirmative nod from the man is worth more than all of the trinkets bestowed by the film industry."

Yet Friedhofer's name never became a household word among the general public. When he died in 1981, his friend Gene Lees called the *New York Times,* offering stories and anecdotes about Friedhofer's significant contributions to the world of film music, his musical erudition, and his role as an articulator of curmudgeonly wit and wisdom. The Arts and Leisure editor of *The New York Times* had never heard of Hugo Friedhofer. This was, in microcosm, the story of Friedhofer's career. Within the film music community, he was regarded as a master craftsman who always pursued artistic excellence over commerciality. Other composers went to him for advice and guidance. Yet in his entire lifetime, he heard his music performed in public only twice.

Friedhofer freely acknowledged the influence of Aaron Copland in his work. Yet Friedhofer himself was pursuing a distinctly American style of composing before Copland's film scores and he continued to explore new horizons in the art of composing for motion pictures. Hugo Wilhelm Friedhofer was born in San Francisco. He came from a family of German musicians who had settled in California. His father was a professional cellist who began teaching his son the instrument when the younger Freidhofer was only 13. After briefly considering a career as an artist, Hugo Friedhofer followed in his father's footsteps as a cellist. He studied composition with the composer Domenic Brescia, a classmate of Ottorino Respighi in Italy. With the advent of sound films, theater orchestras disbanded. Friedhofer found himself unemployed, and moved to Hollywood at the suggestion of his friend, violinist George Lipschultz, who became musical director at Fox Studios. Friedhofer later went to Warner Brothers, where he orchestrated for Max Steiner and Erich Wolfgang Korngold. Friedhofer spoke fluent German and could communicate easily with the demanding Korngold, who appreciated his skill as an orchestrator and used him in that capacity for most of his major classic film scores. He also worked on many of Max Steiner's major scores including *Gone With the Wind.* Unfortunately, Friedhofer was such a fine orchestrator that Leo Forbstein, head of the Warner Brothers music department, never assigned him scores as a composer. But when Alfred Newman recommended him to Samuel Goldwyn for *The Adventures of Marco Polo,* Friedhofer's career as a film composer began in earnest.

Friedhofer believed that music could provide a counterpoint to the visual action of a film. He rejected the idea that a person running on the screen must be accompanied by music which also runs. He suggested that the difference between Brahms and Tchaikovsky was one of objectivity. Friedhofer observed, "Tchaikovsky says 'How unhappy I am' while Brahms says 'How tragic this is.'" Friedhofer was a musician of the Brahmsian variety.

In 1946, Friedhofer scored *The Best Years of Our Lives,* the tale of three veterans returning from World War II. Though the film contained elements of sentiment, emotion, and romance, it did not call for a lush, symphonic score. Friedhofer's approach set the standard for what could be done in the realm of musical Americana. He composed a variety of themes for the characters and situations in the film. His melodies were sturdy and straightforward. Friedhofer could work wonders with the notes of simple, major chords. There were themes for Boone City, for the relationship between Homer, a key character, and the girl next door. One of the melodies Friedhofer wrote, for the character of Wilma, became known as the "Best Years Theme." For one scene, in which Homer smashes a tool shed window, Friedhofer wrote a set of variations on a familiar children's theme. Without the actual sounds of war, he even managed to create a sense of bombing through music, underscoring the memories of the returning veterans. Friedhofer was a lifelong devotee of chamber music, and he loved to use small orchestral combinations to make a musical statement. Unfortunately, director William Wyler had expected a lush, symphonic score filled with romantic melodies. He disliked Friedhofer's score, and the composer was treated like a pariah by most people associated with the picture. Only when composer Marc Blitzstein, a friend of Wyler's, approved of the score did the director soften. When Friedhofer won the Oscar for his *Best Years* score, Wyler and others instantly changed their tune.

Friedhofer followed his success with *The Best of Years of Our Lives* with numerous other scores: lightly satirical music in the Baroque style for *The Bishop's Wife, Joan of Arc* (for which he adapted a medieval-style composition he had written to accompany one of his daughter's college projects) and such varied films as *Above and Beyond, Vera-Cruz, Between Heaven and Hell, An Affair to Remember, The Sun Also Rises, Boy on a Dolphin, The Young Lions, and One-Eyed Jacks.* Friedhofer approached each motion picture with an adventurous spirit, exploring new ideas, testing new boundaries. He remained perpetually curious. Though a finished professional qualified to teach at any university, he continued studying, with master teachers Arnold Schoenberg, Ernst Toch, and Ernest Kanitz, and eventually conducted his own master classes for eager students who came to the small Hollywood apartment where he spent his last years, during a time when serious film composers were not in demand.

For *The Sun Also Rises,* he used the jazz sounds of the 1920s, and Cole Porter's song, "You Do Something To Me." But Friedhofer didn't "plug" the song as a love-theme, he used as a basis for melodic variations. In *Boy on a Dolphin,* he developed themes for Greek instruments and used elements of Greek folk music, and a *vocalise*, a highly unusual wordless melody sung by a single human voice belonging to soprano Marni Nixon, to create a sense of mystery under water. Friedhofer believed that stories set in Mexico should reflect Mexican music, not Spanish music, a subtle distinction. He believed he had finally discovered a new, non-European harmonic language by the time he scored *Vera-Cruz;* his music for Marlon Brando's unusual (and ill-fated) western, *One-Eyed Jacks* also reflected a Mexican mood, but concentrated on the dramatic nature of the film with little references to cowboy music or western clichés.

Together with his friend David Raksin, Friedhofer took delight in exploring the concert works of Hindemith, Copland, and Stravinsky. He said he wanted to pursue simplicity of line, clarity of texture, and an avoidance of overly chromatic harmonies that sounded as if they just got off the boat from Europe. Pupils and colleagues were awed by his knowledge of music. (Colleagues in the studios played a game, trying each day to stump him with a question about music extracted from Grove's Dictionary. They seldom succeeded.) Armed with a photographic memory, he recalled the most obscure names, dates, and facts from every period of music history. Friedhofer was famous for a droll wit and a pungent sense of humor. He disliked self-praise. When faced with the adulation of colleagues (and less recognition from the public and the studio bosses), he quipped "I'm an imaginary giant in a land of real pygmies."

CITIZEN HERRMANN: A GULLIVER AMONG THE LILLIPUTIANS

Many films have been produced since Orson Welles starred in the masterpiece he also directed, *Citizen Kane*. Yet numerous critics still regard the film as the finest of all time. Just as films were never the same after the arrival of the prodigious Welles in Hollywood, the world of motion picture music was changed forever by the arrival of Welles's personal choice as composer, Bernard Herrmann.

Herrmann, like Welles, became a Hollywood legend, and with good reason. Many film composers came to their work with backgrounds in Tin Pan Alley, Broadway musicals, or dance band arranging. Herrmann was a highly original composer and conductor of concert music. He was also a rugged individualist, an iconoclast who had no tolerance of those who placed commerce before art. He was a study in contrasts, a man with a volcanic temperament, outwardly a brash and bombastic New Yorker, privately a scholarly Anglophile. Herrmann had an encyclopedic knowledge of music; he was as comfortable discussing the unfamiliar Baroque chamber music or unperformed 19th century operas as he was reacting to the headlines in the morning paper. He took delight in discovering the work of obscure composers and introducing the public to little-known masterpieces through his activities as conductor of the CBS Symphony Orchestra.

Figure 311 - Bernard Herrmann with his beloved dog, Twilight, in a pose reminiscent of Sir Edward Elgar and his dog. (Photo by John Engstead courtesy Bernard Herrmann Estate, all rights reserved)

Herrmann was born in New York in 1911, and studied with Bernard Wagenaar at the Juilliard School of Music and at New York University with Philip James and Percy Grainger. He found a special rapport with Grainger, a brilliant nonconformist (and some would say eccentric) piano virtuoso from Australia who specialized in the music of Grieg. Like Grainger, Herrmann would, throughout his life, detest those whose approach to music was pedantic or scientific. For Herrmann, music, like life, was an emotional experience. As a teenager, he enjoyed a meteoric rise in music, eventually joining the staff of CBS as composer and conductor. He contributed music to many of the finest radio programs of the times, working with such pioneers as Norman Corwin and Orson Welles. For the latter, Herrmann served as musical director of the famed Mercury Theater broadcasts, including the controversial *War of the Worlds* program which persuaded thousands of listeners that the country had really been invaded by Martians. When Herrmann arrived in Hollywood, he was an exception to all rules. (His friend and colleague Miklós Rózsa would call him "A Gulliver among the Lilliputians of film music.") He had just been appointed conductor of the CBS Symphony, a position he would hold for fifteen years. He approached his film scores with the same expectations of creative achievement and artistic integrity he sought in his concert works. (He had a symphony, a violin concerto, and a cantata to his credit when he began working on *Citizen Kane*.)

Figure 312 - Bernard Herrmann was a composer-conductor of integrity, a rugged individualist, and an irascible genius. (Photo by and courtesy of Alexander Courage)

Herrmann continually sought to exploit, expand, and explore the ranges of orchestral instruments. He never used the same orchestral combination twice, frequently assembling the most unusual ensembles ever seen on a Hollywood sound stage. He always orchestrated his own music, and throughout his career expressed contempt for composers who followed the Hollywood practice of having their music orchestrated by others. While others deferred obsequiously to studio bosses and producers, Herrmann bluntly told them what he thought of them, frequently at the top of his lungs. Herrmann quietly championed the work of composers he admired, but his outspoken nature and explosive temperament made him a standard-bearer for musical integrity, not tact or diplomacy. His scores reflected impeccable taste, musicianship, and artistry, despite a plethora of economic and corporate pressures to the contrary. Many of the films on which he worked became classics, to no small degree because of his contribution. Herrmann had an uncanny ability to express emotions through sound. He added music to film as a painter selects colors for his canvas. Herrmann's first score, *Citizen Kane*, established that his approach was different from anything Hollywood seen before or since.

Although Herrmann was not a devotee of leitmotifs, he knew how to use them. Two musical ideas were created to reflect conflict in the life of Charles Foster Kane, the character derived from the life of publishing tycoon William Randolph Hearst: one, identified with the sled "Rosebud," reflected the lost innocence of Kane's youth, the other, a "power" motif, reflected Kane's driving ambition. The opening shots of the film appear without music; then the somber brass chords create an ominous mood. Herrmann instinctively knew when to use music and when not to use it. For a montage sequence depicting Kane and his first wife at breakfast, Herrmann wrote variations on a sentimental waltz, each more dissonant and frenetic than the last, as the marriage dissolves from wedded bliss to outright hostility. When Susan Alexander, Kane's second wife, pursues a disastrous debut as an opera singer, Herrmann decided to write an original aria for an imaginary opera, *Salammbo*. He selected a soprano with a light voice and had her sing in a key too high for her natural register, creating what he called "a terrified girl lost in the quicksand of a powerful orchestra."

Herrmann's next score, *All That Money Can Buy*, was released in 1941, the same year as *Citizen Kane*. It was based on Stephen Vincent Benét's classic, *The Devil and Daniel Webster*. This is the Faustian fable of an New England farmer who sells his soul to the devil to achieve good fortune, appeals to Daniel Webster to help him break the contract, and ultimately faces trial before a jury of America's worst traitors and scoundrels. Every note of music added something special to the score: a nervously alive, roguish, wily theme for the devil, Mr. Scratch, including a sound-effect derived from a singing telephone wire recorded at 4 a.m., a scherzo for sleigh bells accompanying a diabolical sleigh ride for Mr. Scratch's victims, and an eerie *danse macabre* as the devil claims the soul of Miser Stevens. The pastoral New England countryside, sturdy New Hampshire trees, and frolicking barn dances all received their musical due. Herrmann's score included a violin solo too difficult to be played a single violinist. He arranged for violinist Louis Kaufman to record "Pop Goes the Weasel" several times, each version containing some of Kaufman's own "virtuoso tricks" displaying his technical brilliance. Then he had the solos recorded on top of each other so it sounded as if the piece were being executed by a single musician, described by Kaufman as a "dynamic sonic montage for the violinistic Beezelbub, Mr. Scratch." Herrmann won plaudits (and the Oscar) for *All That Money Can Buy*. The violin solo also won the attention of the world's most famous concert violinist Jascha Heifetz. Unaccustomed to hearing any piece of music that he couldn't execute technically, Heifetz asked Herrmann the name of the violinist who played the solo. Herrmann said, "Oh, a Hungarian fiddler I picked up."

Next came another collaboration with Welles, *The Magnificent Ambersons*, echoing his stylistic approach to *Citizen Kane*. The score magnificently reflects not only the decline of the wealthy Amberson family but 19th century Americana: the ragtime rhythms of a Saturday Night Band Concert and a set of variations on one of Welles's favorite waltzes, Émile Waldteufel's *Toujours ou Jamais*. For the Aldous Huxley-John Houseman adaptation of *Jane Eyre*, Herrmann demonstrated his affinity with Charlotte Brontë. The loneliness of the moors, the gloomy and passionate nature of the novel was reflected in the music. For

Rochester's ride across the moors, the raging fires, and the violent storm sequence, Herrmann's orchestra snarls and trembles with fear and fury.

In 1947, Bernard Herrmann composed music for *The Ghost and Mrs. Muir,* reportedly his own favorite of his scores, undeniably elevating motion picture scoring to the level of high art. For this tale of a young English widow who falls in love with the irascible ghost of a sea captain, adapted in a superb screenplay by Philip Dunne. Herrmann wrote his most romantic music. Gene Tierney starred as Mrs. Muir and Rex Harrison portrayed Captain Gregg. George Sanders played the scoundrel who was the captain's flesh and blood rival. Herrmann's harmonic vocabulary and orchestral colors were stunning. He produced a passionate melody for Mrs. Muir's illusory romance with a suave, but charming cad, and a haunting motif for oboe and strings when the ghost bids Mrs. Muir farewell. Without the music, a fine actor is speaking his lines. With music, he could only be a ghost. The sounds of the sea, the crashing waves against the rocks all seem to emanate naturally from Herrmann's orchestra. In later years, when Mrs. Muir recalls the ghost, Herrmann provides an exquisitely ethereal string accompaniment. The film revealed an element of Herrmann's musical character that is often overlooked. He had a special affinity for the wistful, nostalgic, and ethereal sounds that reflect a longing for another time and place. He expressed this mood again years later while scoring *Walking Distance,* an episode of the television series, *The Twilight Zone,* in which a man tries to go back in time to experience childhood. Herrmann's exquisitely haunting music for strings and harp reflects writer Rod Serling's "little errant wish that a man might never grow old, never outgrow the merry go rounds of his youth." It was one of the finest television scores of all time.

In the 1950s, Herrmann remained active, scoring a wide variety of films, always with his trademarks: a capacity to reflect the inner emotional core of a film and an amazing instinct for orchestration. In *The Snows of Kilimanjaro*, he produced the haunting *Memory Waltz*, a melody filled with yearning for the past. In *The Day The Earth Stood Still,* he looked to the future with his own "science fiction orchestra": two theremins, electric violin, electric guitar, three organs, two pianos, two harps, timpani, and four tubas.

In 1955, Herrmann began an association with director Alfred Hitchcock that resulted in some of the finest film scores ever written. Hitchcock was known as the master of suspense. The element of suspense was frequently sustained or created by the music of Bernard Herrmann. For *The Trouble with Harry,* Herrmann created a score which is alternates between the pastoral sounds of the New England countryside and the comically macabre mischief as villagers ineptly try to conceal a corpse. In *The Man Who Knew Too Much*, Herrmann actually appeared on screen conducting Arthur Benjamin's cantata, *The Storm Clouds.* Herrmann could take an idea and turn it into a musical mood. For *Vertigo,* he composed a dizzying musical main title, as the orchestra turns, twists, and swirls to set the mood for the entire film. (The score also contained Herrmann's *Scene d'Amour,* a soaring musical sequence comparable in intensity to the *Liebestod* from

Wagner's *Tristan and Isolde*.) Herrmann's music for the suspense thriller *North by Northwest* was unprecedented. Instead of typical "big city music," he created a stunning orchestral fandango, with its driving Spanish dance rhythms, and sustained it in scenes from Manhattan to Mount Rushmore. For *Psycho*, a black and white film, Herrmann scared the daylights out of audiences with his "black and white orchestra," an all-string ensemble. Even the terrifying murder in the shower is accompanied by slashing sound effects produced entirely by strings. No composer using sound effects or computers has ever produced anything more frightening.

Herrmann's collaboration with Hitchcock did not end happily. When Herrmann wrote the score for *Torn Curtain,* he took the idea of the Iron Curtain in East Germany literally: an "iron" quality to the orchestra with twelve flutes, sixteen horns, nine trombones, two tubas, two sets of timpani, eight cellos, and eight basses. The famed director succumbed to pressures for a "pop score with a beat." Hitchcock canceled the recording session and the two never worked together again. The studio executives who to whom Hitchcock answered had little sympathy for Herrmann. After the *Torn Curtain* episode, Universal boss Lew Wasserman, displaying the warmth and compassion of a true movie mogul, told Herrmann, "Benny, come see me when you get hungry." Herrmann responded, "Lew, when I get hungry, I go to Chasen's."

Herrmann also worked several times with special effects wizard Ray Harryhausen on such films as *The Seventh Voyage of Sinbad, The Three Worlds of Gulliver, Mysterious Island,* and *Jason and the Argonauts.* For these films of fantasy, Herrmann used his skill at orchestration to bring the figures of mythology and legends to life. In *Sinbad,* he created an astonishing accompaniment for a duel with skeletons, using xylophones, woodblocks, castanets, and whip to depict the wooden nature of these terrifying adversaries. Woodwind trills, string tremolos, and brass flutter-tonguing create a giant orchestral buzz for the giant bee in *Mysterious Island*. The French director Francois Truffaut also worked with Herrmann, on *Fahrenheit 451* and *The Bride Wore Black,* telling him other composers would write 20th century music, but that Herrmann would write music for the 21st. Though Herrmann could be categorized as one of the few geniuses produced by the world of film music, he would have undoubtedly rejected the description. He saw himself as a composer who wrote for films, not as a "film composer." In the words of his friend David Raksin, "He was an artist and warrior in the cause of his art." His film scores set the standard to which others now aspire.

THE BRITISH WERE COMING

British actors contributed greatly to American films. Quite a number, including Ronald Colman and Basil Rathbone, settled in Hollywood and formed "The British Colony," dubbed by author Sheridan Morley, "The Hollywood Raj." They played cricket, enjoyed tea, and maintained thoroughly British customs, led by Sir C. Aubrey Smith. (Actor Robert

Morley once playfully warned actress Gladys Cooper, "There's an American on your lawn.")

During the 1940s, 1950s, and 1960s, there were many fine film scores written by British composers. As we are primarily exploring American films, their accomplishments are a small detour for us. But we shouldn't, under any circumstances, ignore the work of major composers, who worked primarily in Great Britain. Major British composers of concert music found no stigma in London if they wrote for the movies. More often, they did not specialize in film scores. Some worked exclusively in Britain, while others contributed to American films as well.

Scott of the Antarctic, the score that called for a wind machine and a female choir to depict the brutal landscape of the region, is the best remembered film score by Sir Ralph Vaughan Williams, who eventually turned it into the starkly unforgettable *Sinfonia Antarctica*. Although Vaughan Williams scored only a half-dozen feature films, each was accompanied by such distinguished music that he is still recognized as a major film composer. He wrote the scores for *49th Parallel*, *Coastal Command*, *The Flemish Farm*, *The Loves of Joanna Godden*, and *Bitter Springs*.

The film version of Charles Dickens' classic, *Nicholas Nickleby*, was scored by Lord Berners, an English aristocrat, known as a gifted composer who was famous for his eccentricity. His Rolls-Royce had a small clavichord and he kept a sign at the top of the stairs of his home that said, "No Dogs Allowed."

Another Dickens adaption, *Oliver Twist*, was brilliantly scored by Sir Arnold Bax, an English poet and author as well as a musician. Bax dismissed advocates of Schoenberg's twelve-tone technique by declaring that their approach could express neuroses, but not such happy concepts as young love or the coming of spring.

A number of British films contained miniature concertos or rhapsodies that impressed concertgoers as well as movie audiences. *Men of Two Worlds* contained a miniature piano concerto based partly on African rhythms. It was composed by Sir Arthur Bliss. *Love Story* introduced Hubert Bath's *Cornish Rhapsody* and *While I Live* presented Charles Williams' *The Dream of Olwen*. The best-known of the "movie concertos" was Richard Addinsell's *Warsaw Concerto*, first heard in *Dangerous Moonlight*. It reflected the style of Rachmaninoff, who declined to write the piece himself. Ironically, Addinsell's own style was entirely British in such classic films as *Goodbye, Mr. Chips*; *Blithe Spirit*; *A Christmas Carol*; *A Tale of Two Cities*; *Tom Brown's Schooldays*; and *Waltz of the Toreadors*, to mention only a few.

Alfred Hitchcock's production, *The Man Who Knew Too Much*, featured Arthur Benjamin's stunning *Storm Clouds Cantata* which was reused when the film was remade with a classic Bernard Herrmann score. Benjamin was a distinguished Australian composer who also scored the film adaptation of Oscar Wilde's play, *An Ideal Husband*. Wilde's most famous play, *The Importance of Being Earnest*, was scored by Benjamin Frankel, a former dance band arranger who became a serious concert composer and prominent teacher. The film also featured an unforgettable performance by Dame Edith Evans as Lady Bracknell.

Laurence Olivier's adaptations of Shakespeare's plays, *Henry V*, *Hamlet*, and *Richard III*, all featured scores by Sir William Walton, one of Britain's most admired concert music composers. The stirring fanfares, the pathos of the *Funeral March* from *Hamlet*, and the furious music for the Battle of Agincourt in *Henry V* were quite memorable and Walton's film music resurfaced as concert works.

Alan Rawsthorne's family did not want him to become a composer, so he tried studying dentistry. His friend, the composer Constant Lambert, said that Rawsthorne assured him that he had given up dentistry, "even as a hobby." Rawsthorne insisted that the first essential of a good film composer was a talent for composing. Said Rawsthorne, "Film music must be genuine music." His best-known scores were for *The Cruel Sea*, *The Captive Heart*, *Uncle Silas*, and *Sarabande for Dead Lovers*.

Two noted British composers had a special interest in dance. Constant Lambert was a musical prodigy who achieved his greatest successes in early days as a composer. He was also an expert on art and literature. He had a great interest in dance and was best-known for his ballets. He produced a major critique of contemporary music, *Music Ho!*. Lambert also scored several films, including *Anna Karenina*.

Leighton Lucas was a former ballet dancer who became a fine composer. He scored Alfred Hitchcock's *Stage Fright*, which included the memorable "Eve's Rhapsody," *Ice Cold in Alex*, and numerous other British films of the 1940s and 1950s. During the same period, Walt Disney formed a British-based production company that released historical dramas, including *Treasure Island* and *The Sword and the Rose*, scored by the prolific film composer Clifton Parker.

William Alwyn's film scores included *The Mudlark*, *The Crimson Pirate*, *Shake Hands with the Devil*, and a pair of Disney features, *Swiss Family Robinson* and *In Search of the Castaways*. When Alwyn wasn't working on his seventy film scores, he was busy composing numerous symphonies, operas, ballets, and chamber music works, concertizing on the flute, and teaching for three decades.

Not all British films were scored by British composers. Georges Auric was a member of the celebrated group of adventurous young composers (including Darius Milhaud, Francis Poulenc, and Arthur Honegger) known as *Les Six*, who rebelled against tradition in Paris during the 1920s. Auric scored such British classics as *Caesar and Cleopatra*, *Passport to Pimlico*, and *The Lavender Hill Mob*. His Parisian theme from the film, *Moulin Rouge* became an international hit. He also scored numerous French and American movies, ranging from Jean Cocteau's *La Belle et La Bête* to *Roman Holiday*, *Bonjour Tristesse*, and *The Journey*.

Francis Chagrin chose a French-sounding name, but he was originally from Rumania. Eventually, he settled in England and scored such films as *Greyfriars Bobbie* and *The Last Holiday*. For the latter, he wrote what may be one of the saddest and most poignant main titles ever heard in a film. Ironically, it was played not by a large orchestra, but a lonely, mournful solo violin.

Sir Malcolm Arnold's music for *The Bridge on the River Kwai* was his best-known score. It featured the "Colonel Bogey March," ironically composed not by Arnold, but by F. J. Ricketts, known as "The British March King," and writing under the pen name of Kenneth Alford. Malcolm Arnold, one of Britain's most honored composers, provided the scores for many of Britain's most memorable films, including *Hobson's Choice*, *Whistle Down the Wind*, *The Key*, *The Heroes of Telemark*, and *The Chalk Garden*. He also scored a number of films produced through Hollywood studios, including *Trapeze*, *The Inn of the Sixth Happiness*, and *The Lion*, to mention only a few. John Addison, best-known for his film scores, was descended from a military family, fought in the Normandy invasion, and was wounded during World War II. He was trained as an oboe and clarinet soloist and excelled at scoring mysteries with a light, comedic touch. He wrote the music for such films as *Tom Jones*, for which he won an Oscar, and *Sleuth*. Addison also composed the theme music for *Murder, She Wrote*, a popular television series starring Angela Lansbury.

Figure 313 – Sir Malcolm Arnold at work in Denbigh Gardens, 1958 (Photo courtesy of Estate of Sir Malcolm Arnold)

Sir Richard Rodney Bennett was one of the hardest British composers to classify. He wrote concert works under the influence of one of his teachers, Pierre Boulez, the French avant-garde composer; he was also captivated by American jazz. His film scores for both British and American films were eclectic and included *Indiscreet*, *The Devil's Disciple*, *Nicholas and Alexandra*, and *Murder on the Orient Express*.

A serious consideration of British films and the scores that illuminated them would require a whole book. But anyone exploring the world of American film music should be well aware of the influence and contributions of composers on the other side of the Atlantic.

Bernard Herrmann's introduction to Alfred Hitchcock came courtesy of his friend, composer Lyn Murray. Murray, along with fellow British-born composer Cyril Mockridge, was one of several composers from Great Britain who settled in Hollywood, contributed to countless motion pictures and television shows, but never acquired famous names recognized instantly by audiences who appreciated the films they scored. American audiences first became aware of Murray through the widely popular radio program, *Your Hit Parade,* which featured a choral ensemble known as The Lyn Murray Singers. The group also appeared in the Broadway show *Finian's Rainbow*, for which Murray provided arrangements. After a busy career in radio in New York, Murray headed west to Hollywood where he became a prolific composer for films and television. He caught the attention of Alfred Hitchcock, who chose him to score his classic film, *To Catch a Thief*, starring Cary Grant and Grace Kelly. He scored numerous television programs, including *The Alfred Hitchcock Hour*. Murray didn't score other films for Hitchcock after the director began his eleven-year association with Herrmann. But Murray scored many other films, excelling at light, sophisticated comedies such as *Rosie*, starring Rosalind Russell.

Like Murray, Cyril Mockridge was born in England. After serving as a German POW during World War I, Mockridge settled in Hollywood after beginning his career as a pianist and arranger for dance bands. He spent twenty-six years at 20th Century Fox as a mainstay of Alfred Newman's staff. Mockridge was a versatile composer who scored many of Fox's classic films, including all the Shirley Temple films and musicals starring Betty Grable. His credits included everything from sophisticated comedy (*The Late George Apley*) to westerns (*The Ox-Bow Incident*.) He incorporated thematic development of "Jingle Bells" in his most beloved score, for the original *Miracle on 34th Street*, a Christmas classic about a delightful department store Santa Claus, played masterfully by Edmund Gwenn. When Gwenn's character is put on trial after he claims to be the real Santa, even his own lawyer is convinced that his claims might be true, and Mockridge's music has brightened every Christmas since the film was made in 1947.

Figure 314 - Cyril Mockridge was a mainstay at 20th Century Fox for years. His work was long under-recognized by the public. (Photo courtesy of Jeanne Mockridge)

THE ITALIAN INFLUENCE

A thriving film industry in Italy led to involvement by major American studios, stars, and directors. While most of the Italian productions were filmed in Italy, they were responsible for significant musical scores that were certainly part of film music's golden age. Three of the most notable Italian film composers were Mario Nascimbene, Alessandro Cicognini, and Nino Rota.

Nascimbene was a prolific composer of Italian film scores when Hollywood beckoned him to write the music for *The Barefoot Contessa*, the story of the life and loves of a mythical Spanish movie star, directed by Joseph L. Mankiewicz. Nascimbene went on to score such varied films as *A Farewell to Arms*, *Room at the Top*, *Solomon and Sheba*, *Scent of Mystery*, *Romanoff and Juliet*, and *Francis of Assisi*. He was comfortable scoring everything from Biblical epics to romances and was noted for introducing unusual instruments or sound effects into the orchestra.

Alessandro Cicognini was an important contributor to over a hundred Italian films, covering a wide range of motion pictures, often working with director Vittorio de Sica.

His scores included *Bicycle Thief, Indiscretion of an American Wife, Summertime, The Little World of Don Camillo, A Breath of Scandal*, and *It Started in Naples*. Many composers were eager to preserve their film scores; Cicognini was not. He stopped scoring films abruptly and devoted the last three decades of his life to teaching composition. He is also widely believed to have destroyed his records, tapes, and written scores related to his work for films.

Nino Rota was a prolific composer of concert music, a former child prodigy descended from a family of musicians in Milan. He wrote ten operas and five ballets, but this did not prevent him from scoring around 150 films. Most were Italian. He enjoyed a twenty-seven year association with the director Federico Fellini and scored many of Fellini's best-known films. He was an extremely versatile composer; his film scores included the haunting passages for *La Strada*, historical epics such as *The Leopard* and *War and Peace*, Shakespearean dramas, including *The Taming of the Shrew* and *Romeo and Juliet*, and his most commercially successful score for *The Godfather*.

THE NEW YORKERS: JEROME MOROSS AND ALEX NORTH

In the 1950s and 1960s, a number of leading American composers made significant contributions to the development of a new American style of film-scoring. Among the leading composers of the period were Jerome Moross and Alex North. Moross and North had several things in common. Both were New Yorkers, greatly interested in writing music for the concert hall and the theater. Both were also influenced by Aaron Copland.

Jerome Moross, a child prodigy, was born in Brooklyn, New York. He began, composing music at eight and graduated from grammar school at ten. At DeWitt Clinton High School for the Performing Arts, he met Bernard Herrmann in German class. The two became friends, and Moross began playing the piano to Herrmann's violin in a chamber music trio. (Herrmann's brother was a cellist.) The versatile Moross gained a reputation in New York as a fine composer of ballet and theater music, but this very reputation worked against him in Hollywood. Producers, always suspicious of "Carnegie Hall composers," were reluctant to hire him. Copland asked him to orchestrate his score for *Our Town*. Moross was then typecast as an orchestrator, a role he fulfilled on numerous films in the 1940s, including Hugo Friedhofer's classic scores for *The Best Years of Our Lives* and *The Bishop's Wife*. In 1940,

Figure 315 - Jerome Moross, the New Yorker who wrote one of Hollywood's greatest western scores, *The Big Country*. (Courtesy of Susanna Moross Tarjan)

Moross finally got his chance as composer of the score for *Close-Up*. Moross never settled in Hollywood; when not working on a film, he returned to New York, where he resumed writing concert and theater music.

But in 1958, Jerome Moross produced one of the most important and influential scores of all. He wrote what many believe to be the finest western score of all time, *The Big Country*. Moross determined to take an approach to this score, which would be very different from that used in many other westerns. He wanted his music to sound truly western, not, as he described it, "western music from the Hungarian plains or Russian steppes." Musically, he based many of his themes on the pentatonic scale, a five-note scale often used in folk-tunes. *The Big Country* was a huge epic with an all-star cast, a big budget, and lavish location scenes. Moross recalled his first trip west, a long bus trip from Chicago to Los Angeles. He was so excited by the vast plains and empty spaces that he stopped off for a visit to Albuquerque, then a small western town. Moross never forgot the expansiveness of the land. He translated this feeling into music. *The Big Country* opened with a stirring overture scored for full orchestra, beginning with a furiously whirling figuration for strings and winds, and resolving quickly into an original Western melody. From the moment the film opens, it throbs with musical excitement.

Moross used numerous cross-rhythms and irregular phrasing. He wrote a charming "western waltz" which sounds rather like a cowboy tune in 3/4 time. The film contained a dramatic confrontation between two feuding families; the ride into Blanco Canyon was accompanied by a thunderous orchestral finale. Moross started with a few short rhythmic figures and developed them into a percussive fury highlighted by timpani and brass. His sudden starts and stops and asymmetrical figures created a Western awkwardness that lent depth and power to the film. Moross managed to compose a number of sequences for *The Big Country* that are complete pieces of music, as fully developed thematically as anything he would write for the concert hall. Eventually, he adapted his music from the film into a concert suite. A second suite, incorporating excerpts from his other film scores, was titled appropriately, *Music from the Flicks.*

Much of the vitality in Moross's music comes from his sense of rhythmic energy, not surprising in a composer who liked dance forms. After *The Big Country,* Moross went on to score a number of other films. He always maintained his affinity with a wide variety of American music: spirituals, rags, folksongs and dances. Moross had a unique ability to absorb the best of America's own music and use its rhythms and harmonies with the skill of a concert composer. He was not a European trying to sound like an American, but an American speaking his own musical language. Moross's skill was applied to such varied films as *Proud Rebel* (1958), *The Adventures of Huckleberry Finn* (1960), *The Cardinal* (1963), *The War Lord* (1965), *Rachel, Rachel* (1968), and *Valley of the Gwangi* (1968). Moross always approached his film scores with the attitude of an artist, using music to supply elements not already present on the screen. Sometimes, it would be through orchestration, as in his 1956 music for *The Sharkfighters*. He managed to establish the

Cuban locale of the film through dance (a habañera and danzón), and through an unusual percussion ensemble including boobams, timbales, bongo and conga drums. On other occasions, he used thematic development to create a musical mood, as in *The Cardinal,* using a musical conflict between a Viennese waltz and a baroque church theme to accompany the inner conflict of the film's principal character, trying to choose between a secular and religious life. Moross believed that a composer should enable his listeners to experience some of the same emotions he felt. In this, he succeeded admirably.

Just as Jerome Moross revolutionized the western score, Alex North changed the sound of film scoring forever through his use of jazz. North was not a jazz musician, however, and he proved himself equally skilled drawing upon such diverse influences as baroque chamber music and the folk dances of Mexico. Like Moross, North was essentially a New York composer of dramatic and concert music. Through his use of jazz and ability to use small (and quiet) musical ensembles, he blazed a trail for those seeking depart from an exclusively European sound.

Alex North was born in Pennsylvania. He studied at the Curtis Institute and at the Juilliard School of Music. His parents were Russian immigrants and he idolized Prokofiev; so he took advantage of an opportunity offered by the Russian government and studied for several years in Moscow. But he became homesick for American music and his own country.

Figure 316 - Alex North, who brought the sounds of jazz and quiet main titles to the big screen. (Photograph by and courtesy of Alexander Courage)

On returning to the United States, he pursued additional studies with Ernst Toch and Aaron Copland, and for a time, in Mexico with the noted Mexican composer, Silvestre Revueltas. Copland introduced him to colleagues in theater and dance, and North, like Moross, gained a reputation as a composer for the stage. He wrote ballets for such noted dancers as Martha Graham, Agnes de Mille, and Hanya Holm, and composed incidental music for plays like Arthur Miller's *Death of a Salesman* and such Shakespeare classics as *Richard III*. His concert works included *Revue for Clarinet and Orchestra*, commissioned by Benny Goodman, and *Morning Star*, a cantata based on the Nuremberg war crimes trials.

When director Elia Kazan went to Hollywood to develop Tennessee Williams' play *A Streetcar Named Desire* for the screen, he insisted that North with whom he had worked on Broadway, be assigned the score. The 1951 production of *A Streetcar Named Desire* starred Vivien Leigh as Blanche Dubois and Marlon Brando as Stanley Kowalski. Because the story was set in New Orleans, North naturally turned to the music most identified with the setting: jazz, ragtime, and the blues. He decided to use themes as "mental statements" for conflict between various characters. North wanted to reflect the inner tensions of his characters, a technique he used often in film scoring. He also used a little dance tune as an *idée fixe,* a deceptively innocent motif that is repeated over and over whenever reference was made to the suicide of Blanche's husband. North used small jazz ensembles whenever possible. He experimented with music playing *against* a scene, reflecting not what characters were doing, but what they were feeling, sometimes the opposite of their on-screen behavior. North's score for *A Streetcar Named Desire* established the unique potential of jazz elements in a film score.

After *A Streetcar Named Desire*, North had a unique opportunity, to expand and develop the incidental music he had written on Broadway for Arthur Miller's play *Death of a Salesman.* His orchestra highlighted the flute, clarinet, trumpet and cello. Breaking totally with Hollywood tradition, he opened the film not with a huge symphonic orchestra to suggest the personal tragedy of failed salesman Willy Loman, but with a lonely, mournful solo played by an alto flute. North used rhythms derived from jazz and harmonic and melodic ideas drawn from the blues, though his score was neither jazz nor blues. His delicate orchestrations and understated music won praise from Arthur Miller and critics alike.

Next came another collaboration with Elia Kazan, *Viva Zapata!* North had an unusual affinity with this film. Having studied in Mexico, he was fascinated by Mexican folk music, and traveled throughout the country with Kazan gathering musical material. North drew the distinction between authentic Mexican music and the Spanish melodies which were often invoked in Hollywood film scores with Mexican storylines. His score, rich with the rhythms and inflections of Mexican music, was a classic. Alex North proved an exceeding versatile composer throughout his career, scoring such films as *Member of the Wedding* (1953), *Désirée* (1954), *The Rose Tattoo* (1955) and in 1956 alone, *I'll Cry Tomorrow, The Bad Seed, The Rainmaker,* and *Four Girls in Town,* the latter using a "jazz rhapsody" for piano and trumpet as a continuing musical element.

Figure 317 - Alex North (seated right) celebrates his birthday with composer colleagues Leonard Rosenman (seated left) and (left to right standing) Henry Mancini, Jerry Goldsmith, and John Williams. (Photo by Alexander Courage, Courtesy of Alexander Courage Collection, Sibley Music Library, Eastman School of Music)

North could score epics, (*Spartacus* in 1960, *Cleopatra* in 1963, *The Agony and the Ecstasy* in 1965.) North was always a rugged individualist, always interested in the psychological aspects of the characters. In *The Bad Seed,* he used a lullaby to identify with the principal character of the film, a child later revealed to be a murderer. The lullaby was offset by dissonant music to express the torment and emotional disturbance of the child. For

Spartacus, a costume drama about a slave rebellion set in ancient Rome, he elected not to use period music. Instead, he emphasized the cruelty and barbarism of the time through dissonance and a distinctly contemporary sound. Until the thirteenth reel, no violins were used in the score.

North took the opposite approach when he created one of his most unusual scores, for the filmed adaptation of Edward Albee's play, *Who's Afraid of Virginia Woolf?* This 1966 film portrayed a casual get-together of two married couples which turns into a vicious round of shouted accusations and bitter truths. For the time, the language of the film was considered unusually profane and harsh. North could have done the obvious, writing extremely dissonant music. Instead, he decided that the music should offset the dramatic tension created by the actors. He created music in a baroque style. His opening music (reminiscent of *Death of a Salesman*) called for an ensemble of quiet flutes. In another sequence, he scored for harpsichord and strings, in passages that might have been written by Vivaldi.

In 1961, Alex North scored *The Misfits*, the final film for both of its stars, Clark Gable and Marilyn Monroe. The screenplay had been written for Monroe by her former husband Arthur Miller and was directed by John Huston. Huston, who had worked with many of Hollywood's finest, declared North to be his favorite film composer. This was clearly a musical judgment, since no two men could have been more different. North was a quiet, modest, and reflective man, while Huston was famous for his appetites, wine, women, and a pursuit of danger and machismo shared with his friend Ernest Hemingway. North considered Miller's screenplay to be a tapestry of miniature moments and developed a score to tie them together with a dark, yearning theme. The same year, North also wrote the music for *The Children's Hour*, based on a play by another prominent playwright, Lillian Hellman. The film told the story of two teachers whose lives and careers are destroyed by a rumor started by a malicious child. The dialogue was dramatic and tense, and a composer could have been tempted to turn the movie into a melodrama. North, however, wisely chose to write against the tension. His often quiet and introspective score (complete with a variation on a children's nursery theme) was exactly right to express the inner feelings of the story's protagonists.

Alex North was one of the most widely admired and respected composers to work in Hollywood. He achieved this while still being true to his own musical instincts, and demonstrating that a composer can be commercially successful while pursuing high artistic and creative standard.

In 1954, Elia Kazan directed yet another major film, *On the Waterfront*. His composer was Leonard Bernstein, already famous as composer on Broadway and as America's most recognizable conductor. Like Alex North before him, Bernstein drew upon jazz influences to create the dissonant and violent world of the New York waterfront. Bernstein opened the film with a canon, and accompanied murders in the story with a violent three voice fugato scored for percussion. Yet when the tension relaxed (in a love scene or in quiet moments on a rooftop,) Bernstein turned not to a full symphony orchestra, but to sparse, mournful instrumental solos. Like North, he used the solo flute to depict the loneliness and yearning for peace experienced by those subject to the violence and brutality of life among urban gangsters. Like Aaron Copland years earlier, Bernstein wasn't happy to discover that music was often lost during the "dubbing" process in films, as music, dialogue, and sound effects were combined in the final cut of a motion picture. Nor was he amused when the volume of his music was lowered to accommodate a grunt by method actor Marlon Brando. Bernstein was not the first composer to feel a loss of control over his music in Hollywood; nor would he be the last. Composers still face the challenge of music being rewritten or rejected.

THE PREVIN JOURNEY: FROM BERLIN TO BEVERLY HILLS

André Previn was a versatile musician capable of working in many styles. Born in Berlin, Previn was a child prodigy on the piano. When his family settled in California, he studied with his father, a prominent lawyer in Germany who turned into a strict disciplinary piano teacher in Beverly Hills. Previn later studied with Max Rabinowitsch, a classical virtuoso who also recorded for the studios. Previn studied composition, first with Joseph Achron and Ernst Toch, then for seven years with Mario Castelnuovo-Tedesco. (Other pupils included Henry Mancini, John Williams, Nelson Riddle, Jerry Goldsmith, George Duning, Lionel Newman and Johnny Mandel.) Previn went to work at MGM while still a teenager, orchestrating and arranging for musicals and films. He also developed great facility as a jazz pianist, inspired by the work of Art Tatum and Bud Powell.

Previn's skills as a composer of background music equipped him to score everything from the driving, frenetic syncopations that accompany the charlatan-evangelist *Elmer Gantry* (1960) to the dissonant, dramatic scenes of war in *The Four Horsemen of the Apocalypse. (1962)*. He could switch easily from writing racy can-cans for the comedy *Irma La Douce* (1963) to ominous passages for harpsichord in the gothic thriller *Dead Ringer (1964)*. Previn's affinity for jazz naturally lead him to use the idiom in films. In 1960, Previn not only scored *The Subterraneans*, he appeared in the film performing his only unique brand of jazz improvisations at the keyboard. Previn, who found time to study conducting with Pierre Monteux while stationed in San Francisco during his military service, eventually left Hollywood to pursue a successful career as a symphony conductor, directing major orchestras in the

Figure 318 - André Previn, multitalented composer, arranger, conductor, and pianist. (Photo by and courtesy of Alexander Courage)

United States and Europe and making numerous appearances as a concert pianist and chamber musician. Previn also returned to his roots as a composer of concert works. Coming full circle, he also composed an opera based on *A Streetcar Named Desire*, the same work that Alex North used to inspire one of the first jazz film scores, and another opera based on Nöel Coward's *Brief Encounter*.

While Previn was widely known as a jazz performer, a number of musicians for whom jazz was the principal medium of performance also turned their hand to scoring films. John Lewis, pianist with the Modern Jazz Quartet, scored *No Sun in Venice*, with a quiet, cool-jazz treatment. In contrast to Lewis's jazz-chamber music approach, Johnny Mandel used a swinging big band sound for *I Want to Live* (1958), the story of a woman who is executed for murder. Mandel was an accomplished jazz composer-arranger, a trumpet and trombone soloist, and a veteran of the Count Basie big band. He went on to score numerous films including *Emily* and *The Sandpiper*, which contained one of his best-known songs, "The Shadow of Your Smile." Mandel's gift as an arranger led to his being recruited to write arrangements for the world's best-known vocalists who were still performing classics from The Great American Song Book.

Elmer Bernstein, Henry Mancini, Claude Bolling, Calvin Jackson, Jerry Fielding, and Duke Ellington were also among the dynamic composers who incorporated jazz elements in their film scores. In 1959, Duke Ellington scored *Anatomy of a Murder*, using the brilliant brass and saxophone sections from his jazz orchestra. Duke Ellington's score for *Anatomy of a Murder* was particularly notable because Ellington wasn't comfortable with the disciplined timings most composers used as a reference in the scores. MGM sent pianist Harold Gelman to explain some of the timing techniques used in motion pictures to Ellington. But he decided to bring his band into a recording studio and let his musicians perform as they were accustomed to doing in the concerts. Ellington's approach revealed a basic difference between true jazz musicians and composers accustomed to the discipline of notated scores and timing sheets. This made things easy for Ellington and his musicians, but not for the music cutters who had to adapt and edit the music Ellington recorded to fit the timings dictated by screen action.

One of Ellington's admirers was the veteran composer and arranger Earle Hagen. While on the road with bandleader Ray Noble, Hagen composed, a haunting jazz theme invariably played by a saxophone soloist in the style of Johnny Hodges, Ellington's great saxophonist. "Harlem Nocturne" became his best-known composition. Hagen also won wide recognition for the music he composed for *I Spy*, a television series score featuring many jazz elements. In the 1930s, big band jazz was considered dance music. But from the 1940s through the 1960s, jazz, both improvised and composed, set the scene for hard-edged, tough-talking characters in "film noir" crime and mystery dramas. Jazz musicians could be found performing on screen or even in so-called "biopics," screen biographies of jazz musicians themselves.

THE MANY MOODS OF ELMER BERNSTEIN, ERNEST GOLD, AND LAURENCE ROSENTHAL

Elmer Bernstein was a native New Yorker, a prodigious child gifted in music, painting, and dancing. He prepared to be a concert pianist at Juilliard; as a boy, he was presented to Aaron Copland who arranged for him to study composition with one of his own pupils, Israel Citkowitz. Later Bernstein augmented his composition studies with Roger Sessions and Stefan Wolpe and began working as an arranger for Glenn Miller while in the U.S. Army Air Corps. His talents led to assignments in radio and an early film score, *Sudden Fear* earned praise for its harmonic daring. Bernstein was a struggling young film composer in Hollywood when he was asked to score *The View From Pompey's Head*. Bernard Herrmann was originally supposed to score the film, but a commitment to compose the music for an Alfred Hitchcock production imposed a conflicting deadline. So Herrmann suggested Elmer Bernstein. His highly romantic score attracted the attention of powerful director Cecil B. DeMille. DeMille then hired Bernstein to replace Victor Young, who had died suddenly, as the composer for his epic *The Ten Commandments*. Bernstein's score for this Biblical film was in a soaring, sweeping, symphonic style.

Figure 319 - Elmer Bernstein - One of the most versatile film composers for decades. A master in many genres, from *The Ten Commandments* to *To Kill a Mockingbird*. (Photo by and courtesy of Alexander Courage)

While waiting for its release, Bernstein completed another assignment which could not have been more different: *The Man With the Golden Arm*.

This 1955 feature told the tale of Frankie Machine, a drug addict and aspiring jazz drummer, played by Frank Sinatra. Bernstein chose to combine symphonic and jazz elements. This film became one of the very first to use real jazz in dramatic scenes. For the jazz sequences, he was aided by experienced jazz musicians (trumpeter Shorty Rogers and drummer Shelley Manne) and by orchestrator Fred Steiner. Although the score was not a "jazz score," the driving jazz rhythms and obvious sounds of jazz orchestration clearly followed in the footsteps of North's score for *A Streetcar Named Desire*. Hollywood was quick to turn Bernstein's innovation into a standard practice: stories about drug addicts required the use of jazz.

Bernstein himself used jazz elements creatively throughout his career, in such films as *Kings Go Forth* (1958), *Some Came Running* (1958), *The Rat Race* (1960), and *Walk on the Wild Side* (1962). He was versatile enough to simultaneously score films in the symphonic style, including such epics as *The Buccaneer* (1958), *The Miracle* (1959), and *Hawaii* (1966). His throbbing music for *The Magnificent Seven* (1960) became one of the most imitated scores by countless composers writing music for westerns. But his other most original contribution to the genre of screen scoring came from very different types of films. Bernstein had an uncanny ability to write gentle, haunting, nostalgic music for small, quiet combinations of instruments. He created a sense of ornithological wonder in his music for *The Birdman of Alcatraz* (1962).

A year later, Bernstein wrote his landmark score for *To Kill a Mockingbird*. Bernstein's main title opened with a simple piano solo. The folk-like melody reflects the innocence of a distant childhood, wistful and nostalgic in tone. It is followed by a gentle flute solo over an impressionistic background of strings and harp. This represented yet another characteristic Elmer Bernstein sound, alternating the haunting, almost mystical sound of nostalgia with sweeping and romantic melodies overflowing with lyricism. This was apparent in scores for such films as *From the Terrace* (1960), *By Love Possessed* (1961), *Love with the Proper Stranger* (1963), and *A Girl Named Tamiko* (1962). What was unique about Elmer Bernstein was his capacity to create several absolutely distinct styles, all unmistakably his own, and to apply them to nearly every type of motion picture imaginable. Like Kurt Weill, who somehow absorbed and added to the musical vocabularies of the countries in which he lived, Germany, France, and the United States, Elmer Bernstein could move easily from a score requiring a symphonic and romantic style to one throbbing with jazz rhythms to yet another calling for ethereal introspection. There were other composers in Hollywood capable of writing in any of these genres, but it is difficult to imagine anyone fulfilling them all with such ease.

Not all composers made their mark abandoning tradition. Ernest Gold had admired Max Steiner from the time he was a piano student in his native Vienna. Gold came from a musical family, and when his parents moved to New York, he pursued composition studies with Otto Cesana and conducting with Leon Barzin. When critics dubbed his piano concerto "movie music," he headed for Hollywood, where he began scoring films. Ernest Gold was a melodist, a lyrical composer who proved that inspiration did not have to be dissonant or even revolutionary to communicate an emotional message to audiences.

Figure 320 - Ernest Gold continued the tradition of Viennese lyricism in Hollywood. (Photo by Marv Newton Photography, courtesy of Ernest Gold)

Gold worked with his mentor, composer George Antheil, for several years. He served as musical director for the highly unusual 1955 production, *Dementia*, which contained only music by Antheil and no dialogue. The score used the human voice as an instrument, in this case, the voice of soprano, Marni Nixon, receiving a rare screen credit and an original jazz theme by Shorty Rogers. Gold also orchestrated such scores as Antheil's masterful Spanish musical background for *The Pride and the Passion*. Director Stanley Kramer asked Gold to substitute for an ailing Antheil in 1957 for *On the Beach*, beginning his long association with Kramer.

Ernest Gold's scores ranged from the traditional *Too Much, Too Soon*. an homage to the old Hollywood (and the Steiner scores he admired), to his unusually dissonant jazz-oriented score for *Pressure Point*.(1962) His lyricism was ideal for films like *The Young Philadelphians*, (1959) and he achieved phenomenal public success with the symphonic score for *Exodus*. Ernest Gold was perhaps at his finest in scores which recalled the Europe he had left behind, in movies such as *Judgment at Nuremberg*(1961) and *Ship of Fools*(1965). For the latter, he developed an unusual technique. Since the action of the movie takes place on a German freighter, Gold composed nostalgic Viennese waltzes, polkas, and tangos popular in the 1930s. He found a way to make "source music," music coming from a visible source in the scene, provide the dramatic underscoring.

Like Elmer Bernstein, Laurence Rosenthal used delicate, quiet sounds and folk-like harmonies to achieve profound dramatic effect in *The Miracle Worker.* (1962) Rosenthal, a native of Detroit, had pursued his studies with Howard Hanson and Bernard Rogers at the Eastman School of Music and with Nadia Boulanger in Paris. He began scoring films while serving the Air Force, gained a reputation in New York writing music for plays, musicals, and the ballet, and eventually began scoring such films as *Raisin in the Sun.* In *The Miracle Worker,* young Helen Keller, though blind and deaf, realizes in a single moment that words and ideas can be communicated. In the key scene, Rosenthal used gentle flutes and a cascading harp to gradually increase the sense of discovery, moving from musical mystery to musical exhilaration. Rosenthal scored numerous other films, ranging from the use of Gregorian chant in *Becket* (1964) to a frolicking chamber orchestra in the comedy *Hotel Paradiso* (1966) and the sound of Haitian drums in *The Comedians* (1967). In all of these films, Rosenthal demonstrated that small ensembles and unusual instruments could add color and flavor to the spirit of a film. But he was equally comfortable writing full symphonic scores for movies such as *Clash of the Titans*. He also composed scores for many important television programs, concert works, and a Broadway musical, *Sherry*, based on the legendary comedy by George S. Kaufman and Moss Hart, *The Man Who Came to Dinner*.

Figure 321 - Laurence Rosenthal. His scores for many films, such as *The Miracle Worker*, turned movies into classics. (Photo courtesy of Laurence Rosenthal)

LEONARD ROSENMAN: DODECAPHONY IN HOLLYWOOD

Not all the newer composers turned to jazz during this period. Leonard Rosenman was a young composer living in New York. He had gone to California to pursue studies as a painter, but instead concentrated on composition lessons with Ernest Bloch and Arnold Schoenberg. When he returned to New York, he befriended a young actor, James Dean, who became his piano pupil. When Dean was cast in the leading role in *East of Eden*, he urged director Elia Kazan to hire Rosenman to score the film. Rosenman had little ambition to score films. Most young composers would jump at the chance to write the music for a major production in Hollywood. Rosenman simply said to Kazan, "Why don't you ask Aaron Copland?" But he took the job, working closely with Kazan on the film, much as Bernard Herrmann had worked with Orson Welles on *Citizen Kane*.

Figure 322 - Leonard Rosenman (left) plays a duet with his good friend, Alexander Courage, a composer and fine photographer, responsible for far more music than the *Star Trek* theme for which he is best-known to the public. (Photo by Alexander Courage, Courtesy of Sibley Music Library, Eastman School of Music)

Rosenman wanted to write music in a style far more dissonant than usually heard in Hollywood movies. (He not only studied with Schoenberg, but later with Roger Sessions and Luigi Dallapiccola, one of a small number of Italian composers who used the twelve-tone technique of Schoenberg.)

Leonard Rosenman and Elia Kazan found a middle ground; Rosenman wrote tonal music (in traditional keys) for the children on screen, dissonant music for adults. Rosenman took a similar approach in Dean's second film, *Rebel Without a Cause*. He also scored *The Cobweb*, allegedly the first film score thoroughly based on Schoenberg's twelve-tone technique. In this approach, the composer would invent his own 12-tone scale, create many new scales, (inverting the scale and also playing it backwards), and not repeat one note in the scale until all the other notes had been used. The result was usually a musical texture that sounded extremely dissonant and intense to ears accustomed to the more traditional harmonies usually associated with motion picture scores. Ironically, this film was about people in a mental institution, suggesting that the dissonances derived through Schoenberg's serial technique could ideally express emotional distress. Following Dean's sudden death in a motorcycle accident at twenty-four, Rosenman went on to score numerous films in Hollywood, including *The Rise and Fall of Legs Diamond*, *Barry Lyndon*, *Beneath the Planet of the Apes*, and *The Lord of the Rings*. Rosenman continued writing concert works; declaring that they enabled him to enjoy complete musical freedom unavailable in scoring motion pictures.

A PICNIC WITH GEORGE DUNING

The most notable use of "source music" in a dramatic sequence was undoubtedly George Duning's score for *Picnic*. This film was based on William Inge's play about the truths revealed regarding a Midwestern family attending an annual picnic. Duning identified with the characters in the film. A Midwesterner, he was born in Richmond, Indiana, and studied at the Cincinnati Conservatory before pursuing a career as a dance-band arranger that led him to California, where he completed studies with Mario Castelnuovo-Tedesco. Joshua Logan, who directed *Picnic* on Broadway, also directed the film.

In a key scene, a local girl (Kim Novak) and a charming drifter (William Holden) realize they are falling in love while dancing. The superstitious Logan insisted that the couple dance to "Moonglow," a popular song used in the original play. Then he told Duning he wanted an original love theme superimposed on "Moonglow" when the Holden and Novak began to dance. Duning was faced with a dilemma. Playing two pieces at the same time might be acceptable at an avant-garde concert, but the harmonic and melodic clashes would hardly be appropriate for this scene. He solved the problem by composing a melody which could be played by the full orchestra while the small rhythm group on screen played "Moonglow". The combination proved successful, and Duning's "Moonglow and the Theme from Picnic" delighted everyone except Mills Music, the publisher of "Moonglow." The company sued, accusing Duning of merely writing an obbligato, a musical line that depended entirely on their tune. The case was thrown out of court, when two musicologists from Columbia University testified that Duning's melody was completely original and could stand on its own. Then, television star Steve Allen decided to write lyrics to Duning's melody, which became a popular hit, though Allen and Duning never actually collaborated on the piece. Duning displayed great versatility as a film composer, scoring numerous motion pictures, including *Bell, Book, and Candle, Toys in the Attic, The World of Suzie Wong,* and *Cowboy*.

Figure 323 - George Duning, an affable Midwesterner who became the principal composer of the music department for many years at Columbia Pictures. (Photo by and courtesy of Alexander Courage)

SOUNDTRACKS: THE RECORDS OF THE MOVIES

In the early years of film scores, even executives of record companies saw motion picture music as having limited appeal and a short life span. In 1939, producer David O. Selznick was told that Max Steiner's score for *Gone With the Wind* would have little appeal to the public on record. Three years later, a recording of some of Miklós Rózsa's music from *The Jungle Book* did appear on record, followed by recordings of other 1940s classics, including *The Song of Bernadette, Captain from Castile, For Whom the Bell Tolls, Spellbound,* and *Duel in the Sun.* In the 1950s and 1960s, however, two trends began which would indeed prove that motion picture music could enjoy a commercial life of its own away from its original source: an increasing dominance of film scoring by popular songwriters and a radical change in musical styles, beginning with the advent of jazz, and culminating, unfortunately, in the decline of the art of film scoring and the rise of rock music.

No one could have anticipated these trends in 1949, when Anton Karas scored *The Third Man,* a film about intrigues in post-war Vienna, using a zither. This encouraged producers and directors to look for unusual sounds, harmonicas, accordions, even whistlers, for film scores. A score which used a single unusual instrument would be economical and probably gain the film an abundance of publicity. While popular songs originally in musicals often became hits, it was more unusual for a song from non-musical dramatic picture to develop a life of its own outside the film. David Raksin's memorable *Laura* became one of the most popular of all-time. Dimitri Tiomkin wrote a tune for the western *High Noon,* which became tremendously successful as a popular song. But tunes adapted from dramatic scores usually had some reason to be included in the film. They were not being inserted in the score so they could be extracted and promoted for their own sake. With the rise of the long-playing record, an increasing number of original soundtrack albums became available to the public. But soundtrack recordings were considered a specialized market for collectors. This changed dramatically in 1959, when Blake Edwards produced a television show called *Peter Gunn.* He decided to use a "cool jazz" score for the hard-boiled detective series. Edwards hired a composer whose record albums would change the face of film music forever. His name was Henry Mancini.

HENRY MANCINI: THE IMPROBABLE REVOLUTIONARY

Mancini was an unlikely figure to start a Hollywood revolution. He was a staff composer at Universal Studios and worked as a composer, arranger, and orchestrator. Mancini had contributed to a hundred film scores. He was not particularly well-known to the general public and was certainly not considered a musical "star" in the Hollywood pecking order. Mancini, a native of Aliquippa, Pennsylvania had worked as an arranger for the Glenn Miller orchestra. He had moved to California, where he studied with Mario Castelnuovo-Tedesco and developed a reputation as an inventive orchestrator in the big-band style, scoring such films as *The Glenn Miller Story* and *The Benny Goodman Story.*

In 1958, he provided an unusual jazz score for Orson Welles' movie *Touch of Evil.* This dark, somber, off-beat picture was in the genre known as *film noir,* told the tale of a corrupt police officer and a group of drug peddlers in a seedy town across the Mexican border. Mancini's use of jazz attracted the attention of Blake Edwards who wanted the same effects in *Peter Gunn.* The musicians who worked with Mancini included exponents of what had been dubbed "west-coast jazz" in the 1950s. Among them was a gifted

Figure 324 - Henry Mancini, a former Universal Studios staff composer whose jazz sounds revolutionized television and film scores. (Photograph by and courtesy of Alexander Courage)

pianist-composer-arranger then known as Johnny Williams who, many years later, as John Williams, would be responsible for a revival of interest in the symphonic film score. Mancini's music for *Peter Gunn* was created in the same style he had been developing for years: hard-driving big band passages, ballads scored for understated muted trumpets or saxophones, comedy effects created through the use of unexpected instruments like alto flutes playing jazz. But everything changed when *Peter Gunn* was released on record. Not only did Mancini receive an Emmy nomination, the record was named Album of the Year by the National Association of Recording Arts and Sciences. It sold a million copies.

Mancini was suddenly American's best-known film and television composer. No one seemed more surprised by all this than Mancini himself. He was tapped to score *Breakfast at Tiffany's* in 1961. Mancini wrote "Moon River," a song with a modest vocal range for the film's star, Audrey Hepburn. The song ironically almost didn't stay in the film. Paramount Pictures executive Martin Rackin tried to have it deleted after an early preview of the film. But Audrey Hepburn couldn't have been more enthusiastic about Mancini's song. Acclaimed lyricist Johnny Mercer revived his career, under an onslaught from the advocates of rock music, with his lyrics for "Moon River." An inlet near Mercer's home town, Savannah, Georgia, was even named "Moon River" in his honor. "Moon River" became one of the most popular songs ever to emerge from a motion picture. Mancini won an Oscar that year for the best score. In 1962, Mercer and Mancini collaborated again, this time for the title song for *The Days of Wine and Roses*, winning them each a second Academy Award.

Mancini's score for *Breakfast at Tiffany's* won the Oscar despite competition from Miklós Rózsa's magnificent score for *El Cid*. Producers and directors knew that "Moon River" was a fine <u>song</u>. They automatically assumed that it was also a great <u>score</u>. The inability to distinguish between a score and a tune would plague Hollywood for years to come. Producers and executives of studios and record companies were quick to jump on the bandwagon. They concluded that film scores could sell records and the best scores (those that could sell the most records) should be derived from pop music.

Composers of pop music had varying degrees of talent and dramatic instinct. In the best of circumstances, they produced memorable melodious material that appealed to wide audiences and still contributed to the characterization depicted on screen. Michel Legrand, an accomplished French jazz pianist, composer, and arranger, wrote the score for an unusual musical film, *The Umbrellas of Cherbourg*, in which all the dialogue was sung. The score also included a number of Legrand's best melodies, including the haunting "I Will Wait for You" and "Watch What Happens." Legrand also scored the film *Summer of '42* and provided another mournful and pensive melody for this motion picture about a teenager's coming of age.

British composer John Barry scored *Somewhere In Time*, a romantic love story in which the leading character falls in love with the image of an actress and goes back in time to meet her. Although the film featured one of the variations from Rachmaninoff's *Rhapsody on a Theme of Paganini*, the score also included Barry's own "Somewhere in Time" theme. It was a tremendous hit after the movie, not overly successful at the box office, and became a cult favorite after it was released on Videocassette and DVD. Unfortunately, many of the pop composers who began scoring films came from the world of rock music or the decidedly unmusical milieu of current pop singers.

Composers were now faced with a new challenge. Not only must they please the film's director in regard to the role of music on screen. They also had to prove that their work could sell records. During this same period, popular music had changed radically. The rise of rock and roll in the 1950s and the invasion of British rock stars in the 1960s meant that record companies were obsessed with appealing audiences of teenagers. Rock music, harmonically primitive and dependent on a constant, throbbing beat, lacked the subtlety and sophistication for dramatic film scoring. Nor was it capable of expressing a variety of moods which would appear in films; it had only one mood, "loud." Many of its leading stars and "composers" could not read or write a note of music. But producers and executives were not to be dissuaded. If the name of a pop or rock star on a soundtrack album could sell records, that was all that mattered. Scores could be ghostwritten by studio arrangers or hit pop songs could be incorporated into scores written by more conventional film composers. Studios even came up with terms for these musically illiterate stars and their ghost writers. A star that could hum a few notes of an original melody became known as "the hummer." The ghostwriter who actually composed the pop score for which the star was given credit was dubbed "the take-down artist." Composers were expected to provide hit tunes with the scores, preferably those that could be played over and over so the audience would walk out of the theater whistling the melody and proceed directly to a record store to purchase the album. Composers who had been scoring films for decades found themselves suddenly out of work. In some cases, scores already written were thrown out and replaced by pop music credited to rock groups. Even the best composers were now pressured to produce "something with a beat."

When Alfred Hitchcock discarded Bernard Herrmann's score for *Torn Curtain*, it was symbolic of the new emphasis on pop scores. The Board of Governors of the Academy of Motion Picture Arts and Sciences decided that there should only be one award, forcing dramatic background scores to compete with scores for musicals containing popular songs. Ten composers, including Miklós Rózsa, Bronislaw Kaper, and André Previn, resigned their memberships in the Academy in protest. Bernard Herrmann went one step further, tearing up his card and mailing it back to the Academy. He dramatically declared he preferred to be judged by his peers, not his inferiors. The composers in question were outraged by the inability of the Academy to distinguish between a full orchestral score for a film and a series of songs that were included in the score.

Director Otto Preminger, previously associated with David Raksin and Ernest Gold, turned to a folksinger named Harry Nilsson. Some composers compromised, they were eager to compose in "the new sound." Others fought for their principles and found themselves unable to work. Hugo Friedhofer, asked how it felt to have his classic scores discovered by a new generation of admirers at a time when he wasn't offered any jobs quipped, "Now that the ship is sinking, all the rats are climbing aboard." The venerable Miklós Rózsa declared, "Rock music is the most God-awful noise mankind has invented since leaving the jungle. It is thrown into every film. They say 'The kids like it, play it for the kids.' If the kids like sex, violence, and horror, we do not help them change their values. We are merely playing down for the dollar." But Hollywood was not listening to Rozsa or Herrmann; it followed the lead of pop singer Bobby Goldsboro who praised the new style of film scoring because a composer could write whatever he pleased without any regard to the motion picture.

The era of classic film music reached its nadir in 1969 when Las Vegas developer Kirk Kirkorian acquired control of MGM and installed television executive James Aubrey as the studio's supreme boss. Under Aubrey's regime, rock music promoter Mike Curb became president of MGM records. Aubrey sold off the historic MGM backlot and auctioned or destroyed most of the memorabilia associated with classic MGM films. Orders were given for old scores to be burned or thrown away. Truckloads of scores and recordings (including historic outtakes from the musicals that had starred Fred Astaire, Gene Kelly, and Judy Garland) were dumped in a landfill that was eventually covered by part of the Golden State Freeway. A treasure trove of musical history was lost forever. Producer John Houseman dubbed Aubrey "the smiling cobra." MGM wasn't the only studio to liquidate its holdings. Another studio music library compared its list of scores to one in a film critic's book. Scores for films given high ratings for the critic were kept; if the films were given poor ratings, the scores were discarded. While scores in the personal collections of composers and arrangers survived, there is no telling how much irreplaceable material simply vanished into oblivion.

JOHN WILLIAMS AND THE SYMPHONIC RENAISSANCE

The symphonic film score made a comeback in the 1980s. Ironically, the composer most responsible had ties to Mancini's *Peter Gunn* score. Pianist Johnny Williams, a native New Yorker, had originally prepared for a career on the concert stage, including study with the celebrated Russian pedagogue at Juilliard, Mme. Rosina Lhevinne. After time in the Air Force, he settled in Los Angeles, where he studied composition with Mario Castelnuovo-Tedesco. He became active as a composer and arranger for television shows,

Figure 325 - John Williams, though initially known for his jazz style, he sparked a revival of interest in the classic symphonic film score. (Photo by Tash Tish- Public Domain)

including the 1960 series *Checkmate*. He wrote the music for episodes of a wide variety of westerns and comedies on television. One, *Lost in Space*, would anticipate his future role as a leading composer of music for the science fiction epics of the 1980s and '90s.

In 1969, now known as John Williams, he scored a film, *The Reivers*, which won critical acclaim as a fine example of musical Americana. His music for *Jaws* also gained recognition, and in 1977, his score for the epic *Star Wars* made him a household name. Williams admittedly paid tribute to the symphonic style of Erich Wolfgang Korngold and the concert music of English composer Gustav Holst, sparking a revival of interest in the symphonic scores by composers of the golden age. Williams himself went on to score such epics as *Raiders of the Lost Ark, Superman, The Empire Strikes Back,* and *Schindler's List*. He proved himself multitalented as successor to Arthur Fiedler as conductor of the Boston Pops and a versatile composer of many film scores and concert pieces. Williams' music was important not only for its own value, but because it made clear that the symphonic score hadn't lost its potential for new and creative contributions to films. Williams, like Henry Mancini, saw his name become a household word at a time when few legitimate musicians receive attention from the mainstream media. Today some composers are able to write legitimate music for films and avoid writing only an amalgamation of pop, rock, and commercial sounds. But few of the newer composers are producing music comparable to that of Korngold, Rozsa, Herrmann, and the other masters of the art.

JAZZ AND THE AVANT-GARDE: JERRY GOLDSMITH AND LALO SCHIFRIN

Jazz, its harmonies, rhythms, and characteristic orchestral combinations, has played a role, to varying degrees, in the work of numerous other composers for film. Jerry Goldsmith was an eclectic composer who studied with Mario Castelnuovo-Tedesco and Miklós Rózsa. His career began in a most unusual way. In the early 1950s, employees of CBS, even ushers and typists, were allowed to display any talents they might have in a workshop radio show. Only CBS employees could participate. A friend of Goldsmith's thought he would be perfect to provide the show's music, so a faked typing test was used to arrange Goldsmith's status as a clerk-typist employed by CBS. Six months later the CBS music department discovered that Goldsmith's musical talents far exceeded his typing skills and he never looked back. Goldsmith said that scores drew upon such varied influences as jazz, pop music, and the atonal dissonance of the avant-garde.

Jerry Goldsmith scored many popular television series like *Dr.Kildare* and *Thriller,* including "Terror in Teakwood," an episode featuring virtuoso piano compositions by Caesar Giovannini. Then Goldsmith scored *Lonely Are the Brave,* which started him on the road to many other motion pictures, including *Freud*, filled with atonal dissonance, *A Patch of Blue*, *The Sand Pebbles, In Harm's Way,* (in which he made a cameo appearance,) and *Chinatown.* For the latter, Goldsmith used a highly unusual orchestra featuring a trumpet, four pianos, four harps, two percussionists, and strings. He won his only Academy Award for his score for *The Omen*, which created a sense of horror using a choir, not the typical choral sound associated with films. Goldsmith moved easily from the folk-like scores of *Stagecoach* and *Lilies of the Field* (featuring a solo harmonica) to *Planet of the Apes*, a movie for which he created dissonant clusters of sound effects produced by orchestral instruments.

Figure 326 - Jerry Goldsmith. His regular interest in experimental orchestration and his distinct preference for a highly dissonant style changed the sound of film music. (Public domain)

Lalo Schifrin, born in Argentina and trained in Paris, identified himself in the tradition of the French avant-garde composers of concert music. But he also frequented jazz clubs, became an arranger for Dizzy Gillespie, and wrote film scores which reflect influences of jazz, bossa nova, and Latin-Americans dance rhythms. Schifrin's scores included *Cool Hand Luke* and *The Fox.* In recent years, his interest has extended to writing a concerto for the master *of nuevo tango,* Astor Piazzola, a virtuoso on the bandoneon. Nelson Riddle, another pupil of Castelnuovo-Tedesco, was known as one of Hollywood's finest dance-band arrangers, a veteran of many collaborations with Frank Sinatra. When Riddle turned to film scoring, he naturally used the sounds and styles of the jazz ensemble. David Amram is a composer who is at home in many musical styles, drawing upon a background in jazz as well as a composer of dramatic music for Shakespearean dramas and chamber music.

Figure 327 - Lalo Schifrin in Concert with the Big Band of the Kölner Musikhochschule. (Photo by Alexandra Sprük released under Creative Commons license)

The use of true jazz in films offers the composer a dilemma. Jazz, by definition, is simultaneous composition and performance. It calls for the soloists to improvise, to make up their music as they go along. But motion pictures, with precise timings and music absolutely keyed to specific action, do not lend themselves easily to music made up on the spot. Erich

Figure 328 Nelson Riddle, a Dorsey alumnus, also gained fame as one of Frank Sinatra's leading arrangers. (Photo courtesy of Nelson Riddle Collection, University of Arizona Fred Fox School of Music)

Korngold used to improvise at the piano as part of his composing technique, but then his scores were very precisely notated and Korngold's music had no more in common with the rhythms of jazz than chess has with football. It is difficult for improvised jazz to match the precise timings required by motion pictures. Audiences, of course, have no idea whether a score is improvised or meticulously planned. So jazz is more likely to appear in films as music that is composed, note-for-note; but the syncopations, rhythms, and distinct use of instruments can make such composed music sound like jazz improvisation. The throbbing rhythms of jazz create a distinct sense of time and place in films.

THE RISE OF THE MOVIE MUSICAL

Thus far, we have been exploring music used to underscore motion pictures. (Composers typically dislike the term "background music" and film music, whether by accident or design, often comes into the foreground.) But one of Hollywood's greatest legacies was a genre of music in which the music and lyrics became truly the stars of the picture: the movie musical!

When sound came to motion pictures, producers and directors were faced with both the challenges and problems of adding voices to pictures. Some silent-film actors were highly photogenic, but if their voices were weak or their acting skills limited, their careers ended. Since audiences could now hear as well as see screen actors, the film musical became an obvious choice for production. If an audience walked out of the theater whistling the tunes it heard in a movie, popularity and profits were guaranteed.

Movie musicals came in two varieties, adaptations of successful Broadway shows that already had an audience and originals, written specifically for the screen. Since many of the producers and directors in Hollywood came from New York, it was natural for them to draw upon the familiar composers and lyricists of Broadway to write music for their new movies.

In the 1930s, Paramount released musicals featuring the talents of Jeanette MacDonald, a glamorous soprano from Philadelphia, and Maurice Chevalier, a leading star of French music halls. Chevalier made his American debut in *Innocents in Paris*. He was unimpressed with the plot of the film and considering returning to Paris. Convinced that Chevalier would be a major star, the studio executives placated him by inserting into the score some of the musical routines that always won him an ovation in the music halls

Figure 329 - Richard Whiting - a leading composer for movie musicals. (Photo courtesy of My Ideal Music Collection)

of Paris. But when the film was released, the song audiences remembered was "Louise," written especially for the movie by Richard Whiting and Leo Robin.

Richard Whiting grew up in Detroit. He began writing songs for student shows as at Los Angeles military academy. He submitted some songs to the Remick publishing company, and was so eager to own a Steinway grand piano that he made an unusual agreement with the publisher. Whiting traded the rights to his next song "It's Tulip Time in Holland" for a piano. Remick sold over a million copies, enough to buy Whiting a piano many times over. Whiting was a modest man. He once discarded a draft copy of a song, "Till We Meet Again," because he thought the words by lyricist Ray Egan were not patriotic enough to win a songwriting contest held during World War I. A secretary spotted the song in the wastebasket, turned it over to publisher Jerome Remick, who entered it into the contest without Whiting's knowledge. It sold over five million copies and became the biggest hit of the World War I era.

In 1929, Chevalier was teamed with Jeanette MacDonald for *The Love Parade*, directed by Ernst Lubitsch, with an operetta-style score by Victor Schertzinger and Clifford Gray. MacDonald was also the star of *Monte Carlo*, for which Whiting and Robin produced a major hit song, "Beyond the Blue Horizon." For studio bosses, a hit song was pure gold. The public liked to speculate about the relationships of leading men and women they saw regularly falling in love on the screen. But real life didn't always match reel life. Chevalier and MacDonald did not like each other personally, but their screen chemistry made them a popular pair. They were reunited in *Love Me Tonight,* directed by Rouben Mamoulian. The score was provided by one of Broadway's most successful teams, Richard Rodgers and Lorenz Hart. For the film, Hart developed "rhythmic conversation." a type of rhymed dialogue with musical accompaniment. The film contained some of their finest work, "Mimi," "Isn't It Romantic," and "Lover," the latter, ironically sung by Jeanette MacDonald not to Chevalier, but to her horse.

In 1933, Louis B. Mayer achieved a long-sought goal of persuading Jeanette MacDonald to sign with MGM. The following year she again starred opposite Maurice Chevalier in *The Merry Widow*, a filmed adaptation of Franz Lehar's celebrated operetta. Then in 1935, she appeared in *Naughty Marietta,* a milestone for two reasons. The film revived the popularity of the songs by Victor Herbert which had been introduced in the stage version of *Naughty Marietta* twenty-five years earlier and MacDonald had a new leading man, an operatic baritone named Nelson Eddy.

Eddy had worked and struggled to gain recognition as an opera singer. (Early in his career, he supported himself as a newspaper reporter, but was fired for paying too much attention to music.) He was discovered by Hollywood when he substituted at the last minute for famed opera star Lotte Lehmann, ironically later to become Jeanette MacDonald's teacher when she decided to move from film to the operatic stage. Jeanette MacDonald and Nelson Eddy co-starred in seven more films together, *Maytime*, *Girl of the Golden West*, and *New Moon* (all with music by Sigmund Romberg) *Rose-Marie* (with music by Rudolf Friml,) *Sweethearts* (incorporating songs by Victor Herbert,) *Bittersweet* (with music and lyrics by Nöel Coward) and *I Married an Angel* (with music provided by Richard Rodgers and lyrics by his collaborator Lorenz Hart.) Although both stars appeared in other films by themselves (like *San Francisco* based on an Anita Loos screenplay and starring MacDonald as an operatic diva opposite Clark Gable and Spencer Tracy,) they are best remembered as a brilliant team. They made numerous appearances singing together on radio and tried unsuccessfully to develop film projects that would have reunited them on screen after they left MGM. But at the height of their fame, they enjoyed immense popularity as "America's Sweethearts."

Harry Ruby and Bert Kalmar were another very successful team who began their partnership on Broadway and then headed west to Hollywood. Ruby, a native New Yorker, aspired to become a major league baseball player. When he didn't realize his dream, he turned to vaudeville and eventually met his longtime collaborator, Bert Kalmar. Kalmar, like Ruby, worked in vaudeville. He turned to writing songs after appearing as a magician and comedian. Ruby and Kalmar began their collaboration in 1918; by 1923, they had a major hit, "Who's Sorry Now?" Their 1928 song, "I Wanna Be Loved By You," also became a hit for the baby-talking singer, Helen Kane, known as the "Boop Boop a Doop Girl." The song inspired the creation of the animated cartoon character known as Betty Boop. She had a childlike voice while singing lyrics that were provocative in the 1920s. Eventually, Max Fleischer and his animator Grim Natwick created Betty Boop, a cartoon character that immortalized the song by Ruby and Kalmar.

Ruby and Kalmar also had their biggest opportunity in 1928, when they wrote the songs for the stage production of *Animal Crackers*. the production was based on a book by George S. Kaufman and Morrie Ryskind. Groucho Marx's trademark mannerisms, his physical comedy, and his favorite foil, actress Margaret Dumont, were on display for audiences. Two years later, they provided the songs for the film version of *Animal Crackers*, including "Hooray for Captain Spaulding," and the hilarious "Hello, I Must Be Going." The latter phrase was identified with Groucho Marx throughout his career and he used it as the title of his autobiography. "Hooray for Captain Spaulding" became Groucho's signature theme song. They went on to provide songs for other Marx Brothers films, including *Horse Feathers* and *Duck Soup*.

In Hollywood, Ruby and Kalmar had a huge hit when they wrote "Three Little Words," introduced on screen by a trio known as "The Rhythm Boys." The trio consisted of Al

Rinker, Harry Barris, and Bing Crosby. Crosby would eventually pursue a solo career and become one of the biggest stars in history. Ruby and Kalmar also wrote "Nevertheless" and "A Kiss to Build a Dream On." After Kalmar's death in 1947, one of their biggest hits, "Three Little Words," became the title of a biographical film about the pair, starring Red Skelton as Harry Ruby and Fred Astaire as Bert Kalmar.

While many musical films of the period featured plots from operetta and the drawing room: princes and princesses, castles, European locations. In contrast, another genre of musical was inspired by *The Ziegfeld Follies*, lavishly costumed musical reviews produced on Broadway by Florenz Ziegfeld. The Florenz Ziegfeld of Hollywood was a choreographer named Busby Berkeley. His specialties were large ensembles of chorus girls forming elaborate geometric designs through their movements, all designed by Berkeley to look like a kaleidoscope. The leading composer for Berkeley's musicals was Harry Warren.

Harry Warren wrote countless hits at Warner Brothers, and later at 20th Century Fox, for musicals starring Alice Faye and Betty Grable. But throughout his career, he lacked the name-recognition of other top Hollywood and Broadway songwriters. Warren was born in Brooklyn, the son of a bootmaker who had come to the United States from Italy. His musical career was launched while he was working as a property man and extra on the set of a Vitagraph silent film in 1915, when he improvised some piano music that impressed the film's star, Corrine Griffith. After military service, Warren took a job as a song plugger at one of New York's biggest music publishing houses, Remick. When the company was sold to Warner Brothers, Warren headed west to Hollywood.

Figure 330 - Harry Warren and Al Dubin -Their songs lit up the screen through many movie musicals. (Photo courtesy of Harry Warren Entertainment)

Lyricist Al Dubin had arrived in Hollywood before him. Dubin was a larger than life figure who had been named for Alexander the Great. Dubin had been writing songs such as "Tiptoe Through the Tulips with Me" with composer Joe Burke. After Warner Brothers released Burke from his contract, Warren and Dubin formed one of Hollywood's most memorable songwriting teams. They produced at least sixty songs for the studio.

Warren and Dubin provided the songs for *42nd Street*, the 1933 Warner Brothers musical about what takes place behind the scenes of a Broadway show. (The highlight of film was an episode in which a Broadway show is saved by an aspiring young dancer, played by Ruby Keeler, when its intended star, portrayed by Bebe Daniels, breaks her leg. A relatively unknown actress, Ginger Rogers, appeared in a supporting role.) Warren and Dubin provided the songs: "Forty-Second Street," "You're Getting to Be a Habit With Me," and "Shuffle Off to Buffalo." Warren and Dubin made a cameo appearance in the film themselves, portraying two songwriters. Warren and Dubin wrote many hits, including "I Only Have Eyes for You" from another Busby Berkley film, *Dames.*For *Gold Diggers of 1935*, Warren and Dubin wrote one of their greatest hits, "Lullaby of Broadway." It won them an Academy Award. Eventually, Dubin left Warner Brothers to seek his fortune on Broadway. He was a big, gregarious family man who lived life to the fullest, unfortunately indulging in food, drink, and gambling to excess. He died at only fifty-three. One of the Warren-Dubin songs was "The Boulevard of Broken Dreams." It included what would be a prophetic comment on Dubin's life, with reference to the "street of sorrow" where "the joy that you find here, you borrow" and concluding that "you cannot keep it long, it seems." Dubin's death at a young age unfortunately resulted in his not always being remembered for his contributions to the great era of movie musicals.

In the depression, audiences wanted to escape from the grim conditions facing most Americans. They found escape in a series of movies produced by RKO, starring the remarkable dance team of Fred Astaire and Ginger Rogers. Their films featured some of the most elegant dancing ever seen on screen, before or since, and reflected the epitome of taste and style. Music and lyrics were provided by the finest composers working on Broadway, including Cole Porter, Vincent Youmans, Jerome Kern, George and Ira Gershwin, and especially, Irving Berlin. Choreography was developed through a unique collaboration between Astaire and his favorite choreographer, Hermes Pan. Yet the collaboration of Fred Astaire and Ginger Rogers came about quite by accident.

In 1933, RKO released *Flying Down to Rio,* a musical featuring songs by Vincent Youmans. The studio was hovering around bankruptcy and Astaire was billed fifth in the film, behind the ostensible stars, Gene Raymond and Dolores Del Rio. Dorothy Jordan was cast opposite Astaire as his dance partner for the film, but she withdrew when she married the film's executive producer. She was replaced by Ginger Rogers. The score included a title song, a tango, "Orchids in the Moonlight" and a dance number for Astaire and Rogers, "The Carioca." Their chemistry was irresistible, and audiences were soon demanding to see more of them. The Astaire and Rogers musicals all reflected some distinct traits: love stories that

Figure 331 - Vincent Youmans, whose songs for *Flying Down to Rio* helped launch the dance team of Fred Astaire and Ginger Rogers. (Photo courtesy of Vincent Youmans III)

were light and unsentimental, stylized Art Deco settings, first rate Broadway-style scores, and superb dancing. *The Gay Divorcee* (1934) featured Cole Porter songs, but when Porter declined to write new material for the film, Con Conrad and Herb Magidson created "The Continental" which won the first Academy Award for "Best Song." Suddenly everyone, even couples who could barely dance the box step, wanted to imagine themselves dancing like Astaire and Rogers.

Roberta was based on Jerome Kern's Broadway hit. Producer Pandro Berman asked Dorothy Fields and Jimmy McHugh to write lyrics for a melody Kern created for a fashion sequence. Kern had not met Fields, but was delighted when he made her acquaintance and with her effort, "Lovely to Look At." *Top Hat* (1935) established Astaire's trademark of casual elegance, whether dancing or choosing his wardrobe. Irving Berlin created the score, featuring the memorable song, "Cheek to Cheek." Berlin also provided the music and lyrics for *Follow the Fleet* including "Let's Face the Music and Dance," which became the basis for one of the most unique dance sequences ever included in a musical. Astaire and Rogers pretend to be Monte Carlo socialites, both on the brink of suicide. Astaire manages to persuade Rogers that life is still worth living, entirely through dance. This sequence conveyed an emotional seriousness of purposes more often associated with ballet than with the dance of musical comedy.

Swing Time (1936) featured the music of Jerome Kern, including two songs which became major hits, the lyrical melody "The Way You Look Tonight" and the angry love song, "A Fine Romance." Kern, known for the sweeping, lyrical, romantic melodies, had disliked jazz versions of his songs. It took considerable persuasion for him to create a "Waltz in Swing Time" for this film. In 1937, Astaire and Rogers starred in *Shall We Dance?* with music by George and Ira Gershwin. Hollywood executives worried about Gershwin's interest in writing music they considered "long-haired" or "highbrow," especially after several of his Broadway efforts failed to become major hits, while he devoted himself to writing his operatic masterpiece, *Porgy and Bess.* Gershwin actually sent a telegram to his agent declaring, "Rumors About Highbrow Music Ridiculous/Stop/ Am Out to Write Hits."

Figure 332 - George and Ira Gershwin in Beverly Hills, 1937 - In Hollywood, the Gershwins, along with Vincent Youmans, Irving Berlin, and Jerome Kern, provided music for the legendary Astaire-Rogers movies. (Photo by Rex Hardy, Jr. used by special permission of the Gershwin Family Trusts)

Irving Berlin provided the music for the next Astaire-Rogers collaboration, *Carefree* (1938). A highlight of the film was a dance sequence in which Ginger Rogers (under hypnosis) reacts like a puppet on a string to Astaire, who leads her through the dance like a magician. The melody by Irving Berlin, "Change Partners," would prove a prophetic title. In 1939, Astaire and Rogers completed their final film as America's favorite dance duo. *The Story of Vernon and Irene Castle,* a musical tribute to two famed dancers of the World War I era. Rogers pursued a long career as an actress while Astaire danced with many other partners. But the Astaire-Rogers partnership would remain indelibly etched in the public's memory. The scores of the Astaire and Rogers musicals provided the basis for dance routines which would change forever the way dance would be perceived and appreciated by audiences. Astaire and his choreographer-associate, Hermes Pan, had a capacity to use shadows, mirrors, and inanimate objects as props in dazzling displays of artistry. The series of movies would also be responsible for the creation of some of the finest popular songs heard on the screen.

MGM AND THE FREED UNIT

MGM became recognized as Hollywood's finest studio for the production of musicals. Much of this deserved recognition was the result of autonomy for the Freed Unit, which escaped some, but not all of the usual studio politics. Freed's team included such musical producers and arrangers as Roger Edens, Lela Simone, Kay Thompson, Conrad Salinger, Lennie Hayton, Saul Chaplin, Adolph Deutsch, and André Previn.

Roger Edens was a key member of the Freed team working as associate producer, composer, and arranger. He moved to Hollywood from Broadway to work with his friend Ethel Merman at Paramount. Eventually, he went to MGM where he spent two decades contributing greatly to the golden age of MGM musicals. Edens was the original mentor to the studio's prize child star, Judy Garland. In 1913, "You Made Me Love You, I didn't Want to Do It," by composer Jimmy Monaco and lyricist Joe McCarthy, had been a big hit for iconic entertainer Al Jolson. For the musical *Broadway Melody of 1938*, Edens wrote new lyrics and special material for Garland to sing in the form of a letter to the studio's biggest real-life star, Clark Gable. "Dear Mr. Gable" became a sensation and eventually led to Judy Garland being cast in the prize role of Dorothy in *The Wizard of Oz*.

Figure 333 - Harold Arlen, singing "Over the Rainbow," a classic song that was nearly cut from *The Wizard of Oz* by executives who thought no one would remember it. (Photo courtesy of Sam Arlen Music)

In 1939, MGM released an original musical, *The Wizard of Oz*. It established Metro-Goldwyn-Mayer as the leading studio for the production of musicals. Producer Arthur Freed eventually established his own production unit within MGM, "a studio within a studio." The Freed Unit specialized in musicals for more than two decades, producing some of the finest examples of the genre. *The Wizard of Oz* (based on L. Frank Baum's classic tale) starred newcomer and instant child star Judy Garland as a young girl from Kansas who follows the Yellow Brick Road into a magical land of the Scarecrow, the Cowardly Lion, the Tin Man, and the Wicked Witch of the West.

At the suggestion of Jerome Kern, Freed hired composer Harold Arlen and lyricist E.Y. ("Yip") Harburg to write the songs. Freed asked Arlen and Harburg for a ballad to ease the transition from Kansas to Oz. Harburg did not share Arlen's enthusiasm for the idea and when Arlen composed a melody beginning with a wide leap of an octave, Harburg dubbed it suitable for Nelson Eddy, not a little girl from Kansas. The song was always facing expulsion from the score. It was regularly deleted and added after various previews. At a meeting to finally decide the fate of the song, Sam Katz, executive producer of the musical division declared it to be above the heads of children. Publisher Jack Robbins compared it to a children's piano exercise, predicting gloomily that no one would sing it or buy the sheet music. Only Freed's threat of resignation saved "Over the Rainbow" from extinction on the cutting room floor.

If the film had been under the supervision of a less powerful producer than Arthur Freed, "Over the Rainbow" might never have seen the light of day. Of course, as everyone now knows, the song is eternally identified with *The Wizard of Oz*; it became Judy Garland's signature song and one of the best-loved melodies ever to emerge from the movies. "Over the Rainbow" was named best song of the year at the Academy Awards and Herbert Stothart surprisingly took the "Best Score" award in the face of stiff competition from Max Steiner's music for *Gone With the Wind*. The competition between the two scores drew attention to a serious problem in such awards ceremonies. Comparing a musical score based on songs with lyrics and the orchestral score for a dramatic picture was essentially comparing apples and oranges. The conflict wouldn't end in 1939.

Hugh Martin and Ralph Blane were two young composer-lyricists who met in the 1930s. Martin had left Birmingham, Alabama and Blane had come from Broken Arrow, Oklahoma to pursue careers on Broadway where they were both singing in musicals. Martin became known as a vocal arranger when he worked for Richard Rodgers. Blane, born Ralph Hunsecker, was known for his singing on NBC radio. Producer-director George Abbott hired Martin and Blane to write the score for a light-hearted original show about students, *Best Foot Forward*, which attracted the attention of Columbia Pictures. Unlike most teams, Martin and Blane both wrote music and lyrics, but pooled their work when they collaborated. This was a most unusual practice, since people automatically assumed that both men had worked on each song together. When they were added to Arthur Freed's MGM staff, he agreed to buy the rights to *Best Foot Forward* from Columbia. He also gave Martin and Blane a plum assignment, to

Figure 334 - Hugh Martin, hard at work on a new composition, contributed greatly to the golden era of movie musicals, especially those produced by The Freed Unit. (Photo courtesy of Suzanne Hanners)

write the songs for a new film musical, *Meet Me in St. Louis.*

In 1942, MGM released *Meet Me In St. Louis*, a musical based on Sally Benson's *Kensington Stories*, gentle tales about family life in St. Louis in the early years of the century. The score contained three songs that became standards for Judy Garland and added considerably to the fame she had achieved in *The Wizard of Oz.* Although the songs were always credited to Martin and Blane, Martin indicated in his 2010 autobiography that he had written the songs for *Meet Me in St. Louis* by himself.

Garland singing "The Boy Next Door" provided one of her most memorable moments on screen. In one scene, a trolley car leaves a St. Louis depot. It seemed improbable that anyone would take a song about a trolley seriously, so the original plan called for a tune to be sung by passengers and the crowd watching the trolley depart. But Arthur Freed insisted on a song about the trolley. The solution appeared in an unlikely place, the Beverly Hills Public Library. A book on old St. Louis included a picture of an antique trolley captioned, "Clang, Clang, Clang Went the Trolley." It took only ten minutes to dash off the incredibly popular song of that title.

Martin originally struggled with the lyric for "Have Yourself a Merry Little Christmas."

Figure 336 - MGM General Music Director John Green at the head of the table in 1955. (Left front, Hugo Friedhofer, third from front left, Eugene Zádor. Right front, André Previn, third from back right, Bronislaw Kaper. (Photo courtesy of Leslie Zador)

The melody came first; when Blane told Martin that it sounded like a madrigal, Martin was inspired to create the Christmas lyric. But it was originally quite gloomy, containing phrases such as "Have yourself a merry little Christmas, it may be your last." Judy Garland suggested making it more optimistic and said that audiences would think of her as a "monster" if she sang those words to little Margaret O'Brien on screen. Martin resisted pressure from Garland and the studio executives, but he was finally persuaded by his friend Tom Drake over a cup of coffee to change the words. The new hopeful lyric pleased everyone and the song emerged from the film as standard fare for every subsequent Christmas season. Martin and Blane collaborated for many years, although they also continued to work separately. Martin achieved success in a collaboration with Timothy Gray, the Broadway show *High Spirits*, based on Noël Coward's play, *Blithe Spirit*. Blane also worked with others, including Harry Warren, Harold Arlen, and Kay Thompson. Martin died in 2011 at the age of 96. He devoted much of his later musical work to gospel music and lived long enough to see the bizarre decline of standards in popular music. He closed his autobiography by recalling a comparison between the lyrics for two Oscar winning songs, one written in 1936, the other in 2006. The first song was "The Way You Look Tonight," by Jerome Kern and Dorothy Fields, the second, "It's Hard Out Here for a Pimp." The comparison speaks for itself.

Figure 337 - Fred Astaire (left) and Gene Kelly (right) in 1964, while presenting the Screen Producers Guild award to Arthur Freed. (Photo courtesy of The Los Angeles Times Photographic Archive, Library Special Collections, Charles E. Young Research Library, UCLA.)

Frequently the most successful Hollywood musicals were the result of fortuitous accidents. *Easter Parade*, a 1947 musical, seemed a sure-fire hit, with Judy Garland, Gene Kelly, and a score by Irving Berlin. When Freed rejected one of Berlin's comedy songs, he disappeared and came back a few minutes later with "A Couple of Swells," a duet for two tramps lampooning the manners of socialites. The biggest problem facing the film wasn't one of music, but of casting. When Kelly broke his ankle playing volleyball, Fred Astaire agreed to replace him in *Easter Parade*. The film became a tremendous success, and Berlin's title song became a standard sung every Easter throughout the country.

It is impossible to discuss the glorious years of MGM musicals without recognizing the unique contributions of Gene Kelly. While Kelly is best remembered by the public as a dancer and actor, he played an important role behind the camera in his career, as director, producer, writer, and especially as a choreographer who revolutionized the photography of dance in motion pictures.

Kelly's inimitable style brought a strong, athletic approach to the grace associated with dance. He had once aspired to be a professional baseball player. After success on Broadway, he appeared in his first film, *For Me and My Gal*, in which he co-starred opposite Judy Garland. In *Thousands Cheer,* he had the chance to dance to his own choreography, using a mop as his partner. In 1945, Kelly appeared in *Anchors Aweigh*, a film in which he was able to devise his own dance routines. He coached Frank Sinatra to enable the singing star to dance in duets with him and also created a revolutionary dance sequence, combining live action and animation, in which he appeared with a "dancer" he jokingly referred to as his favorite partner—Jerry the Mouse, the star of many "Tom and Jerry" cartoons. Jerry proved up to the task of matching Kelly's athleticism and his demanding work ethic.

Kelly worked with another celebrated partner, Fred Astaire, in *Ziegfeld Follies* that featured a challenge dance scene between the two legendary performers. Kelly broke new ground in another way when he starred in *The Pirate*, again opposite Judy Garland. He was joined in a virtuoso dance sequence by the fantastic Nicholas Brothers. Harold and Fayard Nicholas would have become tremendous movie stars in their own right, but this was a difficult time for black performers, and Kelly's collaboration with them on screen was unforgettable. At the time, it was not acceptable for a white performer to appear in a musical number with black performers, and the number was sadly cut from the movie when it screened in theaters in the South. In *On the Town,* Kelly was one of three sailors, joined by Frank Sinatra and Jules Munshin, who leave their ship in the Brooklyn Navy Yard and literally sing and dance their way around the streets of New York. As Kelly's directorial debut, the film broke new ground by being the first movie musical to shoot on location. Quick cuts and location shots replaced the old-style "dissolves" associated with musicals. In Judy Garland's last musical for MGM, *Summer Stock*, Kelly expressed himself brilliantly through dance using a newspaper and a squeaky floorboard.

An American in Paris featured a ground-breaking seventeen-minute ballet, a *pas de deux* danced by Kelly and French ballerina Leslie Caron. No one could forget Kelly's dance with an umbrella in *Singin' in the Rain* or his remarkable exhibition of tap dancing with Donald O'Connor in "Moses Supposes" in the same film. Kelly's most ambitious project was *Invitation to the Dance*, a film telling three separate stories entirely through dance. There was no dialogue, only choreography. The first story, *Circus*, was presented to music by Jacques Ibert. For this film, André Previn faced an usual challenge: his music for the second story was replacing a discarded score by the English composer Malcolm Arnold. Since the film had already been shot, Previn was handed a volume of timings he described as "thick as the Manhattan telephone directory." Previn managed to compose a highly effective score, *Ring Around the Rosy*, featuring variations on a children's theme and even utilized his skills as a jazz pianist. The final story, *Sinbad the Sailor*, combined live action and cartoons accompanied by the music of Niklolai Rimsky-Korsakov's

Scheherazade. Kelly choreographed and starred in the film, portraying a clown, a tough marine, and Sinbad, a sailor. Kelly's dance routines were not just inserted in films. They were character-driven and always helped to tell and expand the story. Kelly always developed his own style, drawing upon the influences of classical ballet, but also modern dance, tap, folk dancing, and his own natural athleticism. He could present stunning romanticism, as in his *pas de deux* dance duet with Cyd Charisse in *Brigadoon* and his sensuous contemporary jazz sequences with Vera-Ellen. He could also surprise audiences by dancing on roller skates in *It's Always Fair Weather*. In short, Kelly's eclectic and creative style of dance changed the way dancers were perceived and photographed on screen.

From 1949-59, Johnny Green served in a powerful executive position at the studio, General Musical Director. Green was the antithesis of the stereotypical Hollywood producer. An urbane, dapper raconteur, John Waldo Green graduated from Harvard with an economics degree, but turned to music, first as an arranger for Guy Lombardo's orchestra, later as the songwriter of such hits as "Coquette" and "Body and Soul." He was active as a conductor and arranger on Broadway and on radio, moving to Hollywood in 1942. Green always sported a white carnation in his lapel. Staff composers at MGM were required to attend meetings seated at children's school desks while Green explained his policies. A half-century before cell phones were ubiquitous, Green had a telephone in his car and was apt to send instructions to MGM composers, advising the recipient of his call that he was "in traffic at the corner of Hollywood and Vine."

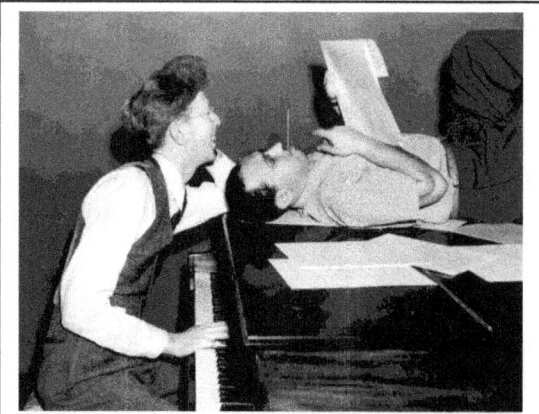

Figure 338 - A young Saul Chaplin at the piano with lyricist Sammy Cahn early in their careers. (Photo courtesy of Tita Cahn)

Green also composed dramatic scores for films like the Civil War epic, *Raintree County* and made appearances as a guest conductor of leading orchestras. He harbored a lifelong ambition to be considered as permanent conductor of a major symphony orchestra. Green eventually dropped the name "Johnny" and said, "You can call me John or you can call me 'Maestro.'" But he is best remembered today for his fine work on MGM classic musicals.

During Green's tenure at MGM, Saul Chaplin became one of the leading members of the Freed Unit. Brooklyn-born Saul Chaplin originally had studied to be an accountant, but decided instead to turn to writing songs when he couldn't resist the lure of music. His early collaborator was lyricist Sammy Cahn. Chaplin and Cahn both moved to Hollywood. In 1946, Chaplin worked on *The Jolson Story* at Columbia Pictures and collaborated with star Al Jolson to write "The Anniversary Song." It was based on a Romanian melody by

Ion Ivanovici. Chaplin eventually settled at MGM and became prominent as a composer, music supervisor, and producer. He contributed to many of the finest musicals produced under the banner of the Freed Unit.

Just as Astaire stepped in to replace Kelly, Ginger Rogers replaced Judy Garland in the 1949 musical *The Barkleys of Broadway*, reuniting her with Fred Astaire. Harry Warren teamed with Ira Gershwin to write the score. Warren and Gershwin were asked to write a song with a Scottish theme. To create "My One and Only Highland Fling," Gershwin searched the Los Angeles telephone book for Scottish names that could be rhymed with other words he wanted to use in the lyric, "McDougal" and "frugal" being typical. Choreographer Hermes Pan was inspired to create the "Winged Shoes" dance for Astaire featuring multiple dancing shoes after watching brooms multiplying in the Disney animated version of *The Sorcerer's Apprentice* in *Fantasia*.

Alan Jay Lerner and Frederick Loewe had completed their stage score for *Brigadoon*. While Loewe took a vacation, Lerner went to Hollywood to develop ideas for movie musicals. He suggested a musical based on the careers of Fred Astaire and his first dance partner, his sister Adele. When Adele Astaire married a titled Englishman, she retired from show business. Lerner used this idea (and the marriage of England's Princess Elizabeth, then in the news) to develop *Royal Wedding*. The plot of the film was clearly adapted from the Astaires' story. Fred Astaire would play a dancer performing with his sister, played by Jane Powell. Romance in *Royal Wedding* would involve Powell's character falling in love with a titled Englishman, just as Astaire's sister Adele had done many years before. Lerner and composer Burton Lane decided to write a vaudeville number for the film. While driving to the studio, Lerner had a sudden inspiration, "How Could You Believe Me When I Said I Love You When You Know I've Been a Liar All My Life?" It has been called the longest song title in history. Lane, however, may have taken the shortest amount of time to compose it. He had the melody in his mind by the time the two reached the studio. Another Lerner and Lane song, "You're All the World To Me," became unforgettable when Astaire performed it apparently dancing on the walls and the ceiling.

Alan Jay Lerner was chosen by Arthur Freed to write the script for *An American In Paris*, an all-Gershwin musical inspired by the orchestral piece of the same name, and featuring the dancing talents of Gene Kelly. Lerner had completed only forty pages of the script when, the night before his own wedding, he accepted a challenge from his collaborator, composer Frederick Loewe, and completed the script overnight. Kelly portrayed an American GI who stays in Paris to paint and falls in love with a pretty French orphan played by ballerina Leslie Caron. The film incorporated numerous classic Gershwin songs, including "Our Love is Here to Stay," the last piece George Gershwin composed before his untimely death, completed by Ira Gershwin and Vernon Duke.

Gershwin's original orchestral composition, *An American In Paris*, was used as the basis for an extended ballet. The music was rearranged in five parts to fit Kelly's choreography, Busy Paris, The Flower Market, The Gay Whirl, Tempo Blues, and Finale. Individual sets were inspired by painters Dufy, Manet, Rousseau, Monet, Utrillo, Van Gogh, and Toulouse-Lautrec. The ballet was a milestone in musicals, using one of the longest dance sequences in films as an essential element of the dramatic plot. The ballet displayed Kelly's graceful, athletic style of dance, quite different from the elegant, urbane approach of Fred Astaire.

One musical highlight was unexpected. The brilliant but often difficult pianist Oscar Levant, who was cast as Kelly's sidekick in the film, came up with the idea for one of the most unusual numbers in a role inspired by his friend, the composer David Diamond. Levant, known for his caustic wit and volatile temperament, emerged from one of his periodic depressions to suggest one of the most remarkable scenes ever to be included in a musical film. In a dream sequence, the "Ego Fantasy," he imagines himself playing one of his own compositions (actually, a movement of Gershwin's *Concerto in F*) with a symphony orchestra. Through photography, Levant appears to be playing the piano and all the orchestral instruments simultaneously, as well as conducting on the podium, and sitting in the audience, shouting "Bravo" as he is overwhelmed by his own genius. More than a few composers had to admit that while the scene might be funny, the fantasy was not far from their own aspirations.

Some of the most famous moments in musical films happened by accident. *Singin' in the Rain* (1951) was a musical about the transition from silent films to sound. The score was based on songs written by Arthur Freed and Nacio Herb Brown. When a new song was needed for a spectacular dance number by Donald O'Connor, Freed and Brown penned: "Make 'Em Laugh." The song was a virtual rewrite of Cole Porter's "Be a Clown," featured in a previous MGM musical, *The Pirate*. Freed proudly had a recording of the song played for Irving Berlin, one of Porter's closest friends. Berlin promptly said, "Who wrote that? That's "Be a Clown!" The film also contained what may be the most famous scene in a film musical: Gene Kelly, umbrella in hand, spinning around lampposts and dancing in the rain to the film's title song. Kelly was searching for a way to lead into the musical number, and Roger Edens suggested that Kelly begin with the musical phrase "doo-de-doo-doo." a "vamp" that remains as familiar as any hit song in the world.

Just as Agnes deMille's ballets revolutionized the use of dance in Broadway musicals, *An American in Paris* changed the way dance was perceived in Hollywood film musicals. *Lili* was a 1953 musical produced at MGM, but not by the Freed Unit. This tale of a French girl traveling with a carnival featured a remarkable score composed by Bronislaw Kaper. He chose to score *Lili* over a major historical epic regarded as much more important by MGM and produced by the head of the studio. Kaper couldn't resist the opportunity to write two intriguing ballets. One, a jazz ballet was developed for the predatory femme fatale (played by Zsa-Zsa Gabor) who was Lili's rival, the other a set of variations on Kaper's wonderful wistful melody, "Hi-Lili, Hi-Lo." It featured individual instruments accompanying dancers who portrayed the puppets who were Lili's only friends. Kaper often quipped that *Lili* paid for his beautiful Spanish-style house in Beverly Hills.

The Band Wagon was a film musical incorporating the songs of Howard Dietz and Arthur Schwartz. A highlight of the film was a dance sequence based on their classic melody, *Dancing in the Dark.* The dance resolved not only the romantic relationship between two dancers, portrayed by Fred Astaire and Cyd Charisse, but their conflicting styles of dance. Still, when Arthur Freed told Dietz and Schwartz that the film needed another song, they complied. Asked to supply something like Irving Berlin's classic, *There's No Business Like Show Business*, the two disappeared into a room and came back a few minutes later with "That's Entertainment." The song became a virtual anthem for MGM's classic musicals and was used as the title of several films highlight the golden era of film musicals. The film included two other especially memorable musical numbers: "Triplets" (in which Fred Astaire, Nanette Fabray, and Jack Buchanan appear to be dancing on baby legs) and "The Girl Hunt Ballet." For the latter, Astaire and Cyd Charisse portray characters derived from a Mickey Spillane detective novel. Roger Edens composed the music for the ballet based on songs by Dietz and Schwartz.

The talented team of the Freed Unit took their high standards with them when they worked elsewhere. In 1957, Paramount released *Funny Face*, featuring some familiar themes: Americans in Paris, (this time Fred Astaire and Audrey Hepburn) and a Gershwin score. Roger Edens and Kay Thompson wrote three new songs, and Thompson appeared in the picture as the *grande dame* of Parisian haute couture.

The Hollywood film musical clearly reached its zenith with the 1958 production of *Gigi.* Alan Jay Lerner was eager to work on the filmed adaptation of a novella by the French writer, Collette, which had been a successful Broadway play by Anita Loos and launched the career of Audrey Hepburn. *Gigi* was the story of a young French girl at the turn of the century, her coming of age, and the conflict caused by her family's expectations that she will become of the unmarried mistress of a rich Parisian playboy. Lerner was eager to fulfill one of his life's ambitions, to work with Maurice Chevalier. But he had difficulties persuading his mercurial collaborator, Frederick Loewe, to agree.

Figure 339 - Frederick Loewe. Though Viennese, his musical ability to reflect a Parisian charm when combined with Alan Jay Lerner's lyrics, made *Gigi* one of the all-time classic Hollywood musical films. (Photograph Courtesy of Estate of Frederick Loewe)

Loewe was, as often, as not, enjoying the pleasures of a casino on the French Riviera. Lerner would cable Loewe with news of projects they had been offered. Loewe often said "no." A proposed musical based on *Gone With the Wind* elicited Loewe's response, complete with Viennese accent, "Vind not funny." A suggested musical inspired by the life of the Trapp Family Singers provoked Loewe's answer, "Dear boy, what do you want me to write, yodel music?" Rodgers and Hammerstein subsequently wrote the show, which turned into *The Sound of Music.*

Though Loewe initially turned Lerner down regarding *Gigi*, he changed his mind and the team which had crafted *My Fair Lady*, the ultimate stage musical, turned their talents to a score that would become one of Hollywood's finest. The cast of *Gigi*, Maurice Chevalier, Leslie Caron, Louis Jourdan, Hermoine Gingold, Isabel Jeans, and Eva Gabor would turn in stellar performances. With Cecil Beaton costumes and the direction of Vincente Minnelli, *Gigi* represented the film musical at its best. Lerner and Loewe produced one of their finest scores for the film, with music arranged and conducted by André Previn.

The songs included "Thank Heaven for Little Girls" and "I'm Glad I'm Not Young Any More" for Chevalier, the poignant duet, "I Remember It Well," as Chevalier plays an aging Lothario reminiscing with Hermione Gingold. Louis Jourdan and Leslie Caron performed "The Night They Invented Champagne." Loewe composed one of his memorable waltzes to match Lerner's comedic lyrics for "She Is Not Thinking of Me." "Say a Prayer for Me Tonight" is indelibly linked to Gigi's preparation for her date with Gaston, the man she loves, at Maxim's, the landmark Parisian restaurant. Few audiences realized that the song wasn't French in origin; it had been cut from Lerner and Loewe's very English stage score for *My Fair Lady*.

Maxim's was closed for several days to the musical sequence could be shot on location. Lerner and Loewe also crafted a soliloquy leading to the title song, "Gigi," for Louis Jourdan. The film, with its stunning costumes and Parisian locations had visual qualities to match the music. Cecil Beaton's costumes earned praise and the location scenes shot in Paris gave the film an authentic Gallic quality. But it wasn't easy. At one point Vincente Minnelli demanded a dozen black swans swimming on a lake to add atmosphere to a scene photographed in the Bois du Boulogne. Minnelli's French was imperfect and his request for *cygnes* was somehow understood as *singes*. When the cast and crew arrived on the scene, there were twenty-four monkeys ready to be photographed. But audiences would never have imagined the temperament and obstacles that were overcome. *Gigi* became the most honored film musical in Hollywood history.

The scores of movie musicals would also be performed by large symphony orchestras, very different from the smaller ensembles working in the orchestra pit of a theater. An adaptation of such a musical score would involve a great deal of dramatic underscoring, frequently requiring the film's musical director to write musical cues adapting passages of the songs written by the Broadway composer. At best, composers like Alfred Newman (in *Carousel* and *South Pacific*) and André Previn (in *My Fair Lady* and *Gigi*) would make major contributions to score. Ironically, when Previn met Frederick Loewe to discuss his orchestrations of Loewe's music for *Gigi*, all did not go smoothly. Previn recalled in his memoir *No Minor Chords* that he tactfully asked Loewe if he would mind a few changes as Previn adapted Loewe's piano sketches for the orchestra. Loewe looked at Previn and said, "Did you attend conservatory?" Previn nodded. Loewe then asked him if he had been given assignments to orchestrate piano sketches? Previn nodded again. Then Loewe said, "And when you did these assignments, did you elect to change Brahms?"

BROADWAY GOES TO HOLLYWOOD

While original musicals emerged from Hollywood, it was only natural that the movie colony would turn east to Broadway for the sources of some of its most successful productions. Throughout the 1930s, 1940s, and 1950s, some of Hollywood's most successful musicals were adaptations of successful Broadway shows. Adapting a hit stage musical and turning it into a film offered a unique set of benefits and problems. A popular score by Jerome Kern, Cole Porter, Irving Berlin, George Gershwin, or Richard Rodgers would virtually guarantee that the film would have memorable words and music, especially since an audience would walk into the theater already knowing and anticipating the score.

But a musical play can't simply be lifted off the stage and deposited on film. Action scenes taking place out of doors, for instance, are depicted in a limited area on stage. *The Desert Song* by Sigmund Romberg may talk about horseman furiously riding over the Arabian desert, but the film version had to *show* them galloping. A substantial difference existed between the Cotton Blossom in the stage version of *Show Boat* (which never came near the water), and the vessel in the various movie versions which had to be seen sailing on the Mississippi River. The surrey with the fringe on top didn't have to really drive over the Oklahoma territory in the stage version of *Oklahoma!* A naval expedition in *South Pacific* or the horse races at Ascot in *My Fair Lady* could be discussed without being shown to the audience.

Figure 340 - Gordon MacRae and Shirley Jones starred in the film version of *Oklahoma!*, bringing the revolutionary team of Rodgers & Hammerstein musical to the wide screen. (Photo courtesy of Rodgers & Hammerstein: An Imagem Company, www.rnh.com)

While action scenes could be portrayed more realistically in the movies, opening up the action scenes could potentially upstage the music and lyrics. Similarly, highly theatrical choreography, such as the "Dream Ballet" in *Oklahoma!*, the depiction of a heaven filled with stars in *Carousel*, and the images of two street gangs confronting each other with choreography instead of weapons in *West Side Story* are good examples. These spectacular dance sequences had to be translated to the screen in ways that wouldn't interfere with the more realistic visual medium of the movies.

When a major studio purchased rights to a stage musical, the studio bosses would frequently order wholesale rewriting of the script. In the original stage version of *Show Boat*, for instance, the leading character of Magnolia and her gambler husband, Gaylord Ravenal, are reunited when their daughter is grown and ready to embark on a theatrical career of her own. In the Kathryn Grayson-Howard Keel film version, the couple is reunited aboard the Cotton Blossom when their daughter is still a small child. In 1958, a film version of Rodgers and Hart's *Pal Joey* received the Hollywood treatment. The original story featured a small time heel carrying on an affair with a married woman in Chicago. The film moved the location to San Francisco, turned the leading lady into a widow, and reformed the villain by the end of the picture. For good measure, eight Rodgers and Hart songs were dropped, replaced by other tunes written by the duo for other shows.

The annals of film musicals are full of major changes, cuts and additions. Producers would think nothing of buying a musical, liquidating many of the composer's original songs (as in the case of Kurt Weill's *Knickerbocker Holiday*) and substituting songs written by others. If the original composer's lyrics were used, they might be altered in ways that changed the original intent of the writers.

A filmed version of Cole Porter's *Anything Goes*, featured one of Porter's sly double-entendres about "four letter words" changed to "three letter words," presumably to not offend the sensibilities of the film audience. Often the studios would regard stage stars as unknowns or lacking box office appeal. Stage stars (and their fans) frequently assume that if an actor has left a personal stamp on a role, it could go to no one else in the movie. (Obvious examples are Yul Brynner in *The King and I*, Rex Harrison in *My Fair Lady*, Robert Preston in *The Music Man,* and William Daniels *in 1776.)*

Yet curiously, producer Jack Warner considered several stars for the role of Henry Higgins in *My Fair Lady.* Improbably, he did not plan on hiring Rex Harrison to play the role that he had created on Broadway in the film Warner was producing. Instead, Warner wanted Cary Grant to portray Higgins, despite a Cockney lilt in Grant's speaking voice which would have rendered him hopelessly miscast as a teacher of textbook aristocratic English. To his credit, Grant told Warner to hire Rex Harrison. Warner also declined to hire Julie Andrews known primarily for her work on stage, to sing the role of Eliza Doolittle in the same film, opting for the better known Audrey Hepburn, an establish movie star. So Audrey Hepburn became a splendid Liza Doolittle on screen; the crestfallen Andrews had to settle for the starring role in a new Walt Disney musical, *Mary Poppins*, which combined music by Disney staff songwriters Richard M. and Robert B. Sherman with scenes using both live action and animation. The brothers' most difficult challenge was to persuade the acerbic British novelist P.L. Travers to accept their score and she was militantly opposed to insertion of songs or animation in the film. After

Figure 341 - The Sherman Brothers. Richard M. Sherman and Robert B. Sherman were among Walt Disney's favorite songwriters for musicals such as *Mary Poppins*. (Public domain)

leaving Disney, the Shermans went on to write scores for such films as *Chitty Chitty Bang Bang* and The *Slipper and the Rose*.

Actors and cartoon characters had worked together before, as when Gene Kelly danced opposite Jerry (the celebrated animated mouse of *Tom and Jerry* fame) in *Anchors Aweigh*. But no one had ever quite seen anything like *Mary Poppins*, which starred Andrews opposite Dick Van Dyke. It was Julie Andrews, not Audrey Hepburn, who won the Oscar (the same year as her stage star Rex Harrison won for *My Fair Lady*), but no one could ever forget her acceptance speech for another award for *Mary Poppins*, the Golden Globe; she sweetly thanked the man who made it all possible, Jack Warner.

THE GHOSTS IN THE DUBBING ROOM

Studios frequently offered major roles in musicals to non-singing stars, necessitating the dubbing of those stars voices by professional singers, usually uncredited. For example, audiences in the 1940s and 1950s would recognize the names of such stars as Rita Hayworth, Claudette Colbert, Loretta Young, Veronica Lake, and Hedy Lamarr. Few would know that when these actresses performed vocal solos on screen, the voice they were actually hearing belonged to a prolific singer named Martha Mears. When "White Christmas" was first heard in the classic musical *Holiday Inn* in 1942, the voice of Marjorie Reynolds was dubbed by Mears.

Studio executives at MGM were undecided about the singing abilities of Ava Gardner, even though she had recorded "Can't Help Lovin' That Man" and "Bill" for the *Show Boat* soundtrack. Before the release of the film, they replaced her singing voice in those songs with that of Annette Warren, an accomplished professional singer. So strangely enough, Gardner's voice is heard on the record, Warren's in the film. The most unusual example of a "ghost voice" in a film had to be the one used for Lauren Bacall in her film debut, *To Have and Have Not*. It was Hoagy Carmichael at the piano when Lauren Bacall's sultry and rather low-pitched singing voice was heard on the screen. Warner Brothers originally didn't think Bacall's singing voice fit the song and arranged to have her solo curiously dubbed by an unknown male teenage singer whose voice had just changed. His name was Andy Williams; in later years, Williams, by then a major recording and television star, confirmed the story, although Bacall insisted that in the end, director Howard Hawks decided to use her recording. Williams, ever the gentleman, said he wouldn't argue with "the formidable Miss Bacall."

Marni Nixon, a soprano with an extraordinary ability to match the singing voices of others, gained fame as the "ghost" voice in many Hollywood musicals, supplying the singing voice of Deborah Kerr in *The King and I*, (and a non-musical film, *An Affair to Remember*, in which Deborah Kerr portrayed a singer.) She also ghosted the singing voices of Audrey Hepburn in *My Fair Lady*, and Natalie Wood in *West Side Story* Although these were her best-known performances in dubbing, she also dubbed for Jeanne Crain, Janet Leigh, and Marilyn Monroe. The talented Miss Nixon could sing anything from Broadway and Hollywood hits to complex concert songs by composers like Arnold Schoenberg. She even recorded an album of rare Schoenberg cabaret songs with his former assistant, pianist Leonard Stein.. *Time* called her "The Ghostess with the Mostest." She finally appeared on screen in

Figure 342 - Marni Nixon, dubbed by *Time*, "The Ghostess with the Mostess," was so successful recording the voices of non-singing stars, that audiences could forget that she was a superb soloist in her own right. (Photo courtesy of Marni Nixon)

the 1965 film version of *The Sound of Music*, as one of the nuns who sing, "(How Do You Solve a Problem Like) Maria?" Despite numerous appearances on stage as a musical theater star, she was never given a major starring role in a film musical of her own. Studio music directors had to deal with predictably mixed reactions when their own voices were not used in musicals. Leslie Caron was not told until the last minute that her voice would be dubbed for songs in *Gigi;* the dubbing voice belonged to singer Betty Wand.

The world of Hollywood dubbing was always rather mysterious. Sometimes the identity of the singing voice was well-known, as when opera star Giorgio Tozzi substituted for Rossano Brazzi in *South Pacific*. In other situations, the identity of the "ghost" voice was kept secret, and even people who worked on pictures may disagree in the recollections of who did the actual work. The singers who dubbed stars voices often had to live with an incredibly frustrating anonymity. In certain cases only their family or close friends might even be aware of their contributions to a film. André Previn was trying to find the right voice to dub the singing of Jean Seberg for the film *Paint Your Wagon*. She had a soft and musical speaking voice, but her singing proved unsatisfactory. Previn felt he had discovered the ideal voice when he watched an old film that starred Jeanne Crain. He finally discovered that Jeanne Crain's singing actually belonged to Anita Conroy, someone of whom he'd never heard. Unable to find a current phone number for her, he called Western Union to send her a telegram. In a turn of events right out of a movie, the phone operator he reached at Western Union turned out to be Anita Conroy herself; her career had slowed down and she had taken a temporary job answering the telephone. She was quickly hired to sing for Jean Seberg. It could only happen in Hollywood.

Filmed adaptations of musicals range from spectacularly successful to dismal failures. At worst, Hollywood studios have taken outstanding musical plays and transformed them into disappointing (and usually very expensive) films that are a pale shadow of their original Broadway sources. At best, some of the finest film musicals ever produced were based on successful Broadway masterpieces.

BROADWAY COMPOSERS IN TINSELTOWN

When Broadway's leading composers worked in Hollywood, they often wrote original film musicals. Some were enormously successfully, financially and creatively. Others were disappointing, especially since the composers and lyricists had much less control over the work under the studio system. Some Broadway masters enjoyed only limited success in Hollywood, while other composers and lyricists enjoyed their greatest successes writing for the screen, not the stage.

No composer was immune from the decisions of producers to drop or delete songs at will. When Irving Berlin wrote the score for *On the Avenue, (1937)* a 20th Century Fox musical starring Dick Powell and Alice Faye, three of his songs were dropped from the film. Did studio boss Darryl F. Zanuck realize that one song that was used, "You're Laughing at Me" had actually been written ten years earlier?

Zanuck could appreciate the fact that Berlin had a valuable trunk filled with his work. If a song by the prolific Berlin was deleted from a show or movie, it would likely turn up somewhere else one day. More often than not, it might become the basis for a whole movie. In 1938, the same year as Berlin's score for Astaire and Rogers in *Carefree,* Zanuck produced *Alexander's Ragtime Band,* a musical filled with vintage Berlin songs. Perhaps the most memorable recycling of Berlin's words and music took place in a filmed version of *This is the Army.* Berlin himself appeared in the uniform of a World War I soldier, singing "Oh How I Hate to Get Up in the Morning."

One of Berlin's best-known songs was "White Christmas," which took the public by storm when it became the big hit of the 1942 musical *Holiday Inn.* The original arrangement of the iconic Christmas song was completed by a veteran Hollywood composer-conductor, Walter Scharf. Scharf transcribed Berlin's dictation and was the first beside the composer to ever play the melody. After watching Berlin struggling to produce the perfect melody and lyric, Scharf reported that the piece didn't come easily to the composer. Nor did anyone working on the film expect it to sell millions of recordings as one of the most popular Christmas songs of all time. After hearing it for the first time, Bing Crosby told Berlin he need not worry about this particular song. Scharf went on to score numerous musicals and comedies which served as vehicles for Bing Crosby, Danny Kaye, and Jerry Lewis.

Figure 343 - Irving Berlin, revered composer of "God Bless America" aboard U.S.S. Arkansas, 1944 (U.S. Government Photo)

Berlin's biggest hits were likely to turn up in films again and again. "Easter Parade" was included in *Holiday Inn* at Paramount before it was included in the MGM classic film of the same name. "White Christmas" returned in another Paramount musical, *Blue Skies,* which (like *Holiday Inn)* starred Fred Astaire and Bing Crosby. After filmed versions of two of Berlin's biggest Broadway musicals, *Annie Get Your Gun* and *Call Me Madam,* Berlin's music was chosen as the basis for yet another Paramount film called *White Christmas.* Bing Crosby was also back again, this time teamed with Danny Kaye. Berlin's last major musical was another film based on one of his song titles, *There's No Business Like Show Business.* As the composer of America's favorite popular Christmas carol, Easter song, celebration of show business, and *God Bless America,* the unofficial national anthem, Berlin would have achieved musical immortality even if he had never written another note.

Jerome Kern moved to Hollywood after the success of the 1936 film version of *Show Boat* and his Astaire-Rogers musical, *Swing Time.* Kern teamed with Oscar Hammerstein to provide the music and lyrics for *High, Wide and Handsome.* The score included such outstanding ballads as "The Folks Who Live on the Hill." Kern's music for the movies contained the same lyrical sweep and stunning melodies as his Broadway scores. This was never more evident than in *You Were Never Lovelier* (1942). This musical, starring

Fred Astaire and Rita Hayworth contained one of Kern's most haunting melodies, "I'm Old Fashioned," completed with lyrics by Johnny Mercer. Kern also provided the score for another Rita Hayworth film, *Cover Girl* (1944), this time collaborating with Ira Gershwin. One of the highlights of the film was a dance routine featuring Hayworth and Gene Kelly moving up and down the steps of a Brooklyn club. Their song was called "Put Me to the Test." Ira Gershwin had written the lyric for *Damsel in Distress*, a 1937 film featuring music by his brother George. When only an instrumental version of the tune survived, he saved the lyric and turned it over to Kern who composed an entirely new melody. One of Kern's best compositions, "All the Things You Are," enjoyed similar revival in the movies. This remarkable melody had unfortunately come from a rare Kern-Hammerstein Broadway flop, *Very Warm for May*. A 1944 movie, *Broadway Rhythm,* used material from the show, however, including "All the Things You Are," which enjoyed a long and happy life as one of the great standards of American popular music.

The music of George Gershwin found its way into movies easily. Not only did the songs of George and Ira Gershwin appear in original musicals, so did various versions of George Gershwin's concert pieces, beginning in 1930 with *King of Jazz,* Universal's tribute to Paul Whiteman, and featuring pianist Roy Bargy performing *Rhapsody in Blue.* George Gershwin composed an instrumental piece, *The New York Rhapsody,* for a dream sequence in the film *Delicious.* It would resurface on the concert stage as his *Second Rhapsody,* though never with the overwhelming popularity of *Rhapsody in Blue.* A highlight of *Shall We Dance* (1937) was a scene (without dialogue) based on walking a dog. Gershwin's music for the scene would also reappear as an instrumental composition, *Promenade.* Gershwin's sudden death in 1937 cut short his Hollywood and Broadway career, but not the life of his music. Ira Gershwin and Vernon Duke completed the score he was finishing at the time of his death, *Goldwyn Follies,* and its theme, "Our Love is Here to Stay." The same could be said for Gershwin's music, which continues to appear in movies to this day. Films like *Strike Up the Band* and *Lady Be Good* were filled with Gershwin music. His opera, *Porgy and Bess* was finally turned into a movie in 1959.

The urbane sophisticate, Cole Porter, enjoyed the parties, nightlife, and activities of Hollywood. But he wasn't spared from dealing with the whims and caprices of producers. When his Broadway show *The Gay Divorce* became the Rogers and Astaire movie, *The Gay Divorcee*, only one of his songs, "Night and Day," was retained by the producers. Porter was also asked to write the score for a projected film project, *Adios Argentina.* Porter agreed to use one lyric by another writer, a poem by Bob Fletcher, a cowboy from Montana. When *Adios Argentina* was canceled, the song took on a life of its own. "Don't Fence Me In" was a tune least-likely to be written the quintessentially cosmopolitan Porter. But in 1944, it made its way into *Hollywood Canteen*, a film featuring an appearance by one of Hollywood's favorite singing cowboys, Roy Rogers; it ironically emerged as one of Porter's biggest hits.

Like Berlin and Kern, Porter learned that in Hollywood, songs became hits in unlikely ways. "Begin the Beguine," extracted from his unsuccessful *Jubilee,* was popularized in a jazz band arrangement recorded by Artie Shaw and his orchestra. As a result, the tune turned up again in *Broadway Melody of 1940,* a movie which teamed Fred Astaire and Eleanor Powell. A dance sequence based on *Begin the Beguine* proved to be one of the most astonishing displays of tap dancing virtuosity ever seen on the screen, and *Begin the Beguine* was established as a legendary film melody. In contrast, Porter's "Dream Dancing" is still one of his least-known ballads. It was used in *You'll Never Get Rich,* a 1941 musical written for Fred Astaire and Rita Hayworth. The fate of a specific song often depended on the success of the movie. Porter continued to write original songs for movies as well as for Broadway, and one, "Be a Clown," performed by Gene Kelly and Judy Garland at the conclusion of *The Pirate (1948)* expressed much of Porter's personal outlook. He didn't take himself or his work too seriously. One of Porter's finest moments on the screen came with "True Love," a nostalgic, sentimental duet sung by Bing Crosby and Grace Kelly while aboard a sailboat in *High Society* (1956). Many of Porter's most memorable tunes were included in film versions of his Broadway successes, including *Silk-Stockings, Can-Can,* and his most popular musical, *Kiss Me, Kate.*

Richard Rodgers inevitably worked in Hollywood, with both of his regular lyricists, Lorenz Hart and Oscar Hammerstein II. Rodgers, accustomed to exercising great control over his work, was never happy with the Hollywood system. His wife Dorothy, in a memoir written years later, recalled their early days in the movie colony where writers were considered "low men on the totem pole." Typical of their experience was an episode involving *Hollywood Party*, a musical which included a few Rodgers & Hart songs. Rodgers & Hart had written a song for a stenographer hoping to become a star. The tune, *Prayer,* was cut from *Hollywood Party*. When asked for a new song for *Manhattan Melodrama,* another film the studio was releasing in 1934, Hart simply wrote a new lyric, *The Bad in Every Man,* to Rodgers' original melody. But when music publisher Jack Robbins balked at publishing the song with a rather somber lyric, Hart asked if he wanted "something corny like 'Blue Moon.'" A few days later, Hart returned with the lyric to "Blue Moon," now a great standard in the Rodgers & Hart songbook.

The team saw a number of their Broadway shows adapted as films, including *On Your Toes* and *Too Many Girls.* When Rodgers achieved his spectacular success collaborating on Broadway shows with Oscar Hammerstein, he concentrated on writing for the stage. Rodgers and Hammerstein did produce a remarkable score for *State Fair,* an original movie musical about an Iowa farm family's adventures at the fair. The score was written in the optimistic, hopeful style of *Oklahoma,* and included such songs as "It Might As Well Be Spring," "That's For Me," and "It's a Grand Night for Singing." The original (1945) was remade in 1962, and adapted as Broadway show years after the death of its two talented writers. For Rodgers and Hammerstein, supreme success in the movies came through adaptation of their great stage masterpieces, *Oklahoma, Carousel, South Pacific, The King and I,* and *The Sound of Music,* among others.

Harold Arlen will undoubtedly be best remembered for the songs he contributed to *The Wizard of Oz.* But Arlen wrote classic songs for other motion pictures as well. In 1941, Arlen teamed with Johnny Mercer to produce the title song for *Blues in the Night.* Arlen's rather complex melody was his highly successful effort to compose a new blues theme that would sound like an authentic blues that had been passed down from one generation to another. The song made its initial appearance in a scene which took place in a jail cell. It became a huge hit and has remained a standard tune to this day.

The following year, another Arlen standard, "That Old Black Magic," became a highlight of Paramount's musical, *Star Spangled Rhythm.* In 1943, Arlen joined with his *Wizard of Oz* lyricist, E.Y. Harburg, to write additional songs for *Cabin in the Sky.* The film was based on a Vernon Duke-John Latouche show, but with both Duke and Latouche in the military, Arlen and Harburg were asked to provide new material for the movie. Ethel Waters, one of the stars of the Broadway show, was furious when one of her songs, "Taking a Chance on Love," was assigned to a younger rival, Lena Horne. Arlen and Harburg promptly wrote a new solo for Waters, "Happiness is Just a Thing Called Joe." Arlen had composed "Stormy Weather" years earlier, but in 1943, 20th Century Fox released a musical using Arlen's tune as the title song, and serving as a showcase for some of the country's finest black performers, including tap dancer Bill Robinson, pianist Fats Waller, Dooley Wilson (who sang "As Time Goes By" in *Casablanca*), the Katherine Dunham Dancers, Cab Calloway and his Orchestra, and Fayard and Harold Nicholas, the two tap dancing brothers whose acrobatic grace left audiences gasping in amazement. The same year, Arlen contributed songs to *My Shining Hour*, including one for Fred Astaire. "One for My Baby," a virtual song-soliloquy in which a lonely drinker pours out his private feelings to a bartender. The song became a standard in the repertoire of Frank Sinatra and several subsequent generations of popular singers.

Like all the best songwriters, Arlen was not immune from the whims and caprices of producers. In 1935, Arlen and Harburg rented a house from opera star Lawrence Tibbett. As a token of appreciation, they penned the song "Last Night When We Were Young." Tibbett wanted this poignant, wistful melody in his film, *Metropolitan*, only to have it cut by studio bosses. Judy Garland recorded the same song for her musical, *In the Good Old*

Figure 344 - *The Sound of Music* became by far one of the most successful Hollywood adaptations of a Broadway musical, starring Julie Andrews in the role created on stage by Mary Martin. (Photo courtesy of Rodgers & Hammerstein: An Imagem Company, www.rnh.com)

Summertime, only to have the song cut again because it was considered "too modern and sophisticated." "Last Night When We Were Young" remains a classic and has been performed and recorded many times by vocalists and instrumentalists everywhere. Garland had better luck with her last song photographed at MGM, the show-stopping "Get Happy." This Harold Arlen song was added at the last minute to *Summer Stock* to add some excitement to the ending of the film. In the movies as on stage, Arlen had an unusual facility for writing the brooding, melancholy songs of lost love. Judy Garland performed another of these Arlen classics, "The Man Who Got Away," this time with lyrics by Ira Gershwin, in *A Star is Born.*

Some leading Broadway figures worked in Hollywood, but never achieved the renown they would win later on Broadway. Frank Loesser wrote his own music and lyrics for both his own songs and those by others. For *Christmas Holiday,* he wrote the wistful "Spring Will Be a Little Late This Year." Of course, another Loesser opus, "Baby, It's Cold Outside," was incorporated in an Esther Williams aquatic musical, *Neptune's Daughter.* Loesser's greatest success in original movie musicals came after his Broadway triumph with *Guys and Dolls.* His score for the 1952 film *Hans Christian Andersen* was outstanding. Similarly, Jule Styne worked actively in Hollywood, but his work for the movies never achieved the success he earned later on Broadway. Styne teamed with lyricist Sammy Cahn who introduced him to Frank Sinatra. At Sinatra's request, the pair were hired to write songs for *Anchors Aweigh,* featuring one of Styne's most popular songs, "I Fall In Love Too Easily." Though Styne would return to Hollywood to compose title songs like "Three Coins in the Fountain" in 1954, his major Hollywood successes were filmed adaptations of his stage shows, including *Bells Are Ringing, Gypsy,* and *Funny Girl.*

THE MASTERS OF MOVIE MUSICALS

Other composers achieved their primary success in Hollywood. Nacio Herb Brown was the son of the sheriff of Los Angeles County. In 1929, together with lyricist Arthur Freed, he wrote hit songs for two of Hollywood's earliest musicals, *The Broadway Melody* and *Hollywood Review.* For the latter, they created "Singin' in the Rain," the song that became a virtual anthem for MGM musicals. This wasn't surprising since Arthur Freed eventually became the studio's most important producer of musical films. In the 1940s, when Freed began his career as an important producer of musical films, Brown continued writing music, but eventually retired from active involvement in films.

London-born composer, Harry Revel, became the piano accompanist for a vaudeville singer and comedian, Mack Gordon, after coming the U.S. Revel and Gordon moved to Hollywood, where they contributed songs to over thirty films. Gordon eventually moved on to collaborate with other composers, especially Harry Warren.

Harry Warren eventually moved from Warner Brothers to Twentieth Century Fox, where he penned the music for *Down Argentine Way* and *Springtime in the Rockies*, films that made the public aware of two new stars, Carmen Miranda and Betty Grable. For *Sun*

Valley Serenade and *Orchestra Wives*, Harry Warren and lyricist Mack Gordon made unforgettable contributions to the Big Band Era. These two films featured Glenn Miller and his orchestra, introducing some of Warren's most popular songs," Chattanooga Choo Choo," " Serenade in Blue," "At Last," and "I've Got a Girl in Kalamazoo." In 1943, Warren and Gordon wrote one of the most memorable songs of the World War II era. "You'll Never Know" won the "Best Song" Oscar for its writers. Warren had good luck writing songs about trains. For the MGM musical, *The Harvey Girls*, he penned "On the Atchison, Topeka, and the Santa Fe," for which he and lyricist Johnny Mercer won an Oscar, Warren's third. Warren continued writing songs for films for years, including the lyrical title song for *An Affair to Remember* in 1957.

When Harry Warren died in 1981, he had written an incredible eight hundred songs, many of which are still performed today. He was one of Hollywood's most prolific songwriters. But perhaps because he never achieved comparable fame on Broadway, his legacy is not nearly so well-known to the public as the work of many of his contemporaries. Ironically, the elusive hit musical, with a score based on the songs of Harry Warren and Al Dubin, arrived on Broadway in 1980. Director-choreographer Gower Champion incorporated many of the hits by Warren and Dubin in a stage version of *42nd Street* produced by David Merrick. The show ran for nearly 3500 performances on Broadway and won the Tony as "Best Musical" of the year.

Ralph Rainger was Paramount's leading composer for movie musicals. Rainger was a New Yorker, born Ralph Reichenthal, whose parents wanted him to pursue a career in law. Rainger had been a gifted young pianist who had studied with renowned pedagogues Paolo Gallico and Clarence Adler. He could have become a concert pianist, but he acceded to his family's wishes and graduated from law school, but he eventually turned his back on a law career to pursue a life in music. When he married Elizabeth Rains, he decided to simplify his own last name to Rainger.

Many songwriters in New York and Hollywood were self-taught pianists who could write good tunes although they lacked classical technique. Rainger, however, was a virtuoso. He gained early attention in 1929 while playing in a pit orchestra for *The Little Show*, a Broadway production starring the actor-dancer Clifton Webb, Fred Allen, and Libby Holman. The production needed a new song. When lyricist Howard Dietz heard Rainger playing an original melody, the two turned the tune into "Moanin' Low." It became a huge hit for Holman and insured that Rainger would never return to his law practice.

In 1930, Rainger collaborated with lyricist Leo Robin to write "I'll Take an Option on You," a song highlighted in the revue, *Tattle Tales*. Leo Robin, a native of Pittsburgh, was a former publicist and reporter who went to New York with ambitions to write plays. Robin and Rainger were both hired as staff composers at Paramount in Hollywood. They formed one of the most successful teams to write scores for movie musicals. They wrote the melodies that became theme songs for two of Hollywood's biggest stars. His 1934 tune, "Love in Bloom," written for a Bing Crosby musical, *She Loves Me Not*, was eventually immortalized as Jack Benny performed it as his theme in unforgettably off-key violin solos. Ironically, Benny was not particularly fond of the song, but he was identified with it for the rest of his career.

Four years later, Rainger and lyricist Leo Robin were asked to write a love song for a divorced couple. They struggled and then came up with "Thanks for The Memory." The star of *The Big Broadcast of 1938*, Bob Hope, used it as his theme throughout his career. The song's success led to an Academy Award for Robin and Rainger. The songwriting pair wrote music for all kinds of pictures and many of Paramount's major stars, including "June in January" for Bing Crosby's film, *Here Is My Heart*; "If I Should Lose You" for the improbable western, *Rose of the Rancho*; the songs for *Little Miss Marker*, which introduced audiences to a remarkable child star named Shirley Temple; as well as the tunes for an animated version of *Gulliver's Travels* created by Max Fleischer. Rainger even teamed with the fabled wit and writer Dorothy Parker to write a song for Bing Crosby, "I Wished on the Moon."

Figure 345 - Ralph Rainger, Leo Robin, Richard Whiting, and vocalist. The team of Robin and Rainger was shattered by Rainger's death in a tragic plane crash. Photo courtesy of the My Ideal Music Collection)

Rainger and Robin seemed to have the brightest future ahead, but fate stepped in when the pair had to return to New York in 1942 for a meeting with a publisher. Robin took the train, while Rainger boarded an American Airlines jet. He had no idea that the pilot of a military plane, a B-34 bomber, was a friend of the co-pilot of the plane on which Rainger was flying. Without changing his flight plan, the military pilot left a day early so he could "thumb his nose" at his former classmate from flight school. The stunt had fatal consequences. The American Airlines plane crashed and all aboard were killed, including Rainger. The military pilot was charged with manslaughter. He was tried and eventually acquitted. Rainger left a wife and three children. He was only forty-one years old. Robin went on to collaborate with other composers, enjoying a long and successful career for four decades; but he never forgot his Paramount partner.

One of Rainger's colleagues at Paramount in the 1930s was Hoagy Carmichael. Hoagland Howard Carmichael, always known as Hoagy, was an Indiana native. Born in 1899 in Bloomington, Indiana, he discovered music early in life because his mother helped support the family by playing in local movie houses. Carmichael would later say that ragtime had been his lullaby. His mother cautioned him that while music was fun, "It don't buy you cornpone." Carmichael was taught by his mother and by Reggie Du Valle, a local black dance hall pianist and bandleader who encouraged him to improvise.

Like Ralph Rainger, Hoagy Carmichael was faced with a choice between the security promised by a career in law or a life of risk and adventure he could encounter in the world of music. Carmichael dreamed of a prosperous family life in Bloomington. But he also fell in love with jazz. Although he went to law school, he was a self-described "jazz maniac" who formed his own band, the "Carmichael Syringe Orchestra." He met the legendary jazz cornetist, Bix Beiderbecke, who inspired him to turn to composing. (Beiderbecke died at a very young age, but Carmichael never forgot him. He would name his eldest son "Hoagy Bix Carmichael.") He had an early success with "Washboard Blues," played by Paul Whiteman's orchestra. (Whiteman's then-unknown singer, Bing Crosby, stood ready to substitute if Carmichael's voice didn't record well.) When Carmichael heard an unfamiliar performance of "Washboard Blues" by Red Nichols's band, he realized that people were discovering his music. He made the decision to abandon the law and pursue music full time.

Figure 346 - Hoagy Carmichael – "Stardust," only one of his countless songs, became the ultimate 'standard' in American popular music. (Photo courtesy of Hoagy Bix Carmichael)

Enduring success proved elusive. When Carmichael arrived in New York to seek his musical fortune, he found himself struggling and paying his bills by working in an uninspiring job as a bond salesman. But he persevered by playing and singing the music he wrote. Audiences in later years would see Carmichael as a homespun musician with an easy, casual manner and a twinkle in his eye. They would never guess that he was not an overnight success. Eventually, leading jazz musicians of the day began recording his songs such as "Rockin' Chair," "Georgia on My Mind," and "Lazy River."

Carmichael said that the inspiration for his most memorable melody, "Stardust," came to him during a visit to his alma mater, Indiana University. He refined it over time, performed it, and eventually it would become one of the most recorded and admired songs of all time. "Stardust" was originally written as a swing tune, but lyricist Mitchell Parish saw its potential as a romantic ballad. Parish supplied lyrics for over six hundred melodies, including jazz standards by various composers, such as Cliff Burwell ("Sweet Lorraine"), Frank Perkins ("Stars Fell on Alabama"), Peter deRose ("Deep Purple"), Glenn Miller ("Moonlight Serenade"), and Duke Ellington ("Mood Indigo"), although credit for the latter lyric was given to publisher Irving Mills. Parish's success in songwriting didn't lead to a life of glamour or riches. For ten years, he augmented his income by working as a court clerk in lower Manhattan and found time simultaneously to earn a college degree in English. In an interview with Stephen Holden, he explained, "Growing up on the Lower

East Side, we didn't see stars. I don't want to psychoanalyze myself, but I sometimes think that all those song lyrics about the moon and stars represented an escape. They expressed a longing for what I couldn't see." Hoagy Carmichael retained a sense of humor. While at the Hotel 1829 on St. Thomas, he signed the guest book with a quote from his most famous song, changing the lyric from "Sometimes I wonder why I spend the lonely nights dreaming of a song" to "Sometimes I wonder why I spend the lonely nights staying in New York."

In 1936, Hoagy Carmichael went to Hollywood, describing it as the place where "rainbows hit the ground for composers." Carmichael worked as a singer and jazz pianist, achieving his greatest success as the composer of hit tunes. Carmichael eventually turned to acting, appearing with the new team of Humphrey Bogart and Lauren Bacall in *To Have and Have Not*. Hoagy Carmichael eventually hosted his own radio and television programs and even acted in non-musical roles. As a result, he became a familiar voice and face in homes throughout America.

Carmichael collaborated with various lyricists over the years. One of his most successful collaborations began when he met the young Johnny Mercer. In 1941, "Skylark" entered the pantheon of the Great American Song Book. Carmichael sent Mercer the melody, which included surprising melodic leaps and chord patterns. Mercer, known for his speed and inspiration, was also a perfectionist; he struggled with the words for a year before producing the lyric for a song which became a jazz standard. Carmichael and Mercer won the Academy Award for "In the Cool, Cool, Cool of the Evening" from *Here Comes the Groom*.

Among others, Carmichael worked with at various times, Jack Brooks ("Ol' Buttermilk Sky" from *Canyon Passage*) and Frank Loesser ("Two Sleepy People" from *Thanks for the Memory*). Loesser also provided the lyrics for "Heart and Soul," a piece with a simple melodic line that became the favorite tune of children playing the piano. But simplicity wasn't Carmichael's hallmark. Alec Wilder, a brilliant analyst and severe critic of many of the most successful popular songs, wrote that Carmichael was "the most talented, inventive, sophisticated, and jazz-oriented of all the great craftsmen." Carmichael produced a large catalogue of songs and made a major contribution to the Great American Songbook.

Johnny Mercer, Carmichael's collaborator, was a Hollywood legend. In 1935, RKO offered Johnny Mercer a contract to write and act in two films. Mercer never became a movie star as an actor or singer. But he moved to Hollywood and in the process became one of the most respected lyricists during the golden age of movie musicals while writing splendid music as well. Mercer continued to sing, performing with Paul Whiteman's band and entertaining troops during World War II. For the next decade, he turned out a string of classic lyrics which remain standards in the Great American Songbook today. Mercer also had a flair for business. In 1942, he teamed with Hollywood record store owner Glenn Wallichs and Paramount executive B.G. (Buddy) DeSylva to found Capitol Records.

By the mid-1940s, the new company was selling one-sixth of the recordings purchased in the United States. Mercer was instrumental in launching the recording careers of a host of new stars, including experimental bandleader Stan Kenton, the gifted pianist and vocalist Nat "King" Cole, and singers Margaret Whiting, Peggy Lee, and Jo Stafford. Stafford was nicknamed "G.I. Jo" for her many performances for troops stationed in the U.S. during World War II. She often collaborated with her husband, composer-arranger Paul Weston.

Figure 347 - Johnny Mercer - David Raksin called him "The Flying Wallenda of Lyricists." The world agreed. (Courtesy of Library of Congress, William P. Gottlieb Collection)

Mercer's list of songs was impressive: "Too Marvelous For Words" and "Hooray for Hollywood" (with composer Richard Whiting), "Jeepers, Creepers" (with composer Harry Warren), "And the Angels Sing" (based on a melody by trumpeter Ziggy Elman and recorded by Benny Goodman), "Day In, Day Out" and "Fools Rush In" (with music by Rube Bloom), and a series of classics with composer Harold Arlen ("Blues in the Night," "One for My Baby and One More for the Road," "That Old Black Magic," "Ac-Cent-Tchu-Ate The Positive," and "Come Rain or Come Shine").

Composer Arthur Schwartz said that "Blues in the Night" was the greatest blues song ever written. Few would argue. "One for My Baby" served as a musical soliloquy for the last, lonely customer talking to his bartender. It became a standard for many singers, most notably Frank Sinatra. Mercer displayed amazing versatility. He could write jazz-oriented words and then shift creative gears completely to write lyrics for the sweeping romanticism of Jerome Kern in "I'm Old Fashioned." He won his first Oscar for "On the Atchison, Topeka, and the Santa Fe" with Harry Warren.

Although Johnny Mercer collaborated with many leading composers during his years in Hollywood, he also wrote music on his own. When Fred Astaire starred in the 1955 film, *Daddy Long Legs*, he was concerned about the thirty-year age gap between him and his co-star, Leslie Caron. The film featured marvelous ballet music by Alex North, but Astaire thought the film needed a popular song. Mercer promptly came up with the words and music for "Something's Gotta Give." Mercer also provided lyrics for songs that were already hits, including songs ranging from "Satin Doll" by Duke Ellington and Billy Strayhorn to "Les Feuilles Mortes," the French hit by Joseph Kosma, a Hungarian composer who settled in Paris. Mercer's English version became "Autumn Leaves." Mercer was one of the most admired and memorable contributors to the Great American Song Book. His own contributions to that musical legacy included more than a thousand songs!

Figure 348 - A 1935 Paramount luncheon honoring movie musical legends: seated, Sam Coslow, Oscar Hammerstein II, Jerome Kern and June Knight; standing, from left, Gerard Carbonara, Irvin Talbot, Max Terr, Victor Young, Phil Boutelje, Boris Morros, Frederick Hollander) (Courtesy Irvin Talbot Collection)

Sam Coslow was another well-known and quite colorful songwriter at Paramount. A New Yorker who worked in Manhattan's "Tin Pan Alley," Coslow headed to Hollywood in 1929. None of the stars or powerful Hollywood figures Coslow met could impress him as much as the man that hired him while he was still a teenager. Coslow answered a classified ad in the newspaper and was hired by Thomas Alva Edison to arrange his favorite 19th century melodies as foxtrots or one-step dance tunes. At Paramount, Coslow teamed with composer Arthur Johnston, Irving Berlin's long-time musical assistant, to write many songs, including early hits for Bing Crosby. In 1934, Coslow and Johnston penned their biggest hit, "Cocktails for Two," to be introduced by Carl Brisson in the film, *Murder at the Vanities*. Coslow and Johnston's misadventures with the film are a good example of what songwriters had to endure in Hollywood. When he first met Coslow and Johnston, Brisson proudly showed them a record of one of his biggest hits in Europe, a song called "Thanks." He had no idea that Coslow and Johnston had written it themselves for a film starring Bing Crosby.

"Cocktails for Two" began inauspiciously. The song was very nearly cut from the film on orders from Broadway impresario Earl Carroll, but it survived and became a popular romantic ballad with a continental flair. Carroll later sang Coslow's praises from the stage of a nightclub he opened in Hollywood; he never mentioned that his initial reaction to the song was to tell the writers "Better luck next time." Finally, Spike Jones, leader of a wildly popular comedy orchestra, recorded "Cocktails for Two" in an outrageous arrangement featuring automobile horns and firecrackers. Coslow hated the arrangement, but tempered his judgment when he collected royalties on sales of five million records. Coslow's career took an unusual turn many years after his greatest hits were sung in Hollywood musicals. By the 1960s, Coslow was still writing songs despite the early years of the rock music revolution. New and younger audiences listened to Dean Martin singing Coslow's song, "Everybody Loves Sombody Sometime," as the theme of his popular television series. But Coslow realized his style of writing would be overwhelmed by the rise of the rock groups. Convinced that he didn't want to suffer the fate of many of his colleagues, who were, in his words, "stranded on the beach," he changed careers. He agreed with singer Tony Bennett who said that the new hit songs were based on only two chords, "both of them wrong." So he turned a hobby, his interest in the stock market, into a new career, becoming a successful Wall Street publisher and securities analyst for ten years.

Edward Chester Babcock was a talented composer working as a disc jockey in his native Syracuse, New York, when he changed his name to James Van Heusen because he liked Van Heusen shirts. His first big hit, "It's The Dreamer in Me," sold 100,000 copies of sheet music thanks to a recording by Jimmy Dorsey. Van Heusen was turning out hit songs in New York, including "Darn That Dream," and "Imagination." He moved west to join lyricist Johnny Burke at Paramount, where the two became favorites of Bing Crosby. Van Heusen and Burke worked together for thirteen years and wrote the songs for the pictures that teamed Crosby and Bob Hope, including *The Road to Morocco* which featured "Moonlight Becomes You." *Going My Way*, in which Crosby portrayed a kindly priest who came to the aid of an older colleague played by Barry Fitzgerald, required a song that taught juvenile troublemakers the virtues of following The Ten Commandments. The result was "Swinging on a Star," including the lines, "All the monkeys aren't in the zoo. Every day you meet quite a few." After dealing with producers and executives in Hollywood, Van Heusen and Burke knew what they were talking about!

Jimmy Van Heusen was known as one of California's most colorful personalities. During World War II, he worked as a Lockheed test pilot. Before he married late in life, he was known as a bachelor and bon vivant who delighted in parties, travel, and friends. He said that he could write music almost anywhere, including his homes in Palm Desert, North Hollywood, and New York. He could take off at a moment's notice and invite friends to join him as he flew coast to coast.

Many of Van Heusen's best songs for the movies were written in collaboration with the effervescent lyricist Sammy Cahn. Cahn had written lyrics for other composers during and after his collaboration with Jule Styne. (His signature song, "I Should Care," also the title of his autobiography, was written with music by Axel Stordahl and Paul Weston. He also worked with Nicholas Brodszky on "Be My Love," for the very operatic tenor Mario Lanza.)

But he formed an enduring partnership with Van Heusen and the two wrote music for numerous pictures that starred Frank Sinatra, including "All the Way" (from *The Joker Is Wild*), "High Hopes" *(from A Hole in the Head)*, "Call Me Irresponsible" (from *Papa's Delicate Condition*), and "Love and Marriage" (from the television special, *Our Town*). In 1960, "High Hopes" became the chosen theme song for John F. Kennedy's campaign for President. They also wrote such varied hits as "To Love and Be Loved" from *Some Came Running*, "The Second Time Around" from *High Time*, "My Kind of Town" from *Robin and the Seven Hoods*, and the title songs for Frank Sinatra's albums, "Come Fly With Me" and "September of My Years."

Figure 349 - Jimmy Van Heusen- bon vivant, pilot, and with lyricist Sammy Cahn, composer of hit songs for Frank Sinatra's musicals. (Photo courtesy of Van Heusen Music Photo Archives)

Van Heusen and Cahn also wrote for Broadway, producing the scores for "Skyscraper" and "Walking Happy." Cahn's greatest Broadway success, however, came when he performed in "Words and Music," a one-man show featuring him performing his own songs and reminiscing about his remarkable life. There were two sides to Sammy Cahn. His wife Tita observed, "Under the finger-snapping, wise-cracking guy who entered the room was a tender-hearted, very sensitive ballad writer."

Although he was one of Hollywood's most successful composers, Van Heusen did not enjoy similar success of Broadway. For an unsuccessful show, however, *Carnival in Flanders,* together with lyricist Johnny Burke, Van Heusen penned "Here's That Rainy Day," one of the best ballads to come from Broadway. It's haunting melody made it a standard for popular and jazz vocalists, and like the Kern-Hammerstein ballad, "All the Things You Are," it continues to enjoy a life of its own long after the show from which it came had closed.

Figure 350 - Jimmy McHugh, the composer of hit songs for motion pictures for four decades. (Courtesy of McHugh music)

Jimmy McHugh was a prolific songwriter for movies. He was born in Boston, the son of a plumber. He turned his back on possible career in classical music to ride around on a bicycle plugging the songs of Irving Berlin, eventually becoming a rehearsal pianist and regular contributor to Harlem's Cotton Club Reviews.

McHugh chose as a partner Dorothy Fields, a young schoolteacher, and the daughter of Lew Fields, a well-known vaudeville comedian. After writing such hits as "I Can't Give You Anything but Love, Baby" for *Blackbirds of 1928,* McHugh and Fields headed for Hollywood, where they continued to write hits; this time for movies like *Every Night at Eight.* One of Jimmy McHugh's favorite collaborators was Harold Adamson, a lyricist who was discovered by composer Vincent Youmans while writing lyrics for Harvard's Hasty Pudding Club. Adamson wrote "Time on My Hands" with Youmans and Mack Gordon, his first hit in 1930. McHugh met Sonny Bragg, a young airman who told him about landing a plane after a combat mission "on a wing and a prayer." McHugh asked Adamson for a lyric and the song they wrote inspired *Wing and a Prayer*, a major film starring Don Ameche. Later, McHugh and Adamson contributed to the war effort with "Buy, Buy, Buy a Bond," which sold millions of dollars in war bonds. They helped launch the career of singer Perry Como with "I Wish I Didn't Have to Say Goodnight" and a marvelous melody sung by Jane Powell in *A Date With Judy*, "It's a Most Unusual Day." Eventually, Adamson began providing lyrics for title songs for non-musical films and television programs including "Around the World in 80 Days" (with music by Victor Young) and "An Affair to Remember" (with music by Harry Warren). Adamson also wrote the lyrics for a song by Eliot Daniel which everyone recognizes, but nearly no one knows: "I Love Lucy," the musical theme for the iconic television series starring Lucille Ball and Desi Arnaz.

In 1944, composer Jay Livingston and lyricist Ray Evans followed the example of so many of their predecessors, heading to Hollywood. They signed a contract with Paramount in 1945 and worked at the studio for eleven years. They won three Oscars for their songs, "Buttons and Bows," "Mona Lisa," and "Que Será, Será" ("Whatever Will Be, Will Be") and contributed songs to over a hundred films.

On occasion, Hollywood paid tribute to its legendary composers and lyricists by producing films based on their life stories *Rhapsody in Blue* (George Gershwin),*'Til The Clouds Roll By* (Jerome Kern), *Words and Music,* (Rodgers & Hart) *Night and Day* (Cole Porter.) Unfortunately, these films were almost always inaccurate and seldom related to the real-life stories of these men. The studios seldom made use of stars who had introduced songs or created major roles in shows by these composers. The composers' lives were more often than not used as the basis of fiction.

One classic example was the casting of Cary Grant as Cole Porter in *Night and Day.* Porter, a thin, rather slight man, was once asked why he didn't protest the casting of Grant, when he obviously bore a much greater physical resemblance to Fred Astaire. Porter allegedly quipped, "Would <u>you</u> have objected to Cary Grant?" Hollywood films implied that composers achieved inspiration by gazing at the moon or listening to the singing birds. It was true that sometimes fate played a hand in inspiring a tune or a lyric, as when Richard Whiting's daughter Margaret walked into his studio carrying a huge lollipop. Whiting was inspired to write "On the Good Ship Lollipop" for Shirley Temple. But by and large, Hollywood's finest movie musicals were created by men who were masters of their craft, drawing upon inspiration and technique to create the songs America sang in the golden era of motion picture musicals. Another Richard Whiting song, "Hooray for Hollywood" (with lyrics by Johnny Mercer from the film *Hollywood Hotel)* sang the praises of the movie colony. It would have been far poorer without the talents of the composers and lyricists who created the best movie musicals.

WISHING UPON A STAR: MUSIC AND ANIMATION

From the earliest days, animated motion pictures played an important role in the development of movie music. In fact, techniques developed by composers scoring cartoons often became standard for those writing the scores for major dramatic motion pictures.

Walt Disney demonstrated the potential combination of music and animation in 1937, when his studio released *Snow White and the Seven Dwarfs,* an animated operetta featuring such unforgettable melodies as "Some Day My Prince Will Come," "Whistle While You Work," "One Song," and "Heigh-Ho, Heigh-Ho." The film opened with an overture based on the songs by composer Frank Churchill and lyricist Larry Morey.

Music always played an important role in Disney films. Albert Hay Malotte, composer of "The Lord's Prayer," scored Disney's *Silly Symphonies.* In *The Reluctant Dragon(1941,)* famed author and actor Robert Benchley took the audience on a tour of the newly built Walt Disney Studio in Burbank, California. A highlight of the film was an operatic duet between Clarence Nash, the original and only voice of Donald Duck for decades, and Florence Gill, the singer whose voice was used for Clara Cluck, an animated hen who clucked her way through the arias she sang.

Disney's full length animated films, including *Pinocchio* (which introduced "When You Wish Upon a Star" by composer Leigh Harline,) *Bambi, Cinderella, Peter Pan, Alice In Wonderland,* and *Lady and the Tramp,* among others, always depended heavily upon both underscoring and memorable songs to achieve dramatic effect.

Leigh Harline had an unusual background for a film composer in Hollywood. He didn't come from the world of Broadway shows or European concert music. His parents were Swedish immigrants who settled in Utah when they joined the Church of Jesus Christ of Latter Day Saints. Harline grew up in Salt Lake City and received his initial musical training from Spencer Cornwall, Musical Director of the Mormon Tabernacle Choir. His splendid work for *Pinocchio* resulted in two Academy Awards, one for Best Musical Score, the other for Best Song. "When You Wish Upon a Star," with Harline's music and lyrics by Ned Washington, became the signature song for the creative world of Walt Disney. Sung by Cliff "Ukulele Ike" Edwards as the voice of an animated Jiminy Cricket, it remains the quintessential Disney theme today. Harline had contributed greatly to early Disney cartoons and films, but he wanted to strike out on his own. He left the studio in 1941 and throughout the next two decades, became a major Hollywood film composer. His film scores proved that he was not only a fine melodist, but highly gifted in writing counter

Figure 351 - Composer Leigh Harline, here at the piano accompanying Cliff Edwards, known as "Ukulele Ike" and the singing voice of Jiminy Cricket, in a performance of "When You Wish Upon a Star." (Photo courtesy of Jo-An Lyman)

melodies and developing thematic material for such diverse films as *Black Widow*; *House of Bamboo*; *Good Morning, Miss Dove*; *The Wayward Bus*; *No Down Payment*; *Ten North Frederick*; and *The Remarkable Mr. Pennypacker*.

British born Oliver Wallace joined the Disney Studio in 1936 and scored numerous Disney shorts. His musical parody of the Nazis' *Horst Wessel* song, "Der Fuehrer's Face," was used in a Donald Duck cartoon heaping ridicule upon America's greatest enemy abroad. Wallace collaborated with Frank Churchill and Paul J. Smith on the score for *Dumbo* in 1941; the composers won an Academy Award for their work. Wallace would remain at the Disney Studio for decades. Smith would later score a number of Disney's "True Life Adventures" featuring astonishing cinematography and depicting real scenes of wildlife around the world. Years later, William Lava would brilliantly score films such as *The Littlest Outlaw* and the *Zorro* television series.

Lesser known Disney classics *Saludos Amigos* and *The Three Caballeros* highlighted the music of Latin-America, while *Make Mine Music* included an animated interpretation of Prokofiev's *Peter and the Wolf.* Disney's most ambitious animated musical project was *Fantasia*. The entire film consisted of animated interpretations of classical music, conducted by Leopold Stokowski. Disney animators created surprising scenes inspired by the music: abstract designs for Bach's *Toccata and Fugue in D Minor*, a classical fantasy set on the slopes of Mt. Olympus for Beethoven's "Pastorale" Symphony, prehistoric dinosaurs for Stravinsky's *The Rite of Spring*, witches and demons for Mussorgsky's *Night on Bald Mountain*, the triumph of light and goodness accompanied by Schubert's *Ave Maria*. The film's two most famous sequences starred Mickey Mouse besieged by an army of runaway brooms in Paul Dukas' *The Sorcerer's Apprentice* and an unlikely ballerina, the improbably graceful Hyacinth Hippo, performing a *pas de deux* with an alligator to the music of Ponchielli's *Dance of the Hours.* Reactions by classical musicians were mixed. While Stokowski became known to new admirers as "the conductor who shook hands with Mickey Mouse," Igor Stravinsky posed for pictures with Walt Disney but denounced alterations in his music. When Paramount's musical director, Irvin Talbot, and his wife Ethel took their friend George Szell, the formidable conductor of the Cleveland Orchestra, to see *Fantasia,* Szell, a traditionalist, abruptly left the theater in protest half-way through the film. *Fantasia* continued to fascinate audiences for generations. The Disney studio released *Fantasia 2000* in 1999, featuring entirely different animated images (including some inspired by legendary caricaturist Al Hirschfeld) and classical pieces which had not been used in the original version a half-century earlier. Ironically, the conductor of the musical accompaniment to the new *Fantasia* was James Levine, a Szell protégé.

Figure 352 - The charismatic Leopold Stokowski served as musical director for Walt Disney's *Fantasia.* (Photo courtesy of Leopold Stokowski Papers, Kislak Center for Special Collections, Rare Books and Manuscripts, University of Pennsylvania)

The Disney Studio wasn't the only one to pioneer techniques in music and animation. The Fleischer brothers, Max and Dave, were eager to produce a full-length animated feature, but they couldn't persuade Paramount to finance such a project until the success of Disney's *Snow White*. Paramount actually built the Fleischers an animation studio in Miami and the result was *Gulliver's Travels,* a delightful full-length feature based on Jonathan Swift's classic book and featuring songs like "Faithful Forever" and "All's Well" by composer Ralph Rainger and lyricist Leo Robin and "It's a Hap-Hap-Happy Day," by Sammy Timberg, Al Neiburg, and Winston Sharples. The underscoring was provided by the mainstay of the Paramount music department, composer Victor Young.

Animator-producer Walter Lantz is best remembered as the creator of Woody Woodpecker (whose voice and trademark cackle were dubbed for years by Lantz's wife, actress Grace Stafford). But before Woody Woodpecker made Lantz famous, he produced a series of animated shorts accompanied by classical music. The music was performed as written, but animals (like a beaver using his tail as a percussion instrument) provided their own inimitable perspective on the classical masterpieces.

While large orchestras were standard in Hollywood, composers David Raksin and Gail Kubik pioneered in the use of small ensembles to accompany UPA animated cartoons. Raksin wrote counterpoint for a shrill soprano saxophone and a clarinet to accompany the argument between a man and his wife in *The Unicorn and The Garden.* (The subject of their disagreement, the mythical unicorn, was played by an alto recorder,

Figure 353 - Gail Kubik, a gifted composer and teacher, adapted concert works from his motion picture scores. (Photo by Ralph Titus, used courtesy of Morse Department of Special Collections, Kansas State University Library)

playing music described by author James Thurber as "exactly right for unicorns.") For Ludwig Bemelmans' *Madeline,* he used an unusual ensemble of eight players.

Gail Kubik scored *Gerald McBoing Boing,* a cartoon based on a tale by celebrated children's author Theodore Seuss Geisel (Dr. Seuss). Kubik was an interesting choice to score the cartoon. Like Erich Korngold, he never changed his style of composition when scoring films. Gail Kubik was a native of Oklahoma who grew up in Kansas and studied at the Eastman School of Music, and later with Leo Sowerby, Walter Piston, and Nadia Boulanger. In the Oscar-winning animated cartoon, Gerald McBoing Boing, a boy who speaks only in sounds, was represented by the percussion instruments. Kubik's widely heralded score was recast as a concert work for narrator, percussion, and nine instruments. It was performed throughout the U.S. and Europe, and significantly elevated the status of cartoon music.

Kubik was quite successful, by the way, in adapting his film music for the concert stage. During World War II, Gail Kubik was Musical Director of the Motion Picture Bureau of the Office of War Information. His documentary score for *The Memphis Belle* reemerged as *Memphis Belle: A Wartime Episode.* He also adapted his music for *The Desperate Hours* as a *Scenario for Orchestra*, this piece featuring two pianos. He gained the greatest recognition of his career when he adapted his brittle and dissonant film score for *C-Man* into a major polytonal concert piece, *Symphony Concertante*. It won the 1952 Pulitzer Prize and Kubik became the youngest composer to ever win the prize at the time.

Kubik distinguished himself as a composer of concert works and as a teacher, but his acerbic style led to few assignments for motion picture romances. On one occasion Kubik said, "If given the chance, I could write music for a love scene." David Raksin responded, "Yes, if it were a scene between two praying mantises."

Figure 354 - Scott Bradley, responsible for countless classic cartoon scores. (Photo by Scott Bradley)

Many animated cartoons were scored by specialists like Carl Stalling, Scott Bradley, Oliver Wallace, and Paul J. Smith. The "click-track"

Figure 355 - David Raksin conducting a concert performance of his classic score for *Laura*. (Photo courtesy of David Raksin)

technique used skillfully by Max Steiner to precisely coordinate music and visual images was developed by Stalling and Bradley for their cartoon scores. Long before Leonard Rosenman's twelve-tone score for *Cobweb*, Bradley used a twelve-tone row for piccolo and oboe to portray Jerry, the mouse in *The Cat That Hated People*. Tom, Jerry's feline nemesis, was accompanied by a bassoon playing the same row in retrograde. Bradley also arranged a version of Liszt's *2nd Hungarian Rhapsody* for two pianos, dubbed *The Cat Concerto*. On screen, Tom displayed his pianistic virtuosity while two noted human pianists, John Crown and Arthur Schutt, provided the sound effects. One of the most memorable depictions of concert music, however, involved a totally human ensemble. Actor John Garfield appeared to be playing the violin in the film *Humoresque*. One violinist was actually providing fingering, another bowing, while a third actually played the music. Pianist Oscar Levant, accompanying the group, quipped, "After this is all over, why don't the five of us make a concert tour?"

FILM MUSIC IN THE 21ST CENTURY: THE DOLLARISTOCRATS

Today, film scoring is a big business. Compact discs of scores, new and old, abound. One could not imagine a studio today destroying, as was attempted with varying degrees of success in the 1960s and 1970s, large portions of its music library. This would not be because the businessmen who control motion picture financing care about music, but

FILM MUSIC | 467

Figure 356 - A luncheon in honor of Bramwell Coles, director of the Salvation Army's International Music Department, organized by Meredith Willson. Seated, left to right, Franz Waxman, Dimitri Tiomkin, Meredith Willson, Bramwell Coles, Earl E. Lawrence, and William Grant Still. Standing, left to right: Abe Meyer, Leith Stevens, William Broughton, Anthony Collins, Johnny Green, Miklos Rozsa, Victor Young, Werner Heymann, Leo Shuken, Arthur Bergh, Alex Steinert, Robert Emmett Dolan, Frank Skinner, Wilbur Hatch, Carlos Morales, and Louis Lipstone. (Friars Club Photo-courtesy of Bobbie Fromberg and the Friars Club)

because music has become an important financial by-product of films themselves. Many years ago Vernon Duke objected to the people he called "Hollywood dollaristocrats." These are the same individuals in control today in Hollywood. Hugo Friedhofer once quipped that the day would come when "First they'll write the song, then they'll make the movie." It did.

One positive development is the fascination of new generations with the classic film scores of the past. Today, audiences are delighted, not surprised, when a piece of classic film music turns up on a concert program.

Have things changed dramatically since the early days? Certainly, digital recording technology represents a long journey from the days of the silent film theater, complete with a lone organist trying to drown out the squeaks and noises of the projectors. Are composers better off today? In the days of the studio system, a powerful producer like Irving Thalberg could write a memo directing composers at MGM to use "no minor chords in their scores." Trained musicians understood that this absurd order was equivalent to telling a writer that he couldn't use specific letters of the alphabet.

Today, we have new studios aligned with computer conglomerates and producers like Jeffrey Katzenberg declaring that "only the music of the Beatles will survive the 20th century." Katzenberg anticipated with evangelical fervor the profits from "records, videos, t-shirts, games and cereals" that would be commercial spin-offs from his remake of *Fantasia* with Beatles' music. Producers such as Jeffrey Katzenberg are in control of the destinies of many a composer and writer, ready to impart their assumed wisdom to those eagerly seeking them as employers. These executives see music not as art; they see it as a commodity. The most gifted film composers must pursue their art in spite of such producers. They view their own preferences and their pursuit of the ubiquitous pop culture as their only standard. The result is that the motion picture industry is dominated, as always, by what one observer called "the morality of hard cash." Jeffrey Katzenberg is wrong, however. The 20th century included not only a rich panorama of composers who failed to impress him with their concert works, but the film composers who frequently made the movies of yesterday into the classics they are today. One would hope that we will one day respond to the Jeffrey Katzenbergs of the world in the words of Sir Thomas Beecham. When approached by a woman who told him that the music of Frederic Delius meant nothing to her, Beecham replied, "Really, Madam? What a terrible loss for you."

For me, film music has been and will always be an important part of my life. After that first momentous childhood discovery of the music for *Anastasia*, I was privileged to know many of the great masters of film music, including the eminent Miklós Rózsa, who wrote the introduction to my own book on the subject, *Soundtrack: The Music of the Movies*. Dr. Rozsa spoke of the composers who had pursued their art and craft in the shadows while studio publicists directed the public's attention elsewhere. Yet their contribution, often misunderstood, was essential. Imagine Fred Astaire and Ginger Rogers dancing without music, Errol Flynn swashbuckling in silence, everyone from *Citizen Kane* to Mickey Mouse, Scarlett O'Hara to Ben-Hur speaking only the accompaniment of noise and sound effects. Among the film composers from whom I sought guidance, I greatly admired the outspoken Bernard Herrmann who said that with few exceptions, motion pictures could not truly express their message without music. Herrmann said this was because music did what actors could not do, supplying a link between the emotions of the characters and the emotions of the audience. As Bach composed cantatas for church services, Mozart and Haydn wrote dinner music for the patrons, many of the finest composers of the 20th century wrote music for motion pictures and its offspring, television.

What is astonishing is not that there have been bad film scores, but that so many good ones were written under such difficult conditions. There was a "Golden Age of Film Music." While the composers who participated were colleagues and often both friends and rivals, when they gathered together, their contribution to the art of film music was clear. Composers of much 20th century concert music lost their emotional connection with their audience. In pursuit of musical fads and fashions, they often discarded emotional content in favor of cerebral theories, intellectual notions, and sheer shock value. In effect, they wrote music for the mind rather than the heart. To be sure, many a film composer (and the executives to whom he answered) thought not of art, but of profit. But the finest film composers, the masters of their craft, revealed that music is an essential part of motion pictures. They remained true to the ideal of a lyrical art in an age of noise and confusion, and their music will continue to deserve the description associated with creative works of lasting value: "classic." For me, the only way to begin shooting a scene for the screen is for the director to say, "Lights, Camera, Music!"

CODA

And so, dear reader, our journey through four great genres of American music has come to an end. *Our Musical Heritage* isn't just a book title; it's a legacy. Time and space would not allow us to explore many elements of this heritage in detail. For instance, folk music and the African American spiritual merit detailed examinations of their own. It is important to remember that any book about music must be augmented by the music itself. I chose not to include lists of recordings. In this high tech age, such lists are dated before they are even completed. Just as you cannot learn all about a country by visiting it once, you must visit great music again and again.

What have we learned?

American music is the result of the American melting pot, a vast and unique combination of influences from the people of many times and places. From the earliest days of our musical Founding Fathers, music in the concert hall evolved and emerged through the energies of master composers, conductors, and instrumental and vocal performers. Jazz added its own special spark, the elements of swing and improvisation. American musical theater gave us a new form of dramatic entertainment embraced around the world and resulted in The Great American Song Book. Film music became an art form on its own and preserved the element of musical lyricism at a time when many suggested that lyrical music would become extinct.

Figure 357 - President Ronald Reagan and Nancy Reagan presenting the Presidential Medal of Freedom to pianist Vladimir Horowitz while his wife, Wanda Toscanini Horowitz, looks on. (White House Photo.)

President Ronald Reagan famously said that freedom is never more than one generation from extinction. The same can be said about great music. In the abysmal 21st century pop culture, we will lose our musical heritage if we do not actively seek to conserve it, preserve it, and pass it along from one generation to another. Each of us can do his or her own part. Ronald and Nancy Reagan acknowledged musical greatness when they invited Vladimir Horowitz to the White House to be honored with the Medal of Freedom. Horowitz, who had emigrated to the United States decades earlier, had embraced his new country with a dazzling piano transcription of John Philip Sousa's *The Stars and Stripes Forever*. Continuity in our history and heritage is important. Francis Hopkinson, the composer who signed the Declaration of Independence, could never have imagined that his *George Washington's March* would be incorporated almost two hundred years later into a cantata performed at the White House and written by modern composer Frank Lewin. The child today who discovers a beautiful string quartet, hears a great jazz solo, attends a brilliant performance of musical theater, or learns the difference between good and bad film music, may be taking the first step in a life that may help preserve, protect, and defend our musical heritage and move it forward. So if you are a parent or grandparent, I urge you to introduce your children or grandchildren to our musical heritage. They may not discover it on their own; it will be their loss, but also ours. Thank you for accompanying me on this exploration of America's music. Whether you are an experienced musical traveler or a first-time explorer, I hope you have enjoyed our journey and that it may inspire you to take many more musical journeys every day.

ABOUT THE PHOTOGRAPHS IN THIS BOOK

It has been said that one picture is worth a thousand words. There are many pictures in this book and their inclusion would have been impossible without the gracious assistance and cooperation of many individuals and institutions. These especially include music librarians (the unsung heroes of research) and members of the families of many of the distinguished musicians discussed in these pages. Photographs under copyright have all been used with permission. Those in public domain do not require clearance. Every effort has been made to insure that no photograph requiring permission has been used without it and should anyone believe that his or her rights to a photo are uncredited, the publisher of this book will certainly attempt to rectify the situation immediately.

It would be impossible to list all the people who helped in this endeavor, but I would like to extend a special thank you to a number of individuals, photographers, libraries, and museums, who provided special help to make many historic photographs and illustrations available, a number of which are appearing in print here for the first time. Photos have come from the Library of Congress, famous museums, small town libraries, colleges, and private collections (including those of the author.) They have come from local sources, throughout the United States, and from as far away as London, Paris, and Vienna.

So a special thank you to:

Abby Burton; Allan Warren; American Composers Alliance; Andrew Stayman, Ellora Management; Annette Warren Smith; Arthur Antheil McTighe and Judith Donoher; Charles Amirkhanian; Associazione Musicale Vincent Persichetti; Dr. Aurelio de la Vega; Azalea Camacho, University Library Archivist, John F. Kennedy Memorial Library, California State University, Los Angeles; Barbara Zeisl Schoenberg; Bobbie Fromberg; Brendan Carroll Collection; Brook Babcock, Van Heusen Music Photo Archives; Carolyn Rossi Copeland; Amanda Dash; Charles Strouse; Cherie Nutting; Claudia Tonge; Curtis Small, The University of Delaware Library Special Collection; Colleen McDonough and Cathy Nevins, ASCAP; Daniel Matusov, Reprise Records/Rhino Entertainment Company; David Amram; Hiroko Sakurazawa, David and Sylvia Teitelbaum Fund; David Loughner, Rodgers & Hammerstein, an Imagem Company; David Newman, Joey Newman; David Peter Coppen, Special Collections Librarian and Archivist, Sibley Music Library, Eastman School of Music; Dean Rogers, Vassar College Library; Debbi Whiting; Kathy Brown, My Ideal Music; Debra Torok; Don and DeeAnne Hunstein; Carol Morrow; Dennis M. Spragg, Glenn Miller Archive, American Music Research Center, University of Colorado, Boulder; Dianne Woods, the George Mann Archive; Dick Hyman; Dr. Emily Ferrigno, Irving Gilmore Library, Yale University; Dr. William Everett; Electra Slonimsky Yourke; Emily Altman, Frederick Loewe Foundation; Erik Huber, The Queens Borough Public Library

Archives, New York Herald-Tribune Photograph Morgue Collection; Ernie Harburg; Fiona Rogers, Estate of Sir Malcolm Arnold; Glen Aitken West; Harvey Schmidt; Heidi Lesemann, Executive Director Piano Spheres; Hoagy Bix Carmichael; Ian Vargas, Harry Warren Collection; Dr. John Bewley, Associate Librarian and Archivist, University at Buffalo Music Library; Irene Haupt; Jim Tuttle; James LaRocca; Janie Ross Coulter; Jerry Herman; Jill Gregg Clever and Laura Voelz, Toledo Lucas County Public Library; Jo-An Lyman; John Pollack, Leopold Stokowski Papers, Kislak Center for Special Collections, Rare Books and Manuscripts, University of Pennsylvania; Jonathan Gourlay, The MacDowell Colony; Josef Astor; Joseph Weiss, Frank Loesser Archives; Katherine Crowe, Curator of Special Collections and Archives, University of Denver Libraries and Valerie Hamlin, Central City Opera; Kevin C. Fitzpatrick, Dorothy Parker Society; Lance Bowling, Cambria Music; Laurence Rosenthal; Leslie Zador; Lisa Kirchner; Lucienne Allen, Ernest Bloch II; Maelos Music, Inc.; Maggie Lee, Sam Arlen Music; Manuelle Pefferkorn Mazerand; Claude Bolling; Marc Mellon; Barry Dougherty; The Friars Club; Margaret Styne; Maristella Feustel, University of North Texas Music Library; Marni Nixon; Michael Curtis Hanna, Rahanna Music; Michael Owen, Gershwin Family Trusts; Miriam and Naomi Lewin; Morse Department of Special Collections, Kansas State University Library; Noble Music; Patricia Bosworth, Estate of Tom Palumbo; Paul Marcorelles; Phineas Newborn III; Dr. Keith Pawlak, Nelson Riddle Collection, University of Arizona Fred Fox School of Music; Portland State University; Randy Weston; Weston Fatoumata; Dr. Diana Burgin, Richard Burgin-Ruth Posselt Family Archives; Rigmor Newman; Robert F.B. Ballard; Robert Tifft; Robin Bell-Stevens, Jazzmobile; Robin G. McElheny and Liza Vick, Harvard University Archives; Sandra Mummert; Sandra Silbert, Ziegler Music Company; Simon Elliott, The Los Angeles Times Photographic Archive, Library Special Collections, Charles E. Young Research Library, UCLA; Steven Smith; Susan Andrews; Carl Rollyson;, Susan Falciani, Abram Samuels Sheet Music Collection, The Trexler Library, Muhlenberg College; Susan Satz, Estate of Benny Goodman; Susan Sukman McCray; Susanna Moross Tarjan;, Suzanne Hanners; Susan Reynolds; Suzanne Merrill; Tad Hershorn, Institute for Jazz Studies, Rutgers University, Terry Harrison, Mason City Public Library; the late Irvin and Ethel Talbot; Raphael Pumpelly; the late Alexander Courage;, the late Annette Kaufman; the late David Raksin; the late Dr. Ernest Kanitz; the late Hugo W. Friedhofer; the late Dr. Joseph Wagner; the late L. Arnold Weissberger; the late Dr. and Mrs. Mario Castelnuovo-Tedesco; the late Dr. Miklós Rózsa;, Therese Muxeneder and Eike Fess, Arnold Schoenberg Center; Tracey Wheeler, Newton and Cowper Museum; Tita Cahn; University of North Carolina School of the Arts Archive; University of Virginia Special Collections Library; Veerle Van de Poel; Vincent Youmans III; Willie Ruff; Woodbury Music Company; Zephorene Stickney, and Madeleine Clark Wallace Library, Wheaton College Norton, MA.

TABLE OF FIGURES

Figure 1 - Francis Hopkinson, designed an early American flag, helped design the Great Seal of the United States, signed the Declaration of Independence, and today is often considered to be America's first composer. (Engraving by James Barton Longacre after painting by Robert Edge Pine, used courtesy of Pennsylvania Historical Society. Public Domain) 6

Figure 2 - John Newton, the composer of "Amazing Grace." (Photo courtesy of Cowper and Newton Museum, Olney UK.) 8

Figure 3 - The glass armonica, invented by Benjamin Franklin. (Photo by and courtesy of Vince Flango) 9

Figure 4 - Billings - *The Psalm Singer's Amusement* 1781. (Public domain) 10

Figure 5 - Former President Harry S. Truman returns to the White House to play the piano with President and Mrs. John F. Kennedy and Vice-President and Mrs. Lyndon B. Johnson in attendance. Music critic Paul Hume is nowhere to be seen. (Photo by Cecil W. Stoughton, courtesy of John F. Kennedy Presidential Library and Museum) 11

Figure 6 - "The Spirit of '76," originally titled "Yankee Doodle." an iconic painting by artist Archibald MacNeal Willard, was exhibited in the U.S. Centennial Exposition. (Public Domain) 12

Figure 7 - The Bombardment of Ft. McHenry inspired our National Anthem, *The Star Spangled Banner*. (Public domain - Courtesy of Maryland Historical Society) 15

Figure 8 - Francis Scott Key, a lawyer and poet, wrote the words for *The Star Spangled Banner*, our National Anthem. (Photograph used through courtesy of EyeonAnnapolis.net) 15

Figure 9 - Lowell Mason, was responsible for introducing music into public schools in the U.S. He also composed hundreds of hymns and produced a famous setting of "Nearer, My God, To Thee." (Public domain) 16

Figure 10 - Theodore Thomas, America's first major symphony conductor and first musical director of the renowned Chicago Symphony. (Public domain) 17

Figure 11 - Ole Bornemann Bull, the famed Norwegian violin virtuoso who dazzled American audiences. (Photo by Abraham Bogardus, courtesy of Bergen Public Library (Norway) public domain, photo taken prior to 1908) 20

Figure 12 - Ignacy Jan Paderewski. In his lifetime, he was the world's most famous pianist and later Prime Minister of Poland. (Public Domain) 20

Figure 13 - Stephen Foster. America's first writer of popular songs. (Public domain photo courtesy of Library of Congress) 22

Figure 14 - Louis Moreau Gottschalk, a pianist, composer, and America's first matinee idol, direct from New Orleans. He performed for President Lincoln. (Portrait by Jacques Reich 1900).. 25

Figure 15 - John S. Dwight, the conservative music critic and champion of German classicism in the New World. (Public domain) 26

Figure 16 - John Knowles Paine was America's and Harvard's first music professor. (Public domain) 28

Figure 17 - George W. Chadwick (1913) was the Director of the New England Conservatory, was a composer, an influential teacher and author. (Public Domain).......... 30

Figure 18 - Daniel Gregory Mason, the composer and teacher who famously declared, "Thank God Wagner is dead and Brahms is alive." (Photo used courtesy of the George Grantham Bain Collection)... 30

Figure 19 - Frederick Converse. His opera, *The Pipes of Desire*, was the first such work written by an American composer to be rewarded by the Metropolitan Opera with a premiere. (Public Domain) 31

Figure 20 - Horatio Parker, Chadwick's most famous pupil, taught for twenty-six years at Yale, all the while, composing. (1913 photograph by Pirie MacDonald, Public Domain) 31

Figure 21 - Amy Marcy Cheney, known as Mrs. H.H.A. Beach, the first American woman to gain international fame as a composer. (Photograph courtesy of the George Grantham Bain Collection, Library of Congress.) 32

Figure 22 - Edward MacDowell, America's most celebrated composer in the nineteenth century and his wife Marian. (Photo courtesy of The MacDowell Colony)....... 33

Figure 23 - Charles Martin Loeffler, an American who was at heart a French composer. (Portrait by John Singer Sargent - Public domain) 36

Figure 24 - Charles Tomlinson Griffes. He was a composer and a painter who was fascinated by the relationship of color and music, photography, and the culture of India and Japan. (Public Domain)... 37

Figure 25 - Antonín Dvořák, who was the most famous Czech composer, came to America to teach in New York and Iowa. (Public Domain) 38

Figure 26 - Arthur Farwell, a composer, teacher, publisher, and advocate of spirituals, folk tunes, cowboy songs, and the music of Native American tribes. (Photo by the Mojonier Studio, Hollywood, CA, 1921. Courtesy of the Arthur Farwell Collection, Sibley Music Library).. 39

Figure 27 - Louis Antoine Jullien, the flamboyant French conductor who pursued stardom by often conducting while facing the audience with a jewelled baton. (Caricature by Benjamin Roubaud, public domain) 41

Figure 28 - Patrick Sarsfield Gilmore, the bandleader whose huge festivals featured 1000 instrumentalists and 20,000 singers. (Photo courtesy of George Grantham Bain Collection, Library of Congress) 42

Figure 29 - John Philip Sousa. He composed *Semper Fidelis* and America's national march, *The Stars and Stripes Forever*, and is known for all time as "The March King." (Portrait courtesy of United States Marine Corps) 45

Figure 30 - *The Stars and Stripes Forever*. An early sheet music version of the most popular march ever written. (Public Domain) 47

Figure 31 - Victor Herbert, Irving Berlin, and John Philip Sousa, three of America's most renowned composers, joined forces on behalf of ASCAP in Washington, D.C. (Photo courtesy of George Grantham Bain Collection, Library of Congress) 48

Figure 32 - In 1881, Henry Lee Higginson, a New England philanthropist, founded and subsidized the Boston Symphony. (Portrait by John Singer Sargent, Public Domain) 49

Figure 33 - Karl Muck, the German conductor who has the misfortune to be conductor of the Boston Symphony and a friend of Kaiser Wilhelm II when the United States went to war against Germany. (Caricature by Arthur George Witherby, known as "wag" and published in *Vanity Fair* 1899- Public Domain) 50

Figure 34 - Pierre Monteux, "Le Maître," returns to conduct the Boston Symphony with soloist Leonid Kogan and concertmaster Richard Burgin. This French maestro and teacher was the mentor to numerous prominent American conductors. (Courtesy of the Ruth Posselt-Richard Burgin Family Archives) 50

Figure 35 - Roland Hayes, the first black soloist with the Boston Symphony Orchestra, triumphed over prejudice on two continents. (Photograph courtesy of Carl Van Vechten Collection, Library of Congress) 51

Figure 36 - Serge Koussevitzky, a Russian conductor who became the devoted champion of American composers. (Photo courtesy of George Grantham Bain Collection, Library of Congress) 51

Figure 37 - Leopold Stokowski, the charismatic conductor whose hands and accent fascinated audiences in Philadelphia. (Photo courtesy of Leopold Stokowski Papers, Kislak Center for Special Collections, Rare Books and Manuscripts, University of Pennsylvania) 52

Figure 38 - Leopold Stokowski conducts the Philadelphia Orchestra in the 1916 performance of Mahler's Eighth Symphony. (Public Domain) 53

Figure 39 - Arturo Toscanini, the fiery Italian maestro who said, "Not all of them hated me, only the bad musicians." (Photo Courtesy of U.S. Office of War Information) 54

Figure 40 - George Szell, the brilliant conductor of the Cleveland Orchestra. (Photo courtesy of Carl Van Vechten Collection, Library of Congress) 55

Figure 41 - Col. Henry Mapleson, a producer who charmed opera stars while fleeing his creditors, as he led the Academy of Music opera. He dismissed the rival Metropolitan Opera as "a yellow brewery." (Public Domain) 57

Figure 42 - Nellie Melba, the Australian soprano who sang during the "Golden Age of the Met." (1914 Metropolitan Opera Photo in Public Domain) 58

Figure 43 - Enrico Caruso, the Neapolitan tenor who remains the most famous opera star of all time through the technology of recording. (Photo courtesy of the George Grantham Bain Collection, Library of Congress) 59

Figure 44 - Heinrich Conried. He changed the emphasis on stars at the Metropolitan Opera, but suddenly found himself promoting the greatest opera star of all, Caruso. (Photograph of Conried by A. Radclyffe Dugmore 1906, Public Domain) 59

Figure 45 - Oscar Hammerstein I started a family dynasty that impacted the entire history of Broadway. (Public domain) 60

Figure 46 - Giulio Gatti-Casazza. The undisputed master and manager of the Metropolitan Opera. (Photo used courtesy of The George Grantham Bain Collection, Library of Congress) 62

Figure 47 - Jan Peerce, Arturo Toscanini's favorite tenor. (Photo courtesy of U.S. Office of War Information) 62

Figure 48 - Robert Merrilll, the baritone who was famous for devotion to the Metropolitan Opera and the New York Yankees. (Photo courtesy of Robert Merrill) 63

Figure 49 - Marian Anderson with Eleanor Roosevelt. The First Lady arranged for Anderson's historic concert at the Lincoln Memorial when she was banned from singing at Constitution Hall because of her race. (Photo courtesy of the Franklin Delano Roosevelt Library) 63

Figure 50 - Todd Duncan created the role of "Porgy" in *Porgy and Bess* and became the first black singer to star with a major opera company. (Photo by Van Damm, courtesy of Todd Duncan) 64

Figure 51 - Rudolf Bing often sat across from operatic divas in his office. The poodle sitting opposite him belonged to soprano Renata Tebaldi. (Photo courtesy of Metropolitan Opera) 64

Figure 52 - Charles Ives, the boldly experimental American composer who anticipated 20th century music in the 19th century and his wife, Harmony Twichell Ives, President of the Mark Twain Society. (Photo by Hallie Erskine, courtesy of the Charles Ives Society and the Irving Gilmore Library, Yale University) 66

Figure 53 - Henry Cowell (left) and Carl Ruggles (right), both major non-conformists who marched to the sound of their own drummers in American music. (Photo by Sydney Cowell, courtesy of the David and Sylvia Teitelbaum Fund, All rights reserved.) 70

Figure 54 - George Antheil, self-proclaimed "Bad Boy of Music," hard at work on a new score. (Photo courtesy of Arthur Antheil McTighe and Judith Donoher) 71

Figure 55 - John Cage, the unpredictable and always startling non-conformist experimenting with a toy piano. (Photo courtesy of Schoenhut Piano Company) 72

Figure 56 - George Gershwin. Decades after his sudden death in 1937, he remains one of the greatest icons of American music. (Photo courtesy Carl Van Vechten Collection, Library of Congress) 73

Figure 57 - - Nadia Boulanger – the legendary teacher of generations of 20th century composers. Her Paris salon became the gathering place for the "Boulangerie," her famed pupils who changed the face of contempory music. (Photo courtesy of la Bibliothèque Nationale de France).. 77

Figure 58 - Aaron Copland. Walter Damrosch said of him, "If a gifted young man can write a symphony like this at twenty-three, within five years, he will be ready to commit murder." (Photo courtesy of... 78

Figure 59 - Roy Harris, born in a log cabin on February 12, Lincoln's Birthday, in Lincoln County, Oklahoma. As a symphonist, he aspired to become "The American Beethoven." (Photo by permission of John F. Kennedy Memorial Library, California State University, Los Angles)... 81

Figure 60 - Roy Harris, composer, and his wife, pianist Johana Harris. Their musical marriage was a unique collaboration in which they traveled the country, all the while composing, teaching, performing, and lecturing to worldwide acclaim. (Photo by permission of John F. Kennedy Memorial Library, California State University, Los Angeles)... 82

Figure 61 - Virgil Thomson. A composer and critic, equally at home in Kansas City, Paris, or New York - inspired by hymn tunes and avant-garde poetry. (Photo courtesy of Virgil Thomson) 86

Figure 62 - Paul Bowles, composer and writer, who spent much of life living as an American expatriate in Morocco. (Photograph by Cherie Nutting, all rights reserved. The University of Delaware Library, Special Collections)... 89

Figure 63 - Ned Rorem, a Virgil Thomson pupil and one of America's best known composer of art songs. (Photo by David Diamond, used courtesy of the David L. Diamond estate - All rights reserved.).. 90

Figure 64 - Randall Thompson was one of America's leading composers of choral music. (Photo courtesy of University of Virginia Special Collections Library) 90

Figure 65 - Edward Levy, co-director, Hanya Holm, co-director and choreographer, Douglas Moore, composer, and John Latouche, librettist, collaborating on a production of Moore's opera, *The Ballad of Baby Doe*. (Photo by Louis Mélançon, courtesy of University of Denver/Central City Opera House)... 91

Figure 66 - George Frederick McKay, a major composer who spent a lifetime writing and teaching in the Pacific Northwest. (Photo courtesy of Fred McKay)..................... 93

Figure 67 - William Schuman. A prolific composer and a major figure in American musical education. (Photo courtesy of Irving Gilmore Library, Yale University) 94

Figure 68 - William Grant Still. The first African-American to conduct and have his work performed by a major American symphony orchestra, with his friends, violinist Louis Kaufman and pianist Annette Kaufman. (Photo courtesy of Annette Kaufman) 95

Figure 69 - Howard Hanson, composer, conductor, teacher, educator and the indefatigable champion of American music. (Photo courtesy of Eastman School Photo Archives, Sibley Music Library) 96

Figure 70 - Bernard Rogers (right) discussing the premiere of his opera, *The Warrior*, with fellow composer Deems Taylor, 1947. (Photo courtesy of the Bernard Rogers Collection, The Sibley Music Library) 99

Figure 71 - Alec Wilder, blowing bubbles, while a bemused Marian McPartland observes. (Photo by Louis Ouzer, courtesy of the Sibley Music Library, Eastman School of Music) 101

Figure 72 - H. Merrills Lewis, Louis Mennini, Wayne Barlow; seated, Howard Hanson, at the annual Festivals of American music. (Photo used courtesy of the Eastman School Photo Archives, Sibley Music Library) 102

Figure 73 - Joseph Wagner, conductor, teacher, and author. Lexicographer Nicolas Slonimsky called him "America's Most Undiscovered Composer." (Photo courtesy of Joseph Wagner) 103

Figure 74 - Composers Martin Mailman and Ron Nelson, both alumni of the Eastman School of Music. (Photo courtesy of Ron Nelson) 104

Figure 75 - Bernard Herrmann with Sir John Barbirolli. Famous for his film scores, he was also a renowned conductor and composer of works including his opera *Wuthering Heights* and his cantata *Moby Dick*. (Photo of recorded CD of *Moby Dick* courtesy of the Sir John Barbirolli Society) 105

Figure 76 - Jerome Moross, a composer whose unique personal style incorporated the rhythms and harmonies of folk tunes and popular songs into major concert works. (Photo courtesy of Susanna Moross Tarjan) 106

Figure 77 - Bernard Herrmann, an Anglophile, was the champion of British music in America. Pictured are (from left) Sir William Walton, Lyn Murray, Victor Bay, Bernard Herrmann, and André Previn. (Photo courtesy of The Queens Borough Public Library, Archives, New York *Herald-Tribune* Photograph Morgue Collection) 106

Figure 78 - Paul Creston - composer, teacher, scholar, and linguist. He was deeply inspired by his desire to write music that reflected spiritual values. (Photo courtesy of Portland State University) 107

Figure 79 - Vittorio Giannini continued the Italian-American tradition of musical lyricism and founded the University of North Carolina School of the Arts, the "Juilliard of the South." (Photo courtesy of University of North Carolina School of the Arts Archives) 109

Figure 80 - Nicolas Flagello. He aspired to challenge the most sophisticated musicians while inspiring the most modest listeners. (Photo courtesy of Maelos Music, Inc. - All rights reserved.) 110

Figure 81 - Norman Dello Joio, a composer who drew upon his heritage of Italian church music. (Photo by (c) Don Hunstein) 110

Figure 82 - Vincent Perschetti. He amazed his students with his ability improvise in the style of any composer, or even in their styles. (Photo courtesy of Associazione Musicale Vincent Persichetti) 111

Figure 83 - Samuel Barber, famous for his operas, art songs, the *Adagio for Strings,* and his neo-romantic style. (Photo courtesy of Carl Van Vechten Collection, Library of Congress) 112

Figure 84 - Gian Carlo Menotti. His operas, including *Amahl and the Night Visitors* and *The Consul*, won rare popularity among audiences of every age and musical taste. (Photo courtesy of Carl Van Vechten Collection, Library of Congress) 113

Figure 85 - Walter Piston, (center) the neo-classical icon whose music and pedagogy defined the study of music at Harvard for decades, with teaching fellow John C. Crawford and Music Department Chairman Randall Thompson. (Photo UAV 605 Box 11, courtesy of Harvard University Archives) 115

Figure 86 - Roger Sessions, an amiable and popular teacher, often described as a "difficult" composer who delighted in dissonance and complexity to express his musicality. (Photo courtesy of Roger Sessions) 116

Figure 87 - Elliott Carter, mentored in his youth by Charles Ives, was still composing at 104. (Photo by Irene Haupt, courtesy of Music Library, University at Buffalo, All Rights Reserved) 118

Figure 88 - Lukas Foss, a pupil of Serge Koussevitzky, was a composer, conductor, pianist, and teacher. (Photo by Jim Tuttle, courtesy of Music Library, University at Buffalo, All Rights Reserved) 119

Figure 89 - David Diamond in Italy. His career took him from working in a Broadway soda fountain to renown as the composer of eleven symphonies. (Courtesy of the Estate of David L. Diamond - All rights reserved.) 120

Figure 90 - Leon Kirchner, as composer and teacher, he spoke out forcefully for modern composers to communicate on an emotional level with their audiences. (Photo by and (c) Lisa Kirchner) 121

Figure 91 Ernest Bloch, composer and renowned teacher. His pupil, Roger Sessions, praised him for expressing "the grandeur of human suffering." (Photo by Ernest Bloch II, 1956, Courtesy Old Stage Studios) 122

Figure 92 - Edgard Varèse, the French composer who came to America, was called "The Father of Electronic Music." (Photo courtesy of George Grantham Bain Collection, Library of Congress) 123

Figure 93 - Darius Milhaud, the serious composer of modern French concert music who was captivated by jazz in the 1920s. (Public Domain) 124

Figure 94 - Bernard Wagenaar, an urbane Dutch-born composer who numbered many of America's finest composers among his pupils at Juilliard. (Photo courtesy of Mary Louise Miller Spang W1933 Collection (MC 035), Marion B. Gebbie W1901 Archives & Special Collection Madeleine Clark Wallace Library, Wheaton College Norton, MA.) 124

Figure 95 - Sergei Rachmaninoff, the logical successor to Tchaikovsky. When this Russian composer settled in the U.S., his romantic style made him one of the most widely beloved composers in the world. (Public Domain - Courtesy of Pictures and Prints Collection Library of Congress) 125

Figure 96 - Igor Stravinsky. A composer of many changing styles, he became the icon of neo-classical music in the 20th century. (Photo Courtesy of Library of Congress, Public Domain) 125

Figure 97 - Arnold Schoenberg conducting an American class. Pupils here include Natalie Limonick, H. Endicott Hansen, Alfred Carlson, Richard Hoffman. He was a celebrated teacher and musical revolutionary, although his twelve-tone technique still remains controversial in the 21st century. (Photo by Richard Fish - Courtesy of the Arnold Schönberg Center, Vienna, Austria) 126

Figure 98 - Gerald Strang, Schoenberg's assistant, was also a prominent composer, teacher, and acoustics consultant, and pioneer in the field of electronic and computer music. (Photo courtesy of The American Composers Alliance) 127

Figure 99 - Leonard Stein, a noted pianist, conductor, lecturer, editor and teacher, was also Schoenberg's assistant. Later, he served for many years as the Director of the Schoenberg Institute. (Photograph by Betty Freeman, Courtesy of Piano Spheres) 127

Figure 100 - Ernst Toch, distinguished as composer, teacher, and author of *The Shaping Forces in Music.* He told his pupils that all secrets of composition could be found in the music of Mozart. (Photo courtesy of the Irvin Talbot Collection) 128

Figure 101 - Ernest Kanitz, noted Austrian composer, spent several decades in Southern California as a teacher specializing in "modern counterpoint." (Photo courtesy of Ernest Kanitz) 128

Figure 102 - Ernst Krenek explores electronic music as fellow composers Aurelio de la Vega and Beverly Grigsby join him. (Photo courtesy of Aurelio de la Vega) 129

Figure 103 - Paul Hindemith a leading neo-classicist who combined a modern European musical vocabulary with the contrapuntal techniques of the Baroque era perfected by J.S. Bach. (Photo courtesy of Irving Gilmore Library, Yale University) 129

Figure 104 - Erich Wolfgang Korngold. When he died, Korngold thought his concert works would be forgotten, eclipsed by his years in Hollywood. Instead, his operas and instrumental works are more famous than ever. (Photo used with the kind permission of the Brendan Carroll Collection) 130

Figure 105 - Béla Bartók. A major Hungarian composer was inspired by true Hungarian folk music. (Public Domain) 130

Figure 106 - Miklós Rósza. He composed concertos for the violin, cello, and viola, among his many concert works, while always maintaining the highest artistic standards and the schedule of a film composer. (Courtesy of New York World Telegram and Sun Collection, Library of Congress) 131

Figure 107 - Eugene Zádor, was a prolific Hungarian composer who wrote important concert works while orchestrating film scores anonymously. (Photo courtesy of Leslie Zador) 131

Figure 108 - Eric Zeisl. His tonal and traditional style and his sudden death at the height of his creative powers at only fifty-three resulted in unjust neglect of his music. (Photograph courtesy of Barbara Zeisl Schoenberg) 131

Figure 109 - Mario Castelnuovo-Tedesco. Polish composer Bronislaw Kaper once said the word "composer" in the 20th century should be redefined to mean anyone who has studied with, is studying with, or will study with Castelnuovo-Tedesco. (Photo courtesy of Mario Castelnuovo-Tedesco) 132

Figure 110 - Mario Castelnuovo-Tedesco, at his writing desk, where he orchestrated in ink. The Maestro's scores required few corrections or changes. (Photograph courtesy of Mario Castelnuovo-Tedesco) 132

Figure 111 - A gathering of composers at the Hollywood Bowl in 1948 included many prominent émigrés and their American colleagues. (L-R, George Antheil, Eugene Zádor, Arthur Bergh, Italo Montemezzi, Miklós Rósza, Richard Hageman, William Grant Still, Igor Stravinsky, Ernst Toch, Louis Gruenberg, Erich Wolfgang Korngold. (Photo courtesy of Leslie Zador) 133

Figure 112 - Nicolas Slonimsky was a Russian composer, musicologist, historian, lexicographer, conductor, pianist, author, and extraordinary raconteur. (Photo courtesy of Electra Slonimsky Yourke) 134

Figure 113 - Aurelio de la Vega, Cuban-American composer, teacher, art historian, writer, scholar, and a voice in the wilderness calling for integrity in the arts and the behavior of nations. (Photo by Lee Choo courtesy of Aurelio de la Vega) 136

Figure 114 - Carlos Chávez, noted Mexican composer, recognized for his percussive music and complex rhythms. (Photo courtesy of the Carl Van Vechten Collection, Library of Congress) 136

Figure 115 - Silvestre Revueltas, a leading Mexican composer and teacher. He drew upon the rhythms and energy of Mexican folklore to create a unique personal style expressing the character of his people. (Photo courtesy of Fototeca Nacional de Mexico) 136

Figure 116 - Deems Taylor became so well known as a writer and commentator that his music was eclipsed by his activities as an author and broadcaster. (Photo courtesy of Carl Van Vechten Collection, Library of Congress) 138

Figure 117 - Robert Russell Bennett, seen with violinist Louis Kaufman. Bennett was a fine composer, but the public often only knew his reputation as the foremost orchestrator on Broadway. (Photo courtesy of Annette Kaufman) 139

Figure 118 - Alan Hovhaness (standing) joins colleagues (from left) John Lessard, Virgil Thomson, Sylvia Marlowe, Vittorio Rieti. (Photo at the Rachmaninoff Society, courtesy of Alan Hovhaness, the official web site) 140

Figure 119 - Leroy Anderson. One of America's most popular composers of light music. (Photograph used by special permission of Woodbury Music Company, All rights reserved.) 141

Figure 120 - Morton Gould, composer, conductor, and pianist. His music transcended labels as he incorporated jazz, blues, popular music, and folk tunes into his concert works before it was fashionable. (Photo courtesy of Abby Burton) 142

Figure 121 - Don Gillis with the most intimidating of conductors, Arturo Toscanini. (Photo courtesy of Don and Barbara Gillis Collection, North Texas University Music Library) 143

Figure 122 - Calvin Jackson. A composer, conductor, and pianist in every genre. He was a true Renaissance man and under recognized genius. (*The Two Sides of Calvin Jackson* (c) by Reprise Records/Rhino Entertainment Company, all rights reserved.) ... 144

Figure 123 - Donald Shirley. A pianist, organist, composer, linguist, painter, and musical philosopher. He combined the classics with spirituals, folk songs, and world music to create a voice unique in musical history. (Photo by Josef Astor) 145

Figure 124 - Donald Shirley after a performance of *New World's A Comin'*, with former Miss America, Jinx Falkenberg, composer Duke Ellington, vocalist Lena Horne, and her husband, musical director Lennie Hayton. (Photo courtesy of Donald Shirley) 146

Figure 125 - Astor Piazzolla, creator of the Nuevo Tango and virtuoso of the bandoneon, with pianist Pablo Ziegler and singer, Milva. (Photo courtesy of Ziegler Music) 147

Figure 126 - David Amram, composer, conductor, French horn soloist, teacher, writer, advocate for world music, comfortable in every musical genre, including symphonic works, jazz, and folk tunes. (Photo courtesy of David Amram) 149

Figure 127 - Frank Lewin, preparing his Mass in memory of Robert F. Kennedy with soloists Sylvia Jones and Leo Geokie in 1969. (Photo courtesy of Miriam and Naomi Lewin) 150

Figure 128- Scott Joplin, the most gifted musician of the Ragtime Era. (Public domain) 156

Figure 129 - Buddy Bolden, known in his time as New Orleans' premier cornetist and bandleader. (Public domain) 157

Figure 130 – "Jelly Roll" Morton, the man who once claimed to have invented jazz. (Public domain) 157

Figure 131 - James P. Johnson. His composition, "Charleston," became the dance anthem of the Roaring Twenties. (Public domain) 159

Figure 132 - Willie "The Lion" Smith. Ferocious as a soldier in World War I and at the piano. (Photo courtesy of William P. Gottlieb Collection, Library of Congress) 159

Figure 133 - Thomas "Fats" Waller began as a church organist, but he gained fame when he wrote the popular song, "Ain't Misbehavin'." (Photo courtesy of New York World Telegram and Sun Collection, Library of Congress) 160

Figure 134 - Donald "The Lamb" Lambert, an unfortunately forgotten giant of the stride era. Transcriptions of his dazzling solos have now been published in France. (Photo courtesy of Paul Marcorelles, all rights reserved.) 160

Figure 135 - Joe "King" Oliver. His band was the first black jazz band to be commercially recorded. (Public Domain) 161

Figure 136 - Nick LaRocca. His Original Dixieland Jazz Band became the first to make a jazz recording. (Photo courtesy of James LaRocca) 162

Figure 137 - Louis Armstrong, known as "Satchmo'" to the public, "Pops" to his friends, became an icon of jazz. (Photo courtesy of New York World Telegram and Sun Collection, Library of Congress) 162

Figure 138 - Earl "Fatha" Hines plays for Private Charles Carpenter. His trumpet and horn lines on the piano changed the jazz style of an era. (Photo courtesy of National Archives) 164

Figure 139 - Bix Beiderbecke, a jazz musician who had a brief, but influential career in the early days of jazz. (Public domain) 165

Figure 140 - Sidney Bechet, soprano saxophonist, Freddie Moore, and Lloyd Phillips. Conductor Ernest Ansermet called Bechet "a genius." (Photo courtesy of the William P. Gottlieb Collection, Library of Congress) 166

Figure 141 - Coleman "Bean" Hawkins. After hearing his solos, musicians took the saxophone seriously during the swing era. (Photo courtesy of the William P. Gottlieb Collection, Library of Congress) 168

Figure 142 - Bandleader Jimmie Lunceford, photographer William P. Gottlieb, drummer Gene Krupa. Lunceford saw himself as a teacher and mentor to other musicians. (Photo by Delia Potofsky Gottlieb, courtesy of William P. Gottlieb Collection, Library of Congress) 170

Figure 143 - Ben Pollack and the Californians. From left, Glenn Miller, Benny Goodman, Gil Rodin, Harry Green, Ben Pollack, Fud Livingston, Al Harris, Harry Goodman, Vic Breidis, and Lou Kastler. (Photo courtesy of Glenn Miller Archive, American Music Research Center, University of Colorado, Boulder, All Rights Reserved) 171

Figure 144 - Benny Goodman with pianist Teddy Wilson and singing star Mel Tormé on drums. (Photo from Metronome magazine, copyright not renewed when Metronome ceased publication.) 172

Figure 145 - Carnegie Hall poster announces Benny Goodman's Historical 1934 Jazz Concert. (Photo courtesy of Estate of Benny Goodman and the Irving Gilmore Library, Yale University. Used by permission) 174

Figure 146 - Benny Goodman (third from left) with musical alumni, left to right, Vernon Brown, George Auld, Gene Krupa, Clint Neagley, Ziggy Elman, Israel Crosby, and Teddy Wilson at the piano. (Photo by Fred Palumbo, courtesy of New York World Telegram and Sun Collection, Library of Congress) 175

Figure 147 - Artie Shaw, proclaimed "King of the Clarinet" and famous for his tone quality. (Photograph courtesy of Glenn Miller Archive, American Music Research Center, University of Colorado, Boulder. All Rights Reserved) 176

Figure 148 - Artie Shaw at the Palomar Ballroom, 1939. (Photo courtesy of Glenn Miller Archive, American Music Research Center, University of Colorado, Boulder, All Rights Reserved) 177

Figure 149 - Jimmy Dorsey and his band at the Panther Room, 1940 - (Photo courtesy of Glenn Miller Archive, American Music Research Center, University of Colorado, Boulder. All Rights Reserved.) 179

Figure 150 - Axel Stordahl, whose arrangements helped make Frank Sinatra a singing idol for the "bobbysoxers," looks on while Sinatra rehearses. (Photo courtesy of William P. Gottlieb Collection, Library of Congress) 179

Figure 151 - Tommy Dorsey leads a rehearsal in 1945. (Photo courtesy of Glenn Miller Archive, American Music Research Center, University of Colorado, Boulder. All Rights Reserved) 180

Figure 152 - Nelson Riddle, a Castelnuovo-Tedesco pupil, naturally incorporated his swinging, big-band style in his motion picture scores. (Photo courtesy of Nelson Riddle Collection, University of Arizona Fred Fox School of Music) 180

Figure 153 - Jimmy and Tommy Dorsey, brothers, rival bandleaders, and giants of the swing era. (Photograph courtesy of Glenn Miller Archive, American Music Research Center, University of Colorado, Boulder. All Rights Reserved.) 181

Figure 154 - Glenn Miller's legacy lives on after his plane vanished during World War II. (Photo courtesy of Glenn Miller Archive, American Music Research Center, University of Colorado, Boulder. All Rights Reserved) 181

Figure 155 -Glenn Miller was a trombonist, but a clarinet lead played over the saxophone section made his band with its signature sound the most popular sweet band in America. (Photo courtesy of Glenn Miller Archive, American Music Research Center, University of Colorado, Boulder. All Rights Reserved.) 182

Figure 156 - Woody Herman - He led "The Band That Played the Blues" and collaborated with Igor Stravinsky. (Photo courtesy of Glenn Miller Archive, American Music Research Center, University of Colorado, Boulder. All Rights Reserved.) 183

Figure 157 - Harry James - His soaring trumpet made him a star during the Big Band era. (Photo courtesy of the William P. Gottlieb Collection, Library of Congress) 185

Figure 158 - Stan Kenton, a lifetime in search of "new sounds." (Photo courtesy of CSULA, The California State University, Los Angeles, John F Kennedy Memorial Library) 186

Figure 159 - Stan Kenton brought an evangelical fervor to musical performances, composing, and arrangements. (Photo courtesy of CSULA, The California State University, Los Angeles, John F Kennedy Memorial Library) 187

Figure 160 - Duke Ellington, justly known as a musician "Beyond Category." (Photo courtesy of Glenn Miller Archive, American Music Research Center, University of Colorado, Boulder. All Rights Reserved) 189

Figure 161 - Billy Strayhorn, a gifted pianist and composer in his own right, was Ellington's musical alter ego. (Photo courtesy of The Carl Van Vechten Collection, Library of Congress) 192

Figure 162 - Duke Ellington (seated at the microphone) and Billy Strayhorn (seated to the left of the microphone) join colleagues in a radio interview with Willis Conover. (Photo courtesy of Willis Conover Collection, North Texas University Music Library).. 193

Figure 163 - William "Count" Basie - His hard-driving bands used "head charts," improvising in their unique way on jazz riffs. (Photo courtesy of Glenn Miller Archive, American Music Research Center, University of Colorado, Boulder. All Rights Reserved.) 194

Figure 164 - Lionel Hampton, was the first major jazz musician to prominently use the vibraphone in his preformance, at The Aquarium, 1946. (Photo courtesy of William P. Gottlieb Collection, Library of Congress) 195

Figure 165 - Xavier Cugat, definitely the best-known Latin-American bandleader of his time, doing a caricature of one of his favorite subjects, himself. (Photo courtesy of William P. Gottlieb Collection, Library of Congress) 197

Figure 166 - Lester Young, known as "Prez." His admirers elected him "President of the Saxophone." (Photo courtesy of William P. Gottlieb Collection, Library of Congress) 198

Figure 167- Teddy Wilson - His lilting phrasing and light touch made him one of the most admired pianists of the swing era. (Photo courtesy of William P. Gottlieb Collection, Library of Congress) 200

Figure 168 - Art Tatum - When Tatum appeared, other pianists whispered, "God is in the house tonight." (Photo courtesy of William P. Gottlieb Collection, Library of Congress) 200

Figure 169 - Art Tatum and Phil Moore at the Club Downbeat, 1946-48. Tatum's dazzling left hand technique and right handed runs at blinding speed left even his most accomplished contemporaries speechless. (Photo courtesy of William P. Gottlieb Collection, Library of Congress) 201

Figure 170 - 52nd Street: In the late 1940s, New Yorkers could hear the world's greatest jazzmen all in a few blocks. (Photo courtesy of William P. Gottlieb Collection, Library of Congress) 204

Figure 171 - Thelonious Monk, Howard McGhee, Roy Eldridge, and Teddy Hill at Minton's, the jazz club where bop was born. (Photo courtesy of William P. Gottlieb Collection, Library of Congress) 205

Figure 172 - Thelonious Monk with his trademark beret and sunglasses, brought whimsy and unpredictability to the bop era as a composer. (Photo courtesy of William P. Gottlieb Collection, Library of Congress) 205

Figure 173 - Charlie Parker, joined by Tommy Potter, Miles Davis, and Duke Jordan. Charlie "Bird" Parker was the leading saxophonist of the bop era. His speed and harmonic daring inspired generations of musicians. (Photo courtesy of William P. Gottlieb Collection, Library of Congress) 206

Figure 174 - Mary Lou Williams, pianist, whose New York apartment became the gathering place for bop musicians to experiment and turn the jazz world upside down. (Photo courtesy of William P. Gottlieb Collection, Library of Congress) 207

Figure 175 - "Dizzy" Gillespie admires a performance by Ella Fitzgerald with colleagues Ray Brown and Milt Jackson, while Danish jazz advocate Timmie Rosenkrantz watches. (Photo courtesy of William P. Gottlieb Collection, Library of Congress) 208

Figure 176 - Bud Powell was called "The Amazing Bud Powell" and with good reason. (Photo courtesy of Carl Smith, Budpowelljazz.com) 209

Figure 177 - Dizzy Gillespie, Tadd Dameron, Hank Jones, Mary Lou Williams, and Milt Orent discuss the state of jazz at Williams' apartment. (Photo courtesy of William P. Gottlieb Collection Library of Congress.) 210

Figure 178 - "Dizzy" Gillespie, famous for his bent trumpet, explored new harmonies and syncopated rhythms to spearhead the movement to bebop. (Photo by and courtesy of Roland Godefroy) 211

Figure 179 - Jazz fans, including widely admired bassist, Al McKibbon, wearing the hat, gather outside The Three Deuces, a popular jazz club of the 1940s. (Photo courtesy of The William P. Gottlieb Collection, Library of Congress) 212

Figure 180 - Pianists Tommy Flanagan and Hank Jones join saxophonist Stan Getz in an ensemble. (Photo by Tad Hershorn, courtesy of the Institute for Jazz Studies, Rutgers University) 213

Figure 181 - Erroll Garner - He became an international jazz star without reading music. (Photograph courtesy of William P. Gottlieb Collection, Library of Congress) 213

Figure 182 - Oscar Peterson, successor to Art Tatum as the ultimate jazz piano virtuoso, with bassist Niels-Henning Ørsted Pederson. (Photo © Claude Truong Ngoc / Wikimedia Commons) 214

Figure 183 - Art Tatum and Oscar Peterson - friends and great icons of jazz piano. (Photo courtesy of the Toledo Lucas County Public Library) 215

Figure 184 - Oscar Peterson at the piano with Voice of America host Willis Conover (Photo courtesy of Willis Conover Collection, University of North Texas) 215

Figure 185 - Nat "King" Cole was an accomplished jazz pianist, but his pianistic skills were often eclipsed by his success as a singer. (Photo by William P. Gottlieb, courtesy of William P. Gottlieb Collection, Library of Congress) 216

Figure 186 - The amazing Dick Hyman excelled not only as a jazz soloist, but as a composer and arranger in virtually every genre of music. (Photo courtesy of Dick Hyman) 217

Figure 187 - Paul Thatcher Smith, known for his brilliant technique and his wife, singer Annette Warren, made music together for decades. (Photo courtesy of Annette Warren Smith) 218

Figure 188 - Marian McPartland, pianist, broadcaster and advocate for women in jazz. (Photo courtesy of the Kurland Agency) 218

Figure 189 - Claude Thornhill, together with arranger Gil Evans, brought French horns into the jazz world. (Photo courtesy of William P. Gottlieb Collection, Library of Congress) 219

Figure 190 - Lennie Tristano, experimental pianist and jazz teacher. (Photo courtesy of William P. Gottlieb Collection, Library of Congress) 220

Figure 191 - Miles Davis, trumpeter, led the "Birth of the Cool." (Photo by and copyright by Tom Palumbo) 220

Figure 192 - Bill Evans, famous for his harmonic voicings at the piano, said that jazz could not be explained—it had to be felt. (Photo courtesy of Institute of Jazz Studies, Rutgers University) 221

Figure 193 - André Previn, the classical prodigy who made his mark as a jazz pianist and film composer before devoting his time to symphonic conducting and composing operas. (Photo by Bert Verhoeff / Anefo courtesy of Dutch National Archives) 222

Figure 194 - Dave Brubeck startled audiences with daring jazz improvisations in unusual time signatures such as 5/4. (Photo courtesy of Carl Van Vechten Collection, Library of Congress) 223

Figure 195 - George Shearing brought classical sensibilities to his solo jazz improvisations. (Photograph courtesy of The Institute of Jazz Studies, Rutgers University) 223

Figure 196 - George Shearing - Famous for his Quintet, but one of the finest ballad soloists in jazz history. (Photo by James Kriegsmann for Associated Booking Corporation, courtesy of George Shearing.) 224

Figure 197 - The Modern Jazz Quartet combined the rhythms and harmonies of jazz with the genre of chamber music. (Photo by Tad Hershorn, courtesy of Institute of Jazz Studies, Rutgers University) 225

Figure 198 - Ahmad Jamal. His use of contrapuntal lines in jazz has won him a worldwide audience of admirers for decades. (Photograph by Jacques Beneich, used by special permission courtesy of Ellora Management. All rights reserved) 225

Figure 199 - Randy Weston, a pianist who explored the musical heritage of Africa while building a reputation in jazz. (Photo by Ariane Smolderen, courtesy of Randy Weston) 226

Figure 200 - Sir Roland Hanna, renowned as a soloist and ensemble player in the jazz world, found time to compose four hundred original works combining classical and jazz elements. (Photo courtesy of Rahanna Music, Inc. All Rights Reserved.) 227

Figure 201 - Phineas Newborn, Jr., the dazzling jazz pianist from Tennessee whose career was sadly cut short by illness and circumstances. (Photo courtesy of Phineas Newborn, III) 228

Figure 202 - Billie Holiday -"Lady Day." (Photo by William P. Gottlieb and courtesy off The William P. Gottlieb Collection, The Library of Congress) 229

Figure 203 - Ella Fitzgerald everyone's favorite jazz vocalist, famed for flawless intonation and as the Queen of "Scat," welcomed to the White House by President Ronald Reagan. (U.S. Government Photo) 230

Figure 204 - Sarah Vaughan, known to her close friends as "Sassy." (Photo by William P. Gottlieb and used courtesy of The William P. Gottlieb Collection, Library of Congress) 230

Figure 205 - Jackie Cain and Roy Kral, known as "Jackie and Roy," were collaborators for fifty-six years in a happy musical marriage. Photograph taken at Bach Dancing & Dynamite Society, Half Moon Bay CA, 1982. Brian McMillen (Used under Creative Commons license.) 231

Figure 206 - Mel Tormé initially disliked his nickname, "The Velvet Fog." He was a brilliant vocalist, but also a drummer, composer, arranger, and author. (Photo courtesy of Alan Light) 232

Figure 207 - Toots Thielemans, the Belgian harmonica virtuoso. (Photo by Jos L.Knaepen, courtesy of Veerle Van de Poel) 235

Figure 208 - Art Van Damme, regarded as the leading exponent of jazz on the accordion. (Photo courtesy of Sandra Mummert) 235

Figure 209 - Sam Saxe, one of America's finest piano pedagogues, was a major pioneer in the teaching of jazz. (Photo courtesy of Sam Saxe) 236

Figure 210 - Billy Taylor, pianist and the greatest ambassador for jazz in the classroom and around the world. (Photo courtesy of Jazzmobile) 239

Figure 211 - Pomping Vila. He discovered American jazz in pre-war Shanghai as America's own music traveled the globe. (Photo courtesy of Pomping Vila) 240

Figure 212 - The Mitchell-Ruff duo featured Dwike Mitchell on piano and Willie Ruff on bass and French horn. Mitchell and Ruff gave historic performances of American jazz in the Soviet Union and China. (Photo courtesy of Willie Ruff) 241

Figure 213 - Willis Conover. Through the Voice of America, he became the voice of American jazz behind the Iron Curtain. (Photo by Voice of America) 241

Figure 214 - Claude Bolling, a French pianist and composer, named by America's Duke Ellington, his "spiritual son." (Photo courtesy of Claude Bolling) 244

TABLE OF FIGURES | 491

Figure 215 - Ornette Coleman startled the jazz world by improvising without key signatures in an atonal style, the same one used by many experimental European avant-garde composers decades earlier. (Photo by Geert Vandepoele) 246

Figure 216 - Duke Ellington at the White House - Jazz comes full circle. Duke Ellington is honored by President Richard M. Nixon as a guest in the White House where his father once worked as a butler. (U.S. Government Photo) 248

Figure 217 Victor Herbert. Irish-born, he composed the scores for many of the most popular and successful Broadway productions of the early 20th century. (Photograph courtesy of Library of Congress, Public Domain) 254

Figure 218 - Victor Herbert, at the piano, joined by colleagues and charter members of ASCAP, Gustave Kerker, Raymond Hubbell, Harry Tierney, Louis A. Hirsch, Rudolf Friml, Robert Hood Bowers, Silvio Hein, Alfred Baldwin Sloane and Irving Berlin. (Photo courtesy of ASCAP) 255

Figure 219 - "Give My Regards to Broadway" by George M. Cohan became the anthem of Broadway. (Photograph used Courtesy of Abram Samuels Sheet Music Collection, The Trexler Library, Muhlenberg College) 256

Figure 220 - "Over There" by George M. Cohan, literally inspired millions of Americans in World War I. (Photograph Courtesy of Abram Samuels Sheet Music Collection,Trexler Library,Muhlenberg College) 256

Figure 221 - Franz Lehar, composer of the post-Strauss "Silver Age" in Vienna. He composed *The Merry Widow*, still today the most popular operetta of all time. (Photo courtesy of the George Grantham Bain Collection, Library of Congress) 257

Figure 222 - Rudolf Friml, the composer whose romantic scores were among the most popular on Broadway in the 1920s, had his musical roots in 19th century operetta, as is clear in this 1905 sketch by Czech artist Alfons Mucha. (Public domain.) 257

Figure 223 - Sigmund Romberg - His scores, inspired by Viennese operetta, set the tone of romantic musicals in the years following World War I. (Publicity photograph-public domain) 258

Figure 224 - Otto Harbach, lyricist and mentor to Oscar Hammerstein II in the early days of his career. (Public domain) 259

Figure 225 - Irving Berlin in 1906. Jerome Kern said that Berlin does not have a role in American music, he IS American music. (Public Domain) 260

Figure 226 - A rare view of many of America's leading popular composers and lyricists in 1920: from left, Gene Buck, Victor Herbert, John Philip Sousa, Harry B. Smith, Jerome Kern, Irving Berlin, George W. Meyer, Iving Bibo, Otto Harbach. (Photo by Al Aumuller, courtesy of New York World Telegram and Sun Collection, Library of Congress) 261

Figure 227 - Vincent Youmans, who made his mark on Broadway with melodies of fine quality that are widely admired today, was devoted to fishing and sailing.(Photo courtesy of Vincent Youmans III) 262

Figure 228 - Irving Caesar early in his career with the junior partner in his Broadway publishing company, Incy, (pronounced "Inky.") (Photo courtesy of the ASCAP Foundation) 262

Figure 229 - Noble Sissle was a gifted songwriter who collaborated with his friend, pianist Eubie Blake. Sissle was a singer, a musician, and later in life a popular disc jockey in New York. (Photo courtesy of Carl Van Vechten Collection, Library of Congress) 264

Figure 230 - "I'm Just Wild About Harry," originally a waltz, became a toe tapping hit in the 1920s and in1948, Harry S. Truman selected it as his campaign song when he ran for President of the United States. (Photo Courtesy of Abram Samuels Sheet Music Collection, The Trexler Library Muhlenberg College) 265

Figure 231 - Eubie Blake, pianist, composer, and the last surviving figure of the Ragtime Era. (Photo courtesy of Institute of Jazz Studies, Rutgers University) 265

Figure 232 - Andy Razaf, nephew of the Queen of Madagascar, became a prominent songwriter in America. (Photo courtesy of the Institute of Jazz Studies, Rutgers University) 266

Figure 233 - Producer Morris Gest, writers P.G. Wodehouse and Guy Bolton, producer F. Ray Comstock, and composer Jerome Kern at the time *of Leave It to Jane* in 1917. (Public domain) 267

Figure 234 - Edna Ferber, whose sprawling, vibrant novel inspired Jerome Kern and Oscar Hammerstein II to write the score for *Showboat*. (Photo courtesy of Kevin C. Fitzpatrick, and the Dorothy Parker Society, dorothyparker.com) 268

Figure 235 - Helen Morgan, who introduced the song "Bill" in *Showboat* on Broadway and sang it in the 1929 and 1936 film adaptations. Ava Gardner performed it in the 1952 film, although her voice was dubbed by Annette Warren. (Photo by Carl Van Vechten, courtesy of the Van Vechten Collection, Library of Congress) 269

Figure 236 - George and Ira Gershwin, New York 1928. As brothers and collaborators, they had a unique rapport that made a tremendous impact on America's musical history. (Photo used by special permission from the Gershwin Family Trusts) 271

Figure 237 - George Gershwin, Dubose Hayward, Ira Gershwin, discuss their score for one of the great American operas, *Porgy and Bess*. (Photo by VanDamm Studio, 1935, used by special permission from the Gershwin Family Trusts) 273

Figure 238 - Richard Rodgers and Lorenz Hart - The disciplined, meticulous Rodgers and the mercurial, unpredictable Hart were improbable collaborators, but they produced one brilliant score after another throughout the 1920s and 1930s. (Photo courtesy of New York World Telegram and Sun Collection, Library of Congress) 275

Figure 239 - Cole Porter, an extraordinary composer and lyricist brought a dazzling sophistication to the musical theater with wit, style, elegance, and astonishing rhymes. But when asked to describe himself, he just said, "I'm Broadway." (Public Domain) 277

Figure 240 - Noël Coward, urbane, sophisticated, world-weary, playwright, actor, composer, lyricist, wit, bon vivant, was simply described by his colleagues as "The Master." (Photo by Allan Warren. Used by special permission. All rights reserved.) 279

Figure 241 - Arthur Schwartz, originally an attorney, with lyricist Dorothy Fields. Schwartz's dark and haunting melodies were memorable, as was his long time collaboration with another lyricist, Howard Dietz. (Photo by Walter Albertin, staff of New York World Telegram and Sun, courtesy of Library of Congress) 281

Figure 242 - Howard Dietz, standing, with collaborator Arthur Schwartz and actress Cyd Charisse at the piano. Dietz, a brilliant lyricist, also was also the publicist responsible for creating Leo the Lion, MGM's roaring mascot and the studio's on-screen motto, "Ars Gratia Artis." (Photo courtesy of Robert F.R. Ballard) 282

Figure 243 - Vernon Duke (left) with his collaborator Ira Gershwin. (Courtesy of New York World Telegram and Sun Collection, Library of Congress) 283

Figure 244 - Blitzstein's work was a scathing attack on the capitalist system. (Poster courtesy of The Federal Theater Project) 288

Figure 245 - Harold Rome switched from architecture to music and became the composer of hit Broadway shows. (Photo Courtesy of Irving Gilmore Library, Yale University) 290

Figure 246 - *Oklahoma!* became one of the greatest hits ever produced on Broadway and changed musical theater history forever. (Photograph appears courtesy of Rodgers & Hammerstein: An Imagem Company, www.rnh.com) 292

Figure 247 - Rodgers & Hammerstein moved the setting of *Liliom* to New England and created *Carousel*, one of the finest scores ever written for Broadway. (Photo courtesy of Rodgers & Hammerstein: An Imagem Company, www.rnh.com) 293

Figure 248 - Gordon MacRae and Shirley Jones performed the famous "Bench Scene" in the film version of the Rodgers & Hammerstein's masterpiece, *Carousel*. (Photograph appears courtesy of Rodgers & Hammerstein: An Imagem Company, www.rnh.com) ... 295

Figure 249 - *South Pacific,* starring Mary Martin and Ezio Pinza, combined characters from several stories by James Michener in a brilliant, well-crafted and most memorable musical. (Photo with permission of Rodgers & Hammerstein: An Imagem Company, www.rnh.com) 296

Figure 250 - Mary Martin, the All-American Broadway star from Weatherford, Texas and Ezio Pinza, the Italian operatic basso, singing the "twin-soliloquy," providing an enchanted evening for all. (Photo courtesy of Rodgers & Hammerstein: An Imagem Company, www.rnh.com) 296

Figure 251 - *The King and I* combined a favorite Rodgers & Hammerstein theme, East meets West through music. (Photograph appears courtesy of Rodgers & Hammerstein: An Imagem Company, www.rnh.com) 297

Figure 252 - It is hard to imagine anyone other than Yul Brynner, not the first choice, as the King, as he and Gertrude Lawrence perform "Shall We Dance? in *The King and I.* (Photo courtesy of Rodgers & Hammerstein: An Imagem Company, www.rnh.com) 297

Figure 253 - Mary Martin and Theodore Bikel share a musical moment in *The Sound of Music,* the last Rodgers & Hammerstein collaboration, ended only by Hammerstein's death. (Photo appears courtesy of Rodgers & Hammerstein: An Imagem Company, www.rnh.com).. 298

Figure 254 - Alan Jay Lerner proved up to the challenge of adapting George Bernard Shaw's *Pygmalion.* His lyrics combined with music by Frederick Loewe made *My Fair Lady* one of the greatest Broadway shows. 302

Figure 255 - Leonard Bernstein was drawn to Broadway as a comoser despite objections from his classical mentors. (Photo by Al Ravenna, Courtesy of New York World Telegram and Sun Collection, Library of Congress) 306

Figure 256- Betty Comden and Adolph Green, with one of their later collaborators, composer Cy Coleman (left.) (Photo courtesy of Noble Music)... 307

Figure 257 - Composer Jule Styne (right) and lyricist Bob Merrill (left), collaborators on the hit show, *Funny Girl.* (Photo courtesy of Margaret Styne and Suzanne Merrill) ... 310

Figure 258 - Sammy Cahn, the master of the finger-snapping lyric and the sentimental ballad, celebrating several of his most successful songs. (Photo courtesy of Tita Cahn) 310

Figure 259 - The remarkable Frank Loesser had a major impact on Broadway as both composer and lyricist. (Photo courtesy of Frank Loesser Archives) 313

Figure 260 - Frank Loesser at his desk, hard at work. (Photo courtesy of Frank Loesser Archives) 314

Figure 261 - "I'll Know," one of the fine love songs from *Guys and Dolls.* (Photo courtesy of Frank Loesser Enterprises) 315

Figure 262 - "My Heart is So Full of You," sung in *The Most Happy Fella* by operatic star Robert Weede to soprano Jo Sullivan in the original New York production. (Photo courtesy of Frank Loesser Enterprises) 316

Figure 263 - Richard Adler (seated) and Jerry Ross (at the piano), the brilliant team whose brief collaboration, cut short by Ross's sudden death, produced Broadway classic shows. (Photo by Paul Radkai, courtesy of Janie Ross Coulter.) 318

Figure 264 - Meredith Willson never forgot his roots in Mason City, Iowa. He turned his hometown into River City, the mythical setting of his biggest hit musical, *The Music Man.* (Photo courtesy of Mason City Public Library) 319

Figure 265 - Irving Berlin, composer of *Annie Get Your Gun*, attends auditions with producers Richard Rodgers, Oscar Hammerstein II, and choreographer Helen Tamiris. (Photo by Al Aumuller. Courtesy of New York World Telegram and Sun Collection, Library of Congress) 320

Figure 266 - Cole Porter in 1955 receiving an honorary doctorate from Williams College. He composed the score for *Kiss Me, Kate* on a Bechstein piano, today residing in the Williams

College chapel. He received another honorary doctorate from Yale University five years later. (Photo courtesy of the Irving Gilmore Library, Yale University, Cole Porter Papers, Box 50, Folder 307s) 322

Figure 267 - Kurt Weill (center) with author Alan Paton and playwright Maxwell Anderson collaborating on the musical version of *Lost in the Stars*. (Photo by Hagelmeyer, courtesy of New York World Telegram and Sun Collection, Library of Congress) 324

Figure 268 - Jerome Moross (in the center), choreographer Hanya Holm, and lyricist John Latouche during a rehearsal of *The Golden Apple*, a highly experimental musical show that deserved a longer life. (Photo courtesy of Susanna Moross Tarjan) 327

Figure 269 - Harold Arlen. On Broadway and in Hollywood, colleagues said that Arlen was their musical role model. (Photograph courtesy of the Carl Van Vechten Collection) 329

Figure 270 - Harold and Fayard Nicholas, the Nicholas Brothers, dazzled audiences through their incomparable appearances on stage and screen. (Photo courtesy of Rigmor Newman) 331

Figure 271 - Composer Burton Lane and lyricist E. Y. Harburg achieved their greatest success on Broadway with a musical combining Irish folklore and Southern social satire. (Photo by L. Arnold Weissberger, All Rights Reserved, courtesy of Ernie Harburg.) 331

Figure 272 - Sammy Fain, a gifted melodist, wrote many of the most memorable songs heard in the movies. (Photo by George Mann, courtesy of Dianne Woods, the George Mann Archive.) 332

Figure 273 - Jerry Bock and Sheldon Harnick - Their lyrical style resulted in a huge success for *Fiddler on the Roof*, a show which broke the record as the longest running musical on Broadway, a record which lasted for ten years. (Photo courtesy of Broadway to Vegas) 334

Figure 274 - Jerry Herman with two of his favorite leading ladies, Angela Lansbury, the original Mame, (left) and Carol Channing, the original Dolly (right.) (Photo courtesy of Jerry Herman) 335

Figure 275 - Cy Coleman was a classical child prodigy and jazz pianist, but he made his greatest mark on Broadway. He teamed successfully with lyricist Dorothy Fields. She had been writing lyrics on Broadway before he was born. (Photo courtesy of Noble Music Inc.) 336

Figure 276 - Composer John Kander and lyricist Fred Ebb enjoyed many years of happy collaboration together, resulting in shows such as *Cabaret* and *Chicago*. Photo by Marc Mellon, courtesy of the Friars Club) 337

Figure 277 - Charles Strouse at the piano with lyricist Lee Adams (left,) and playwright Clifford Odets (right,) during collaboration on *Golden Boy*. (Photo courtesy of Charles Strouse) 337

Figure 278 - Harvey Schmidt and Tom Jones, both Texans, seen here with Anne Bancroft, wrote *The Fantasticks*, which ran off-Broadway for forty-two years. One of the most popular musicals in history, the show continued for over 17,000 performances. (Photo courtesy of Harvey Schmidt) 338

Figure 279 - Stephen Sondheim. He revolutionized American musical theater with new forms and styles. (Public domain publicity still) 339

Figure 280 - William G. Blanchard at the console of a large theater organ. (Photo courtesy of William G. Blanchard) 351

Figure 281 - Paramount Theater in New York. The Paramount Theater, like many of the 1920s "movie palaces" featured a full-length vaudeville show as well as motion pictures accompanied by a live orchestra. (Photo courtesy of the Irvin Talbot Collection) 352

Figure 282 - Irvin Talbot. For forty-five years, he set the highest musical standards conducting the Paramount orchestra. (Photo courtesy of the Irvin Talbot Collection) .. 353

Figure 283 - Irvin Talbot conducting the musical score for a sound film in the early days of Paramount Pictures. (Photo courtesy of Irvin Talbot Collection) 355

Figure 284 - Walt Disney, whose Magic Kingdom, on screen and in life, all started with a mouse. (Photo courtesy of New York World Telegram and Sun collection, Library of Congress, public domain) 356

Figure 285 - Erich Wolfgang Korngold. The greatest musical prodigy of the century who became a pioneer film composer. (With the kind permission of the Brendan Carroll Collection) 359

Figure 286 - Erich Wolfgang Korngold conducted his film scores as if he were spontaneously conducting the score of one of his operas. (Photo used with the kind permission of the Brendan Carroll Collection.) 360

Figure 287 - Max Steiner – He composed over 300 film scores. His score for *The Informer* established the coordination between music and images on screen. (Photo by and courtesy of Alexander Courage) 363

Figure 288 - Ernst Krenek at work. (Courtesy of Archives and Special Collections, Vassar College Library) 367

Figure 289 - A luncheon at MGM as composers adjust to life at Hollywood's largest studio. From left, Eugene Zádor, Charles Wakefield Cadman, studio executive Nat Finston, actor and composer Lionel Barrymore, Mario Castelnuovo-Tedesco, Daniele Amfitheatrof. (Photo courtesy of Leslie Zádor) 368

Figure 290 - Alfred Newman, composer, conductor, and creator of the "Fox String Sound," with a collection of his Oscars. (Photo courtesy of Thomas Newman) 370

Figure 291 - A Party at the Home of Alfred Newman. 20th Century Fox colleagues include, from left, Franz Waxman, Alfred Newman, Bernard Herrmann, Ken Darby, Vinton Vernon, Alex North, Hugo Friedhofer. (Courtesy of Hugo Friedhofer) 371

Figure 292 - Victor Young. Friends said he looked like a prizefighter, but he is still regarded as one of the greatest romantic melodists ever to score films in Hollywood. (Photograph courtesy of Bobbie Fromberg) 374

Figure 293 - Harry Sukman, pianist and composer, known for his keyboard virtuosity and rich, melodic style of scoring for films and television, accepting a well-deserved Academy Award from presenters Sandra Dee and Bobby Darin. (Photo courtesy of Susan Sukman McCray.) 376

Figure 294 - Frank Skinner - Film composer, big band arranger, and author. His talents enabled him to score every genre of film at Universal Studios for decades. (Photo courtesy of Frank Skinner) 377

Figure 295 - Joseph Gershenson, for many years, conducted and supervised numerous musical scores as the director of Universal Studios' music department. (Photograph courtesy of Joseph Gershenson) 377

Figure 296 - Russ Garcia, the amiable composer-arranger who gave up life in Hollywood to pursue his dreams in New Zealand. (Photo by Kaiwhakahaere) 378

Figure 297 - Roy Webb, pioneer film composer, spent two decades scoring motion pictures at RKO. (Photo courtesy of Roy Webb) 379

Figure 298 - Franz Waxman - Composer, conductor, and founder of the Los Angeles Music Festival. Waxman was the first to win the Academy Award two years in a row. (Photo by and courtesy of Alexander Courage) 379

Figure 299 - Puccini in Japanese. Soprano Michiko Sunahara, center, joined by Franz Waxman and Irvin Talbot to her right. A team was required to suggest that Shirley MacLaine was singing opera in Japanese. (Photo courtesy of Irvin Talbot Collection) ... 382

Figure 300 - Bronislaw Kaper. He excelled at scores of wit and charm during nearly three decades in the Music Department at MGM. (Photo by and courtesy of Alexander Courage) 383

Figure 301 - Dimitri Tiomkin (far right) joins colleagues at Paramount, from left, Richard Hageman, Boris Morros, Albert Coates, Irvin Talbot, Pietro Cimini. (Courtesy of The Irvin Talbot Collection) 385

Figure 302 - Dimitri Tiomkin spoke English and scored the most popular westerns with his inimitable Russian accent. (Photo by and courtesy of Alexander Courage) 386

Figure 303 - Miklós Rózsa through his 'double life,' scaled the heights of both film scoring and concert music. (Photo by and courtesy of Alexander Courage) 387

Figure 304 - Miklós Rózsa, a rare composer who retained his principles and musical integrity while achieving great public recognition and commercial success. (Photo from the collection of Janos Sebestyen courtesy of Robert Tifft) 390

Figure 305 - Aaron Copland scored only a few films and protested the excesses of Hollywood, but he influenced film scoring through his pupils and admirers he influenced. (Photo by and courtesy of Alexander Courage) 392

Figure 306 - Virgil Thomson made his mark in motion pictures scoring documentary films. (Carl Van Vechten collection. Courtesy of Library of Congress Public Domain) 393

Figure 307 - The team from *Modern Times*: Charles Dunworth, conductor Alfred Newman, star Charlie Chaplin, composer David Raksin, sound engineer Paul G. Neal, orchestrator Edward B. Powell. (Photo by Autrey, all rights reserved. Courtesy of David Raksin and Paul G. Neal).. 394

Figure 308 - *The Timeless Melodies of David Raksin*. The composer's photo, substituted for iconic picture of Dana Andrews gazing at a portrait of Gene Tierney and listening to "Laura." (Photo courtesy of Susan Andrews, used by special permission. Collection (c) 1996 by EKay Music, Inc. All rights reserved).. 395

Figure 309 - Two composers known for the scores for films starring Dana Andrews: David Raksin *(Laura)* and composer colleague Leith Stevens (*Night Song*) at an awards ceremony. (Photo by and courtesy of Alexander Courage) 396

Figure 310 - Hugo Friedhofer, called by David Raksin, 'the most learned of us all." (Photo courtesy of Hugo Friedhofer) 397

Figure 311 - Bernard Herrmann with his beloved dog, Twilight, in a pose reminiscent of Sir Edward Elgar and his dog. (Photo by John Engstead courtesy Bernard Herrmann Estate, all rights reserved) 400

Figure 312 - Bernard Herrmann was a composer-conductor of integrity, a rugged individualist, and an irascible genius. (Photo by and courtesy of Alexander Courage)... 401

Figure 313 – Sir Malcolm Arnold at work in Denbigh Gardens, 1958 (Photo courtesy of Estate of Sir Malcolm Arnold) 407

Figure 314 - Cyril Mockridge was a mainstay at 20th Century Fox for years. His work was long under-recognized by the public. (Photo courtesy of Jeanne Mockridge) 408

Figure 315 - Jerome Moross, the New Yorker who wrote one of Hollywood's greatest western scores, *The Big Country*. (Courtesy of Susanna Moross Tarjan) 409

Figure 316 - Alex North, who brought the sounds of jazz and quiet main titles to the big screen. (Photograph by and courtesy of Alexander Courage) 411

Figure 317 - Alex North (seated right) celebrates his birthday with composer colleagues Leonard Rosenman (seated left) and (left to right standing) Henry Mancini, Jerry Goldsmith, and John Williams. (Photo by Alexander Courage, Courtesy of Alexander Courage Collection, Sibley Music Library, Eastman School of Music) 412

Figure 318 - André Previn, multitalented composer, arranger, conductor, and pianist. (Photo by and courtesy of Alexander Courage) 414

Figure 319 - Elmer Bernstein - One of the most versatile film composers for decades. A master in many genres, from *The Ten Commandments* to *To Kill a Mockingbird*. (Photo by and courtesy of Alexander Courage) 416

Figure 320 - Ernest Gold continued the tradition of Viennese lyricism in Hollywood. (Photo by Marv Newton Photography, courtesy of Ernest Gold)... 417

Figure 321 - Laurence Rosenthal. His scores for many films, such as *The Miracle Worker*, turned movies into classics. (Photo courtesy of Laurence Rosenthal).................... 418

Figure 322 - Leonard Rosenman (left) plays a duet with his good friend, Alexander Courage, a composer and fine photographer, responsible for far more music than the *Star*

Trek theme for which he is best-known to the public. (Photo by Alexander Courage, Courtesy of Sibley Music Library, Eastman School of Music) 419

Figure 323 - George Duning, an affable Midwesterner who became the principal composer of the music department for many years at Columbia Pictures. (Photo by and courtesy of Alexander Courage) 420

Figure 324 - Henry Mancini, a former Universal Studios staff composer whose jazz sounds revolutionized television and film scores. (Photograph by and courtesy of Alexander Courage) 422

Figure 325 - John Williams, though initially known for his jazz style, he sparked a revival of interest in the classic symphonic film score. (Photo by Tash Tish- Public Domain) 425

Figure 326 - Jerry Goldsmith. His regular interest in experimental orchestration and his distinct preference for a highly dissonant style changed the sound of film music. (Public domain) 426

Figure 327 - Lalo Schifrin in Concert with the Big Band of the Kölner Musikhochschule. (Photo by Alexandra Sprük released under Creative Commons license) 426

Figure 328 Nelson Riddle, a Dorsey alumnus, also gained fame as one of Frank Sinatra's leading arrangers. (Photo courtesy of Nelson Riddle Collection, University of Arizona Fred Fox School of Music) 427

Figure 329 - Richard Whiting - a leading composer for movie musicals. (Photo courtesy of My Ideal Music Collection) 428

Figure 330 - Harry Warren and Al Dubin -Their songs lit up the screen through many movie musicals. (Photo courtesy of Harry Warren Entertainment) 430

Figure 331 - Vincent Youmans, whose songs for *Flying Down to Rio* helped launch the dance team of Fred Astaire and Ginger Rogers. (Photo courtesy of Vincent Youmans III) 431

Figure 332 - George and Ira Gershwin in Beverly Hills, 1937 - In Hollywood, the Gershwins, along with Vincent Youmans, Irving Berlin, and Jerome Kern, provided music for the legendary Astaire-Rogers movies. (Photo by Rex Hardy, Jr. used by special permission of the Gershwin Family Trusts) 432

Figure 333 - Harold Arlen, singing "Over the Rainbow," a classic song that was nearly cut from *The Wizard of Oz* by executives who thought no one would remember it. (Photo courtesy of Sam Arlen Music) 433

Figure 334 - Hugh Martin, hard at work on a new composition, contributed greatly to the golden era of movie musicals, especially those produced by The Freed Unit. (Photo courtesy of Suzanne Hanners) 434

Figure 335 - Hugh Martin, hard at work on a new composition, contributed greatly to the golden era of movie musicals, especially those produced by The Freed Unit. (Photo courtesy of Suzanne Hanners) 435

Figure 336 - MGM General Music Director John Green at the head of the table in 1955. (Left front, Hugo Friedhofer, third from front left, Eugene Zádor. Right front, André Previn, third from back right, Bronislaw Kaper. (Photo courtesy of Leslie Zador) 435

Figure 337 - Fred Astaire (left) and Gene Kelly (right) in 1964, while presenting the Screen Producers Guild award to Arthur Freed. (Photo courtesy of The Los Angeles Times Photographic Archive, Library Special Collections, Charles E. Young Research Library, UCLA.) 436

Figure 338 - A young Saul Chaplin at the piano with lyricist Sammy Cahn early in their careers. (Photo courtesy of Tita Cahn) 438

Figure 339 - Frederick Loewe. Though Viennese, his musical ability to reflect a Parisian charm when combined with Alan Jay Lerner's lyrics, made *Gigi* one of the all-time classic Hollywood musical films. (Photograph Courtesy of Estate of Frederick Loewe) 441

Figure 340 - Gordon MacRae and Shirley Jones starred in the film version of *Oklahoma!*, bringing the revolutionary team of Rodgers & Hammerstein musical to the wide screen. (Photo courtesy of Rodgers & Hammerstein: An Imagem Company, www.rnh.com) 443

Figure 341 - The Sherman Brothers. Richard M. Sherman and Robert B. Sherman were among Walt Disney's favorite songwriters for musicals such as *Mary Poppins*. (Public domain) 445

Figure 342 - Marni Nixon, dubbed by *Time*, "The Ghostess with the Mostess," was so successful recording the voices of non-singing stars, that audiences could forget that she was a superb soloist in her own right. (Photo courtesy of Marni Nixon) 446

Figure 343 - Irving Berlin, revered composer of "God Bless America" aboard U.S.S. Arkansas, 1944 (U.S. Government Photo) 448

Figure 344 - *The Sound of Music* became by far one of the most successful Hollywood adaptations of a Broadway musical, starring Julie Andrews in the role created on stage by Mary Martin. (Photo courtesy of Rodgers & Hammerstein: An Imagem Company, www.rnh.com) 451

Figure 345 - Ralph Rainger, Leo Robin, Richard Whiting, and vocalist. The team of Robin and Rainger was shattered by Rainger's death in a tragic plane crash. Photo courtesy of the My Ideal Music Collection) 454

Figure 346 - Hoagy Carmichael – "Stardust," only one of his countless songs, became the ultimate 'standard' in American popular music. (Photo courtesy of Hoagy Bix Carmichael) 455

Figure 347 - Johnny Mercer - David Raksin called him "The Flying Wallenda of Lyricists." The world agreed. (Courtesy of Library of Congress, William P. Gottlieb Collection) 457

Figure 348 - A 1935 Paramount luncheon honoring movie musical legends: seated, Sam Coslow, Oscar Hammerstein II, Jerome Kern and June Knight; standing, from left,

Gerard Carbonara, Irvin Talbot, Max Terr, Victor Young, Phil Boutelje, Boris Morros, Frederick Hollander) (Courtesy Irvin Talbot Collection) 458

Figure 349 - Jimmy Van Heusen- bon vivant, pilot, and with lyricist Sammy Cahn, composer of hit songs for Frank Sinatra's musicals. (Photo courtesy of Van Heusen Music Photo Archives) 460

Figure 350 - Jimmy McHugh, the composer of hit songs for motion pictures for four decades. (Courtesy of McHugh music) 460

Figure 351 - Composer Leigh Harline, here at the piano accompanying Cliff Edwards, known as "Ukulele Ike" and the singing voice of Jiminy Cricket, in a performance of "When You Wish Upon a Star." (Photo courtesy of Jo-An Lyman) 463

Figure 352 - The charismatic Leopold Stokowski served as musical director for Walt Disney's *Fantasia.* (Photo courtesy of Leopold Stokowski Papers, Kislak Center for Special Collections, Rare Books and Manuscripts, University of Pennsylvania) 464

Figure 353 - Gail Kubik, a gifted composer and teacher, adapted concert works from his motion picture scores. (Photo by Ralph Titus, used courtesy of Morse Department of Special Collections, Kansas State University Library) 465

Figure 354 - Scott Bradley, responsible for countless classic cartoon scores. (Photo by Scott Bradley) 465

Figure 355 - David Raksin conducting a concert performance of his classic score for *Laura.* (Photo courtesy of David Raksin) 466

Figure 356 - A luncheon in honor of Bramwell Coles, director of the Salvation Army's International Music Department, organized by Meredith Willson. Seated, left to right, Franz Waxman, Dimitri Tiomkin, Meredith Willson, Bramwell Coles, Earl E. Lawrence, and William Grant Still. Standing, left to right: Abe Meyer, Leith Stevens, William Broughton, Anthony Collins, Johnny Green, Miklos Rozsa, Victor Young, Werner Heymann, Leo Shuken, Arthur Bergh, Alex Steinert, Robert Emmett Dolan, Frank Skinner, Wilbur Hatch, Carlos Morales, and Louis Lipstone. (Friars Club Photo-courtesy of Bobbie Fromberg and the Friars Club) 467

Figure 357 - President Ronald Reagan and Nancy Reagan presenting the Presidential Medal of Freedom to pianist Vladimir Horowitz while his wife, Wanda Toscanini Horowitz, looks on. (White House Photo.) 471

INDEX

A

Abbey, Henry, 57-58
Abbott and Costello, 377
Abbott, George, 314, 317, 334, 434
Achron, Joseph, 414
Adam, Adolphe, 24
Adams, Abigail, 14
Adams, Franklin P., 138
Adams, John, 10, 21
Adams, Lee, 337
Adamson, Harold, 263, 461
Addinsell, Richard, 405
Addison, John, 407
Adler, Clarence, 317, 453
Adler, Larry, 145, 235
Adler, Luther, 287
Adler, Mortimer, 242
Adler, Richard, 317-318
Adler, Samuel, 103
Ajemian, Maro and Anahid, 140
Alden, John, 91
Aleichem, Sholem, 334
Alexander, Van, 230
Ali, Bardu, 169
Allen, Fred, 453
Allen, Lorraine, 197
Allen, Maude, 122
Allen, Moses, 170
Allen, Steve, 420
Almeida, Laurindo, 186
Amato, Pasquale, 62
Ameche, Don, 461
Amfitheatrof, Daniele, 368
Amram, David, 148-150, 426
Anderson, Leroy, 141, 143
Anderson, Marian, 30, 63-64
Anderson, Maxwell, 287, 324-325
Anderson, William Alonzo "Cat," 190
André, Maurice, 244
Andrews, Dana, 395-396
Andrews, Julie, 299, 303-304, 444-445, 451
Anouilh, Jean, 150
Ansermet, Ernest, 166
Antheil, George, 71, 87, 133, 353, 417
Anthony, Ray, 181
Anthony, Susan B., 87
Arbuckle, Matthew, 45
Ardlow, Dorothy, 135
Arlen, Harold, 230, 328-329, 332-333, 433-434, 436, 451-452, 457
Armstrong, Louis "Satchmo," 63, 154, 162-166, 168-169, 186, 195, 198, 207, 210, 228, 249-250, 265, 357, 378
Arnaud, Leo, 358
Arnaz, Desi, 197, 461
Arnold, Samuel, 15
Arnold, Sir Malcolm, 407
Arthur, Chester A., 46
Ashby, Irving, 214
Astaire, Adele, 261, 281, 439
Astaire, Fred, 261, 263, 278, 281, 364, 424, 430-431, 436-437, 439-441, 448-451, 457, 461, 468
Aubrey, James, 424
Audubon, John James, 23
Auld, George, 175
Auric, Georges, 166, 357, 406
Avakian, George, 158
Axt, William, 354
Ayers, Lemuel, 321

B

Babbitt, Milton, 340
Bacall, Lauren, 445, 456

Bach, Johann Sebastian, 28, 34, 53, 82-83, 85, 104, 111, 123, 129, 137, 144, 148, 155, 168, 209, 216, 221, 224. 232, 243, 251, 313, 397, 463, 468
Bach, Karl Philip Emmanuel, 14, 28
Bailey, Buster, 172
Bailey, Pearl, 330, 332, 335
Baird, Bil, 331
Baker, Chet, 221
Baker, David, 244
Baker, Dorothy, 165
Baker, John, 281
Baker, Theodore, 35
Balanchine, George, 88, 275, 314, 332
Baldwin, Billy, 279
Ball, Lucille, 336, 461
Bampton, Claude, 223
Bancroft, Anne, 338
Bankhead, Tallulah, 108
Barber, Samuel, 112-113
Bargy, Roy, 449
Barlow, Wayne, 102, 104
Barnet, Charlie, 208
Barras, Charles, 253
Barrett, Mary Ellin, 4
Barris, Harry, 430
Barry, John, 305, 423
Barry, Philip, 92
Barrymore, John, 354
Barrymore, Lionel, 368
Bart, Lionel, 338
Bartók, Béla, 130-131, 147, 175, 187, 387
Barzin, Leon, 417
Basie, William "Count," 161, 175-176, 191, 194-195, 197, 203, 209, 225, 232, 415
Bates, Abigail and Rebecca, 13
Bates, Bob, 222

Bates, Katherine Lee, 4
Bath, Hubert, 405
Bauer, Billy, 220
Bauer, Harold, 310, 354
Bax, Sir Arnold, 405
Bay, Victor, 106
Beach, Henry Harris Aubrey, 32
Beach, Sylvia, 71
Beal, Eddie, 240
Beames, William, 15
Beatles, 3, 188, 468
Beaton, Cecil, 304, 442
Becce, Giuseppe, 351-352, 357
Bechet, Sidney, 161, 166
Beecham, Sir Thomas, 107, 358, 468
Beeson, Jack, 65
Beethoven, Ludwig van, , 9, 18, 23-24, 26, 33-34, 42, 54-56, 68, 81-82, 84-85, 123, 135-136, 148, 242, 247, 387, 463
Beiderbecke, Bix, 165, 172, 198, 218, 455
Beissel, Conrad, 8
Belafonte, Harry, 333
Belford, Joe, 182
Belgrave, Marcus, 213
Bellison, Simeon, 175
Bellow, Saul, 121
Bemelmans, Ludwig, 465
Benét, Stephen Vincent, 92, 402
Benjamin, Arthur, 403, 405
Bennett, Robert Russell, 139
Bennett, Sir Richard Rodney, 407
Bennett, Tony, 229, 317, 459
Benton, Thomas Hart, 71
Berg, Alban, 121, 377
Berg, Billy, 208
Berger, Arthur, 105, 116
Berger, Dr. Ludwig, 388
Bergh, Arthur, 133, 467

Bergsma, William, 102
Berk, Lawrence, 237
Berlin, Ellin, 272
Berlin, Irving 2, 4, 48, 73, 139, 230, 253, 255, 260-261, 266, 272, 278, 284, 299, 320-322, 336, 344-346, 366, 370, 384, 431-432, 436, 440-441, 443, 447-448, 450, 458, 460
Berlioz, Hector, 25
Berman, Pandro, 432
Berners, Lord, 405
Bernier, Conrad, 146
Bernstein, Artie, 198
Bernstein, Elmer, 117, 349, 415-418
Bernstein, Leonard, 17, 28, 52, 65, 76, 83, 116, 118-119, 140, 150, 253, 271, 299, 305-306, 324-325, 340-341, 345, 413
Berry, Chu, 175, 204
Bertrand, Jimmy, 196
Best, Denzel, 223
Bibo, Iving, 261
Bigard, Barney, 189, 191
Bikel, Theodore, 298
Bilbo, Theodore, 331
Billings, William, 10-11, 94
Bing, Rudolf, 56, 63-64
Bishop, Joe, 183
Bissell, Richard, 317
Bizet, Georges, 380
Blair, Janet, 229
Blake, Eubie, 95, 156, 160, 264-266
Blakely, David, 46-47
Blanchard, Terence, 250
Blanchard, William G., 351
Blane, Ralph, 434
Blanton, Jimmy, 197-198
Blind Tom, 156
Bliss, Sir Arthur, 405
Blitzstein, Marc, 284, 288, 325, 399

Bloch, Ernest, 71, 90-91, 99, 117, 121-122, 419
Bloom, Rube, 457
Bloomer, Dolly, 329-330
Bloomgarden, Kermit, 319
Blumenfeld, Felix, 384
Bock, Jerry, 334
Bock, Richard, 221
Bogart, Humphrey, 456
Bolcom, William, 93
Bolden, Charles "Buddy," 157
Bolling, Claude, 244, 415
Bolm, Adolf, 38
Bolton, Guy, 267, 278
Bonds, Margaret, 30, 144
Bonfá, Luiz, 246
Bonney, J. William ("Billy the Kid"), 79
Bontemps, Ara, 330
Borden, Lizzie, 143
Bordoni, Irene, 277-278
Borodin, Alexander, 326
Bosch, Hieronymus, 114
Boswell, Connee, 162
Boublil, Alain, 339
Boulanger, Lili, 77
Boulanger, Nadia, 77-78, 81, 86, 91, 99, 104, 116, 118, 120, 139, 148, 167, 288, 418, 465
Boulerin, Jacques, 285
Boulez, Pierre, 283, 407
Boutelje, Phil, 458
Bowers, Robert Hood, 255
Bowes, Major, 354
Bowles, Paul, 89
Boyette, Lippy, 201
Brackeen, Joanne, 237
Bradley, Scott, 365, 465
Bragg, Sonny, 461

Brahms, Johannes, 18-19, 21, 30-31, 38, 55, 123, 136-137, 194, 247, 273, 387, 398, 443
Brain, Alfred, 358
Brando, Marlon, 399, 411, 414
Brant, Henry, 72, 105
Brattle, Thomas, 9
Brazzi, Rosanno, 341
Brecht, Bertolt, 284
Breeden, Leon, 237
Breen, Robert, 333
Breidis, Vic, 171
Breil, Joseph Carl, 352
Brescia, Domenic, 398
Breton, Nicholas, 106
Brice, Fanny, 312, 352
Bristow, George F., 24
Britten, Benjamin, 380
Brodszky, Nicholas, 460
Brontë, Charlotte, 402
Brontë, Emily, 106
Brook, Peter, 332
Brooks, Jack, 456
Broughton, Mary Selena, 37
Broughton, William, 467
Brown, Clifford, 212
Brown, John Mason, 286
Brown, Nacio Herb, 440, 452
Brown, Ray, 208, 211, 214-215, 224, 230, 234, 238
Brown, Vernon, 175
Brubeck, Dave, 203, 222-223
Bruce, Richard, 95
Brynner, Yul, 297-298, 319, 349, 444
Buchanan, Jack, 441
Buchanan, James, 42
Buchanan, Scott, 118
Buck, Dudley, 29-30, 66
Buck, Gene, 261
Buckner, Milt, 224

Buhlig, Richard, 121, 127
Bull, Ole, 19, 40
Bumbry, Grace, 64
Burgin, Richard, 50
Burke, Joe, 430
Burke, Johnny, 188, 459-460
Burleigh, Henry Thacker, 38
Burns, Ralph, 183-184
Burrell, Kenny, 211, 213
Burrows, Abe, 311, 315, 317
Burton, Richard, 304
Butler, Frank, 320
Butler, Nicholas Murray, 35
Byas, Don, 211
Byrd, Charlie, 234

C

Cadman, Charles Wakefield, 41, 352, 368
Caesar, Irving, 262
Caesar, Sid, 336
Cage, John, 72-73, 93, 140
Cahn, Sammy, 188, 283, 310-311, 438, 452, 459-460
Cahn, Tita, 310, 438
Cain, Jackie, 231
Callas, Maria, 64
Calloway, Cab, 204-205, 357, 451
Calvé, Emma, 58
Campanini, Italo, 57
Candoli, Pete and Conte, 183
Cantor, Eddie, 352
Capalbo, Carmen, 325
Capeau, Placide, 24
Capote, Truman, 332
Capp, Al, 302
Capp, Frank, 215
Cappa, Carlo, 45
Capra, Frank, 385
Carbonara, Gerard, 458
Carerras, José, 64

Carlisle, Kitty, 300, 304
Carlson, Alfred, 126
Carmichael, Hoagy, 1, 169, 313, 445, 454-456
Carney, Harry, 175, 190, 192
Carnovsky, Morris, 287
Caron, Leslie, 437, 439, 442, 446, 457
Carpenter, Charles, 164
Carpenter, John Alden, 29, 36
Carr, Benjamin, 14
Carreño, Teresa, 27, 33-34
Carreras, José, 64
Carroll, Brendan, 130, 359-361
Carroll, Diahann, 332
Carroll, Earl, 329, 458
Carroll, Lewis, 138
Carson, Johnny, 263
Carter, Benny, 144, 168-169, 192, 196,198, 212, 231
Carter, Betty, 231
Carter, Elliott, 98, 116, 118
Carter, Lou, 234
Caruso, Enrico, 59, 197
Casals, Pablo, 372
Casella, Alfredo, 104
Castelnuovo-Tedesco, Clara, 132
Castelnuovo-Tedesco, Mario, 132-134, 222, 253, 347, 349, 368-369, 414, 420- 421, 424-427
Castillo, Carmen, 197
Castle, Vernon and Irene, 260, 432
Cendrars, Blaise, 193
Cesana, Otto, 417
Chadwick, George W., 30, 33
Chagrin, Francis, 406
Chaliapin, Feodor, 62
Chaloff, Serge, 184
Champion, Gower, 338, 453
Chanler, Theodore, 91
Channing, Carol, 335

Chaplin, Charles, 41
Chaplin, Saul, 310, 433, 438
Chapman, John, 333
Charisse, Cyd, 282, 438, 441
Charlap, Moose, 311
Charles, Teddy, 245
Charnin, Martin, 299, 338
Charo, 197
Chase, Stanley, 325, 333
Chasins, Abram, 53, 203
Chauvin, Louis, 156
Chávez, Carlos, 79, 135-136
Cheney, Amy Marcy (Mrs. H.H.A. Beach,) 32
Chevalier, Maurice, 352, 427-428, 441-442
Chodorov, Jerome, 307
Chopin, Frederick, 25- 26, 82, 201-202, 221, 250, 263, 383
Christian, Charlie, 174, 197-199, 233
Christlieb, Don, 358
Christy, E.P., 22
Christy, June, 186
Churchill, Frank, 356, 462-463
Chute, B. J., 316
Cicognini, Alessandro, 408
Cimini, Pietro, 385
Citkowitz, Israel, 89, 105
Clarke, Herbert L., 47
Clarke, Kenny, 205, 224
Clay, Henry, 170
Clayton, Buck, 195, 199, 240
Cleveland, Grover, 46, 70
Clift, Montgomery, 381
Clooney, Rosemary, 179, 229
Clurman, Harold, 286
Coates, Albert, 385
Cobb, Lee J., 287
Cobb, Ty, 99
Cocteau, Jean, 86, 202, 406

Cohan, George M., 254, 256, 275, 288
Colbert, Claudette, 445
Cole, Cozy, 211
Cole, Eddie, 216
Cole, Freddie, 216
Cole, Ike, 216
Cole, Nat "King," 179, 214, 216-217, 234, 249, 457
Coleman, Cy, 307, 333, 335-336
Coleman, Ornette, 245-246
Coles, Bramwell, 467
Collette, 441
Collier, James Lincoln, 164, 191
Collins, Al "Jazzbo," 146
Collins, Anthony, 467
Collins, Russell, 287
Colman, Ronald, 389, 404
Coltrane, John, 211, 245
Comden, Betty, 306-307, 309, 318
Como, Perry, 199, 229, 461
Comstock, F. Ray, 267
Connelly, Marc, 138
Conover, Willis, 193, 215, 241, 249
Conried, Heinrich, 59, 61
Conroy, Anita, 446
Converse, Frederick Shepherd, 29, 31, 103, 352
Cook, Barbara, 308, 319, 331, 334
Cook, Joe, 284
Cook, William Marion, 166
Cooke, James Francis, 48
Cooper, Gary, 374, 386
Cooper, Gladys, 405
Coote, Robert, 303, 305
Coots, J. Fred, 354-355
Copland, Aaron, 27, 39, 52, 65, 69, 76, 78, 81-82, 84, 86-89, 103-105, 107, 116, 119, 121, 140, 167, 176, 292, 307, 391-392, 398, 409, 411, 414, 416, 419

Cornwall, Spencer, 462
Cortot, Alfred, 251
Corwin, Norman, 93, 99, 109, 401
Coslow, Sam, 458
Cotton, Reverend John, 7
Coué, Emil, 345
Courage, Alexander, 363, 379, 383, 386-387, 392, 396, 401, 411-412, 414, 416, 419-420, 422
Coward, Sir Nöel, 192, 259-260, 279-281, 298, 303, 338, 345-346, 415, 429, 436
Cowell, Henry, 69-71, 98, 118
Cowper, William, 8
Crain, Jeanne, 446
Crawford, Cheryl, 287
Crawford, Jimmy, 170
Crawford, John C., 115
Crawford, Robert 4
Crawford, Sam, 99
Creston, Paul, 98, 107-108, 233
Crosby, Bing, 171, 185, 199, 229, 352, 430, 447-448, 450, 454-455, 458-459
Crosby, Bob, 171, 178, 185
Crosby, Israel, 175
Crouch, Stanley, 226, 250
Crouse, Russell, 278
Crown, John, 121, 466
Cugat, Xavier, 173, 197
Cukor, George, 389
Cullen, Countee, 330
cummings, e.e., 121
Curb, Mike, 424
Custis, Nelly, 14
Cutner, Sidney, 374
Cutter, Murray, 367

D

Da Costa, Morton, 319
Dali, Salvador, 71

Dallapiccola, Luigi, 419
d'Amboise, Jacques, 150
Dameron, Tadd, 209-210
Damrosch, Leopold, 19, 58
Damrosch, Walter, 50, 58, 74, 78
Dance, Stanley, 193
Daniel, Eliot, 461
Daniels, Bebe, 430
Daniels, William, 444
Darby, Ken, 371
Darin, Bobby, 376
Darion, Joe, 338
Davis, Jefferson, 22
Davis, Miles, 206, 219-221, 226, 245, 250
Davis, Peter, 163
Davison, Archibald T., 90, 116
Dawson, Mary Cardwell, 225
Dawson, William Levi, 30
Day, Doris, 229, 264
De Carlo, Yvonne, 342
de Forest, Lee, 357
de Gorgoza, Emilio, 112
de Havilland, Olivia, 360, 393
De Koven, Reginald, 254
de la Vega, Aurelio, 128-129, 136
De Luca, Giuseppe, 62
de Mille, Agnes, 80, 292, 295, 301, 330, 339, 411
de Moraes, Vinicius, 246
de Reszke, Jean and Édouard, 58
Dean, Christopher, 336
Dean, James, 419
Debussy, Claude, 31, 33, 38, 60, 77, 84, 106, 120, 122, 137, 165-166, 191, 200, 219, 224, 233, 243, 246-247, 280, 380
Dee, Sandra, 376
deFranco, Buddy, 223
del Rio, Dolores, 431
Delius, Frederick, 106, 144, 150, 218, 224, 232, 468
Dello Joio, Norman, 65, 110
DeMille, Cecil B., 351, 416
Dennis, Patrick, 335
Desmond, Paul, 222
Dessaline, Jean-Jacques, 95
Dessau, Paul, 357
DeSylva, George Gard "Buddy," 389, 456
Dethier, Gaston, 107
Deutsch, Adolph, 433
Deval, Jacques, 285
Diamond, David, 98-99, 120-121, 440
Dietrich, Marlene, 311, 323, 357, 380, 388
Dietz, Howard, 274, 281-282, 441, 453
D'Indy, Vincent, 31, 91, 276
Disney, Roy, 356
Disney, Walt, 3, 53, 356-357, 406, 444-445, 462, 464
Ditson, Oliver, 44
Dodds, Johnny, 158, 163
Dodge, Joe, 222
Dohnányi, Erno von, 131
Dolan, Robert Emmett, 467
Domingo, Placido, 64
Donaldson, Walter, 264
Donegan, Dorothy, 202
Donizetti, Gaetano, 160
Donnelly, Dorothy, 258
Doolittle, Amos, 13
Dorham, Kenny, 246
Dorsey, Jimmy, 176, 179-180, 229, 237, 459
Dorsey, Tommy, 171, 179-181, 185, 199, 217, 229, 234, 263
Dortort, David, 376
Douglas, Tommy, 206

Drake, Alfred, 298
Drake, Ervin, 180
Drake, Tom, 436
Draper, Paul, 145
Drew, Martin, 216
Du Valle, Reggie, 454
Dubin, Al, 430, 453
Dukas, Paul, 463
Duke, Vernon, 181, 282-283, 330, 439, 449, 451, 467
Dumas, Alexandre, 25
Dumont, Margaret, 429
Dunbar, Paul Laurence, 96
Duncan, Todd, 3, 64-65, 273-274, 325
Dunham, Katherine, 451
Duning, George, 414, 420
Dunne, Philip, 54, 403
Dunworth, Charles, 394
Dupré, Marcel, 388
Durbin, Deanna, 53
Dvořák, Antonín, 5, 21, 34, 38-39, 77, 201, 258, 351
Dwight, John Sullivan, 24- 26, 28, 32, 44, 47

E

Eager, Edward, 328
Eames, Emma, 58
Eastman, George, 97
Ebb, Fred, 337
Eberle, Ray, 229
Eberly, Bob, 179, 229
Eckstine, Billy, 207, 209, 212, 230, 237
Eddy, Nelson, 383, 428-429, 434
Edens, Roger, 433, 440-441
Edison, Harry "Sweets," 195
Edison, Thomas Alva, 48, 458
Edwards, Blake, 421
Edwards, Cliff "Ukulele Ike," 463
Edwards, Eddie, 162
Edwards, Jonathan, 8
Edwards, Sherman, 338
Egan, Ray, 428
Eichberg, Julius, 44
Einstein, Albert, 123
Eisenhower, Dwight D., 103
Eisler, Hanns, 357
Eldridge, Roy, 168, 198, 204-205, 244, 246
Elgar, Sir Edward, 400
Elinor, Carl, 352
Eliot, Charles W, 29
Eliot, T.S., 193
Eliscu, Edward, 263
Ellington, Edward Kennedy "Duke," 79, 146, 154, 158, 161, 170, 172, 174-176, 187-194, 197, 209- 210, 213, 226, 229-231, 236, 238, 241-245, 248, 250, 273-274, 395, 415, 455, 457
Ellington, Mercedes, 194
Ellington, Mercer, 194, 231
Ellis, Herb, 214, 233-234
Ellison, Ralph, 189
Elman, Mischa, 197, 354, 372
Elman, Ziggy, 175, 457
Elwell, G. Herbert, 77
Emerson, Ralph Waldo, 29
Emmett, Dan, 22
Epstein, Dave, 386
Escoffier, Auguste, 58
Europe, James Reese, 73, 264
Evans, Bill, 221
Evans, Dale, 229
Evans, Dame Edith, 406
Evans, Gil, 219-221
Evans, Herschel, 194, 198
Evans, Maurice, 334
Evans, Ray, 461
Ewen, David, 138

F

Fain, Sammy, 331-332
Falkenberg, Jinx 146
Farmer, Art, 196
Farwell, Arthur, 38-40, 81-82, 99
Fauré, Gabriel, 221
Fay, Charles Norman, 20
Faye, Alice, 229, 430, 447
Feather, Leonard, 157, 187, 193, 223, 227-229, 231, 238, 242, 247, 249
Fellini, Federico, 409
Ferber, Edna, 268-269, 333
Ferguson, Maynard, 186
Feuer, Cy, 315, 317
Fiedler, Arthur, 425
Fiedler, Max, 49
Fielding, Jerry, 415
Fields, Dorothy, 281, 320, 336, 432, 436, 461
Fields, Herbert, 291
Fields, Joseph, 307, 320
Fields, W.C., 377
Finck, Henry T., 29
Fine, Sylvia, 288
Fine, Vivian, 105
Finston, Nat, 354, 368
Fisher, Eddie, 317
Fisher, William Arms, 38
Fitzgerald, Barry, 459
Fitzgerald, Ella, 169, 179, 208, 213, 217, 229-231, 235, 378
Fitzgerald, F. Scott, 86, 165, 263, 276
Flagello, Nicolas, 108-109
Flanagan, Tommy, 212-213
Flaster, Karl, 109
Fleischer, Dave, 357
Fleischer, Max, 356-357, 429, 454
Fletcher, Bob, 449
Fletcher, Lucille, 106-107
Flowers, Martha, 146, 226
Floyd, Carlisle, 65
Flynn, Errol, 360, 468
Fontanne, Lynne, 321
Foote, Arthur, 29-30
Forbstein, Leo, 398
Ford, John, 364-365
Forrest, George, 326
Forrest, Helen, 178, 229
Foss, Lukas, 119
Fosse, Bob, 336-337, 339
Fox, Felix, 237
Fox, Gilbert, 14
Fox, William, 353
Fradon, Dana, 176
Frankel, Benjamin, 405
Franklin, Benjamin, 9, 24
Franklin, Lidia, 330
Freed, Arthur, 433-436, 439-441, 452
Freeman, Bud, 165
Friedhofer, Hugo, 128, 349, 367, 371, 393, 397-400, 409, 424, 435, 467
Frigo, Johnny, 234
Friml, Rudolf, 255, 257-258, 268, 429
Friskin, James, 144
Frost, Robert, 71
Fry, William Henry, 23, 25
Fuchs, Robert, 363
Furth, George, 341, 343

G

Gable, Clark, 383, 413, 429, 433
Gabor, Eva, 442
Gabor, Zsa-Zsa, 440
Gallico, Paolo, 453
Galli-Curci, Amelita, 62
Gannon, Kim, 366
Ganz, Rudolph, 138, 375
Garcia, Gina Mauriello, 378
Garcia, Russell, 378
Gardel, Carlos, 147

Garden, Mary, 60
Gardner, Ava, 178, 269, 445
Gardner, Isabella Stewart, 37
Garfield, James A., 46
Garfield, John, 287, 466
Garland, Judy, 332, 424, 433-437, 439, 450-452
Garland, Red, 212
Garner, Erroll, 160, 213
Garrett, Betty, 314
Gatti-Casazza, Giulio, 62
Gay, John, 12, 284
Geer, Will, 288
Geisel, Theodore Seuss ("Dr. Seuss",) 465
Gelbart, Larry, 340
Gelman, Harold, 415
Geokie, Leo, 150
George, Yvonne, 166
Gericke, Wilhelm, 49
Gershenson, Joseph, 377
Gershwin, George, 3, 5, 39, 72-75, 79, 124, 127, 135, 138, 145, 166, 173, 179, 181, 230, 253, 261, 263, 270-274, 282-284, 286, 294, 306-307, 310, 316, 324, 328, 345, 357, 363, 370, 385, 394- 395, 431-432, 439--441, 443, 449, , 461
Gershwin, Ira, 73, 75, 173, 181, 253, 261, 271-274, 282-283, 287-288, 323, 329-330, 344-345, 395, 431-432, 439, 449, 452
Gest, Morris, 267
Getz, Stan, 184, 213, 246, 378
Giannini, Dusolina, 108-109
Giannini, Euphemia, 108
Giannini, Vittorio, 65, 108-110, 148-149
Giddens, Gary, 208, 210
Gilbert and Sullivan, 254, 271, 274, 288, 329
Gilbert, Henry Franklin Belknap, 39-40
Gilberto, Astrud, 247
Gilberto, João, 246-247
Gill, Florence, 462
Gillespie, Dizzy, 144, 192, 205, 207, 210-212, 220, 224, 230, 235, 238, 240, 245, 426
Gillis, Don, 143
Gilman, Lawrence, 74
Gilmore, Patrick Sarsfield, 42
Gingold, Hermione, 442
Gingold, Josef, 55
Ginsberg, Allen, 149
Giovannini, Caesar, 426
Gitler, Ira, 245
Giuffre, Jimmy, 184, 221, 231, 238
Glazounov, Alexander, 384
Gleason, Jackie, 319
Gleghorn, Arthur, 358
Glière, Reinhold, 282
Gluck, Alma, 73
Goddard, Chris, 166
Godowsky, Leopold, 160, 202
Goetschius, Percy, 40, 97, 99
Goetz, Ray, 277
Gold, Ernest, 416-418, 424
Goldfarb, Howard "Chubby," 184
Goldkette, Jean, 165
Goldmark, Aaron "Goldie," 184
Goldmark, Rubin, 38-39, 77, 370
Goldsboro, Bobby, 424
Goldsmith, Jerry, 412, 414, 425-426
Goldstone, Nat, 329
Goldwyn, Samuel, 371, 398
Gonsalves, Paul, 190, 211
Goodman, Al, 394

Goodman, Benny, 80, 165, 171-177,
    181, 184-185, 188, 191, 196-200,
    217, 225, 229, 234-237, 394, 411,
    421, 457
Goodman, Harry, 171
Goosens, Eugene, 80
Gordon, Dexter, 196, 211
Gordon, Mack, 263, 452-453, 461
Gordon, Max, 281
Gorney, Jay, 329
Gottlieb, William P., 14, 159, 166,
    168, 170, 179, 185, 195, 197-198,
    200-201, 204-208, 210, 212-213,
    216, 219-220, 229-230, 457
Gotto, Louise, 108
Gottschalk, Louis Moreau, 25, 28
Gould, Morton, 142-143
Goulet, Robert, 305
Gounod, Charles, 57
Grable, Betty, 185, 229, 408, 430, 452
Grabner, Hermann, 387
Graedner, Herman, 363
Graettinger, Bob, 187
Graham, Martha, 80, 108, 113, 140,
    411
Grainger, Percy, 400
Granados, Enrique, 221
Grant, Cary, 408, 444, 461
Grant, Ulysses S., 65
Granz, Norman, 214, 240
Grappelli, Stephane, 234
Grau, Maurice, 58
Graupner, Johann Christian Gottlieb,
    14
Gray, Clifford, 428
Gray, Glen, 171
Grayson, Kathryn, 444
Greeley, Mary Elizabeth, 28
Green, Adolph, 306-307, 309, 318
Green, Benny, 145

Green, Freddie, 195
Green, Harry, 171
Green, John, 367, 435
Green, Paul, 287
Grieg, Edvard, 20, 97, 160, 243, 326,
    352, 356, 400
Griffes, Charles Tomlinson, 37-38
Griffis, Elliot, 31
Griffith, Andy, 358
Griffith, Corrine, 430
Griffith, D.W., 352
Grigsby, Beverly, 129
Grofé, Ferde, 74
Gruber, First Lieutenant Edmund L.,
    3
Gruenberg, Louis, 133
Guardino, Harry, 341
Guilmant, Alexander, 39
Gwenn, Edmund, 408

H

Hadley, Henry, 354
Hadley, Jerry, 308
Hageman, Richard, 133, 385
Hagen, Earle, 415
Haig, Al, 211
Haines, Connie, 179
Halasz, Laszlo, 65
Hall, Adelaide, 201
Hall, Gene, 237, 239
Halliday, Richard, 303
Hamilton, Chico, 221
Hamilton, Jimmy, 189
Hamlisch, Marvin, 338
Hammell, John C., 382
Hammerstein, Dorothy, 270
Hammerstein, Oscar II, 2, 80, 253,
    258-259, 267-270, 272 274, 282,
    290-300, 302, 305-306, 309, 320,
    336, 339-341, 345, 347, 552-443,
    448-451, 458, 460

Hammerstein, Oscar, 60-61
Hammond, John, 173, 193, 198, 225
Hampton, Lionel, 174, 176, 195, 212, 240, 244
Handel, George Frederick, 9, 24
Handy, W.C., 95, 157-159, 164, 168
Hanna, Sir Roland, 212, 227
Hansen, H. Endicott, 126
Hanson, Howard, 2, 51, 82, 93, 96-100, 102-104, 107, 120, 418
Harbach, Otto, 259, 261, 268, 290, 340
Harburg, E.Y., 283, 302, 328-330, 434, 451
Hardin Armstrong, Lil, 163
Hardwick, Otto, 191
Hardy, Emmett, 165
Harline, Leigh, 462-463
Harnick, Sheldon, 299, 334
Harris, Al, 171
Harris, Barry, 212-213
Harris, Bill, 183
Harris, Johana, 82-85, 155
Harris, Roy, 1, 5, 30, 40, 52, 81-87, 92, 94, 98, 111, 115, 150, 167, 307
Harrison, Benjamin, 46
Harrison, Donald, 250
Harrison, Lou, 140
Harrison, Rex, 298, 303-304, 403, 444-445
Hart, Lorenz, 253, 261, 272, 274-276, 282, 293, 344, 428-429, 450
Hart, Moss, 275, 279, 287, 300, 303-305, 319, 343, 418
Hatch, Wilbur, 467
Haubiel, Charles, 94, 137
Haupt, Karl, 28
Havoc, June, 312
Hawes, Hampton, 237

Hawkins, Coleman, 144, 168, 198, 213, 246
Hawks, Howard, 385, 445
Hawthorne, Nathaniel, 98, 109
Hayes, Edgar, 204
Hayes, Jack, 374
Hayes, Roland, 51
Hayes, Rutherford B., 46
Haymes, Dick, 185
Hayton, Lennie, 146, 433
Hayward, Dubose, 272-273
Hayworth, Rita, 197, 445, 449-450
Heath, Jimmy, 227
Heath, Joyce, 92
Heath, Percy, 224
Heifetz, Jascha, 73, 83, 132, 197, 362, 372, 390, 402
Hein, Silvio, 255
Heinrich, Anthony Philip, 23
Helburn, Theresa, 292
Hellinger, Mark, 390
Hellman, Lillian, 308, 413
Hemingway, Ernest, 71-72, 374, 413
Henderson, Fletcher, 163, 167-168, 173-175, 196, 198
Henderson, Horace, 174
Henderson, Stephen "The Beetle," 159
Hendricks, Jon, 231
Henry, Patrick, 10
Henschel, George, 49
Hepburn, Audrey, 422, 441, 444-446
Hepburn, Katherine, 341
Herbert, Victor, 48, 50, 73, 254-255, 258, 261, 267, 271, 363, 428-429
Herman, Woody, 176, 182-184, 199, 221, 231, 240
Herrmann, Bernard, 69, 105-107, 298-299, 349, 355, 371, 379, 395,

400-405, 407-409, 416, 419, 423-425, 468
Herz, Henri, 44
Herzig, Sig, 330
Hewitt, James, 13
Heyman, Edward, 263
Heyman, Karl, 33
Heymann, Werner, 467
Higginson, Henry Lee, 37, 49, 57
Hill, E.B., 31, 73
Hill, Teddy, 204-205
Hiller, Wendy, 302
Hilliard, Harriet, 229
Hilton, James, 385
Hindemith, Paul, 103, 110, 119, 129-130, 150, 176, 187, 353, 399
Hines, Earl, 163, 172, 186, 209, 212-213, 217, 230, 240
Hirsch, Louis A., 255
Hirschfeld, Albert, 283
Hitchcock, Alfred, 349, 355, 378, 381, 385, 389, 403, 405-408, 416, 423
Hitler, Adolf, 129
Hodeir, André, 244
Hodges, Johnny "Rabbit," 175, 190, 196, 415
Hoey, Evelyn, 283
Hoffman, Richard, 126
Holden, Stephen, 455
Holden, William, 420
Holiday, Billie, 174, 178, 199, 229, 231
Holiday, Clarence, 174
Hollander, Frederick, 357, 379, 458
Holliday, Judy, 306, 310, 312
Holloway, Stanley, 303
Holm, Hanya, 91, 304, 327, 411
Holman, Bill, 187
Holman, Libby, 453
Holmes, Oliver Wendell, 29, 254

Holst, Gustav, 425
Holtzman, Fanny, 297
Homer, Louise, 112
Honegger, Arthur, 86, 166, 353, 357, 380, 388, 406
Hoover, Herbert, 16, 284
Hope, Bob, 219, 279, 283, 352, 387, 454, 459
Hopkinson, Francis, 6, 10-11, 14, 471
Horne, Lena, 146, 192, 199, 237, 330, 333, 451
Horowitz, Vladimir, 112, 202-203, 372, 384, 471
Horowitz, Wanda Toscanini, 471
Houseman, John, 288-289, 402, 424
Hovhaness, Alan, 139-140
Howard, Leslie, 302
Howard, Sidney, 315
Howe, Julia Ward, 43
Hubbell, Raymond, 255
Hughes, Adela Prentiss, 55
Hughes, Langston, 30, 150, 183, 226, 324
Hugo, Victor, 25, 198
Hume, Paul, 11
Humperdinck, Engelbert, 37, 39, 284
Hunter, Ross, 377
Hurok, Sol, 64
Huston, John, 413
Huston, Walter, 287
Hutton, Betty, 229, 237
Hyams, Marge, 223
Hyland, William, 346
Hyman, Dick, 217

I

Ibert, Jacques, 233, 353, 437
Ibsen, Henrik, 150
Ickes, Harold, 64
Inch, Herbert, 100
Inge, William, 420

Irving, Henry, 34
Irving, Washington, 24, 287
Ito, Michito, 38
Ivanovici, Ion, 439
Ives, Charles, 31, 65-66, 68, 70-71, 118
Ives, George, 65-66
Ives, Harmony Twichell, 66-67

J

Jackson, Andrew, 21
Jackson, Calvin, 144-146, 415
Jackson, Chubby, 183
Jackson, Milt, 208, 211, 224-225
Jackson, Tony, 158
Jacobi, Frederick, 39, 138
Jacquet, Illinois, 196
Jamal, Ahmad, 225-226
James, Harry, 174, 184-185, 199, 237
James, Henry, 92, 392
James, Jimmy, 240
James, Lilith and Dan, 329
James, Philip, 39, 138, 400
James, William, 29
Jarrett, Henry C., 253
Jeans, Isabel, 442
Jefferson, Thomas, 6, 9-10, 15, 91, 150
Jenkins, Gordon, 180, 182
Jessel, George, 352
Jobim, Antônio Carlos, 246
Johnson, Edward, 62
Johnson, Howard, "Stretch," 200
Johnson, J. J., 211-212, 222
Johnson, James P., 159-160, 189, 201, 266
Johnson, Lady Bird, 11
Johnson, Lyndon B., 11, 150
Johnson, Palmer, 240
Johnson, William Geary (Bunk), 157
Johnston, Arthur, 458

Jolson, Al, 107, 272, 353, 433, 438
Jones, Elvin, 213
Jones, George Thaddeus, 146
Jones, Hank, 202, 212-213, 227
Jones, Isham, 182, 264
Jones, Jennifer, 366, 386
Jones, Jo, 195
Jones, Jonah, 206
Jones, Shirley, 295, 319, 443
Jones, Spike, 459
Jones, Sylvia, 150
Jones, Thad, 213, 227
Jones, Tom, 338, 407
Jones, Vincent, 142
Joplin, Scott, 156, 167
Jordan, Dorothy, 431
Jordan, Eben, 44
Jordan, Joe, 156
Jourdan, Louis, 442
Joyce, James, 71, 92, 146
Juhan, Alexander, 14
Jullien, Louis-Antoine, 18, 42

K

Kahal, Irving, 331-332
Kahn, Gus, 264
Kalmar, Bert, 429-430
Kander, John, 337
Kanitz, Ernest, 128, 399
Kanner, Hedwig, 237
Kaper, Bronislaw, 132, 338, 349, 383, 423, 435, 440
Karas, Anton, 421
Kastler, Lou, 171
Katz, Fred, 237
Katz, Sam, 434
Katzenberg, Jeffrey, 3, 468
Kaufman, Annette, 95
Kaufman, George S, 138, 271-272, 275, 281, 315, 323, 343, 418, 429

Kaufman, Louis, 95, 139, 358, 372, 375, 402
Kay, Connie, 224
Kay, Ulysses Simpson, 102
Kaye, Danny, 288, 319, 447-448
Kazan, Elia, 150, 287, 411-413, 419
Keel, Howard, 444
Keeler, Ruby, 430
Keene, Constance, 203
Kell, Reginald, 175
Keller, Helen, 418
Kelley, Edgar Stillman, 39
Kelly, Gene, 276, 424, 436, 439-440, 445, 449-450
Kelly, Grace, 408, 450
Kelly, Paula, 229
Kelly, Wynton, 211-212
Kendall, Edward "Ned," 43
Kennedy, Jacqueline, 305
Kennedy, John F., 11, 81-82, 145, 305, 460
Kennedy, Robert F., 150
Kenton, Stan, 176, 185-188, 221, 239, 242, 247, 457
Keppard, Freddie, 157, 172
Kerker, Gustave, 255
Kern, Jerome, 61, 65, 139, 230, 253, 260-261, 267-270, 272, 275, 281, 290-291, 293, 320-321, 336, 363, 370, 380, 431-432, 434, 436, 443, 448, 457-458, 461
Kerouac, Jack, 149
Kerr, Deborah, 446
Kessel, Barney, 178, 214, 233
Key, Francis Scott, 15
Khachaturian, Aram, 384
King George III, 11, 13
King George V, 51
King Sisters, 311
King, Martin Luther, 30, 110

Kirchner, Leon, 120-121
Kirkorian, Kirk, 424
Kirkpatrick, John, 69
Kirstein, Lincoln, 80
Kitt, Eartha, 332
Kleban, Edward, 338
Kleinsinger, George, 63
Kneisel, Franz, 197
Knight, June, 458
Kodály, Zoltán, 131, 387
Koehler, Ted, 329
Kogan, Leonid, 50
Kolodin, Irving, 56
Konitz, Lee, 220
Korda, Alexander, 388
Korngold, Erich Wolfgang 129-130, 133, 349, 358-363, 365-366, 370-371, 373, 387, 398, 425, 427, 465
Korngold, Julius, 358-359
Kosma, Joseph, 457
Koussevitzky, Serge, 51-52, 78-79, 81-82, 116, 119, 135, 306-307
Kral, Roy, 231-232
Kreisler, Fritz, 372
Krenek, Ernst, 129, 166, 367-368
Kretzmer, Herbert, 339
Krupa, Gene, 173-175, 198, 221
Kubelik, Jan, 258
Kubik, Gail, 99, 464-465

L

LaFaro, Scott, 221
Lagoya, Alexandre, 244
LaGuardia, Fiorello, 65, 88, 334
Lake, Veronica, 445
Lamarr, Hedy, 72, 445
Lamb, Joseph, 156
Lambert, Constant, 406
Lambert, Donald "The Lamb," 159-161
Landowska, Wanda, 251

Lane, Abbe, 197
Lane, Burton, 305, 313, 321, 328, 331, 333, 439
Lang, Eddie, 234
Lang, Fritz, 380
Langan, Jim, 165
Langdon, Dory, 231
Lanier, Sydney, 29
Lansbury, Angela, 335, 341, 407
Lantz, Walter, 464
Lanza, Mario, 52, 60, 460
Lapine, James, 343
LaPorta, John, 245
LaRocca, James, 162
LaRocca, Nick, 161-162, 165
LaRue, Grace, 370
László, Miklós, 334
Latouche, John, 91-92, 283, 308, 327, 451
Lauder, Harry, 310
Laurents, Arthur, 308-309, 341
Lauri-Volpi, Giacomo, 62
Lava, William, 463
Lawrence, Earl E., 467
Lawrence, Gertrude, 287, 297-298, 352
Lawrence, Jerome, 335
Lawrence, Robert, 124
Le Pera, Alfredo, 147
Lee, Ann, 8
Lee, Gypsy Rose, 276, 312
Lee, Peggy, 174, 179, 199, 229, 457
Lee, Robert E., 335
Lees, Gene, 182, 216, 398
Legay, Charles, 27
Léger, Fernand, 353
Leginska, Ethel, 251
Legrand, Michel, 422
Lehar, Franz, 257, 428
Lehmann, Lilli, 58

Lehmann, Lotte, 429
Leigh, Carolyn, 311, 336
Leigh, Janet, 446
Leigh, Mitch, 338
Leigh, Vivien, 411
Leinsdorf, Erich, 55
Lenya, Lotte, 285, 325-326
Leonowens, Anna, 298
Lerner, Alan Jay, 253, 276, 280, 282, 299-302, 309, 325, 327, 346, 439, 441
Leschetizky, Theodor, 41
Lessard, John, 140
Leuning, Otto, 98
Levant, Oscar, 364, 372, 394, 440, 466
Levine, James, 464
Levy, Edward, 91
Levy, John, 223
Levy, Jules, 45
Levy, Morris, 223
Lewin, Frank, 150-151, 472
Lewis, H. Merrills, 102
Lewis, Jerry, 447
Lewis, John, 167, 211, 219, 224, 238, 242-243, 245, 247, 249, 415
Lewis, Mel, 227
Lewis, Robert, 287, 333
Lewis, Sam M., 264
Lewis, Ted, 172-173, 175
Lhevinne, Rosina, 424
Lieberson, Goddard, 93
Limonick, Natalie, 126
Lind, Jenny, 91
Lindsay, Howard, 278
Lindsay, Vachel, 92
Lipschultz, George, 398
Lipstone, Louis, 467
Liston, Melba, 226

Liszt, Franz, 20-21, 25-27, 33-34, 60, 71, 146, 155, 159, 225, 227, 263, 361-362, 376, 466
Little, William, 11
Livingston, Fud, 171
Livingston, Jay, 461
Lloyd Webber, Andrew, 339
Locke, Alain, 95
Lockridge, Richard, 286
Loeffler, Charles Martin, 37
Loesser, Arthur, 312
Loesser, Frank, 93, 253, 299, 312-317, 319, 345, 452, 456
Loesser, Henry, 312
Loesser, Lynn Garland, 313
Loesser, Susan, 313
Loewe, Edmond, 300
Loewe, Frederick, 139, 253, 299-302, 304, 439, 441-442
Logan, Joshua, 298, 320, 420
Lombardo, Guy, 171, 438
Long, Avon, 328
Loomis, Harvey Worthington, 38
Loos, Anita, 311, 383, 429, 441
Lorentz, Pare, 393
Lorillard, Elaine, 237
Loring, Euene, 79
Losch, Tilly, 281-282
Low, Bill, 303
Low, Seth, 35
Lubitsch, Ernst, 334, 428
Lucas, Leighton, 406
Lumière Brothers, 350
Lunceford, Jimmy, 144, 169-172, 180, 195-196, 198, 209, 214
Lyles, Aubrey, 264
Lyon, James, 10, 16
Lyons, Marv, 48

M

Ma, Yo-Yo, 244
MacDonald, Jeanette, 383, 427-429
MacDowell, Edward, 33-36, 40, 165
MacDowell, Marian, 33-36
Macero, Teo, 245
MacGrath, Leueen, 323
MacLaine, Shirley, 382
MacMurray, Fred, 389
MacRae, Gordon, 295, 443
Maeterlinck, Maurice, 37, 60
Maganini, Quinto, 139
Magidson, Herb, 431
Mahler, Gustav, 130, 359, 363, 367
Mailman, Martin, 104
Mainbocher, 323
Malko, Nikolai, 262
Malotte, Albert Hay, 462
Mamoulian, Rouben, 325, 428
Mancini, Henry, 397, 412, 414-415, 421-422, 425
Mandel, Johnny, 414-415
Mandyczewski, Eusebius, 55
Mankiewicz, Herman, 274
Mankiewicz, Joseph l., 337, 408
Mann, Herbie, 246
Manne, Shelly, 211, 234
Mapleson, Henry, 57-58
Marable, Fate, 163
Marcy Cheney, Amy, 32
Marlowe, Sylvia, 140
Marowitz, Sam, 184
Marquette, Père, 84
Marsalis, Wynton, 242-243, 250
Marsh, Wayne, 220
Marshall, Arthur, 156
Martin, Dean, 179, 459
Martin, Ernest, 315, 317
Martin, Hugh, 434-435
Martin, Mary, 296, 298-299, 303, 320, 323, 335, 451
Martinelli, Giovanni, 62, 354

Marx, Groucho, 429
Mason, Daniel Gregory, 29-31
Mason, Henry, 44
Mason, Lowell, 16-18, 21, 31
Massenet, Jules, 160
Mathieson, Muir, 387
Maugham, W. Somerset, 373
Mayer, Louis B., 266, 369, 383, 428
Mayerl, Billy, 218
McCarthy, Joe, 433
McCarthy, Sen. Joseph, 331
McDonald, Harl, 138, 394
McDougall, Alexander, 12
McGhee, Howard, 205
McGlohon, Loonis, 100
McHugh, Jimmy, 313, 336, 432, 460-461
McKay, George Frederick, 93, 98
McKibbon, Al, 211-212
McLaglen, Victor, 365
McPartland Brothers, 165
McPartland, Marian, 100, 218
McRae, Carmen, 227, 231, 233
McShann, Jay, 206
Mears, Martha, 445
Mehegan, John, 236
Meisner, Sanford, 287
Melba, Nellie, 58, 61
Melchior, Lauritz, 62
Melton, James, 352
Mel-Tones, 232
Mencken, H.L., 91, 183
Méndez, Rafael, 386
Mendoza, David, 351, 354
Mennin, Peter, 103
Mennini, Louis, 103-104
Menotti, Gian Carlo, 113-115
Mercer, Johnny, 188, 230, 328-330, 332-333, 395, 422, 449, 451, 453, 456-457, 462

Mercer, Mabel, 100
Meredith, Morley, 332
Merman, Ethel, 279, 312, 320-321, 335, 340, 352, 433
Merrick, David, 333, 335, 338, 453
Merrill, Bob, 310, 338
Merrill, Robert, 62-63
Messter, Oscar, 350
Mesta, Perle, 321
Meyer, Abe, 467
Meyer, George W., 261
Michener, James A., 295
Miles, Alfred Hart, 4
Miley, James "Bubber," 189-190
Milhaud, Darius, 27, 86, 124, 134, 166, 222, 357, 406
Milhaud, Madeleine, 124
Miller, Arthur, 150, 412-413
Miller, Flournoy, 264
Miller, Glenn, 171, 173, 176-183, 189, 194, 229, 234, 237, 416, 421, 453, 455
Miller, Marilyn, 268
Miller, Mitch, 100
Millevoye, Charles-Hubert, 25
Mills, Irving, 455
Milva, 147
Mingus, Charles, 149, 196, 245
Minnelli, Liza, 337
Minnelli, Vincente, 442
Mitchell, Dwike, 240-241
Mitchell, James, 330
Mitchell, Red, 215
Mittolovski, Leopold, 146
Mockridge, Cyril, 407-408
Modern Jazz Quartet, 167, 213, 224-225, 247, 415
Modernaires, 229
Mole, Miff, 165
Molnár, Ferenc, 294, 380, 384

INDEX | 521

Monaco, Jimmy, 433
Monk, Thelonious Sphere, 205
Montalban, Ricardo, 314
Montaner, Rita, 197
Montemezzi, Italo, 133
Monteux, Pierre, 50, 104, 118, 414
Moore, Douglas, 52, 65, 91-93, 98, 104
Moore, Freddie, 166
Moore, Phil, 201
Morales, Carlos, 467
Morello, Joe, 222
Morey, Larry, 462
Morgan, Helen, 269-270
Morgan, Justin, 13
Morley, Robert, 404-405
Morley, Sheridan, 404
Moross, Jerome, 65, 105-107, 327, 349, 409-411
Morris, Audrey, 214
Morris, Marlowe, 202
Morros, Boris, 385, 458
Morse, Robert, 317
Morton, Benny, 195
Morton, Ferdinand "Jelly Roll," 157-158
Mostel, Zero, 334, 340
Moten, Bennie, 167, 194
Motian, Paul, 221
Mozart, Wolfgang Amadeus, 9, 19, 23, 34, 48, 55-56, 103, 110, 119, 128, 175, 200, 203, 224, 247, 257, 304, 337, 357-358, 362, 468
Muck, Karl, 49-50
Mulligan, Gerry, 148, 187, 219-221
Munch, Charles, 52, 307
Mundy, Jimmy, 174-175
Munshin, Jules, 437
Murphy, Lyle "Spud," 174
Murray, Kel, 173

Murray, Lyn, 106, 373, 407
Murrow, Edward R., 121
Mussolini, Benito, 54

N

Nanton, Joe "Tricky Sam," 190
Napoleon, Phil, 165
Nascimbene, Mario, 408
Nash, Clarence, 462
Nash, Ogden, 151, 283, 323
Nash, Ted, 381
Natwick, Grim, 429
Navarro, Fats, 212
Neagley, Clint, 175
Neal, Paul G., 355, 394
Neiburg, Al, 464
Nelson, Louis Delisle "Big Eye", 157
Nelson, Ozzie, 171, 217, 229
Nelson, Ron, 102, 104
Nero, Peter, 203
Nesbitt, Cathleen, 303
Newborn, Phineas, Jr., 212, 227-228
Newman, Alfred, 1, 39, 313, 349, 358, 369-371, 373, 394-395, 398, 408, 442
Newman, Emil, 373
Newman, Lionel, 373, 414
Newton, John, 8
Niblo, William, 57
Nicholas, Fayard and Harold, 330-331, , 437, 451
Nichols, Red, 165, 173, 198, 455
Niles, John Jacob, 91
Nilsson, Christina, 57
Nilsson, Harry, 424
Nimmons, Phil, 238
Nimoy, Leonard, 334
Nixon, Marni, 399, 418, 446
Nixon, Richard M., 189, 248
Noble, Ray, 415
Noone, Jimmy, 161

Nordenstrom, Gladys, 129
Nordica, Lillian, 58-59
Normand, Mabel, 335-336
North, Alex, 128, 242, 349, 371, 393, 409, 411-413, 415, 457
Norvo, Red, 174
Novak, Kim, 420
Nureyev, Rudolf, 314

O

Oakley, Annie, 320
O'Connell, Charles, 54
O'Connell, Helen, 179, 229
O'Connor, Donald, 437, 440
O'Day, Anita, 198
Odets, Clifford, 140, 337
Offenbach, Jacques, 3, 25, 45, 308
Oglethorpe, James, 8
O'Hara, John, 276
O'Hara, Maureen, 332
Oliver, Joe "King," 102, 161-163, 165, 172
Oliver, Sy, 169-170, 180
Olivier, Laurence, 406
Orent, Milt, 210
Ørsted Pederson, Niels-Henning, 214
Ory, Kid, 158, 161, 163
Ostrowska, Djina, 77
Ouzer, Louis, 100

P

Pachelbel, Karl Theodore, 9
Paderewski, Ignacy Jan, 20, 370
Page, Oren "Hot Lips," 194-195
Page, Walter, 195
Paget, Debra, 49
Paine, David, 28
Paine, John Knowles, 28-29, 33, 36
Paine, Robert Treat, 15
Paine, Thomas, 15, 28
Paine, William, 28
Palmer, Harry, 253

Palmgren, Selim, 93
Papas, Sophocles, 234
Parish, Mitchell, 181, 455
Parker, Charlie "Bird," 150, 203, 106-210, 212-213, 219-220, 223, 230, 235, 245, 250
Parker, Clifton, 406
Parker, Dorothy, 138, 268, 308, 454
Parker, Horatio, 30-31, 66, 91, 117
Parkman, Francis, 29
Pascal, Gabriel, 302
Pass, Joe, 233-234
Pathé, Charles, 350
Paton, Alan, 325
Patti, Adelina, 19, 57
Paulsen, Harold, 285
Paur, Emil, 49
Pavarotti, Luciano, 2, 64
Peck, Gregory, 386, 389
Peerce, Jan, 62
Pennario, Leonard, 128
Pepper, Art, 186
Perelman, S. J., 283
Perlman, Itzhak, 203
Persichetti, Vincent, 111
Persin, Max, 94
Peters, Bernadette, 335
Peters, Brock, 226
Peterson, Albin, 97
Peterson, Daniel, 202
Peterson, Oscar, 145, 202-203, 214-216, 227, 233-234, 238, 243, 251
Petri, Egon, 384
Pettiford, Oscar, 149, 190, 198, 208, 214
Phile, Philip, 14
Phillips, Burrill, 99
Piatigorsky, Gregor, 84, 132, 372
Piazzolla, Astor, 147-148
Picasso, Pablo, 71, 86, 88

Pickford, Mary, 41
Picou, Alphonse, 157
Pied Pipers, 229
Pinza, Ezio, 296
Piron, A.J., 191
Piston, Walter, 103, 115, 118, 121, 141, 465
Plautus, 340
Pollack, Ben, 171-172, 185
Pommer, Erich, 380
Pons, Lily, 62
Porter, Cole, 1-2, 139, 177, 190, 210, 230, 253, 261, 266, 276-277, 280, 284, 299, 302-303, 320-322, 399, 431, 440, 443-444, 449, 461
Porter, Quincy, 91, 98
Posselt, Ruth, 50
Potter, Tommy, 206
Poulenc, Francis, 406
Pound, Ezra, 71
Powell, Baden, 246
Powell, Dick, 229, 447
Powell, Earl "Bud," 202-203, 208-214, 222, 246, 414
Powell, Edward B., 372, 394
Powell, Eleanor, 450
Powell, Jane, 143, 439, 461
Powell, John, 41
Powell, Richie, 212
Powell, Rudy, 204
Pozo, Chano, 150, 208
Presley, Elvis, 337
Preston, Robert, 319, 335, 444
Previn, André, 3, 106, 128, 203, 215, 222, 231, 300, 305, 362, 369, 414, 423, 433, 435, 437, 442, 446
Price, Florence, 30
Price, Leontyne, 64
Priestley, J.B, 281
Prima, Louis, 175

Prince, Harold, 335, 343
Princess Hitachi of Japan, 261
Princess San Faustino, , 278
Prokofiev, Sergei, 51, 115, 166, 282, 366, 380, 384, 386, 396, 411, 463
Prout, Ebeneezer, 280
Pryor, Arthur, 46
Puccini, Giacomo, 5, 130, 294, 359

Q

Queen Elizabeth II, , 192-193, 224
Queen Rànavàlona III, 265
Queen, Mary of England, 51
Quilly, Dennis, 335

R

Rabinowitsch, Max, 365, 414
Rachmaninoff, Sergei, 2, 51, 73, 125-126, 134, 140, 144, 146-147, 202, 216, 326, 386-387, 405, 423
Rackin, Martin, 422
Raderman, Lou, 358
Raff, Joachim, 33, 36
Ragas, Henry, 162
Rainger, Ralph, 453-455, 464
Rains, Elizabeth, 453
Raitt, John, 317
Raksin, David, 349, 351, 367, 371, 393-397, 399, 404, 421, 424, 457, 464-466
Raleigh, Sir Walter, 102
Rankin, John, 331
Rapée, Ernö, 351
Rasch, Albertina, 384
Rathaus, Karol, 357
Rathom, John R., 50
Ravel, Maurice, 5, 31, 77, 120-121, 165-167, 186, 191, 200, 219, 224, 246-247, 280, 342
Rawsthorne, Alan, 406
Raymond, Gene, 431
Razaf, Andy, 175, 265-266

Read, Daniel, 13
Reagan, Nancy, 471
Reagan, Ronald, 178, 230, 377, 471
Redgrave, Michael, 303
Redmon, Don, 167-169, 357
Reger, Max, 131, 387
Reinagle, Alexander, 14
Reiner, Fritz, 119, 306, 370
Reinhardt, Django, 225, 235, 243
Reinhardt, Max, 359
Remick, Jerome, 428
Remick, Lee, 341
Respighi, Ottorino, 97, 398
Revel, Harry, 452
Revueltas, Silvestre, 79, 135, 411
Rexroth, Kenneth, 183
Reynolds, Marjorie, 445
Rheinberger, Joseph, 31
Rice, Elmer, 324
Rice, Thomas Dartmouth "Daddy," 22
Rich, Buddy, 178, 180
Ricketts, F. J, 406
Riddle, Gladys, 196
Riddle, Nelson, 179-180, 414, 426-427
Riegger, Wallingford, 98
Riesenfeld, Dr Hugo., 351
Rieti, Vittorio, 140
Riggs, Lynn, 290
Rimsky-Korsakov, Niklolai, 437
Rinker, Al, 429-430
Rivera, Chita, 337
Roach, Max, 211-212, 238
Robbins, Jack, 434, 450
Robbins, Jerome, 306, 309
Robert, Richard, 55
Roberts, Charles Luckeyeth, 159
Robertson, Dave, 238
Robeson, Paul, 93
Robin, Leo, 311, 428, 453-454, 464

Robinson, Bill "Bojangles," 451
Robinson, Earl, 93
Robyn, William, 42
Rodgers, Dorothy, 450
Rodgers, Richard, 2, 80, 139, 179, 253, 261-262, 270, 274-277, 290-300, 302, 305-306, 312, 320, 327, 334, 336, 340-342, 345-346, 378, 428-429, 434, 442-444, 450-451, 461
Rodin, Gil, 171
Rodzinski, Artur, 55
Rogers, Bernard, 91, 99, 102-104, 120, 418
Rogers, Ginger, 263, 335, 364, 430-432, 439, 468
Rogers, Milton "Shorty," 183, 186-187, 221, 416, 418
Rogers, Roy, 229, 449
Rogers, Will, 261
Rollins, Sonny, 212
Romberg, Sigmund, 257-258, 268, 362-363, 429, 443
Rome, Harold, 289-290
Ronell, Ann, 356
Roosevelt, Eleanor, 64
Roosevelt, Franklin D., 275, 356
Roosevelt, Theodore, 20, 50
Rorem, Ned, 89-90, 339
Rose, Al, 191
Rose, Billy, 263
Rosenfeld, Paul, 69
Rosenkrantz, Timmie, 208
Rosenman, Leonard, 419, 466
Rosenstock, Milton, 311
Rosenthal, Laurence, 416, 418
Ross, Annie, 231
Ross, Arnold, 234, 237
Ross, Harold, 154
Ross, Jerry, 317-318

Rostand, Edmond, 338
Rota, Nino, 408-409
Rothier, Leon, 353
Rowland, Gene, 184
Rowles, Jimmy, 233
Royce, Edward, 100
Royle, Edwin, 255
Rózsa, Dr.Miklós, 349, 380, 387, 390, 401, 420, 422-425, 468
Ruby, Harry, 429-430
Rudel, Julius, 65
Rufer, Josef, 359
Ruff, Willie, 240-241
Ruggles, Carl, 70-71
Rugolo, Pete, 186
Rumsey, Howard, 221
Runyon, Damon, 311, 314
Russell, George, 219
Russell, Henry, 60
Russell, Jane, 229
Russell, Rosalind, 408
Russo, Bill, 238
Ruth, Babe, 1, 353
Ryskind, Morrie, 271-272, 274, 429

S

Saidy, Fred, 302, 330-331, 333
Saint-Saens, Camille, 77, 352
Saint-Subber, Arnold, 321
Salinger, Conrad, 433
Salter, Hans J., 377
Salzedo, Carlos, 123
Samaroff, Olga, 111
Sampson, Edgar, 174-175
Sandburg, Carl, 145
Sanders, George, 303, 403
Sanderson, James, 16
Sanga, Tuntemeke, 226
Santayana, George, 29
Santisi, Ray, 238
Saroyan, William, 89

Satie, Eric, 353, 357
Sauguet, Henri, 88
Saxe, Sam, 236-237
Scalero, Rosario, 112-114, 137
Schabas, Ezra, 17, 21
Scharf, Walter, 447
Scheel, Fritz, 52
Scheff, Fritzi, 254
Schenk, Joseph M., 370
Schertzinger, Victor, 428
Schifrin, Lalo, 148, 211, 244, 425-426
Schillinger, Joseph, 181
Schmidt, Harvey, 338
Schnabel, Artur, 251
Schoeffel, John B., 58
Schoenberg, Arnold, 76, 81, 85, 110, 117-119, 121, 126-128, 130-131, 140, 246, 288, 357, 359, 362, 367, 391, 397, 399, 405, 419, 446
Schoepp, Franz, 172
Schreker, Franz, 129, 377
Schubart, Mark, 117, 193
Schubert, Franz, 11, 210, 258, 273, 372, 463
Schulberg, Budd, 319
Schuller, Gunther, 149, 163, 170, 194, 244-245
Schuman, William, 94, 313
Schumann, Robert, 82
Schumann-Heink, Ernestine, 58
Schutt, Arthur, 466
Schwartz, Arthur, 281-282, 441, 457
Schwartz, Jonathan, 179
Scott, James, 156
Scott, Raymond, 174
Scott, Sir Walter, 16
Scriabin, Alexander, 38, 51
Seberg, Jean, 446-447
Segovia, Andrés, 132, 234
Selby, William, 14

Selznick, David O., 365, 386, 389, 420
Sembrich, Marcella, 58
Sennett, Mack, 335-336
Serafin, Tullio, 114
Serling, Rod, 403
Sessions, Roger, 78, 89, 91, 116, 118, 120-121, 416, 419
Seurat, Georges, 343
Severinsen, Doc, 263
Sevitzky, Fabien, 148
Shakespeare, William, 29-30, 87, 132, 149-150, 193, 250, 276, 278, 309, 321-322, 334, 384, 406, 409, 411, 426
Shank, Bud, 186
Sharaff, Irene, 323
Sharples, Winston, 464
Shavers, Charlie, 144
Shaw, Artie, 95, 176-178, 232, 237, 450
Shaw, George Bernard, 257, 301-302
Shearing, Sir George, 155
Shepherd, Arthur, 39-40
Sherman, Richard M., 444-445
Sherman, Robert B., 444-445
Shettler, Charlie, 357
Shevelove, Burt, 340
Shields, Larry, 162
Shilkret, Nathaniel, 134
Shirley, Dr. Donald, 144-147
Shirley, George, 64
Shore, Dinah, 197, 199
Shostakovich, Dmitri, 166, 262, 353, 347, 380, 381, 384
Shuckburgh, Richard, 12
Shuken, Leo, 374, 467
Sibelius, Jean, 71, 92, 97, 99, 106, 140
Siegmeister, Elie, 98, 105
Sills, Beverly, 65
Silver, Horace, 212

Silvers, Phil, 311
Simon, George T., 169
Simon, Neil, 336
Simone, Lela, 433
Sims, Lee, 200
Sims, Zoot, 184
Sinatra, Frank, 93, 100, 179, 185, 199, 229, 310, 312, 343, 416, 426, 437, 451-452, 457, 460
Sinding, Christian, 92
Sissle, Noble, 95, 264
Sisters, King, 311
Skelton, Red, 314, 430
Skinner, Frank, 376-378, 467
Slenczynska, Ruth, 251
Sloane, Alfred Baldwin, 255
Sloane, Carol, 233
Slonimsky, Nicolas, 69, 103, 134
Smith, Bessie, 164
Smith, Cecil, 126
Smith, Harry B., 261
Smith, Henry "Buster," 195, 206
Smith, John Stafford, 15
Smith, Kate, 352
Smith, Melville, 77
Smith, Paul J., 463, 465
Smith, Paul Thatcher, 217-218
Smith, Samuel Francis, 16
Smith, Sir C. Aubrey, 404
Smith, Steven, 105
Smith, William, 11
Smith, Willie "The Lion," 159-160, 189, 201
Smith, Willie, 170
Sokoloff, Nikolai, 55
Sondheim, Stephen, 268, 299, 309, 312, 324, 339-341, 344
Soubirous, Bernadette, 372
Sousa, Antonio, 45

Sousa, John Philip, 3, 45-46, 48-49, 158, 261, 318, 471
Sowerby, Leo, 465
Spargo, Tony, 162
Spencer, Herbert, 358
Spewack, Bella and Samuel, 321
Spillane, Mickey, 441
St. Cyr, Johnny, 163
Stafford, Grace, 464
Stafford, Jo, 179, 199, 229, 457
Stalling, Carl, 365, 465
Standish, Miles, 91
Stanwyck, Barbara, 389
Starr, S. Frederick, 27
Statlovsky, Roman, 373
Staunton, Imelda, 335
Stearns, Marshall, 183, 238
Stein, Gertrude, 71, 86-87
Stein, Leonard, 127, 446
Steinbeck, John, 151, 193, 298, 391-392
Steinberg, Michael, 98
Steiner, Fred, 416
Steiner, Gabor, 363
Steiner, Max, 349, 358, 362-367, 370, 373-374, 378, 383, 385, 391, 398, 417-418, 420, 434, 466
Steinert, Alex, 467
Stengel, Casey, 63
Stevens, George, 381, 385
Stevens, Leith, 396, 467
Steward, Herbie, 184
Still, William Grant, 65, 93, 95, 98, 133, 467
Stitt, Sonny, 212
Stockhausen, Karlheinz, 283
Stojowski, Sigismond, 370
Stokes, Richard L., 98
Stokowski, Leopold, 17, 52-53, 188, 202, 463-464

Stordahl, Axel, 179, 460
Stothart, Herbert, 434
Strang, Gerald, 127
Strasberg, Lee, 287
Strasberg, Paula Miller, 287
Straus, Oscar, 388
Strauss, Johann, 44, 46, 342, 363, 387
Strauss, Richard, 21, 55, 130, 285, 359, 361, 370, 387
Stravinsky, Igor, 5, 31, 51, 77, 85, 88, 110, 112, 117-118, 120, 125-126, 130, 133-134, 141, 146-147, 166, 183-184, 188, 208, 283, 288, 357, 366, 369, 380, 384, 399, 463-464
Strayhorn, Billy, 191-193, 243, 457
Strelitzer, Hugo, 379
Stritch, Elaine, 342
Strouse, Charles, 305, 337-338
Styne, Jule, 310, 312-313, 318, 340-341, 343, 452, 459
Styne, Margaret, 310
Sukman, Harry, 358, 375-376
Sullivan, Ed, 305
Sullivan, Jo, 316
Sullivan, Pat, 356
Sumac, Yma, 331
Sunahara, Michiko, 382
Suskin, Stephen, 283
Swerling, Jo, 315
Swift, Jonathan, 464
Swift, Kay, 284
Szell, George, 53, 55, 464
Szigeti, Joseph, 175

T

Taillefaire, Germaine, 166
Talbot, Ethel, 369
Talbot, Irvin, 128, 318, 349, 351-355, 358, 360, 369, 373, 382, 385, 391, 458, 464
Tamiris, Helen, 320

Tansman, Alexandre, 134
Tarchetti, Iginio Ugo, 343
Tarjan, Susanna Moross, 327-328, 409
Tatum, Art, 1, 144, 199-203, 214-218, 222, 225, 227, 231, 239, 246, 263, 414
Taylor, Billy, 154, 202-204, 211, 239, 244
Taylor, Cecil, 244, 246
Taylor, Deems, 99, 138
Taylor, Elizabeth, 381
Taylor, Samuel, 316
Tchaikovsky, Pyotr Ilyich, 19, 21, 125, 243, 247, 288, 373, 387, 398
Temple, Shirley, 263, 310, 408, 454, 461
Terr, Max, 354, 458
Terry, Clark, 196
Terry, Ellen, 34
Teschmacher, Frank, 165
Tetrazzini, Luisa, 61, 352
Thalberg, Irving, 368, 467
Thayer, Alexander Wheelock, 24
Thielemans, Jean "Toots," 235
Thigpen, Ed, 215, 234, 238
Thomas, Brandon, 314
Thomas, Danny, 264
Thomas, Johann, 18
Thomas, Linda Lee, 276
Thomas, Theodore, 17-21, 29, 34
Thompson, Kay, 433, 436, 441
Thompson, Randall, 90-91, 103, 115
Thomson, Virgil, 70, 77-78, 86-90, 104, 121, 140, 167, 393
Thoreau, Henry David, 31
Thornhill, Claude, 219-220
Thumb, General and Mrs. Tom, 92
Thurber, James, 465
Tibbett, Lawrence, 356, 385, 451

Tierney, Gene, 395, 403
Tierney, Harry, 255, 363
Timberg, Sammy, 464
Tio, Leonard, 191
Tiomkin, Dimitri, 384-387, 421, 467
Tizol, Juan, 190
Toch, Ernst, 121, 128, 133-134, 368, 399, 411, 414
Toch, Lilly, 128
Todd, Mike, 292
Tomlinson, Ralph, 15
Tormé, Mel, 172, 178, 224, 229-230, 232, 237, 378
Torvill, Jayne, 336
Toscanini, Arturo, 17, 54-56, 61-63, 83, 88, 112-113, 143, 193, 248, 471
Tough, Dave, 165, 183
Tourjée, Eben, 44
Tozzi, Giorgio, 446
Tracy, Spencer, 429
Trapp Family Singers, 299, 442
Trapp, Baroness Maria Von, 299
Tremblay, George, 127
Tristano, Lennie, 187, 219-220, 236
Troilo, Anibal, 147
Truman, Harry S, 11, 265
Truman, Margaret, 11
Trumbauer, Frankie, 165, 198
Tucker, Richard, 62
Tucker, Sophie, 311
Tufts, Reverend John, 7
Turner, Frederick Jackson, 21
Turner, Lana, 178
Turner, Ray, 354, 358
Twain, Mark, 66, 119, 138, 217, 262, 366

U

Ulanov, Barry, 202

V

Valentino, Rudolph, 197
Vallee, Rudy, 171, 317
Van Boskerck, Captain Francis Saltus, 4
Van Buren, Martin, 16
Van Damme, Art, 235
Van Doren, Carl, 242
Van Dyke, Dick, 337, 445
Van Heusen, James, 188, 310, 459-460
Vansittart, Sir Robert, 388
Vardaro, Elvino, 147
Vardill, John, 12
Varèse, Edgard, 95, 118, 123
Vartabed, Komitas, 140
Vaughan Williams, Sir Ralph, 106, 405
Vaughan, Sarah, 207, 227, 230-231, 237
Vengerova, Isabella, 111, 119, 306
Venuti, Joe, 234
Vera-Ellen, 438
Verdi, Giuseppe, 44, 61-62, 109, 114, 368
Verdon, Gwen, 336
Vernon, Vinton, 371
Verrett, Shirley, 64
Vila, Pomping, 240
Villa-Lobos, Heitor, 246, 384
Vinding, Terkild, 160
Voltaire, 308
Von Tilzer, Harry, 256

W

Wagenaar, Bernard, 89, 124, 144, 400
Wagner, Joseph, 98, 103-104
Wagner, Richard, 18-19, 21, 30-31, 44, 49, 58-60, 123, 151, 160, 302, 333, 352, 372, 380, 387, 404
Wagner, Robert, 49

Waldteufel, Émile, 402
Walker, Robert, 366
Wallace, Oliver, 463, 465
Waller, John L., 265
Waller, Maurice, 201
Waller, Thomas, "Fats," 160, 172, 194-195, 201-202, 240, 249, 265-266, 451
Wallichs, Glenn, 456
Wallop, Douglas, 318
Walton, Harry, 265
Walton, Sir William, 106, 380
Wand, Betty, 446
Warburg, James P., 284
Ward, Samuel A., 4
Warner, Harry, 354
Warner, Jack, 369, 444-445
Warren, Annette, 218, 269, 445
Warren, Harry, 430, 436, 439, 452-453, 457, 461
Washington, Dinah, 196
Washington, George, 6, 14, 16, 23, 36, 91, 94, 255, 330, 471
Wasserman, Lew, 404
Watanabe, Butch, 238
Waters, Ethel, 228, 451
Waxman, Franz, 349, 365, 371, 379-380, 382, 467
Wayne, Chuck, 223
Weatherford, Teddy, 240
Webb, Chick, 169, 176, 230
Webb, Clifton, 49, 282, 453
Webb, Jack, 390
Webb, Kenneth, 378
Webb, Roy, 363, 365, 378-379
Webern, Anton, 69, 246
Webster, Ben, 190, 199
Webster, Daniel, 92, 402
Webster, Noah, 13
Webster, Paul Francis, 332

Wechsler, Lawrence, 368
Wedge, George, 370
Weede, Robert, 316
Weeks, Anson, 229
Weidman, Jerome, 334
Weill, Kurt, 166, 222, 233, 253, 284, 286, 299, 301, 323-324, 326, 329, 345, 417, 444
Wein, George, 237
Weingartner, Felix, 103, 363
Welles, Orson, 87-89, 289, 321, 400-401, 419, 421
Wells, Dickie, 195
Werfel, Franz, 372
Wesley, Charles, 8
Weston, Paul, 457, 460
Weston, Randy, 226
Wheatley, William, 253
Wheeler, Francis, 331
White, Paul, 98
White, T.H., 304
White, Walter, 64
Whiteman, Paul, 73, 165-166, 169, 173, 234, 449, 455-456
Whiteman, Wilberforce J., 169
Whiteside, Abby, 142
Whiting, George, 264
Whiting, Margaret, 378, 457
Whiting, Richard, 428, 454, 457, 461-462
Whitlock, Bob, 221
Whitman, Walt, 84, 98
Wieprecht, Friedrich, 28
Wilber, Bob, 178
Wilbur, Richard, 308
Wilcox, Edwin, 170
Wilda, Bela, 147
Wilde, Oscar, 132, 405
Wilder, Alec, 99-100, 218, 232, 277, 283, 456

Wilder, Billy, 389
Wilder, Thornton, 335, 391
Williams, Andy, 445
Williams, Charles Melvin Cootie," 174-175, 190
Williams, Charles, 405
Williams, Esther, 197, 314, 452
Williams, Joe, 196, 232
Williams, John, 142, 412, 414, 422, 424-425
Williams, Mary Lou, 199, 206-207, 210
Williams, Tennessee, 89, 150, 411
Williamson, Claude, 237
Willson, Meredith, 4, 318-319, 467
Wilson, Dooley, 451
Wilson, Gerald, 211
Wilson, John, 330
Wilson, Mortimer, 353
Wilson, Teddy, 144, 173-175, 199-200, 203, 217, 236
Winchell, Walter, 292
Winters, Morgan, 145
Winters, Shelley, 381
Wittke, Paul, 89
Wodehouse, P.G., 267, 270, 278
Wolpe, Stefan, 416
Wood, Natalie, 446
Woollcott, Alexander, 138, 269, 279
Woolley, Monty, 278-279
Wright, Eugene, 222
Wright, Robert, 326
Wyler, William, 385, 399
Wyman, Jane, 378

Y

Yoder, Walt, 183
Yon, Pietro, 107
Youmans, Vincent, 262-263, 329, 431-432, 461
Young, Joe, 264

Young, Lester, "Prez," 194, 197-199, 206-207, 229-230
Young, Loretta, 445
Young, Victor, 373-376, 416, 458, 461, 464, 467
Ysaÿe, Eugene, 123

Z

Zádor, Eugene, 131, 133, 368, 435
Zamcenik, J.S., 352
Zanuck, Darryl, 99
Zeisl, Eric, 131
Zemlinsky, Alexander von, 359
Zerrahn, Carl, 44
Ziegfeld, Florenz, 260, 363, 430
Ziegler, Pablo, 147
Ziffrin, Marilyn J., 71
Zimbalist, Efrem, 73, 197, 354, 372
Zimmermann, Charles A., 3
Zukerman, Pinchas, 244
Zukor, Adolph, 355
Zweig, Fritz, 379

www.ingramcontent.com/pod-product-compliance
Lightning Source LLC
Chambersburg PA
CBHW080721230426
43665CB00020B/2570